Canada since 1945:
Power, politics, and provincialism

UNIVERSITY OF TORONTO PRESS   Toronto   Buffalo   London

ROBERT BOTHWELL, IAN DRUMMOND, JOHN ENGLISH

Canada since 1945:
Power, Politics, and Provincialism

© University of Toronto Press 1981
Toronto Buffalo London
Reprinted in paperback 1982, 1984
Printed in Canada
ISBN 0-8020-2417-3 (cloth)
ISBN 0-8020-6478-7 (paper)

Canadian Cataloguing in Publication Data

Bothwell, Robert, 1944-
Canada since 1945

Bibliography: p.
Includes index.

ISBN 0-8020-2417-3
ISBN 0-8020-6478-7 pbk.

I. Canada – History – 1945- 2. Canada –
Politics and government – 1935- *3. Canada –
Economic conditions – 1945- I. Drummond, Ian,
1933- II. English, John, 1945-
III. Title.

FC600.B68   971.06   C80.094860-2
F1034.2.B68

This book has been published with the assistance of block grants from the Canada Council
and the Ontario Arts Council.

To Charles Stacey,
scholar, colleague, and friend

Contents

Contents viii

Preface

A visitor seeing Canada for the first time since 1939 might well conclude that Canada, even more than nations devastated by war, has become another country. On the surface so much remains the same: the Liberals prevail in Ottawa; the provinces quarrel with Ottawa and among themselves; and we worry about Americans in our future. But most of the pieces have been rearranged, and the effect of the picture is quite different. In 1939 the prairie provinces were mostly dustbowls clouding over the nation's economic future. These one-time mendicants are now our new plutocrats, threatening long-established balances by the ferocity of their prosperity. Although nationalist sounds still emanate from Quebec City, their nuances would make them unrecognizable to the parochialists of 1939. To many Ontarians (and other English-speaking Canadians) in 1939, French Canada's problems lay primarily in its relationship with God: believing too much and breeding too often, French Canada was mired in the Middle Ages. Someday it would grow up, like its Anglo-Saxon brethren. But when it did grow up, the adult was wildly unexpected. So, for that matter, was the Ontario counterpart. By the 1970s over forty per cent of Torontonians had been born outside Canada. Many more had come from the countryside and small towns, and had left much of their old lives behind. The sights, sounds, and smells of many city streets were new; only the street names remained to recall an older and very different time.

This is a book about our own times, and as such it expresses definite views. No reader will agree with everything we say. We have not tried to end debate; we have tried to clarify and broaden. We trust that our readers will be encouraged to seek for themselves a better understanding of where Canadians have been and what they have become.

If we were to thank all of those who have influenced this book, the list would be longer than the book. There are some who have worked on this manuscript who merit special thanks, especially Virgil Duff. Virgil gave early encouragement to this project and hastened its completion through frequent advice and generous advances. He is a model editor, a good friend, and as much a part of this book as the authors. Beverley Beetham, Margaret Woollard, and Jean Wilson were extremely competent editors who removed many stylistic abuses and corrected some egregious errors. It is often said that a picture is worth a thousand words and by this token the designer and our cover artist are responsible for a very significant and welcome addition to this volume, and we warmly acknowledge the splendid co-operation and imagination of Laurie Lewis and Don Evans. Others to whom we owe thanks for research assistance and timely help are Senator Carl Goldenberg, W.J. Bennett, Paul Evans, Catherine Barclay, Louise Driedger, and Dr Gerald Campbell. Much of the research on which the sections written by Bothwell and English are based was supported by the C.D. Howe Foundation, the Killam Foundation, and the Social Sciences and Humanities Research Council of Canada. We also want to thank Gail Heideman and Murielle Labrie for stalwart help with the typing.

Every reasonable precaution has been taken to trace the owners of copyright material and to make due acknowledgment. Any omission will be gladly rectified in future editions.

RB, ID, JE

PART ONE

Patterns of Change

I

Beginnings

Canadian history is a success story – an account of coping with troubles and, now and then, triumphing over adversities. The years since 1945 have been more successful than most. At first glance it may seem that Canada's recent successes have been mostly economic, and that even in that realm the record, marred as it is by uncomfortable inflation, is not perfect. But in political, social, and cultural matters Canada has much to be proud of. Nor should the nation's economic achievements be undervalued or ignored. Living standards have risen to heights undreamt of thirty years ago. Thanks to its economic achievements, Canada can afford a social welfare system that few believed possible in 1945. The country now has the apparatus of a humane and urbane society; that was not present in 1945 either. Canadians are now a well-schooled and fairly thoughtful people, even though in education and learning – as opposed to schooling – a good deal may still remain to be desired. Canadians are certainly much less pious than in 1945, but perhaps they are a little more humane and a little less self-righteous. They give little to overseas missionaries, but much to economic development in poor countries. Their cities have grown and changed without turning into hellholes of poverty, dirt, and insecurity. They worry about pollution, and actually do something to restrain it. They have grown more concerned about the preservation and conservation of national resources, both physical and intellectual.

These things are at once familiar and surprising. Once voiced, they are obvious, and yet in the atmosphere of shrillness and crisis that is created around every Canadian every day, they are very seldom said. If they sound banal, it is because the familiar is so seldom newsworthy. But a conscientious history of post-war Canada should stress them, as this book tries to do. If Canada suffers from a failure of nerve, it is partly because Canadians are so seldom told how much they have done, and how well.

It may seem odd to call Canada's recent history a success story when the very existence of the country, in its present form, is still uncertain even as this book goes to press. Naturally, the authors would be sorry to see the rupture of the nation-state, and not simply because historians are understandably anxious to preserve that entity which they study. We are sentimental enough to believe that one great nation – ocean to ocean, in the old phrase – is a better thing than an assemblage of squalling mini-states. There was a time when Canada was significant in world affairs, and perhaps it may be again. The authors must confess a preference for the relatively centralized but outward-looking Canada of the forties and fifties; later chapters detail with sadness the turns of events, some avoidable, some unavoidable, that have brought the country to its present pass. But even if the nation-state should break up – and some observers think that the first fragmentation would not be the last – there would be a past of achievement to look back on, and much of the good would remain. Canadians would not change. They are, on the whole, rather nice people, and quite happy people. So visitors tell us; and we believe them. The developments of the past thirty-five years may or may not have made them nicer; they have certainly made them happier. Canadians have built the great cities, laid the pipelines, learned to be diligent and skilful. These habits and attitudes would remain, and the machines and equipment – the fabric of civilized life in the late twentieth century – would also survive. Even if Canadians were so unlucky as to slip a little way down the economic slope – something that one would not expect to happen – the halt would be a long way above the bottom, and far above the level of 1945. In other words, even if the nation-state were to disintegrate Canadians would probably continue to live in much the same way as they do now. And it is the lives of persons, not nations, that really matter. However pessimistic one may sometimes feel about the latter, one should be optimistic about the former so far as Canada and Canadians are concerned.

Canada's history is not only a success story. Much of Canada's recent past is very funny indeed, and usually the humour is accidental, the humour of incident and situation. Harold Adams Innis once remarked that the principal danger in being a social scientist in Canada is that one might die of laughter. As usual Innis overstated his case, but as usual there was some truth in what he said. The history of post-war Canada is replete with pomposity, and therefore with absurdity. Naturally the 'pomposity co-efficient' varies from year to year and, therefore, in the following pages, from chapter to chapter, as the reader who perseveres will discover. However nice and happy Canadians in general are, the country has its quota of fools and windbags; such people are most prominent in politics, where their inherent weaknesses seem less glaring and attract less ridicule than they would in other walks of life. Hence, in political history-writing they get more of the limelight than their importance really justifies. And so does the element of the absurd in Canadian life.

War, of course, is not funny at all, and no one in Canada has ever found it so, although much of the popular culture was once firmly rooted in war-based humour and in that legacy of war, the Canadian Legion hall. But Canada has been called the 'peaceable kingdom,' and since 1945 it has been just that. The nation managed rapid demobilization, reluctant rearmament to meet the Russian and Chinese threats in the early fifties, and then gradual and rather thoughtless re-disarmament for almost a quarter of a century. Intermittently, Canadians dreamed of middle-power status and fancied themselves as world peacekeepers. But when it was clear not only that soldiers could get killed but that no one loves a peacekeeper, the national temptation was to retire to gardens, cottages, and the endless elaboration of the social welfare state, a game that the provinces as well as Ottawa could play. Fortunately for Canada, the international balance of terror held, and no one actually asked Canadian troops to do anything much until, in 1970, they were used to pacify – some would say, subjugate – Quebec. Not for Canada an overseas empire of military power and influence both economic and political. Not for Canadians the complex careers, replete with risks and opportunities, that flowed to Americans from that nation's imperial role. Not for Canadians the dislike and detestation that that role so often produced. Did Canadians wear the maple leaf pin so that people would know they were not Americans? Or so that they could recognize one another? Whatever the reasons, no one would accuse Canadians of cultural imperialism. They laughed about the 'American way of life' but rarely referred to their own, perhaps because it was so like the American. But whenever some American talked of exporting freedom, democracy, capitalism, free enterprise, or that American way of life, some Canadian could be found in the background, quietly chuckling. And however much Canadians might dislike the 'other side' in the Cold War, on the whole they refused to preach at it.

On the other hand, when surveying non-democratic regimes that were on 'our side,' Canadians were far more critical, not to say moralistic, than Americans, for whom considerations of power politics reinforced worries about Communism. No doubt many Americans did not like Spain, South Africa, Iran, or Saigon. Nevertheless, except with respect to South Vietnam, Canadians were much more likely to stand up and complain and ask awkward questions about democracy and freedom of speech, and also to worry about racial discrimination.

At first, it may be thought, moralizing came easily to Canadians, who could all too readily believe that their own country was not merely democratic but also unprejudiced. As time passed, there was less assurance about the home base. Canadians gradually learned that their own society did impose some barriers to upward mobility, that ethnicity did sometimes matter, that some of their fellow citizens – Inuit, Amerindian, Métis, even Ukrainian, not to mention the relatively new but rapidly growing communities of East and West Indian origin – did face discrimination in some directions and believed they faced it in others. Also, in the sixties and especially in the seventies, anglophone Canadians heard much more about the unhappiness of the francophones, whose leaders, both in Quebec and elsewhere, spoke increasingly not just of misunderstanding but of grievance.

The response was interesting, and really quite encouraging. Canadians did not stop moralizing about racism and oppression abroad, but at home they began to take matters in hand, profiting, perhaps, from the American example. In this respect, the landmarks, although not the only measures, are Diefenbaker's Bill of Rights and Trudeau's language legislation. Whatever one may think of these measures in and of themselves, they were steps in a direction of which most Canadians approved, no matter how their viscera might respond to the sound of French and the sight of 'colour.' In some respects too little, perhaps too late, possibly misconceived in detail, the new laws nevertheless represented part of a humane adaptation not only to change but to a reality that had been present, although incompletely perceived, for a long time. Many other measures, both federal and provincial, tended in the same direction; it is hard to think of any retrograde steps, except for the Quebec language legislation of the late seventies. In these important respects the legal evolution of the sixties and seventies is part of Canada's success story, while unilingual language laws are blots on the national escutcheon, from whatever province they may have emanated.

This is not to say that all has been for the best in the best of all possible Canadas. There are many things to deplore besides linguistic bigotry. Compared with their fellow Canadians of the late seventies, Canadians in the nineteen-forties may appear boring and limited, but in many respects they were probably less confused and less uncertain. Two authors of this book deplore the retreat of mainstream, organized religion; all three deplore the advance of formless cults and the tidal wave of self-seeking not only among politicians, where it has never been absent, but among artists, intellectuals, and other public subsidiaries and employees who must serve not only themselves but all Canadians. Some professions, both learned and semi- or pseudo-learned, show similar tendencies, to the obvious detriment not only of personal dignity but also of the standing of all professionals in the community.

But even here there are shreds of a silver lining inside the cloud of greed. When teachers strike, for instance, they are certainly behaving just like any other body of workers that wants more. The dedicated pedagogue has vanished, and in his stead is the suburbanite who wants the same things his college buddies have. But is it altogether bad for teachers to make demands on the community? In the past, Canadians could all too readily congratulate themselves on the splendours of their educational system while shamelessly underpaying and exploiting the teachers who ran the schools and taught the kids. Those days will not come again. No one should be sorry to see them gone.

In the pages that follow, readers will find assessments and judgments about recent events – events through which the authors have lived. Many readers will have lived through these events as well, and their recollections may differ from the account of events that is put together here. This does not necessarily mean that the authors are wrong and the reader is right; memories can be faulty, as any reader of memoirs or writer of contemporary history must readily admit. Many things in the book may surprise the reader, therefore; some of them surprised the authors too. Time may have altered perceptions of events, and, especially for the events of the sixties and seventies, far more documentary material than any historian or journalist is now allowed to see will eventually be available. In particular, these thirty-five years may come to look darker, or perhaps brighter, than the authors have found them. Still, it is important to assess the recent past, if only so that Canadians may better understand the present; whether history illumines the future only time will tell.

No part of Canada's history is as neglected or as misunderstood as that of the past thirty years. This is partly because people remember things selectively and often remember them wrong, and partly because most people did not and could not know very much about what was really happening. The job of the contemporary historian, therefore, is partly to check recollections and partly to fill in gaps by diligent research, or simply by the careful exploitation of published but neglected materials. While checking and filling in, one often has cause to be critical of the mass media. In part this is just the snobbishness of university people. But it does appear that the media have deteriorated. They have become increasingly disinclined to give the Canadian people accurate and unbiased information in sufficient quantity. Also, one can detect a tendency to personalize, and therefore to trivialize, almost everything. Here is one of the darker sides to Canada's recent history. Was it inevitable? Did things have to go that way? It may be that television, compared with radio, is a trivializing medium. Perhaps Canada's media people learned too much from the great neighbour to the south, and learned the wrong things. Or perhaps, if better men had been in charge at the top – whatever the reasons, it is partly because of the media that the reader of contemporary history, like the writer of it, is forced to reassess and relearn the past he has lived through.

Although this book concentrates on political developments, which have been so important for the shaping of post-war Canada, what follows is neither a straight-forward narrative history nor a purely political history. The book tries to bring together political, economic, social, and cultural developments since the end of the Second World War. It has seemed useful to divide the material among chapters on the basis of the various governments – Mackenzie King, St Laurent, and so on. This does not mean that the authors believe political events have priority. In particular, political events *per se* have not much to do with the direction of social and economic change, where governments often respond but seldom lead or cause. Neither does it mean that politics can simply be considered a reflection of economic forces. Economic developments run right through the period with a continuity that is impressive or depressing, depending on one's point of view. Hence, Part I of this book offers a survey of economic and demographic change, and, in addition, assembles some information about the monetary system and Canada's international economic obligations. As for cultural and social developments, this material is distributed through the other parts. It also seemed convenient to follow common usage and speak of the culture of the forties, the fifties, and so on. Somewhat to the authors' surprise, on looking into the matter we found that in many important respects the decades really *are* different from one another. Why this should be so remains a mystery.

Much that some would find important has had to be omitted. It is to be hoped that nothing really crucial has been left out. Because the authors believe that the past is relevant to the present and the future, it is also to be hoped that this volume will enrich memory and stimulate thought. If the book causes controversy we shall not be surprised; if it causes nothing but controversy we shall be disappointed.

The next four chapters of Part I survey some of the more important economic developments in post-war Canada: the growth of the economy and the money supply, the changing financial system, rising living standards, and the development of Canada's financial relations with the rest of the world. These topics, especially insofar as government policy affected the details of economic development and insofar as economic questions became matters for political controversy, will be discussed in Parts II through VI, although the reader should remember that this book does not try to give a minutely comprehensive account of economic developments since 1944. The opening chapters emphasize economic affairs for several reasons. First and most important, in Canada political arguments have largely been about economic affairs. Second, most Canadians have only the vaguest ideas of what has really been happening in the economy, and a necessary part of the historian's job is to peel away the confusion, illusion, and misinformation that have clustered so thickly around Canada's recent economic evolution. Third, by beginning with these durable and deep-seated movements in economic life the reader may be able to put political disputations in a more appropriate perspective. Finally, it would be both arbitrary and misleading to divide up economic evolution into the political compartments with which the rest of this book is concerned.

2

Economic Growth and Change

Canadians can rarely bring themselves to praise their own economic performance.[1] Yet if we compare our performance since 1945 with that of earlier decades or with that of many other countries, we must conclude that our record, though occasionally flawed, is still impressive. Our production and consumption have risen substantially faster than our population, and this rise has been almost without interruption. Only in 1945, 1946, and 1954 did our output actually fall, and these declines were very small indeed. Only in 1948 did consumption decline, and this decline was also of little moment. In the sixties and seventies living standards rose even more rapidly than in the late forties and fifties, although there were years, such as 1977 and 1978, when things slipped back a little.

Naturally this economic expansion was accompanied by a considerable growth in employment. In 1945, 4.4 million Canadians had civilian jobs; in 1979, over ten million. Only in 1945, 1954, and 1958 did employment actually fall. The first of these declines reflects the aftermath of the Second World War, when the economy was converting to peacetime activities; the second reflects the slight recession after the Korean War of 1950-3; the third reflects the recession that ended the economic boom of the mid-fifties.

The newspapers and parliamentary debates of the period give this remarkable progress and improvement relatively muted coverage, perhaps on the assumption that good news is not really news; instead they concern themselves primarily with gloomier topics – inflation, unemployment, and regional disparities – and, in the seventies, with energy problems. There is no doubt that on all of these scores the national performance was less splendid than many observers and critics would have

---

1 The numbers in this chapter come almost entirely from Statistics Canada, *National Income and Expenditure Accounts*, 1926-74, and later annual compilations. Methodology, coverage, and definition are all treated exhaustively in that publication.

liked. In 1979, as in 1947, incomes and living standards were much lower in the Atlantic provinces and Quebec than in the rest of the country. Furthermore, for much of the period there was a deterioration in Saskatchewan relative to Canada as a whole. As for inflation, by 1979 prices were much higher than in 1945, while unemployment had also tended to increase both absolutely and in relation to the labour force. Like the rate of inflation, the level and rate of unemployment changed in jerks and jolts. In twelve of the post-war years the number of unemployed actually fell and, because the labour force was rising steadily, the percentage of unemployed naturally fell too. As an absolute magnitude, unemployment fell in 1947, 1948, 1951, 1955-6, 1959, 1962-6, and 1973; as a percentage of the labour force, unemployment fell in all these years and also in 1969 and 1974. But as an absolute magnitude unemployment rose in 1945-6, 1949-50, 1952-4, 1957-8, 1960-1, 1967-8, 1970-2, and 1974-9, and as a percentage of the labour force it rose in all those years except 1972 and 1974, when rising employment outran rising unemployment.

These developments are summarized in Figures 1 through 4. The first figure shows the movement in total output and consumption; the second shows total employment and total unemployment; the third shows the movement in the general price level, that is to say, the rate of inflation; the fourth shows unemployment as a percentage of the labour force. In the first two figures one can readily perceive the smooth progress described above, while in the last two one sees the irregular and painful developments on which political controversy concentrated. Figure 4 also shows a sort of broad wave-like pattern, as unemployment rises from a low of 2.5 per cent in 1944 to a high of 8.5 per cent in 1978. Although the percentage falls to a low of 3.6 per cent in 1967, this was still higher than at any time in the late forties, or in the fifties before 1958. Thereafter the percentage rises once more, declines, and rises again, ending our period well above the level of 1961. Statistical analysis of this series reveals a slight upward trend, but the fit is not very good, and the picture may be distorted by unusually high numbers at the end of the period, and unusually low ones at the beginning.

Our figures seem to show a steady upward progress in output, employment, and prosperity. This is not a misleading impression. Since 1944 most Canadian families have been improving their situations most of the time, and the economy has grown almost fast enough to absorb the rapidly expanding labour force, which rose from 5.2 million in 1945 to nearly 11 million in 1979. Population rose from 11.9 million to 23.6 million, while output rose from $29.7 billion to $126.1 billion in 1978 (in both years outputs are valued at 1971 prices). It is not surprising, then, to find that the average income was much higher by the mid- to late-seventies than in the mid-forties. In 1944 it was $2,486 per head; in 1978, $5,388. In thirty-four years, hardly more than a generation, the average Canadian's living standard doubled. If we have

Figure 1 Growth in national output and some of its components (1971 dollars)

Billion $

Source: Statistics Canada, *National Income and Expenditure Accounts*
(recent years subject to revision)

Figure 2 Employment and unemployment

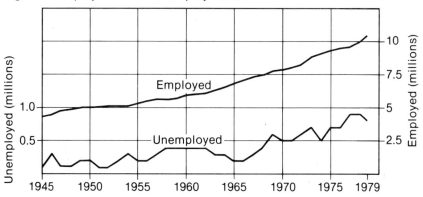

Source: Statistics Canada, *National Income and Expenditure Accounts* (recent years subject to revision)

Figure 3 Price index of national output (1971 = 100)

Source: Statistics Canada, *National Income and Expenditure Accounts* (recent years subject to revision)

Figure 4 Unemployment as a percentage of labour force
Per cent

Source: Statistics Canada, *National Income and Expenditure Accounts* (recent years subject to revision)

lost ground with respect to pollution and congestion, we have certainly gained a great deal along more mundane and more measurable paths. This basic fact lies behind the cultural and social transformations of our time, no less than the economic.

Of course Canada's progress did not occur quite as smoothly as the figures' broad outlines suggest. The economy did not grow at the same rate year after year. Since the labour force was expanding remorselessly year after year, and more rapidly in the sixties and seventies than in the forties and fifties, the economy sometimes failed to grow in step with its labour force, although sometimes it grew more rapidly. Hence the fluctuations in the number of jobless.

Why did the economy not grow more smoothly? In an economy like Canada's, citizens and businesses plan their own spending and over one-quarter of the nation's production is sold abroad. It is to be expected, economists agree, that these private spending plans, both domestic and foreign, will accumulate to produce periods of rapid growth and periods of slower growth, or even of slump. It is probably just good luck that Canadian output slumped only in the post-war readjustment of 1945-6 and in the readjustment of 1954 that followed the Korean War. It is also lucky that even in those three years, output fell very little.

These 'mysterious' spurts and lags are usually linked to the behaviour of two big items – exports and investment outlays on new buildings, housing, plant, equipment, and inventories. Export volume and value depend on foreigners' willingness to buy Canada's goods and services. This will change from time to time, depending on many things: the levels of economic activity in the United States and elsewhere, prices and the exchange rate, tariffs and import controls in other countries, and the discovery of new productive possibilities within Canada, especially in the resource-based industries such as oil and forest products. Investment outlays also vary. Some are made by governments, but in Canada most are made by businesses, and these businesses act with an eye to the chance of profit. These chances change from time to time, and so do both businessmen's perceptions of them and their assessments of the risks. Other changes, like those that occur from time to time in the cost of finance or its availability, can also affect businessmen's eagerness to build new things – new factories, perhaps, or new houses and apartment buildings. It is hardly surprising, then, that investment outlay, what economists often call 'capital forma-tion,' does not simply rise every year, or that it sometimes falls. As for the other kinds of spending, the only important ones are household consumption outlays and government outlays on current operations. Although in principle each could change in such a way as to affect the growth rate, in practice both continue monotonously upward, and, for the purposes of this discussion, can be safely ignored.

The following paragraphs trace the interactions among exports, new investment outlays, growth, and unemployment between 1944 and 1978. The data used in these paragraphs have been adjusted so as to eliminate the distorting effects or price increases. (Statistics Canada has produced a series of output and expenditure data in which the prices of 1971 are applied to the physical outputs of other years, and the results are then added up, year by year.) Naturally this calculation involves a good many estimates and some guesses; but the results are reliable enough for most purposes, including those of the present argument.

From 1944 until 1957, recovery and expansion were fuelled by business spending on new plant and equipment, and by new house building. In the late forties, export volumes diminished sharply and almost continuously from the extremely high levels to which wartime demands had pushed them. After falling 21 per cent from 1944 to 1950, only in 1955 did export volumes pass the 1943-4 level: the increase from 1954 to 1957 was only 17 per cent and from 1944 to 1957 only 6 per cent. As national output rose 64 per cent over the same thirteen-year period, it was obviously not export volumes that were providing the engine for growth. On the other hand, export *prospects* were good, especially in the non-agricultural, resource-based industries; this fact was reflected in the high and rising level of new investment in plant and equipment which, by 1953, had risen 253 per cent above the depressed wartime level of 1944. From 1952 to 1957 the level of new investment rose another 66 per cent, or 249 per cent over-all. Meanwhile, governments were spending ever more on schools, roads, and other buildings and equipment; they were even spend-ing a little on housing. Though still far smaller than the comparable sorts of private investment outlays, the volume of such government purchases was rising steadily and quickly – 776 per cent from 1944 to 1957.

Just as the expansion of 1946-57 was fuelled by investment outlays, so the deceleration of 1957-61 can be blamed on a falling away of investment. Admittedly national output did not fall. Neither did national consumption. Except in 1958, employment also increased with convenient speed in the late fifties and early sixties. National output grew 2.9 per cent per year, while consumption rose 3.4 per cent per year, comfortably outgrowing both population and labour force. Nevertheless, from 1946 to 1956 the record had been considerably better. Output had grown 5.3 per cent per year, and consumption 5.1 per cent; unemployment had been much lower.

What went wrong after 1956? The performance of exports was not to blame. Although export volumes fell in 1958, they revived thereafter, and in 1961 they were 16 per cent higher than in 1957, a better record than in the forties or the early fifties. As for other types of investment outlay – government spending on construction and equipment went up 35 per cent and, in the private sector, house building went up 5 per cent. Unfortunately, the private sector was spending less on new non-residential structures, plant, and equipment. Such outlays declined in 1958, 1959, and 1960; in 1961 they were 9 per cent lower than they had been in 1957.

Since the Liberals gave up office to the Conservatives in 1957 and did not return to power until 1963, it might seem that the Conservatives were responsible for the slowdown of the late fifties and the Liberals for the revival in the sixties. But it would be inaccurate to distribute praise or blame in this way. Although the Liberals were still in office during the first half of 1957, the slowdown had already begun before the Conservatives took power: output in 1957 was only 2.3 per cent larger than in 1956, while unemployment was already rising. The Tories inherited a retardation, but they did not cause it. Whether their actions made it worse is a question which will be scrutinized in Part IV. Similarly, in the early sixties there were already signs of a change during 1961, although unemployment peaked in that year. Business was already spending a little more on plant and equipment, and there was a further increase in 1962, when total investment grew 4.5 per cent, exports 3.9 per cent, and total output 6.8 per cent. In 1962 unemployment was markedly lower than in 1961. The Liberals, then, inherited the beginnings of a boom; they did not create one, although perhaps their later actions may have prolonged it or increased its size. This question also is explored later, in Part V.

Once the boom of the sixties was under way, its progress was impressive. From 1961 until 1966, exports and business fixed investment rose together at rates of growth close to the rate at which investment had grown in the early fifties. The propulsive force was remarkably strong and, thanks to this double propulsion, output and employment rose steadily and rapidly, while unemployment fell. For a while, the growth of the economy once more outstripped the labour force. Between 1961 and 1966 the unemployment percentage fell from 7.2 to 3.6 per cent of the labour force.

After 1966, while exports continued to rise steadily to 1973, fixed investment fell in 1967 and 1968, entirely because business was spending less on new non-residential plant and equipment. Because of this decline the unemployment rate began to rise once more, and although investment recovered in 1969 and thereafter, the expansion was not enough to absorb all the new workers. Thus employment, output, living standards, and unemployment all rose together. By 1971, 6.4 per cent of the labour force was out of work. Matters improved in 1972-4, when the economy grew 4.8 per cent per year and unemployment fell to 5.4 per cent, even though in 1974, for the first time since 1958, export volumes actually fell a little. Thereafter exports, investment, and output all faltered together. In 1975 export volumes fell still more, and the recovery in 1976 left the volume still below the 1974 level; but there were strong recoveries in 1977 and 1978, when export volumes rose 10 per cent per year. Investment outlays, unfortunately, were less accommodating. Total investment outlays rose strongly through 1973-5, rose a little more in 1976 and 1977, and then fell a little in 1978, when business did not raise its spending on new plant and equipment enough to offset the decline in spending on new housing. At the same time, physical output was rising, and the increase, though varying from year to year, was substantial, averaging 3.1 per cent per year from 1975 through 1978. Employment grew also – from 9.1 million in 1975 to 10 million in 1978 – but the labour force was growing still faster; and so the number of unemployed rose from half a million in 1974 to nine hundred thousand in 1978 and the unemployment rate rose from 5.3 to 8.4 per cent.

The economy's impressive growth during this period was paralleled by an equally dramatic change in its structure. Although few industries declined absolutely, some became less important relative to others. Not only have production patterns altered; there have also been far-reaching changes in the things Canadians do and in the industries where they work. Figures 5 through 7 summarize the changing patterns of production and employment. The reader should remember that all three figures are calculated in terms of percentages, which may decline when the absolute magnitude is increasing. Thus, for instance, in Figure 5, it would be quite wrong to conclude that Canada is becoming 'de-industrialized' simply because manufacturing and construction are now somewhat less important *relative to other industries* than they were in the late forties.

In these figures two things stand out. First of all, agriculture is far less important than it was in the 1940s, both as a producer of output and as an absorber of labour. Indeed, the mining industry, though an insignificant employer, now produces more than agriculture does. Second, the real Canadian 'growth industry' is 'public administration plus defence plus service activities' – that is, government offices, education, health, miscellaneous service industries, and in principle the armed forces, although these have actually declined since the war. In 1944-6 this sector was inflated in

Figure 5 Industrial origins of national output

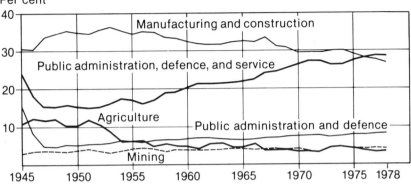

Source: Statistics Canada, *National Income and Expenditure Accounts*
(recent years subject to revision)

Figure 6 Employment in industry group: percentages of total employment

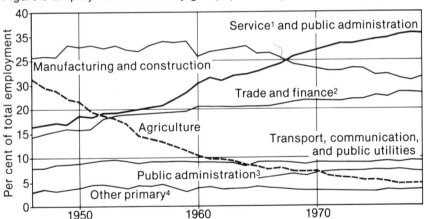

1 Business, community, and personal service (including education, medicine, and law)
2 Wholesale and retail trade, finance, insurance, and real estate
3 Not separately estimated before 1965, except in census years
4 Forestry, fishing, mining, oilwell drilling, trapping, quarrying

Sources: *Historical Statistics of Canada,* Statistics Canada *The Labour Force* (71-001), and *Historical Labour Force Statistics* (71-201)

Figure 7 Changing mix of occupations:
          percentages of total employment 1948-79

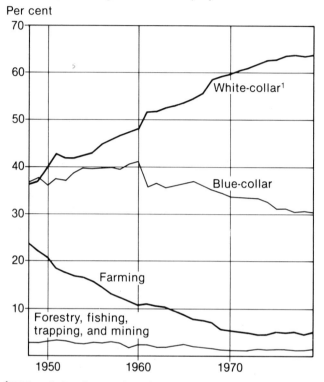

Per cent

[1]'White-collar' workers are those in managerial, professional, clerical, commercial, financial, and service occupations. 'Blue-collar' workers are all others, except those in farming, forestry, fishing, trapping, or mining occupations.

Sources: *Historical Statistics of Canada;* Statistics Canada, *The Labour Force; Canada Year Book*

importance because the war was still under way. Once it was over, the sector accounted for only about 15 per cent of output, and relatively few Canadians laboured in it. In 1946, public administration and defence contributed only 4.5 per cent of national output. By 1975, however, it accounted for 7.8 per cent of output, while the whole 'growth industry' produced 28.4 per cent, only slightly less than the 28.9 per cent that came from manufacturing and construction, a sector that in the 1940s and 1950s typically accounted for 32 per cent of output or more.

Compared with agriculture or manufacturing the great national 'growth industry' employs a disproportionately large number of white-collar workers, especially highly educated labour, because so few of its tasks can be mechanized. This is in part why the transformation of employment, recorded in Figure 6, is even more striking than the transformation of production. Because of the expansion of white-collar jobs and the fact that so many of the white-collar workers have to be extensively educated and trained, the well-educated have usually had little trouble finding attractive jobs in post-war Canada. The occupational pattern is affected not only by the growth of these service and administrative industries but also by the increasing importance of wholesale and retail trade and finance, and by a change in the nature of production in manufacturing, transportation, and many other sectors, which demand ever more skilled workers, ever more white-collar workers, and ever fewer labourers. In Canada, as in other well-developed industrial countries, economic growth has gone hand in hand with a changing pattern of work and life. Figure 7 shows just how drastic the change has been.

These changes produced remarkably few stresses or strains. Because more and more young people were seeking more and more schooling, the expanding economy was generally able to get the sorts of worker it needed. Where gaps appeared, immigrants filled them. Cities grew because so many of the expanding activities were based in cities; and, although land and housing prices rose, this urbanization was noticeably trouble-free, especially in comparison with developments in some other countries. Agriculture had to shed labour, but in most parts of the country it could do so by attrition; the older farmers retired, and their children, better schooled than their parents, moved off to city jobs. In some parts of the country agricultural depression speeded the process because the new urban jobs paid much better than the old agricultural work. In other places, notably around the larger cities, the value of agricultural land rose dramatically, often because it was in demand for non-agricultural uses. This provided many farmers with an added incentive to retire – with very substantial nest eggs. And even where farm prices and incomes were depressed, land prices often seemed tied to the general prosperity of the country, not to the troubled agricultural economy. Perhaps land-buyers hoped for better times. If so they were not disappointed; by the early 1970s agricultural prices were rising relative to other prices, and agricultural incomes had begun to rise dramatically relative to urban incomes.

This is not to say that everything adjusted itself with perfect smoothness. For agriculture there were certain troubles, chiefly in areas where land was not very good, where it had always been hard to make a decent living from the soil, and where alternative, non-agricultural uses did not appear. In such zones, largely in Quebec, the Atlantic provinces, and northern Ontario, the agricultural shrinkage was far from painless, and by the early sixties the national government had become concerned about the problem. Before 1957, other parts of the economy were hit by labour shortages: some businesses had trouble finding the skilled workers they wanted at the wages they were willing to pay, and it was hard for school boards to find enough teachers. These troubles reflected the fact that in the fifties the Canadian labour force was growing rather slowly; they may also have reflected some deficiencies in the educational system, which has always had trouble producing skilled tradesmen. Politicians responded to these problems in various ways, and there is some discussion of the responses in Parts IV and V.

Although a rise in average living standards and in per-capita input are evidence of economic progress and health, the accuracy of such a diagnosis is always open to question without evidence that the distribution of income has also improved. At the same time, conclusive proof about changes in the distribution of wealth is hard to come by, because not everyone agrees about what is meant by 'improvement.' Did all persons or groups share equally in the advance? Did anyone lose absolutely? Did the incomes of various groups come closer together, or move farther apart? Even if everyone gained, did some people – capitalists? city-dwellers? doctors? – gain by an unfair amount? Finally, what about the people of the various regions?

To make matters worse, one may examine the 'distribution of income' from various angles. One can simply set up a list of categories – for instance, incomes below $1,000, between $1,000 and $10,000, over $10,000 – and then ask how many people or households fall into each category. Such results, drawn up for various dates and corrected for inflation, can then be analysed in various ways. On the other hand, one can take the average income of some group – farmers or Inuit or Newfoundlanders or coalminers – and compare it with the average income of some other group – mill workers or Indians or Ontarians or 'capitalists.' Canadians specialize in such comparisons, which can be trusted to breed resentment. Since different observers are interested in different groups this operation can go on forever. Further, since the comparison can be made in various ways there is no guarantee that any two observers will agree on the answer even if they are asking about the same groups.

Hypothetical questions often complicate the issue further. What would have happened to the distribution of income if the economy had not grown, and if consumption per head had not increased? Conditions in other, less well-off countries suggest that all Canadians have benefited from growth. The example of the aged is instructive here. With the passage of time, people move through an income cycle that parallels their life cycle. Usually the young adult earns less than he or she can expect to earn in middle life, while the elderly, whether employed or not, typically receive less than they did in their fifties. No one really expects that economic growth will somehow prevent this decline, although some reformers sometimes talk as if they think it ought to. In fact, by the seventies, Canada was making far better provision for the elderly than it had made in the forties or fifties, and the country could afford this, both economically and politically, because of economic growth.

The same is true of unemployment insurance and other forms of support for the able-bodied. Canada does far better under these headings than it did in the forties.

Again, growth has provided the resources for an improvement in welfare and income-maintenance. Without such improvements pensioners and the unemployed would be far worse off *than they are now*, whether or not they have become better off or worse off relative to the able-bodied employed or to capitalists or to some other reference group. It is widely thought that if a society does not use some of the fruits of growth to provide for the elderly and helpless in a more humane way there is something badly wrong with that society – whatever the indices of growth or distribution may say. Judged by that criterion, Canada has not done badly in the past thirty years.

In general, it seems clear that all the regions and most identifiable groups have shared in the economic advance of Canada since 1945. Living standards have risen everywhere, and the vast majority of Canadians are far better off than their parents were thirty years ago. They are also better off than they would have been or could have been if the income levels of 1945 had continued to 1964 or 1979. The fruits of growth have been widely shared and widely enjoyed. Whether the sharing has been fair, just, or equitable is of course another question.

It would be foolish, however, to claim that *everyone* is better off or that *nobody* has lost, whether absolutely or relatively. The most obvious losers have been the wheat farmers, whose earnings have not always kept up with their costs. Here and there, too, workers and capitalists have been unable to extract themselves and their funds from declining industries. Such people cannot be called the victims of economic growth, since it was not the growth that caused their troubles. But certainly the growth has done little for them, except in so far as government has become more able and willing to pay subsidies, unemployment insurance, welfare benefits, and so forth.

Because the economic structure has been evolving in such a way as to create more openings in the white-collar and professional occupations, more and more Canadians have found such jobs. In them, incomes are often relatively high and working conditions are almost invariably better than in labouring or in routine factory work. It is true that for some of the lower-level white-collar skills, earnings have fallen relative to the earnings of factory workers. But hours of work have generally been shorter and the working environment usually more pleasant, while fringe benefits have often been better. The professional and managerial groups, whose earnings were unequivocally higher than the average and whose working conditions were generally much more pleasant, increased in number relative to the total population, thus giving relatively high earnings to a comparatively large and fast-growing group. Indeed, for some components of this group (teachers and doctors, for example) earnings rose relative to the national average just when numbers were also growing unusually fast. Thus, the period in question has seem a dramatic shift of population into higher-income occupations where working conditions are comparatively attractive. This shift has absorbed much of the increase in output per head because society

Figure 8 Distribution of income in Canada,[1] 1951 and 1977[1]

Cumulative percentages of income

Cumulative percentages of spending units

1977

1951

[1] Data cover families and unattached individuals, but 1951 data omit those on farms.

Sources: Statistics Canada, *Income Distributions... 1951-1965*
(13-529) and *Income Distributions... 1977* (13-207)

was using so much more of these comparatively expensive kinds of labour. Most people would approve of the result. It is one of the ways in which the fruits of economic growth were spread among larger numbers of Canadians. But whether this change could be said to have resulted in a more 'equal distribution of income' is questionable.

Figure 8 summarizes the information about the distribution of incomes among the population at various dates. The incomes include such payments as old-age pensions and unemployment insurance benefits. Income taxes have not been deducted. Each line shows what proportion of total family income accrues to each fraction of the population in a particular year. If income were equally distributed, so that every family had the same income as every other family, the dotted line would lie along the diagonal line. If income were distributed in a perfectly unequal way, so that one family got all of it, the dotted line would lie along the horizontal axis and would then climb the right-hand margin. Thus the more deepy bowed the dotted line the more unequal the income-distribution – in the sense that the lower-income groups receive a comparatively small share of total income, and the higher-income groups receive a relatively large share.

It would appear that Canada had much the same distribution of family income in 1977 as in 1951. The poorer groups seem to get a slightly smaller share in 1977, but this is only because the 1951 data do not cover farm families. For those who want the situation to become more egalitarian the result will not be altogether attractive. On the other hand, things have not become more unequal either.

To compare the differences in incomes among the various regions, average personal income – a figure that the national statisticians regularly produce – is used. It includes all sorts of pre-tax family income. There is no adjustment for differences in living costs, which may vary widely from region to region. Figure 9 summarizes the events.

For those who worry about regional disparities the general picture ought to be encouraging. In Newfoundland, Prince Edward Island, New Brunswick, and Quebec, incomes have risen toward the national average; in British Columbia and Ontario they have fallen relative to that average, while rising substantially in absolute levels. In Nova Scotia and on the prairies the picture is more mixed, but in 1944 these provinces were by no means the poorest in the country. On the prairies we see the joint effect of agricultural difficulty and mineral wealth. The result is fluctuation relative to the national average. In 1978 the citizens of Saskatchewan were worse off in comparison to that average than they were in 1944, while the citizens of Manitoba and Alberta were somewhat better off. In Nova Scotia the situation worsened for twenty years and then improved, leaving the typical Nova Scotian no worse off in comparison to the national level in 1978 than in 1944. But the populations of Nova Scotia and Saskatchewan, where matters have grown no better, are small in comparison to the total population of the rest of the country, where incomes have moved closer to the national average.

Why has Canada done so well for more than thirty years? In general, it appears that Canadians have simply made good use of fundamentally favourable conditions. The nation's labour force has been growing; new raw materials and new uses for old ones have been discovered; much of the time world markets have been favourable to Canada's exports; the country has accumulated new, more productive, and more efficient plant and equipment; its workers have grown more skilful and its managers more effective; and Canada has eagerly imported new technical knowledge from the United States and elsewhere while developing more than a little for itself.

These are the normal processes by which an industrial economy raises its power to produce, and Canada, like the United States, western Europe, or Japan, has benefited from these processes, which have been at work here for a very long time.

Figure 9 Personal income per capita: provincial data as percentage of
national average

Source: Statistics Canada, *National Income and Expenditure Accounts*
(recent years subject to revision)

Nor has Canada's recent history been particularly unusual. It closely parallels the American experience, and although Britain has done less well and Japan and continental western Europe have done very much better, the same sort of growth has been happening throughout the industrialized countries of the capitalist world. By using more 'inputs' – labour, machinery, natural resources – Canada raises its output; by using 'inputs' more efficiently it can raise its output per unit of input, thus getting a double return, so to speak. It is this double return that accounts for the rise in living standards. To achieve this all-important efficiency, up-to-date technology applied correctly in light of the supplies and costs of the various inputs and Canada's marketing opportunities is essential; the abiity to adapt despite the dislocation that a new machine or a new production process or a new arrangement may entail is also crucial. Where such changes have been resisted, as in the United Kingdom, the country has lost much of the benefit from technological progress and even from the accumulation of new plant. As a result, outputs and living standards have risen more slowly than they might have done. Where changes have been swallowed readily and eagerly, as in West Germany or Japan, outputs and living standards have risen very rapidly indeed. Relative to Britain, Canada and the United States have responded reasonably well to technological change and dislocation. At least, that has been so during most of the period since 1944. By 1979, however, some observers were wondering whether Canada might not have caught the 'British disease.' Although some signs do point in that direction, the evidence is conflicting and inconclusive.

Finally, a word about the relation between economic growth and the quality of life. In some circles it is now fashionable to assert that economic growth is a bad thing because, we are told, it causes pollution, congestion, and the depletion of natural resources, or because it creates pressures for change or for hard work that make people unhappy. Such criticisms, though not altogether empty, are frequently made by people who know no history. It must be remembered that for the great masses in Canada economic growth has provided an escape from a life of grinding poverty. That escape must be placed in the balance, along with the costs of congestion, stress, urbanization, and change. Also on the postive side of the balance must go many 'non-economic' benefits. Increased wealth permits Canada to subsidize the arts, run a decent social security system, look after the poor and the aged, deal with pollution if it chooses to do so, and develop new technologies that will offset, wholly or in part, the depletion of natural resources. The 'golden age' of the past was at best a pretty tarnished piece of silver plate with a large admixture of base metal. Rather than longing for it, Canadians would do better to seize the opportunities for betterment – personal and national – that the nation's economic success now offers them.

3

The Demographic Background

Demographic developments influenced society profoundly.[1] So did 'demographic echoes,' especially from the late 1920s and 1930s. It was births rather than deaths that mattered most. Admittedly there was a general tendency for people to live longer. In 1951 a male baby might expect to live sixty-six years and a female baby seventy-one years. By 1966 life expectancies had increased to sixty-nine years for males and seventy-five years for females. The death rate fell from 8.5 per thousand in the early fifties to 7.3 per thousand in the early seventies. These improvements were noticeable in all parts of the country. In the Yukon and Northwest Territories they were especially dramatic. In Saskatchewan and two Atlantic provinces death rates did not fall because young people tended to leave these provinces, but life expectancies increased.

In a general way we know why people were living longer. The body and its functions were better understood. The chemical industry had developed new and more effective medicines. The federal and provincial governments had introduced insurance schemes which reduced or removed the financial barriers to medical care. Relative to population there were more doctors and more dentists. As people became more prosperous they were more likely to be properly fed, clothed, and sheltered. These improvements offset the negative effects of prosperity on life expectancy because of drink, tobacco, food additives, pollution, and the risk of a car crash.

Although the elderly became more numerous, the population did not age very much. In 1951 7.7 per cent of the population was aged sixty-five or more; in 1972 the percentage was still only 8.1. As the economy was becoming much more produc-

---

1 Demographic data in this chapter are based on material in M.C. Urquhart and K.A.H. Buckley, eds, *Historical Statistics of Canada* (Toronto: Macmillan 1965), the *Canada Year Book*, and *Statistics Canada Daily*.

tive it could easily provide for the elderly. In this regard two things were especially important. One was a contributory and relatively generous pension scheme, the Canada Pension Plan. Another was medical insurance, which is of special importance to the old. In addition, governments and private agencies did something to provide decent housing and other services for 'senior citizens.' Such things were needed because many urban families could not, and some families would not, care for their own elderly relatives. Detecting a 'crisis of the elderly,' social workers and publicists worked mightily to sway public opinion in the right direction; governments were impressed by the results, and they were not unaware that old people had votes.

Men were living longer chiefly because they were less likely to die in childhood or adolescence: from 1941 to 1966 the life expectancy of a twenty-five-year-old male increased by less than two years, and for a sixty-five-year-old man the increase was only ten months. Over the same period the young female gained more than five years, and the elderly female, more than two. In terms of life expectancy, therefore, women increased the lead that they had long enjoyed.

As infectious diseases were controlled by vaccination and drugs, while deficiency diseases were controlled by better nutrition and housing, some diseases dwindled in importance while others became much more important causes of death. By the early seventies almost no one died of syphilis, tuberculosis, cholera, typhoid, diphtheria, polio, or smallpox. The diseases of the young had been reduced almost to statistical insignificance. The principal killers were now heart disease, cancer, and accidents, including motor accidents.

All these developments imposed strains on the medical services and on the ingenuity of governments and officials, who had to devise schemes first for financing health care and pensions and then for controlling the costs of the new programs. But the pressures and strains built up slowly. Because the changes were gradual, regular, and easy to predict, society digested them with relative ease. Unfortunately for Canada's governments, neither births nor migrations behaved in so helpful a way.

When discussing births, demographers use a private terminology that incorporates some important distinctions. Before looking at Canada's experience with fertility we should stop and define the terms that we have had to borrow from the demographers. First and most basic is the 'crude birth rate.' This is calculated by dividing total population into total births. It is called 'crude' because it gives only a rough indication of fertility as it is affected by two things – the proportion of women in the population, and the size of the childbearing age group – that have nothing to do with what an economist once called 'the propensity to have children.' Hence demographers have devised 'age-specific fertility rates,' which divide the babies up according to the age of the mothers; they then relate each group of babies to the number of women in that age category. Finally we encounter the 'gross and net reproduction rates.' These show whether the population is producing enough girl-babies to maintain itself, given the age-specific fertility rates at a particular time. The gross rate ignores the possiblity that some girl-babies will die before they reach childbearing age; the net rate is adjusted to allow for this event. Whenever the net reproduction rate is one or higher, the current pattern of fertility ensures that the population will not fall. But in calculating the rate for, say 1970, the demographers have to assume that 1970 fertility rates will continue to apply, at least until the girl-babies of 1970 are in their forties. History shows that this expectation is unfounded. Thus the reproduction rates cannot rightly be used to make population forecasts. On the other hand, they are the only means for summing up all the relevant data – actual births, the size-distribution of the population by age, and age-specific fertility rates – as these exist at a particular moment of time.

In this century, the gross reproduction rate has fluctuated dramatically. In 1926 it was 1.6, a figure that implies a considerable rate of natural increase. The rate then fell to about 1.3 in the thirties, as fertility rates declined in a striking way. In 1946 it had risen to 1.64; although among older women fertility rates were still lower than in the 1920s, among women in their twenties fertility rates were very much higher than they had been for many years, and for women in their early thirties fertility was almost as high as in the 1920s. The 'post-war baby boom' was underway.

In the forties and fifties young women became steadily more fertile although older women became steadily less so. The peak was reached in 1959 when the gross reproduction rate was 1.915. The chances were better than one in five that if a woman was in her twenties, she would produce a baby in the year 1959! Further, if the 1959 pattern had continued the typical girl-baby of 1959 would in due course have produced 1.915 girl-babies. Population obviously would have grown very fast indeed, even if people lived no longer and even if Canada repelled all immigrants.

Fortunately the young women of Canada quickly came to their senses. Early in the 1960s they became much less fertile. Throughout the sixties and early seventies, the age-specific fertility rates fell spectacularly. By 1971, the rates among young women were only 50 to 60 per cent of what they had been in 1961. The gross reproduction rate had fallen to 1.061. That is, if the fertility patterns of 1971 were to become permanent, by 1971 the women of Canada were barely producing enough babies to reproduce the population.

Crude birth rates followed the same general pattern. Although they add little to our knowledge we shall glance at them, because some readers will probably find them easier to understand. In 1937 the crude birth rate was 20.1 births per thousand inhabitants, and in 1946, 27.2. The rate stayed at or slightly above that figure for the balance of the 1940s and through the 1950s. Then it fell steadily, reaching 16.8 in 1971 and 15.3 in 1978.

In all provinces and territories the same general movements occurred. In the Northwest Territories fertility started higher, rose much higher, and stayed higher longer than elsewhere. In the Maritime provinces and Alberta, fertility rose so high as to pass the level of Quebec, which, with Newfoundland, had long possessed relatively high fertility. But in the 1960s Quebec's collapse was extraordinarily speedy and complete. By 1969 the crude birth rate was lower in Quebec than anywhere else in Canada.

Why does fertility change so much? No one really knows. Historians and demographers can provide some explanations for particular periods, but no one has a general theory that is worth much, especially because many countries seem to experience the same sorts of swing at the same times. Thus birth rates were low in the United States and western Europe during the 1930s, and the baby boom hit those countries just as much as Canada.

Scholars generally agree that the Depression of the 1930s had a depressing effect on fertility, and that to some extent the post-war baby boom was a catching-up process. Similar booms have followed other great wars. But few such post-war booms have gone on for as long as fifteen years. Hence economists have devised an explanation that bases iself on the 'echo effect' from the low birth rates of the 1930s.

Recall that the babies of the thirties are the new workers of the fifties. Because so few children were born during the Depression, young workers were relatively scarce in the fifties. Therefore they could get good jobs quickly, and their pay was often remarkably high compared with starting pay in earlier decades or with the earnings of older and more experienced workers. Also, the 1950s were good years to set up housekeeping. Thanks to technological change, cars and household durables were becoming cheaper relative to incomes. Gasoline and fuel were also relatively cheap. Compared with current incomes, land and housing were much less expensive than they later became, because technological change was affecting construction to some extent and because few new families were being formed. Hence the temptation to acquire two cars and four babies, and adopt the suburban style of life.

If the economists are correct, things should have begun to change once the babies of the 1940s began to enter the labour force. If the old pre-war patterns had persisted, that would have begun to happen on a large scale at or around the age of fifteen, that is, around 1960. Becoming more plentiful, young workers would have placed strains on the economic fabric that would have made marriage and child-bearing costly compared with the 1950s. The result would have been a fall in fertility. But if any such effect was present it was damped and delayed as more and more teenagers stayed on in school or continued their educations in universities. Thus it cannot have been important until after 1965, although fertility was already falling by 1960.

In popular culture the fall-off is blamed on the 'pill,' which for the first time provided an almost foolproof, invisible, dignified contraceptive that women themselves could control. The first such pills became available late in the 1950s, and soon they were in common use. Perhaps if the country had been poorer they would not have been taken up so quickly. After all, in really poor countries they are not much used, even in the 1970s. Perhaps, too, if the churches had maintained their authority and their opposition to contraception, the pill would have had less effect. But in the 1960s the Roman Catholic Church was rapidly losing its authority in such matters, and Roman Catholics were increasingly willing to use the pill; other churches had long since abandoned their opposition. For Quebec, in particular, the attitude of the Church had once been of extreme importance in maintaining the birth rate. But the pill arrived just when the worldwide Church was trying to appear more flexible and up-to-date. At the same time, in Quebec, the role of the Church was changing, as ecclesiastical authorities turned over their institutions and programs to lay people and to the provincial government. By 1970, admittedly, Rome had thundered once more against birth control in general and the pill in particular. But by then the pope's words were falling on deaf ears.

Finally one must observe the effect of 'women's liberation' and the 'women's movement.' After all, it is very hard for a woman to have four or five babies and a career as well. Prosperous though Canada had become, few couples could afford the servants that would make such a life possible. As for day nurseries, these came only much later, in the sixties. Thus the educated housewife of the 1950s was often trapped in a world of green lawns, barbecues, and diapers which offered little challenge and less diversion. It was not unusual by 1960 for newly married couples to think of limiting their family size so as to have a more pleasant and interesting style of life. By the mid-sixties the women's movement was on hand to provide an ideology and a justification that could only move things in the same direction.

These demographic developments created opportunities as well as problems. Before 1957, when the Canadian-born labour force was growing relatively slowly, it was fairly easy for the government to maintain full employment and also to admit large numbers of immigrants. For practical and humanitarian reasons immigration was a 'good thing': Canada could absorb displaced persons in the forties, refugee Hungarians in the mid-fifties, and disgruntled Britons throughout. Even after 1957, when the boom of the mid-fifties faded, for Canada's university graduates prospects remained relatively bright. For this there were two reasons. First, the elementary and secondary schools were expanding rapidly and more and more often the schools insisted on hiring graduates. Second, business continued to hire new, qualified graduates. And because births had been few in the late 1930s, in the late 1950s such graduates were also few relative to demand.

In the 1960s the events of the late fifties produced an echo that might have been predicted. Observing that the better-educated had passed through the fifties unscathed, schools and parents tried to convince pupils to stay in secondary school and to seek higher education. Noticing that the economic expansion of the fifties had depended heavily on the importation of skills, the dominion government decided that Canada must have more technical and vocational education. These developments kept people in school longer, made the secondary schools bigger, and thus delayed the movement from school to work while supporting an ever larger demand for teachers, especially in secondary schools and universities. Thus for graduates the job prospects remained good, and once the economy began to grow faster the government felt justified in admitting more immigrants. In the forties and fifties Canada had digested them by the thousands; why not in the sixties and seventies?

The answer came with chilling directness. By 1970 the elementary schools had begun to shrink, and it was already clear that, as the smaller classes of the sixties worked their way through the school system, secondary schools would shrink too. So would the universities and community colleges, unless they could attract a larger fraction of each cohort. But now the market for graduates had softened, partly because the economy was growing more slowly and irregularly and partly because schoolteaching could no longer absorb many new graduates. Because such developments reduced the rewards from further study, they weakened the incentive to stay on in school, college, or university. The boom babies of the forties and fifties began to push their way onto the labour market. In any event they would not have stayed in school forever; sooner or later they would have emerged and looked for jobs. And on the labour market they met a tide of immigrant workers that the national government seemed unable or perhaps unwilling to control.

Canada has long been a country both of immigration and of emigration. Before 1914 the settlement of the prairies generated a wave of immigration that peaked in 1913, when 400,870 people were admitted. That figure has never since been approached. But in the late 1920s immigration again became substantial, only to fall away to almost nothing in the 1930s. Indeed, it is estimated that during that decade of depression Canada lost more by emigration than it gained by immigration. During the Second World War immigration dwindled still further, but it revived sharply after the end of hostilities, partly because Canada agreed to absorb refugees and displaced persons from continental Europe. Between the end of 1946 and the end of 1958 we absorbed 223,299 such people – chiefly Czechs, Germans, Jews, Hungarians, Poles, Ukrainians, Russians, and Yugoslavians. During those years refugee migration was only 13 per cent of the total; most migrants were of other sorts.

In the years since 1945 immigration has fluctuated, reflecting changes in government policy and variations in employment prospects here and abroad. The numbers rose from 12,000 in 1944 to 125,000 in 1948, then fell to 74,000 in 1950, only to rise to a post-war peak of 282,000 in 1957. In the slower growth of the late fifties and early sixties immigration fell to 72,000 in 1961. It then rose to 223,000 in 1967 and remained well over the 100,000-person mark until 1978, when it fell to 70,000. Emigration has been important also, although one cannot be precise about the fluctuations because Canada does not keep any emigration statistics. Fortunately, by

TABLE 1
Sources of Canada's Population Growth 1941-78 (thousands)

	Increase	Natural increase	Immigration	Emigration	Territorial growth[1]
1941-51	2,503	1,992	548	382	365
1951-61	4,228	3,148	1,543	463	0
1961-71	3,330	2,608	1,415	693	0
1971-8	2,032	1,346	1,034	348	0

SOURCES: *Canada Year Book, Bank of Canada Review*
1 Accession of Newfoundland and Labrador, 1949

combining natural-increase, immigration, and population-growth figures one can estimate emigration and use the results to trace the movement of Canada's population and the sources of its change. The result is Table 1.

Throughout the post-war years natural increase accounted for most of the growth in Canada's population, which increased by more than 105 per cent between 1941 and 1978. Net migration provided 7.7 per cent of the increase in the 1940s, 25.5 per cent in the 1950s, 21.7 per cent in the 1960s, and 33.8 per cent in the 1970s. By 1971 only 15.3 per cent of the population had been born abroad. In 1941 the proportion had been 17.5 per cent, and in 1911, 22 per cent. Nevertheless, the immigration had been sufficiently large and diverse to change Canada's ethnic mix. In the late forties, half of all Canadians were of British and Irish descent and 31 per cent were French. By 1971 these percentages had fallen to 45 per cent and 29 per cent. Those of other European extractions had become relatively numerous, rising from 18 per cent of the population to 23 per cent. Most prominent in this group were the German and Italian communities, but the Greek and Portuguese communities, although still very small in 1971, had grown from virtually nothing in the late 1940s. The same thing happened to the West Indians, who entered Canada in some numbers for the first time in the 1960s. Relative to those of European origin, Canadians of Asiatic background were still very few in 1971, but their numbers had increased quite rapidly, especially in the 1960s. Since 1951 the Chinese population had quintupled, the Japanese population had increased by nearly 50 per cent, and the population of other Asiatic backgrounds – largely Indian and Pakistani – had increased sevenfold.

The new migrants affected the texture of Canadian life. Partly because they concentrated in the great cities, especially in Toronto and Montreal, the impact was much greater than the raw numbers might lead one to suspect. Toronto in particular became a genuinely multiracial and multicultural society, while in Montreal the immigrants, who generally wanted to learn English and work in that language, appeared to threaten the demographic dominance of the francophones. In Vancouver the long-established communities of Chinese and East Indians were reinforced, and many other ethnic backgrounds were represented in some numbers for the first time. The result was a much more varied and interesting urban scene. The change was most noticeable in matters of shopping, eating, and drinking. Here, admittedly, it is hard to distinguish two causes: on the one hand, ethnic diversity; on the other, rising prosperity. Nevertheless it is clear that many of the new arrivals wanted to eat and drink the sorts of things they were used to. Other Canadians could, so to speak, go along for the ride. And a joyful adventure they often found their first excursions to be.

Among native-born Canadians there was one development of such importance that it must be singled out for special attention. After many decades of decline, the Eskimo and the native Indian peoples began to increase in numbers. In 1951 there were 9,733 Eskimo and 155,874 native Indians – only 1.2 per cent of Canada's population. By 1971 there were 18,000 Eskimo and 297,000 Indians. The Eskimo had kept pace with the national population growth and the Indians had outstripped it. Thus in 1971 the two groups jointly accounted for 1.5 per cent of Canada's population. The result, for the Indians, was an extremely peculiar age structure, in that a remarkably high proportion of the Indian population was under twenty-one years of age. Such a pattern is characteristic of underdeveloped countries, and it generally reflects the impact of modern medicine, which reduces infant mortality without at once reducing the birth rate. Of course there was little likelihood that the native peoples could achieve a 'revenge of the cradle.' However rapidly they might increase, they were simply too few to be other than a small minority group. Indeed, even in 1971 they were outnumbered within Canada by the Ukrainians, the Italians, the Norwegians, the Dutch, and the Jews. Similarly the West Indians and the other Negroes outnumbered the Eskimo, and so did such groups as Indians and Pakistanis, Estonians, and Finns. Nevertheless, the demographic resurgence was both sign and cause of a renewed self-confidence and assertiveness among the native peoples. Further, in the native economies this demographic pressure could often be serious, especially as the white man's economy pressed ever more closely on the areas where traditional hunting and gathering could be continued. In the 1930s it might have been expected that the 'Indian problem' would solve itself as the Indians gradually died out. In the 1960s and 1970s no such expectation could be entertained, and Canada's whites were obliged to confront a series of questions and problems for which neither history nor attitude had prepared them.

4

The Exchange Rate,
Money, Banks, and Inflation

Since the end of the Second World War Canadian politicians and media people have
been agitated by questions of monetary policy: what interest rates should be, what
the exchange rate should be, why prices have been rising so fast and so regularly.
Because these subjects are closely intertwined with the political history of our
period, we shall often have to discuss them in the chapters that follow. The present
chapter provides a general overview that treats various things which do not neatly fit
into any of the later chapters. This overview begins with the exchange rate, proceeds
to the banks, and then treats monetary policy and inflation in a general way. More
details will follow in later chapters.

With the outbreak of war in 1939, transactions in foreign moneys were centralized in the Foreign Exchange Control Board. Because the government could not be
sure that it would earn enough foreign money to pay for the imports from the United
States that our war effort would require, it was thought necessary to ration foreign
money; the system of rationing survived until 1951 although it varied in stringency,
as we shall see in Part II. Through the fifties, sixties, and seventies Canadians were
free to buy and sell foreign money – dollars, pounds, marks, yen, or whatever –
whenever they liked and it whatever quantities they liked. Citizens of other countries, where exchange rationing lingered on, were by no means always so fortunate.
For example, only in 1979 did Britain finally abolish the last of the foreign exchange
controls that had been introduced in 1939.

In the forties the government also controlled the price of foreign money, using the
US dollar as a yardstick. From 1939 to 1946 an American dollar cost about $1.10
Canadian. Then until 1949 the exchange rate was one for one, sometimes called
'par.' In 1949 the government returned to the wartime rate, which lasted until 1950,
when it was decided that supply and demand should determine the price of Canadian dollars in terms of foreign moneys. This system lasted until 1962, when the
government once more pegged the exchange rate, this time choosing a price of 92.5

American cents. This rate lasted until 1970, at which time the government once more allowed supply and demand to determine the price. This system, called a 'floating exchange rate,' was still operative in 1980. In later chapters we discuss the reasons for these changes in policy, and the movements of the Canadian dollar during the periods when it was a floating currency, the fifties and the seventies.

During the late seventies, when the Canadian dollar had fallen far below the American, it was sometimes suggested that the government might reintroduce exchange control, rationing and allocating foreign money as it had done in the forties. By autumn 1980 it had not done so, and most serious observers thought that it would not and could not. Since 1950, when the rationing of foreign money had been abandoned, the world financial system had become much more complicated, and by 1979 Canada's international financial interconnections were far more complex than they had been in the forties. Rationing would be hard to work, and the administrative apparatus for it had long since passed away, as had most of the officials who had run the system in the forties.

At no time during this period was the Canadian dollar based on gold, or related to it in any very simple way. Not since 1914 had there been any connection between the quantities of gold in the government vaults and the paper money in the hands of the public. Not since the early thirties had the government been willing to buy and sell gold at a fixed price in paper money. From January 1934 until August 1971, American dollars could be converted into gold at a fixed price of about thirty-five American dollars per ounce. Thus whenever the Canadian dollar was pegged to the American, as in the forties or the sixties, the price of gold was indirectly fixed in terms of Canadian dollars also. In addition, by joining the International Monetary Fund at the end of the war, Canada had pledged itself to peg its own currency to the American dollar and to keep its dollar within a narrow range in relation to the American. When Canada floated its dollar in 1950 it needed Fund permission. But in the seventies the Fund arrangements had broken down, and Canada could float its dollar without worrying about the Fund rules. After all, by contrast with the preceding two decades, the seventies were a time of considerable *laissez-faire* in currency regulation; most moneys floated in relation to the US dollar which itself floated – in fact, although not quite always in theory – relative to gold. In the fifties the Canadian dollar was unusual because it was one of the few floating currencies; in the seventies Canada was just one of the crowd. Throughout the post-war period the Canadian government was willing to buy gold and hold it, but not because there was any particular relation between gold and the Canadian dollar: gold was useful because foreign money, especially American money, could always be bought with it.

Whether the exchange rate was fixed or floating the national authorities had to act with respect to the rate. When the exchange rate was fixed they had to supply foreign money or buy foreign money if other supplies and demands did not happen to balance at or very near to the fixed rate. When the rate was floating they had to buy and sell so as to prevent big day-to-day changes in the rate and, from time to time, especially in the seventies, they might be active buyers or sellers so as to prevent the forces of supply and demand from pushing the rate to a level that, for political or economic reasons, the government might not like. Given the levels of prices and costs at home and abroad, the exchange rate affects all sorts of things. When the Canadian dollar rises in value in relation to foreign moneys the export trade suffers and Canada tends to import more. More exports mean more jobs; more imports mean fewer jobs. But when Canada's dollar is worth more, imports cost less in terms of Canadian dollars. So a high exchange rate restrains inflation, others things being equal. As we shall see in later chapters, governments had to worry about such things when choosing both a system (fixed or floating rate) and a rate (high or low relative to other moneys).

In the market for foreign exchange, Canadians and foreigners were buying foreign money with Canadian, or vice versa. Until 1951, when the government wound up the Foreign Exchange Control Board, there really was no market, because the Board was the ultimate buyer and seller. Since then there has been a very large and active market in which the principal dealers are banks, importers, exporters, governments, and multinational enterprises both foreign and Canadian. Ordinary Canadians did not encounter this market directly when they exchanged currency across the counters of their banks, but increasingly they were aware of the results – a fluctuating price for foreign currency. In the seventies as in the fifties, the public was very interested in these fluctuations.

An important actor in the market was the Bank of Canada, established in 1934, which bought and sold in the foreign-exchange market as the executor of government policy. Besides its responsibilities with respect to foreign exchange, the Bank had important duties with respect to the domestic monetary system. Although it has never fixed the rates of interest at which ordinary banks borrow from the public or lend to it, the Bank does fix the rate at which it itself will lend to the ordinary banks (in Canada, always called 'chartered banks'). In regard to its day-to-day operations, the Bank of Canada always operated quite independently and, except for a brief period in the late fifties and early sixties, which we shall examine in Part IV, it always co-ordinated its monetary policy with the general direction of government economic policy. Before 1954 and after 1961 it was clear at all times that, if the government wanted one thing and the Bank wanted another, the government would eventually get its way, even if the Governor of the Bank had to resign.

So far as the domestic monetary system was concerned, the Bank's main role was to provide the 'reserve base' on which the chartered banks could operate. Ever since 1934 Canadian law has required definite ratios between the public's claims on the banks – the banks' deposit liabilities – and the banks' claims on the Bank of Canada – the 'reserve base.' From time to time, as banking law has changed so have the ratios, but the basic arrangements have not been altered. The Bank can control the growth of the commercial banks, and therefore the growth of the credit the banks can offer, by controlling the increase in the reserve base.

Besides the changes in these ratios, from time to time there have been changes in the lending powers of the banks, in the charges they may collect, and in the arrangements for the protection of depositors. The general tendency since 1945 has been to widen the banks' powers, remove the controls on the interest they may charge, and provide new schemes to protect depositors. Each is considered here in turn.

In 1954, for the first time, banks were allowed to lend on the security of motor vehicles and other consumer goods and to make mortgage loans under certain restrictive conditions. In 1967 this restrictive arrangement was removed, and after a slow start the banks moved massively into mortgage lending, as the government had intended when Parliament changed the law. Throughout the period, the banks were also extending their consumer lending, a field they had once left to the specialized instalment-finance companies, household-finance companies, and loan sharks. In the seventies the media were full of advertisements from banks, urging households to rush in and borrow. The sedate and nervous bankers of the forties, perhaps remembering the Depression of the thirties, could not have imagined any such development, and certainly would not have tolerated it.

Until 1967, the banks could not charge more than 6 per cent interest, and they were allowed to agree among themselves on the interest they could charge borrowers and pay on deposits. These rules had originally been devised to protect borrowers and banks in equal measure. Then the law was changed: the banks could not longer collude, and they could charge or pay whatever rates of interest they thought right and proper. The result was a sudden outbreak of competition that quickly extended from charges to such important matters as opening hours and such unimportant ones as personalized scenic cheques. As for the ceiling on bank charges, there was much protest when its abolition was proposed, but by 1980 it had been long forgotten and the public was accustomed to a situation where banks, like supermarkets and car dealers, eagerly sought their business while charging and paying what the traffic would bear.

There had never been any doubt that Canada's banks were secure, safe, and solvent. None had failed since 1923; in case of need, any bank could borrow from the Bank of Canada. In 1965, however, the government decided to make assurance doubly sure. It was seriously worried not about the banks but about the 'near-banks' – trust companies, mortgage companies, and credit unions – which did bank-like business but which were less closely regulated and which could not borrow from the Bank of Canada. In the fifties and sixties near-banks mushroomed all over Canada. Some were ancient and well managed; some were new but well run; some were neither.

In 1965 a financial house, Atlantic Acceptance Corporation, collapsed noisily and messily. This collapse involved a large and long-established near-bank, British Mortgage and Trust of Stratford, Ontario, which had lent a lot to Atlantic. The Ontario government and the Ottawa authorities were afraid that the public would lose confidence in near-banks and try to withdraw their deposits, quickly producing a wave of near-bank failures. The Bank of Canada provided emergency help and urged the chartered banks, some of which had close links with the near-banks, to do likewise. Another trust company absorbed British Mortgage, and to preserve public confidence in banks and near-banks the national government introduced deposit insurance.

The Canada Deposit Insurance Corporation (CDIC) was modelled on lines that had been followed in the United States since 1933. All banks and all federally incorporated near-banks were obliged to insure their smaller deposits; provincially incorporated companies could join so long as their provincial authorities approved. Nine provincial governments did so, while the tenth, Quebec, set up its own deposit insurance plan. Credit unions were not covered.

The CDIC made no difference to the banks, but it must have helped the near-banks to expand still more quickly. By the mid-seventies they were very much in evidence, competing energetically with the chartered banks. Most striking in some regions were the credit unions. Long established in Quebec and in a few French-speaking areas elsewhere, by the seventies credit unions had come out of the closet almost everywhere and were making a major splash with handsome new buildings and massive advertising campaigns. Relative to the chartered banks the credit unions and the other near-banks were still rather small, but in the sixties and seventies they had a considerable impact. Did they produce 'finance with a human face,' as some observers thought? Only time would tell.

Although the near-banks were numerous and rather decentralized, the chartered banks remained few and large. In 1945 there were a few smaller banks and four very large ones: the Bank of Montreal, the Bank of Nova Scotia, the Royal Bank, and the Bank of Commerce. With the merger of the Dominion Bank and the Bank of Toronto into the Toronto-Dominion Bank, the Big Four became the Big Five. Meanwhile the Commerce absorbed the Imperial and Barclay's. During the rest of the period new foundations roughly balanced departures, although none of the new creations – the Mercantile Bank, the Bank of British Columbia, and so on – made any effort to set up a nation-wide branch system. Nor were all new flotations successful. Indeed, there was a noticeable tendency for new creations, such as the Unity

Bank, to vanish by amalgamation with remarkable speed. Sometimes a new bank did little or no business. Among the most striking of these was the Bank of Western Canada, devised in the mid-sixties by James Coyne (former Governor of the Bank of Canada) and Sinclair Stevens (later President of the Treasury Board in the Clark government of 1979). The BWC vanished from the scene almost at once, leaving rather a bad odour behind itself. But at least it had not failed. Meanwhile in Quebec there were interesting developments. The Banque Provinciale, one of the 'French banks' based in Montreal, made a serious effort to expand its business, especially in Ontario. In 1979 it merged with the Banque Canadienne Nationale to form the Banque Nationale du Canada, known in Quebec simply as la Banque Nationale.

Whether this merger had turned the 'Big Five' into a 'Big Six' remained to be seen. There was no sign that the Royal or the Montreal was quaking in its boardroom – at least, not for that reason. By 1979 these two banks, based as they were in Quebec, had other things to fear. The Bank of Montreal began in the early seventies to prepare a possible line of retreat. It began to promote a subtitle – the 'First Canadian Bank.' Erecting a huge regional office building in Toronto, it named the structure First Canadian Place. Rumour asserted that the inside of the Place was designed so that it could become the bank's head office on a few days' notice.

Meanwhile other banks built glass towers and decorated city centres with plazas and art works. Toronto acquired the Toronto-Dominion Centre and Commerce Court, in addition to First Canadian Place. Social commentators thought the glass was symbolic: banks were now open, welcoming, eager to see and be seen, no longer the costive, introverted institutions of the old days.

While the banks were sheathing themselves in glass, consumers were bedecking themselves in plastic. At the end of the war it was still quite difficult for households to borrow money. Of course there were mortgage loans and instalment plans, but the latter were closely regulated with respect to downpayments and terms of repayment, lest consumers create inflationary pressure by trying to buy too much. The department stores ran charge accounts and some oil companies were beginning to issue credit cards, but both systems were small in scale and impact, and neither made much provision for extended credit. In the fifties things began to change. As wartime inflation receded the government stopped controlling instalment credit. As stores and oil companies competed harder they spread their plastic manna more widely and paid less attention to the credit-worthiness of cardholders. By 1960 American Express, Diners' Club, and Carte Blanche had begun to distribute general-purpose credit cards; even so, their standards were high, they insisted that accounts be paid when rendered, and there were still relatively few places that would accept the things. American Express said that you could go around the world on your card without spending a dollar in cash. True, but only if you wanted to travel first class.

The breakthrough came in the sixties with Chargex and Mastercharge, the first really general-purpose cards that also allowed for extended payment. These were also the first credit cards to be distributed quite widely.

Plastic money had reached Canada. Like most good things it arrived a little late. Some observers thought that the stuff must be inflationary. They forgot that the users would always have to pay with real money in the end. Economists argued that the change from a cash society to a cashless one could indeed be inflationary, because for a short while it could raise demand without raising supply. The extra demand would come because people would be able to reduce their holdings of cash in the transition from paying cash day by day to paying cash once a month when the Chargex account comes in. But the effect is once and for all. Once society has fully adjusted to the plastic money there can be no extra inflationary effect. So 'plasticization' may have raised prices a little but we can hardly blame it for the much higher inflation of the seventies.

Because the chartered banks and near-banks ran the new credit cards, plastic money slipped neatly not only into the Canadian way of life but also into the Canadian financial fabric. Other developments, less obvious to ordinary people, were digested with equal smoothness. As Canadians grew richer and Canadian business grew more sophisticated the financial scene became much more complex. There were new kinds of specialized financial business and new sorts of instruments for borrowing and lending. In a sense there were even branches of foreign banks. Although such firms could not do a full banking business they could open 'representative offices' from which they were increasingly active as lenders. Meanwhile Canadian chartered banks expanded their external operations in some directions, such as western Europe, while cutting back in others, such as Cuba and the Caribbean where the political climate had become increasingly uncomfortable. At the same time, within Canada there was a gradual westward drift of financial institutions and some diffusion of control. Toronto rose relative to Montreal and largely at Montreal's expense, as banks and insurance companies found it prudent to transfer their activities or to prepare to do so. But in Alberta and British Columbia resource-based riches created new self-confidence and new institutions. The Bank of British Columbia was floated off with gusto. So was Alberta's Heritage Fund, fed and fertilized by a flow of petrodollars.

By 1980 Westerners were heard to assert that the centre of finance, like the centre of wealth, would migrate to the Rockies. Would this really happen? Few observers thought so. Central Canada, after all, still contained most of the wealth, people, and financial institutions. Montreal might sink further, but it was hard to suppress the suspicion that Toronto, not Edmonton or Calgary or Vancouver, would be the chief gainer. After all, if one aspires to be a major financial centre it is helpful to be in the same time zone as New York, and not to be so far from London and Zurich that one is shut down whenever they are working.

Having looked at the development of the financial institutions, we must now examine the things with which the banks and near-banks were most intimately concerned – money and prices.

Everyone agrees that since the end of the Second World War prices have been rising with inconvenient speed. By 1980 most prices were very much higher than they had been in 1944. By the early seventies people had come to expect that prices would rise, and more and more people were adjusting their behaviour accordingly. In particular they were trying to allow for future inflation when negotiating wages, salaries, and professional fees; also they were seeking to buy assets, such as houses, land, and gold, whose value might be expected to keep pace with inflation. Furthermore, on any kind of asset whose value was fixed in terms of money, such as a Canada Savings Bond, any other sort of bond, or a mortgage, lenders demanded much higher rates of interest to compensate them in whole or in part for the loss of purchasing power that would happen between the time of lending and the time of repayment, while borrowers were often happy to pay such interest charges because they expected their own earnings would rise in step with inflation. In the seventies, when prices rose much more rapidly than in the fifties or sixties, such adjustments and demands were especially noticeable, although by that time people had come to recognize that some plausible assets, such as common stocks, might very well not rise in step with the general price level.

Although inflation has afflicted various countries at different rates, since 1944 the inflationary experience has been common throughout the western world and throughout the 'third world' also. Canadian inflation, therefore, has been part of a worldwide process, and the roots of the inflation are not to be found solely in Canada, which is a small part of the world economic system. Because the United States is Canada's major market and source of supply, Canadian prices are especially sensitive to developments south of the border. On the other hand, Canada is quite capable of adding its own fuel to the inflationary bonfire.

How quickly have prices been rising? There are various ways to measure the general price level, and commonly they give somewhat different answers. Figure 3 in Chapter 2 plots one price index, the one that statisticians call the 'implicit price deflator of gross national expenditure.' It tries to measure the prices of everything that is produced and used, and it adds them together, weighting each price in relation to the importance of that commodity in economic life. The data show that the immediate post-war inflation was concentrated in the years 1946-8, and that prices jumped upward once more in 1951-2; in 1946-7 prices rose 10 per cent, in 1947-8, 13 per cent, and in 1950-2, 16 per cent in two years. Thereafter prices rose a little through 1957 and still more gradually until 1968, when inflation accelerated. Compared with the developments in 1972 and thereafter, however, the inflation of 1968-71 looks quite gentle. From 1971 to 1972 the general price level rose 5 per cent, from 1972 to 1973, 9 per cent, and so on. The worst year of all was 1974, when this price index rose 15.3 per cent. In 1968-71 the average annual increase was 3.9 per cent, and in 1972-8, 9 per cent, while in the first half of 1979 prices were rising at an annual rate of more than 11 per cent.

During the Second World War most prices and wages had been controlled, but the government was anxious to dismantle the system, and after the war was over it soon began to do so. Although rent controls lingered on in a few places for many years, during most of our period the inflation was an unregulated one until 1975, when price and wage controls were imposed for a three-year period. These controls are discussed in a later chapter, when we deal with the Trudeau government.

Why do prices rise? Although economists argue about the balance of forces in any particular case they are in general agreement about the three basic pressures. Most obviously, costs may rise, pushing prices up. Because wages are the dominant cost-item it is natural to look first at wage-push pressures, although other costs, such as the price of oil, may be at the root of the trouble from time to time. A second element may be on the side of demand, which can pull prices up. For example, if a town is booming but for some reason no one is building new houses there, we would expect house prices and rents to rise in that town. The same thing can happen in a whole country or in the world, if demand is growing faster than supply. Third, producers or sellers can sometimes combine to raise particular prices, as Canadian farmers do through their marketing boards or as OPEC does with oil.

Whichever of these three pressures are at work, and in whatever combinations, money is also an important actor in the inflationary story; without extra money the pressure won't get very far, whereas the supplying of new money can itself fuel the inflationary fire. In the first instance, when costs rise business will need extra money just to keep the wheels turning; in the second, if the new money gets spent by government or business it adds directly to demand but adds nothing to supply, causing prices to rise as the economy adjusts to the new and larger quantity of money. Or if wages are rising more rapidly than national output, extra money allows the economy at large to pay those wages.

In Canada, as in other developed industrial countries, there are three kinds of money: paper currency, coin, and chequable deposits in chartered banks and near-banks. If a deposit can be drawn on or transferred by means of a cheque it is said to be 'chequable,' and to be 'bank money,' thus part of the 'money supply,' the quantity of money in existence. At any given time there is far more 'bank money,' that is to say chequable deposits, than any other kind of money. Thus at the end of 1978 there was almost $70 billion worth of bank money in the form of chartered-bank deposits alone, while the public held only $8 billion in currency and the chartered banks held only another $1.4 billion.

All these definitions of money may seem somewhat abstract and uninteresting, but they matter, because there is a close connection between the quantity of money in existence and its growth on the one hand, and the movement of prices on the other. In a general way everyone suspects this. But ordinary people are very muddled about the origins of the money supply. Why is it what it is, and why has it been rising so much?

Economists know that bank money does not originate with the depositing of paper money or coin, except to a very minor extent. In the economy as a whole, the banking system *creates* deposits by crediting accounts in the process of making loans and buying securities. Once created in this way, deposits can be transferred, drawn out in the form of currency, and generally handled exactly as if they were currency or coin. But the chartered banks are obliged to maintain a minimum ratio between their deposit liabilities to the public, which they can create, and their claims on the Bank of Canada – the 'reserve base' – which they cannot. Thus the rate at which money can grow is fundamentally controlled by the rate at which the Bank of Canada creates claims on itself, that is to say, chartered bank deposits with the central bank.

How does the Bank create these claims? Basically it does just what the chartered banks do. That is, it makes loans and it buys securities. But rule, law, and custom restrict the kinds of loans and purchases the Bank can make. It can make loans to the chartered banks, and it can buy federal government bonds, either from the public or from the government itself. But the banks do not like to borrow from the Bank. So the rate at which the money supply can expand is fundamentally controlled by the rate at which the Bank buys government bonds. And even if the government itself does not want to sell any new bonds, there are always lots of bonds on offer from the public at large. An additional element is this. When the Bank buys foreign money – US dollars, pounds, or whatever – it pays by crediting the seller's account. The result is just like the purchase of a government bond – more claims on the Bank of Canada, and so more potential for monetary growth.

Although these arrangements have changed in detail from time to time, in all essentials they date from 1935, when the Bank of Canada actually began to operate. Thus the historian can write the monetary history of the post-war years in terms of the Bank's changing willingness to fuel the inflationary fires by creating a larger 'reserve base' for the chartered banks. (This history is described in later chapters on the basis of the preliminary definitions and explanations given here.) But since the management of the monetary system is entrusted to the Bank, whose managers decide when to increase the reserve base and by how much, the monetary history of our period could also be organized around the four governors of the Bank.

Graham Towers, the first governor, came to the central bank from the Royal Bank in 1934. He remained in office for twenty years, until J.E. Coyne, his deputy, succeeded him late in 1954. Coyne had been a member of the central bank's staff since 1938 and deputy governor since 1950. He retained his high office until 1961, when the national government asked Parliament to relieve him of it. The parliamentary stench was considerable, as we shall see in Part IV, and although the measure passed the House it was rejected in the Senate. Coyne, however, resigned and was succeeded by his deputy, Louis Rasminsky, who held the governorship and the government's confidence until his resignation early in 1973. He was succeeded by Gerald Bouey, who had to face a series of slings and arrows when, in 1979, interest rates rose to unprecedented heights.

The governors were very different and they had to deal with very different situations. Towers, Rasminsky, and Bouey worked closely with the various governments, accepting that final power over monetary policy must rest with the cabinet. The Bank might propose its own targets for the growth of the reserve base and thus of the money supply. Indeed, in the late seventies the Bank did exactly this. But if Bank and government were at odds it was government that would win in the end. Coyne, however, believed that the governor could and should ignore the government when he thought it right to do so. Hence the eventual collision between governor and government in 1961. Towers had to handle the inflationary aftermath of the Second World War and the pressures of the Korean War, when there was almost no unemployment and when the chartered banks could expand money and credit almost as fast as they liked because they held far more reserves than bank custom or national law required. But Coyne had to deal with a period in which prices were almost stable and when unemployment was inconveniently high. As for Rasminsky, he was governor during the decade when worldwide inflation took off once more and when the world system of stable exchange rates collapsed in disorder. Bouey has had to handle ever-stronger inflationary pressure, the general floating of exchange rates that followed the collapse, and, in and after 1975, disorder in Ottawa's own budget – a disorder so profound that for the first time since 1945 the federal government was obliged to borrow heavily from the Bank of Canada.

As the Bank and the banks grew up, so did the money supply, from at least $5.9 billion in 1944 to over $78 billion in 1978. National output, meanwhile, rose from $29.7 billion at 1971 prices to $126.1 billion.[1] Thus output quadrupled while the money supply increased thirteen-fold. It is hardly surprising that prices rose!

1 Data on money supply from M.C. Urquhart and K.A.H. Buckley, eds, *Historical Statistics of Canada* (Toronto: Macmillan 1965) and *Bank of Canada Review*. Data on output from Statistics Canada, *National Income and Expenditure Accounts*.

As the Canadian economy grew, so did the Bank of Canada. In the late thirties there had arisen a modest stone structure on Wellington Street in Ottawa – something Prime Minister King doubtless thought would add a new classic perspective to the capital. But the building was soon far too small and, at long last, late in the seventies, the old stone structure was surrounded by and embedded in an immense structure of reflecting glass that filled a city block. The net effect, one cynic remarked, resembled a Mack truck that had launched itself part way through a very large shop window. But by now Canada was a grown-up country, and its central bank presumably deserved the same sort of glass-walled sanctum that the chartered banks were pushing ever higher in Toronto.

5

Trade, Imports of Capital, and the Question of Foreign Ownership

Developments since 1944 with respect to Canada's trade, borrowing, and lending suggest that, with a few exceptions, foreign investment has been a good thing for Canada.[1] It is argued here that, contrary to popular opinion, the evidence does not support the view that the inflow of foreign capital or the changing trade pattern has Americanized Canada, emasculated its foreign policy, or made the country any less distinctive. If these things have happened the causes are to be found elsewhere. Indeed, without injections of foreign money Canadians would have been somewhat poorer than they are, and the economy would have grown a little more slowly than it has, although there is no agreement about how big these effects might have been. It is certainly true that, in comparison with Canada's growing economy, the cost of interest and dividends on the growing external obligations has been tending to fall, and that at no time in the entire post-war period has this burden been painful. In short, not all nationalists – since the authors think of themselves as nationalists – accept the criticisms that are directed against Canada's involvement with the American market, or against capital importation from the United States. Most economists agree that the weight of the evidence contradicts the pessimistic nationalists' claims.

Any attempt to argue this case in detail requires some definition of the terms which will appear in this and later chapters. These are the standard labels that economists and statisticians use when discussing international trade and finance. Historians have tended to be less careful and less consistent than economists in the use of these labels, with confusing results, so that although the reader and the writer may think they know what certain words mean, both may be wrong, and each may read certain key words differently. It is hoped that such confusions may be avoided by defining these terms at the outset and sticking to the definitions.

1 Data in this chapter are drawn from three Statistics Canada publications: *National Income and Expenditure Accounts, Balance of International Payments,* and *Balance of International Indebtedness.* In some instances the most recent data have been drawn from *Statistics Canada Daily.*

When discussing international borrowing, lending, and direct investment, economists and statisticians usually use two frameworks of definition. The first is the balance of payments, more properly called the balance of international payments; the second is the balance of international indebtedness. Let us take each in turn.

The balance of payments records the international flow of funds into or out of a country within a single year, or some part of a year. There are three main categories of transactions. First, imports, exports, international payments and receipts of interest and dividends, and international gifts are recorded in the *current account*. Second, when the Canadian government buys or sells gold or foreign money, these transactions are recorded in *official monetary items*. Third, all other flows belong to the *capital account* of the balance of payments. If receipts exceed payments under the first category one speaks of a *surplus on the current account*, or simply of a *current-account surplus*; a *current-account deficit* means an excess of payments over receipts so far as the current account is concerned. The third category, the *capital account*, includes international borrowing, lending, and the purchases of common stocks. One instance would be a British Columbia Hydro bond issue in New York. Another would be a Swiss purchase of Noranda shares on the Toronto Stock Exchange. Such operations are called *portfolio investments* because the international capitalist is imagined to carry around the bonds and stock certificates in his portfolio. In addition the capital account contains *direct investment*. This occurs when an individual or a business buys or expands a business in another country – for instance, when General Motors expands its St Hubert plant near Montreal, or when Massey-Ferguson builds a new factory in Scotland. If direct investment is financed by the reinvestment of profits or by borrowing in the country where the investment is made, Canada's balance of payments does not record the transaction, on the grounds that the investment does not affect the markets where one kind of money is traded for others, what economists call the *foreign exchange market*. But if direct investment is financed from abroad then it, like external borrowing, gives rise to an *inflow of capital funds*, or simply a *capital inflow* or *capital import*. Of course these flows can go both ways. Thus if Canadians invest abroad, as when Inco builds plants in Central America or when the Bank of Commerce makes loans to South Africa, the result is a capital outflow, from Canada's point of view.

These are the main entries in the capital account of the balance of payments. The other entries, although interesting to specialists, can safely be ignored, except for the 'errors and omissions,' a balancing item to ensure that all the receipts and payments add up correctly. Because capital-account transactions are hard to record and trace, this item can often be quite large.

The balance of payments records receipts and payments during a particular period of time. If it shows a current-account deficit, it must also show a capital inflow and/or a reduction in Canada's holdings of gold and foreign money, because there is no other way through which the foreign money to pay for the excess imports can be found. But one can also take a sort of inventory of external claims and obligations at a particular moment of time, typically December 31. In such a stock-taking one adds up all foreigners' claims against the Canadian economy and all Canadians' claims against the rest of the world. The result is the *balance of international indebtedness*.

Thanks to the media and to the controversy over foreign ownership that has raged in Canada since the mid-fifties, many Canadians have become accustomed to one item in our balance of international indebtedness. This is the value of foreign claims on the Canadian economy. Another familiar figure is the value of foreign direct investment in Canada. These numbers are somewhat suspect. For example, when pricing factory buildings, machines, or real estate, it is very hard to know just what a foreign-owned asset is really worth. Canadians are often further misled by an even cruder and simpler device: they are told how much Canada owes the world, but not how much the rest of the world owes Canada. The distinction is important. Canadians own shares in foreign companies, such as General Motors, Dupont, and Imperial Chemicals, and they own businesses and real estate in foreign countries – and not only in Florida! There are Canadian multinationals, such as Massey-Ferguson, Falconbridge, and Northern Telecom, and many other Canadian firms that do not qualify for multinational status have branch plants abroad.

In 1946 Canada's gross liabilities were $7.8 billion, but the rest of the world owed Canadians $4 billion, so our net liabilities were $3.8 billion, or 32 per cent of gross national product (GNP). In 1969 Canadians owed the rest of the world $48.8 billion – 59 per cent of GNP. But the rest of the world owed Canadians $20.7 billion. Thus our net indebtedness was $28.1 billion, or 35 per cent of 1969 GNP. Should one have worried about those extra three percentage points? Many observers thought not, although some influential people disagreed. In the seventies things rapidly became still more complicated. Canadians became even more substantial direct investors in other countries, while the inflow of foreign direct investment first slowed and then, in 1976 and 1978, reversed itself, so that in every year after 1974 Canadians' new direct investment in other countries exceeded foreigners' new direct investment in Canada. Although Canadians were not 'buying back Canada' in any very simple way, the net position was obviously changing, and in a way that nationalists ought to have approved of. At the same time, while still importing large amounts of capital funds on a long-term basis by selling bonds in foreign markets, Canadians were exporting large amounts of funds that were being lent on foreign markets. In effect, from the financial point of view national boundaries had come to mean very little, making it difficult to draw conclusions about policy, Americanization, or anything else from the fact that the value of Canada's gross liabilities and of foreign direct investment in Canada went up. Between 1969 and 1977 gross liabilities rose from $48.8 billion to $106 billion, and from 1969 to 1975, the last year for which detailed data are available, the value of foreign direct investment rose from $24.4 billion to $36.1 billion. Meanwhile, however, the value of Canadians' direct investments in other countries rose from $5.2 billion to $10.7 billion, and in 1977 Canada's net liabilities, after deducting its claims on foreigners from foreigners' claims on the Canadian economy, were worth $53.5 billion or 25.5 per cent of GNP – in percentage terms, very much less than in 1946 or in 1969.

Canada has still not dispensed with foreign-controlled enterprises, which by 1979 were accounting for 48 per cent of new investment outlays in manufacturing, 66 per cent of such outlays in mining, quarrying, and oil drilling, and 42 per cent in forestry. But many activities, most obviously in the resource industries, showed a changing balance in the course of the seventies, as some major firms passed from foreign to Canadian control. Also, of course, there were still important manufacturing industries, such as steel and textiles, where foreign ownership and control had always been insignificant. Although the changing situation was not really well known, by the late seventies there were signs that the general public, which had never cared much about the topic, now cared even less. Although some publicists and politicians were worried about the sheer size of the obligations, on the whole Canadian officials and politicians have tended to be much less concerned about the burden, and have normally looked at net indebtedness, not at gross indebtedness. It appears that they have been right to do so, and that the facts justify the nonchalance with which official Ottawa is accustomed to regard the whole matter of foreign investment. When eminent politicians – Walter Gordon in the sixties and Herb Gray during the early seventies – attempted to make foreign control an issue, they seemed eccentric; now, in retrospect, given further changes in the climate of public opinion, they seem even more so, though in the eighties things may change.

Two other types of commentators, the Marxists and the cultural nationalists, deserve mention. The Marxist argument is that, since governments are the creatures of capitalists, it follows that when many of those capitalists are foreigners the Canadian government will be largely controlled from abroad. But in Canada few of the nationalists have been Marxists, and few of the Marxists have revealed their model of the political process. The arguments of the second group, which likes to bring political and cultural matters into the debate about foreign investment, have been weakened by the discouragingly metaphorical and allusive nature of their complaints.

In 1978 Canadians paid $5.5 billion in interest and dividends to the rest of the world, while receiving $1.1 billion. The net payment, $4.4 billion, was 1.9 per cent of Canada's GNP in that year, when in terms of current prices GNP was growing by 10 per cent per year, and in terms of constant prices, by 3.4 per cent per year. In other words, eight months' growth in Canada's output was more than enough to service all the nation's external obligations, both public and private. Similarly, relative to exports the burden was quite small – only 8 per cent in 1977. Although these percentages fluctuate a little from year to year, they have been tending downward for many years. In 1963 they were 2 and 9.3 per cent, and in 1926, 4.6 and 14.5 per cent.

Although Canada normally has run a current-account deficit in its balance of payments, in our period it has not always done so. In 1944 exports equalled imports, and in 1945-9, 1952, 1970-1, and 1973 exports were larger than imports, which resulted in current-account surpluses. Indeed, throughout the thirties and forties surpluses had been the usual thing, and they also had appeared in the twenties, although not in every year. In terms of the movement of capital funds, however, the period since 1949 harks back to the years before 1914, when Canada was normally importing capital funds.

Why, after nearly forty years of current-account surpluses, did Canada begin in 1950 to run large deficits? Why did these deficits continue for twenty years and then, after a brief respite in 1970-3, reappear in the seventies? The cumulative current-account deficit of the years 1951-69 was $15.5 billion, and in 1974-8 the cumulative deficit was $22.4 billion, while in 1970-3, when there were three surpluses and a deficit in 1972, the cumulative surplus was only $1.2 billion. There is no doubt about the pattern; the problem is to explain it.

As the Canadian economy has grown almost every year since the end of the war, it has pulled in more imports: consumer goods, machinery, raw materials, foodstuffs. Also, Canada has had to pay increasing amounts in interest and dividends, and Canadians, as they became more prosperous, tended to spend more on foreign travel. If one plots the volume of imports against the volume of Canada's output, the result is a graph that shows a reasonably stable and regular relationship between output and imports, especially since 1961. On the average for the whole post-war period, each extra $10 billion of output has sucked in about $3 billion of extra imports. As the economy grew so did the import bill. Export earnings, however, depend not on Canada's production but on foreign demand – especially American demand – for Canada's goods. Although Canada has been lucky in discovering and arranging for new markets for old exports, such as wheat and automobiles, and very fortunate in finding new things that can be exported in quantity, such as natural gas and uranium, there is nothing in the nature of things that will ensure a convenient growth of export earnings that will just match the growth of Canada's spending on imports. In fact, as we saw above, the volume of Canada's exports hardly rose in the late forties and mid-fifties; from 1957 until 1973 export volumes moved upward in a fashion that just about matched import growth, but then in 1974 and 1975 export volumes fell sharply, and although they moved upward relative to imports in 1976-8 they were moving up from an uncomfortably low level. Thus one might say that Canada ran persistent current-account surpluses because in the early fifties imports leapt ahead while exports stagnated; thereafter the country could seldom push export revenues high enough to close the gap, even though relative to GNP that gap changed remarkably little. From 1955 to 1979 the import surplus averaged about 1.75 per cent of GNP; in 1975 it was almost 3 per cent, but then it fell to about 2 per cent in 1978.

This explanation is not really a very profound one, because it does not dig beneath the figures for total exports and imports to explore the reasons for these movements. In later chapters we shall have something to say about these reasons, although a work of general history cannot devote a great deal of space to Canada's foreign trade. Certainly the post-war years have seen some dramatic developments: the diminishing importance of the British market, new opportunities for wheat sales in the USSR and China, new demands from the United States for forest products, iron ore, oil and natural gas, uranium, aluminum, and other non-ferrous metals, and, after 1965, motor cars and parts. Without these new export markets Canada would not have been able to pay for its imports. It is unlikely that it could have borrowed all the foreign money needed to fill the gap, and growth would have been throttled had it not been able to pay for the imports the country wanted. As it was, Canada filled the remaining gap by importing capital funds and by welcoming a large amount of direct foreign investment.

In this whole process Canada's trade became ever more closely bound up with the American market, in spite of the new opportunities in Japan and the socialist world. In 1946 Britain took 26 per cent of our exports and the United States 38 per cent; in 1978 the percentages were 3.8 and 70, while continental western Europe's total share had risen to 7 and Japan's from less than 1 per cent to 5.5. On the import side the changes were less dramatic, but they were equally significant. In 1946 the United States provided 75 per cent of our imports, and in 1978, 71 per cent; Britain's shares were 7.5 per cent in 1946 and 3.2 per cent in 1978, while Japan's share had risen from almost nothing to 4.5 per cent, and continental Europe's to 8.3 per cent.

These changing percentages reflect many things. The British economy, although growing, found itself outgrown by all the other western European economies, and Japan grew faster still; in terms of design, quality, and price many British goods lost the competitive edge that they had had in the late forties and fifties; American multinational firms often preferred to draw supplies from their parents and to send their exports there; continental Europe and Japan emerged as producers of machines, equipment, and consumer goods that were highly competitive in design, quality, and price – not merely with British goods but also with American; as Britain gradually withdrew into the protective agricultural arrangements of the European Economic Community after 1973, the British market became less open to Canadian grain and other foodstuffs; once the stresses and strains of war and reconstruction had been surmounted, Britain naturally drew more of her foodstuffs from continental Europe and more primary products from Scandinavia and even from the Soviet Union, because these supplies were close by.

As the years passed Canadians were vaguely aware that Britain mattered less and Japan mattered more. They certainly noticed when the Soviet Union and China began to buy Canada's wheat. Nor could they ignore the extent to which American goods and American opportunities had become pre-eminent in the nation's external trade. Without doubt they would have noticed that American firms were very much present in the Canadian marketplace even if publicists and politicians had not regularly reminded them of the fact.

By 1968 foreign-owned corporations held 62.8 per cent of the assets in Canada's mining corporations and 58 per cent of the assets in manufacturing. In other sectors foreign ownership, which was chiefly American, was less striking; it ranged from 7.8 per cent of assets in transport, communication, and public utilities (where most installations are government-owned) to 12.6 per cent in financial corporations, 13 per cent in construction, 20 per cent in services, and 31 per cent in wholesale trade. The foreign-owned sector had grown partly by new investment and partly by purchase; it had financed its growth partly by importing capital funds, partly by borrowing within Canada, and partly by accumulating earnings from its Canadian operations. In the seventies the percentages fell a little especially in the resource industries, as some foreign-owned firms shifted to Canadian private control while others were taken over, directly or indirectly, by governments.

It can be argued that the numbers of foreign-owned firms do not matter very much. Admittedly they have dominated some parts of the resource industries and some parts of manufacturing, although certainly not all. But in the resource industries they have chiefly used resources, like oil and timber, that Canadian governments owned. In managing manufacturing, exports, and energy policy, Ottawa had learned by the mid-sixties that foreign-owned firms could be bent to the national will – indeed, that they could be instruments of Canada's national purpose. So far as jobs were concerned foreign firms mattered much less than people seemed to think. Very few people worked in the relevant resource industries. In manufacturing, employment was shrinking in comparison with the growing labour force, and the new jobs were chiefly in the service sectors – everything from banking and selling to education, medicine, and the civil service – where foreign ownership was insignificant or altogether absent. The vast majority of Canadians did *not* work for a foreign-owned firm. For most Canadians foreign ownership really meant little more than the chance to buy and sell American-designed consumer durables produced in Canada with something less than American efficiency and costing considerably more than they would have in the United States. No doubt Canadians were increasingly steeped in American ideas and increasingly inclined to adopt American styles and attitudes both in life and in politics. But the blame, if that is the appropriate word, belongs with prosperity, travel, family contacts, the media, and the absence of any persuasive alternative models for life and conduct – not with foreign investment.

Many years have now passed since George Grant sang his *Lament for a Nation.*[2] Perhaps Grant is right to regret that Canadians are now so very like their great neighbours to the south. It is open to anyone to imitate Grant in imagining hypothetical histories of Canada, historical trajectories different from the one on which the Dominion of the North launched itself so long ago. And anyone can deplore some of the things that some foreign-owned firms have done or left undone. But it is equally important to criticize the native product. Most of what has gone wrong with post-war Canada has been inevitable, unavoidable, or Canada's own damn fault. The later chapters marshal evidence and argument that will support this assertion.

2 (Toronto: McClelland & Stewart 1965).

PART TWO

The End of Mackenzie King 1945-8

6

Canada Adrift

'The sequence for sane Canadian thinking,' a foreign affairs commentator wrote in 1941, 'is, first, the British Commonwealth, second, the Anglo-Saxon union, and finally a world order, beyond the war, based on co-operation and justice.' Canadians reading these words nodded sagely. Thus it had always been; thus, once Hitler was disposed of, it would be again. The sentiment stands in poignant contrast to another observation, made about the same time, by Britain's ambassador in Washington. 'Boys,' he told a group of reporters, 'Britain's broke.'

A worried Mackenzie King reflected on what one of his dinner guests had just told him. 'Britain,' King was told, 'is a bankrupt country ... He had not conceived that England could ever be bankrupt ... but that was where she was now.' True in 1941, those words were truer in 1945. Some Canadians knew it. Speaking in August 1940, a University of Toronto professor of history, Frank Underhill, uttered these prescient words: 'We now have two loyalties – one to Britain and the other to North America. I venture to say it is the second, North America, that is going to be supreme now. The relative significance of Britain is going to sink, no matter what happens.' Underhill's candour was premature; he was almost fired for his pains, and was saved only because his friends persuaded the premier of Ontario that his departure would be inexpedient. Britain, as far as public opinion was concerned, was still best.

The resultant gap between the ideal and the real in Canada's perception of the outside world bedevilled Mackenzie King's Liberal government. Ever since 1763 Canadian external relations had been dominated by one country – Britain. 'Foreign affairs' were in Canada styled 'external affairs' so that relations with the mother country could be included. Twice in the twentieth century Canadians had plunged into world wars at Britain's side, and between 1939 and 1945 over a million Canadian men and women disrupted their lives to serve in a cause whose symbol was, as always, Britain. In 1945 victory crowned British arms. The Empire still stood: why should things be any different?

But things were very different. Six years of war had disrupted the European economy and demoralized Europe's political society. At the war's end, the Soviet Union had advanced out of its Eurasian fastnesses and occupied the centre of Europe. The largest Soviet armies encircled Hitler's last bastion in Berlin, now to be governed jointly by the four major allies, Britain, France, the Soviet Union, and the United States.

Britain in 1945 disposed of large armies too, though never as large as the Soviet Union's. British troops occupied a vast swath of territory from Saigon to Hamburg, not to mention those parts of the empire recovered from enemy occupation. But the bright colours of the victory parades were soon forgotten. Soldiers returning to England after four or five years' absence found a very different country from the one they had left. Grey bread, tea served in jam jars, meagre rations of meat and butter, dilapidated rolling stock on the railways, all testified to the sacrifices the civilian economy had made for victory.

Britain's new Labour government, contemplating the dismal scene, decided that it could not afford the luxury of the empire very long. The Neilson's Chocolates map of the empire, for so long a feature of Canadian classrooms, began to shrink and change colour as the blotches of pink that represented the empire were replaced by unfamiliar greens and yellows. India was the Indian Empire no longer, but the Dominion of India – just like Canada – and then, in 1949, a republic. Beside it was another Moslem dominion, Pakistan, a testament to India's civil strife and religious disagreements. Burma left the empire entirely, and Palestine, with its warring Jewish and Arab factions, was abandoned altogether in the spring of 1948. Only in Africa did the empire hold on for a few more years, but even there its days were numbered.

These developments were presented to Canadians in the cheery guise of liberal progress. Most of the newly independent Asian states remained in the Commonwealth; all had properly constituted parliamentary governments, like Canada's, free of the embarrassing encumbrances of British colonial rule. Canadians, who believed themselves to be a model for the Commonwealth's constitutional development, expected that the new nations would in time become exotic reproductions, modified for local colour, of Britain abroad. The Canadian government sat back approvingly, tendering much sympathy but little advice, as the British packed up and moved out.

The focus for the government's external perceptions was the Department of External Affairs, headed as was the custom, by the prime minister himself. Its officers had matured under Mackenzie King's shadow. A highly intelligent group, they added tone to Canada's representation abroad, and lustre to the reports the government received. Inside Ottawa, foreign-service officers were admired as an élite corps in the civil service. But their influence did not match their prestige.

Mackenzie King took it to be axiomatic that external events, although they might affect Canada, were nevertheless beyond Canada's capacity to control, and usually beyond its ability to influence. King had, over the years, met most of the world's leading statesmen, from Theodore Roosevelt and Sir Edward Grey to Winston Churchill, Clement Attlee, and the new American president, Harry Truman. The Prime Minister prided himself on this accomplishment. He believed that it gave him a unique insight into the workings of the world and the preoccupations of its leaders. Liberal propagandists informed the electorate that King's influence, acquired over two generations, was irreplaceable.

It was an influence that King carefully conserved. Not for him the high-flying diplomatic exploits of his Conservative predecessor, Sir Robert Borden. Borden's turn as a world statesman in the First World War had done his party little good on the home front. Canada, Borden believed, had paid for its status in the world through the blood of its soldiers. Borden believed that sacrifice cemented national unity. King, however, suspected that blood was a pretty effective solvent. He dismissed the substance of influence abroad as a will o' the wisp; far better, he concluded, to enjoy the appearance of influence, posing happily for the photographers at the Quebec Conference beside American President Roosevelt and British Prime Minister Churchill. Only King and his closest staff knew that the Canadians then left the scene.

In the election of 1945, King was presented as a beacon of stability and sense in a world which had to be set to rights. In fact, he was puzzled and disheartened by the chaos he perceived around him. In education and upbringing, Mackenzie King was a good Ontario Victorian, with family and racial roots deep in British colonial soil. For King, London was the centre of the political and intellectual universe, the place outside Canada where he felt most at home and at ease. King's library was lined with British biographies and books on British politics and British thought – most of them unread, to be sure, but nevertheless a sure sign of their owner's tastes and affections. When King held his pre-war 'at homes' for the spirit world, it was British ghosts who came to call and proffer advice.

The ghosts could not tell the Prime Minister what to do, only reflect on what they, and he, had done. In 1945 there was a new addition to the pantheon, President Roosevelt, the first American spectre to be admitted to the charmed circle. There, at least, was one American who could listen to and reassure King. King could reflect that Roosevelt was the only American president who took any time for Canada and who had even taken the trouble to advise King on the subjects that interested him most: national unity and Canadian politics. Roosevelt's advice, to assimilate the French Canadians to the English majority, was, of course, eccentric and politically unfeasible.

The new American president, Harry Truman, liked Canadians. He even knew one or two, and one of his first requests was that Canada appoint an old ex-Canadian crony of his a consul in Kansas City. From time to time Truman bestowed new marks of his esteem: Canadians were to be admitted to West Point, the military academy, just like Americans, Truman decided, and it took much bureaucratic shuffling by his embarrassed subordinates to bury the proposal. Relations between Truman and Mackenzie King, however, remained formal, polite, and minimal.

Fortunately other people in Washington liked Canadians, and some of them were in important posts. Professional diplomats admired the competence of Canada's fledgling foreign service, and envied the compact tidiness of the Canadian government's ability to make decisions and then ratify and implement them, without messy reference to a fractious and ignorant legislature. In a war which was, on the American side, largely run by a powerful and increasingly arrogant military, American bureaucrats discovered fellow-feeling with their Canadian counterparts in Washington: both were usually on the outside looking wistfully in. Common interests reinforced shared experience. During the war it had become increasingly common simply to pick up the phone and dial one's counterpart in the other capital. Almost always the Americans had something the Canadians wanted; less frequently, but still profitably, the Canadians could satisfy American demands.

Watching the United States go to war was an impressive experience. The Americans had, in 1945, over twelve million men and women in uniform. In 1947 the Americans produced over one-half of the manufactures of the whole world. In the same year they generated 43 per cent of the world's electricity and pumped 62 per cent of the world's oil. American productive capacity had determined the outcome of the Second World War, dethroning the Germans, the previous masters of the art of turning production into military predominance. With the American example so close and so obviously effective, it was natural and inevitable for Canadians to imitate the American model. Using American technology, American management skills, and largely American designs, Canadian industry surged ahead during the war, even surpassing, from time to time, American production records. Canadian achievements were, however, usually in terms of unit costs – making something quicker and cheaper than the Americans could, such as standardized merchant ships or artificial rubber. There was little question of making *more* of anything than the Americans, who were still ten times bigger and fifteen times richer than their northern neighbour.

The Americans also had the atomic bomb. The bomb was the war's most closely guarded secret, known only to a handful of British and American statesmen, military officers, and scientists – and to Mackenzie King and a handful of Canadians. Canada's participation in atomic research during the war derived from possession of a previously neglected metal, uranium, and from Britain's need for atomic research facilities. These Canada provided, first in Montreal and then in Chalk River, Ontario, and secured in return priceless training in the most advanced science and technology.

When the bomb was dropped on the Japanese cities of Hiroshima and Nagasaki in August 1945, and the war came to an abrupt end, the timing, but not the fact, was a surprise to the Canadian government. While the existence of the bomb was no longer concealed, the United States embarked on an elaborate secrecy program, designed to preserve the atomic monopoly, with all its military and security advantages, for the United States alone. The American program was a fallacy, since the British too had the know-how, if not the facilities, to construct a similar device, and the Russians, not to be left behind, were hot on the trail.

So hot were the Russians that the Soviet government could not contain its eagerness to know as much as possible, as soon as possible, about the new wonder weapons. Fortunately for Moscow, some of the scientists engaged in atomic research were well disposed toward the Soviet cause, and some of these men worked in Canada. The revelation of this fact came all too quickly for Mackenzie King. On September 6, 1945, Norman Robertson, the Under Secretary of State for External Affairs, met the Prime Minister at his office. Something was terribly wrong, Robertson told King: 'A man had turned up, with his wife, at the office of the Minister of Justice. He asked to see the Minister. He said he was from the Russian Embassy.' It was not an official call, as could be seen from the Soviet official's observation that 'the Russian democracy was different from ours.'

How different Canadians were soon to learn. A shocked Prime Minister discovered that the Russian, Igor Gouzenko, had brought with him embassy documents proving the existence of a Soviet spy ring in Canada which had as its object the discovery of information on the making of the atomic bomb. It was a shattering awakening for a Victorian Canadian, even one as worldly and politically astute as Mackenzie King. King confided his shock and distress to his diary; Robertson, more practically, began to assemble one of Canada's finest collections of the literature of espionage. A royal commission was appointed to discover what it could about the spy ring. The findings were startling: a Member of Parliament, a prominent scientist, and minor members of the military and civil service were implicated. The suspects were rounded up in the early morning under the authority of the War Measures Act, Canada's emergency constitution, jailed, and interrogated. When brought to trial, about half of the accused, including Canada's only Communist MP, were convicted and sentenced to prison.

That was only the beginning. The Soviet Union professed to regard the publicity surrounding the spy scandal as a malicious provocation by the Canadian government, part of an anti-Soviet strategy orchestrated by the Americans. As such, it was a nine-days' wonder internationally; for Canadians it was the end of innocence.

It was not difficult to connect what was happening domestically with what was going on internationally. Canadian diplomats stationed in Moscow had been sounding cautionary notes for some time. Even before the war was over, in April 1945, a

Canadian despatch from the Soviet capital called 'for a firm diplomatic line to be taken by the Western Powers in their dealings with the Soviet Union, and it is also desirable to consider building up those areas in Europe and elsewhere where Western influence is, or can be, dominant.'

Canada's advice on such an issue could not be decisive: that was left to the larger powers, the United States and Great Britain. What is noteworthy is the fact that most of the currents of the internal American debate over foreign policy were faithfully reproduced in a Canadian context. There were even some optimists who argued that it would still be possible for the great powers, including the Soviet Union, to agree among themselves, provided all parties kept their heads. But embedded in the optimism was a strain of bleak realism. Dana Wilgress, Canada's ambassador to Moscow, concluded that the chief interest of the Soviet Union was stability, domestically and internationally. That, he told Ottawa, was because Russia was the home of a 'new privileged class.' To preserve its dominance at home, the Soviet leadership required to be left alone, safe from interference from abroad. But would it be? Russia's new class was uncertain and fearful of western intentions and influences, anxious to preserve its utopia from comparisons with western freedom and affluence. When the Russians constructed a *cordon sanitaire* along their western frontier, establishing their own puppet governments under reliable personalities, the western powers carped and balked. Russian diversions in the Far East and the Mediterranean, Wilgress explained, could be seen largely as a response to western initiatives in Poland and the Balkans. They should not be taken seriously. 'On the whole,' he concluded, 'the interests of the Soviet privileged class are bound up with the maintenance of a long period of peace....'

If Wilgress was right, the world was in for a long period of division between two mutually exclusive economic and political systems. If there was little to fear, there was nothing to hope for. There would soon be a term for the situation, the Cold War, and a description of the boundary between West and East: the Iron Curtain. In the East there would be monolithic Communist regimes, firmly under the thumb of the spiritual grandfather of all Communists, Josef Stalin. In the West, there were the surviving traces of free economies and societies in western Europe and North America. In such a system, Canada's place was axiomatic: it belonged with its elder Anglo-Saxon partners.

The nub of the matter had been stated by Mackenzie King in 1938: 'We, too, as a good friendly neighbour, have our responsibilities. One of them is to see that our country is made as immune from possible invasion as we can reasonably be expected to make it, and, that should the occasion ever arise, enemy forces should not be able to make their way, either by land, sea or air, to the United States across Canadian territory.' That policy remained in effect in 1945; it would remain in effect for the next generation.

7

The End of the War

When General Alfred Jodl stepped out of a French schoolhouse on May 7, 1945, after signing the surrender of Nazi Germany, the western world went wild with excitement. It hardly mattered to Canadians that their country was still at war with the Japanese and that the bloody battles of the Pacific might have another year to run. 'The war' was the war against Hitler, and Hitler was dead, his armies prisoners, his cities smashed, his people beaten, his country occupied.

Across Canada people celebrated according to their mood. Everyone left work, some heading for taverns to drink, others for the main streets to wave Union Jacks. In Ottawa, there was a solemn ceremony of thanksgiving. In Halifax, there was a riot.

It had been a long war. In five and a half years some 41 per cent of Canada's male population of military age (eighteen to forty-five) had passed through the armed forces – over a million men out of a total population of just over twelve million. The size of Canada's armed forces made Canada, temporarily, the fourth military power in the world in 1945, a significant factor in any equation of power.

The Canadian armed forces had a fine fighting record. Forty-two thousand had been killed during the war (fewer than during the First World War). Canadians had fought their way through Sicily and up the Italian peninsula, as well as across the lowlands of northern Europe. On May 7, Canada's own army, the First Canadian Army, on the allies' northern flank, was preparing to advance into the German fortress of Holland, to liberate the starving cities of Amsterdam, Rotterdam, and The Hague.

The Canadian government and the Canadian army had no intention of keeping Canada's military power in being. Canadian mobilization was an occasional thing, a temporary outing for a deeply civilian society. In 1944, with victory imminent, preparations for demobilization had been accelerated. The Canadian government informed the British that Canada would maintain a few formations in Europe to assist in the occupation of Germany – an offer the British gratefully accepted – but otherwise Canada's soldiers were to come home on the first available ships. And they did: 15,665 soldiers in June, and more thereafter. By the end of December, 184,000 had made the homeward voyage. Some brought new brides: in 1945 almost 7,000 adults and 3,700 children were admitted to Canada as 'soldiers' dependents.'

Some units were to be shipped to the Pacific theatre; otherwise priority was given to those who had served longest: first in, first out. Not everyone accepted the principle with equanimity. Riots broke out in overseas camps, with attendant publicity. A scandalized government decided to be quit of the whole matter as soon as possible. All troops would be brought home, previous pledges notwithstanding. In December 1945 the British were told that Canada's army would leave Europe no later than the summer of 1946. And by the autumn of that year it had.

On reaching Canadian soil military units were disbanded as quickly as possible. From a strength of 478,000 in May 1945, the army was reduced to 31,000 at the end of September 1946. The hopes of the generals, admirals, and air marshals that the government would show its gratitude for their military prowess by maintaining a military strength of 105,000 in peacetime were quickly dashed. Late in September, the Cabinet Defence Committee decided that the army would have to live with a force level of between 20,000 and 25,000 soldiers, instead of the 55,000 it had requested. The air force received 15,000 to 20,000, and the navy 10,000. The military budget contracted, in spasms, until by fiscal 1947-8 (the Canadian fiscal year is measured from April 1 to March 31) it touched bottom at $240,000,000. This represented 12 per cent of the budget, a level dearly won against the opposition of more civilian-minded ministers by the Minister of National Defence, Brooke Claxton.

During the war, the civilian side of government had necessarily taken second place. Now the lid was off. Gross national product, in current dollars, had been $5.6 billion in 1939; it was $11.8 billion in 1945. Unemployment was negligible: 163,000 in 1946, out of a civilian labour force of 4.8 million. Those who were unemployed benefited from the new unemployment insurance system.

Retrospectively, the picture looks rosy, but that was not the impression at the time. Canadians at the end of the war were deeply worried. 'What will we do if there's a slump after the war?' one young mother asked. 'I don't want my children to have the hardships I had.' Economists, businessmen, labour leaders, social workers, and politicians all worried. 'Discontented youth formed the vanguard of revolutionary movements abroad after the last war,' the Canadian Youth Commission reported in 1945. 'They might well play a similar role here should prolonged unemployment destroy their faith in democratic institutions.'

With an eye to the future, businessmen and workers, free enterprisers and socialists alike, rushed to join what C.D. Howe, the Liberal Minister of Reconstruction, scornfully called 'the Security Brigade.' Fear of depression stimulated elaborate planning for the dreadful future. Typical was the proposal by Canada's tiny democratic socialist party, the Co-operative Commonwealth Federation (gratefully abridged by press and public to CCF) for a 'National Planning Commission, consisting of a small group of economists, engineers and statisticians assisted by an appropriate technical staff,' to advise the government what it could do with the economy and discover what would make a socialized Canada run. After all, the argument ran, it had been done in war; now it could be done in peace. Canadians, the CCF believed, would order 'Left Turn, Canada,' in the words of a party pamphlet.

The voters appeared to give their support to the CCF's analysis when they turned out two discredited provincial Liberal regimes, in Ontario and Saskatchewan, installing the CCF as official opposition in Ontario and as the government in Saskatchewan. The voters had chosen the CCF, and the CCF stood for planning and socialization. Surely the signposts pointed left. Some of the signs, however, were deceptive. Part of the problem was that the public was undecided about which of its desires it wished to emphasize. On the one hand, the Canadian public wanted security; but it also craved material prosperity, consumer goods, cars, and a house in the suburbs. It had had a taste of prosperity during the war: personal expenditure on goods and services rose from $10.6 billion in 1938 to $14.1 billion in 1944 (in constant 1971 dollars). It wanted more of the same.

Alone of King's ministers, C.D. Howe seized the mood of the public, and combined his perception with a grasp of the practicalities of planning. The real problem with the civilian economy after the war, he told King, would be shortages. Industry would be strained to the utmost to make up for fifteen years of depression and war. The facilities to exploit the potential boom were ready to hand, in capital investment in war industry. Indeed, in Howe's view, the true reconstruction of the Canadian economy had already taken place. All that was needed now was 'reconversion' to make the best new use of what existed.

King's preference did not go immediately to Howe or his program. There were alternatives, promoted by Ian Mackenzie and social planners under his patronage in the Department of Pensions and National Health. Mackenzie had sponsored the Committee on Reconstruction, chaired by Principal Cyril James of McGill University, to uncover the trouble spots in the Canadian economy and prescribe remedies that the government should adopt. From the James Committee's perspective, the chief post-war desideratum was employment; its chief premise, that there would be an economic slump. The government would, therefore, have to intervene in the economy to create employment, cushioning the shock with social welfare benefits such as unemployment insurance and health insurance. Meanwhile a committee of Mackenzie's own officials worked out a plan for a national health insurance scheme.

The problem with both the James Committee's plan and with the more modest health insurance scheme was that they were constitutionally unfeasible. 'I am inclined to think,' one of Mackenzie's French-Canadian colleagues warned in April 1942, 'that in considering the future policies of the Country we should not entirely forget the system which has been prevailing in our federal administration up to the present time.' Moreover, the minister added, 'I am somewhat doubtful as to the advisability of creating an entirely new organization of public activities which, among other things, would mean a rather complete condemnation of the present responsible system which we are defending and which young men of Canada are being asked to fight for.' In the opinion of some the gospel of centralized social welfare was not all-powerful. In Quebec, at least, it might be politically dangerous.

The country wasn't ready, and neither was King. When the James Committee's research director, Leonard Marsh, issued a report on social planning early in 1943, it was firmly trodden on. The politicians found Marsh's proposals strange, and the civil servants found them actively offensive.

The civil servants knew, better than Marsh or James, how to make their opinions count. Their nerve centre was the Department of Finance. In pre-depression days the finance department had been a sleepy accounting office, periodically spewing out new taxation and keeping the government's finances roughly in balance. All that had changed when, in 1932, King's Conservative predecessor, R.B. Bennett, had summoned W. Clifford Clark from Queen's University to become deputy minister of finance. Clark was a youngish man who had worked for the government at the end of the First World War, and who had then left for the United States to make his fortune in private banking. That business had turned sour with the Depression, and Clark returned to academe to await better times. But Dr Clark (as he became when Queen's awarded him an honorary degree) turned out to have talents, seldom found in an academic, which were more reminiscent of New York finance than of the university's dreaming spires. Clark combined his banker's flair with a talent for intrigue and a passion to arrive, and remain, at the centre of things. King, who shared many of the same qualities (besides a real PHD in economics), no doubt appreciated a kindred spirit, and kept Clark on when he returned to power in 1935. Dr Clark and Dr King together made a formidable combination, as the cabinet discovered when King placed proposals for family allowances before them in January 1944. King summoned Clark to the council table (in the absence of the Minister of Finance, who had pressing business elsewhere) to explain matters. 'I think,' King later wrote in his diary, 'most of the Ministers who have been opposing the idea did not feel equal to debating the matter with Clark.' Those who did were squelched.

Family allowances were just one of the opportunities the war brought to Clifford Clark. The budget expanded fivefold during the war (from $2.9 billion in 1939 to $19.4 billion in 1944, in constant 1971 dollars). Finance had to find how to raise it. To handle the problem, Clark assembled a formidable team. First to come, just before the war, was R.B. Bryce, a product of John Maynard Keynes's seminar at

Cambridge, who combined a firm belief in the possibilities of government action with a clear and rational explanatory style. J.H. Perry and A.K. Eaton devised taxation policies, and for more specialized tasks Clark summoned an old colleague, W.A. Mackintosh, from Queen's.

Mackintosh was no stranger to Ottawa or governmental problems. His work for the pre-war Royal Commission on Dominion-Provincial Relations had helped to shape that group's perceptions of Canada's fundamental economic problems. Brilliant and persuasive on paper, Mackintosh was down-to-earth and blunt in person. Fertile in expedients and indefatigable in work, he became a much more powerful figure than his title, 'special assistant to the deputy minister,' indicated. 'Twin' or 'alter ego' would have been closer to the truth.

Mackintosh functioned most effectively on a special interdepartmental committee, created and chaired by Clark, called the Economic Advisory Committee. Its function was to purvey sound counsel to the cabinet on thorny economic problems on occasions when the Minister of Finance could not cope with them by himself. For the first three years of the war these problems were war-related. On topics such as taxation, wage control, or the balance of payments the ministers were used to listening and deferring to Clark's arguments. By 1942, however, the war was in principle won, and Clark could turn his attention to less immediate matters.

One such matter was the James Committee's report. When preliminary rumblings reached the cabinet in the autumn of 1942, they were referred to the Economic Advisory Committee. James recommended that a special department be established to guide reconstruction planning, or that at least a minister without portfolio be assigned the task of co-ordinating the government's reconstruction program. The Economic Advisory Committee poured cold water on James's proposals. It was then that James authorized Marsh to proceed with his famous report. It was ready on February 17, 1943.

Marsh failed to impress the civil servants. W.A. Mackintosh pointed out the defects in an early comment, observing that 'the full programme of social insurance here discussed is not at present within the powers of the Parliament of Canada.' Marsh was not deterred. His report plumped for a 'comprehensive' scheme – health insurance, family allowances, unemployment insurance, children's allowances, and workmen's compensation – to be implemented by Ottawa alone. His sole concession to political reality was the observation that 'There should be no danger if the whole situation were canvassed and agreed on in advance – possibly through the medium of a special conference of federal and provincial representatives....' Besides social welfare, Marsh prescribed a dominion 'works development programme' which would combat unemployment in the inevitable economic downturn. The total cost of social security was estimated at $500 million, while public works might go as high as $1 billion. But even so, it would cost less than the war was costing in the fiscal year 1942-3.

Marsh was naturally proud of his creation, viewing it as an intellectual *tour de force*. It had not taken very long to complete, he told the press. Marsh's immodest observation provoked derision. Marsh's 'thinking was squeezed into a period of one week,' one of Mackintosh's friends, Walter Gordon, observed. 'Having in mind the "pie in the sky" era to which we are all looking forward,' Gordon added, 'I presume he means a working week of four or five days of perhaps six hours per day or a total of, say, thirty hours per one billion dollars.' Mackintosh reassured his friend. 'The so-called Marsh Report did not emanate from any of the Government departments,' he wrote, 'and I am afraid that it is likely to prove a boomerang.' Or a dead duck.

It was the sponsorship of the James Committee and the publicity which the Marsh Report received that helped to bury its proposals. But the spirit it represented had a profound effect on government thinking. James's and Marsh's views had a long and respectable ancestry in the writings of social workers and some economists. Britain's Beveridge Report, published the previous fall, had achieved bestseller status, and was referred to by countless individuals, including Prime Minister King, who had never read it.

King moved slowly. Family allowances, recommended by the National War Labour Board as a means to circumvent wage control for the worst-paid in the work force, were brought before Parliament in 1944 and passed, though not before the Conservatives uttered some harsh thoughts about the French-Catholic families, with their unlimited breeding potential, for whom it was undoubtedly destined. A Department of Reconstruction was authorized, to serve as a co-ordinating agency for the government's reconstruction program. A cabinet committee was established to prepare for a dominion-provincial conference on reconstruction. A new Department of National Health and Welfare was established, and a special agency for veterans, the Department of Veterans' Affairs, created. But the government's action was strictly circumscribed. No one questioned its ability to clean up after the war: war-making was a dominion responsibility. Family allowances arguably belonged within the dominion's sphere of action too. But the other schemes advocated by the enthusiasts for social welfare, planning, and government intervention in the economy did not.

While a cabinet committee wrestled with this problem (and while the committee's chairman, T.A. Crerar, a provincial rights' enthusiast, wrestled with his conscience and his colleagues), King was forced to come to a decision on reconstruction. The only possible appointee for the job was C.D. Howe, he decided, and in October 1944 Howe duly assumed the duties of Minister of Reconstruction. Reconstruction, he insisted, would follow the lines that he prescribed, and not those laid down by the woolly proponents of state planning. Reconstruction in fact would be reconversion.

Reconversion was in full swing, under the aegis of the wartime Department of Munitions and Supply. Under a 1944 budget provision, Howe was able to grant accelerated depreciation to companies converting their facilities to peacetime production. The accelerated depreciation would permit a quick write-off of extra expenses against current taxation; at the same time, if the economy turned downward, they would already have paid off their gamble on the future. If, as luck would have it, economic conditions were favourable after the war, they would be paying full taxes on their new, but productive, plant. Under Howe's program, funds for capital expansion were readily available.

Mackintosh, who had joined the Department of Reconstruction, was uneasy. A cautious and prudent man, he was opposed to putting all the reconstruction eggs into Howe's reconversion basket. Squeezing a reluctant approval from his minister, Mackintosh set to work exploring a different line of country. From his labours emerged a general statement of the government's post-war economic policy, the White Paper on Employment and Income.

There had never before been a White Paper in Canada. Such a document committed the government to doctrine and policy, yet had no legislative effect. It could, however, attract attention and focus debate, both public and parliamentary. Mackintosh's first draft, when he laid it before Howe, took a spacious view of the government's capacities. There would be 'full employment' after the war, Mackintosh promised: the government would make it so. Howe bridled. 'Full employment was impossible,' he snorted, and any government that promised it would be a sitting duck collecting the pot shots of the press and the opposition. Far better, he thought, to take refuge in the circumlocution, 'high and stable level of employment.' That looked good, and yet promised nothing in particular. 'High and stable level' it was. Under that lumbering banner the Liberals marched out to the first post-war election, on June 11, 1945. Party orators had no hesitation in translating the 'high and stable level' into 'full employment' – after the election that would be forgotten. The Liberals, after all, had 'a plan.' But the plan they had was not necessarily the one the electorate expected or, perhaps, voted for.

The real Liberal plan, whether by accident or design, was Howe's. It was based on optimism about the economy, and scepticism about the potentialities of planning. It would not be the economic abstractions of doctrinaire planners in Ottawa that would shape post-war Canada. That would be left to business's self-interest, guided, prodded, and shaped by incentives that businessmen could understand. Post-war Canada would be a free enterprise society.

8

The Legacy of War

As Canadians struggled to regain their feet in civilian life and as their government endeavoured to inculcate the unfamiliar spirit of optimism in the electorate, certain phenomena remained constant. Among them was the Canadian constitution, the British North America (BNA) Act. That Act divided Canadian government into pockets of authority and sovereignty labelled federal (or dominion) and provincial. Eighty years of interpretation by the courts had fixed clear limits to the ability of the central authority to exercise its powers.

Such a limitation could be a political convenience. During the thirties Mackenzie King's Liberal government was only too happy to slough off responsibility for the unemployed and the destitute on to the provinces and municipalities. It was only after the outbreak of war that the King government acted on the problem of unemployment, securing the provinces' consent to the transfer of authority over unemployment insurance to the central government, which alone possessed the necessary financial resources to grapple with the problem. As for the recommendations of the Royal Commission on Dominion-Provincial Relations, which in 1940 had suggested a much more fundamental restructuring of federal-provincial relationships, they were placed in a deep freeze for the duration of the war.

The staff of the Royal Commission dispersed to war work – more urgent and more necessary under the circumstances. The war took care of unemployment, and the emergency transferred ultimate authority to the central government (only in national emergencies did the central government's residual powers become active and effective).

The operative instrument of the dominion government's emergency powers was (and is) the War Measures Act, passed in 1914 to cope with the First World War emergency. The Act is a simple one. In a specified emergency the governor-in-council (the cabinet) may make 'orders and regulations [which] shall have the force of law' on any subject or for any purpose deemed 'necessary for the security, defence, peace, order and welfare of Canada.' During the Second World War the dominion government enacted 6,414 orders under the War Measures Act, orders which had the force of law and circumvented parliamentary debate. Using these orders, an army of civil servants, controllers, directors-general, and commissioners fanned out across the country, calculating, enforcing, regulating, and sometimes arresting persons or confiscating products.

The civil service expanded to match its growing powers. In 1939, the dominion bureaucracy totalled 46,000; in 1945 there were 116,000 civil servants. But that was not all. Unable to cram all of its administrators or functions into the tiny city of Ottawa, the central government set up specialized crown corporations to run essential aspects of the war effort. Crown corporations bought and stockpiled silk; mined uranium; built bombers; imported machine tools; refined fuel; ran telephone companies.

What the government did not ordain directly, it regulated through an army of controllers. That included transport, air, road and rail, petroleum products, hydro-electricity, and construction materials, among others. Supplies for the war effort, scarce commodities for civilian life, all came under federal jurisdiction. Those who could demonstrate a valid need for one of the scarce commodities controlled by the Department of Munitions and Supply could apply for permission to use it. Those who could not, whether they wanted to put stainless steel railings in an office building or a new metal roof on a church, were told to wait until the end of the war.

Howe's controllers were principally concerned to supply raw materials to Canada's hungry factories. However, the government could not entirely ignore the needs of the rest of the economy, those parts that fed the war workers, clothed them, and kept public services in repair. Munitions and Supply symbolized what Minister of Finance James Ilsley called the 'real costs' of the war, 'the goods and services which have to be sacrificed out of our current production to meet the needs of war.' Those things that could not be sacrificed were doled out, and their prices controlled, by a parallel organization, the Wartime Prices and Trade Board under its hard-driving chairman, Donald Gordon.

Gordon was by any standards a remarkable man. He had to be to face down the contending special interests that demanded his personal concentration and attention. Gordon enjoyed confronting his opponents, and he usually carried the day. The only exception to the rule was agriculture, where the Minister of Agriculture, Saskatchewan's Jimmy Gardiner, and the particular interests of farmers, reigned supreme. Gordon's attempts to integrate farmers into his system were seldom successful. But as Gardiner pointed out, farm production was booming ($570 million in 1939, it reached $1,320 million in 1944). Gordon wasted his profanity on Gardiner.

In other spheres, the hard-drinking Gordon (he consumed a bottle of scotch a day, according to legend) was much more successful. His principal task, to keep the cost of living down, was achieved. The index of wholesale prices in December 1945 was a paltry 11.1 per cent over that of December 1941, while the cost of living reached only 120.1 (using the period 1935-9 as an average). Officials travelling out of their Ottawa fastnesses were pleasantly surprised at the relative absence of public complaint or resentment. The galloping inflation of the First World War had created an industrial crisis in Canada; there was hardly any repetition in the Second. Indeed, Canadians as a whole were better off than they had been before the war. For most, standards of living and disposable income had increased during the war. Only the business and professional classes and those on fixed incomes resented the large bites taken out of their salaries by stringent taxation. Gordon's organization proudly pointed out that food and clothing actually cost less in 1945 than they had in 1919, while fuel, home furnishings, and services cost just slightly more; only rents were substantially above 1919 levels.

Controls did not vanish with the end of Hitler's war. Servicemen released into the civilian economy created heavy demands on still-scarce supplies. Overseas, the liberation of Europe brought in its train millions of starving mouths to be fed. It was the same in the Far East. In July 1945 meat rationing had to be reintroduced (it had been abolished in 1944). Henceforth, Canadians could buy from one to three pounds of meat per person per week, depending on the type of meat. Butter, too, was rationed, and the allotment kept going down: in March 1946 it stood at four ounces per person per week. Sugar and preserves were also rationed, and so was clothing. There the object was to ensure that each newly discharged veteran got a new suit of clothes on leaving the service, and that meant hundreds of thousands of new suits. There was good news in one area, however: gasoline rationing was wound up in late 1945, and so was tire rationing. Canadians were released into the countryside for the first time in years. There were complications, of course. Since no new automobiles had been produced since 1942, Canada's highways looked like ambulatory motor museums. But shabby or not, it was one of the fruits of victory – liberation.

Other controls were lifted as soon as supplies became available. It was not always easy, however, to dispense with restrictions that had become customary and popular. The most important of these was rent control. This had been instituted early in the war to prevent landlords from gouging luckless tenants forced by war work to move into areas where housing was scarce. The end of the war naturally placed even greater strain on limited accommodation as soldiers returned to join their families and landlords struggled to escape from the web of wartime regulations in which their investments were enmeshed. The easiest device was to evict a tenant in order to occupy the premises oneself, although in some cases six months' notice would serve. There was, predictably, a flurry of eviction notices – 3,500 in Toronto, 1,100 in Vancouver, and 700 in Winnipeg in the summer of 1945 alone. Evicting an unwelcome tenant simply shifted the burden of accommodation to other shoulders, usually those of the government. In the first years after the war the dominion acted as landlord to thousands, using emergency shelters converted from barracks. More stringent controls on evictions naturally followed.

Housing was just one area where Canadians looked to Ottawa for solutions. Controls, for example, were good when it came to rent, and bearable when it came to meat and butter. Restraining private enterprise from gaudy excesses was justifiable in the public interest, whether or not that interest was enlightened. Socialists marvelled at the sight. Writing in 1945, the CCF intellectual Frank Scott observed that 'a central government which could not provide three square meals a day to the hundreds of thousands on relief ... now pours its billions annually among the astonished citizens and calls forth miracles of production from old and new enterprises.'

Wartime centralization did not stop with regulating business, large and small. Before the war Canadian labour had been governed under a crazy quilt of ten separate jurisdictions (one for the dominion and one for each of the nine provinces). Railways were under federal jurisdiction, so railway workers were regulated by the dominion's Industrial Disputes Investigation Act; but a Quebec streetcar conductor or a British Columbia hydro lineman came under the respective labour acts of those provinces. War's centralized economy could not tolerate jurisdictional particularities in labour law. Within a few months after the declaration of war, the federal government had brought war-related industries under its own jurisdiction. By the end of the war, this meant that 85 per cent of the non-agricultural work force fell under the federal sway. The dominion government prescribed union recognition, compulsory negotiation, and compulsory conciliation for employers and employees. It was a rational system, which was generally well administered. Most of the time it worked. It worked well enough to serve as a model for most provinces at the end of the war; their subsequent labour codes were based on the federal wartime regulations, rather than on pre-war experience.

Centralization had more indirect effects as well. All foreign-exchange transactions were placed under dominion control on the outbreak of war. Regulations were tightened drastically in 1940, and then supplemented by a series of special-priority arrangements between Canada and the United States governing the supply of goods essential to both countries' war effort. Spending on luxuries and tourism was strictly curtailed, although an inspection of import figures reveals that not all consumer cravings were prohibited. Oranges, for example, tipped the scale at twelve million cubic feet in 1945, while Scotch whisky reached Canada at the rate of 730,000 gallons in 1942. (Scotch, however, was a casualty of the battle of the Atlantic, dipping to 468,000 gallons in 1945.)

What interfered with provincial jurisdiction (for example, over liquor imports) also naturally affected provincial revenues and spending. The scope of provincial politics shrank, as their content was trivialized. Naturally the ferocity of provincial political contests grew in inverse relation to their actual importance, and federal issues played an ever larger part in provincial elections. Mackenzie King's temperance sentiments, normally strong, fierce, and sanctimonious, wobbled when confronted with the Ontario and Quebec provincial elections in 1943 and 1944. Could there not be, King mused, some means of easing controls? Provincial Liberals fervently agreed, out of hope before the elections (which they lost), and afterward from despair.

For most provinces the war provided a welcome respite from financial burdens. Capital projects now lay mostly within the federal sphere. Even if the provinces could procure the supplies necessary to carry out their own projects, it was by no means certain where they could find the money. As a consequence, provincial government departments quietly mouldered between 1939 and 1945. Comparisons between the levels of dominion and provincial spending are quite startling. Federal expenditure on goods and services, including capital formation, reached its wartime maximum in 1944 at $4,488 million. In the same year, provincial spending amounted to only $200 million ($539 million if local spending is added in).

For ordinary needs, the central government provided. The Wartime Tax Agreements of 1941 allowed the dominion government to 'occupy' the corporation and income-tax fields, which were 'vacated' by the provinces. In return, the dominion paid the provinces either the revenues they would have raised from the 'occupied' sources in the fiscal year 1940-1, or the service on the provincial debt, less certain amounts. In addition, the dominion paid the statutory subsidies under the BNA Act and 'fiscal-need subsidies' where a province could demonstrate an urgent need for extra funds. These grants went to the poorest provinces: Saskatchewan, New Brunswick, Manitoba, and Prince Edward Island. In general, the provinces were able to pocket the federal compensation, run surpluses, and begin to retire their debts.

In the meantime Canadians got used to paying their taxes to the central government. A new fiscal device allowed the government to extract the money directly from the citizen's paycheque, eliminating, as far as possible, the direct pain of involuntary transfer from the subject to the Chief Magistrate. The effect in Ottawa was rather heady. From 1941 until 1945 Mackenzie King steered clear of any dominion-provincial gatherings, restricting his provincial contacts to occasional consultations with friendly Liberals. Most of his ministers came to view the provinces, not as rivals or antagonists, as they had been during the thirties, but as irrelevancies to be stroked or prodded according to whether they had a Liberal government or not. In an era of expansive action it was enough to contend with fellow ministers in the Treasury Board without worrying about parochial difficulties in one or another of the provinces.

Much of the central government's aggressive self-confidence derived from its collective belief that it monopolized the progressive ideas and the active intelligences of Canada's administrative system. You could look far in any single province, or in all the provinces put together, before spying the equals of Ottawa's mandarin team. With a successful record of wartime administration behind them, with all its invaluable and instructive experience, Clark and his colleagues were well placed to tell the King government what to do next. After devising national standards and policies that had been tested in war there could be no doubt that they could do it in peace as well. And what Clark and company could assemble would, or should, be superior to anything the provinces could imagine – or anyway, as with CCF Saskatchewan – afford.

Paradoxically, and despite Howe's strong confidence in the post-war economy, the central government's strongest card in its negotiations with the provinces was the general uncertainty over what to expect. It would take strong medicine to banish the miseries of unemployment – strong centralized medicine. Masterful management of the economy by the dominion could not be achieved in the pre-war vacuum of power and initiative. Governments after the war would have to 'incur huge expenditures for housing and various construction projects' with or without help from the provinces, so as to fuel the economy and 'maintain a high level of national income.' It would therefore be, as the Minister of Finance explained to his colleagues in 1944, 'quite impossible for the Dominion Government to manage ... if we have to go back to our pre-war taxing system.'

If Canada's antiquated constitutional system could be cranked up to provide the necessary resources, then the Department of Finance had the answer. If the 'high and stable level of employment' promised by the White Paper was to be achieved, the government would have to promote the main sources of employment and income. These were four in number: export trade, private investment, consumption expenditure, and public investment. This was in conformity with the doctrines of the British economist, Lord Keynes, whose ideas had so profoundly influenced Ottawa's own economic specialists.

Clark and Mackintosh undertook to translate Keynes for their political masters. It all, in the end, came down to one thing: Ottawa had to concentrate taxing and, to a large degree, spending authority in its own hands in order to provide a stable rudder for the economy. There must be a change in the rules by which peacetime Canada was run. As the White Paper said, 'when unemployment threatens,' the government would incur the necessary deficits to promote job creation, 'whether that policy in the circumstances is best applied through increased expenditures or reduced taxation.'

The war had accustomed many Canadians to thinking in national terms. Large problems, such as unemployment, must be solved on a large scale, and the largest

Canadian dimension was the dominion government. Certain provinces whose finances were most threatened under a return to pre-war fiscal autonomy were anxious to assign some of their most onerous responsibilities to Ottawa. Liberal intellectuals, whose friends were in any case already in power in Ottawa, added their voices to the centralizing chorus. So did many businessmen, stirred by the memory of what had been done in the war. Canada, a business publicist pointed out in 1946, had enjoyed 'the most centralized – and perhaps the most efficient – war production organization in the world.' The experience had converted some reluctant businessmen to change their politics from reliable Tory blue to Liberal red, for, as long as C.D. Howe held the reins of economic power, business knew that it had a friend in Ottawa.

Next to King himself, and to St Laurent in Quebec, Howe was the best-known member of the cabinet. He had been the visible manifestation of the domestic war effort, criss-crossing the country to preside at the christening of the thousandth tank, the ten-thousandth plane, the millionth shell – jobs which Howe hated but tolerated for their considerable publicity value. Howe incarnated the business approach to administrative problems, contemptuous of theory, concentrating always on facts and specifics. Howe possessed manifest advantages. He had, in the first place, a quick mind and a decisive and impressive personality. 'When C.D. entered a room you knew it,' one of his business friends recalled. Howe caught people's attention with his pithy phrases (though he never uttered the one most often attributed to him, 'What's a million?') and his succinct summaries of problems too complicated, even insoluble, for everyone but himself. Howe sometimes horrified his colleagues, and his subordinates, by his willingness to speak off the cuff. Speaking one evening in the House of Commons, he unwittingly reversed the policy he was supposed to be defending. The next morning his assistant deputy minister came to tell him so. Howe was unperturbed. 'Fred,' he said, crossing his legs and lifting his feet to his desk, 'I've got news for you. Our policy changed at 9:57 last night.' Howe had the personal force to make his decisions, even the unconscious ones, stick. But he also had the information to formulate sensible policies. Using the statistics cranked out by his departmental economists, and combining them with the word-of-telephone by which he flourished, Howe knew in advance of most major investment decisions in Canada. He also knew, from the war, the men who would be making them, men like E.P. Taylor or Eric Phillips in Toronto, Frank Ross in Vancouver, or R.E. Powell in Montreal. Some though by no means all of Howe's business friends were Liberals: they became the backbone of the fund-raising system he perfected to fuel the Liberal party. But prominent Conservatives like Henry Borden, the president of Brazilian Traction, also supported Howe, if not his party.

Howe's closeness to business, his fishing trips and golf and bridge games with the Canadian rich, were part of his attraction to the economic élite. They were not designed to appeal to other segments of society. As Howe's colleague, Brooke Claxton, caustically observed, 'The mental climate of the businessman is ... unintellectual ... If a group of businessmen meet together for an afternoon or evening or for a week-end, the chances are that time will pass very enjoyably but that there will not be a moment's talk about politics, books or any serious subject.' Mackenzie King heartily agreed. When Howe lent his name to a book describing business leaders as 'Canadian strength,' King lamented that his minister showed a 'curious lack of proportion.' 'It is rather surprising,' the Prime Minister added, 'that any colleague should indicate that from his point of view Canadian strength was composed primarily of the heads of large corporations....' It was not the large corporations that voted, King knew, and the imposition of a corporate viewpoint on the Liberal party could bring in its train electoral dangers. Howe and the Minister of Finance (Douglas Abbott after 1946) were all too ready, in King's opinion, to 'impose their own will much too strongly through having a knowledge of certain matters respecting finance and trade and relations to the United States etc.' Howe scorned ignorant objections from colleagues too lazy or self-interested to see his point.

That was hurting the party, a delegation of Liberal Members of Parliament told the Prime Minister. The government 'was getting the reputation with the people of being icy cold; really not being in touch with the people at all.' The cabinet deferred too much to the wisdom of the finance department rather than to the sense of the caucus. But could the finance department garner votes?

It was not Howe, who despite his short temper was popular with backbenchers and the party rank and file, who epitomized the problem, but Douglas Abbott. Jaunty and cheerful, sensible and politically astute, Abbott had decided opinions on what was right and wrong in economic policy. Appearing before the Resolutions Committee at the national Liberal Convention in August 1948, Abbott lost no time in setting his audience straight. 'It doesn't matter,' Abbott told the party faithful, 'what resolutions you pass here. Pass any resolutions you like. But I am Minister of Finance and so long as I am, I will do what I think is right.'

It is normal for any party long in power to develop a hardening of the arteries in communications from bottom to top. The Canadian Liberal party was no exception. Through no particular fault of its own, it became a neutered cat, perfumed, brushed, belled, and fat (thanks to Howe's contribution system). As the cabinet's occasional pet, the party dragged its overweight carcass from election to election; in between, the cabinet's rigid propriety ensured that the party languished, without status or influence, on the sidelines. It was the civil servants, not the party, who had the ideas and the knowledge of how to run a country. In 1945, Mackintosh's White Paper was no mean banner to follow – a formula for national success that beat anything the grass roots could devise. The bush leagues would have to wait until after the election.

9

A Strategy for Economic Survival

In 1939 Canada ranked sixth among the world's trading nations. In terms of per capita trade, Canada was seventh, and in terms of per capita income also seventh. Canadians knew it well: their country was founded on trade and must trade to survive. 'It is only,' the Royal Commission on Dominion-Provincial Relations warned in 1940, 'by playing this role that Canada can maintain anything like her present standard of living and can support the great capital investment which has been made to equip her for this role.' That depended on international co-operation, for as the Commission observed, 'Canada is one of the least self-sufficient countries in the world.' It had paid the price during the thirties, along with other trading nations, suffering under the reign of 'Beggar my neighbour.'

There were no substantial alterations in Canada's official trade policy during the war. The policy was simply put in mothballs, superseded by innumerable practical arrangements between Canada and its principal trading partners, Britain and the United States. For five years, Canada had guaranteed exports, a market for all the war material the country could produce. The wartime bonanza had limited prospects, a fact which depressed the government's economic advisers. 'Adequate employment,' W.A. Mackintosh predicted, could not be achieved unless other countries co-operated to help 'maintain our external trade.'

The United States was Canada's best customer. In 1944 Canada bought $1,447,226,000 worth of imports from the United States, and sold $1,334,554,000 in return. Britain was next, buying $1,238,078,000 worth of Canadian products, but selling Canada only $110,599,000 in return. The imbalance between British purchases and sales in Canada was a source of great concern. The Americans, when they bought from Canada, paid US dollars, which Canada needed to make up its purchases in the United States. The British, however, financed their Canadian imports with loans and credits from the Canadian government. Without governmental assistance, British purchases in Canada would have been next to nothing.

During the war the King government had become used to the British returning, time and again, to the Canadian treasury in quest of more finance. It was provided, sometimes over the protest of parochially minded politicians who regarded Britain as the eternal incarnation of ill-gotten imperialist wealth. For them, enlightenment would be late in dawning, if it ever came. For the Liberals, dependent as they were on a suspicious Quebec delegation, assistance to the descendants of Wolfe and Durham posed a particular problem.

But the government had to try. It was axiomatic, as Mackintosh told Mackenzie King, that 'only by promoting and participating in a collaboration between the United States and the United Kingdom, with the threefold object of developing co-ordinated policies for maintaining employment, ensuring relative freedom of trade, and contributing to productive international investment, [could] Canada ... find after the war the larger world economy necessary to her tolerable existence.' Any such collaboration could scarcely be expected to develop out of private initiative. Over the course of the war, the government had appropriated most of Canada's private trading system. Most recently, in September 1943, the government had suspended private trading in wheat in order to curb rising prices and speculation on the Winnipeg Grain Exchange.

Wheat was a staple export whose markets were not easily destroyed. The same could not be said of Canada's manufactured exports. Shipping controls, foreign exchange restrictions, and alternative war production had reduced civilian exports to a low ebb by the end of the war. It was partly the government's (especially C.D. Howe's) anxiety to secure post-war markets for Canadian products that stimulated its stubborn insistence on membership in several allied combined-supply boards toward the end of the war. What went to the military today could go to refugees tomorrow and to reconstructed buyers the day after. It was important, while Europe's industries lay prostrate, to encourage Europeans to think Canadian. It was pleasant to combine self-interest with altruism.

Canada would not define the terms, nor secure the arena, for post-war trading planning. That was the prerogative of the two senior allies, Britain and the United States. During the war the Americans had freely dispensed aid to virtually all comers, as long as they were fighting the Germans. There would be no repayment. In return for this startling generosity, the Americans asked only one small consideration: signature to a clause in the Lend-Lease (aid) agreements committing the signatory to try to reduce its discriminatory trade practices and to join, after the war, in a free multilateral trading system. Discussions (called Article VII talks, after the numbered clause in the Lend-Lease master agreement) were to take place before the end of the war, so as to be ready for a better trading world as soon as hostilities ceased. Canada had remained aloof from Lend-Lease (though it gladly cashed in some British benefits under the scheme) in order to emphasize its independence from American charity. But the dominion could hardly afford to be left outside the Article VII talks, so crucial to Canada's trading future. Canadian representatives gladly signed a separate note accepting the principles of Article VII, and thereby qualifying, it was hoped, for the great trading pow-wow.

Multilateral tariff reductions represented the best of all possible trading worlds from the Canadian point of view. A free flow of goods across one customs frontier was, of course, a distinct advantage to a trading nation, but a free flow across as many frontiers as possible was even more desirable. A diversified Canadian trading pattern would avoid undue reliance on a single customer, the United States, with all the dangerous political consequences that might entail.

Canadian officials during the war were not reluctant to urge their vision of multilateral trading on their American and British counterparts. They met a warm response among American officials, who also believed the goal of a multilateral, low-tariff or no-tariff world well worth pursuing. Unhappily, those Congressmen responsible for legislating American tariff policy were unlikely to take as broad or altruistic a perspective; discussions with the Americans therefore had a quality of fervent unreality all their own. The British also took the Canadian point. Their difficulty was not a divorce between an enlightened bureaucracy and a benighted Parliament, but the very real dangers of Britain's international economic position. Britain's standing in international trade had so far eroded by 1944 or 1945 that the British were forced to contemplate a variety of unpleasant alternatives, involving restricting trade with dollar countries, in order to stave off total collapse. Nevertheless, the British remained firmly committed, *in theory*, to multilateralism in trade. All they asked was that someone give them the means to put multilateralism into practical terms.

A distinct second best, from the Canadian perspective, was the possibility of some special bilateral trading arrangement with a powerful economic partner. Canada already participated in such an arrangement – known as Empire Preference – a system of reduced tariffs exchanged by the several parts of the British empire. Until true multilateral trade was achieved, Empire Preference had its uses, not least as a bargaining counter with the suspicious and fearful Americans with whom the abolition of Empire Preference was a veritable grail of policy. Britain's economic weakness made it unrealistic to place too much reliance on the efficacy of imperial trading arrangements after the war. Dire necessity might make it imperative to contemplate another kind of special arrangement, this time with the United States. The concept was scouted in talks between Canadian and American diplomats toward the end of the war, but always as a highly theoretical possibility. Nevertheless, should the world slide into economic chaos, economic union with the United States might well become inevitable.

It was decidedly a time for bold initiatives. When Canadian ministers and their advisers considered the matter at a meeting in January 1945 their mood was gloomy. Clifford Clark as usual set the tone. 'The developing prospects ... [appear] to be so serious,' he argued, 'that they [justify] the Canadian Government doing what it could at the present time to improve matters.' Canada could not equably contemplate a British withdrawal into economic isolation inside a 'soft currency' bloc made up of those states which could not afford to see their money converted into American (or Canadian) dollars. The British dilemma was real. To win the war, they had dissipated their foreign assets and piled up a mountain of debt, less with the Americans and Canadians than with the Indians, Egyptians, and South Africans. In the face of this terrible prospect, Canada should be prepared to loosen the national purse strings. One immediate measure was to write down most of the British debt accumulated during the war: it was traded off against costs incurred by Canadian soldiers and airmen abroad. Then, in the spring of 1945, the Canadians went further.

The British were offered a Canadian loan to tide them over their worst post-war troubles. The loan would allow the British to continue buying in Canada until their economy righted itself, even if that happy day were as much as two years away. The British were not unreceptive, as discussions in May 1945 indicated, but details were left until later. The continuation of the war against Japan ensured a continuing flow of American aid for the immediate future at least.

The unexpected conclusion of the war against Japan brought with it the immediate termination of American wartime aid. British missions swiftly sped across the Atlantic. There they found the climate distinctly chilly. The Americans were not in a giving mood, and British hopes for a multi-billion-dollar aid program shrank under the icy impact of self-interested American parochialism. It took all of Keynes's persuasive powers to extract a grudging $3.75 billion from the Americans, to be repaid, with interest, over the next fifty years. In exchange, the British agreed to return the pound sterling to convertibility against the American dollar no later than the middle of 1947. They also agreed not to accept loans from other countries on terms more favourable than those received from the United States.

It would have been politically impossible for the Canadian government to offer better terms than those the British had received from the Americans. The American conditions were known: and the cabinet was not disposed to go one better than Uncle Sam. The British could expect essentially what they had got in Washington, a long-term loan, at low interest. What did cause comment was the size of the Canadian proposition. Canada would lend $1.25 billion, a third of the American subvention. It was as if the United States had proffered $12.5 billion (or more, considering the comparative magnitudes of the Canadian and American economies). The Canadians would have preferred such a larger amount: both the Canadian and British negotiators regarded the American loan as dangerously small. Domestically, the Canadian loan was justified on the grounds of long-term trading benefits. Both government and business, the US embassy reported to Washington, hoped the loan would help restore 'a normal volume of trade' with the United Kingdom, Canada's 'best market.'

By plumping for a vast loan to Britain, along with large credits to other European governments, Canada was trying to restore the pre-war balance of trade, in which Britain and Europe served as a counterweight to the United States. The Canadian government was also trying to preserve export markets retained or acquired during the war. By 1946 it had become apparent that there would be no revolutionary changes in the world trading system. The United States, the chief supporter of liberalized trade, had surrendered its lead in 1945 when President Truman agreed to a simple continuation of the American reciprocal trading formula. Across-the-board cuts were ruled out: each tariff reduction would have to be bargained for individually. Ottawa was deeply disappointed.

Canadian negotiators thereafter had to make do with salvaging what they could from the wreck of the war's multilateral hopes. An attempt to found an International Trading Organization (ITO) foundered in futility on an American refusal to ratify its covenant. While the ITO millennium was still under discussion, the world's trading nations met in Geneva to explore ways of reducing tariffs on an interim basis. The American delegation, its hands partially tied by American legislation, worked closely with Canada's exceptionally competent delegates, led by Dana Wilgress. The chief American objective, loudly trumpeted, was to eliminate the British preference in empire trade. That had been anticipated. What had not been was the skill with which the Canadian delegates talked round the thorny preferential issue, to emerge both with an agreement and, equally important, a method of reaching an agreement. The agreement was called the General Agreement on Tariffs and Trade, better known today as GATT. The method evolved in the course of the Geneva talks became known as the 'principal supplier rule,' whereby countries negotiate tariff concessions with the principal supplier of a given commodity. Canada, which was mainly interested in reducing American tariffs, thus assumed responsibility for certain primary products; European countries, more interested in supplying manufactured goods, took on the burden of those negotiations. The success of the Geneva negotiations also hinged on the willingness of the empire countries to make a gesture to the United States on imperial preference. Canada was not unwilling to do away with preference, and in an exchange of letters between the Canadian and the British governments, the bargain was struck: both countries undertook not to extend the preferential system to any new products, and to reduce or abolish it if that were at all possible. (It was – but it took until December 1979.)

The results of the Geneva conference were unexpectedly favourable for Canada. Tariffs on Canadian-American trade, the largest items in both countries' trade baskets, were reduced. In Canada's case, however, as one economic analyst has commented, there were 'only a limited number of reductions which have had a significant effect on the prices and competitive conditions' of Canada's protected industries. The British preferential system survived the Geneva negotiations virtually intact. An orderly forum for future negotiations, operating on the principle of non-discrimination, was established. The spectre of the tariff wars of the thirties was appeased, if not finally laid. All this was measurable, valuable progress. But it was still a far cry from wartime visions of a great multilateral, low-tariff, trading system.

The key negotiations at Geneva were between the United States and the members of the British Commonwealth. (The terms Commonwealth and Empire were still used interchangeably, with Commonwealth gradually predominating.) The Commonwealth countries, and especially Britain, were important parts of Canada's economic world. Britain's balance of payments difficulties were important to Canada in a way that those of a later generation would not be, and the viability of Canada's external trade policy was measured as much in terms of its effect on Anglo-Canadian trade volumes, as of its impact on Canadian trade with the United States.

The area most immediately affected by changing post-war trading policies was agriculture. Canadian agriculture had done well out of the war. Canadian farmers sold all they produced, and grew more. There was a startling recovery in farm prices, especially in wheat. As we have seen, the government responded by becoming more and more involved in the grain business, an involvement which culminated in the establishment of the Canadian Wheat Board monopoly in September 1943.

Would the wheat boom be permanent? There had been such a boom in the First World War, and then a smash. Memories of hard times soured Canadian farmers' enjoyment of present prosperity, and they communicated their anxiety to the federal Minister of Agriculture, Jimmy Gardiner.

Gardiner had represented Saskatchewan in the King cabinet since 1935. A former premier of the province, he was totally committed to serving what he perceived to be its interests, high farm prices and the supremacy of the Liberal party. Since for Gardiner there could be no contradiction between these principles, he was untroubled by qualms or political confusion. The same, the minister ruefully admitted, could not be said of Saskatchewan voters. In the 1945 general election only two Liberals were returned from the province to the dominion House of Commons; Gardiner was one. That September, welcoming the new CCF MPs from Saskatchewan to Ottawa, Gardiner observed that he should also congratulate himself on being there at all.

Gardiner knew that he would not be back after the next election unless the rural voter were reassured that the good times of war would not give way to the hard times of peace. Security and stability were the watchwords of farm interest groups, as they were of the rest of the population. Farmers appreciated the intervention of the central government during the war, and concluded that more of the same might be beneficial. In particular, Ottawa might help guarantee better markets and higher prices, and work to iron out the fluctuations of price so as to produce a stable and predictable income for risk-prone farmers, especially those dependent on export markets.

If Canadian farmers wanted security, Gardiner was ready to oblige. The options before the Minister of Agriculture were much the same as those presented to Canada's other trade negotiators. In the case of wheat, the most attractive prospect was a multilateral wheat agreement between the producing countries (Canada, Australia, the United States, and Argentina) and the consuming countries (Britain and the European continent). That would bring an end to cutthroat competition of the kind that had made the thirties so very unpleasant for primary producers. Unfortunately, the prospects in this area were dim. An international wheat agreement was stalled for the indefinite future, or so it seemed. And so Gardiner turned to the alternative. A bulk purchase agreement between Canada and Britain, its best customer, along the lines of wartime contracts, might prove useful for shoring up both the volumes of wheat exports, and wheat prices. The British, now ruled by a socialist Labour government, were interested. In the spring of 1946 Gardiner accordingly rushed negotiations to a conclusion. So eager was the minister to reach a settlement that he swallowed the British terms virtually unaltered. After a feeble fluttering of multilateral pieties the cabinet went along with the Minister of Agriculture. On July 25, 1946, the Anglo-Canadian wheat agreement was revealed to a delighted Parliament.

The terms were straightforward. In the 1946-7 and 1947-8 crop years, the British government would buy 160 million bushels of wheat, at $1.55 a bushel. In the next two crop years, 1948-9 and 1949-50, the British would buy 140 million bushels. In 1948-9, the price was set at $1.25, and for the last year, 1949-50, it would be not less than $1.00 a bushel. These prices presumed that world wheat prices would fall over the term of the contract. In case they did not, the British offered, and Gardiner accepted, a clause which stipulated that the British government would 'have regard to' any price advantage it might secure in the first two years at some later point. In Gardiner's view, this meant that the prices paid by the British between 1948 and 1950, the last two years of the contract, would balance off any difference between higher world prices and the contract in the first two. Soon the innocuous words 'have regard to' became an essential ingredient in any discussion of wheat marketing.

The trouble was that 'have regard to' was not specific. It seemed to promise much, but in fact delivered little or nothing. More careful drafting might have ironed out the problem, but in his haste Gardiner refused to take the trouble. And thereby hung a tale of political woe.

The announcement of the wheat sale was coupled with the government's decision to retain the Canadian Wheat Board as the sole agency for the purchase and sale of Canadian wheat. That and the contract, the Canadian Federation of Agriculture proclaimed, were 'what organized agriculture ... had been urging upon the government for a long time.' In the seventies, when the Wheat Board was more than a little unpopular, farmers would have cause to remember their wartime demands and the government's response. From the beginning the private grain interests were naturally disgusted. Nobody worried about that; the Winnipeg Grain Exchange was sufficiently unpopular among farmers to make its denunciations a positive electoral blessing. The Grain Exchange did make one unpalatable and painful point, however: the bulk purchase price of $1.55 a bushel was considerably below world market values. Canadian farmers had gained security at the price of a windfall profit.

Over the next four years this realization gnawed away at the satisfactions of the wheat agreement. When Gardiner belatedly tried to recoup for the farmers what he thought he had been promised, the British politely told him to read the contract. Gardiner's publicly expressed irritation and frequent admonitory visits to the United Kingdom did nothing to move the British government. Finally, in 1951, the Canadians and British agreed to bury the whole issue by applying the unspent residue of the British loan – some $65 million – to the financial wounds of the wheat farmers.

In 1946, however, Gardiner had successfully sensed the public mood, and had exploited it. Nor was he alone in doing so. As the war contracts unwound and servicemen and women returned home, unemployment grew a little, and exports shrank. The autumn of 1945 looked bleak and the future, if these trends continued, looked worse. But unemployment was cushioned by the Unemployment Insurance Act, now really useful for the first time, and many veterans were siphoned out of the labour market into retraining or education provided by courtesy of the government. When, in the spring of 1946, the country paused to catch its breath, the shadow had passed. Employment was up, factories were reconverting smoothly to peacetime operations, and new investment was establishing new industry. Most important, consumer expenditure was beginning to rise. In 1944 the government had accounted for fully 40 per cent of national expenditures. In 1945 this fell abruptly to 29 per cent, and in 1946 to just under 16 per cent. Consumer expenditure rose from $14.1 billion in 1944 to $17.3 billion in 1946 and $18.5 billion in 1947 (it had been $10.9 billion before the war).[1] It continued to rise for the rest of the decade.

Investment increased too. Expenditure on durable goods such as machinery rose steadily between 1945 and 1953, totalling $1.37 billion in 1945 and $2.5 billion in 1946. Some of this represented the purchase of war surplus. It was C.D. Howe's

1 Measured in constant 1971 dollars.

policy, as Minister of Reconstruction, to sell government's outmoded property to anyone who would guarantee to put it to productive use. Government telephone lines, aircraft plants, optical factories, and other facilities were knocked down to the best prospect and the highest bidder, although at a rate of return that exceeded the American government's on similar sales. Sometimes government plants were sold or leased to foreigners, the two best known being A.V. Roe of Great Britain, which took over the Victory Aircraft plant at Malton, Ontario, and the Electric Boat Company of Cleveland (despite its name, an aircraft company), which bought Canadair in Montreal. In both cases Howe was sure he had made a good deal: without a continuous infusion of foreign technology (and foreign technicians) the prospects for Canada's aircraft industry were dim. Howe had no wish to tie up government money in the hopeless pursuit of non-existent markets for costly Canadian planes. And, as Howe realized, factories for making bombers and fighters were no more than junk once the demand for their product ceased.

Having made the decision to continue the Canadian aircraft industry, Howe supported it to the utmost. Canadair married the American DC-4 airliner to the British Rolls-Royce engine. The result was a serviceable and reliable aircraft (dubbed the North Star), which Howe's Trans-Canada Airlines promptly bought. The North Star had only one slight defect: noise and vibrations from the engines deafened its passengers and loosened the fillings in their teeth. As the North Stars lumbered across Canadian skies, perceptive observers must have reflected that Canada had not quite achieved technological maturity.

More generally, however, Canada had trouble attracting foreign capital between 1944 and 1949. There was little foreign direct investment, and little borrowing abroad by Canadians. On the securities markets of the United States Canada was a net lender, not the borrower it has been almost ever since. Perhaps Canadian exchange controls made Americans reluctant to move funds northward, or to buy or build new plants here. It was true that the controls as they existed would not have prevented Americans from taking their money home whenever they liked. But who could be sure things would stay that way? After all, in other countries the trend seemed to be in the other direction – ever tighter controls, and ever more stringent regulations on the movement of funds and the interest and dividends those funds had earned.

The lack of foreign investment was barely remarked in the late forties. The domestic economy was booming; but as it boomed, Canada's foreign exchange position started to slip. In 1946-9 the country was actually running a surplus on the current account of its balance of payments, a surplus of $1,040 million. There was, however, a very large deficit with the United States and a very large surplus with Britain and Europe. The deficit with the United States seemed inescapable. Canadians wanted to buy what had been denied them during the war. Businessmen, converting to new lines, turned to American suppliers. At first this was not thought to be a problem. Canada's export position was strong, and its reserves of convertible foreign exchange (gold or American dollars) ample. In 1946, however, exports were off by almost a billion dollars, and the trade balance declined still more, by $1.3 billion. Exports would not again reach the levels of 1945 until 1951. The British began to draw on their huge loan, and simultaneously the government decided to revalue the Canadian dollar.

The problem with the dollar began with domestic decontrol. As price and wage controls were lifted, prices began to rise. Slowly at first, Canadians discovered that necessities were costing more. Inflation re-entered the political arena, and it did not take great perspicacity to predict the political problems it could cause. One contributing factor to Canadian inflation was price rises in the United States. With Canada dependent on a wide variety of American imports, any American inflation had drastic implications for Canada. To make matters worse, an American dollar cost $1.10 Canadian, so that prices of imports looked much higher than the original American price. In July 1946, therefore, the Canadian dollar was revalued to parity with the American.

Inflation continued to advance, however, and dollar reserves naturally continued to drop, since the cost of American goods was lower than before. And there was still the British loan to take into account. That had been intended to last for five years; by the spring of 1947, half had been drawn. Worst of all, it appeared that the loan was not enough. When the British fulfilled their part of the American loan bargain and made sterling convertible into American dollars, there was a run on the pound. After six weeks, the British suspended convertibility indefinitely. International trade was back where it had been in the summer of 1945.

The Canadian government was in a ticklish position. British needs were great, but Canada's own exchange position was precarious. The British were told to go more slowly in their drawings on the Canadian loan, but that was a palliative, not a cure. Finally, firm action could be avoided no longer. In November 1947, just after Mackenzie King announced the conclusion of the GATT agreements, finance minister Abbott came on the radio to proclaim economic measures of a different kind. The loss of exchange reserves had reached crisis proportions, Abbott told Canadians. To halt the drain the government had decided on a series of unpalatable, but essential, measures. Imports would be drastically reduced. Luxury items were banned altogether, and other imports would be subjected to quotas. Capital goods, machinery, and other imports essential to industrial reconversion would be admitted subject to special licences to be doled out by C.D. Howe, Minister of Reconstruction. To tide things over, the dollar would be supported by an emergency loan of $300 million from the American Import-Export Bank. In the understatement of the year, Abbott told his audience that he knew that his new policy would come as 'something of a shock,' but it would be temporary. Improvement was just around the corner.

Permanent improvement could only come if Washington willed it. The fundamental economic problem facing the western world was a dollar shortage, a situation to which Congress had proved impervious the year before. But the American legislative logjam was shifting slightly. Britain's troubles and the fear of Soviet Communism had finally convinced the American government and, more important, Congress, that something more imaginative would have to be tried if the United States were not to be isolated – rich and friendless in an impoverished world. Despite their ravished appearance, Britain and Europe still had immense reserves of skills, equipment, and technology; all that was needed was to get them started, with a substantial injection of American dollars to pay for imports of food, raw materials, and essential equipment for repair and modernization.

In the summer of 1947 the American government nerved itself to prescribe the magic elixir. Europe would, according to the Truman administration's plan, receive American aid on an unprecedented scale: money to buy capital goods and rebuild industry; money to buy supplies to feed and clothe the population; money to re-establish the European economy. Early in 1948 Congress approved the program, with the Canadian government watching anxiously from the sidelines. At the very least, the American proposals, called the Marshall Plan after their sponsor, Secretary of State George Marshall, would restore the self-respect of the democratic nations of western Europe and prevent them from becoming a group of mendicants. Also, the money might save them from Communism.

While the Canadian government approved the American initiative, it worried about its implications for Canadian trade. Next only to solvency, diversification was the watchword of Canadian trade policy. It was easy to imagine what would become of Canada's exports if European purchases of goods under the Marshall Plan were restricted to the United States. Fortunately American officials took a broad view. American nations were eligible to become 'off-shore' suppliers for the Europeans (in American geography all foreign nations are 'off-shore'). Canada was, of course, an American nation. There would be a place for Canada in the Marshall Plan, allowing Europeans to buy Canadian goods with American dollars. It was, the Canadian ambassador in Washington reported, 'as generous an attitude towards Canada as I think we could possibly hope for.' The American attitude was not entirely altruistic: the United States wanted to preserve Canada as a strong ally, and its government hoped that Canada would keep it company in furnishing aid through the Marshall Plan (Canada escaped by pleading that the British loan and the wheat contract were enough foreign aid for a country of Canada's size).

Had the Marshall Plan not appeared, one stillborn proposal of the desperate autumn of 1947 might have come closer to realization. As Canada's dollar difficulties mounted, Canadian and American officials gave prolonged consideration to another approach to Canada's trade and balance of payment problems. One idea that struck both sides was a return to the wartime integration of the two economies. Then, American and Canadian agencies had freely purchased one another's supplies with little thought for the border. By removing tariffs along the frontier, perhaps the same end could be achieved. At least some officials thought it was worth a try.

The proposal commended itself to high Canadian civil servants, especially John Deutsch of the Department of Finance and Lester Pearson, the recently appointed Under Secretary of State for External Affairs. The Minister of Finance, Abbott, and the Minister of Reconstruction, Howe, were also interested, and Prime Minister Mackenzie King gave his officials the go-ahead to see what they could produce. But when, in March 1948, discussions did produce a tentative plan, the Prime Minister got cold feet. It reminded him too much of Sir Wilfrid Laurier's fatal reciprocity project of 1911, King confided to his diary, and it would be better to drop it. Drop it he did, to the incredulous dismay of his officials.

It would be comforting to believe that this was all there was to it. King had 'saved' Canada from economic annexation by the United States which in 1948, as always, drooled over the prospect of inveigling its northern neighbour into economic servitude. Unfortunately American behaviour during the reciprocity negotiations, not to mention American self-interest, does not stand up to this analysis. Enthusiasm for free trade with Canada was confined to a small group of State Department officials, professional friends of Canada, who saw it as their professional duty to shore up the dominion as a bastion of democracy. The reciprocity project barely reached the political level in the American government; if it had surfaced, it would probably have been shelved for the duration of 1948, an election year, if not forever. It is difficult to imagine any situation in which the many special interests on the American side of the line could have been brought into harmony with their Canadian counterparts. Aborted on the Canadian side, continental free trade had few mourners on the American.

For better or worse, Canada was left to pursue an autonomous commercial policy in a fractious world. There was no permanent solution to Canada's economic dilemma, just the hope that the workings of the Marshall Plan would restore something of a balance in Canada's commercial relations with the outside world. That, as contemporary commentators pointed out, was an unstable and improbable contingency. More likely Canada's attraction to the United States market would continue and grow, as has actually happened.

Yet Canada's post-war economic adjustment can be rated a qualified success. The Canadian government, coping simultaneously with western Europe's economic troubles, inflation at home, the reconversion of industry, and pent-up consumer demand, muddled through as best it could. Its reconstruction program was generally successful, maintaining high output and employment while effectively removing the government from the large sectors of the economy it had ruled so masterfully between 1939 and 1945. By underestimating the extent of Britain's needs and the imports Canada's reconstruction boom would suck in, the government had exposed Canada's foreign exchange weakness, exacerbated through the premature revaluation of the Canadian dollar in 1946. As a result, 1948 saw a return to some of the stringent economic controls of wartime and a perpetuation of the dominant role of the central government in the shaping of the Canadian economy.

10

Making a Better Country

When Prime Minister Mackenzie King rose in his place to open the Dominion-Provincial Conference on Reconstruction on August 6, 1945, he carried a heavy burden. In his hand King held a small green booklet, the proposals of the Government of Canada for the economic well-being of the country, a comprehensive plan to restructure Canadian federalism to give the central government the financial power and the legislative authority to guide the economy through the perils of depression, while insuring individual Canadians against disease, old age, and extended unemployment. It was an unusual moment. Never before had the King government laid such a comprehensive and audacious program before the public. Never before, King's advisers and colleagues believed, had there been such a heaven-sent opportunity to rescue Canada from constitutional stalemate and spare the country the baneful repetition of the squabbling of the thirties. Finally Canada could shape a central government fit to cope with the uncertainties and dangers of the twentieth century.

Mackenzie King was alive to the potential of the moment. Never before, the Prime Minister told himself, had he placed so much at risk, and Mackenzie King hated risks and uncertainties. For over four years he had put off this moment, and its arrival left him fretful and perturbed. Perhaps this was neither the moment, nor the place, to attempt something of the magnitude of constitutional reform.

The sight that greeted King could scarcely have been encouraging. Around him sat the sleeping dogs of provincial power, yawning and stretching after five years in mothballs. Among the nine provincial premiers were some of Mackenzie King's bitterest political enemies. George Drew, the Conservative premier of Ontario, was a familiar foe. A passionate, self-assured, and strikingly handsome man, Drew could easily imagine himself in the place of the pudgy little fellow who occupied the prime minister's chair. And high time too, he liked to assure Ontario audiences. Drew's style had long since become frozen in bombast: attractive and interesting in small groups, he turned every gathering of over three people into a public meeting. On King's left sat another Tory, Maurice Duplessis, the Union Nationale premier of Quebec. Duplessis had started out as a Conservative, but had discovered that a judicious mixture of nationalism with his *bleu* principles furnished just the right formula for winning elections. Duplessis stood four-square for the stability of Quebec's traditional institutions and society; he was uninterested in new designs for Canada. But if Duplessis could not be counted on to promote a renewed Canada, he might not hinder it if events took their proper course. The same might have been said for Manning of Alberta, the youngest man at the conference table. Quiet, earnest, and efficient, Manning was an exponent of Social Credit evangelism. Could it be wedded to the central government's new economics? Tommy Douglas of Saskatchewan headed Canada's first (and last) CCF government. King liked Douglas, and philosophically there was no great gulf between them. But Douglas was also closer to the federal proposals in spirit than was the prime minister. Saskatchewan had suffered cruelly from drought and depression and well knew the value of a strong federal treasury.

The Liberal premiers were King's official allies. Stuart Garson of Manitoba was the best known. With a strong reputation for his work as Manitoba's provincial treasurer, Garson had a detailed understanding of the financial intricacies of dominion-provincial relations. His experience and his province's weak economic position made Garson a strong exponent of a strong central government. John Hart of British Columbia had been in office since 1941 as the chief of a Liberal-Conservative coalition. Tall, dry, dispassionate, Hart was not a dominating or disturbing element. The three Maritime premiers, all Liberals, were anything but colourless. John McNair of New Brunswick was an old political hand, raised in a political system that expected government to be the visible patron of the unfortunate, or at least of the unfortunate who voted for the right party. Five dollar bills were the welfare policy of New Brunswick. A.S. MacMillan of Nova Scotia was the oldest premier present, older even than Mackenzie King. He dozed gently next to Drew, waiting out the months until he retired to make way for Angus L. Macdonald, Nova Scotia Liberalism's legendary leader, who had recently returned to his native province from wartime service in Mackenzie King's cabinet. Macdonald was no friend of King's, and held strong views on provincial rights, but for the moment he was unable to derail proceedings directly. Finally, there was Walter Jones, the farmer-premier of Prince Edward Island. Those who knew Jones suspected that farming came before politics in his personal order of priorities. 'There is not a worry on Prince Edward Island except tomorrow's hockey match and possibly the price of potatoes,' Jones told an interviewer.

In the final showdown, King knew the Liberal premiers would follow his lead – if he looked like winning. But he could win only if he neutralized his two greatest opponents, Drew and Duplessis. That, King suspected, was a very doubtful proposition. Drew represented an Ontario tradition of assertive provincial rights – Ontario first, others last – which was deeply embedded in the province's political and administrative history. Even Drew's Liberal predecessor, Mitchell Hepburn, stood squarely in that tradition, although whether he did so for reasons of state or personal spite remains a mystery. Drew, like Hepburn, strongly disliked Mackenzie King, and even King's masterful diplomatic skills usually failed on his marble exterior. Drew, however, depended on others, the provincial treasury department, and his provincial treasurer, Leslie Frost, for the details, if not the substance of his policy.

So did King. The dominion government's proposals had their origins in the Department of Finance, with an assist from the Bank of Canada. Finance spoke for what had already been achieved. Thanks to the Wartime Tax Agreements Canada had for the first time a common, although temporary, tax system. Ottawa's decisions directed investment, shaped consumption, and secured resources for national goals. As things stood, there was no danger of competition from the provinces. In the King cabinet, Ilsley spoke up for Finance, and Ilsley was a powerful and effective advocate who had given his department's proposals his heart and soul. But Ilsley was not alone. Co-ordination of the dominion's proposals meant bringing together a coalition of agencies and talents: that task King delegated in 1944 to his own parliamentary secretary, Brooke Claxton (later the Minister of National Health and Welfare) and to Alex (Sandy) Skelton of the Bank of Canada. Skelton had served as secretary to the Royal Commission on Dominion-Provincial Relations, and had brought away from the experience a burning commitment to see the Canadian federal structure reformed and cleansed of petty provincialism and jurisdictional rivalries. Claxton, a consultant to the same royal commission, had come to believe that only a strong dominion government could cope with the welfare policies that the times demanded. A former Conservative, Claxton had become the most fervent, and one of the most politically astute, of Liberals. He combined his political passions with a strong administrative sense and indefatigable energy; his only defect, though a large one, was an unappealing public personality.

Claxton and Skelton had first to convince the King cabinet that reform was essential, politically desirable, and safe. Some members of the cabinet proved most reluctant. T.A. Crerar, after King the most senior minister, was the most conservative and the most provincially minded of the group. Crerar had grown up in a world where the 'brains trust' of the finance department and the Bank of Canada were unknown quantities; as W.A. Mackintosh once quipped to the minister, 'You don't think we have any brains, and you don't trust us.'

For Crerar, a redistribution of federal and provincial powers and responsibilities would risk crippling the central government under a too vast weight of administration and expenditure. Crerar's views could be ascribed to an outdated and discredited view of the proper functioning of government, and they could be ignored as the prejudices of a minister whose political influence was in descent. The hesitations of the Minister of Justice, Louis St Laurent, were in a different category. St Laurent was no crank. His detailed knowledge of dominion-provincial problems derived from service as the counsel to the Rowell–Sirois Commission in the late thirties, as well as from extensive experience in corporation law. He spoke, too, as the senior representative of Quebec and, in a Mackenzie King government, views from such a source were listened to with respect.

St Laurent's orderly mind had an unusual capacity for assimilating facts and arguments quickly and then rendering judgment in a concise, pungent form. He had no use for timidity, and no patience for arguments that simply sought to avoid conflict. When, at a meeting of the cabinet committee on dominion-provincial relations in March 1945, Crerar advanced the familiar argument that an activist federal policy would 'precipitate acrimonious disputes with the provinces,' St Laurent readily agreed. But that was no reason not to go ahead, he told his colleagues: 'acrimonious dispute was inevitable with Quebec in any case.' Crerar persisted. 'In a conflict,' he told the other ministers, 'the majority of the people would support the provincial governments against the Dominion.' 'Not at all,' St Laurent replied. The reason most Canadians turned to provincial governments first was because 'people were made constantly aware of the services which provincial governments render while they tended to think of the central government as the one imposing burdens such as taxation and conscription.' Family allowances would correct this situation, as would the other programs now contemplated by Ottawa.

By the time the dominion-provincial conference convened in August, St Laurent's side had prevailed. Crerar was gone from the cabinet, dismissed by King in April and promoted to the Senate. The needs of the finance department, newly rationalized in the White Paper on Employment and Income, and ably summarized by Alex Skelton and Brooke Claxton, shaped the conference's agenda. The dominion proposals set before the provinces in a green-covered pamphlet (quickly nicknamed 'The Green Book') were sweeping, logical, and uncompromising.

The dominion's proposals began by reviewing the progress made during the war and the expectations the war had raised among the Canadian people. What the people wanted, Ottawa told the provinces, was security and stability. The central government knew how to provide these, and had already outlined its strategy in the White Paper. There were four basic points: the encouragement of export trade, private investment, consumer expenditure, and a program of public investment. There would also be encouragement of technological development, and social security for the individual against 'large and uncertain risks' – those of old age, sickness, and unemployment. To finance the central government's prospective expenditures on social security and public investment, it must secure an adequate base in taxation. Ilsley's officials proposed that in return for federal participation in and contribution to social security expenditures (many of which were located in provincial jurisdiction) the provinces should surrender the right to levy income, corporate, and succession taxes to Ottawa. In return, the provinces would receive an annual per capita grant indexed to the fluctuating value of the gross national product. Because the latter had grown substantially since the last adjustment in 1941, there would be an immediate and large increase in provincial revenues.

As King stressed to the premiers, Ottawa's proposals relied on co-operation, not coercion. No constitutional amendment was contemplated; instead, there would be joint agreements enforced by little more than the power of public opinion. But that public opinion, in the minds of King's officials, was now firmly on the side of the dominion government.

August had seemed a likely time for a conference, at the beginning of the breathing space provided by the end of the war against Germany and before the end of the war against Japan. That event might be as much as a year away, and during that year Ottawa's ideas could be circulated and popularized. But within a month the war was over, Japan surrendered, and the emergency powers of the central government were soon due to expire. Within a measurable and very short space of time Ottawa would have to hand back to the provinces what it had appropriated in 1939.

Some of the provinces were determined to turn the clock right back to the thirties. Ontario's Premier George Drew took the lead. First, he secured a delay in the conference's proceedings. The federal proposals were so sweeping and so sudden, he maintained, that he would have to take them home to Toronto for study. Even on brief acquaintance they looked unpromising. They were little more than a scheme to replace the provinces with a unitary government, contrary to the expressed federalist wishes of the hallowed Fathers of Confederation. The dominion's jurisdiction did not need rounding out; rather, the provinces should be on their guard against centralizing encroachments. In Drew's view, the provinces would bear the primary responsibility for post-war social policy, and for that purpose they would need more, not less, revenue. Certainly Ontario would not agree to surrender its rights to income and other direct taxes. After Drew's salvo, it was Duplessis' turn: the Quebec premier happily followed where his Ontario ally had led.

Immediate agreement being impossible, the dominion delegation had no option but to send its proposals to a Dominion-Provincial Co-ordinating Committee for study and elaboration. There followed a winter of hope and uncertainty. Drew was actually encouraging, so federal officials believed, and for a time it seemed that he might be persuaded to go along with a redistribution of taxation and, subsequently, the dominion's social security package. Duplessis, according to Alex Skelton, who served as Ottawa's roving ambassador, did not appear even to have read the federal proposals. But that might be taken as encouraging: if he hadn't read them, presumably he had not finally made up his mind on the subject. Premier Hart of British Columbia provided an unexpected snag. Ottawa's financial proposals worried him, and they continued to perturb his mind even after plentiful reassurances were provided. Naturally, Nova Scotia's attitude took a distinct turn for the worse after Angus L. Macdonald's return as premier. Macdonald sympathized with provincial rights and nursed a healthy distrust of any propositions that bore the imprint of Mackenzie King's cloven hoof.

The uncertainties of the autumn surfaced in January 1946. Drew, King, and the premiers met in Ottawa to examine the provinces' reactions to the dominion proposals. Drew's counter-proposal grudgingly accepted the utility of the central government as the collection agent for income tax (it would reap thereby the unpopularity that derives from visible taxation), but he insisted on the right of the individual provinces to charge their own rates. In exchange for this dubious concession, Drew insisted that the dominion promise never to return to or to invade any new fields of direct taxation. As for the federal proposal that the central government serve as the economic balance-wheel of the federation, Drew would concede only that 10 per cent of the proceeds of provincial income taxes be placed in a fund to be administered jointly by the dominion and the provinces. The poorer provinces could petition the fund for relief according to their needs. Drew's proposals stimulated a further need for contemplation; the conference adjourned until April.

The last session of the Dominion-Provincial Conference on Reconstruction met on April 25, 1946. It was a depressing day. Drew denounced centralization and its socialistic spawn, health insurance. Duplessis chimed in, beating the drum for provincial autonomy and comparing the dominion proposals to the works of Hitler and Mussolini. Angus L. Macdonald hymned the virtues of autonomy and locality. Stuart Garson's indignant protests were swept away in a rhapsody of provincial rights.

For Minister of Finance James Ilsley it was a tragic moment. He had hoped that his six years as finance minister would end triumphantly in the recasting of Canadian fiscal federalism, only to be baulked by parochial obstruction that he considered ridiculous and unworthy. King adjourned the conference *sine die*. Clifford Clark scornfully characterized Drew's final proposals as 'full of misstatements and half-truths' and with his External Affairs counterpart Norman Robertson mournfully told an American diplomat that, 'If the selfish interests of the two principal Provinces are going to hamstring the Federal Government in its efforts to provide machinery which will permit it to fulfill the functions of a central government in this modern age, then Confederation is a failure and Canada cannot be a nation.' Clark's words were prophetic. Yet his handling of the delicate and complicated dominion proposals had not been without fault. As Mackenzie King commented, as the con-

LaPalme, 1948

Le Canada

The Pimp: 'Mais, mon frère, en sommes-nous rendus là?'
Premier Duplessis, seated at table, rents Quebec to American investors, thereby affirming
provincial control over resources (LaPalme, 1948). Reproduced with the permission of
Robert LaPalme

ference was collapsing around him, 'you cannot get Clark, whose mind is wholly academic, to realize that no matter how theoretically accurate you may be or in accord with strict financial rules that [sic] what you are doing is no good unless you can get the public to understand and support it.'

Canada, in any case, survived Clark's disappointment. In the revised agenda of dominion-provincial relations (King steadfastly refused Drew's demands to reconvene the conference) the first item was to regularize the fiscal relations between the dominion and the provinces. Emergency powers were gradually wound up and returned to the provinces. Instead of the comprehensive taxation and social security scheme of 1945, the national government offered 'tax rental' to the provinces. Under this scheme, the federal government would occupy completely the fields of income, corporation, and succession taxes. In return for their abstention from taxing these fields, the provinces received payments based on complicated formulas designed to provide both a per capita grant and their statutory subsidies under the BNA Act. The per capita grants varied, with Nova Scotia and Saskatchewan receiving higher amounts than the other provinces. Quebec and Ontario predictably rejected the federal terms and in 1947 re-established their own autonomous taxation systems. The remaining provinces did accept, and in 1949 they were joined by the newest province of Newfoundland. Through tax rental, Ilsley hoped, the poorer provinces would escape the worst consequences of their unequal tax bases and unequal resources.

The dominion's case might have had more force, and more point, had Canada been facing a genuine economic crisis in 1945 or 1946. If a real crisis of unemployment had developed, then popular support might have been mobilized behind national control of government taxing and spending. In the event, without a completely co-ordinated economy, the nation's income recovered and then began to grow. The real problem, as C.D. Howe informed his colleagues in September 1945, was not going to be labour surplus but labour shortage. Lacking a crisis and a focus, the popular mood changed, and with it Canada's political imperatives.

Nor was the dominion government, despite the gloom of some of its officials, prepared to wither away. St Laurent was right when he observed that a government with a tangible presence and a real function attracted attention and focused loyalty. Many federal programs did not depend on provincial co-operation for their implementation, and these proceeded. Where provincial co-operation was constitutionally inescapable, the lesson of 1945 was thoughtfully applied. Sensible co-operation being impossible, it was best to present the provinces with financial inducements to go along with predetermined national initiatives. If a province was prepared to do without a dominion program with its attached subsidy, then it could justify the lack to its own electors.

The most prominent programs of the post-war era did not infringe very much on provincial rights, nor did they excite much controversy. Veterans were the government's first concern. Legislation in 1944 and 1945 established a framework of demobilization grants based on time served in the armed forces and time served overseas. Incapacitated veterans received full medical care, and invalids were pensioned to the full extent of their individual disability. Those veterans who wished to go on to university or technical schools received free tuition and a living allowance that corresponded, month for month, with the time they had spent in the armed services. Veterans wishing to take up farming or to buy land for small businesses were assisted under the Veterans' Land Act. Those who wished to return to their pre-war jobs were handed their old jobs back, with seniority as if they had never been away to war. Unemployed veterans received out-of-work allowances. At first it seemed as if this last category would be alarmingly large: in January 1947 over 50,000 veterans of the Second World War were registered as seeking work. By September of the same year, however, only 15,000 were still jobless, and even the seasonal rise in unemployment failed to reproduce the previous winter's large figures. In any case the Department of Labour preferred to look on the bright side, emphasizing that almost a million people had been discharged from the armed forces by September 1947, and that 810,000 placements had been made.

If the education and employment of veterans produced few serious complaints, the same was not true of the homes they proposed to occupy. The problem was of long standing. In 1930, the Dominion Bureau of Statistics later concluded, Canadians had been under-housed: there were not enough dwelling units to accommodate the number of families available to occupy them. During the 1930s this condition was masked because large numbers of families doubled up in single units to make ends meet; thus, vacancy rates did not reflect real needs. The war, which placed large amounts of money for the first time in the hands of many families, resulted in an explosion of housing demand and, until rent control was imposed, in skyrocketing rents. Rent control proved popular, and was difficult to get rid of after the end of the war. The central government eventually offered to vacate the field in favour of any province willing to take up the burden, and slowly some provinces responded, first Saskatchewan and then, in 1951, Quebec. Not surprisingly, rent controls directed capital into houses for sale rather than into new apartment buildings. Housing construction was, nevertheless, extraordinary. Measured in constant (1971) dollars, private residential construction totalled $713 million in 1944, $1,033 million in 1945, and $1,342 million in 1948 (the government accounted for about $3 million worth in each year). In 1947, for the first time, new dwelling units exceeded the rate of family formation, no small boast, since the number of marriages in that boom year was 130,000 (1938: 90,709). Between 1945 and 1949, no less than 367,900 new dwelling units were completed.

To help people pay for their new homes, the national government made mort-gages available under the National Housing Act of 1944. Between 1945 and 1947 over 19,000 loans were approved under the new legislation. Most interesting of all, of the 76,738 dwelling units built during 1947, no less than 76 per cent were for single-family dwellings. Whatever else Canada became during the post-war years, one thing was clear: it would be a country of individually occupied and owner-occupied homes.

The first consequences of this became immediately apparent. Cities began to spread into subdivisions and suburbs. Some subdivisions were built especially for veterans according to government specifications. Profiting from wartime experience, the government's Central Mortgage and Housing Corporation promoted a National Building Code to simplify its financial tasks in evaluating new housing. And so across Canada distinctively 'Canadian' suburbs began to appear: solid, well-built, and generally unimaginative houses of wood or brick, conforming to the 'Canadian federal' style of architecture. Canadian cities sprawled, and municipalities spread outward to follow their inhabitants.

Had visiting sociologists wished to examine the beliefs of the average Canadian, or the typical Canadian family, they might have done worse than to study the largely unregarded growth of the central government's housing policy. Possibly because there was so little conflict between that policy and what the electorate thought was natural, it passed without much in the way of general comment. 'Today,' an English visitor wrote in 1961, 'about three-quarters of all Canadians own their own houses.'[1] Canadians, he added, also tended to move out of rented accommodation as soon as they could. With such aspirations, and such a lifestyle, it was not surprising that few Canadians were ablaze with resentment of social injustice, or that political ferment should be a rarity.

Despite the setbacks of the 1930s, Canada remained a country of homeowners scattered across miles of suburbs and preoccupied with the arrival of the next sewer line in the vicinity, or with the paving of the streets. Along those streets drove the diaper service to help with another post-war phenomenon: the baby boom. In 1948, Canada's total population was estimated at 12,850,000. Of that total, over two and a half million were aged nine and under, born since the outbreak of the Second World War. The birth rate had risen during the war; it rose still further when the war was over (23.5 births per thousand between 1941 and 1945; 27.4 per thousand between 1946 and 1950). 'To-day,' a caustic critic lamented, '... the five-room bungalow [is] the object of life and every woman in sight [is] pregnant....'[2]

1 Alistair Horne, *Canada and the Canadians* (London and Toronto: Macmillan 1961), 235.
2 A.R.M. Lower, *Canadians in the Making* (Toronto: Longmans 1958), 417.

Housing, by national standards, can be accounted a success. There was a reasonable national consensus on goals and agreement on guidelines. But other forms of social programs did not fare so well. Health insurance, one of the centrepieces of social security, survived the dominion-provincial debacle of 1946 only in a much muted form. The central government made health grants for certain diseases, as well as hospital grants, available to the provinces for the improvement of their health-care facilities. The Department of National Health and Welfare acquired a new minister when, in December 1946, its founder, Brooke Claxton, moved to the Department of National Defence. Paul Martin, the new minister, strongly believed in the appropriateness and the inevitability of national health insurance. But the obstacles – stubborn and conservative provincial governments, and a preference for other forms of economic action in Ottawa – hobbled him. Martin discovered that the cardinal virtues of a Minister of National Health and Welfare in an increasingly conservative society were patience and tolerance. For health insurance, 1946 had been the opportunity of the decade, and probably of the next one too. Martin settled down to wait.

II

Making a Better World

Word of Germany's surrender reached Mackenzie King at a hotel in San Francisco. The California city had been chosen to host the founding conference of the new international organization which would replace the failed League of Nations. This time, nothing was left to the imagination: the new world body would be called the United Nations.

As King heard the news, he uttered 'a prayer of thanksgiving.' Then he added, 'and of rededication to the service of my fellow-men.' Most international bodies had need of rededication and renewal that spring. Few had managed to survive the war, and those that had were safely peripheral to great events. A start had already been made on restoration, however. Attention had turned first to economic reconstruction.

It is difficult to imagine any world economic order on which the Grand Alliance that won the war against Hitler could have agreed. Britain, the Soviet Union, and the United States were deeply divided in their notions of what the ideal world economy would be. When the representatives of the allied nations met in Bretton Woods, a New Hampshire resort, in the summer of 1944, the British and Americans had enough trouble in agreeing among themselves about the reform of the international monetary system. The Russians, who arrived late, sat dourly on the sidelines and waited for the results. What capitalists did among themselves did not greatly concern the Soviet Union, which knew, as an article of faith, that the West was doomed to economic stagnation and depression as soon as the war was over.

Although the main action at Bretton Woods involved the British and the Americans, Canada was there too, represented by an exceptionally capable delegation headed by Louis Rasminsky of the Bank of Canada. The Canadians were well informed about the respective states of mind of the Americans and the British; they arrived in Bretton Woods determined to bridge any gaps that might open between Canada's two principal allies. It was one occasion in which Canada's self-designated role of 'helpful fixer' or 'linch pin' actually worked. The competence and diligence of Canada's representatives won them the confidence of both sides, and helped bring about a solution which both sides perceived as respectable and viable. Canadian suggestions, a British observer wrote, 'were intelligent and constructive, and the British and Americans were always anxious to have them.'

The Bretton Woods agreements established an International Monetary Fund (IMF) and an International Bank for Reconstruction and Development (later called the World Bank). The agreements had various purposes: one was to establish a means for regulating the currencies of the world. To this end the governments subscribing to the IMF agreed not to allow their currencies to deviate more than 1 per cent from their par values and to consult about larger changes. The values were expressed in American dollars, and the currency of the United States accordingly became the world's prime monetary unit. To help its members manage their currencies, the IMF provided short-term credits.

The American government conceived of the Bretton Woods agreements as the best response available to the monetary wars of the thirties. Accepting the arrangements would benefit all nations by removing one of the causes of economic instability. Canadian officials agreed, in general, with this point of view. There was, Louis Rasminsky later pointed out, a 'great increase in international consultation and collaboration' as a result of the establishment of the Fund. The mere existence of an agreed international forum for the discussion of economic policies was a great advantage. Relief and guarded optimism notwithstanding, there were still some forebodings. The IMF and the Bank would not be enough to help finance countries through their reconstruction difficulties; but the United States had been unwilling to pledge more, and the Americans had their way. W.A. Mackintosh was worried by the manner in which the United States had achieved its goals, and perturbed at the American assumption that the United States could now benevolently prescribe what rules the rest of the trading world should follow. This was familiar stuff to a Canadian raised in the British Empire, and it amounted, in Mackintosh's view, to 'imperialism.' Mackintosh did not, of course, regard imperialism as the ultimate political sin that the term now implies, but he did question the practicality and desirability of its American variant. 'The United States,' the economist wrote, 'with its inevitable minorities, is incapable of following any consistent imperialistic policy. It would also be defeated by the Fifth Column within its own country. What it could, and may, do is to defeat any adequate programme by abortive imperialism.'

Mackintosh's views found an echo mainly among Canadians with direct experience with the American government. Canadian diplomats in Washington smarted when Canada was left out of discussions preparing for the future world security organization. Although Canada would have to accept the consequences of great-power decision-making, the dominion was seldom consulted. External Affairs officials dug into the theory of international relations and came up with a concept that fitted, or appeared to fit, the Canadian case: 'functionalism' or functional representation. Broadly speaking, functionalism was interpreted to mean that Canada had a right and a capacity to be consulted about decisions for which this country would later have to take responsibility. This, as John Holmes has noted, was linked to a belief in the efficacy of international action in reducing the level of international conflict.[1]

Functionalism found a home in some Canadian international negotiations (for example, in aviation conferences), but never in high-level political discussions. On that lofty plane, King knew, the smaller powers were expected to show their appreciation and not indulge their own peculiar ideas. Canada's contribution to the drafting of the charter of the new world security organization was a minor one.

The United Nations was born for all that. Like the old League of Nations, it had a Security Council, housing the great powers, with permanent seats, and elected representatives chosen from among the other members of the organization. Some votes in the Security Council were more equal than others, for the great powers could veto any substantive (as opposed to procedural) motion. Without the insurance of a veto it is doubtful if either the Soviet Union or the United States would have consented to join. In the General Assembly, which included all members, things were theoretically more equal. The same was true of the various specialized agencies belonging to the UN. To reflect the new realities of power, the United Nations would not have its seat in Geneva, but in New York. A site was donated by the Rockefellers and a new ultramodern building was soon under construction. Canada's contribution was a set of metal doors.

As the new UN building rose above the East River, high diplomacy made a last perambulation around Europe. The early sessions of the UN were held in London and Paris, and in Paris, too, was convened the first post-war peace conference. The conference was meant to restore the formalities of peace between the allies and Germany's former satellites. In the end it did so, but that was not its lasting achievement. What the Paris Peace Conference did do was to make people think of a new war. Soviet, British, French, and American diplomats and ministers growled and spat and snarled for the benefit of the world's press. It was the first time the world (or that part of it with a free press) had been furnished such an instructive vista of the gulf between the wartime allies, but it would not be the last.

Canadian sympathies lay with the United States and Great Britain. The revelation of a Russian spy ring in March 1946 helped. So did a speech by Winston Churchill at a small college in Fulton, Missouri. On a continent-wide radio hook-up, Canadians heard Churchill intone: 'From Stettin in the Baltic to Trieste in the Adriatic,

---

1 See the discussion in John Holmes, *The Shaping of Peace* (Toronto: University of Toronto Press 1979), 72.

an iron curtain has descended across the continent.' On all sides, Churchill told his audience, the Russians and their Communist sympathizers constituted 'a growing challenge and peril to Christian civilization.' The Russians had no intention of going to war while they could get what they wanted by bluff: 'What they desire is the fruits of war and the indefinite expansion of their power and doctrines.' Only by strength could the Russians be stopped, and the only powers in a position to show strength were the British Commonwealth and the United States. Mackenzie King, whom Churchill consulted about the speech, was deeply moved. 'I confess,' he wrote in his diary, 'I personally believe that as regards Russia the rest of the world is not in a very different position than other countries in Europe were when Hitler had made up his mind to aim at the conquest of Europe.'

King soon got a taste of Soviet diplomacy at first hand. Travelling to Paris for the peace conference, King had a front-row seat as the great powers quarrelled among themselves. A Canadian reporter watched the prime minister sit fascinated through a diatribe by the Soviet delegate, Vishinsky. 'Oh Smith,' King later lamented to the reporter, 'I'm aghast. Isn't this ghastly.' 'And in his eyes,' Smith commented, 'were sadness, fear and disillusion.'[2]

King's reaction might have been duplicated across Canada as citizens followed in their papers or on the radio the progress of the Sovietization of eastern Europe. It all sounded very familiar: rigged elections, arrests, show trials, and the steady growth in power of the local Communist parties. The news made a profound impression in Ottawa as well.

In Ottawa there had been a cabinet shuffle. Mackenzie King, who had been both minister of external affairs and prime minister, handed over the former to the Minister of Justice, Louis St Laurent. As St Laurent's deputy, King chose Lester B. (Mike) Pearson, Canada's ambassador to the United States, and sent Hume Wrong, one of the country's ablest diplomats, to replace Pearson in Washington. St Laurent, Pearson, and Wrong were only the most visible level of an exceptionally competent team. The team's first and most important task was to confront the problem of Soviet expansion in Europe and to assess its implications for Canada. The problem seemed obvious: very recent history had shown what could happen if aggression were not resisted and if totalitarian states were allowed to run roughshod over their weaker neighbours. By tolerating or countenancing Soviet expansion in Europe, Canada would only be weakening its own position in a showdown with the Soviet Union. Canada's liberal democratic institutions, its economic welfare, and its hope for political survival were all bound up in the fate of Europe.

St Laurent expounded the External Affairs viewpoint in a speech at the University of Toronto in January 1947. Canadian policy in external relations, he told his audience, was founded on five basic principles: national unity, political liberty, the

2 I.N. Smith, *A Reporter Reports* (Toronto: Ryerson 1954), 28.

rule of law, the values of Christian civilization, and a 'willingness to accept international responsibilities.' All these principles were at stake in western Europe and that, St Laurent added, was a matter of the gravest concern to Canada. 'We have realized,' St Laurent told his listeners, 'that a threat to the liberty of western Europe, where our own political ideas were nurtured, was a threat to our own way of life.'

If that was the threat, what should be the response? New manifestations of the Soviet threat arose daily. In February 1948, there was a coup in Czechoslovakia, placing a Communist regime in firm control. Within months, Czechoslovakia's democratic parties and institutions were suppressed, and its most prominent non-Communist politician, the foreign minister Jan Masaryk, was mysteriously dead on the pavement outside his apartment. 'Suicide,' the Czech government claimed. Further north, around Berlin, the Soviet grip tightened. Berlin was occupied by the four principal allies, deep inside the Russian zone. Access depended on land, water, and air corridors across East Germany. When the Western allies implemented a currency reform, in June 1948, these routes were blocked – all except the air corridor. There followed the Berlin airlift, a symbol of Western determination and initiative in the face of Soviet pressure. Britain, France, the United States, even Australia and South Africa sent planes and pilots. Canada, virtually disarmed, could only send sympathy.

The government in Ottawa, and especially Mackenzie King, pondered what to do. In December 1947, after a trip to England, where British reports on the European situation thoroughly alarmed him, King disclosed the secret to his cabinet, telling them 'perhaps more than I should have about inside of situation in Europe as I knew it and believe is about to break.' The cabinet was 'stunned,' King wrote. 'It is just too terrible to contemplate, but it does look increasingly to me as if the men at the head of affairs in Russia have got it into their minds that they can conquer the world.' Typically, however, King hesitated to take any final or irrevocable action.

The first reaction to the Communist coup in Prague came from western Europe. There, the British, French, Dutch, Belgian, and Luxembourg governments signed the Treaty of Brussels on March 17, pledging mutual aid in case of aggression. A week before, British Prime Minister Attlee had sent Mackenzie King an important message noting the dangers posed by Soviet pressures on Norway, and proposing, as a counter-measure, the establishment of 'a regional Atlantic pact of mutual assistance in which all the countries threatened by a Russian move on the Atlantic could participate.' King promptly convened an urgent meeting of his foreign policy advisers – St Laurent, Claxton, and Pearson – in his office on the afternoon of March 11, 1948. A prompt and affirmative reply was despatched at once to Attlee. 'Collective measures seem to me to be essential to establish some sense of security and to preserve the peace. Such collective measures will, of course, require the active leadership of the United Kingdom and of the United States.' To assist in Anglo-American deliberations King arranged for immediate Canadian participation in secret talks in Washington. Though no commitments had as yet been made, they were now clearly envisaged.

As discussions proceeded in Washington, Louis St Laurent and his officials undertook the delicate task of selling an Atlantic alliance to Canadian public opinion. Most Canadians were by this time firmly anti-Communist and deeply mistrustful of the Soviet Union. The Canadian Communist party (then travelling under the name of Labour Progressive party) collected a negligible handful of votes in national elections. Its influence, and that of allied 'peace' groups, could be discounted. But there were others besides Communists who found the prospect of a peacetime military alliance with the United States less than alluring. A few intellectuals, among them a trio from the University of Toronto – Harold Adams Innis, Donald Creighton, and Frank Underhill – poured scorn on the idea of an alliance from a variety of perspectives. Innis disgustedly wrote that 'Pearson seems to be as active as possible in selling us down the river to the United States.'[3]

The Toronto trio spoke for few besides themselves. But there were other, and more significant, sources of opposition. French Canada, with its history of isolationism, was a likely source of dissent. Even there, however, disagreement with Ottawa's alliance policy was scattered, confined to a few fractious politicians and the Montreal newspaper *Le Devoir*. St Laurent, it appeared, spoke for Quebec as well as Canada when he preached his alliance crusade. As for the non-Communist left, it had little choice but to follow the leadership of the national CCF in support of an Atlantic alliance. With battles against domestic Communists in the labour movement just behind them, it was natural for the CCF to extend the fight to the realm of external affairs.

With these minor exceptions, Canadian opinion on foreign policy was remarkably coherent: a consensus had gradually been established that would last, without serious opposition, for the best part of the next decade. When St Laurent spoke to the House of Commons of a 'dynamic counter-attraction of a free, prosperous and progressive society ... opposed to the totalitarian and reactionary society of the communist world,' he was addressing the converted.

In his wake the vigorous and firmly committed Minister of External Affairs dragged a reluctant Mackenzie King. It was not that King was unimpressed by the Soviet threat, nor that he regarded a Western grouping as unnecessary. But he was getting old, tired, and depressed at the awful prospect of an indefinite Cold War (as the new bi-polar international system was beginning to be called). Increasingly,

---

3 Public reaction is ably discussed in James Eayrs, *In Defence of Canada*, IV (Toronto: University of Toronto Press 1980), 51-8.

King's leadership in cabinet seemed directed to demonstrating that he was, indeed, still leader and prime minister: 'the last bellows of the leader of the herd before he cashed in his cheques,' as Brooke Claxton unkindly put it. At the end of 1947 King announced his impending retirement and summoned a Liberal convention, the first since 1919, to meet in Ottawa and choose his successor. The choice was purely formal. King knew, and most Liberals knew too, who the choice must be. The convention ratified the choice, making St Laurent the new Liberal leader and, on November 15, 1948, prime minister of Canada.

Mackenzie King shuffled off into retirement. He had good reason to be content with his legacy. He had handed on a prosperous country with a sound administration. The Liberal party was flourishing. Its successful leadership during the war had stimulated a wave of national pride and self-confidence which the Liberals were not slow to exploit. The central government and its policies were in the forefront of the nation's consciousness; it was to Ottawa that Canadians looked for direction and, given the unhappy world situation, protection. It was, after all, better to be united against an uncertain future than to resume domestic quarrelling on the model of the 1930s.

Under firm and strong leadership, Canadians could turn their attention to domestic concerns.

12

Popular Culture

In 1948 Canada was still a relatively pious country compared with Britain, France, or other European states. In this respect, as in so many others, its residents resembled the Americans with whom they had such close connections. Whether Roman Catholic, Protestant, or Anglican, Canadians went to church on Sunday. Unless they were Roman Catholics, they met a sermon-dominated liturgy that had much to say about piety and obligations, and not much to say about anything else. For Roman Catholics, whose liturgical tradition centred on the mass and on Mariological devotional exercises, the experience was rather different. But this difference was less important than the fact that almost all Canadians professed some religion. Both for believers and non-believers religion was a serious matter. Faith was a spur to action, although it did not necessarily point unequivocally in any one direction. Among Roman Catholics there were plentiful recruits for the religious orders, whose members staffed hospitals and schools throughout the dominion. In other denominations there was a perpetual war between the 'social gospellers,' who wanted to enlist Christianity in the service of socioeconomic reform, and the devotionally and sacramentally inclined, who were more interested in individual purification and sanctity. All denominations, however, believed in 'mission.' Hence the Canadian churches supported Indian and Eskimo work at home, and medical missions abroad. The Canadian churches, like the American, were deeply involved in China. Unlike the American, they had also committed themselves to India, while the Roman Catholics had many projects in Latin America also.

Regardless of denomination, people looked to their priest, minister, or pastor for spiritual guidance. They might think the minister odd, they often told themselves that they paid his salary, but they did not ignore him. Often, of course, the clergyman was the only educated person with whom ordinary people had contact. However irrelevant that education to the mid-century situation, or to the perplexities of the parishioners, it helped to strengthen the clergyman's ex-officio authority. Conscious of their followings and of their influence, clergymen of all denominations were inclined to say that Canada was a Christian country. The state schools reflected this influence. There were Bible readings, prayers, and, in some provinces, formal religious instruction. Indeed, during the period 1944-8 such exercises became more numerous, and in many places they were enforced more rigorously than before. The churches, in effect, were enlisting the power of the state, hoping that governments could do what the churches themselves had not managed to achieve.

Christianity is chiefly meant to turn man toward God. There are various aspects of this turning – worship, prayer, alms-giving, good works, respect for one's fellows, and love of them. Canada's churches were reasonably good at worship. Some had a good record of alms-giving and other good works. As for respect and love, the record was mixed, and certainly it was much less satisfactory. All the churches tended to convert love into law. Thus, for instance, the Roman Catholic Church tried to ban birth control and divorce, while the United Church tried to ban 'beverage alcohol.' In such matters the flocks may or may not have heeded their pastors. But governments certainly did.

Broadcasting, too, was permeated by a rather simple sort of morality, the doctrine of uplift. In the 1930s the Canadian Radio League had propagated this doctrine, and the CBC had been founded largely to embody it. Canadian broadcasting was supposed to unify the country, displace American programming, and improve the cultural and moral condition of the people.

During the war, CBC radio had come of age. Admittedly, both in production and in transmission the arrangements were often primitive. For the English network the main programming centre was a derelict girls' secondary school in one of the less savoury parts of Toronto. The French network was no better served. The ambitious framework of 50,000-watt transmitters adumbrated in 1936 had barely been commenced when war began, and it could not be further expanded until after 1945. Many CBC stations, therefore, had rather limited ranges. On the other hand, the AM band was then much less crowded than it later became, and, especially at night, a relatively weak AM signal could often be heard for considerable distances. The CBC also had the power to affiliate privately owned stations to itself, and this power was used with vigour, especially for the networking of news, public affairs, drama, and music. In Toronto, Watrous, Saskatchewan, Montreal, and Sackville, New Brunswick, the CBC did own four high-power transmitters. As yet there were no television transmitters, no cable systems, and no FM; but through landline linkages between its owned and affiliated stations, CBC AM radio reached a large proportion of Canada's population.

Broadcasting was regulated by the legislation of 1936. This stated that there was a single national system, in which privately owned elements co-operated with the state-owned element and were regulated by that element. Private stations depended on advertising revenues, but if affiliated to the national network they got CBC programming free, or very cheaply indeed. The CBC also got some revenue from advertising, but it depended chiefly on the licence fees which radio listeners paid. That licence system was cumbersome and costly to enforce, but it had been designed to ensure that government could not influence programming: since Parliament did not vote any money to the CBC, in theory the state-owned system was independent of government control. In fact, of course, things could never have been quite so simple; Parliament did determine the size of the licence fee and, especially in wartime, there must have been many occasions when government ministers made suggestions to broadcasters. On the whole, however, CBC broadcasters evinced a sturdy independence, not just of government but also of public opinion. Like the British broadcasters on whom so many of them had modelled themselves, they were concerned to purify and improve the public taste, not slavishly to follow it.

The CBC aimed at 'balanced programming' – a mixture of information, entertainment, and uplift, with something for everyone in the course of a week. In the big cities, unaffiliated private stations provided alternatives. But these stations were not allowed to form networks, or to link themselves with the American chains: Columbia Broadcasting, Mutual, or the Red and Blue Networks of NBC. Nor could they be foreign-owned. However, most Canadian cities were within range of American AM transmitters, and so American programming was widely available in the dominion. The CBC itself transmitted a certain amount of American material and it drew a good deal of news from the British Broadcasting Corporation. But although there were no 'Canadian content' regulations, the CBC concentrated on Canadian programming, almost all of which went out 'live.'

For much CBC programming the audience was massive. All over the dominion people huddled around their loudspeakers on Saturday nights to hear Foster Hewitt narrate 'Hockey Night in Canada.' For news and public affairs there was also a mass audience, especially while the war continued. In these spheres, CBC programming showed seriousness together with thoroughness and attention to the large and important issues. Commentators treated the issues as if they thought the public wanted to understand important questions and think about them.

Here, one supposes, the war itself was a considerable help. Most Canadian families – at least the English-speaking ones – had relatives on the battlefields; everyone cared about the conduct of the war and the shaping of the post-war scene. But other forces were at work too, traditions of popular education and uplift that were partly borrowed from the BBC and the Fabian tradition, and partly generated from the native soil of populism, puritanism, protestantism, the Grange, and the labour movement. Hence the intense seriousness of such programs as Citizens' Forum and National Farm Radio Forum; hence, too, the considerable audiences for such things.

The privately owned broadcasters cared little about the arts and letters, or about public affairs. The CBC, however, cared passionately, and it compelled many private radio stations to carry some of the programs that it produced or purchased. From the United States the CBC acquired the Metropolitan Opera and New York Philharmonic programs, which it networked throughout the dominion. From Canadian sources it picked up the Toronto, Montreal, and Vancouver symphony orchestras, the only substantial symphony orchestras that the country possessed. It aired immense amounts of music for small orchestras and for soloists. It developed a remarkable offering of drama, including morning soap opera – *Laura Limited* and her friends and relations, modelled closely on American prototypes. Some was aimed at particular audiences, the regional family dramas modelled on BBC programming and aimed solely at farm families. But a great deal was meant to be culture and high art, and many remember it with admiration and gratitude. Every Sunday night in Toronto, on *CBC Stage*, Andrew Allan produced a major play. Some were new plays, the works of such Canadian authors as Lister Sinclair and Len Petersen. Some were adaptations, borrowings from the great plays and novels of world literature, past and present. From other centres came similar though less ambitious series. Such programming provided invaluable opportunities for Canadian authors and actors. On Wednesday nights, from 1947 until 1963, the CBC transmitted a full evening of serious music, talks, and drama. Modelled on the BBC Third Programme, CBC Wednesday Night never achieved a mass following, but it did not aspire to one. Its producers were confident that they were doing good and useful work, no matter how small the audience ratings might be. In a sense, such programming was 'broadcasting for the sake of the broadcaster.' But it was also broadcasting that treated the radio audience with respect. And although American commercial radio then broadcast somewhat more serious matter than American commercial television would later manage to transmit, CBC radio had no competitors, and no parallels, south of the border. At that time, there was no 'public broadcasting' in the United States.

In its more relaxed and less serious moments, the CBC joined with Canadian private broadcasters and American stations in the transmission and diffusion of North American popular culture. In such matters there was some effort at Canadian programming, but it is hard to find much that was distinctive. From Charlottetown every afternoon for fifteen minutes came Don Messer and his Islanders; from the West came Wilf Carter and his cowboy friends and relations. Here and there, too, one detected the beginnings of a perhaps slightly self-conscious cult of the folk song. Nevertheless, Canadian popular music prospered insofar as it assimilated itself to American models: in Canada there was a mass audience for the staples of American network programming: *The Hit Parade*, Bob Hope and Francis Langford, Fred Allen, Jack Benny, *Fibber McGee and Molly*. Thanks to the CBC there was Canadian content, and Canadian competition, from such worthies as Juliette, or the Happy Gang, or Wayne and Schuster. On New Year's Eve, as the American networks followed the old year across the continent from New York to San Francisco, the CBC moved, time zone after time zone, from Halifax to Vancouver. On both sides of the border, the big band sound was much the same, but the Americans were better at it; on both sides of the border enthusiasts followed the evolution of jazz, but few Canadians tried to play it.

Like present-day television programming, radio programming was based on the assumption that audiences would actually settle down and pay attention. There were identifiable separate programs, typically lasting fifteen minutes or half an hour. Advertising breaks, where they occurred, intervened every ten or fifteen minutes. Many CBC programs, especially the cultural ones, carried no advertising at all, and many ran for an hour or more.

By 1944 the North American radio and record industries had established the symbiotic relationship that has characterized them ever since. In the 1920s and early 1930s the new phenomenon of radio had almost destroyed the much older recording industry. But in the late thirties record sales gradually revived. The Depression was passing; the quality of the records had dramatically improved; people were beginning to buy recordings they heard on the radio. As RCA Victor explained in its advertising, records gave you 'the music you want, when you want it.'

Although the electronically recorded discs of the forties were spectacularly better than the acoustically processed discs of the twenties, by the standards of the 1970s they were nasty, brutish, and short. Because records revolved at 78 rpm, the standard ten-inch disc played for only three minutes per side, and the standard twelve-inch for five. Records were pressed out of highly breakable wax or slightly less breakable laminates and played with fibre or steel needles. Reproduction systems were unable to reproduce a wide range of sound, and recording technique was adjusted to this fact. High fidelity, therefore, was unknown, and stereophonic sound was inconceivable. Records, too, were expensive relative to current earnings. In 1945 an RCA Victor Red Seal disc cost $1.35, and yielded only ten minutes of music; lower-quality ten-inch discs might cost as little as $0.85. Popular music was tailored to the three-minute format that the ten-inch disc imposed, and to the sound the discs were capable of reproducing.

By present-day standards the recording companies were few and catalogues were thin. While some discs were pressed in Canada, almost no masters were produced here; the masters came from Britain and the United States. In Canada, Columbia and RCA Victor – both subsidiaries of American record and radio conglomerates – dominated the industry.

As classical albums were heavy, bulky, and extremely expensive relative to earnings, few people could attempt to build a large collection of serious music, and in most parts of the country classical discs were almost unavailable, except on special order. Popular discs, especially dance discs, were more widely sold, but even here the range was limited and was dominated by the radio programming of the *Hit Parade* and its imitators. Disc jockeys existed, but their influence was relatively slight, because nationally networked live programming absorbed so much of the broadcast week.

As for the printed media, the war had given them an unexpected fillip. As Canada tightened its exchange controls, Canadians were unable to spend American dollars on the more frivolous American publications – specifically, comic books – and the result was the short-lived flowering of the Canadian comic-book industry. For a few years Adrian Dingle could make a living out of *Johnny Canuck.* The war itself provided the basic scenario: upright and clean-cut Canadian youths confronted the slimy and corrupt 'Fascist beast.' But such efflorescences did not long survive the arrival of peace and the easing of exchange controls.

As for the more serious periodicals, the war provided a new relevance for such newsmagazines as *Maclean's* and *Saturday Night*. The specialized trade publications, as always, did well. So did the women's magazines. The *Canadian Forum* soldiered on, as it had done since 1922, bringing uplift and a vague socialism to its 2,000 subscribers. In Toronto, Kingston, and Halifax the universities produced literary quarterlies that aspired unsuccessfully to interest the literate public. However, *Time* and *Life* had already penetrated deep into the Canadian scene, and *Reader's Digest* was not far behind. Such periodicals were too 'serious' to be excluded under the exchange control.

More durable publishing was modest in quantity and uncertain in quality. In the forties, as for many years previously, the Canadian publishing industry rested on two pedestals. The typical company made most of its living from the distributing of American or British books. Some did well, instead or in addition, by producing school texts. The more earnest firms used the proceeds to subsidize the publication of Canadian material: poetry, fiction, and works of scholarship. Many such firms were owned abroad: Macmillan of Canada and J.M. Dent were British-owned, although both firms published and distributed – often at a loss – many Canadian scholarly books.

Radio mattered, partly because the population was still so dispersed, and partly because even in cities there was so little else. As a French diplomat said of wartime Ottawa, 'Le cinéma! Toujours le cinéma!' But for the Canadians who lived on farms and in small towns, even the cinema was a rare and exotic treat, and the only recreation was likely to be found in the Canadian Legion bar or the Orange Lodge. As for the city-dweller, by present-day standards the fare was remarkably sparse.

The discothèque had not yet been invented. In the larger cities there were a few 'supper clubs,' where cabaret could be seen. But outside Quebec these led a dim and sequestered life because they could not serve alcoholic drinks. They could and would sell 'mixers'; their tables were all equipped with floor-length tablecloths; and when patrons came bearing anonymous brown paper bags, the managements were understanding. Here and there the Canadian Legion clubs offered entertainment of a sordid and derivative kind.

Many cities had theatres, often built for vaudeville and once used by touring players and repertory companies. But in the 1930s most of these buildings had been converted into cinemas, and some were derelict. Not much theatre or vaudeville had survived the onslaught of the talkies; because the war made touring impossible it administered the *coup de grâce*, and live professional theatre did not revive promptly with the coming of peace.

In music the situation was better, but only slightly. Vancouver and Toronto had professional symphony orchestras, and Montreal had a semi-professional one. But Toronto was the only Canadian city to have a proper concert hall. In Vancouver the symphony performed sometimes in a cinema and sometimes in a hockey rink; Les Concerts Symphoniques de Montréal used a high school auditorium. Canadian musical audiences were timid in the extreme. In 1946, for example, a rendition of Jan Sibelius' Fourth Symphony by the Toronto Symphony Orchestra was prefaced by a plea from the podium for tolerance for this new and strange work.

Nor were museums and art galleries numerous or impressive. In Ottawa the National Gallery had lived since 1907 in the National Science Museum, where the lighting was bad and the ambience depressing. In Montreal and Toronto there were substantial galleries, but private donors had provided the buildings and the contents. Toronto had the Royal Ontario Museum, where a distinguished collection had been accumulated. Vancouver had a small municipal art gallery. Other cities had little or nothing.

On the other hand, in big cities and towns the movies were everywhere, and they were available in profusion. Every suburb had its local cinema, where films were shown cheaply within weeks after they had opened in the big downtown palaces. These palaces, in turn, were numerous and immense. Dating from the 1920s or before, some had begun as proper theatres or as vaudeville houses; but many had small stages or no stages at all and these had been built and designed as picture palaces.

In a downtown theatre, a film would often run for several weeks. In the suburbs, on the other hand, the typical run was two or three days, so that in a single week a suburban theatre would show two or three complete programs, each including a main feature film, a supporting full-length production, a newsreel, a cartoon, and sometimes a travelogue or other short subject. Most suburban theatres also had a Saturday 'kiddy matinee' – one or two features, lots of cartoons, and an exciting serial such as *Batman* or *Captain Marvel*.

People went to the movies a great deal, sometimes two or three times a week. Movies were not only exciting and undemanding, they were cheap, too. In Vancouver, in 1947-8, for example, the suburban kiddy matinee cost twelve cents – about the price of two bottles of Coca Cola or two rides on the street car. The sociologist may suspect that the age of the movie was based on escapism; the economist is fairly sure that it was based on cheapness. Hence its vulnerability to the competition of television, which *appears* to be even cheaper – indeed, free. By 1948 there was still no television in Canada, but its arrival was foreshadowed.

Regular television broadcasting began in 1936, when the BBC commenced transmission in London. These broadcasts ceased in 1939 when war broke out. By then, the National Broadcasting Company had begun experimental broadcasting near New York. When the United States entered the war in 1941 its transmission ended. In North America, therefore, commercial television began only in 1946, when the American Federal Communications Commission defined and allocated twelve VHF channels.

Television is different from AM radio in that the TV signal does not follow the curvature of the earth. Hence the height of the transmission tower really determines the range of the signal. American radio could penetrate Canada readily; American TV could do so only with difficulty. Montreal could receive Plattsburgh, Toronto could get Buffalo, and Vancouver could receive Bellingham, but only with expensive equipment and tall antennas. By 1948, Canadians were beginning to watch the 'box in the corner' (by 1949, there were at least 3,600 sets in the dominion), but these sets were inconvenient to tune and their pictures were small: the ten-inch picture tube was the standard. They were still extremely expensive, too, so that the TV set was a luxury and a status symbol. So long as TV sets were few there was little economic justification for cable connection, even though all programming came from relatively remote transmitters in the United States. Cable systems came later, when the sets were more common and when the signals were more numerous.

When they went to the movies, Canadians saw British and American films. The war had cut off the supply of films from continental Europe, but even before 1939 such films were rarely seen. After 1945 the Soviet Union sent one or two art films, which achieved critical acclaim and very limited exposure. Canada's National Film Board laboured worthily, producing a torrent of short subjects, but there was no Canadian feature film industry, and no sign of one.

Most of the cinemas were grouped in a few great chains. The largest, Odeon, was British-owned. Famous Players and Twentieth Century belonged to American interests. The British and American owners, in turn, had close links with the great film studios of Hollywood and London. Some observers have deduced from this that the chains conspired to show foreign films, suppressing Canadian talent and corrupting the Canadian consciousness, but the claim has only dubious plausibility.

Naturally each chain tried to release the products of its parent studio, but there were many more studios than chains, and no chain showed only the products of its parent. Moreover, no studio produced enough feature films to satisfy the demand from its own chain. The suburban cinemas, it should be remembered, showed from four to six feature films every week and almost never showed re-runs or revivals. Each chain offered the products of all the great American studios – Twentieth Century Fox, Warner Brothers, Universal-International, and the rest. Although Rank films might appear first in Odeon cinemas, they were shown also in Famous Players and other movie houses. It is reasonable to suppose, therefore, that if there had been a Canadian feature film industry, and if theatre-managers had thought its products saleable, the films would have been shown.

In recent years, Canada has developed a feature film industry, just when the feature film, as a form of mass entertainment, is declining. As so often in our history, the timing is wrong. It might well be argued that if the government had provided some subsidies in the 1940s, as seed money, Canada might have developed a film industry at a time when there was a genuine mass market for film – at a time, that is, when film-making was really part of popular culture. But the government of the day did not see things in that light. It did not subsidize the arts, music, drama, or sport; it subsidized higher education only with extreme reluctance. How could it have been expected to subsidize film-making? Symphony orchestras and operas, at least, were recognized money-losers the world over, but the movies were an enormously remunerative business, not just for the studios but for the distributors. A less plausible field for subsidy it would have been hard to imagine.

In the film era, and especially during the war and immediately after it, the newsreel had an importance that the TV newscast would later assume. Like the feature films, the newsreels came from British and American companies. Most of the footage came from abroad, but for Canadian distribution the producers usually added a good deal of 'Canadian content.' The newsreels also gave some attention to sport, both professional and amateur; although the coverage of sport, as of other matters, was far more sketchy than that which TV would later provide. The newsreel was short, and was assembled with considerable trouble. Typically it covered all the events of a week in twenty minutes or less. It assembled its raw materials by train, ship, and airplane, but not by satellite or by landline; it distributed its finished product in the same pre-electronic way. It could hardly aim at immediacy, depth, or thoroughness, but at least it gave ordinary people the feeling that they had actually seen what was going on in the great world.

Vying with the movies for popular attention were the sports arena and the beer parlour. In Canada, sports-madness grew with television, which exposed Canadians to an intensive dose of sport both commonplace and exotic and converted national sports and many foreign sports into nation-wide events. In the era of radio and film, however, such things could not occur. The range of sports, too, was more limited than it has later become; few schools had the facilities for such things as gymnastics or swimming, for example, and skiing was both exotic and expensive. Although some cities provided parks, no one did anything to subsidize the amateur. In each age group, only a small number completed secondary school or attended university, so that participation was limited largely to sandlot baseball and local hockey. Few people persevered in either sport after the end of formal schooling. As for professional sport, the range was less complete and the atmosphere less intense than it became in the 1950s and 1960s. Of course, Torontonians and Montrealers flocked to football and hockey. The National Hockey League comprised six teams, of which two were Canadian; many people could remember the time when there were no American teams at all. But the season for professional football was short and the teams were few. Neither hockey nor football reached the west coast until later.

On the other hand, there was a great deal of baseball. In this, as in so many other respects, Canadians showed their identification with the North American culture. Canadian cities fielded teams in various American leagues, not the National or the American, but various second- or third-level gatherings such as the International or the Western International leagues. In Canada, as in the United States, the baseball stadia were often rickety and primitive; nevertheless, Canadians found baseball a suitable diversion for the hot Saturday afternoons of midsummer. And if they kept away from Maple Leaf Stadium or Capilano Stadium, they followed the American major-league broadcasts on the Liberty Broadcasting System. Admittedly, Liberty had no outlets in Canada, but its American affiliates were nearby.

To the observer of the 1970s the spectator sports of the forties, like the movies, look cheap relative to incomes. Drink, however, was neither cheap nor plentiful. By 1944, everywhere in Canada except in Prince Edward Island, where until 1948 drink was available only on prescription, the days of prohibition were long past. Even so, everywhere the buying of drink was inconvenient, and, except in Quebec, the buyer was astonishingly made to feel slightly daring. No one could drink, or buy drink, before the age of twenty-one. Through the outlets of the provincial liquor control boards one bought spirits, wine, and, in most provinces, beer. During the war spirits were rationed and watered. After the war the rationing ended but the watering has continued to this day. Only in Quebec were there cocktail bars; only there could one get a drink with a meal. Elsewhere there was nothing but the 'licenced premises,' or 'beverage room,' or 'beer parlour.' These remarkable places were always attached to hotels. In them one could buy a glass of beer, and usually nothing else – not even food. Normally an unattached man was not allowed to drink beer in the same room as a woman, attached or not; in some cities it was impossible for a man and a woman to drink beer in the same room at all. About many other things, too, there were regulations. One of the more notorious related to the number of draught glasses that could rest on a table at any one time. Outside Quebec, no one was allowed to sell wine or spirits by the glass, and bottles could be bought only in provincial outlets or, in some provinces, in the wineries' own stores as well. Hence it was impossible to have wine with one's meal, unless one were eating at home. On Sundays, nothing was sold and nothing was open. No wonder the average Canadian consumed only a few litres of wine in a year. One province even employed a teetotaller to handle its wine buying.

To Americans and Europeans these arrangements were incredible. Canadians, however, were inclined to accept them as inevitable, if not altogether natural. And, as the country was still relatively poor, they did have certain advantages. Simply because drink was so hard to come by, drunkenness must have been less common than it would have been if beer, wine, and spirits had been widely available.

In the 1970s many observers have been inclined to be nostalgic about the popular culture of the 1940s. Many things *were* a good deal simpler, often extremely cheap, and often, too, less commercialized than they have since become. But fundamentally things were pretty bleak. Even in 1944 the Toronto Maple Leafs were a money-making proposition. The Vancouver Capilanos were run for profit, not for fun. Commercial radio was as blatantly commercial as commercial television was later to become. In popular music, in cinema, and in all sports but hockey, Americanization was all but complete. The CBC had not yet abandoned the battle for standards and sense, but its impact was probably small, except when it was participating in the diffusion of North American mass culture. In the forties, broadcasting was certainly more imaginative than in the seventies; it aired a great deal of Canadian material, and much of this material was very good indeed. But of this programming most Canadians knew little and cared less. As for high culture and the arts, Canada had precious little of either.

Among those who lived through the war and its aftermath, 'the sounds of the forties,' and the sights of that depressing decade can often produce a *frisson* of excitement. But the 'big band sound' could grow monotonous when little else was available. Frank Sinatra was embarrassingly sentimental, while 'Shep Fields and his Rippling Rhythm' was simply embarrassing. Jitterbugging or jiving was fun but formless, while the 'slow fox trots' of the era were soporific – though at a time when sexual continence was still the norm, cheek-to-cheek dancing had an obvious place in the scheme of things. It is as well to remember that, in the last years of the Mackenzie King era, most Canadians were rather poor, extremely busy, and more than a little timid. There was little time and less income to give to frivolities. Also, the young were relatively few. In the late twenties and throughout the thirties Canadian birth rates had been low, while in the thirties immigration had been slight;

thus by 1945 there were remarkably few teenagers or young adults. Compared with the late sixties or the seventies, the population was middle-aged. The dominion looked grey partly because so many of its people were greying.

What, then, has changed since 1948? First and most important, we are all a great deal better off. We spend casually on things that our parents and grandparents would have thought unattainable luxuries. There are many more of us, too, and the age distribution has changed a great deal. In 1945 there were about eleven million Canadians; in 1972 there were over twenty-two million. In popular and high culture, as in many other things, opportunities expand with the growth of the market. Relative to the total population there are far more adolescents and young adults who, in turn, are far more prosperous than their predecessors. Governments are more willing to subsidize and control, and the public is more willing to bear the costs of the former and the irritations of the latter. Relative to incomes some things have become very much cheaper. Television bathes us in free entertainment. Thanks to technical change and progress, records and televisions are no longer the luxuries that they were in the late forties, and the quality of sound-reproduction and transmission has improved dramatically. In 1978 it was simply impossible to find anything as ghastly as the standard five-tube superheterodyne table radio of 1948. But such a radio could cost fifty dollars or more, at a time when few families made five thousand dollars per year. Travel, too, is now cheaper: air and bus transport have perfected themselves, and car travel became steadily cheaper relative to incomes throughout the fifties and sixties. Conversely, many older pleasures, such as streetcar rides and sermons, have become relatively costly, either in money or in time and effort. Popular consumption responds accordingly, and popular culture is transformed.

13

Education

For many years, enrolments in most provinces had been growing very slowly, or declining. In Ontario, between 1934 and 1946 enrolments fell by nearly 30,000, or 4 per cent. In the prairie provinces the declines in percentage terms were more dramatic – 18 per cent in Manitoba, 22 per cent in Saskatchewan, and 9.5 per cent in Alberta. It is true that, in British Columbia, enrolments rose by 13 per cent in twelve years, and in Newfoundland and the Maritimes by 7.2 per cent; but Quebec enrolments, having risen in the 1930s, then declined by 11.6 per cent from a 1938 peak. These patterns reflected the demographic developments of the late twenties and thirties, when birth rates had been relatively low in most parts of the country. They also reflected the fact that high-school attendance was little more fashionable in 1946 than it had been in 1939. It was also no less expensive, whether the measure is sacrificed income or out-of-pocket costs relative to family earnings.

Where enrolments had been rising, as in the Atlantic provinces and British Columbia, the expansion had been so slow that the provincial and local authorities could provide extra teachers and facilities with very little extra strain: new buildings were rarely necessary, instructional media were simple and cheap, and teachers could readily be found, although a remote and unattractive area might have to settle for an 'unqualified' person. Where enrolments had been falling, as in Ontario, the decline was so gentle that it posed few problems for the educational authorities. Rather, it provided opportunities: by lowering the pupil-teacher ratio, and by lengthening the period of teacher-training, the authorities could perhaps raise the quality of education. In all provinces such developments can be traced during the years before 1944 or 1946. Even where enrolments were falling, teachers became more numerous. Everywhere, on average, they became better qualified. In Quebec, for example, in 1930 only 14 per cent of all teachers had any training beyond junior matriculation, the end of high school, and 64 per cent had not completed high school; in 1950 only 23 per cent had not completed high school and 44 per cent had progressed beyond junior matriculation. Although in other provinces teachers had been better qualified than in Quebec, in all provinces there was a movement in the same general direction. In Ontario, in 1930, 63 per cent of teachers had studied for only one year past junior matriculation, and only 10.6 per cent had university degrees; in 1950 the former figure had fallen to 16 and the latter was 17.

In eight of the nine provinces, Canadian schools operated under provincial regimes which generally gave relatively little power to local schools and teachers and relatively great power to provincial education departments. The provincial authorities, not the schools, set the curricula and chose the textbooks. They also arranged for exit examinations – junior matriculation after eleven or twelve years of schooling, and senior matriculation after twelve or thirteen years of schooling. In Quebec, where there was no department of education, the Protestant schools operated in the same way as the public schools elsewhere in Canada. That is, they prepared pupils for matriculation examinations which admitted graduates directly into university. Matriculation examinations were set and marked by provincial authorities, not by schools. High-school teaching often centred on these external examinations because a teacher was often judged by his success in getting pupils through them.

In some of the western provinces, the matriculation examinations were no longer compulsory by 1946. A promising candidate could be 'recommended' for university entrance on the basis of his high-school work. Nevertheless, even in such provinces the provincial examinations remained in existence. They had to be sat by any pupils who had not earned 'recommendation,' and no one could receive a provincial university scholarship without competing in them. Such scholarships were few, and neither the dominion nor the provinces ran any general scheme of student aid.

Each provincial system bred up its own officialdom and produced most of the instructors for its own teacher-training institutions. A teacher of teachers might go away for higher studies, but he would generally return to the province where he had commenced. Thus each school system had a career ladder – teacher to principal to inspector to government official, with a branching path into teacher-training. This self-containment helped to make each system rather stable and tradition-minded, and public attitudes tended in the same direction. In 1946, most people appear to have demanded much the same things from the school system as their parents and grandparents had demanded in the 1920s or even before 1914.

These centrally regulated systems made a great deal of sense when teachers were badly schooled and when parents and children were badly informed, or timid, or both. The arrangements had developed at a time when the typical teacher could not have been trusted to devise a program of study, choose textbooks, or maintain standards, and when pupils and parents were ignorant and knew it. The arrangements also rested on an implicit assumption that most pupils would leave school before matriculation. In some provinces, and in some cities, efforts had been made to provide various sorts of secondary school, not only academic, but also vocational, technical, and commercial. These non-academic schools and streams did not lead to matriculation and university entrance; they were meant to give a more practical training that would lead directly into work. But such schools could not be established everywhere, and when obliged to choose, the educational authorities would set up an academic high school – in some provinces, a 'collegiate institute.' Few citizens expected that the typical adolescent would stay in school, any kind of school, until he or she had completed some sort of course. It was expected that the vast majority would leave school as soon as the law allowed. Thus the external apparatus of academic curriculum and external examination was never meant to process more than a small fraction of each age group. It was implicitly assumed, too, that numbers would rise slowly, or not at all. Although elementary schooling was compulsory everywhere by 1945, no one was compelled to complete a secondary education of any sort. Teachers and parents might worry about 'drop-outs,' and hope that the more promising adolescents would stay in school, but the authorities, as yet, were not really concerned.

In time, all these circumstances changed. With more education and more self-confidence, teachers became more assertive. With more training and more mobility came more knowledge of other arrangements, systems, and assumptions, especially American ones. Parents and pupils grew less docile and the schools were asked to do more sorts of things: to develop personality, treat neuroses, instruct in the right use of the automobile and the right attitudes toward alcohol and the opposite sex. Schools and politicians now began to share teachers' worries about 'drop-outs' and their worryings affected curricula. Most important of all, perhaps, was the rising tide of high-school students. In later decades, and especially in the 1960s, these and other pressures transformed both the English- and the French-speaking school systems, but in the forties they were not much in evidence.

Admittedly, numbers were increasing, and compared with the thirties or earlier forties these increases were considerable. But compared with the 1950s they were small. The 'baby boom' of the forties had started to affect enrolments, but the pressure had only begun. From 1945 to 1950 elementary enrolments rose 12 per cent and secondary enrolments 13 per cent; in the next quinquennium the increases were 27 per cent and 29 per cent. In the forties it was possible to go on much as before. One hired more teachers; one worried about their qualifications; one put more pupils into the same school buildings, many of which had been under-utilized since their construction two or more decades before.

The Catholic schools of Quebec provided almost all of the province's French-language teaching and a very little of its English. They were not at all like Quebec's Protestant system, or like the public-school systems in the other provinces.

In the first place, Quebec's local primary schools were generally staffed by members of religious orders, and normally the parish priest took a special interest in the school and its work. Such arrangements could and did occur elsewhere. British Columbia had independent Roman Catholic parochial schools. Ontario and Alberta had tax-supported 'separate schools' that were fitted into the provincial education systems. But although monks and nuns might staff such schools, and although public-school supporters might fulminate against them, the provincial educational authorities controlled both the separate and also the parochial schools, where enrolments relative to public schools were small.

In the second place, Quebec really had no general integrated system of secondary schooling. The provincial authorities had established various special schools for technical and agricultural training. But the ordinary or academic schools went to mid-adolescence and no further. At that point, aspiring Catholic pupils transferred to the 'classical college.' There they might remain for one to five years. Having completed the course they would receive the baccalaureate degree and could proceed to university, having got somewhat beyond senior matriculation on the English-Canadian scale. Although aided by government grants, the classical colleges were independent institutions. Almost all of them were owned and staffed by members of religious orders. Their curricula were severely academic, and somewhat more specialized than those of the English-speaking systems. Typically they concentrated on theology, philosophy, and languages; few made any effort to teach science.

Outside Quebec there were some classical colleges. Usually these were based in a French-speaking area, and generally they wre affiliated for purposes of credit and transfer to a francophone university, often the University of Ottawa, which the Oblate Order owned and operated. English-speaking Canadians found the classical colleges puzzling. The more virulent Protestants saw them as yet another agency of Catholic thought-control. Such criticisms were understandable but rather unfair. Admittedly, the colleges taught theology and usually ignored science. Admittedly, too, although they attempted some university level work they probably did not always attain that level in fact. But in Quebec the public authorities were not yet concerned to suggest an alternative, much less to devise and introduce one. It would be better to praise the monks and nuns whose efforts filled a gap in the state system.

UNIVERSITIES

Beyond the secondary schools and the classical colleges Canada had universities and almost nothing else. There were military colleges at Kingston and Victoria. Some provinces had created higher schools in such things as agriculture and forestry which did not grant degrees. Most provinces had teacher-training colleges which took and processed both high-school and university graduates. Here and there, too, one found colleges which were affiliated to some university and which did some university-level teaching. In the Maritimes there were specialized professional colleges that granted degrees. In Ontario and elsewhere there were Bible colleges that did not. Everywhere there were theological colleges, most of which had affiliated themselves to universities. But there were no full-blown community colleges, junior colleges, or institutes of technology. As for the universities, because so few Canadians sought university degrees in 1944, the universities were few and small. They had always been that way, and little had changed for a long, long time.

In 1920 Canada contained 21,869 full-time undergraduates and an insignificant number of postgraduate and professional students. By 1930 the total had risen to 30,209, and by 1944 to 35,132, of which about one-quarter were women. Full-time faculty numbered 4,503. Through the twenties and thirties enrolments had grown steadily, but slowly – 61 per cent in twenty-four years, or less than 2 per cent a year on the average. The universities, like the schools, were thus adjusted to an extremely gradual pattern of growth. Further, the Depression had hurt them severely because provincial grants and private benefactions had fallen together.

The universities of Canada originated in different ways. Some were provincial foundations; others came from the efforts of religious groups – Roman Catholic and Anglican bishops, Protestant churches, various sorts of pious conventicle; a few had been founded by private benefactions on a non-sectarian basis; and many had severed their church ties wholly or in large part. But in Ontario, Quebec, Manitoba, and the Maritime provinces the religious dimension was still very much in evidence, and it was not altogether absent elsewhere. Universities received no federal funds, and provincial governments financed them in various ways. However, some universities received nothing from the government. A few, such as McGill, had large endowments. A few received subventions from churches, and the Roman Catholic colleges and universities gained from their ability to employ a clerical and monastic staff whose pay was small. But many universities depended to a quite remarkable extent on tuition fees, and for all universities this fee revenue was important.

This tranquil scene was transformed when the dominion government announced that it would send veterans to universities. Tuition fees would be paid; there would be a subsistence allowance; each university would get a federal government grant, the size dependent on the number of veterans who had enrolled. This grant was meant to help the universities hire extra staff, buy books, and provide for other current expenses.

No one expected, or hoped, that there would be time to construct new buildings. Indeed, because the 'veteran bulge' was bound to leave the universities before many years had passed, the new program did little to justify such building. Nor could it justify an expansion of the permanent staff. The universities, therefore, were forced into a series of heroic improvisations. Temporary lecturers joined the somewhat frail and elderly permanent staffs, most of whom had been appointed in the 1920s or before. Branch campuses were set up in old army camps. Prefabricated army hutments were moved from camps to campuses, where some are still to be found. Lecturers spoke in theatres, churches, and halls of all sorts. Classes became enormous.

In the academic year 1945-6, Canadian universities had enrolled 38,776 full-time undergraduates. In 1946-7 the figure was 61,861, and at the peak in 1948, there were 79,346 full-time undergraduates. In three years, enrolments had almost doubled.

Fortunately the veterans tended to prefer arts and commerce courses, where equipment was of little importance and where lecturers could to some extent be substituted for the books that the university libraries did not have. There was pressure in science and engineering also, but the pressure was less severe. This was just as well, since the heroic improvisations would have been much less practicable, and much less successful, in the laboratory-based subjects.

The university staffs found the veterans stimulating and refreshing. One wonders whether the veterans thought the same of the professors. Most Canadian universities were then rather dim and limited places. For generations the provincial authorities had been pinching pennies, and private benefactions had not made up the deficiency. Of the churches' contributions the less said the better. Libraries, therefore, were often very incomplete, and the array of courses was limited in quantity, while quality was at best variable. Although some professors tried to keep up with current scholarship in the humanities and social sciences there were no funds for research or travel. As university staffs were miserably paid, few professors were able to attend learned gatherings, or to finance their own investigations. Many were unable to purchase current learned journals, or to follow current developments in other ways. In terms of purchasing power, from 1938 until 1955 the average professorial stipend *fell*, before taxes, even though from 1939 until 1944 the tax burden increased substantially, and even though after 1945 most Canadians became steadily better off. Although there were a few private scholarships for postgraduate study, in the arts and social sciences there were no government scholarships, and no loan funds. The aspiring scholar could only hope to capture an American university award or one of the three sorts of grant that might take him to Britain. Canadian governments contributed nothing to any of these grants or awards. As for the results of scholarly investigations, in 1948 there were still no government grants to aid scholarly publication in the arts and social sciences. The dominion contained one university press, whose operations were subsidized only by the profits of the printing plant with which that press was affiliated.

In medicine and the natural sciences matters were somewhat better. Since 1917 the National Research Council had provided some funds for university research and helped to finance graduate fellowships; it also operated several learned journals. There were similar arrangements for medicine. In agriculture and in some other specialized subjects the dominion and the provinces did something to finance and aid research. But on most Canadian campuses such subjects were not predominant, and on some they were absent entirely.

However dim the universities may have seemed, and however dedicated solely to teaching their staffs may have appeared, some interesting work was underway. University physicists had been deeply involved in the wartime atomic-energy program. After the war this involvement continued. In literature, universities provided the bases from which artists like Birney, Klein, and Child produced works of imagination and power. Although in history the dominant tendency was a sort of curricular boredom, here and there scholars were at work, forming and reshaping the several national myths. In economics the eccentric genius of Harold Innis was already attracting attention in Britain and the United States. Here and there, scholars brooded on the significance of the prairie wheat economy, on dominion status, on democracy in the British dominions. However great their physical isolation, and however deep their poverty, Canadian university people felt they belonged to an international community of learning. So far as they could, they contributed to that corpus of knowledge.

In universities, as in schools, the staffs of the forties had formal qualifications that were relatively low and extremely various. Outside of the sciences, few professors had doctorates, and many had the sort of British MA that is earned not by formal work but by the effluxion of time. On the other hand, typically they took their teaching responsibilities very seriously, and many took a great interest in the later careers of their students. Perhaps they were serious about teaching because they could not hope for recognition as researchers. Perhaps they simply manifested and transmitted a seriousness of purpose that then manifested itself in many aspects of Canadian life. We shall see more of this seriousness in Part III.

PART THREE

The St Laurent Years 1948-57

14

A New Cabinet and Its Foreign Policy

The new prime minister, Louis St Laurent, was a late-comer to politics, but no stranger to public life. Sixty-six when he took office as prime minister, he had been a practising politician for not quite seven years. In his cabinet he was dwarfed in seniority by C.D. Howe and James G. (Jimmy) Gardiner, the Ministers of Trade and Commerce and of Agriculture, respectively, and by James MacKinnon, Alberta's representative in the government. MacKinnon, an amiable and respectable lightweight, would soon shuffle out of active politics into the Senate. Howe and Gardiner, however, were the St Laurent government's heavy artillery, as they had been in the King administration. Fortunately, St Laurent and Howe were fast friends and firm allies, for Howe had no ambition to become leader or prime minister, tasks for which he felt unsuitable and unsuited. Gardiner was a different matter. A former premier of Saskatchewan, Gardiner was raised in the heavily partisan politics of a bygone age. He was a professional politician and proud of it. 'I don't think Mr St Laurent was a politician at all,' Gardiner once commented. 'He was a lawyer's lawyer ... but that isn't politics.'[1]

Many of St Laurent's colleagues, then and later, would have agreed. St Laurent was a good and faithful Liberal, to be sure (his *Who's Who* entries noted the fact long before he entered partisan politics), but he had no experience in political organization and little interest in learning about it. That he left to the more overtly political members of his cabinet, C.D. Howe, the party's chief fund raiser, and Brooke Claxton, its chief electoral strategist. St Laurent's strong points were administrative and personal. Endowed with a clear and quick understanding, St Laurent had an uncanny ability to grasp and epitomize the essence of an argument, an

---

1 Quoted in R. Bothwell and W. Kilbourn, *C.D. Howe: A Biography* (Toronto: McClelland & Stewart 1979), 226.

invaluable attribute in a period when cabinet agendas were becoming longer and more complicated, and when the questions placed before cabinet were becoming increasingly technical. Although others might shine more brightly in the House of Commons and on the hustings, St Laurent was master of his cabinet, and of the civil servants who appeared before it.

The links between the cabinet and the civil service were strong, and becoming stronger. The Liberals had grown grey in office during their thirteen years in the East Block. Howe and Gardiner had been around longer than the 'permanent' heads of their departments. It was small wonder that the civil servants relied on their ministers for tradition and guidance, or, where they did not, freely exchanged advice on policy for advice on political impact. St Laurent's ministers had their politics – and their administration – well under control. A case in point may be found in the finance department, the citadel of economic power in St Laurent's Ottawa. There the deputy minister, Clifford Clark, still reigned supreme. Journalists specializing in financial or economic questions regarded Clark with unstinting admiration: 'brilliant,' one wrote; 'gentle and civilized to his fingertips,' another recorded, 'perhaps the most lovable of Ottawa's top-flight officials, utterly free of "side" or pomposity and incapable of pettiness.' Equally formidable, however, was the minister, Douglas Abbott. Abbott, a Montreal lawyer, had scant knowledge of economics; but he was a skilled politician, with abundant confidence in his own abilities and common sense. Abbott acted as a valuable brake on his economists' enthusiasms. On one occasion, shortly after the end of the war, Abbott's officials informed the minister that the government should run a large surplus in the next budget to combat inflation. 'You fellows tell me we should have surpluses, in inflationary conditions,' Abbott is said to have replied. That, he told the officials, was out of the question. If he predicted surplus, his backbenchers would expect it to be shared out in the form of tax relief. The thing to do, Abbott explained, was to forecast a small surplus, rather than the large one actually anticipated. Then, when the large surplus occurred, it could be put down to good fortune and good management. And so it was.

For the first six months of the St Laurent government's life it seemed that Abbott's surpluses would make little difference to the Liberals' political fate. They would not, pundits decided, be around much longer. The Conservatives had a bright new leader, George Drew, newly translated from his Ontario fastness. What Drew had done for the Ontario Tories, his supporters reasoned, he could repeat on the national level. He looked like a leader: tall, handsome, authoritative, and experienced; and the leader had an issue – Communists in government. Ottawa was full of them, Drew told a startled House of Commons. The country's first priority should be to fire the Reds and outlaw their party. Secure at home, Canada could then turn to face the enemy abroad. The only trouble, Drew explained, was that the government refused to take the situation as seriously as he did.

It looked like a winning issue. 'Communists in government' was playing to packed political houses south of the border; soon it would become even more popular. When Drew unlimbered his parliamentary big gun in the parliamentary session of January 1949, he was firing the first salvo of a campaign which would shortly blow the Liberals out of office altogether. St Laurent, caught off guard, was initially hesitant and uncertain. Suddenly, just as his troops were losing heart, he rallied. No, St Laurent affirmed, Canada would not outlaw the Communist party, however repugnant its beliefs might be. There was no real threat and no excuse for such drastic measures. As for the Communists in government, they hardly existed. St Laurent's reasoned reply to Drew's charges probably had less impact than another exchange that occurred at about the same time. When Drew tried to pin the spectre of Karl Marx on the Liberal cabinet, Abbott easily replied that Drew reminded him of Marx, too: 'Groucho, not Karl."

Drew's charges were dissolved in ridicule. The minor chord of Communism disposed of, the Liberals introduced the main theme of their electoral hymn: prosperity. When Parliament was dissolved on April 30, 1949, the Liberal symphony was in full blast under Brooke Claxton's skillful direction. Drew, thumping the stale Communist issue, was overwhelmed. The Liberals attracted 49 per cent of the popular vote in the June election (not counting Liberals who won their seats by acclamation), and 193 of the 262 seats in the House of Commons. Only in Alberta, where they elected five members, did the Liberals receive less than half the total number of MPs. Louis St. Laurent, who had shed his lawyerly shyness to become everybody's favourite 'Uncle Louis,' proved to be an unbeatable electoral asset. Canadians liked him, they liked his cabinet, and they approved of his party. They decidedly did not like George Drew, who earned a meagre forty-one seats, or the CCF, which fell from twenty-eight members in 1945 to thirteen in 1949. The CCF would be in the future a minor electoral sect, distinguished mostly for its earnestness and its parliamentary skills.

For the next eight years Canadian politics followed the line set down in 1949: a powerful government, sustained by an overwhelming majority in the House of Commons, dominated the political world. The proposition that it could not, if it wished, push any legislation it desired through Parliament was unthinkable, even laughable; and since the Liberals consistently led in the public opinion polls there was no prospect of change. At the time of the next election, in 1953, a Toronto philosopher, Marcus Long, explained to a television audience why this should be so: 'I pointed out,' he wrote to a prominent Liberal, 'that change is of no value unless it represents improvement. ... I then suggested that there was no point in changing a government that had done so much for Canada, nationally and internationally. ... Finally I expressed the opinion that I could not see Mr Drew and his Conservative Party as an improvement.' Most Canadians agreed. Eighteen years into office, the Liberals won another resounding victory in August 1953.[2]

The cabinet took the electorate's endorsement as a well-deserved compliment. Some of the cabinet's stars began to believe that their term in office was limited only by mortality. Canada had never had a finance minister as smooth and cheerful as Douglas Abbott, a trade minister as capable and commanding as C.D. Howe, or an external affairs minister as charming and plausible as Lester Pearson. St Laurent gave his colleagues their head, subject to his overall supervision. In St Laurent's systematic and orderly government there were few surprises. The circulation of cabinet papers warned ministers of their colleagues' plans and saved tedious exposition. It had another, unexpected effect. The power of the finance minister, already great, was increased. Forewarned, Abbott or his successor, Walter Harris, could come to cabinet and deliver instant opinions on the financial soundness of any ministerial proposal. The system guaranteed that the St Laurent government would pay a great deal of attention to the voice of responsible finance, and it confirmed the already great power of the Department of Finance.

That institution shared some of its authority with other agencies and departments. Clifford Clark, together with the 'cool, detached, objective' Graham Towers, governor of the Bank of Canada, with an assist from Mitchell Sharp at the Department of Trade and Commerce, shaped and implemented Canada's fiscal and monetary policies. These men, assisted by a corps of senior officials, were the top rung of what came to be called the Ottawa 'mandarinate.' The civil service mandarinate is a mysterious concept, evoking visions of languid, broad-browed intellectuals formulating government policy in between sips of tea. This picture is naturally overdrawn, but there are some elements of truth in it.

Most of the mandarins were not the scions of Canada's privileged urban élite. Of the government's top officials, the Clerk of the Privy Council, J.W. Pickersgill, was raised in rural Manitoba; Mitchell Sharp, Winnipeg-born, was anything but privileged in background; while Clifford Clark, the dean of the mandarinate, hailed from a tiny Ontario hamlet just outside of Cornwall. Though predominantly Anglo-Saxon and Protestant, the mandarins were not exclusively so: the prominence in their ranks of John Deutsch (Catholic), Louis Rasminsky (Jewish), or Jules Léger would indicate that government, more than business, furnished a road open to all talents.

The most obvious common characteristic of the higher civil servants was that they were educated far above the average. At a minimum, the senior public servants

---

2 Results of the 1953 general election: Liberals: 172; Progressive Conservatives: 51; CCF: 23; Social Credit: 15; Others: 4.

had earned an undergraduate degree, most frequently at the University of Toronto, Queen's University, the University of British Columbia, or, less frequently, one of the western provincial universities. There were few French Canadians. Of the 201 foreign service officers employed in the Department of External Affairs in December 1949, only 43 were of French origin. And External Affairs fared better than most Ottawa departments in its French-Canadian recruiting.

What was true of the Department of External Affairs was generally true of other government departments. They were officered by men (very few women reached senior levels) usually recruited direct from the university into the civil service. Even at the highest level, the average age was comparatively low. At the most senior level, only Clifford Clark himself and the president of the National Research Council, C.J. Mackenzie, exceeded sixty in 1949; most of their peers ('the juniors') had not even reached fifty. There was, as a result, surprising stability and continuity in the senior civil service. To a large extent, the history of the central government between 1945 and 1970 is the story of a single and coherent group.

In 1945, it had been expected that the central government's preoccupation would be social security and domestic improvement. Instead, it was defence. In 1948 Canada was practically disarmed. The defence budget in fiscal 1947-8 touched a post-war low of $240 million; in mid-1948 all the armed services were below their authorized strength. Spending on defence had dropped to 12 per cent of the government's total budget, and although some increase was contemplated, it would not be swift in coming. There were other priorities for the moment: winding up reconstruction, expanding national services (the St Lawrence Seaway and the Trans-Canada Highway were in the offing), and, above all, re-establishing Canada's shaky foreign exchange balance. Social services, a gleam in the eye of the health and welfare minister, Paul Martin, were deferred, and defence would have to take its turn.

It was a safe projection, however, that defence spending would be in the offing. In October 1948, shortly before the change of government, external affairs minister Lester Pearson placed before his cabinet colleagues the recommendation that Canada join an Atlantic alliance. Such an alliance, Pearson stated, 'would provide the basis for the organization of an overwhelming preponderance of force – military, economic and moral – over the Soviet Union and a sufficient degree of unity to ensure that this preponderance of force may be so used as to guarantee that the free nations will not be defeated one by one.'[3] The security of Europe was vital to Canada's defence, in Pearson's view; and it was vital in other ways as well. A world without a democratic and friendly Europe would throw Canada into the arms of the United States. Reviewing Canada's established policy, Maurice Lamontagne wrote in 1948 that 'the only long-run solution compatible with our national independence'

3 Cited in James Eayrs, *In Defence of Canada*, IV, 97.

was to help Europe to reconstruct itself so that it might once more become a viable trading partner for Canada.[4] If a true Canadian national identity was ever to emerge, it had to balance itself on something other than a unilateral dependence on the friendly southern neighbour.

In negotiations in Washington late in 1948, Canadian negotiators tried to define what they meant by an Atlantic alliance. It would, in the first place, be restricted to the democracies of northwestern Europe: Britain, France, Benelux and Scandinavia. It would exclude dictatorships, and it would not extend to areas outside the North Atlantic sphere. And it should, if possible, be more than a military alliance.

Canada's strictures on membership did not survive intact. Portugal, a functioning dictatorship, was included because of its highly strategic location. Italy, a democracy far from the Atlantic, was included because its omission would have disheartened democratic forces in that country. The Algerian departments of France were included at French insistence. Ireland, a genuine North Atlantic democracy, had to be excluded because it insisted on an immediate settlement of the problem of Northern Ireland (and settlement, in Irish eyes, meant the inclusion of the North in the South, whether the majority of northerners wanted it or not).

The proposition that the Atlantic pact should be more than a military alliance was vigorously pursued. A North Atlantic treaty, the Canadians proposed, should include 'some general provision which would encourage economic and social collaboration between the members. ... The Treaty should be something more than a defence treaty or a defensive military alliance.' It could be an instrument for the pursuit of broad multilateral objectives: trade, economic development and investment, and cultural exchanges. Perhaps, ultimately, it could become the framework for a new trans-Atlantic superstate, in which the overwhelmingly dominant power, the Americans, would be more equal than they were at present. This conception, which later travelled under the name 'Atlanticism,' drew much of its strength from wartime idealism. Its proponents laboured under the strain of knowing that what might just be possible in critical times would be forgotten in more normal ones. The winter of 1948-9 was such a critical time.

Some Americans shared the vision, but many did not. Those who did not were more important. Their leadership was located in the American congress, fearful as always of turning over the keys of the American treasure chest to a horde of untrustworthy foreigners, themselves one short step removed from Communism. Congressional complaints perturbed officials in the executive branch, accustomed to the dangerous consequences of ignoring legislative whims. The Secretary of State, Dean Acheson, classified the Canadians' Atlantic dream as a time-wasting delusion. Even

---

4 M. Lamontagne, 'Some Political Aspects of Canada's Trade Problem,' in J.D. Gibson, ed., *Canada's Economy in a Changing World* (Toronto: Macmillan 1948), 37.

the Canadian ambassador in Washington, Hume Wrong, had his doubts. But under pressure from his own government Wrong persevered, and eventually Acheson gave in. The North Atlantic Treaty would have a Canadian clause, Article 2, which promised economic co-operation (and cultural too). It would come to nothing, Acheson predicted, and it did.

When the North Atlantic Treaty was signed, on April 4, 1949, by Canada, the United States, the United Kingdom, France, Italy, Portugal, Norway, Denmark, The Netherlands, Belgium, and Luxembourg, Canada committed itself to the defence of western Europe against Russian attack. The western Europeans, less plausibly, were pledged to come to the aid of Canada and the United States should those countries be attacked separately; in any case it was assumed that the defence of one would be the defence of all.

But how to organize the defence? That was the concern of the generals, and in particular the concern of the Chief of the General Staff, General Charles Foulkes. A competent officer and a canny negotiator, Foulkes had his plans ready before the ink on the treaty was dry. 'It is interesting to note,' he later wrote, 'that the organization of the military aspects of NATO suggested in our proposal of 7 March 1949, is very similar to the present organization.'[5] There would be a supreme military commander, an American, and a series of staff committees, some strategic, some regional in character. Eventually a Standing Group was decided upon, consisting of the principal military powers in the Alliance, the United States, Britain, and France. The other members, including Canada, had a right to be consulted before the Standing Group disposed of their forces or resources.

For the moment, Canadian forces were a notional concept. Canadian resources, however, were not. Article 3 of the treaty provided for mutual aid among the allies on Second World War lines – equipment for the allies to help them, as the treaty put it, to 'maintain and develop their individual and collective capacity to resist armed attack.' In Ottawa it was decided that Canada should contribute in kind, obsolescent British-type equipment now being discarded in favour of up-to-date American lines. In fiscal 1950-1 this Canadian mutual aid amounted to almost $200 million; as stocks were drawn down, and as Canada's balance-of-payments position eased, other types of aid would become possible.

The Americans and the Europeans were anxious for more. Canada, cautiously balancing its budgets, was reluctant to pledge more for the immediate future. Armament and rearmament proposals were calculated to furnish a rational and long-lived re-equipment of the armed forces; those forces would total less than 50,000. That calculation was thrown overboard in the wake of a most unexpected event in June 1950.

5 Quoted in Eayrs, *In Defence of Canada* IV, 133.

On June 25, the army of North Korea invaded South Korea. North Korea was a state on the Soviet model, complete with local dictator, an omnipotent Communist party organization, and an insatiable desire to fulfil its destiny by absorbing the southern half of the divided country. South Korea, established by the Americans under United Nations auspices, was an overpopulated and impoverished piece of rocky real estate ruled by a less efficient (and therefore more benign) autocrat named Syngman Rhee. In January 1950 the American government had indicated to those who wanted to hear that it considered that South Korea lay outside its strategic perimeter. It would not, presumably, be defended at all costs. It is at least possible that this news was taken very seriously in North Korea, and in Moscow, which was handling the equipment of the North's oversized army. Whether with Moscow's collusion or not – the absence of contemporary documentary research in the Soviet Union is an obstacle to those who wish to understand its policies with any certainty – the North Koreans decided that the time was opportune for an excursion.

Initially, their attack delivered all that could have been hoped. The South Korean army, poorly equipped and badly led, crumbled. American reaction was initially uncertain. Soon, however, that reaction took shape. President Truman and his advisers decided that North Korea's aggression was intolerable and must be stopped. To Truman, it was the 1930s all over again: then, dictators had been permitted to escape with their loot in order to avoid a wide and destructive war. That reasoning had proved fallacious, and it was high time that the proper deductions were drawn from the experience. North Korea had to be stopped; Truman appealed to the United Nations to stop it.

Because the Soviet Union was boycotting the Security Council in order to secure Nationalist China's replacement by Communist China in the international body, the Americans were able to get speedy agreement from the international organization. No other Communist state, besides the Soviet Union, had a veto over UN action; soon, North Korea was branded an aggressor and a United Nations force was being organized to put it in its place.

Most of the United Nations force was American. No other country had the army, air force, sea transport, or money that action in a far-off Asian country required. Other countries sending troops and equipment found their contributions integrated into a larger, American command. Although a coalition in form, the United Nations side in the Korean conflict inevitably leaned heavily in the direction of what the United States desired and expected.

The Canadian government, like the American, was taken by surprise at the outbreak of hostilities in Korea. Parliament was about to adjourn for the summer; the nation's attention was riveted on domestic matters. Even after the American response became clear, the Canadian government temporized; it would send some aid, but no ground forces. It would, naturally, support the United Nations in attempting to end aggression. For July, the principal deployment for Canadian troops was the state funeral of Mackenzie King, who was given a magnificent send-off that must have gratified his hovering spirit.

On the train back to Ottawa from King's burial in Toronto, the cabinet discussed the Korean situation. Newspapers were demanding that Canada contribute something more tangible than a few ships and transport planes, and public opinion was not opposed to firmer action. Action there would have to be, the cabinet decided: on August 7, Prime Minister St Laurent and the Minister of National Defence, Brooke Claxton, went on the radio to announce that Canada would raise a special army brigade to go to Korea, or anywhere else that necessity might dictate. For, as St Laurent warned his listeners, 'No one can guarantee that, through the action we are now taking, the free nations will succeed in preventing a general war.'

What perturbed the cabinet was the possibility that the conflict in Korea was the first stage in a general Communist assault on Western defences. Korea, after all, was at best of marginal importance to Western strength, but if crucial resources were diverted there and bottled up, it would be all the more difficult to respond to a real offensive by the Red Army in Europe. It was obvious that Canada would have to do more than send troops to Korea; through the winter of 1950-1 defence planners, economists, and politicians laboured to decide just how much more was required.

When the planners got through, Canada's armed forces had doubled in size, to 100,000, and the massive sum of $5 billion was earmarked for rearmament, over three years. As Claxton explained to the House of Commons, 'It is the view of this and the other allied governments that the vital centre of our global defence is in Western Europe.' Accordingly, Canada agreed to send a brigade group (some 6,670 strong) and an air division (eleven, later twelve, squadrons of fighter aircraft). A NATO command structure was established, with an American general on top. Canadian troops in Europe, however, would serve not with the Americans, but with the British, a sign of Canada's traditional associations, as well as of Claxton's mistrust of the US army.

As Canadian troops set sail for Europe, their colleagues in Korea were bogged down in a hopeless, seemingly endless war. There was no longer any possibility of a Communist victory: the North Koreans had been stopped and their army virtually destroyed in the autumn of 1950. The victorious United Nations troops, spurred on by the Americans, unwisely pressed their advantage too far, and were defeated in their turn by a Chinese offensive over the Manchurian border. The US government hesitated to take the war into China; the United Kingdom and Canada begged the American government not to use its nuclear weapons to rescue its hard-pressed ground forces. President Truman had had no serious intention of doing so and in any case a front was soon stabilized across the waist of the Korean peninsula. There it rested from late 1951 until mid-1953, when a ceasefire was finally declared. When the war ended, on July 27, 1953, 1,557 Canadians were casualties and of these 312 had died.

Much of the last stage of the war was taken up by diplomatic wrangling among the Western allies as to how best to make peace. Pearson, who was also president of the United Nations General Assembly in 1952-3, played a key role in the discussions. His object was to bring a quick end to the conflict, which he saw as an increasingly unnecessary diversion of attention and resources from the central, European front. He had his doubts on the wisdom of American policy, which he found too belligerent and unyielding. The Americans, in turn, were furious at the ingratitude and obstruction of an ally whose contribution to the Korean War was minuscule. Pearson's relations with some of his American diplomatic counterparts would never be the same again.

Relations with the British were more cordial. The British economy was staggering back to its feet after the catastrophes of the post-war period and soon it would be possible to contemplate normal relations with the mother country again. And, after the truncating of the British Empire in 1947 and 1948, when India, Pakistan, Ceylon, Burma, and Israel had become independent, the rest of the colonial empire seemed momentarily contented and healthy. In October 1951, St Laurent and the cabinet were the proud hosts to Princess Elizabeth, the heiress to the throne, and her consort, Prince Philip. Canada wallowed in royalist ecstasy as the handsome young couple proceeded from coast to coast. Editors loosed their fashion writers, starving for prey, in the direction of the royal party; the Canadian Broadcasting Corporation, not to be outdone, tried to make up in purple prose and breathless enthusiasm for Canada's continuing lack of television.

Elizabeth and Philip were received, like previous visiting royalty, by a British aristocrat serving a term as Canadian Governor General. But a change was in the offing. The next Governor General would not be British at all, St Laurent decided. Canada's next head of state would be a Canadian. The Prime Minister toyed with the idea of making C.D. Howe Governor General, a selection which would surely have provoked howls of Conservative outrage from Halifax, Westmount, Toronto, and Victoria – and some points in between. Circumstances came to St Laurent's rescue. Howe was unavailable; he liked politics, and power, too much. The next Governor General, therefore, would be Vincent Massey, Canada's long-serving High Commissioner in London, a man who, in habits and attitudes, was more British than the British themselves. Massey succeeded to his new dignity in February 1952.

Massey's appointment was overshadowed by yet another royal event. George VI died that month and his daughter succeeded him as Elizabeth II. Her coronation was scheduled for June 1953. That year, the Canadian Parliament was wound up early and a general election postponed so that platoons of politicians and other dignitaries could sail to London – few people, even then, preferred to fly – for the social event of the decade. Among their numbers were a select few who had been allowed to purchase their admission through generous donations to one or another of Canada's impoverished universities – the useful inspiration of a former university lecturer, now the secretary to the cabinet, J.W. Pickersgill.

The festivities surrounding Elizabeth II's coronation reflected more than a simple loyalty to the Crown, although there was plenty of that. They represented a hope, almost a faith, on the part of millions of Canadians that Britain had recovered from the war and was now back near the top of the international heap. The Commonwealth Conference that coincided with the coronation showed that Canada was still an important member of a functioning international organization, the most important after Britain itself. The Commonwealth, representing Britain and the 'old dominions,' Canada, Australia, New Zealand, and South Africa, as well as the new members, India, Pakistan, and Ceylon, held out the promise that it would be a genuine bridge between the underdeveloped world and the Western powers.

Canadians prided themselves on the fact that the Commonwealth had successfully made the transition from a colonial body to a post-colonial association, from centralized control to decentralized co-operation. But that change implied another: old Commonwealth institutions lost their significance. Defence co-operation, for example, gradually unravelled. It was generally admitted that the Commonwealth would never fight again as a single body, because its members could hardly be expected to agree on what would be important enough to fight about; as it later developed, several members of the Commonwealth would war against each other. It could no longer be pretended that external policies were co-ordinated, although that realization was slower in coming. During the Korean War India's foreign policy differed markedly from that of the older Commonwealth states, and as the fifties wore on the difference widened.

The Commonwealth's internal contradictions remained on a family basis in the mid-fifties. It was possible to dream that Canada and India had formed a Commonwealth axis; in support of that dream, and in recognition of India's unceasing preaching of peace, Canada furnished the Indians with a nuclear reactor. It was simultaneously a celebration of Canadian technology, Canadian good intentions, and Canadian faith in the permanence of India's pacific internationalism.

Some of Canada's good intentions were discharged on the Americans. American politics in the early fifties were a discouraging sight. Prominent politicians fought Communism and won popularity with the weapons of bombast and defamation. The Democrats lost the presidency and control of Congress in the 1952 elections. The new American president, Dwight D. Eisenhower, was a certified war hero, uncertain of his directions in domestic politics. The politicians in his Republican party including his Secretary of State, John Foster Dulles, were only too willing to guide his steps. Dulles, who came from northern New York state, even knew where Canada was, and where it should be. Treating a congressional committee to a *tour d'horizon* of American foreign policy, Dulles started with Canada. 'He takes a few slams at Canada,' one State Department official remembered, '– their inferiority complex, their ambivalent attitude to the U.S. – but points out that it's a very important piece of real estate that should be humored along.'[6] Dulles's testimony had to be sanitized by his horrified aides before it could be released to an unsuspecting public.

Sure of itself and conscious of its rectitude, the Eisenhower administration treated Canada with friendly unconcern. Sometimes the unconcern turned into uncomprehending annoyance, as in disputes over membership in the United Nations or discussions of the West's obligations to Nationalist China's refugee regime on Taiwan. On economic matters Eisenhower did not bring back old-fashioned high-tariff Republicanism, but he did enforce a blind devotion to domestic economic interests to the exclusion of those of America's allies. Giveaways of American surplus wheat gratified American farmers, disrupted world wheat markets, and brought pain to the heart of C.D. Howe, who as minister responsible for selling Canadian wheat abroad now faced horrendous political problems at home.

Surface tranquility was preserved, however. It was with the British rather than the Americans that obvious trouble first surfaced. The likelihood of a serious difference increased after the replacement of the Labour party by the Conservatives in the 1951 British general election. The returning Conservatives, under the wartime hero Winston Churchill, still tended to believe in the great power status of Great Britain. Churchill's successor, Anthony Eden (who became Prime Minister in 1955), was more conscious than his elder colleague of Britain's precarious economic position and its weakened defence forces, but he hoped through skilful negotiation to make the illusion of power last a little longer. And for a while he did. The most painful pressure on Britain's strained resources was at the Suez Canal in Egypt, where 70,000 British troops were tied down defending a line of navigable water and its connecting ports and water supplies. It was a terrible drain on the British army, which had problems elsewhere, and on the British Treasury. It seemed sensible to seek a negotiated solution with Egypt, which wanted the canal, and was encouraging terrorist attacks to make trouble for the British.

In 1954, while serving as British Foreign Secretary, Eden found what he was looking for – an agreement with the Egyptian leader, Gamal Abd-al Nasser, providing for the withdrawal of British troops but the preservation of the Suez Canal as the property of a private foreign company. In case of war, Nasser promised to let British troops back in to protect the canal. The last of the British garrison left Egypt in June 1956.

6 Quoted in Leonard Mosley, *Dulles* (New York: Dell 1979), 358.

Barely a month later Anglo-Egyptian relations were inflamed anew when the British and American governments announced that they could not agree to furnish Egypt with a loan to build a new dam across the Nile at Aswan. In response, Nasser nationalized the Suez Canal. Eden, now British prime minister, decided that Nasser had been allowed to go too far. If the Egyptian dictator could not be persuaded to disgorge the canal, he would have to be compelled to do so. The effort of returning to Egypt so soon after leaving it was almost beyond Britain's resources, but the French were happy to help, and so were the Israelis. Gradually an allied plan of attack was worked out, and combined forces moved into position.

Canada had no direct role in these events. The Commonwealth prime ministers met in London at the end of June 1956, too early to have anything to say about Egypt or the Suez Canal. When the crisis emerged later in the summer, it was obvious that the Commonwealth could not hope to meet it as a united body. India, bastion of ostentatious neutrality, was consolidating its position as the leader of a third force in world politics, the 'non-aligned nations.' Its partner in this enterprise was none other than Gamal Abd-al Nasser. Clearly India would oppose any move that could result in the humiliation or deposition of its Egyptian ally. The Canadian government required no great perspicacity to see that the future of the Commonwealth was at risk. British intervention in Egypt, Pearson wrote to Norman Robertson, would 'split the Commonwealth.' Worse still, it might fracture Britain's alliance with the United States, which had absolutely no intention of going along with Eden's scheme. It seemed impossible that Eden did not realize what he had to lose, in comparison with the doubtful and expensive gains his troops could secure; nevertheless, he persisted.

Eden's irresponsibility became even more galling when, in October 1956, serious rifts appeared in Russia's eastern European sphere of influence. In Poland, the government was toppled, to be replaced by a more secure (but ostensibly more liberal) nationalist Communist regime. In Hungary, a similar process began, and then began to go farther than the Soviets could imagine. Hungary actually wanted to throw off Russian control and assert its national independence. Western correspondents, including a CBC team, scented a story and rushed to Budapest. They sent back dramatic reports of the mass rejection of ten years of Communist indoctrination, best symbolized by the free-standing bronze legs which had recently supported a statue of Stalin. ('He stooped to pick up a stolen wristwatch,' the Hungarians helpfully explained.)

It was infuriating that just as the Soviet Union faced international embarrassment and imperial disruption, the British were fumbling back into their discarded colonial costumes, picking up the imperial elephant gun, and going hunting for an 'emerging nation.' Third World countries were not impressed. Egypt was much closer to them in fact and spirit than Hungary, and it was about Egypt that they proposed to excite themselves. As the British and French landed in Egypt, at the beginning of November, international attention swung away from Hungary – just as the Russians completed their preparations to reinvade their erstwhile satellite. The United Nations demanded immediate action in Egypt to throw the imperialists out. The Americans ostentatiously stood aside. In Ottawa there was consternation and incredulity.

Commonwealth consultation, such as it was, had completely broken down. The British hoped that the Canadians would endorse their action but, fearing that they would not, had not bothered to inform them of its details. Despite this lack of consultation, the Commonwealth connection was still strong at the level of public opinion, where old memories and older sentiments compensated for the lack of substantial common interest. A Gallup Poll showed that 43 per cent of Canadians thought that the Anglo-French invasion was a good idea, while only 40 per cent opposed it. St Laurent and Pearson would not be able to count on the support of a united public opinion if they publicly differed with the British.

Pearson knew that Canada's international standing would suffer if his country associated itself with the British action. He knew, too, that the Anglo-French invasion had little chance of long-term success, regardless of what might be achieved in the short run. Worst of all, a permanent Western occupation of the Suez Canal zone could drive wavering non-aligned countries to conclude that the West, not the Soviet Union, threatened their essential interests. Pearson was not alone on the issue; many, even in Britain, agreed that there was no point in the British seizing something that events had shown they neither wanted nor controlled.

Fortunately Pearson had several assets (besides a clear understanding of the circumstances) at his disposal. His own standing was high, both at the United Nations and in Great Britain. So was Canada's, thanks largely to the superior diplomatic skills of Canadian representatives abroad. Pearson therefore put all his considerable negotiating skills to work in the cause of covering an Anglo-French withdrawal from Suez. There should be a United Nations force sent to Suez to keep the peace, and incidentally provide a face-saving cover for the withdrawal of British, French, and Israeli troops. After several tense days and sleepless nights, Pearson's emergency diplomacy paid off. The British and French invasion was floundering, economic pressure was mounting, and American displeasure was increasing. The Anglo-French invasion was halted. Shortly thereafter, a United Nations Emergency Force (UNEF) was organized and dispatched to Egypt. It later took up positions along the Egyptian-Israeli border, hoping to separate the two perennial combatants. Canadian troops participated; indeed, for the sake of the St Laurent government's internal prestige it was essential that they should.

Pearson later won the Nobel Prize for his efforts, but many at home failed to applaud his performance. Prime Minister St Laurent, who completely supported his external affairs minister throughout, made matters worse by letting slip a damaging phrase, 'the supermen of Europe,' to describe the British and French. Their day was over, St Laurent told the House of Commons, whether people recognized it or not. Many Canadians refused to. The Conservatives introduced a motion deploring the government's policy; although defeated by the Liberals with CCF support it evoked ancestral memories inside and outside of Parliament – some of them acutely dangerous to the government's political health.

The classic expression of English Canada's folk memories was given by Howard Green in a speech in the House of Commons. Canada, the Conservative MP for Vancouver–Quadra proclaimed, had turned its back on Great Britain and France. This was no surprise; in fact it was the logical conclusion of the whole external policy of the Liberals, from Mackenzie King forward. Now Canada was nothing more than 'a chore boy' for the United States. 'In the last ten years,' Green declaimed, 'this government has been currying favour with the United States. Ever since the Second World War, that has been the policy of the Canadian government.' Many Canadians agreed. The Americans were the wrong people to work with.

That feeling became well-nigh irresistible the next spring when the Canadian ambassador to Egypt, Herbert Norman, jumped to his death. Norman had been publicly accused, not for the first time, of Communist sympathies because of his membership in a Communist group before the Second World War. Investigated and cleared by Canadian security authorities, Norman was denounced by an American Senate committee. Pearson, who had also been denounced by American Communist-hunters, was appalled at the tragic waste of Norman's life. In a note to the American government he condemned the public smears on Norman's integrity as 'unfair and indeed intolerable.'

Pearson's statement signalled a twenty-year low in Canadian-American relations. Pearson's statement was far too moderate for many. Americans were everywhere, circling around the world, dominating NATO, humiliating Great Britain, affronting Canadian intellectuals with their loud Hawaiian shirts and breezy Bermuda shorts. As one Calgary matron exclaimed, there were now so many Americans in Alberta that 'I feel like staying away from the club; there are so many Americans here. ... *They're forever trying to make me feel at home in my own club!*'[7] Once an American, always an American, a Conservative MP reminded the House of Commons in the summer of 1956. He was referring to the Minister of Trade and Commerce, C.D. Howe, an American by birth. The listener was left to infer that Howe's American origins had determined his choice of an American-financed consortium to build the new Trans-Canada Pipeline. The fact that the Pipeline would run entirely in Canada

7 Quoted in Joseph Barber, *Good Fences Make Good Neighbors* (Toronto: McClelland & Stewart 1958), 67.

and help make Canada less dependent on American gas supply was not stressed. The Americans were everywhere!

And if the Americans were not, their dupes were. When Pearson spoke in Florida, the Conservative Toronto *Telegram* interpreted his words for its readers. Pearson's speech was 'a public renunciation of Canadian sovereignty' that ranged Canada 'among the banana republics, a satellite state proclaimed by Pearson.'[8]

But while the Canadian élite knew what it didn't like, it could hardly agree on what it wanted. American investment, American culture, and American alliances were condemned by some intellectuals, and even a few politicians. Yet the alternatives were most unclear: the fuzzy Commonwealth, even less significant or united since the Suez fiasco, the forlorn hope of a closer relationship with Europe, perhaps a retreat into a monarchist bastion in the northern half of North America. *Freedom Wears a Crown* was the title of a book widely read and discussed in Conservative and intellectual circles in the fifties. But while freedom and royalty were hob-nobbing in the common rooms of Canadian universities, most Canadians were watching *I Love Lucy* from the United States. Would freedom survive the removal of the United States' protecting armed umbrella? Most Canadians thought not.

A later commentator observed that Canada's foreign and defence policies enjoyed unusual support – 'consensus' – in the decade from 1948 to 1957. That support was remarkably uniform geographically and racially, both coast to coast and among French and English. From the CCF on the left to the Social Credit on the right, the political parties agreed that NATO was a good thing, and Communism a bad thing, that a close association with Europe was desirable, and that the Commonwealth embodied a glorious past. It could not be denied that Canada's international standing was high, and would remain high until war-devastated Europe recovered completely. There were differences over techniques, but none over objectives. It was not until 1956, when the controversy about American leadership and American investment merged into the pipeline debate and then into recriminations over Suez, that public support for Canada's foreign policy came unstuck. Foreign policy, from being a winning issue for the Liberals, was fast becoming a losing one.

8 Judith Robinson, *This is on the House* (Toronto: McClelland & Stewart 1957), 59-61.

15

Liberal Centralization

External relations are only a part of the diplomatic life of a Canadian government. Canada, as a country, is fully equipped with a collection of jealous local sovereignties: four in 1867, nine in 1945, and ten in 1949.

The tenth was the island of Newfoundland, Britain's oldest colony, which had stood out against the Confederation tide in 1867 and which ever since had viewed the possibility of union with Canada with the deepest suspicion. Newfoundland's fish- and forest-based economy had collapsed completely during the depression of the 1930s, so completely that its government had to be bailed out by the British, who underwrote most of the colony's budget in return for a suspension of the island's constitution. The truce on political activity lasted through the Second World War, as Newfoundland's economy gradually righted itself under the stimulus of high prices and demand. Newfoundland was the gateway to North America, and a strategic link on the air and sea routes connecting Canada and the United States to Great Britain; to defend the island, the Canadian and American governments poured in thousands of troops whose spending power also helped to restore the local economy. The Canadian government made sure that a Canadian officer was the senior commander on Newfoundland.

Canada's plans for Newfoundland were indefinite. Clearly the dominion did not want to see its large eastern neighbour pass under the control of the United States. But it was not sure that it wanted Newfoundland to become part of Canada either. That had been tried three times before, in the 1860s, in the 1890s, and in the 1910s, and each time the proposition was wrecked on the shoals of Newfoundland particularism and demands for money, which provoked a reciprocal Canadian meanness. It could happen again. Generations of Newfoundlanders had proudly sung, 'Draw near at your peril, Canadian wolf.' Some Canadians did not see things quite that way; Canada was in their eyes a sheep in wolf's clothing; union would entail shearing the sheep.

The initiative for union did not come from Canada, but from Newfoundland. It came from one man, Joseph R. ('Joey') Smallwood, a frustrated ex-politician and failed pig farmer who had honed his remarkable oratorical talents as a radio announcer during the war. Smallwood was a born orator, a master of vivid, earthy imagery, and he proved to be no mean political strategist. When a convention was convened in St John's to consider the colony's future government, Smallwood became a delegate. The convention's proceedings were broadcast and Smallwood took advantage of his familiarity with the medium to drum into his listeners' ears his own preferred solution: confederation with Canada. Most of the convention was hostile to the idea, but Smallwood knew that they were not his real audience. That audience was sitting every night in the parlours and kitchens of Newfoundland waiting for the latest news from St John's.

Smallwood contrived to have a delegation sent to Ottawa to explore terms of union with the Canadian government. With the help of Mackenzie King's secretary, J.W. Pickersgill, a cabinet committee drafted proposals. These were a combination of Canadian social security and special financial compensation for the loss of Newfoundland's existing revenues. In addition, Canada would pick up most of Newfoundland's debt, and Labrador, the subject of covetous glances from Quebec, would remain an indisputable part of the new province.

Initially, these proposals were badly received in Newfoundland. Two plebiscites were held to test public opinion. In the first, confederation with Canada ran second (41.13 per cent) among three possible options. Because there was no clear majority, a run-off was held, and on July 22, 1948, the cause of confederation prevailed, 78,323 to 71,334. Starting virtually from nothing, Smallwood had created a winning coalition which had reversed Newfoundland's history, overturned its traditional political leadership, and reoriented the province's economy to the west and away from the Atlantic.

At the time it seemed that Newfoundland had hardly any choice. The province's historic export industries – fish, timber, pulp and paper, and iron ore – were often precarious. It was the decline in world market prices for fish and forest products that had undermined Newfoundland's autonomy in the 1930s. Even with the return of prosperity Newfoundland could not afford a Canadian level of government expenditures, and the British, beset with their own economic troubles, were unwilling to foot the bills of a distant, dollar-consuming economy. Confederation indeed performed what it promised: there were family allowance cheques, a system of unemployment insurance, and federal grants-in-aid for various provincial projects, including the province's famous, rickety, narrow-gauge railway. With the help of federal subsidies, Smallwood dragged the province out of the isolation of centuries. It became a commonplace, in the 1950s and 1960s, as Smallwood's roads reached previously roadless fishing villages, for the inhabitants to take to those same roads, heading for St John's or points west, away from the way of life of their ancestors.

Everyone was affected. Some of the province's traditional élite, beaten at their own game of politics, adapted to the times. One of the leaders of the anti-confederation movement was pensioned off with the federal position of director of civil defence for Newfoundland; another, Don Jamieson, joined the national Liberal party and eventually became Canada's Minister of External Affairs. Not everything worked well, however. Ottawa's fisheries' policy was unsatisfactory: help for the fishing industry came too late to help it modernize or to preserve its fishing grounds and markets abroad. The latter was a problem shared by other Canadian export industries; but, short of detaching parts of the country and towing them next to Ireland, it was difficult to see what fundamental changes in Canadian policy would have kept Newfoundland's economy in its traditional orbit. In any case, it was not enough to sustain all the Newfoundlanders that a high birth rate (consistently the highest in the country) turned out. In 1971, out of 594,000 persons born in Newfoundland and still residing in Canada, no less than 98,000 had moved outside the province.[1]

Newfoundland's entry into Canada on March 31, 1949, was generally welcomed. The St Laurent government easily secured approval from Parliament for the financial terms, and brushed aside protests from the provincially-minded Conservatives (their leader was, after all, a very recent provincial premier) that the other provinces should be consulted and allowed to give their consent. The same point was repeated, more strongly, by Quebec's Premier Maurice Duplessis, who had claims of his own – the ownership of most of Labrador – to enter against the new province. But St Laurent refuted their arguments. The Ottawa government represented all of Canada, and it had no reason to go running to the provinces for ratification of a national act. It was in the national interest that Newfoundland be admitted to Canada, and the national government would not shirk its responsibilities.

St Laurent's government was among the most nationally minded that Canada had ever seen. Its national direction reflected Ottawa's strong position *vis-à-vis* the provinces. In 1948, Ottawa spent $1.767 billion compared with the $810 million spent by all the provinces taken together, and the $715 million spent by Canada's municipalities – over 50 per cent of all government expenditures in Canada. By 1952, with the Korean War and rearmament in full swing, the imbalance was even greater: $4 billion as against a combined provincial and municipal total of $2.3 billion. Of the federal total, defence and mutual aid accounted for $1.9 billion – almost half.

Few questioned the necessity of heavy defence spending in the face of a powerful Red Army in Europe and war in Asia. Such heavy national spending seemed like the natural order of things, although as recently as 1939 spending by the provinces

---

1 It should be pointed out, in fairness, that Saskatchewan had the largest out-migration: in 1971 some 371,000 Saskatchewanians lived outside their native province, inside Canada.

alone had far surpassed that of the central government. That, perhaps, was a better definition of normality.

St Laurent, with his confident belief in Ottawa's ability to act, and in its right to act, was hardly the man to dismantle the national government's administrative apparatus. As far as he could, he strengthened it. In 1949-50 he turned his attention to the question of the Canadian constitution. The British North America (BNA) Act, Canada's fundamental constitutional document, still required amendment in Britain. True, the British freely amended the act on request, but it was embarrassing and inconsistent with Canada's national stature to have to beg favours from another country, however friendly and closely related, in order to have the country's internal affairs set to rights. St Laurent's solution was simple. For matters that lay inside the national sphere, as defined by the BNA Act, the federal government would act alone: Canada's Parliament would in future handle its own amendments. Where it was a question of provincial jurisdiction, the additional consent of all the provinces would be required. At the last moment, however, St Laurent drew back. On the advice of J.W. Pickersgill, who had been passed on by King to his successor, he decided to let sleeping dogs lie; only the federal government's power to amend its part of the constitution was enacted. It was a missed opportunity. St Laurent had the power and the prestige to override opposition both in Ottawa and in the provinces. Most Canadians were probably in favour, even though they might not have assigned constitutional amendment a very high place on their list of governmental priorities. But once abandoned, the idea of repatriating Canada's constitution was dormant for a decade. When it was revived, ten years later, it was under very different circumstances.

Canada's bifurcated constitution was still a manageable and generally comfortable framework for government. Duplessis periodically ranted about the waste of Quebec dollars on aid to unbelievers and Communists abroad ('Duplessis donne à sa province, St-Laurent donne aux autres,' read one slogan) but for the moment he undertook no serious moves to challenge the federal dominance. Between St Laurent and Leslie Frost, George Drew's successor as premier of Ontario, there was positive warmth. Frost did not care much for Drew, his methods, or his policies. A warm, practical, and friendly man, Frost had no ambition to promote Ontario's local concerns into full-dress constitutional battles. Instead, Frost let the federal Liberals know that he, for one, was willing to live and let live politically. If that meant abandoning George Drew and his federal party, Frost could live with that. Frost kept Ontario's taxes down and its expenditures low, and he ended the tax feud with Ottawa. In 1952 Ontario officially entered Ottawa's tax rental scheme. Henceforth only Quebec remained outside the single, national, income tax system.

Quebec levied no income tax, so that Quebec taxpayers were not penalized for remaining outside the tax rental system. Duplessis made it clear that this was a matter of convenience, not of principle. In his reading of the constitution, the provinces had priority in direct taxation, including income tax, and by occupying the field the federal government was usurping provincial prerogatives. When, in 1954, Duplessis did impose a Quebec income tax, to be collected separately by the provincial government, he embodied his constitutional argument in the preamble to the legislation.

Although St Laurent remained a strong Canadian nationalist, he was no longer sure that the voters of Quebec would share his view that all provinces should enter Ottawa's existing tax rental agreement, or, as he put it, that 'Quebec can be a province like any other.' He preferred to manoeuvre to avoid a head-on collision over taxation. Duplessis remained obdurate, refusing to grasp any of the olive branches tendered by Ottawa in the spring and summer of 1954. Annoyed, St Laurent put aside his misgivings and took his case directly to the Quebec people. In a speech in September 1954, he told his audience: 'in certain parts of the province of Quebec, the idea that there should be a Canadian nation, united and strong, holding an important place in the family of nations, does not please everybody.' St Laurent repeated his assertion in an even stronger speech before the Reform Club in Quebec City on September 18. He stressed his belief that Ottawa's policies did not constitute centralization, as his opponent claimed, but added that his government also believed that the provinces were not more important, singly or collectively, than the whole country. St Laurent again offered a compromise, if Duplessis would take it.

Duplessis, sensing that he now had a lively and possibly advantageous political issue, sent off a counter-blast instead. At the same time, he asked St Laurent for a personal meeting, which took place in Montreal's elegant Windsor Hotel early in October. At the meeting, Duplessis made some concessions. His provincial income tax act would be amended to remove his claim to provincial priority in direct taxation. He assured St Laurent that Quebec's income tax would not amount to more than 10 per cent of its federal counterpart. In return, once Duplessis' figures were in, St Laurent agreed to amend the federal income tax act to allow inhabitants of a province outside the tax rental system (ie, Quebec) to reduce their federal tax by 10 per cent.

This defused the confrontation. The two contending governments had chosen the path of co-operation, and had found a workable solution. But there were some disquieting elements, nevertheless, in St Laurent's ready agreement with Duplessis. There was no disguising the fact that Duplessis had secured terms which made Quebec, in fact if not in law, a province different from the others. He claimed that this was because of Quebec's special need to safeguard its language and particular institutions. St Laurent, of course, admitted no such thing, but his dry defence of equity and reasonableness had less impact than Duplessis' intonations on the theme of provincial sovereignty and Quebec's special situation. Some of St Laurent's followers in Quebec believed that he should have pursued his fight with Duplessis to the end. By pitting his own considerable prestige against that of the Quebec premier, the federal champion must prevail. By pandering to Duplessis, St Laurent was bowing before precisely those nationalist elements he had so caustically denounced in September. In a serious political confrontation, Ottawa had shied away from defending its predominance as the national government over the demands and interests of a provincial government. It did not augur particularly happily.

The breach in the tax rental agreements opened by Quebec's decision to impose its own income tax system raised the possibility that other provinces, for their own reasons, would do the same. If that happened, the federal grants to the poorer provinces under the tax rental system would be jeopardized. In any case, some of the provinces were complaining that their burdens were growing and that the tax rental payments designed to meet their needs were simply inadequate. The national government had already promised to help with provincial unemployment assistance; now it was forced to contemplate further measures to supplement and stabilize the revenues of the 'have-not' provinces. The brainchild of John Deutsch, a lively and imaginative economist serving in the finance department, the new financial proposals were summed up under the title, 'equalization.' What equalization meant was comparatively simple. In the first place, the old tax rental system would be abandoned. In its place there would be a system of tax points, equivalent to a percentage system. A province would be allowed to collect 10 per cent of the federal personal income tax, 10 per cent of the taxable income of corporations, and 50 per cent of federal succession duties. Then an average would be taken of the amounts which could be collected by the two wealthiest provinces, Ontario and British Columbia, and grants to the remaining provinces would be 'equalized' or brought up to that standard.

With the substantial advantages promised by the equalization grants, it was unlikely that the 'have-not' provinces, even Quebec, would stand out against them; and they did not. When the last tax rental agreement expired, on March 31, 1957, the new arrangement came into effect. It was not, it is true, without its detractors, principally Premier Frost of Ontario, who wanted the federal government to raise its basic tax rate so that Ontario could garner more from its 10 per cent of federal corporate and personal income taxes. St Laurent, facing a federal election within the year and mindful of larger fiscal considerations, refused, arguing that the tax level was already high enough. Frost would have to seek his extra revenue elsewhere – if not from his taxpayers, then from his political friends in Ottawa, the Conservatives.

The end of tax rental has been severely criticized as a sell-out of federal power and the beginning of an auction of federal tax points for momentary political advantage to the government of the day. Worse, it has been portrayed as a political ransom to buy off the insatiable provinces for a year or two at a time. But in context equalization looks very different. Its proponents arguably took a more realistic view of taxation and expenditures than did their opponents. The absolute federal dominance of Canada's finances that characterized the post-war period was an exceptional phenomenon. It existed because of a war emergency which began almost twenty years before. It was sustained because of the critical problems – economic, military, and political – that Canada faced in its dealings with the outside world. Under these circumstances, it would have been difficult for any province to decry the federal government's large budgets and its strategy of economic management. But, as the years passed, it was becoming easier to discover provincial priorities which were either distorted or suppressed by the dominant position of Ottawa in the country's tax fields. The provinces saw the lush green grass of revenue and yearned to graze in the federal field; like any good political husbandman St Laurent opened the gate before the beasts kicked down the fence.

16

Roads and Resources

The St Laurent years were a time of high employment, a high birth rate, and high immigration. From an estimated 12,823,000 in 1948, the population grew to an estimated 16,610,000 in 1957. Some of the increase derived from more than 1.5 million immigrants; the rest from more than 4.1 million births. Few Canadians left; of those who did, most went toward the United States. These tended to come from the better-educated technical and professional classes. There were 46,000 emigrants from Canada to the United States in 1957; of these, some 32,000 were Canadian-born.

But there were plenty of Canadians to go around. The birth rate soared, hovering above twenty-seven per thousand for the whole nine-year period. Within Canada, the largest number of births was in the province of Quebec, some of whose publicists hoped by this means to overcome English Canada's numerical advantage, founded as it was merely on immigration and a lower (though not much lower) birth rate. The census of 1941, taken after a decade of minimal immigration, had pointed in the right direction, but the hopes aroused were doomed to disappointment in the 1951 census. The flow of immigration after the Second World War landed hundreds of thousands whose sole desire was to adapt as quickly as possible to English-speaking society, whether by residence in an English-speaking province or within the English minority inside Quebec. The census of 1951 also disclosed another trend: Canadians migrating within Canada were congregating in just two provinces, Ontario and British Columbia. Every other province lost population, from the 150,000 leaving Saskatchewan between 1941 and 1951 to the trickle of 5,000 departing from Prince Edward Island.

Leaving Saskatchewan meant, in most cases, leaving the farm. Canada's rural blood was perceptibly thinning, in proportionate if not absolute terms. While, in 1941, 4.9 million Canadians lived in rural areas and 6.5 million in urban centres, by 1956 urban dwellers totalled 10.7 million, and rural inhabitants 5.3 million (of

Bell, 1948

Sask. Leader Post

'Doesn't seem to scare them any more ...'
Premier T.C. Douglas of Saskatchewan discussing his campaign strategy (Bell, 1948).
Reproduced with the permission of Charles E. Bell

whom only 2.6 million actually lived on farms). The cities offered manifold advantages. To begin with, there were modern conveniences such as electricity, no small matter as late as 1951 when 44 per cent of all homes in Saskatchewan were heated by gas or kerosene. Even where electricity lines reached, it is difficult to know what appliances existed. In 1951, of 3,409,295 Canadian homes (or 'dwelling units' as the census put it: a dwelling unit, to adapt a phrase of the time, need not be a home), 1,485,055 relied on wood stoves for cooking, and 1,136,585 had no refrigerators whatsoever, not even the time-honoured ice box still employed in over 621,000 others.

The absence of modern appliances was not an exclusively rural or farm phenomenon, but it was nevertheless true that the quality of rural life as a whole suffered by comparison with its urban cousin. To take another revealing statistic, in 1951 some 885,690 'occupied dwellings' in Canada had neither hot nor cold running water (583,835 had only cold): of these, 758,950 were rural. Similarly, 998,660 dwellings had 'other' than a flush or chemical toilet, and of these 845,810 were in rural areas. There was, it was true, much evidence of progress, as the statisticians pointed out. In 1941 only 61 per cent of Canadian homes had running water; in 1951, 75 per cent; and by 1961, 89 per cent. It was hard not to see 'Canada's century' – the boom of the industrial age and the improvements in life style that it brought in its train – as an urban phenomenon. In the 1950s many thousands, indeed several millions, of Canadians still lived in many respects as their ancestors had: not surprisingly they did not want to live that way any more.

The number of Canadian farms steadily declined during this period. Between 1951 and 1961 the number of farms sank from 623,000 to 570,000. Perhaps as a consequence, the normal trend to home ownership among Canadians in general was not as pronounced between 1951 and 1961 as it had been between 1941 and 1951. Yet in all provinces except Quebec the majority of homes were owner-occupied. Many were brand-new: almost a million new dwellings were constructed between 1948 and 1957. Most were single-family dwellings: Canadians liked the feeling of space and independence that owning their houses gave them.

As a result, Canadian cities sprawled, overflowing their pre-Second World War municipal boundaries and invading the surrounding rural townships. The townships were hard-put to keep abreast of the invasion, even where their own hunger for revenue had encouraged it. One early consequence was the development of metropolitan government. In the case of Toronto, the city's population grew from 667,500 to a scant 675,800 in 1951, while its suburban satellites positively blossomed in the same period from 242,500 to 441,700. By 1961 they would grow further, to 946,000, and thereby outnumber the city itself. The suburban municipalities proved unable to handle the strain separately. Chaos in sewage facilities, road building and maintenance, and water supply finally forced the province to intervene. As a result, in

1953, Metropolitan Toronto was established, a federation of the city and twelve suburbs (later reduced to the city and five boroughs), enjoying centralized services for important regional matters (such as the water supply) while preserving local autonomy on other matters.

The drift to the suburbs helped to accentuate another development: the growing use of the automobile. Between 1941 and 1951 automobile ownership increased only marginally: 36.7 per cent of Canadian households reported owning one in 1941 as compared to 43 per cent in 1951. But by 1961 the automobile boom was on in earnest: 68.4 per cent of Canadian homes boasted at least one car, although ownership varied from a low of 37.8 per cent in Newfoundland to a high of 76 per cent in Ontario. Cars soon came to occupy a central place in the Canadian life style: the convenience absolutely essential to recreation, travel – and commuting. So central, so obvious, had automobile traffic become that when a social historian analysed recent trends in Canadian life in the late 1950s he could find none so representative as 'the god CAR.' CARS, according to A.R.M. Lower, 'invaded every urban open space and threatened to destroy every blade of urban grass. They knocked down houses. They called imperiously for straight, wide roads to be carved out of our diminishing fertile fields.' They were also, as Lower could not fail to note, ostentatious and vulgar to a degree.[1]

But they were inescapably, ineluctably popular, as more and more Canadians took up the challenge to 'tour the broad highway in a Chev-ro-let,' or selected the Chrysler Corporation's hideous fin-tailed 'forward look'; vast chrome-encrusted vehicles belched their way over the landscape, or more often than not treated their owners to traffic jams on overcrowded highways and arterial roads. And so the several provincial governments girded themselves for a renewed highway-building program. They had a long way to go. In 1949, Canada boasted some 10,000 miles of paved roads and 540,000 miles of unpaved roads (improved or unimproved). The total cost of building and maintaining such a highway system was vast, and it fell almost entirely on the budgets of the provinces (and, to a much lesser extent, on those of their subordinate municipalities). It was, therefore, something of a godsend when, in 1948, the central government decided to contribute some $150 million to the construction of the Trans-Canada Highway according to an agreed national standard. If the provinces agreed to co-operate in such a project, the federal government would meet 50 per cent of the construction costs, and indeed 50 per cent of the cost since 1928 of any existing part of the route that the provinces chose to donate. The St Laurent government optimistically set the date for completion as 1956. It took nine years longer. When the final segment of the Trans-Canada Highway was officially opened in November 1965, it had cost $924 million, of which the federal

---

1 A.R.M. Lower, *Canadians in the Making* (Toronto: Longmans 1958), 424.

government had contributed $587 million. All the provinces eventually joined in the program, even Quebec, which held out until the early 1960s and joined in only when it discovered that the fiscal lures were great enough to overcome the most rigid constitutional scruples.

A joint project of a different kind was the St Lawrence Seaway, a deep-water system to link the Great Lakes with tidewater. Long the subject of negotiations between Canada and the United States, the Seaway was finally given top priority by the St Laurent government in 1951. Unless the United States stopped dragging its feet in this matter, the government announced, Canada would proceed by itself in digging the deep-water ditch; ancillary power benefits would be shared by Ontario and New York State, which was only too happy to co-operate. Even the province of Quebec, loud and fierce in its opposition in the 1930s, agreed to stay mum. Canada's case was reinforced from the American side by the report of a presidential commission on raw materials, which urged that it was in the American national interest to proceed as soon as possible to bring Labrador iron ore to the steel furnaces of the Middle West. With the lukewarm support of American President Eisenhower, the pro-Seaway forces finally prevailed in Congress, and a treaty was signed in 1954 providing for joint construction and ownership of the Seaway works.

This news was greeted with relief in Ottawa, where the Minister of Trade and Commerce, C.D. Howe, was looking about for a 'big project' to fuel the Canadian economy. As for the stricter meaning of fuel, the Seaway's hydro development would come in handy as well, because southern Canada, and especially Ontario, were running out of sites for hydro-electric plants. The St Lawrence would be the last; thereafter southern Ontario would have to rely on steam generators, burning coal or oil, for new electricity – or possibly using a newer energy source, uranium.

Canadian uranium development went back to the beginnings of the atomic age, to the development of the atomic bomb during the Second World War. At that time, Canada's allies, Britain and the United States, had approached Mackenzie King with two requests: first, that the Canadian government secure control of an obscure and inactive uranium and radium mine on the shores of Great Bear Lake in the Northwest Territories, and second, that the Canadian government welcome to its shores a British atomic research team. The mine was a relatively simple proposition. Eldorado Mining and Refining Limited became a Crown corporation, and eventually the exclusive agent for uranium sales within Canada, sending its product south to the American nuclear laboratories to be fashioned into atomic weaponry. Uranium sales began modestly, only $4,050,000 in 1948, but as American demand expanded the Canadian and American governments jointly raised the incentives they were prepared to offer for uranium development. A uranium boom followed, first in northern Saskatchewan and then in northern Ontario. At one time, uranium contracts with the United States totalled over $1.5 billion, and annual deliveries reached the very large sum of $331 million in 1959.

The other side of atomic development was equally intriguing, though less immediately profitable. During the war Canada had co-operated closely with British atomic scientists, thereby acquiring basic information and technology that made the dominion, in 1945, one of the three 'atomic powers.' Canadian atomic research was centred at a new laboratory and reactor complex up the Ottawa River at Chalk River, Ontario. The potential use of atomic energy for electrical generation had always been regarded as possible, but by the 1950s it was on the threshhold of economic feasibility. Putting together a consortium of Canadian utilities with his own Atomic Energy of Canada Limited, C.D. Howe instructed his officials to begin the active development of atomic power. By 1957, Atomic Energy of Canada Limited was ready to start work on a prototype commercial reactor, later known as the CANDU (Canadian Deuterium-Uranium).

Although the government now knew that atomic power was feasible, it was obvious that large-scale nuclear power plants were little more than a gleam in an engineer's eye. More fuel would be needed before atomic energy became widespread, and the most obvious was natural gas, found in large quantities in Alberta. It seemed to make sense to bring Alberta's gas straight to the major Canadian market – southern Ontario – and C.D. Howe began in the early 1950s to encourage gas promoters to think in terms of a trans-Canada pipeline, running exclusively in Canada. Rival groupings soon formed, some to compete for the pipeline on Howe's terms, others to argue that to be economically viable, such a pipeline would have to pass through the United States. Still others argued that it made more sense to pipe Alberta gas directly south and west, to the United States, and to supply Ontario with American gas from the south and southwest. Though Howe solved most of the organizational problems of the projected gas line by merging two rival groups (one of them American) into a single company, Trans-Canada Pipelines Limited, he was unable to solve its difficult financial problems. As a result the Liberal government confronted the thorny problem of furnishing the company with emergency financial aid to allow it to buy pipe and start construction. But only Parliament could provide the money.

What had seemed to Howe and his cabinet colleagues to be a straightforward economic proposition was for the opposition in Parliament the opportunity of a political lifetime. By filibustering the pipeline bill they would either force the powerful Liberals to back down and hand the pipeline over to a purely Canadian company (which for the CCF meant a national Crown corporation, or in the case of the Conservatives a private company with different principals), or force the government to push the bill through Parliament using closure, the parliamentary device which limits debate and forces a vote on issues before the House of Commons. As a royal commission later observed, the government had few alternatives. If Howe wanted the pipeline built he had to choose closure. The pipeline company needed its money in early June. By the time the government nerved itself to apply the device, in mid-May 1956, it had only sixteen days left for debate: ample time, under ordinary circumstances, for ventilating the most controversial legislation. But the legislation, as such, was hardly discussed. Instead the Commons chamber rang with points of order, accusations that the Liberals, slavishly pro-American as they were, were selling Canada out to a bunch of Texas oil buccaneers, and arguments that the whole thing could have been done differently, in some unexplained way. It was a pyrotechnic parliamentary circus for the opposition, whose sole object was to perform death-defying feats of oratory to talk out the government bill. The press was impressed, and when the Liberals brought in closure, the nation's newspapers reported that democracy was in danger at the hands of the Liberal majority in Parliament. Although Howe's pipeline bill finally passed, under closure, the debate proved a public relations disaster for the government.

Construction of the pipeline started immediately. Trans-Canada Pipelines surmounted its financial problems, and in February 1957 repaid the government its loan. Far from ending up as the fief of Texas oil buccaneers, Trans-Canada Pipelines became a majority Canadian-owned company. And in October 1958 natural gas reached Toronto and Montreal. That was cold comfort for the Liberals: by then they – and Howe – were out of office.

17

Building the Welfare State

While C.D. Howe was preoccupying himself with industrial stratagems, worrying over fuel supplies, and weighing the reports his economists gave him for signs of boom or bust, other Liberals worried about a very different problem.

Abandoned in the wreckage of the dominion-provincial disputation in 1946 were the government's plans for an expanded and comprehensive welfare system to ensure Canadians against want. As far as most members of the Liberal cabinet were concerned, those plans were now museum pieces, relics of bygone hopes which were now, because of the economic boom, fortunately outdated. But not everyone took that view. The flame of welfare burnt bright inside the Department of National Health and Welfare in Ottawa, in the hearts of its minister, Paul Martin, and its deputy minister, George Davidson, and in regional chapels on the Prairies and the west coast.

For while Ottawa paused, dallied, and then dozed, the first stages of health insurance went ahead in Saskatchewan and British Columbia. In Saskatchewan, the CCF government of T.C. Douglas determined that, despite the collapse of the federal proposals for a national scheme, Saskatchewan ought to enjoy hospital insurance as soon as possible, and at any rate before the next provincial election. Accordingly a Hospital Insurance Act was introduced and passed in the legislature in 1946, to take effect on January 1, 1947. On that day the first universal, compulsory system of medical insurance in Canada with a uniform rate of contribution began. It was not the last such program; indeed, it became the model. Saskatchewan's plan proved successful, though costly – far costlier than its proponents had imagined. In this too Saskatchewan set a precedent.

Barely a year after Saskatchewan, the coalition Liberal-Conservative government of British Columbia also took the plunge into hospital insurance. The BC plan proved to be an administrative nightmare: those who paid their insurance might nevertheless be left without coverage; those who did not pay might receive an entitlement card anyway. For delinquents, the government reserved powers to garnishee wages and prosecute offenders. None of these features was popular: they helped to bring about the resignation of the responsible minister, and then the chaos of the program as a whole served as a principal factor in the defeat of the coalition by the maverick Social Credit party in 1952.

Hospital insurance in BC survived the change of government. Understandably, the new Social Credit regime of W.A.C. Bennett became an enthusiastic supporter of a national program of hospital insurance, if only to relieve some of the political burden of the BC plan. But the Ottawa Liberals remained obdurate, taking refuge in the formula that they would, and could, only agree to a national plan when they had enough money and when a majority of the provinces agreed to join. That, they were confident, would never be.

The stronghold of conservatism in Canada was the 'blue' province of Ontario, governed for most of the time since 1905 by the Conservative party. Ontario had been in the forefront of the opposition to the federal proposals in 1945 under the leadership of its blustering premier, George Drew. But while the premier was thundering his anathemas at Liberal centralization, his provincial treasurer, Leslie Frost, was taking a longer and quieter look at the whole situation (one story even holds that Frost sought advice from the Liberal premier of Manitoba, Stuart Garson).

When Frost succeeded to the Ontario premiership in 1949, a new day dawned, politically and administratively, for Canada's largest province. Frost got on well with St Laurent, ideologically, politically, and personally. Tax rental held no terrors for 'old man Ontario,' and he negotiated reasonable terms for joining the national program in 1952. Projects like the Trans-Canada Pipeline likewise appealed to the Ontario premier: he and C.D. Howe saw eye to eye on that, although Frost's influence was not enough to prevent his Conservative brethren in Ottawa from running amok. He and St Laurent agreed about something else too. After a conversation with Frost in January 1956, St Laurent turned wonderingly to a companion and remarked: 'you know, Mr Frost doesn't like health insurance either.'

But it was Frost who made national hospital insurance in Canada politically inevitable. Although personally uninvolved in the health insurance advocates' enthusiasm, Frost seems to have perceived that hospital insurance, at least, was a sign of the times, an idea whose hour had very nearly struck. He had no particular commitment or attachment to the private insurance companies (on his sixtieth birthday, in September 1955, two of his personal health insurance policies were thoughtfully cancelled) and was unmoved by their claim that the government should confine itself to insuring the uninsurables, while the private companies skimmed off the cream of the crop.

Accordingly, in 1955, Frost opened a public campaign to push the federal government into a national hospital insurance scheme. Except for Maurice Duplessis of

Quebec, Frost's fellow premiers supported him with varying degrees of warmth, urging that Ottawa make an immediate commitment to hospital insurance and back up its pledge with federal funds. Frost's *démarche* struck an answering chord in the federal cabinet, where Paul Martin bluntly informed St Laurent that he could not remain in the government if it failed to take up Frost's challenge. St Laurent's response to Frost was a careful and qualified 'maybe' instead of the flat 'no' he would doubtless have preferred.

Martin had been briefing himself for seven years in readiness for this moment. He had already implemented a health grants program, and had prepared an authoritative survey of the health needs of Canadians. His officials were willing and able to move on hospital insurance as soon as he gave the word. After prolonged and frustrating negotiations, agreement was reached between the national government and the provinces in the late winter of 1957. In April Martin introduced a national hospital insurance scheme, the Hospital Insurance and Diagnostic Services Act, to the House of Commons. It was unanimously passed.

One other major welfare proposal reached fruition during this period. Since 1927, Canada had had an old age pension, a joint federal-provincial affair which, since Quebec's accession in 1936, was national in scope. But the pension, which was low, was dependent on a means test, and it was limited to the over-seventy age group. The test was inefficient and humiliating, and there was considerable agitation during the 1940s for its abolition. St Laurent and the finance department would have preferred a contributory scheme (one financed directly by individuals), but the agitation inside and outside the Liberal party was too much to withstand. In the 1949 general election all parties promised to do something about the means test. A joint committee of the Senate and House of Commons examined the issue, and eventually recommended a universal pension for Canadians over seventy, and the introduction of a means test pension for those between sixty-five and sixty-nine. The St Laurent government was surprised, but acquiesced. The consent of the provinces to a limited constitutional amendment (necessary because welfare was basically a provincial field) was secured, and a new old age pension regime came into operation in 1951. Special Old Age Security taxes were enacted to pay for it.

Throughout the St Laurent government's tenure of office, it could rely on a ginger group to the left to push it further than it might have been willing to go. The CCF party, largely confined to its prairie base in Saskatchewan, was generally admitted to have no hope of securing power. Its members, most of them sedate and responsible, recalled St Laurent's phrase that the CCF were really only 'Liberals in a hurry.' But if the CCF was hurrying anywhere, it was not toward the seats of power.

This fact perturbed both the professional CCF politicians and their allies in the Canadian Congress of Labour, one of the country's three umbrella labour organizations (the others were the Trades and Labour Congress and the Confédération des

Travailleurs Catholiques du Canada). Both the CCF and the CCL stood for a democratic-socialist-labour party in Canada; to that end, both had weeded Communist sympathizers out of their ranks, or expelled unions which remained obdurately Communist-dominated. In a futile attempt to attract the attention of voters whose sympathies were wedded to the political centre and the existing economic system, the CCF even undertook to modify the socialist rhetoric that had enveloped its platform since the 1930s. All in vain: by the 1957 election the CCF was sinking in the public opinion polls and was moving further from the prospect of power than ever before.

If the CCF was floundering, its union affiliates were flourishing. Union membership was going up, and passed the million mark for the first time in 1949. Expanding membership was reflected in strike action, action which was, however, firmly directed toward amelioration of wages and working conditions and which conspicuously lacked the revolutionary verbiage that had accompanied the strikes of the post-First World War period. The issue of compulsory union membership for all employees in a unionized company was met by the system of compulsory check-offs of dues (a formula devised by Mr Justice Ivan Rand and consequently known as the Rand formula), whether or not the individual concerned belonged to a union.

Although the fifties were not lacking in bitter and sometimes violent strikes, observers noted a decline in basic conflict between unions and most management, and between unions and government. There was also a reduction in inter-union hostility, as the Trades and Labour Congress (affiliated with the American Federation of Labor) and the Canadian Congress of Labour (affiliated with the Congress of Industrial Organizations, or CIO, in the United States) grew closer together. In 1953 both organizations appointed a Unity Committee which in 1954 produced a No-raiding Agreement and then in 1955 a Merger Agreement. The latter was implemented in April 1956 when the Trades and Labour Congress and the Canadian Congress of Labour officially merged into the Canadian Labour Congress (CLC), under the leadership of the veteran labour leader, Claude Jodoin.

Jodoin's physique, large and solid, and amiable appearance reassured a public still skittish of 'radical' innovations. Harmony among the unions prefigured harmony in society in general. The economic order no longer demanded fundamental reform, and virtually no one was asking for it any more. Progress and prosperity seemed to have obliterated discontent almost everywhere, leaving only a few isolated pockets of misery and malcontents. In the fullness of time these too would join the past where, so it seemed, they already belonged.

18

Stratford, Elvis, and the Happy Gang

The effects of prosperity were most evident in a sector where Canada had little past to live down – culture. Culture was a matter of bookstores, a couple of theatres (some professional, but many more amateur), and literary salons. The state, whether federal or provincial, had little business there.

Indirectly, the Canadian government had slowly and almost accidentally acquired a galaxy of cultural institutions. Out of the Department of Agriculture, for example, there had sprung the Public Archives. Since the early part of the century there had been the National Gallery – housed, it is true, behind the dinosaur collection in the National Museum. There was the National Film Board and, above all, the Canadian Broadcasting Corporation. Over-all, support for these institutions was meagre, for there was no Canadian tradition of state support for the arts as in Europe. Worse, the private foundations which so generously contributed to artistic endeavours in the United States were also lacking. Canadian philanthropists and American foundations had built some concert halls and libraries and endowed some scholarships. But there was still little to boast of, and the cultural facilities of Canadian cities compared badly with those of their American counterparts and even with those in the bombed-out European cities. Symphony concerts in hockey rinks, movie theatres, or high-school auditoriums were common, as we have seen, and great performers all too often shunned Canada on North American tours. George Bernard Shaw refused to visit Canada lest he die of intellectual starvation in a land of primitive ruffians.

Shaw's comments were an exaggerated reflection of a common view of Canadian development. Canada was a coarse-grained adolescent still clearing the land, lacking the leisure and taste for refinement. After the war, many Canadians were embarrassed by this image, and prominent among these were two internationalists (and Liberal ministers), Brooke Claxton and Lester Pearson. Claxton was irritated when the National Liberal Convention in August 1948 failed to support a resolution for a commission on the arts. Once Mackenzie King was out of the way, however, Claxton believed that such a commission was both possible and workable. He spoke to

Pearson and Jack Pickersgill about the idea, and both enthusiastically supported it. Louis St Laurent had his doubts – he told Pickersgill that he was sceptical about 'subsidizing "ballet dancing"' – but eventually he came round. For chairman of the Royal Commission on National Development in the Arts, Letters and Sciences, Claxton suggested Vincent Massey, the most apparently cultured Canadian of his day. It would give Massey something to do, Claxton argued; without this job, the former diplomat might leave for England for good. Massey's appointment was announced on April 8, 1949; the other commission members were Laval social scientist Father Georges-Henri Lévesque, Montreal engineer Arthur Surveyer, Saskatchewan historian Hilda Neatby, and the president of the University of British Columbia, Norman MacKenzie.

The Massey Commission, as it soon became known, examined the work of numerous federal agencies, including the Canadian Broadcasting Corporation, the National Research Council, the National Film Board, and the National Gallery. It also confronted a difficult constitutional problem on federal aid to universities, and even the old question of what kind of honours Canadians should receive. Massey, characteristically, approached these tasks with broader, grander aims in view. The report would be an official statement on Canadian 'culture' – what it lacked, what it could and should be. The report, submitted to St Laurent on June 1, 1951, took an appropriately large view of its subject. Canadian culture, the commissioners reported, existed on the margin of society. It was time to end the isolation and irrelevance of the Canadian writer and the Canadian artist and make them 'an integral part' of the Canadian environment. Only then could 'the spiritual foundations' of our national life be secured.

To that end, the report recommended that a 'Canada Council for the Encouragement of the Arts, Letters, Humanities and Social Sciences' be established. In general, traditional institutions such as the Canadian Broadcasting Corporation and the National Gallery should also be more generously supported lest American cultural influence become, for Canada, 'permanent dependence.' Federal grants must strengthen Canadian universities in order to strengthen their role in the life of the nation. Otherwise the nation would not long endure. In fact, as N.A.M. MacKenzie later explained, 'I was the only member of the Commission who felt that this should be done and that it was possible under the general terms of our constitution despite the importance of education to the provinces.' Understandably, however, MacKenzie's views were popular with his fellow university presidents, many of whom viewed the possibility of federal aid to their institutions with an anxiety born of years of budgetary starvation.[1]

---

1 One minor indication of the state of the universities may be found in the real income of faculty. A senior economist at the University of Toronto, Vincent Bladen, calculated that his disposable income in 1971 dollars was less in 1951 ($11,000) than it had been in 1941 ($11,900) or indeed

The tone of the Massey Report sounds archaic today. The state now promotes Canadian culture to a degree that the Massey commissioners could never have imagined and probably would not have fully approved. Their criticisms, then, are no longer valid. Neither, it seems, is the particular notion of 'culture' which Massey so carefully defined and employed. The Massey Commission reflected not only post-war nationalistic optimism, but also a conservative view of the western cultural tradition, a view which had appeared in the wake of, and in response to, the holocaust. Massey's fear of 'mass culture,' his identification of culture and art, his confidence in the continuity and the excellence of the western intellectual tradition were Canadian counterparts of T.S. Eliot's post-war enquiry into the meaning of our cultural tradition and Friedrich Meinecke's call for a return to the traditional values of 'civilization,' which he claimed were the strongest barricades against the return of the barbarians of the 1930s. The Massey Report was as much an echo of the past as it was a forecast of the future. Most of the institutional recommendations of the report have been followed, but the institutions created have not shaped Canadian cultural life into the forms which the commissioners expected. The nationalism of the Massey Report is as different from the English-Canadian radical variant of the 1960s as is traditional French-Canadian nationalism from Lévesque separatism. They are related, but not fraternally.

The Massey Report was greeted with acclaim by most of the Canadian artistic and intellectual community. There were dissenters: Frank Underhill complained of the identification of mass culture with the United States, claiming that mass culture was an inevitable concomitant of modern democracy and not some peculiar 'American' evil. More troubling to the government was the attitude of the Quebec government, which attacked the commission as an infringement of the province's rights in the field of culture. The conception of federal grants to the universities was repugnant not only to Premier Duplessis (although he accepted them for a year) but also to some of his strongest opponents, such as the Montreal editor and publisher Pierre Trudeau. Nevertheless, St Laurent decided to make the grants; as he told a University of Toronto audience in 1950, 'some means must be found to ensure to our universities the financial capacity to perform the many services which are required in the interest of the nation.' The government established the National Library in 1953 as called for in the report, but it delayed action on Massey's most important recommendation, the Canada Council. Members of the government, including Claxton, were nervous about the impact such a purely cultural policy would have on the electorate. When a windfall from succession duties did make the Canada Council possible in 1957, a Social Credit MP predicted that it would subvert religion and the family. Claxton blamed a popular backlash

in 1933 ($11,100). *Bladen on Bladen: The Memoirs of a Political Economist* (Toronto: privately printed 1978), 218.

against the new body for some of the Liberals' unpopularity and defeat in the 1957 election.

The Canada Council survived to become the major federal government commitment to the support of Canadian culture and a forerunner of many other agencies and programs created to make the Canadian artist and intellectual 'an integral part' of the Canadian environment.

Whether the Council has played a major role in the appearance of a sophisticated Canadian cultural life is debatable, as are all historic relationships between patrons and scholars and artists. *The Literary History of Canada*, for example, stresses the continuity between the 1940s and the 1950s in the development of Canadian literature since the war. One might also point to many Canadian writers who spurn the Council's largesse but who produce many of our finest works. It does seem, then, that the rise of a distinctive Canadian literary world and consciousness owes less to official patronage than to a general improvement in the level of education and what George Woodcock calls 'the shift in national tone from the bucolic to the urbane.'[2]

The most dramatic indication of the shift occurred in the small city of Stratford, Ontario. Tom Patterson, a Stratford native, thought that Stratford, whose best days seemed to have passed with the decline of the railway, might find in culture what it lacked in industry and trade. He persuaded the practical burghers on the city council to pay Tyrone Guthrie, a distinguished English director, five hundred dollars to come to Stratford to consider founding a Shakespearean theatre. At first glance Stratford offered only its name and that of its river – the Avon – but Guthrie soon caught Patterson's enthusiasm. In 1953 the Stratford Shakespearian Festival opened in a circus tent with Alec Guinness starring in *Richard III*. The performance was good; Stratford became a pleasant summer diversion for thousands of North Americans and the source of employment and income for a few actors and actresses, as well as for the city.

In a sense Stratford was premature because Canadians had not yet acquired the training which distinguished theatre demands. The casts of early plays were sprinkled with Canadians among more eminent imports. No one complained much. Theatre in the 1950s, after Stratford, was consumer-oriented. The audience got what it wanted; after all, who would have travelled to an Ontario country town for a Robertson Davies or Merrill Denison festival?

For the time, it was enough that new facilities were being built. Other theatre companies appeared, and not only at Stratford. Gratien Gélinas's and Jean Gascon's Théâtre du Nouveau Monde in Montreal did much to reinvigorate French-language theatre, and Gascon was soon making links with Stratford. The small number of people involved in Canadian theatre in the 1950s meant that such

---

2 George Woodcock, *Canada and the Canadians* (Toronto: Macmillan 1970), 253.

links were important and possible. While this could lead to an 'in-group' atmosphere – and in the 1960s all too often it did – it endowed Canadian theatre with the excitement that derives from new discovery and growth. Moreover, there were some critics, most notably Nathan Cohen of the *Toronto Daily Star*, who would not tolerate the second-rate even when produced by friends. Inexperience was no excuse.

Stratford did not eclipse other equally notable cultural developments. The Canadian Ballet Festival, beginning in 1948, led to an increasing interest in and support for the dance in Canada. In ballet Winnipeg took the lead with a professional company established in 1950. Gweneth Lloyd's efforts in Winnipeg were soon followed by British-born Celia Franca's work in building the National Ballet Company centred in Toronto. These professional companies, which toured widely, soon overshadowed the amateur Ballet Festival, which died out in the middle of the decade. Canadians were less willing to accept amateur performances when professional ones were readily accessible on radio or television. Television was to become an additional means of support for the arts, but not so strong a support as many had hoped. Television as a medium is best discussed under the heading of popular culture.

A more enduring prop for the arts in Canada was the university. An extremely high proportion of Canada's functioning writers and critics were associated with the universities. The most prominent example was Northrop Frye, who evaluated the efforts of Canadian writers year by year in the *University of Toronto Quarterly*. There was, nevertheless, much scepticism when George Woodcock and the University of British Columbia established *Canadian Literature* in 1959. This quarterly presented serious criticism of Canadian writing, past and present, and from its first issue it strove to avoid a narrow nationalism which might impair critical standards. Its endurance testifies to its success.

The universities contributed to a general atmosphere where the arts were tolerated if not encouraged. All too often there was an intellectual barrenness to the fervour civic leaders brought to the promotion of the arts. The 'edifice complex' – buildings being constructed without much thought for their eventual function – affected too many Canadian cities and the institutions within them. The origins of this complex may be discerned in the perception of the future held by Canadians of middle age in the fifties. For them the task was to accommodate wealth and progress; for their children there would be a different and richer life, one in which leisure and refinement would be possible as the hard edges of Canadian life wore off. The post-war generation would not only be better housed and fed; it would also be university-trained (if not better educated). University administrators sensed this mood early in the fifties, and when they scanned the post-war birth-rate figures they realized that their classrooms might soon be overwhelmed. Their enthusiasm for the federal grants advocated by the Massey Commission may be gauged accordingly. University presidents sounded dire warnings about the future, predicting that enrolments would and must double between 1955 and 1965. Where would these students find their professors, much less their residences? This time Cassandra was believed, but only late in the day and after much incidental help from the Russians.

On October 4, 1957, the Soviet Union launched the first global satellite, and the heavens seemed to confirm the worst fear of all: 'The Russians are ahead of us.' Suddenly penny-wise politicians began to orate about millions and even billions for engineers, for scientists, and for the universities which would train them. Beer, football, and fraternity frolics now began to seem slightly seditious, and certainly irrelevant. Educators began to stress how serious education must be. Hilda Neatby who, in 1953, had published *So Little for the Mind*, an indictment of Canadian pre-university training, now became a prophet whose all-too-accurate warnings about child-oriented progressive education had been unwisely ignored. Now serious purpose must return to the classroom, from the kindergarten through to the university; otherwise, in the continuing struggle of freedom against darkness, freedom would perish. One indication of the shock inspired by the Soviet menace was the statement by University of Toronto political scientist James Eayrs that Canada should consider merging with the United States if that proved necessary for the defence of the 'free world.' University administrators began to envisage themselves as the leaders of a national mission. No argument for funds was so effective as national security, and it was widely and loosely used. New universities sprang up on muddy Waterloo cow pastures, the barren plains of Downsview, and even on a small mountaintop in Burnaby. Bulldozers became a normal feature of the campus scene in the late fifties and early sixties, as the 'edifice complex' spread to the universities.

The baby boom had other effects as well. There were acute teacher shortages, first at the elementary and secondary levels, and then at the universities as well. To stock the universities there was an inflow of American and European academics. Canadian graduate schools, comparatively underdeveloped, could not meet the demand. Canadians who went abroad to finish their education often did not return. In the pure sciences, many aspiring PHDs found the research facilities inadequate – and moved; in the social sciences, many liked where they studied – and stayed. Canadian universities responded by raising their incentives in the form of salaries and research grants.[3] Besides money, there was deference, an intangible but enjoyable 'perk' for the professoriate. Still, as universities expanded, many found that their staffs were less than 50 per cent Canadian. Given that expansion must occur, and no one seemed to disagree, there was simply no alternative.

There seems to have been a curious hiatus of scholarship in Canada as the universities prepared for the deluge. Several distinguished individual works appeared

---

3 Using Vincent Bladen's figures (above, p 166, note), we find his salary in 1971 dollars rising from $11,000 in 1951 to $23,000 in 1960.

during the fifties, but, as in literature, scholarship seemed to take few new departures from the patterns of the previous decade. Historians were probably the most productive scholars. Donald Creighton's two-volume biography of Sir John A. Macdonald attracted much public attention, a reflection of a reawakened interest in Canada's past as well as of the popular taste for biography. Interestingly, at a time when history as an academic discipline was adopting more frequently a neo-positivist approach, Creighton's study emphasized the traditional linkage of history with narrative and imaginative literature.

Creighton's work attracted few disciples and even fewer successful imitators. Harold Innis, Creighton's friend and colleague at the University of Toronto, produced some stimulating works (*Empire and Communications*, 1950, *The Bias of Communication*, 1951, and *Changing Concepts of Time*, 1952) just before his untimely death in 1952, but, as Carl Berger has observed, Innis's abrupt departure from his earlier field of economic history was met with 'a mixture of admiration for his intellectual daring and courage and bewilderment over what he was driving at.'[4] One who seemed to sense where Innis might lead was the literary scholar Marshall McLuhan who, along with other academics, was studying the problem of technology, communications, and culture in his book *The Mechanical Bride* and the journal *Explorations*. McLuhan's impact, however, was minimal in the fifties, when his work was viewed mainly as a manifestation of quixotic curiosity.

The curiosity of English-Canadian social scientists seemed to focus upon deviant cases in the Canadian consensus. Social Credit in Alberta received more attention than any other topic as the Social Science Research Council endowed an excellent series on that subject. Social Credit lay outside the mainstream of Canadian political thought and tradition, and the reasons for its appearance and survival seemed important to an understanding of what the mainstream might be. Even Canadian socialism was being assimilated to the Canadian liberal consensus, as we have seen above (p 164). The thirties, seen from the prosperous fifties, seemed an aberration, and the CCF's Regina Manifesto of 1933 appeared to some to be little more than an outdated collection of anti-capitalist ravings. Such sentiments were often expressed in the *Canadian Forum* in the fifties when that traditionally left-wing periodical generally supported American leadership in the world struggle against Communism and, in domestic affairs, an 'end of ideology' approach to Canadian politics which emphasized the absence of sharp class division and class conflict in Canadian politics. Not all agreed. When Seymour Martin Lipset, an American who had studied the 'anomaly' of agrarian socialism in Saskatchewan, contended that ideology was irrelevant to North American politics and that the Canadian and American political cultures were fundamentally similar, a young prairie socialist and

4 *The Writing of Canadian History* (Toronto: Oxford University Press 1976), 194.

Forum contributor, Ramsay Cook, strongly dissented, expressing his belief in the separate historical identity of Canadian socialism and the autonomy of the Canadian political tradition. And yet Canadian social science and social philosophy did not clearly identify what that unique tradition might be. Attempts to uncover the tradition in the British connection (as in John Farthing's book, *Freedom Wears a Crown*) or in a new conservatism were unconvincing when not simply hackneyed.

French Canada's intellectual life was considerably livelier. There was little tendency to minimize political and social antagonism as the province of Quebec's young intellectuals expressed their hostility to Maurice Duplessis and actively sought to break up the foundations of the old premier's conservative sway. Among French-Canadian social scientists and historians there was a distinct decision to break with the past, a recognition that their tasks were new, and, in the context of the 1950s, perhaps even revolutionary. Scholarly detachment and reserve had little appeal for scholars like Guy Frégault, Fernand Dumont, Maurice Séguin, or Jean-Charles Falardeau. Epitomizing the view of the past held by so many Quebec scholars during the fifties, Pierre Trudeau declared that 'in Quebec, during the first half of the twentieth century, our social thinking was so idealistic, so *a priori*, so far removed from reality and to be blunt, so ineffectual, that it practically never became a real part of the community's living and evolving institutions.'[5] This, of course, naturally exaggerated the sins of the past and it ignored the consequences for scholarship of the commitment to change that such remarks seemed to demand. But it is undeniable that in the debates about church and society, man and politics, the meaning of modernization and nationalism, French-Canadian intellectuals outshone their English-Canadian counterparts in originality, depth, and, most of all, vitality.

In Quebec, too, academic discourse and popular debate were not widely separated. After all, change required popular support and that demanded public education. Thus academics took up their pens and wrote political pamphlets, and on the French-language CBC (a federal institution where Duplessis's long arm could not reach) Pierre Trudeau was a commonplace figure, along with other intellectuals and critics of the Quebec regime, exhorting the people to awaken and accept responsibility for their political fate. Other CBC programs were less obviously political but equally didactic. René Lévesque, for example, became familiar as a lecturer on international affairs on the television program, *Point de Mire*. From this time the relationship between the media and public life took a different form than in English Canada. Journalists who saw themselves primarily as educators often became politicians, and the distinction between the crafts was often blurred. The 'new journalism' and the reporter *engagé* were seen in Quebec long before the term became popular

5 From 'Quebec on the Eve of the Asbestos Strike,' in Ramsay Cook, ed., *French-Canadian Nationalism* (Toronto: Macmillan 1979; 1st ed. 1970), 32.

in the United States in the mid-sixties. (Duplessis recognized the phenomenon when he barred a reporter from *Le Devoir* from his office.)

Quebec led in other ways as well. The painters Alfred Pellan and Paul Emile Borduas had brought to Canada from Paris a post-impressionist experimental mood which rejected representational art. In English Canada, the influence of the Group of Seven and landscape art remained strong, but in 1953 a group of Toronto abstract expressionists formed Painters Eleven. Influenced by American art theory and practice, but possessing strong individual traits, these painters (among them Harold Town and Jock Macdonald) attracted much attention and, naturally, criticism. The National Gallery under the directorship of Alan Jarvis became a patron to the abstract artists and gave them a respectability which a cautious Canadian art market might not otherwise have afforded.

Respectability, however, was less definable by the end of the fifties than at the beginning. The Massey Report had followed the traditional distinctions between high culture and popular culture and, for the commissioners, high culture was associated with refinement, with education, with taste. These provided critical standards against which artistic effort could be clearly measured. Yet what happened when artistic effort was directed against these same standards, as was the case with some modern artists? How, too, did one judge films now that they had passed beyond slapstick and melodrama and had 'serious' intentions? And finally, what was one to make of the challenge to traditional restraints and to the puritan ethic which could be found in what most agreed was 'good' literature?

These questions were not answered directly, but their declining relevance was to be discerned in the crumbling support for censorship. The most spectacular censorship case of the decade, Quebec's banning of the film *Martin Luther*, gave critics of censorship a 'respectable' point of departure. As the decade advanced, the rules of censorship became perceptibly more liberal. Grace Metalious's *Peyton Place*, a steamy novel of life and lust in rural New England, was doubtless junk, but what could one say of Vladimir Nabokov's *Lolita* or James Joyce's *Ulysses*, both modern classics but both affronts to the censorship laws? Fort William and Port Arthur citizens publicly burned D.H. Lawrence's *Lady Chatterley's Lover*, but thousands of others simply bought and read it. By 1960 the majority seemed clearly on the side of liberalization and the courts and politicians were quick to respond.

Their response, unfortunately, did not arise from a mature consideration of the relationship between what people read and saw and what it made them do. Traditional controls on public information broke down with mass education, affluence, and the appearance of new means of communication, especially television. In the United States, television programming had been from the beginning a medium for entertainment. Dependent on advertisers, the American networks needed consumers. The Massey commissioners had feared Canada would follow such a pattern and had urged strict control over the growth of Canadian television. The experience of Canadian radio should have been enlightening, but it was not. Instead of the strictly regulated and edifying fare envisaged by the Massey Commission, Canadian television, when it took to the airwaves in 1952, proved to have much more in common with raucous American television than with any abstract educational model. With antennae facing south, Canadians indicated their preference for *I Love Lucy* (considerately carried by the CBC as well as the American networks), *Jackie Gleason*, and, after Gleason on Saturday nights, *Hockey Night in Canada*. Where the CBC did not directly buy American programs, it imitated them. Thus the Canadian program *Space Command*, complete with cardboard sets, challenged American space operas, and a Canadian *Howdy Doody* disputed conclusions and audiences with the celebrated American puppet. Perhaps the most successful original Canadian programming came from the CBC's French network. It was noticed that one French program was attracting an unusual amount of attention in English Canada: *La Famille Plouffe*, a creation of the novelist Roger Lemelin. Duly translated and re-baptized *The Plouffe Family*, it proved capable of attracting English-language audiences to its own homely version of French-Canadian family life.

Although the CBC directed some of its attention to the provision of high quality cultural fare to its audiences (Nathan Cohen's *Fighting Words* and the CBC's drama flagship *Folio* are examples) its pandering to Americanized Canadian audiences distressed academics and potential performers. Would it not be better to take a stand on principle, rejecting American mass culture for the next generation? The answers to these question must have been unpleasant for those who asked. From every juke-box playing popular music, for every watcher of *American Bandstand* or *Trans-Canada Hit Parade* (playing American songs, though with Canadian performers), the sound of a common North American experience burst forth. Popular music sounded the same in Chicago, Vancouver, Moose Jaw, or Toronto, and Canadians rushed to buy the latest records and the latest styles that American pop stars produced. The most shocking to the sedate tastes of the fifties was the Tennessee singer Elvis Presley, whose visits on tour to Canada stimulated the same crowds of shrieking teenagers that an earlier idol, Frank Sinatra, had enjoyed. Canadian parents worried, and Canadian pundits pondered: was rock 'n' roll uniquely bad, or was it just the most recent example of a deplorable and inevitable drift of the young into American mass culture? Some Canadians were appeased when Canadian singers appeared to show that they could do it too. A young Ottawa resident, Paul Anka, was the first, with his gold record 'Diana.' There would be many more for Anka, but few other Canadians had such success in these years. Many radio stations turned to continuous music programming, usually 'rock,' but, on the 'Top 40,' only one or two at most were Canadian efforts.

No one cared very much. Radio survived the shock of television by becoming specialized. The CBC gradually brought its popular Dominion Network to an end (the flag station, CJBC in Toronto, turned French in the early sixties). *The Happy Gang*, an afternoon diversion since the thirties, finally broke up. CBC radio began to concentrate on reaching specialized audiences (the 'highbrows' through CBC 'Wednesday Night') or catering to regional or special interest groups. The CBC at least had solid financing behind it. For radio stations that didn't, the way was clear: maximum audiences, with maximum advertising impact, could only be achieved by catering to youth. Without the 'Top 40' many stations simply could not have existed. They survived, and their frenzied, sometimes raucous, voices became the inescapable background music for Canadian beaches and drive-in restaurants.

As younger Canadians adopted the tastes of young Americans in music, food, and dress, they became less doubtful of American behaviour than their parents had been. Divorce, for example, seemed less an indication of a decadent American society than an effective, though drastic, solution to marital incompatibility. The number of divorces went up at the end of the Second World War, and it stayed up, between 6,000 and 7,000 a year compared to 1,000 to 2,000 in the thirties. Canada's divorce laws were increasingly condemned as archaic; so were Sunday closing laws and drinking restrictions outside Quebec. The opponents of change hung on, fighting every plebiscite, hoping that the temper of the times would change. But despite ostentatious displays of public and official piety, it never did. The reward of the moral conservatives was cruel caricature, and for none more than the United Church's James Mutchmor. Mutchmor, a serious and intelligent critic of contemporary society, was depicted as a foe of human happiness, a relic of the age of Carrie Nation and her axe-carrying disciples.

The real trend was up: up for alcoholic beverages and Sunday movies and other forms of public indulgence. Cocktail lounges opened and spread. More restaurants listed wine on their menus. Yet, by international standards, Canada remained an abstemious society. In 1953 Canadians drank 13.72 gallons of beer, 0.74 gallons of spirits, and 0.36 gallons of wine per capita. By 1960 beer consumption had dropped to 13.41, although spirit consumption rose to 0.82 and wine to 0.44 gallons. It was still a mild trend. In large cities, except Montreal, it was exceedingly difficult, if not impossible, to get a drink on Sunday. Canadians could still not read a Sunday paper, unless they bought the *New York Times* or another American paper. It would be in the next decade that the real changes would be felt.

19

Crosscurrents in
Economic Affairs and Policy

The heart of the St Laurent government's policy structure lay far from the rhythms of 'ballet dancing' and closer to cycles of a different sort. Down Parliament Hill from the House of Commons, in a Gothic office tower, dwelt the Department of Finance, the focus of the capital's mandarinate, the conduit through which all other departments' spending projects must travel. Many of Finance's proceedings were classed as secret and jealously guarded: the making of the budget was the most secret process of all, revealed only to the prime minister himself, and that at a late date. If some of Finance's workings were not secret, they were judged so arcane as to be beyond the understanding of the average citizen or bureaucrat. Into the language of the officers of the finance department were creeping terms like 'macroeconomic policy,' puzzling to a cabinet consisting largely of lawyers, and more puzzling still to the press outside, which began to interpret the doings of the government's economists as a kind of benign wizardry.[1]

Today the wizardry would be interpreted rather more easily. 'Macroeconomic policy,' the conundrum of the fifties, is quite simply that area of government policy that tries to manage the level of unemployment, inflation, and the balance of payments. In restraining inflation and combating unemployment the St Laurent government could use standard textbook weapons: engineering changes in tax rates and outlays, increasing or decreasing the flow of credit from the Bank of Canada, cutting or raising tariff rates, lowering or raising the exchange rate, imposing or removing exchange controls, or other sorts of direct regulation. Economists studying the matter have usually argued that although the St Laurent government's actual actions were not always correct, at least the administration was fully committed to this kind

---

1 The untimely death of Kenneth R. Wilson, the *Financial Post*'s economic correspondent, appreciably lowered the level of economic reporting in Canada.

of macroeconomic management, and tried hard to do the right thing. The pattern was different in the United States, where the Truman administration of 1945-53 understood such matters only dimly, and the Eisenhower administration of 1953-61 did not understand them at all. Of course these things were more easily managed in a parliamentary system like Canada's or Britain's than in a congressional one, especially when the government enjoyed a secure majority in the House of Commons. On the other hand, because 'junior governments' – provinces and municipalities – bulk so large on the Canadian scene, macroeconomic policy-making has always been more difficult in Canada's federal system than in unitary countries like Great Britain. Indeed, during the St Laurent years the 'federal problem' became much more awkward as the junior governments waxed larger and more importunate. Furthermore, with the dismantling of wartime controls in Canada and elsewhere the Canadian economy became more closely integrated with the others, especially with the American economy, whose share in Canada's import and export trade rose steadily. Trade with Britain grew absolutely but diminished relatively; as yet continental Europe and Japan mattered little, and neither mainland China nor the Soviet Union was yet buying Canadian wheat. By 1957 Canada's trading pattern made it plain that this was a North American country whose trade and financial connections would be with the United States. Not all Canadians rejoiced at the prospect. Imperial longings were not extinct, as the Diefenbaker years were to show. Ignoring the repeated attempts of the Canadian government to encourage Anglo-Canadian trade, some commentators and mythmakers began to chatter about the American dominance of the Canadian economy. In the prosperous and complacent fifties, their warnings had little impact. Canadians enjoying the rising, American-style standard of living were not inclined to listen to prophets of economic and political doom; if anything, they were inclined to overestimate the contribution of American money and American markets to the new national prosperity.

The economy was functioning well: trade and investment figures proved it. If anything could reinforce the belief in the effortless superiority of the Ottawa mandarins, this was it. All that a perceptive observer had to do was witness a dominion-provincial conference to mark the difference in competence between the Otttawa civil servants and their provincial counterparts. Saskatchewan had a competent group of administrators, but their horizons were limited. In the Atlantic provinces, as always, politicians ran things, and they did not better and no worse than ever. In Newfoundland and British Columbia, where they followed the wizard principle, governments had some disastrous experiences with 'special advisers' whose advice cost millions and who occasionally vanished without trace or landed in jail. Although the provinces were spending more than ever before, they had yet to develop the expert bureaucrats who could meet their Ottawa opposite numbers as equals. Thus, although provincial revenues and expenditures were rising, and Ottawa's were falling relatively, the central government's dominant expertise allowed it to retain the financial leadership of the Canadian federation for a little while longer.

Yet the grasp of Ottawa was far less all-embracing than it would later become. Compared with the Pearson or Trudeau governments, the St Laurent administration appears almost 'minimalist' in its approach to the role of government in the national economy. There was no regional development program, and there were few shared-cost programs (in which the national and provincial governments jointly finance projects). Major initiatives were comparatively few, the St Lawrence Seaway and the Trans-Canada Highway being the biggest and the most important. Nothing was done to stimulate competition, except insofar as tariff reductions and the ending of exchange control had this incidental effect. The feeble Combines Investigation Act, inherited from the King era, was amended in 1952, but it was not strengthened. Ottawa did support a few agricultural prices under 1944 legislation, and it ran the Canadian Wheat Board for the marketing of prairie grain, but the wheat crop was sold without government guarantee and the provinces ran all the other marketing boards. Pressure from wheat farmers to get Ottawa to pay more attention to their economic plight was either resolutely ignored, or responded to grudgingly.

By 1957 federal price and rent controls had long been things of the past, and no one yet talked of an 'incomes policy' that would regulate wages. With the return of peace the provinces had regained their authority in this area, and in other aspects of social policy as well. Only 5 per cent of the labour force was subject to federal regulation (although that 5 per cent was in key areas, as the railway strike of 1950 demonstrated); in labour as in agriculture Ottawa did not try to encroach on the provincial sphere. No one doubted that the provinces were entitled to collect revenue from the natural resources they owned, and to control resource development if they wished. Off-shore oil was another matter, because no one was sure who owned it, but before 1957 no one very much cared. Ottawa had assumed control over uranium, it was true, but in the atomic age that power was not yet seriously questioned. The central government did regulate energy exports, and was still reluctant to allow the sale of electricity abroad; on one notable occasion, C.D. Howe used his power over energy exports to block an American aluminum plant in Alaska that would have competed with a Canadian facility, Kitimat, just across the line. But when it came to oil and gas, Ottawa was more eager to find United States markets than to limit development. As for subsidies to universities, the central government justified its action as an aspect of the spending power. The provinces were not obliged to accept federal grants (and after a year Quebec refused them); Ottawa was merely topping up inadequate provincial funding. When the government set up the Canada Council in 1957 the constitutional logic was the same, and to this federal initiative no one objected.

The provinces, it might be observed, had problems of their own. Expenditures were surging upward as governments built more things, schooled more children, spent more on old age security, and, in British Columbia and Saskatchewan, began to spend on hospital insurance. Fortunately, by 1950 it was possible to borrow, not only at home but in the United States. The rigid limits on provincial spending and revenues during the Second World War had had their beneficial side: provinces and municipalities, relieved from spending, improved their financial standing. Better credit ratings and the abolition of Canadian exchange control reopened American money markets to Canadian borrowers, and after 1950 the Bank of Canada pursued a financial policy that encouraged them to go there. Everyone believed that to maintain a decent pace of development and modernization Canada would have to draw money from abroad. Nevertheless, in spite of their borrowings, the junior governments needed more current revenues – from taxes, natural resources, and their increasingly profitable liquor monopolies.

Naturally the provinces criticized the dominion, which, they claimed, took too much in taxation and gave back too little. The tax agreements of 1947 (see above, page 98), though acceptable, did limit provincial taxing powers. Tax rental payments steadily grew, as did other forms of federal transfers to the provinces. Unconditional grants to the provinces totalled $103.9 million in 1949, $338.7 million in 1952, and $382.6 million in 1957.[2] During the same period conditional transfers fluctuated between $115.9 million in 1949 and $144.8 million in 1957. To give the provinces some leeway, the central government repealed its own taxes on gasoline and amusements, and the provinces soon occupied these fields wholly or in part. In 1950 the St Laurent government offered an amendment to the BNA Act that would have permitted the provinces to levy 'indirect' sales taxes at the retail level. Ontario, however, refused, and the proposal lapsed. The provinces could and did impose 'direct' retail sales taxes. Saskatchewan had been doing so since 1937, and in Quebec there had been municipal sales taxes since 1935. Ontario held out against the trend until 1961, and Alberta, oil-rich since the late 1940s, has never needed a retail sales tax at all. But in most provinces the fiscal stresses and strains of the St Laurent years forced governments to tap this one remaining source of funds.

In some provinces resource revenues could help float the ship of state. After the Leduc discoveries Alberta's oil production rapidly increased, and so did the province's output of natural gas. The same thing happened, although to a lesser extent,

2 Here and elsewhere in this book data on government receipts and expenditures are presented on a calendar-year basis, using the definitions that Statistics Canada employs in its *National Income and Expenditure Accounts*. Although the numerical results can be reconciled with the *Public Accounts* they are almost never the same. Increasingly, when discussing budgets, taxes, and estimates, finance ministers have used both the National Accounts basis and the Public Accounts basis, thus recognizing that the former is more meaningful than the latter.

in British Columbia and Saskatchewan. Pipelines opened new markets in Ontario and the United States. Economic growth stimulated buoyant markets. By the mid-fifties Alberta was debt-free, an achievement which some attributed to the exotic effects of the Social Credit doctrine, but which others, more realistically, ascribed to frugal financial management and the oil bonanza. In British Columbia and in some other provinces the North American construction boom produced active demand for forest products, and mining developments provided royalties from provincially owned minerals. But some provinces liked to tax the resource industries relatively lightly so as to encourage development, and perhaps to pay off political obligations. Thus only in Alberta were the resource revenues really large enough to meet the public demand for government services – roads, schools, public buildings, sewers, water mains, hospitals, welfare services, and pensions – areas where nothing much had been done since the 1920s.

There was talk of other initiatives. In 1950 Ontario dallied with a provincial income tax before joining the tax rental system, and, as we have seen (above, page 151) Quebec actually did impose one in 1954.

All these developments created problems for Ottawa's mandarin macroeconomic managers. In 1947 the dominion collected 70 per cent of all government revenue and spent 60 per cent of all government outlay. By 1957, in spite of the defence build-up and the new old age pensions, the percentages were 62 and 55. Worse, the provincial and local share in government capital outlays, always high relative to the federal share, was now 83 per cent. Worse still, the ten provinces and the thousands of municipalities made their own spending plans, without any kind of central co-ordination. Thus if Ottawa were to raise taxes or cut spending so as to restrain inflation, the junior governments could and did offset the impact. In principle Ottawa might press harder, offsetting the offsetting, as it were. But there were limits to this. By 1957, 73 per cent of the outlays of the national government consisted of wages, salaries, interest on debt, and other payments to persons and junior governments. In the remaining 27 per cent only 4 percentage points came from capital outlay – the easiest sort to turn on and off – while the rest was spent on the raw materials of government, everything from electricity and paper to the fuel for Canada's mighty air force and the red tape with which to bundle reports on government spending. On the other side of the account, tax hikes were unpopular with everyone except the provinces, since it was the central government which did the collecting everywhere except Quebec. Whenever Ottawa ran a surplus, the provinces could be relied on to ask for a larger handout. By 1957 the optimistic statements of the 1945 White Paper and Reconstruction conference seemed remote and unreal. If any ministers ever thought about them, they must have been thankful that C.D. Howe had forced his officials to speak not of 'full employment' but of 'high and stable levels of employment.' Nor is it surprising that Ottawa was increasingly inclined to rely on old-style monetary management, not only on new-style Keynesian fiscal management, to control the inflationary pressures of the 1954-7 boom.

Throughout the St Laurent period the central government sought to combat the menace of inflation. Hence the government deliberately ran surpluses and managed expenditures so as to reduce the inflationary pressure. Only in 1953-4, when there was a brief recession, was the fiscal engine used to create extra jobs. In 1948-53 and in 1955-7, the national government's surpluses were very substantial – 15 per cent of total revenues in the first period and 7 per cent in the second. The funds were mostly used to finance Crown agencies, such as the Central Mortgage and Housing Corporation (CMHC), and to reduce the national debt. In and of themselves the surpluses certainly reduced inflationary pressure, although it has sometimes been argued that they could have been used in ways that would have reduced that pressure still more. In particular, it was probably a pity that so much of the retired debt belonged to ordinary citizens instead of to chartered banks and the Bank of Canada. It was also a pity that Ottawa was still pumping funds into the housing market through CMHC.

When the National Housing Act was modified in 1954, Ottawa had hoped to end the direct mortgage loans that it had been providing, under one guise or another, since 1935. But the authorities were reluctant to face the possibility that fewer houses would be built. During the minor recession of 1954 these worries were especially understandable. And of course the housing shortage was still a very live political issue. Thus CMHC drifted back into the business of direct lending. By the end of 1957 it had been authorized to draw up to $400 million from the public purse for this purpose. The impact was considerable: $400 million was 40 per cent of the federal surplus in 1955-7. In principle, of course, CMHC activity was subject to government control. In practice, it was rapidly becoming another means of offsetting the tax-changing and expenditure-planning with which Keynesian fiscal policy is chiefly concerned.

By 1948-9 it appeared that the major taxes had been reduced far enough from their wartime peaks. Although personal income tax was further reduced in 1949, and although various commodity taxes were reduced in both years, the government seems to have been chiefly concerned to encourage new investment not just in the resource industries but throughout the economy. Thus there were various tax changes to that end, but no changes of macroeconomic direction. To fight inflation the government continued to run surpluses, as it had done in 1947. In terms of the goods and services it actually used up, government expenditure fell noticeably in 1948 and rose only a little in 1949. A measure of government expenditures may be found in the force levels of the armed services – 35,000 in 1948. The Korean War was required to reverse the trend.

In February 1951 the government unveiled its plans for rearmament. The strength of the armed forces would rise from 90,000 full-time employees (service and civilian) to 148,000. The government would modernize and upgrade military equipment, and the changes would cost $5 billion. Defence as a percentage of federal budgetary outlays rose from 16 per cent in 1950 to 45 per cent in 1953.

The rearmament program coincided with the new old age pension scheme (above, page 163), which added another $250 million a year to federal outlays. Although these were apparently vast sums, they could have been absorbed without much difficulty. There had been a budgetary surplus of $484 million in 1949. But war had rekindled the fires of inflation around the world; in order to combat that menace the government decided to raise its tax rate. In the fall of 1950 Parliament approved rises in corporation taxes and various commodity taxes. In April 1951 the government raised them again, and added a 20 per cent surcharge on personal income taxes. When, in the autumn of 1951, the government made fiscal provision for old age pensions, costs went up, but revenues went up still more. As a result, in 1951 the federal surplus was almost $1 billion. This vigorous Keynesian fiscal policy nevertheless failed to halt inflation. From 1949 to 1952 consumer prices rose 17 per cent, and from 1951 to 1952, the period of greatest pressure, they rose 10 per cent. Modest though these increases now appear, by the standards of their time they were shocking. But if the government had not deliberately counteracted inflation by running large surpluses, they would have been larger still.

By 1952 prices were rising very little, and, in 1953, for the first time since the early 1930s, the price index actually fell a little. Hence in 1952 Ottawa could reduce some commodity taxes, and in 1953 it reduced income taxes to the 1949 level while also lowering commodity and corporation taxation. The provinces were handed a little more room for income taxation. In 1952 and 1953 the national government still ran surpluses, but these were smaller than those in 1950 and 1951, and relative to federal outlays or national production they were too small to be interesting – less than 1 per cent of gross national product in 1952, and still less in 1953.

In 1954 there was actually a federal deficit – a small one, less than 1 per cent of total federal outlays. The deficit helped, in a minor way, to offset the recession of that year, when gross national product actually declined a little. Since the risk of recession had been foreseen, the Minister of Finance had already cut personal and corporate income taxes and reduced or removed various sales and excise taxes. Because the rearmament effort was winding down, government outlays actually fell somewhat, but the tax cuts and the recession itself reduced government revenues still more.

The last years of the St Laurent government, 1954-7, saw an inflationary expansion, but Ottawa's expenditures provided none of the fuel. Although the national government was spending more on goods and services, thanks to inflation it was actually buying less: in 1957 the national government bought less, in physical terms, than in 1954. Revenues, on the other hand, rose sharply both in terms of current dollars and in dollars of constant purchasing power; hence the rising surpluses, which peaked in 1956 and then shrank in 1957 as the economy decelerated. Ottawa fought inflation by controlling its own outlays, while growth and inflation were automatically pushing its revenue up. Tax cuts would have been perverse in an inflationary environment, and nobody pressed for them. But tax increases would have been unpopular, especially as the 1957 election drew near, and they were not imposed.

Ottawa's restraint was a contrast to, not a model for, the activities of the provinces and municipalities, whose capital and current outlays rose sharply. And so Canadians were presented with a paradox that – outside the cloistered inner circles of government – was only dimly understood. Ottawa was helping to restrain inflation, while the provinces were helping to create it.

Of course, taxes were not the government's only weapon in a war on inflation. The St Laurent government had the option of choosing a relatively high exchange rate and enforcing a policy of monetary restraint – high interest and tight credit. But high interest rates were unpopular with borrowers, and a high exchange rate did not hold much appeal for hard-pressed exporters. Accordingly, after 1954 the government increasingly relied on a novel interpretation of the Bank of Canada Act. By following the letter of the Act, it appeared that the governor of the Bank, rather than the government of the day, determined monetary policy.

Under the first governor, Graham Towers, it was always understood that in any ultimate confrontation over monetary policy the Bank would have to take direction from the cabinet. But James Coyne, who succeeded Towers in 1954, was as inclined to demand his statutory independence as the government was to emphasize it. Yet one may reasonably suppose that if the Bank's 'tight money' policy had actually annoyed the responsible ministers in 1955-7 they would have taken steps to dispose of the governor, just as the Diefenbaker government eventually had to do in 1961. On the one hand, Coyne really believed that Canadians should tighten their belts, borrow less, pay more for their borrowings, and live within their collective means. On the other hand, the government found it politically convenient to have a governor who would carry the can for a monetary policy that the government would in any event have wanted to follow.

In the early 1950s, Governor Towers had provided extra reserves so that the banking system could expand credit in step with higher prices. But in 1952 Towers applied the brakes. Thereafter, banks' reserves rose very little indeed, and in 1953 and 1954 actually fell. It would seem that Towers was determined to pump out the extra dose of reserves that he had injected, and in a sense he may be said to have succeeded. Between 1945 and 1954, reserves rose at an annual average rate of 1.9 per cent, while output rose 1.96 per cent a year. Thus monetary policy was modestly contractionary throughout, although these averages mask the year-to-year changes in growth rates that were such a marked feature of the Towers regime, as of those of his successors. Thus there were years in which the reserves and the money supply outgrew output and years in which they lagged behind, deflating output and employment as well as inflation.

When James Coyne took office in 1954 he changed central bank policy in two obvious respects. First he began to change the bank rate – the Bank's charge for credit to the chartered banks – far more frequently. In the central bank's first twenty years, Towers had only once altered the rate. Since the banks did not need to borrow and preferred not to do so, this stability was perhaps understandable. But the bank rate was changed three times in Coyne's first year as governor, and he was just as active during 1956. Indeed, he arranged in November 1956 that it would move up and down weekly, in a fixed relation to the cost at which the government could borrow. Indirectly, the Bank could affect that cost, because it entered the government bond market regularly as a buyer or seller of government bonds. But to the uninformed, bank rate now looked like a piece of automatism, as divorced from the Bank's control as from the government's. To Harris, one supposes, the advantages were obvious.

Second, the new governor began to use his annual reports as a means of self-justification. He was anxious to explain his policies, much more so than his predecessor. For reasons that never became explicit, he wanted to influence inflationary pressure by controlling the money supply itself, not just interest rates or other aspects of credit conditions. The idea, which became familiar and fashionable once more in the late seventies, was really quite simple and sensible. By first fixing the supply of credit through its decisions about the growth of the money supply, the Bank would affect the financial markets, where, given the demands for credit, interest rates would be fixed in an automatic way by the interaction of supply and demand. Coyne, unlike his successors in the late seventies, never stated what rate of growth he thought appropriate, but if we are to judge by his performance we must conclude that he thought the money supply should rise less rapidly than output, thus applying upward pressure on interest rates and downward pressure on prices. That was the pattern from 1954 until 1957, and indeed for most of Coyne's remaining years as governor.

The Bank's tight-money policy encouraged Canadians to borrow abroad, chiefly in the United States. Thus it tended to raise Canada's foreign indebtedness, which would in any event have been rising because of the attractions Canada held as a place for Americans to build new factories and develop new industries, especially in the resource field. But the Bank's policy was deflationary in three respects.

It provided the foreign money with which to pay for imports, thus reducing the pressure on Canada's own productive capacities. It caused the floating Canadian dollar to float higher, thus reducing the Canadian-dollar price of imports. Because it made exporting less profitable this high Canadian dollar tended to discourage exports, thus releasing labour and machinery to produce more for the domestic market. For the government there were obvious political advantages: it helped to have the exchange rate of the dollar determined by unseen market forces, and not by government policy.

This had not always been so. During the war, the external value of the Canadian dollar had been strictly controlled at 90.9 cents (US). In July 1946 the government changed the peg, making one Canadian dollar equal to one American. As we have seen above (page 87), Canada's foreign exchange reserves dribbled away in the next two years, leading directly to the emergency program of November 1947, which imposed heavy taxation and import control. The Marshall Plan helped: in 1948-9 Marshall Plan procurements in Canada totalled $1,027 million when net direct American investment amounted to only $145 million. From the end of 1947 until early 1950 Canada's gold and exchange reserves rose by nearly $500 million. The emergency restrictions by themselves do not account for this improvement; at best, they prevented some erosion that would otherwise have occurred during 1948. Their loosening during 1949 reflected the new exchange position.

In 1949 various things changed. Net direct American investment jumped from $84 million in 1949 to $200 million in 1950, and although American investment in bonds and stocks was now negative Canada attracted an enormous flow of short-term capital, largely from the United States but also from elsewhere. It seems that people expected the Canadian dollar to rise relative to other currencies, especially the American. Presumably the speculators believed that the 1949 devaluation of the Canadian dollar (back to 90.9 cents, US) had fixed too low a value. So they were buying Canadian money as fast as they could. Thus in the first nine months of 1950 Canada's reserves rose from about $1 billion to about $1.7 billion, even though for the first time in twenty years Canadians imported more than they exported.

For the government the situation was a difficult one. Having joined the International Monetary Fund, Canada was supposed to keep its exchange rate fixed relative to the American dollar. Only the narrowest fluctuations were permissible: Canada could change the peg on the dollar unilaterally only to a small extent; beyond the limits set by the IMF the Canadian government was supposed to consult the Fund, whose arrangements did not provide for floating exchange rates at all. But the inflow of foreign money was an embarrassment. It was producing extra inflationary pressure just when Korean War inflation was beginning. Because it was not embedding itself in new plant and equipment, or bonds and stocks, it might leave just as quickly as it had come. The obvious solution was to give in to the speculators and peg the Canadian dollar higher. But then the speculators would have won their gamble. They might then remove their funds from Canada, producing downward pressure on Canadian reserves and creating renewed demands for a change in the exchange rate, this time in the opposite direction. Thus the government might face an absurd oscillation whereby it would first raise the value of the dollar only to be forced to reduce it shortly afterward.

It is surely not surprising that the government decided to avoid the whole problem by floating the rate, returning in effect to the regime of the 1930s. The decision, taken in October 1950, was meant to be temporary. The IMF acquiesced on the understanding that Canada would fix its rate as soon as it could. But the floating rate became a habit, and it was not until 1962 that it was pegged to the American dollar once more.

For more than eleven years the Canadian authorities entered the foreign exchange market only to prevent large day-to-day fluctuations. As a result Canadian foreign exchange reserves changed very little: the government was neither piling up heaps of United States dollars nor spending its hoard. But the price of the Canadian dollar changed a great deal. It rose from 90.9 US cents in September 1950 to 95 US cents in November. Then, after fluctuating, it rose again to $1.04 US in the third quarter of 1952. After falling to par with the American dollar in 1956, it rose again, touching $1.05 US in the third quarter of 1957. Under the Diefenbaker government these oscillations continued, but, as we shall see below (page 225), the dollar remained well above par until after 1960.

After 1950 the Canadian dollar danced to the tune of supply and demand. But who had written the score? The answer to that question lies buried in Canada's export and import figures, interpreted in the light of Canadian commercial commitments and American trade policies. We must also explore the reasons why the Canadian economy was booming in 1950-3 and 1954-7. Finally we must examine the policy of the Bank of Canada, increasingly independent under Coyne's governorship.

From the beginning of 1950 Canada was exporting less than it was importing. In 1952, there was a small surplus, but that was swamped by the deficits of other years. In 1951 and 1953-7 Canada even ran a deficit on merchandise trade – purchases and sales of goods and services not counting interest and dividends. In 1950 there was a merchandise surplus, but the weight of interest and dividend obligations converted this surplus into a current account deficit.

Fundamentally Canada ran a deficit because the great boom of the fifties was based on domestic spending – consumption, domestic accumulation of plant and equipment, new building, and, especially in the later stages, the spending programs of junior governments. As noted in Part I (above, page 14), the boom was not export-led. That is to say, it was not a growth in Canadian export receipts that was responsible for the country's increasing prosperity; instead it was based on domestic spending. Indeed, some export industries were in serious trouble. This was most obviously true of the prairie wheat economy, where the revival of European production combined with the advent of subsidized American competition to produce a collapse of prices and farm incomes. Admittedly, much domestic spending, especially in the resource industries, was made with an eye to *future* export prospects. In this regard the American Paley Report, which had underlined American needs for resources from abroad, certainly played a part. But these investment programs did nothing for *current* export earnings, while directly they demanded large imports of machinery and equipment; indirectly they also stimulated the importation of consumer goods and services. It was in the later St Laurent years that Canadians first became really noticeable at tropical resorts in Florida, Hawaii, and the Caribbean.

Meanwhile, developments in commercial policy, both Canadian and foreign, may have hindered rather than helped Canada's current account position. The Marshall Plan ended in 1953. European production was reviving, and, although the dollar shortage was disappearing, this revival implied further competition for Canadian exports. In the United States, thanks to a system of domestic price supports there was now an ever-growing heap of produce that the world would not accept on ordinary commercial terms. In response Congress passed Public Law 480, a measure which provided for the subsidized export of agricultural products, especially grain. For Canada the impact could have been exaggerated because many of the buyers were poor countries which might not have bought our grain in any event. But Public Law 480 certainly did not help Canada's export trade, and at least at the margin it harmed us more than a little.

In the area of tariffs the St Laurent years also saw some changes made. In 1948 the Canadian tariff was lowered so as to implement the General Agreement on Tariffs and Trade (GATT) signed the previous year (above, page 82). The reduction of Canada's emergency barriers to trade also served to encourage trade, as did the end of the rationing of foreign exchange in 1950. In 1950-1 there were new GATT negotiations at the English resort town of Torquay, and in 1953-4 at Geneva again. Thanks to these negotiations the Canadian tariff fell further. So far as imports were concerned, these changed opened the Canadian market more widely to foreign competition, even though for many goods the Canadian tariff was still prohibitive. Although other countries also reduced their duties, so many Canadian products already enjoyed duty-free entry, especially to Britain and the United States, that on balance the GATT agreements probably raised imports rather than exports for Canada. Meanwhile, although the United States welcomed ever more Canadian goods, on certain agricultural products there were exceptions, and on fish sticks American duties were actually raised. Continental Europe, now recovered, was also returning with a rush to its immemorial habits of agricultural protectionism.

Given this pattern imports could be expected to rise relative to exports, pushing the Canadian current account into deficit, just as the actual experience of the fifties indicates. But why, then, did the floating dollar not fall? What kept it up was the inflow of capital funds. Some of the inflow was directed at raising Canada's export capacity, but most was not. Much direct investment was aimed at the domestic market, while little of the junior governments' borrowings was aimed at helping Canada to produce more.

The Bank of Canada is relevant to this story because its policies made external finance more attractive. If the Bank had allowed credit to expand more rapidly within Canada, domestic credit would have been cheaper and more plentiful, relative to American credit, than in fact it was. In the immediate post-war years the Bank had not worried much about these matters. Whenever extra money was needed to support the prices of Canadian bonds, the Bank had created credit with gay abandon. In effect, whenever the public wanted to sell inconvenient quantities of the bonds it had bought during the war the Bank simply printed extra dollars with which to buy the bonds. Gradually, however, the Bank awoke to the fact that by controlling the supply of credit it could restrain inflationary pressure. Thus in 1948 it allowed the prices of dominion war bonds to sag a bit, and in 1950 it declared its monetary independence by raising its own lending rate to 2 per cent – the first increase since the rate was fixed at 1.5 per cent in 1944. The increase was a signal that the Bank would try to control money and credit so as to reduce inflationary pressure. The Bank also convened the chartered banks and insurance companies, both of which agreed to restrain their lending. Meanwhile the government imposed a ceiling on bank credit and acted to prevent an undue expansion of consumer credit. By autumn 1953 the authorities were more worried about unemployment than about inflation, and so in 1954 the Bank Act was modified in an expansionary direction. But in 1955, when inflationary pressures were visible once more, the Bank asked the chartered banks and other lenders to restrain credit. Although the Bank did let the chartered banks lend a good deal more, interest rates rose, to the embarrassment of the government and the delight of the opposition.

With the election of 1957 the end of the inflationary boom was already in sight. In 1956 prices rose 4 per cent, and in 1957 only 2 per cent. But of course the government was blamed not just for the inflation, which its actions had helped to moderate, but for the 'high rates' (translated for the electorate into the slogan 'tight money') that had helped to control the inflation. Ministers responded by blaming the Bank for the credit squeeze, and the world situation for the inflation. The electorate, it seemed, was not convinced.

It was a salutary lesson for textbook economists. In the textbooks of macroeconomics, governments are imagined to make policy – manipulate taxes, spending programs, and the monetary system and exchanges – without regard to elections. It is assumed either that a government does not have to worry about re-election or that the electorate understands the game the government is playing and rewards the government that plays it properly. Clearly neither assumption is true, as finance minister Abbott understood, and few governments have behaved as if they believed them. In Britain it has been shown that since the war there has been a 'political cycle' in macroeconomic policy. Governments often have cut taxes and developed new spending programs just before elections, regardless of the economic climate. Of course all democratic governments must be tempted to behave this way; the problem about modern macroeconomic policy is that governments now think they can more readily get away with it. Fortunately for the St Laurent administration, in Canada the political and economic imperatives often pointed in the same direction. In 1949 and 1953 it made economic sense to cut tax rates, but because elections were on the way it also made political sense. The results produced such massive Liberal majorities that the government might well have concluded that it was as safe to heed its technocrats as it was to consult its ward heelers. In 1955-6, and especially in 1956, the situation was altogether different. In an inflationary boom with elections in the offing the political and economic imperatives pointed in opposite directions, and it is not surprising that the government's attack on inflation was something less than wholehearted. Nevertheless, as we have seen, it did move in the right direction, and on the whole the Bank of Canada was helpful. In the 1957 elections, did sensible policy win votes or cost votes? Or did the pipeline battle plus prairie populist rhetoric add up to a winning combination that would have swept the Liberals from office regardless? We shall never know.

20

The Twilight of the Grits

It is an axiom of politics that oppositions do not win elections; governments lose them. Most observers did not expect the Liberals to lose the general election of June 10, 1957; when they did, by a margin of seven seats (112 Conservatives, 105 Liberals, and 48 MPs from the minor parties), it seemed as if the foundations of the earth had shifted.

For two decades after 1957 commentators and political scientists have laboured to explain the inexplicable. Why did a government that had ruled for so long, and generally so well, with such a minimum of fuss and bother, suddenly collapse? What did it portend for the Canadian political system, and what did it demonstrate about the nature of Canada?

The simplest explanation for the defeat may be the one offered by a former member of the St Laurent cabinet: 'The electorate got bored,' he said. 'St Laurent made it seem so easy to govern Canada that the electorate decided that anybody could do it. And so the people elected anybody.' Equally simple is the reverse proposition: the Liberals were afflicted with incurable arrogance, *hubris*, the quality of blind conceit that invites divine retribution which was administered, in this case, by the votes of an aroused populace. There is some truth in both arguments.

The art of government seemed easy under St Laurent. St Laurent's own qualities had something to do with the phenomenon – his grandfatherly appearance, his mastery of his cabinet, the grace and apparent effortlessness of his administrative style. So did the political balance within Canada. The federal government was still politically predominant, a predominance reflected in comparisons of the over-all sizes of federal and provincial budgets. But, as we have noted, the figures of expenditure on capital account tell a different story, particularly if defence expenditures are excluded. The tale of Canada's capital expenditures prefigured a different kind of politics, although what kind could as yet hardly be guessed at. The age of masterful management of a disparate federal system was clearly coming to an end. Its approaching conclusion was masked only by the mystique of power that wafted along the grey corridors of Ottawa: hence, in some sense, the *hubris* that commentators have depicted.

A more complicated explanation would point out that in twenty-two years in power any democratic government will necessarily offend a large variety of interest groups across the country, especially in a country as large (spatially) and diverse as Canada. It was the Liberals' fate, during their last ten years in office, to offend many. The party's heaviest losses occurred in the western wheatfields where farmers cherished an acute sense of grievance at the government's inability to sell their wheat on glutted international markets, or to offer them compensation for their efforts comparable to what their American cousins were getting. In social policy, despite Paul Martin's best efforts, the Liberals had patently lost the initiative to the provinces, even to Conservative Ontario, where the ideological commitment to social reform was even less, if possible, than that of the majority of the St Laurent cabinet. And, as we have seen, when the government tried to follow the prescriptions of Keynesian finance, it eventually reaped a whirlwind of popular abuse and hostility. 'The Liberal dynasty had simply run out of ideas,' C.D. Howe heavily concluded, after the fall.

Yet it is still possible to view the St Laurent government's legislative program and administrative style, right up to the end, as relatively successful and efficient, certainly by comparison with what came after. St Laurent and his colleagues perceived what most of his critics then and since did not, that the bases for the federal government's predominance were shifting and that, short of attempting a formal constitutional revolution, some accommodation had become inevitable. The flexible attitude to Duplessis's Quebec income tax, the new fiscal arrangements, the willingness to reach an agreement over medicare with Leslie Frost, all betokened the government's conviction that it should be possible to reach a *modus vivendi* with their several opposite numbers in the provinces. They were all partners in administration, after all.

And so they were, over the short term. Because the Liberal government negotiated from a position of strength, it was still able to offer its planning and co-ordinating services to the provinces, to integrate its bureaucrats with their bureaucrats, and to rely on the stronger federal team to prevail. If there was no longer an overt colonial dominance between the national government and its provincial satellites, there might be an administrative colonial bond, sustained by a subterranean administrative politics in which the true actors did all the real bargaining offstage, behind closed doors, in joint co-ordinating committees whose existence the electorate, and most of the politicians, only dimly suspected.

Such a system of accommodation, rather than confrontation, suited St Laurent's personal style – that of the corporation lawyer. It did not appeal to his more politically minded colleagues. 'Mr St Laurent was a lawyer's lawyer,' as Jimmy Gardiner commented. 'He wasn't a politician at all.' St Laurent as prime minister and party leader was indifferent to the needs and well-being of the Liberal party's local organization; though a partisan when he had to be, he interpreted his partisan responsibilities strictly, and in a limited fashion. They did not include close cohabitation with the Liberals' provincial branches, and it is remarkable that during the nine years of St Laurent's term of office the Liberal governments of British Columbia, New Brunswick, and Nova Scotia went down to defeat, while the Liberal parties of Ontario, Quebec, Saskatchewan, and Alberta regularly suffered drubbings at the polls. In a peculiar way the dismal records of the provincial parties brought them closer to the national organization: they became its pensioners, demoralized but docile.

The real dangers of the erosion of the Liberals' provincial bases were concealed by the phenomenal federal election victories of 1949 and 1953. It seemed self-evident that voters could maintain one allegiance provincially and vote, without self-contradiction, for another party in Ottawa. If that were true, then the fate of the provincial parties was indeed a matter of little moment for the Liberal chieftains in the national capital. But it was not so. The cases of Ontario and Quebec are particularly instructive. Leslie Frost, premier of Ontario, was a natural complement to St Laurent. As we have seen, Old Man Ontario took the path of co-operation rather than confrontation with the national government. His cool relations with the national leader of the Conservatives, George Drew, fostered the view that Ontario had, late in the day, discovered the path of true statesmanship that would mute partisan loyalties and provincial entanglements. That proved true in the late forties and early fifties, but only until some other conflict arose between the government of Ontario and the government of Canada. That conflict did arise in the mid-fifties over the proportion of the tax dollar that should go to the provinces, and to Ontario in particular. In the 1957 election Premier Frost's Conservative partisanship reasserted itself, and, while the subsequent loss of thirty Liberal seats cannot be blamed entirely on the weight of the provincial Conservative organization, there were many Liberals who wished that they had more viable provincial allies in the struggle against a revived Conservative party.

The situation in Quebec was even more serious, although its consequences were delayed until the 1958 federal election. There, the provincial Liberal party had been left to perish by the national leadership. And perish it did, annihilated in the 1948 provincial election by Maurice Duplessis's Union Nationale. The Liberals' provincial remnant was itself infiltrated by the Union Nationale (the party caucus in the mid-fifties had to take the unusual step of expelling some disguised Unionistes from its legislative ranks), while federal Liberal MPs often took refuge in electoral pacts with their provincial Union Nationale counterparts: neither, it was agreed, would campaign against the other. And neither did, until Duplessis's organization undertook a pre-emptive strike in 1958, reducing the Liberals in Quebec to a corporal's guard of twenty-five.

The Liberals' provincial weakness was compounded by another oddity. Although the Liberal government enjoyed closer relations with Canadian business than any other twentieth-century Canadian administration, it had not secured business's electoral support. Indeed, one of the keys to C.D. Howe's success as the government's link to the financial and industrial community was his utter indifference to partisan considerations where economic affairs were concerned. The businessmen with whom he dealt admired him, sought his advice, and fed him information; some even followed him into the Liberal party. But not all, and, indeed, not most. Howe continued to enjoy the company of his business friends after the 1957 Liberal débâcle, never more than when his lunch table of bank presidents and mining directors began grumbling about the new Conservative prime minister they had helped to elect. 'Well,' Howe would say, smiling sweetly, '*I* didn't vote for him.'

It is tempting to conclude that the Liberal party marched into its electoral Armageddon imbued with the primitive belief that partisan bullets could not touch it. Secure in its administrative non-partisanship, its co-operative competence, and its credo that most problems could be resolved administratively, it met an enemy for which it was totally unprepared. Psychologically disarmed, bereft of their provincial militia, the Liberals were easy prey. With their defeat the post-war period came to an end; a new era of doubtful, contentious politics had arrived.

PART FOUR

The Diefenbaker Years 1957-63

21

The Shape of Things

On June 21, 1957, John Diefenbaker became prime minister of Canada. He was the first Conservative to have led the country since 1935, when R.B. Bennett's five-year rule had ended. Canada had grown accustomed to Liberal rule. So had Ottawa. Eventually there were fourteen members in the new government including the prime minister himself. In forming a cabinet there were special problems about Quebec because the Tories had won so few seats there. An anglophone prime minister is expected to have a francophone lieutenant, but Quebec had supplied only nine Tory MPs, of whom few were distinguished and some were anti-Diefenbaker. In the end there were just three ministers from Quebec of whom only two were francophone, and neither of these ministers received an important portfolio. The significant ministers were Donald Fleming (finance), George Hees (transport), George Pearkes (defence), Gordon Churchill (trade and commerce), Davie Fulton (justice), Douglas Harkness (agriculture), Michael Starr (labour), and Alvin Hamilton (northern affairs and natural resources). When the cabinet membership was announced the press became especially excited about Starr: the Oshawa MP was the first Canadian of Ukrainian origin to sit in cabinet. Later Sidney Smith left the presidency of the University of Toronto, to take up the external affairs portfolio, which at first Diefenbaker had retained for himself. All the ministers were inexperienced, and many were suspicious. None of the members had held cabinet office, either federally or provincially, although some had run other things. George Hees, the new transport minister, for instance, had operated the family business before entering politics; George Pearkes, the new Minister of National Defence, had been a senior army commander.

The new ministers were suspicious of the senior civil service; the officials were nervous about the new ministry. The Conservatives knew that most officials were Liberal-appointed and Liberal-trained; the officials suspected that some ministers were madmen and that others were incompetent. In the event, things went better than might have been expected. Mandarins and ministers came to respect one another. But there were troubles, none the less. Some ministers wanted officials who could tell them how to do things and were not happy when officials told them why something could *not* be done. During the long Liberal regime, civil servants had learned to propose and dispose. It was not easy for them to convert themselves into mere executors of cabinet desires. But they tried and, on the whole, they succeeded.

Among the most suspicious was the prime minister himself. In his memoirs Diefenbaker reveals just how deeply he distrusted the officials, especially in External Affairs. While in office, he behaved in ways that clogged the diplomatic machine while confusing his associates. Presumably these things happened because he did not trust the officials. George Drew, Canada's new High Commissioner in London, communicated directly with the prime minister, instead of through the external affairs department. And, as one adviser later reported, when President Kennedy sent confidential messages from Washington they went directly to Diefenbaker, who would open them, 'look mysterious,' and then lose them. The same thing happened when Harold Macmillan, the British prime minister, sent confidential messages. Nor were such letters answered, by Diefenbaker or by anyone else. After a few awkward encounters between the American embassy and the department, the adviser trained the maids in the Diefenbaker home to trace down the missing papers – 'between his mattress, or ... in one of those deep drawers, or ... in a pocket in a clothes cupboard somewhere, or under the blotter.'[1]

Thanks to Liberal co-operation, during the session of 1957-8 things in Parliament went well. The new government was able to legislate, and it shoved masses of paper through the House machine. In this first year the prime minister appeared dynamic and decisive. In 1958, thanks to a maladroit Liberal manoeuvre, Diefenbaker was able to call a snap election; and, partly because of Union Nationale support in Quebec, the Conservatives swept the country, winning 208 seats out of 265. Henceforth Diefenbaker was much less decisive. It was almost as if he were afraid that his immense majority might become a steamroller. After all, he had long defended the rights of Parliament and in 1957 the Conservatives had campaigned largely on that issue. From 1958 until 1963 there would be plenty of time for debate; the opposition would be given enough rope; everything would be referred to the House of Commons. In other words, although the parliamentary machine continued to grind out new matter at an impressive rate it seemed to have slowed down. Media people, anxious to denigrate Diefenbaker, made the most of the chance with which he had presented them.

1 Peter Stursberg, *Diefenbaker: Leadership Gained 1956-62* (Toronto: University of Toronto Press 1975), 172-3.

In 1962 the Conservative government went to the country once more, but its popularity had melted away. In much of the country the leader no longer exerted the magnetism he had displayed in 1957 and 1958. Only on the prairies did the folk hold to the true Tory vision. Perhaps in the cities people had lost their taste for populist oratory; perhaps people were dismayed by the evidence of economic mismanagement, and, in defence policy, by signs of confusion or worse. In Quebec, the Liberals were in power and the Union Nationale machine had crumbled in disarray. Thus, in the election of 1962, the Tories garnered only 116 seats – 17 short of a majority. For a few months more, propped up by the Social Credit members, Diefenbaker clung to office. Then in 1963 another election was forced upon him, and this time, although no party won a majority, the Tories were defeated as definitely as the Liberals had been in 1957.

22

Delusions Complete or Partial

In the 1957 election campaign, and much more forcefully in 1958, Diefenbaker and the Conservatives spoke of a national 'vision.' Some of this related to social welfare measures and to the equalization of opportunity and development throughout the dominion. But most related to the North, and it was Diefenbaker's northern vision that captured the national imagination. Reminding us that he had already thought of this in 1956, Diefenbaker has written, 'In emphasizing the question of northern development and northern vision, I advocated a twentieth-century equivalent of Sir John Macdonald's national policy, a uniquely Canadian economic dream.'[1] Thanks to the intervention of Dr Merril Menzies, the northern dream acquired new substance. Menzies was a Saskatchewan-born economist who had written a doctoral dissertation on Canada's grain trade. Early in 1957 he had sent Diefenbaker a long brief on the development of the North. This, Diefenbaker tells us, captured his interest, inspiring 'the dream of opening Canada to its polar reaches.'[2] For the 1957 campaign he made Menzies a speechwriter, and later Menzies was assistant and economic adviser. In office, Diefenbaker discussed Menzies's ideas with Alvin Hamilton, a devoted Saskatchewan supporter who first entered Parliament in 1957. Hamilton became the Conservatives' Minister of Northern Affairs and National Resources, and held this portfolio until he moved to agriculture in 1960. He devoted himself to the 'vision' with vigour.

There is every reason to believe that the prime minister and Alvin Hamilton took the vision seriously. Certainly Merril Menzies did; once the campaign was over, he worked as an adviser who could help make it come about – whenever he was not advising Diefenbaker directly. As for the Conservative party, it is hard to believe

---

1 John G. Diefenbaker, *One Canada: The Crusading Years 1895 to 1956* (Toronto: Macmillan 1975), II.
2 *Ibid.*, 12.

that it did not detect the wonderful opportunities for regional patronage that the vision could present. Linking 'regional development' with a 'drive to the North' made everything possible – the South Saskatchewan Dam, a bridge at Prince Albert, a railway to Pine Point where Cominco had discovered a new mine, not to mention a host of branch railway lines and 'roads to resources.' Menzies thought Canada needed national goals and priorities together with some definite developmental projects, such as a national energy policy with a grid that would cover both power and pipelines. He and Diefenbaker also wanted to build an inventory of all Canadian resources, so as to plan their development. Out of these ideas came the Royal Commission on Energy, the National Energy Board, the roads to resources program, and a conference called 'Resources for Tomorrow.' The government also became interested in the prospects of finding Arctic oil and gas. From Ottawa's perspective, of course, Arctic resources had one great advantage: because they were not in any province they were wholly under dominion control. To Diefenbaker in particular, a vision of national development was especially appealing because of the tradition of Sir John A. Macdonald, on whom the prime minister was increasingly inclined to model himself.

But what really happened? Menzies was unable to bring Diefenbaker to the point, and in 1959 Menzies became an ordinary civil servant, working hard on the marketing of grain. An energy policy did come, but chiefly because it was politically essential to secure a protected vent for Alberta's overpriced oil. A power grid was discussed, and in the Columbia and Peace River conversations with British Columbia it played some part, but by 1962 the scheme had vanished without trace. Of course some dams, railways, and roads were built, often in co-operation with the provinces. At Frobisher and Inuvik work continued on the planning of modern townsites. During the Diefenbaker years there was plenty of oil exploration in the Arctic, thanks to the incentives with which the government had tried to encourage this, but there was no new production. A good deal was done for icebreaking, harbours, and airports in the North, and for Eskimo (Inuit today) education. Thanks to the new railway, the Pine Point lead-zinc mine began to produce. In the Northwest Territories explorers found one great tungsten deposit and an immense mass of iron ore. But in all the Diefenbaker years there were only two new northern mines – one gold and one tungsten – while in the North the two uranium mines and the one copper-nickel mine all shut down. In short, although by 1963 the vision had given Canada some useful and expensive new facilities, it had not transformed the economy or even significantly changed it. Moreover a serious national development strategy was still undefined.

In 1958 the Liberals made fun of the vision. They spoke of roads from igloo to igloo – good politics perhaps, but sketchy analysis. They did not ask the questions that now arise: what of the fragile ecology? What of the native peoples and their land claims? What of the markets for Arctic products and the prudence of early development? Indeed none of the parties, including the CCF, worried about these things or mentioned them. As for foreign ownership, the government had considered this matter, and tried to exclude foreign control by devices described later in Part IV. But as there was little more than exploration in the Arctic during the Diefenbaker years, these could not affect the balance between domestic and foreign control. In fact, the vision was the last gasp of Canadian developmentomania. In the eighties Canadians can still get excited about great projects, like a gas pipeline from Alaska, but nowadays they ask hard questions about need, impact, cost, and pay-off. In Diefenbaker's North the costs would have been immense, the need debatable, the impact destructive, and the pay-off negligible. The North is full of blackflies and mosquitoes. Its winter climate is appalling. It has little soil and not much by way of timber. In present-day terms, it is good only for oil drilling and mining. But mines and oil wells do not support a large or closely settled population, so it is not surprising that so few white Canadians want to live in the North.

For the masses who would linger in the south, cuddled up for warmth close to the American border, Mr Diefenbaker offered something else – a bill of rights. He had demanded this since the mid-thirties; he placed it in campaign platforms in 1957 and again in 1958; at length, in 1960, his Bill for the Recognition and Protection of Human Rights and Fundamental Freedoms received the royal assent. In no time Conservative MPs assisted by a patriotic toothpaste manufacturer were scattering the Act broadcast. Whether it would take root remained to be seen.

A dominion statute, the Bill of Rights could apply only in the federal sphere, and in principle it could be amended, repealed, or overruled by any later Parliament at any time. It also contained escape clauses to protect the security of the state. On the other hand, as Diefenbaker himself loved to explain, in Britain such parliamentary enactments had stood for centuries without anyone's trying to repeal them or supersede them; besides which the bill was so drafted as to give itself a certain primacy over other laws. Unless some other dominion statute stated that it was to 'operate notwithstanding the Canadian Bill of Rights,' then that other statute was to be 'construed and applied' on the basis of the new bill.

In 1960 Professor Edward McWhinney wrote that the bill might or might not be effective; if it were, it would work by strengthening the tendencies toward libertarianism that had been present in the courts since 1949. Ten years passed before a 'Bill of Rights case' reached the Supreme Court. Writing in 1976 Diefenbaker himself was still proud of his bill, although he observed that the courts had been shying away from it and he noted that in their recent judgments the courts had shown a 'desire to chisel away at some of the freedoms Parliament intended to protect.'[3]

3 John Diefenbaker, *One Canada*, II (Toronto: Macmillan 1976), 263-4.

What it all has meant is hard to say. Pierre Trudeau's subsequent proposal of a Charter of Rights binding both Ottawa and the provinces went one better than Diefenbaker. Of course, within the federal sphere Parliament is sovereign, and any parliament may repeal the acts of its predecessors. The provinces, meanwhile, have jurisdiction over 'property and civil rights,' while the courts have access to a long stream of precedents to defend the rights of the individual, not just in Canada but in Britain, and may in addition draw upon certain normative British statutes such as *habeas corpus*. But despite the fact that the Bill of Rights' usefulness has not been conclusively demonstrated, in the sixties and seventies, province after province has passed explicit 'human rights legislation.' Perhaps, as Diefenbaker believed, the provinces have been following his example.

Paralleling virtue at home there was virtue abroad. From 1959 until the fall of the Conservative government, Howard Green and Diefenbaker laboured long and hard, although not particularly helpfully, to produce world disarmament and the liberation of captive peoples. The United Nations provided them with a forum, but little was accomplished. When the United Nations tried to stabilize the newly independent Congo (now Zaire), Canada sent a signals unit, and helped to finance the UN airlift. Much further north, Canadian troops lingered in the sands of the Middle East hoping to keep the Egyptians and the Israelis apart. Through the Commonwealth Scholarship Plan (1960), the Colombo Plan (1950), and various bilateral and multilateral arrangements Canada gave modest sums to educate the poor countries and to help them grow. The totals were small – by 1961-2, $69.32 million per year in grant aid, or 0.19 per cent of GNP – far, far below the 1 per cent figure that had already begun to circulate as an aid target. But the Canadian public, Diefenbaker believed, would not willingly shell out more. As yet Canada had no 'aid community' that could lobby for larger subventions and sway public opinion. That would come in the sixties – first CUSO, then CIDA, then a steadily rising aid budget.

Diefenbaker was genuinely attached to the British connection, and genuinely distressed about the ever-closer integration between the Canadian and American economies. He worried about the extent of American direct investment and about the increasing importance of the United States as market and supplier. In the 1957 election campaign he announced that he would try to increase Canada's trading links with the United Kingdom, so as to reduce its dependence on the United States. He must also have been meditating about ways by which to control the inflow of American capital.

With respect to Anglo-Canadian trade, the Conservatives faced a difficult task. In 1872, Britain had supplied 60 per cent of Canada's imports and the United States, 32 per cent; in 1938 the percentages had been 18 and 63, and in 1957, 9 and 71. As for exports, over the same period Britain's importance had shrunk from 47 per cent to 41 per cent and then to 15 per cent, while the American share had changed from 44 per cent to 32 per cent and 59 per cent. These developments occurred in spite of the system of preferential tariffs, whose elaboration Canada had begun in 1897. During the period 1919-32, both Britain and Canada expanded their mutual tariff concessions. Canada acquired a protected British market for certain goods, especially foodstuffs, in exchange for tariff cuts on some British manufactures. The Ottawa Agreements of 1932 did something for some Canadian farmers and processors, but little for Britain, as the British share of Canadian import trade continued to fall. After the Second World War Britain mounted an export drive which increased its total sales on the Canadian market. This drive was helped by the preferential tariffs, which accorded duty-free entry to some British products, such as cars and parts. Even so, Britain's share still drifted downward. In addition, for many British manufacturers there were serious problems about quality control, spare parts, delivery dates, design, and after-sales service.

The American market was close and familiar; many Canadian producers depended on parts and components from American suppliers, often their own parent firms; Canadian consumers were more accustomed to American designs; Canadian businesses tended to buy American machinery because they could expect speedy and convenient after-sales service, and spare parts, from nearby American sources. These considerations militated against any easy switch from American to British suppliers. Further, nothing could be done by way of new preferential tariffs. The General Agreement on Tariffs and Trade (GATT), which both Canada and Britain had signed, prohibited any extension of preferential tariffs. During the war and the postwar years, Britain made further unilateral commitments to the United States, in which it promised not to invent any new preferences. In the brave new world of multilateral non-discrimination free trade zones could be created, but new preferential concessions could not be granted or the preferential margins widened. Thus tCanada could not extend the privileges that Britain already enjoyed. Nor was it obvious how Canada could divert its own exports from American markets to other places, either in Britain or elsewhere. Because the UK economy ws the slowest-growing in the industrialized world, and because its economy was in any event relatively small, Britain could not absorb much more of the traditional Canadian exports – wheat, minerals, and forest products. Nor could it buy large quantities of Canadian manufactures, many of which were not price competitive even after preferential concessions had been made. Moreover, from 1940 to 1958 Britain, Europe, and Japan had been obliged by their shortages of dollars to discriminate against goods from the dollar zone. As for the Communist economies in Europe and Asia, they practised rigorous exchange control, buying only what they absolutely required to feed their people and to industrialize. Neither salesmanship nor competitive pricing could make much difference when trying to sell to the Soviet Union, China, or

Albania. In Britain, western Europe, and Japan, dollar discrimination was already fading, but there was little Canada could do to speed its departure, except by purchasing more from these countries, something no protectionist government could readily contemplate.

In July 1957, responding to press questions, Diefenbaker proposed to divert 15 per cent of Canada's import trade from the United States to Britain. It seems that the figure occurred to him in the course of the interview. The United Kingdom responded by offering to form an Anglo-Canadian free trade area, the only sort of thing that the GATT rules would have permitted. Britain's idea was that over a fifteen-year period duties would be gradually reduced to zero. Neither Diefenbaker nor Fleming was prepared to consider the idea, which by late 1957 had sunk without trace. In his memoirs, Diefenbaker implies that the proposal was never intended seriously. For the rest of his administration, nothing more was heard about trade diversion; indeed, in its later years the Diefenbaker administration took certain measures that discouraged Canadian purchases in the United Kingdom.

Export trade was another matter. Coming from the prairies and believing himself to be at one with the small merchants and farmers of Canada, Diefenbaker was especially sensitive to the proposals for a European common market that had already begun to circulate when he became prime minister. What would happen in Europe was still obscure. The United Kingdom was pressing for a free trade area that would cover only manufactures, and that would not have a common external tariff. Such a scheme would have let Britain retain its own system of external duties, the imperial preferences on Canadian goods, and the free entry for wheat and other agricultural products. Britain could also have kept its own system of agricultural assistance, a system that could readily co-exist with large-scale imports of grain, meat, dairy products, apples, and other fruits. France and Germany, on the other hand, wanted a genuine economic integration with a common external tariff, and internal free trade not just in manufactures but also in agricultural goods. No one knew just how agriculture would be protected in such a common market, but as France and Germany already had high tariffs and quotas it was clear that Canadian foodstuffs would have hard sledding if Europe should integrate on the Franco-German model rather than the British.

When the Conservatives came to power in 1957, the Treaty of Rome had just been signed, establishing the European Economic Community on the Franco-German model, with Britain outside. The United Kingdom proceeded to form a Free Trade Area with the Scandinavian countries and some of the other European states that had not joined the Community. However, the British authorities quickly decided that their future lay inside the Community, not outside it, and in 1961 the United Kingdom applied for entrance. Many years afterward, Diefenbaker maintained that French President General de Gaulle had told him that France would never allow Britain to join. If so, it is difficult to understand the barrage of hostility with which the Conservative government of Canada greeted Britain's request. Canada, it seemed, could accept Britain's membership only if all Canada's preferential trading privileges remained intact. When the Commonwealth's prime ministers met at London in September 1962, Diefenbaker criticized not only Britain's application but the 'common market' itself. Fortunately for the Canadian government but unhappily for Britain, France did indeed veto Britain's membership; only in 1973 did the United Kingdom finally win entry, taking Denmark and Ireland with it.

Regrettably, although Ottawa officials had expected some sort of European economic union since the early 1950s, there is no sign that Diefenbaker or his ministers understood or tried to understand the forces that were impelling Britain into Europe. The rapidly growing markets were on the continent, where the post-war economic miracle had already been under way for more than a decade. Even if the Commonwealth markets had been fully open to Britain's goods, such markets as Canada and Australia could never be as receptive to Britain's manufactures as France, Germany, or Italy might prove to be. In any event, the Commonwealth countries wanted to industrialize too, and all of them pursued protectionist policies that limited Britain's ability to suply their markets. Admittedly the common market would raise the price of food in Britain. But the British standard of living had risen so high that the typical British family did not spend much of its income on food – at least, not on the raw imported component thereof. When food prices rose, living standards would drop, but only a little and only temporarily; on the other hand, when British manufactures enjoyed duty-free access to the immense European market there might well be a boom in British industry whose effects would soon swamp the effect of the more expensive food. In any event, ever since 1931 Britain had wanted to protect its own farmers against competition, and Commonwealth foodstuffs were not exempted from this desire. Even if the British were to stay out of the Community there was no guarantee that Britain would continue to allow relatively free access to Canada's foodstuffs. For Canadian grain growers the dynamic markets would be in the Communist countries and in the Third World, not in Britain or in western Europe. In defending the Commonwealth preferences Diefenbaker was simply defending the past.

The prime minister's Commonwealth trade initiatives were crowned, in a sense, by a Commonwealth Economic Conference which met in Montreal in autumn 1958. This conference was meant to devote itself to commodity agreements and economic development, not to tariff arrangements. But the government had other fish to fry. As Diefenbaker has written: 'From my point of view, the Commonwealth Trade and Economic Conference became a success the moment the British agreed to sweep away the greater part of their trade discrimination against dollar countries. This made the system of preferences, within the Commonwealth, so far as they applied to

Canada, a reality.'[4] Once again, as so often in trade and tariff bargaining, Canada had tried to get without giving. This time it succeeded.

Soon after the Conservatives took office the Gordon Commission issued its final report. In this report Walter Gordon expressed his concern about the size of American direct investment in Canada, and made a few mild and tentative suggestions for ensuring that Canadians could have access to jobs, research opportunities, and shareholdings in foreign-owned businesses. In his memoirs written nearly twenty years later, Diefenbaker echoed Gordon's concerns: too much American capital, too few export orders, too little Canadian control. Whatever one may think about Diefenbaker's own feelings while actually in office, there is no doubt that some members of his government did worry about these things. In September 1957, Diefenbaker himself told an American audience that American firms should offer stock to Canadians and should not regard Canada as an extension of the American market. In framing new regulations for resource development in the Northwest Territories, the Diefenbaker government insisted that firms should be controlled in Canada and that the majority of shares be owned in the dominion also. The regulations of 1960 required that oil and gas leases be granted only to Canadian citizens and residents, or to Canadian incorporated companies whose shares were either listed on a Canadian exchange or at least 50 per cent owned by Canadian residents and citizens. Of course these rules did not apply to the provinces, where provincial authorities determined policy with respect to resources. Nor was anything similar done with respect to manufacturing, finance, or real estate. In other words, the Diefenbaker government took some steps down the path recommended by the Gordon Commission, but the steps were tentative and timid. Nor did the government recognize, until after 1960, that the monetary policies of the central bank were encouraging exactly the sort of capital inflow that Gordon and Diefenbaker seemed to deplore. This topic is explored more fully in Chapter 23.

The prime minister believed in personal diplomacy and in world travel. Regrettably, the public became increasingly sceptical about the value of these adventures, and Diefenbaker himself eventually lost interest in them. It was all very well while President Eisenhower was installed in the White House, because the two old men understood and liked one another. It was different when the young and energetic John Kennedy came to power. Nor was the prime minister altogether happy in his Commonwealth relationships, seriously though he took them.

Beginning in June 1957, a few days after his installation, Diefenbaker travelled to numerous Commonwealth conferences. Then, in October 1958, he set off on a world tour that would take him to New York, London, and various European and Com-

---

4 John G. Diefenbaker, *One Canada: The Years of Achievement 1957-1962* (Toronto: Macmillan, 1976), 264.

monwealth capitals. After forty-eight days he returned to Ottawa, having visited fourteen countries. In his memoirs Diefenbaker described his travels and his conversations with the great in loving detail. It is far from clear that he accomplished anything, but in this he was not unique: such world junketings are rarely productive. In later years he addressed the United Nations, where he spoke eloquently in favour of freedom and self-determination in eastern Europe. These speeches did nothing to change Soviet policy, and they did the Conservatives no harm with Canada's 'ethnic communities,' but there is no reason to believe they were insincere.

Diefenbaker also made many trips to the United States, where he conferred with both Eisenhower and Kennedy. He found the former congenial, but soon fell out with the latter, whose brashness offended him. Perhaps, in addition, he was surprised to discover that Kennedy was as concerned to defend and advance American interests as he himself was anxious to advance Canadian. The Canadian position was admittedly difficult. Anxious to assert an independent national direction, in contradistinction to the 'Pearson pattern' which they saw as unduly acquiescent, the Conservatives none the less had no particular goals that they wished to attain in international affairs. They were, in fact, consistently negative. Canada would not join the Organisation of American States; it would not recognise Communist China; it would not approve the American response – nor the Soviet initiative – in the Cuban missile crisis of 1962, when the USSR installed ballistic missiles in Cuba and President Kennedy used a naval blockade to get them removed. As for its own defences, Canada would neither withdraw from NATO, nor increase its contributions to the alliance; Canada would cancel the production of its own interceptor-fighter and buy American Bomarc missiles, but it would not purchase the atomic warheads for which these missiles were designed. It would not force South Africa out of the Commonwealth, but would devise a form of words that would induce the South Africans to withdraw and not apply for readmission.

Apart from the problem of the EEC, which we have treated elsewhere, the main item on the Commonwealth agenda was the South African perplex. At the end of the Second World War the Commonwealth consisted of Britain, Ireland, Canada, Australia, New Zealand, and South Africa. Ireland quickly departed, but India, Pakistan, and Ceylon were soon admitted, and in 1957 Ghana and Malaya became members also. It had been established that if a Commonwealth country became a republic it could remain a member so long as it acknowledged the British sovereign as head of the Commonwealth; Eire withdrew before that fact had become clear. Formally, on becoming a republic a country had to reapply for Commonwealth membership. In 1961 South Africa became a republic. At that time its racial policies had long been a world scandal; the question was whether it should, or could, be readmitted, given these policies. The Commonwealth tradition was one of non-interference in the internal affairs of the members; it was different, however, if a country was applying or reapplying to join the club. Also, it was possible to argue that if South Africa were inside the Commonwealth it might be more amenable to suggestion. Perhaps in time it might be led to adopt less dreadful policies. At the Commonwealth Prime Ministers' Conference of May 1960, Diefenbaker did his best to convince the South African delegates that their nation's racial policies were repugnant to civilized opinion everywhere. Soon thereafter, South Africa asked to be assured that if she became a republic she would be welcomed back into the Commonwealth. Diefenbaker argued that no such assurance could be given in advance, but that an application could certainly be considered.

Later in 1960, South Africa held a referendum on the question of republican status, toward which it moved early in 1961. The South African authorities told their electorate that they would apply for readmission to the Commonwealth and suggested that other countries would welcome South Africa back. However, Diefenbaker later wrote that he did not see how he could support South Africa's readmission if the Union government would not even pay lip service to the concept of racial equality. He was not anxious to drive South Africa out of the club, but when the Commonwealth leaders reassembled in March 1961 he supported a passage in the draft communiqué that labelled apartheid as inconsistent with Commonwealth ideals and that committed Commonwealth countries to work for equality of opportunity, 'irrespective of race, colour, or creed.' Unable to accept such a declaration, the South Africans withdrew their proposal to rejoin the club. At the time, Diefenbaker regretted their decision, but he later wrote, 'in retrospect I consider it fortunate that the South Africans withdrew their application.'[5]

American wheat policy was a worry to the Conservative government. For some time, the United States had been producing surplus wheat, because it supported wheat prices at a level which consistently produced an excess of supply over demand. The US government bought the excess and stored it. This accumulation was worrying in and of itself; more worrying was the fact that the United States had begun to give food aid, and to sell wheat in exchange for 'soft currencies.' Such sales were, in effect, gifts. Although Canada did not support the price of wheat, the Canadian Wheat Board controlled the marketing of the crop, and as it was not willing to sell wheat at very low prices it piled up surpluses first in the elevators and then on the farms, once the elevators were full. In Britain and Europe, governments were ever more inclined to protect their own farmers; in Asia and the rest of the Third World, Canadian grain met competition from subsidized American grain and from American food aid. In December 1957 Diefenbaker suggested to the NATO council that there should be a World Food Bank which would hold stocks and supply them to countries that were in need. The Bank would also protect the world

5 *Ibid.*, 209-21.

against the risk of future crop failures or shortages. Of course the Bank would acquire food from Canada and the United States, thus reducing the weight of the surpluses. Who would pay the farmers was not altogether clear.

Unfortunately, in 1957 the United States was not interested in a food bank, although by 1960 there was a new secretary of state in Washington, and a new Food for Peace program. In 1958, the United States believed that to store all the food would cost too much. In 1960, when Diefenbaker and Eisenhower met once more, Eisenhower was more forthcoming, and later that year Canada and the United States jointly sponsored a UN resolution for a food bank. The resolution was adopted unanimously, but, like most UN resolutions, came to nothing.

In May 1961, three months after his inauguration as president, John F. Kennedy came to Ottawa. Having explained his worries about Cuba, he pressed Canada to join the Organization of American States. The Canadian elder statesman was not impressed by the young American leader, nor did Kennedy enjoy Diefenbaker. Visiting Ottawa in May 1961, the President mislaid a memorandum that fell into Diefenbaker's hands. Rather than return it, Diefenbaker used it to charge Kennedy with interference. Kennedy, we are told, vowed never to meet Diefenbaker again. It has also been suggested that he smoothed the path that led an eminent American public relations firm onto the Liberal payroll.

Such manoeuvres were not the best way to create confidence between the two great countries of North America. No doubt there was guilt on both sides, or perhaps one should say errors of judgment. But there were also substantive problems, and these really were not affected by the histrionics with which Diefenbaker loved to decorate the sober fabric of Canadian-American diplomacy.

Like other Canadian administrations, the Diefenbaker government loved royal commissions. Among those it established were the Glassco Commission, which looked into the organization of the public service, the Borden Commission on energy, the Hall Commission on health care, the Macpherson Commission on transportation, the Porter Commission on banking, the Carter Commission on taxation, and the O'Leary Commission on the problems of Canadian magazines. The Glassco Commission's report led to some rearrangements in the federal administration. The Hall and Carter commissions, which reported long after the Pearson administration had taken office, embarked on enormous research programs and produced voluminous reports that have not markedly affected events. The Porter Commission, which also reported after Diefenbaker's fall, did affect our banking arrangements. The Borden Commission developed a plan to reserve the Ontario market for Alberta oil. As for the O'Leary Commission's report, when it appeared in June 1961 it embarrassed the government greatly.

The 'magazine problem' had arisen because some American publications, especially *Time* and *Reader's Digest*, were producing special runs for Canadian distribution for which they solicited Canadian advertising. At that time there was already a Canadian edition of *Reader's Digest*, and *Time* was planning to print in Canada and to bring out a distinctive Canadian edition. Canadian mass magazines complained that such editions, plus the overflow of American magazines into Canada, amounted to unfair competition. Canadian magazines had to bear editorial costs but could not attract much advertising revenue; American magazines did not have very heavy editorial costs relating to Canada, but because they had large Canadian circulations they could and did draw advertising revenue away from the Canadian magazines.

No doubt the Americans were doing well out of selling magazines in Canada. But there was no reason to believe that Canadian advertisers would stick to the Canadian media, so long as the American media were so widely read in Canada. The O'Leary Commission suggested that Canada should prohibit the importation of any magazine that contained advertising for the Canadian market. Thus if Imperial Oil advertised in *Newsweek*, the Canadian Customs would bar *Newsweek* at the frontier. They also suggested that if a Canadian taxpayer advertised in any 'foreign' periodical, whether printed abroad or in Canada, his advertising outlays should not count as a business outlay for tax purposes. Canadians would still be able to buy foreign magazines so long as these did not have any advertising that was specifically directed at the Canadian market. As for the change in tax treatment, it was reasonable to suppose that Canadian advertisers would swallow the extra outlay for the sake of the circulation, and that to counter the tax change American publishers might lower their advertising rates in their 'Canadian editions.' If, as was alleged, they were doing so well out of their Canadian operations, presumably they could have afforded to do so, although of course they did not want to tell the government so. In his memoirs Diefenbaker explains that he received strong representations from *Reader's Digest* and *Time*. He mentions no pressure from the US government, and it is reasonable to suppose that if there had been any pressure he would not have concealed the fact.

The government adopted the O'Leary recommendations, but it made special provisions for the foreign periodicals that were already established in the country. When Canadians advertised in *Time* or *Reader's Digest*, they could count *half* of their advertising costs as business expenses. However, before the government could do anything about its decision, it fell from office. Like so many other matters, the 'magazine question' remained to perplex the Pearson government – and its successor as well.

The St Laurent government had set up a royal commission on broadcasting, under the chairmanship of Robert Fowler. In October 1958 it reported, and the government based much of the new Broadcasting Act on that report. No longer would the CBC license and regulate the private stations. Henceforth this would be done by the Board of Broadcast Governors or BBG, the ancestor of the present CRTC. Now there could be private television networking, and private TV stations in the big cities as well as in the small towns. New licences were eagerly sought and quickly awarded. No one was surprised that some new licences, such as the Toronto one, went to ardent Conservatives.

There was also the Bladen Commission on the automobile industry. Formed because the Canadian car industry had lost its export markets and much of its domestic market too, it recommended various inducements that might produce a more extended integration of the North American car industry. Although the Auto Pact of 1965 did not resemble the Bladen Plan, it originated with the Bladen Commission's report. Professor Bladen also wanted the government to put an import duty on British cars and remove the excise tax from Canadian-made cars. He got the latter but not the former. Not that it mattered much; already the British competitive position was eroding, and soon that erosion would have gone far enough to do the work for which Bladen suggested an import duty. On December 11, 1979, another Conservative government announced that it was ending the preferential tariff concessions to Britain, not just on cars and parts but across the board. By then, however, almost no one noticed, and certainly no one cared. Like Britain's imperial power, imperial preferences had faded into the woodwork, and as foci for debate they now mattered not at all. Other and more pressing economic issues perplexed the Conservative cabinet; to these issues we now turn our attention.

23

Managing the Economy:
Budgets, the Bank, and the Diefenbuck

Like most Canadian prime ministers, Diefenbaker was not particularly interested in economic affairs except insofar as they might affect his fate at the polling stations. But like most of his Liberal predecessors he was genuinely anxious to apply the power of the state to help the downtrodden and the disadvantaged. He was, in other words, a populist or a Red Tory, not a neo-conservative of the sort that surfaced in the late seventies. Coming as he did from Saskatchewan, the Prime Minister was especially interested in the fate of the farmers, the one group that seemed to have gained nothing and lost something in the great post-war boom. At first, it seemed, Diefenbaker was content to leave the problems of macroeconomic management – monetary policy, taxing, and spending – to the officials and to his competent and respected Minister of Finance, Donald Fleming. Unfortunately for Diefenbaker, the economy would not be left alone. Unemployment was inconveniently high. The management at the Bank of Canada soon revealed itself to be both inflexible and intractable. Finally, in 1961-2, the government itself provoked a flight from the Canadian dollar, after which it was obliged to pick up the pieces in an embarrassingly public way. In this chapter we present the story of these misadventures: the Conservative budgets; the crisis at the Bank of Canada; the dollar crisis; and Tory agricultural policy.

In 1957 the economy had already begun to turn downward. After taking office Diefenbaker was able to make parliamentary play with the evidence that the Liberals had known what was afoot. But there was little point in blaming the Liberals for their failure to prevent unemployment if the Conservative government could not manage to dispel it. Thereafter, although the unemployment rate fluctuated from time to time it remained inconveniently high throughout the Diefenbaker years.

Things were further complicated for the Tories by the fact that James Coyne was governor of the Bank of Canada. A Liberal appointee and a friend of Liberal ministers, Coyne was a man the Tories would instinctively distrust. Worse, he had his own views on economic policy, and these proved not to be the same as the new cabinet's, although within the cabinet Coyne certainly had some supporters. Worst of all, although Coyne would manage the Bank's affairs to accommodate the government's needs he would not co-operate in any program of fiscal and monetary expansion – the medicine that some ministers and most economists would have prescribed at the time, given the slow growth and rising unemployment of the late fifties.

At least as serious were the troubles of the resource industries, whose development had helped to fuel the expansion of the early and middle fifties. The market for uranium did not develop as rapidly as governments and companies had hoped. By 1960 mines were closing, and in the new mining towns life had become alarmingly insecure. The Americans were still subsidizing the export of wheat. As a consequence grain piled up on Canada's farms and prices fell disconcertingly. Thanks to competition and the ever-growing tanker fleet the oil of Venezuela and the Middle East was becoming cheaper, and it penetrated ever more deeply into the American and Canadian markets, with painful effects on Alberta's oil industry. The emerging European trade blocs would do further damage to Canada's metals industries, lumbering, and wheat; although Britain and Europe were dismantling the discriminations against dollar goods that had survived the years of post-war reconstruction, there was no reason to be optimistic about the future European demand for Canada's staple exports.

As these storm clouds gathered on the horizon the government was much more preoccupied with a tempest in a teapot – what to do about the unemployment insurance system. At March 31, 1957, the unemployment insurance fund held a surplus of $871 million. The surplus had accumulated because in planning the contributions in the early forties the actuaries had assumed that unemployment would be higher than it had proved to be from 1940 to 1957. Although the St Laurent government had revised the scheme so as to make the payouts larger, nevertheless the fund had continued to grow. Since the end of 1952 unemployment benefits had been larger than current contributions, but until the end of 1956 the fund had been earning enough interest to maintain itself and even to increse. Then, with rising unemployment, the fund began to shrink; and thereafter it declined inexorably throughout the Diefenbaker years. Although the government raised the rates of contribution it also made the payout easier and more generous, while at the same time unemployment stayed inconveniently high. Hence annual outlays rose from $210 million in 1956 to $494 million in 1962, while the fund shrank away to nothing.

It was easy for opponents and journalists to claim that there was something wrong about all this. Was not the government dissipating the unemployment insurance fund? Economists saw the matter rather differently. When people received unemployment benefits they spent the money, creating extra demand and extra jobs at a time when there were not enough jobs to go around. If government had tried to 'protect the fund,' it would have had to raise taxes. But the extra taxation would have reduced the after-tax income that people could spend. Certainly, if jobs and output are seen as being of paramount importance, then the government was right to spend the fund, and it would have been wrong to find the money for additional benefits by raising taxes.

The same general argument applies to the old age security payments, which also fell outside the ordinary budget. Here, too, the special tax collections did not cover the outlays, and this had been the case since 1952, when the special old age security fund was set up. Unlike the unemployment insurance fund, however, this 'fund' had never contained anything, and had always required subsidy from the ordinary budget. The Diefenbaker government raised the old age pension without raising old age security taxes. When unemployment was relatively high, both decisions were certainly wise.

So much for the largest extra-budgetary items. What of the budgets themselves?

During the Diefenbaker years there was constant conflict both within the cabinet and among the government's advisers with respect to taxing and spending policy. Donald Fleming, the Minister of Finance, preferred to balance his budgets, although he was never able to do so. Many advisers, especially those in the Department of Finance, argued in the same way. Afraid of inflation, they disliked new spending and they hoped the government would cut taxes. On the other hand, Dr Merril Menzies thought the government should try to eliminate unemployment by cutting tax rates and by new spending, especially on national and northern development. The prime minister and many members of the cabinet thought the same. Thus before the end of 1957 the Conservatives had asked Parliament to cut the income tax and to authorize various new kinds of spending programs. In later years the government did more of the same, although it was more and more inclined to concentrate on extra spending, not tax cuts.

It was easy to make fun of the results. On the one hand, the finance minister was known to want balanced budgets; on the other hand, the accounts were never balanced, and only twice did Fleming dare even to forecast a surplus. As time passed, Fleming himself became even less attached to the idea of a balanced budget, and from December 1960 through spring 1962 he wanted to cut taxes and raise spending so as to create new jobs. Although the budgetary expenditures were consistently higher than budgetary revenues, in only one of his seven budgets did Fleming actually raise tax rates; in all the other budgets, rates were reduced. Fun was also made of the fact that things never came out the way Fleming said they would. When he made his first budget statement on December 6, 1957, he forecast a surplus of $152 million for the fiscal year 1957-58; in reality, there was a deficit of $39 million. On March 31, 1960, he forecast a $12 million surplus for 1960-61, but in that period there was a $340 million deficit. And these figures do not include the deficits on such things as unemployment insurance and old age security. Including these and other adjustments, the total deficit in 1958 was $767 million, although the budget deficit

Tory cakewalk.
Prime Minister Diefenbaker, Minister of Finance Donald Fleming, and Minister of
Trade and Commerce George Hees (Macpherson, 1961). Reproduced with the
permission of the *Toronto Star*

was only $38 million. Similarly, in 1961 the total deficit was $410 million, although the budget deficit was $340 million. But there was nothing really discreditable about all this. Fleming's forecasts went wrong partly because the economy grew rather slowly, and partly because his colleagues kept inventing new ways to spend money. Thanks to the latter, spending ran ahead of the estimates; thanks to the former, revenue rose less rapidly than one might have hoped. What would have been really discreditable would have been to make reality march with the forecast by cutting expenditure or raising tax rates. Given the high unemployment and the slow growth, neither medicine would have been a good prescription.

Because unemployment was inconveniently high, while prices were barely rising and the economy was growing rather slowly, it was sensible for the Conservative government to cut tax rates and to devise new spending schemes. Relative to government spending or national output the results were far from bad. In the event, of course, these measures were not enough to get rid of all the unemployment, although they were certainly large enough to reduce it. But should the deficits have been larger? Or could they have been?

It is always easy for Parliament to cut tax rates and to give citizens more grants and larger subsidies. The same goes for intergovernmental payments – transfers from the dominion to the provinces and municipalities. And it is always easy to prescribe such medicine when unemployment rises. But history has taught us that after unemployment has risen it generally falls. At such times a prudent government may want to *raise* the tax rates and *reduce* the subsidies to citizens and junior governments, although politically that is a much harder thing to do. And, of course, the grants and subsidies and benefits and welfare payments get built into the economic and social system so that people come to depend on them. Thus a prudent government, hoping to fight unemployment by cutting tax rates and by pumping out grants and subsidies, might do well to restrain itself. Indeed, some observers think that the Conservative government was not sufficiently restrained. One is left with new kinds of government spending on goods and services, especially on such installations as roads, canals, public buildings, and the like. The Conservatives were very interested in such things. Diefenbaker, prompted by Merril Menzies, had seen a 'northern vision,' and he did not just dream dreams about it; he set out to build railways and roads in northern Canada, and he meditated on a second Trans-Canada Highway. Under his leadership the government began to spend much more on technical surveys, so as to map Canada's natural wealth. In the 1962 election campaign he came near to enunciating a still more grandiose developmental vision.

As anti-unemployment weapons such schemes have one important advntage: they need not go on forever. One can build a few 'roads to resources' without committing oneself to build a thousand miles or so, every year, indefinitely. As regional and personal patronage they are ideal, too. But the projects take time to work out, and at any given time there may only be a limited number of projects that a government can sensibly undertake. It is easy to talk of extra spending, but sometimes it is hard to find anything useful to spend on. And compared with the St Laurent administration, the Diefenbaker government was certainly an ingenious and imaginative spender!

It is also important to remember that in the late fifties there was a good deal of confusion about the *source* or *origin* of the unemployment. When unemployment is too high because demand is too low, it makes sense to cut tax rates, devise new spending programs, and pay larger subsidies to citizens and junior governments. When output and employment have fallen from a previous peak, it is reasonable to suppose that the trouble is deficient demand. But as shown in Part I, output and employment *rose* during the Diefenbaker years. It was certainly not a depression, or even a recession, but rather a deceleration. This fact worried politicians and officials who thought the standard Keynesian medicine too crude. Moreover, many observers thought there was something odd about the unemployed themselves. Inside and outside government it was noticed that the unemployed were chiefly those who had few skills and little or no education. The better educated, it seemed, had no trouble finding or holding a job, so perhaps the real trouble was a lack of education. The Department of Labour had discovered that in the post-war expansion, Canada had drawn many skilled workers from Britain and Europe, but relatively few from its own native-born population. Perhaps the real trouble was a mismatch betwen labour supply and labour demand, they reasoned. Or perhaps the real trouble was 'automation,' the replacement of men by machines. In the late fifties, automation was a vogue word in the media and among the literati; its function was much the same as 'ecology' or 'energy crisis' in the late sixties and seventies.

These conflicting counsels inspired the Diefenbaker government to try various things. Grants to universities were doubled, and arrangements were made by which the Quebec universities, for the first time, might receive dominion funds. In 1960, legislation was passed to allow the dominion to help bear the costs of technical and vocational education. Co-operating with the provinces and sharing the costs, the dominion financed many new technical and vocational schools and gave large grants for school staff and equipment. A propaganda campaign, aimed at keeping pupils in school, was also instituted. About automation nothing could be done, although by increasing the period of entitlement to unemployment benefits from sixteen to fifty-two weeks the government may have helped to cushion its impact.

The problem of winter unemployment had always been a serious matter in Canada, but now it, too, attracted still more attention. Strictly speaking, it cannot have affected the average level of unemployment, which was adjusted for seasonal variation; there was no reason to believe that winter unemployment was more severe under Diefenbaker than under St Laurent or King. But it was a distressing social problem, and one that the public was less and less willing to accept as a fact of life.

The St Laurent government had introduced a system of 'seasonal unemployment benefits,' which allowed workers to receive special assistance even if they had not contributed enough to qualify for the ordinary unemployment benefit. The Diefenbaker government made the terms more generous and extended seasonal benefits to farm labourers and fishermen, but by subsidizing municipalities and the construction trades it tried to encourage winter *work* as well. These subsidies were withdrawn under Pearson, but they seem to have changed the behaviour of the Canadian construction industry, which learned a good deal about year-round working.

Of course these educational and climatic schemes had their impact on the budget, and therefore on the level of spending in the economy. But they were not introduced for that reason. Rather, they were meant to improve the economic *structure*, making the economy perform better in the longer run. Indeed, years would pass before the university funding and the vocational education plan could affect the labour market in any important way. The Conservatives must have realized this fact, but it did not deter them.

Nor should one forget George Hees, the Minister of Trade and Commerce, who mobilized our trade commissioners and businessmen in the interest of the export trade. No one knows just how effective Hees' razzle-dazzle methods may have been, but certainly they were pushing in the right direction. It is a pity that until 1961 they were impeded by the exchange rate: when the Canadian dollar stood relatively high while productivity was relatively low and wage rates were not low enough to offset these two facts, Canadian manufacturers had difficulty keeping their domestic markets, to say nothing of finding new foreign ones.

Fleming himself later explained that he knew unemployment was growing 'into '59.' He argues, however, that the government's approach was 'realistic. ... We did take measures to increase direct employment by government programs.' Michael Starr, then Minister of Labour, has said that the winter works and the school programs were meant 'to relieve unemployment.' Fleming has also explained that although he was proud of the balanced budget that he introduced in 1960, three weeks later things were looking much worse. 'It was necessary then, as we thought, to resort to more fiscal measures to accompany any measures in the monetary field that the Bank of Canada might see fit to take.' Alvin Hamilton has asserted that the 'tight money budget' of 1959 actually stopped a recovery.[1] It was only when devaluation began in mid-1961, he argues, that Canada really began to absorb this unemployment. But Hamilton exaggerates the effect of Fleming's tax increases – foolish though these doubtless were, given the levels of unemployment and prices. There is no doubt that by June 1961 the government was consciously planning to force the

---

1 Peter Stursberg, *Diefenbaker: Leadership Gained 1956-62* (Toronto: University of Toronto Press 1975), 210-11, 213, 214.

dollar down so as to make jobs, a sensible step which might well have been taken sooner.

As Fleming explained to Diefenbaker shortly after making his first budget speech on June 17, 1958, the government would have trouble borrowing the sums that would be needed both to pay its current bills and also to retire or roll over $19 billion in old loans. Matters would quickly get even worse since, between the beginning of 1959 and mid-1966, Ottawa would also have to repay some $10 billion in old Victory Loans. For the time being the government would not be able to borrow on a long-term basis; instead, it would have to raise $400 million from the Bank of Canada. Fleming also suggested that the government might convert $6.4 billion of the old 3 per cent Victory Loans into new bonds. These would pay higher interest, and would have various terms; there would be cash bonuses for those who agreed to convert their holdings of the old bonds into new ones. As Diefenbaker later explained: 'This proposal ... would lift from the market the burden of the substantial amount of early maturities. For years afterward, debt management would be simpler. Above all, this would restore confidence and give us the opportunity to carry on with our development plans.'[2]

The conversion involved an immense selling effort, and this was successful in that by September 15, 1958, some 90 per cent of the old Victory Loans had been converted into the new government bonds. Unfortunately, the new terms were not attractive enough to make people hold the bonds, once converted. Thus at once the public began to sell the new paper. For a time the Bank of Canada supported the market by buying government bonds. But early in October 1958 it decided that it could not go on doing so: to buy up the bonds the Bank had to create new money, and this it was unwilling to do on the necessary scale. Thus, as interest rates went up, the bonds depreciated. The people who had converted their Victory Bonds were annoyed, and criticized the government for 'mismanaging the conversion.' For those who had held relatively short-dated Victory Bonds the complaint had some merit: they could have held their old bonds to maturity, cashed in each $100 bond for its full face value, and started again; now if they wanted to get the face value they would have to hold the new bonds for some time, often for a good many years, as the new issues ranged in term from three and a quarter to twenty-five years.

More serious was the economists' complaint that because the conversion had replaced short-term bonds with longer-term ones it lengthened the average term of the national debt. Because short-term bonds feel more like money, if the average term rises the public is likely to spend and buy less – hardly what one should prescribe for a recession. On the other hand, to facilitate the conversion and to support

---

2 John G. Diefenbaker, *One Canada: The Years of Achievement 1957-1962* (Toronto: Macmillan 1976), 276.

the new bonds for a couple of weeks the Bank of Canada had had to create $1 billion of new money. By expanding the money supply, the Bank may well have offset the contractionary effect that would normally have followed from the conversion itself. If the Bank had allowed the money supply to rise further there would be no reason to criticize the conversion operation, or even to mention it. As things were, however, the operation is interesting not only for its effects but also for what it revealed about the relations between the Conservative government and the governor of the Bank of Canada.

During Coyne's term as governor, the Bank allowed chartered bank reserves to rise by 4 per cent per year, while output grew 3.1 per cent per year on the average. Thus it would seem at first sight that money was outgrowing output, contributing to inflationary pressure rather than restraining it. However, the extra reserves were concentrated in the single year 1958, when the central bank was financing both a massive bond issue and the conversion plan that has just been described. Coyne regretted the resultant increase in the reserves and in the money supply. Although he thought it 'justified and unavoidable' that the Bank should help to finance the government's deficit and its conversion plan, he believed that the increase was 'substantially greater than would have been necessary for monetary and economic reasons alone.'[3] This statement appears to mean that he would have preferred to see the money supply grow more slowly, in spite of the rising unemployment rate, which he knew was becoming a social and economic problem in 1958, and in spite of the fact that the general price level was no longer rising.

The following year, having explained once more that 'the primary function of the central bank is to regulate the total quantity of money,' Coyne went on to say that he had kept chartered bank reserves 'on a broadly stable basis.'[4] In fact, although prices were still stable and unemployment was still high, bank reserves *fell* by 4.7 per cent while output *rose* nearly 4 per cent! The Bank was applying a genuine squeeze. It is hardly surprising that in Canada the cost of credit rose, both absolutely and in comparison with American interest rates. With respect to the cost and availability of credit, government and governor were already on a collision course.

Coyne knew that too many Canadians were out of work. He knew that many Canadians, inside and outside government, blamed him. But he refused to accept any blame. Since unemployment rates had been rising for a decade, he argued that the cause must be some long-standing underlying structural deficiency, not Bank of Canada policies. There was no shortage of money, he said, and no deficiency of demand. The problem, he wrote in 1961, was an excessive deficit on the balance of

---

3 Bank of Canada, *Annual Report of the Governor*, 1959.
4 Bank of Canada, *Annual Report of the Governor*, 1960.

payments. What was needed was a tighter control over imports so that Canada could live within its means.[5]

Unfortunately, by tightening credit relative to the situation in the United States Coyne had indirectly and probably unintentionally helped to create the problem of which he complained. In 1959 short-term loans earned 4.81 per cent in Canada and 3.42 per cent in the United States, while long-term government bonds paid 4.93 per cent in the former country and 4.06 per cent in the latter. It was hardly surprising that, whenever possible, Canadian businesses and junior governments were raising funds abroad. When they brought their borrowings home they had to exchange American dollars for Canadian, thus forcing up the exchange rate – the price of Canadian dollars – and encouraging Canada to import more goods and to export less. Since the exchange rate was floating, any extra inflow of money tended to force up the rate, generating an extra current-account deficit. For an underemployed economy a more unwise policy would have been hard to devise. It would have been more sensible to use monetary policy in the reverse direction, making credit cheaper in Canada relative to the United States so as to discourage foreign borrowing and encouraging the exchange rate to float down. But this sensible policy Coyne would not countenance.

During 1958-61, Canadian productive capacity rose much more rapidly than production. Hence the level of unemployment went up, hovering between 6 and 7 per cent for four years. Yet during those years Canada imported $4.9 billion in foreign capital. Believing that the unemployment problem was deeply rooted in Canada's economic structure, Coyne asserted that it was 'unsound and dangerous' to increase the money supply fast, or at all. Thus he continued to fight inflation because he thought it was right to do so, even though prices had been almost stable since mid-1957.

Among Canadian economists the policies of Governor Coyne created a rage and dismay so strong that, in 1961, many of them signed an open letter that requested his dismissal on grounds of incompetence. In Ottawa, government mandarins closed ranks, defending one of their own against outside criticism. To ensure that none of the offending economists would ever receive government employment, a black list was prepared and extensively circulated. However, the government itself was becoming alarmed. Coyne's monetary policies were creating difficulties that were as much political as economic.

Coyne had always made Diefenbaker unhappy. Not only was the governor uncommunicative and an 'unregenerate Grit,' he was also unsympathetic in that he was a 'tight money' man, who worried much more about inflation and foreign control than about unemployment.[6]

---

5 Bank of Canada, *Annual Report of the Governor*, 1961.
6 *One Canada ... 1957-1962*, 274.

Early in 1960, having failed to convert ministers to his views, Coyne began to make public speeches; at the same time his 1959 *Annual Report* appeared. The governor wanted Canadians to live within their means. In this desire it is hard to avoid seeing an extrapolation of the extreme thriftiness that characterized his own style of life. Canadians, Coyne thought, should save more, so as to reduce their dependence on foreign capital by reducing their living standards. Imports should be cut and/or restricted. Tax rates should rise. The Canadian dollar should be pegged at par but not lower. Governments should spend less. Foreign investment should be discouraged. Thus Coyne, to the intense embarrassment and irritation of the cabinet, was expounding on economic policy in general and fiscal policy in particular. And he was not consulting the government before doing so.

Ever since Coyne's appointment there had been troubles about the meshing of fiscal and monetary policy. But the speeches were deeply troubling. So was Fleming's discovery, early in 1960, that Coyne was not willing to co-operate in government policy; he would continue to make speeches about a fiscal policy that was not the government's, and he would not manage credit in the ways that the government thought right and proper. Insult was added to injury when Fleming and Diefenbaker discovered that the Bank had voted the governor a pension of $25,000 a year, for life.

At the time it was argued by observers that Donald Fleming was relatively close to the Coyne position. He was willing to act against capital inflows; he seemed to distrust the idea of Keynesian deficit financing. Other cabinet members, such as Alvin Hamilton, Gordon Churchill, and Diefenbaker himself were thought to oppose Coyne. By now it is reasonably clear that Coyne had little support within the cabinet. Fleming had defended the governor because he was a public servant; and the finance minister acted against foreign investment simply to bring down the value of the Canadian dollar. It was the question of the governor's pension that was the last straw. Fleming was so incensed that he took the matter to cabinet, where it was quickly agreed that Coyne would have to go. Not only was the pension unconscionable; as Fleming later explained: 'I was at last convinced that it was no longer possible to reconcile Mr Coyne's tenure and the policies that he was following and the fiscal policies that he was advocating with the responsibilities of the government.'[7]

Fleming tried to shift Coyne by stealth. The governor, whose term would end in six months, refused to go quietly. Instead he rushed to the press. On June 13 he refused to resign; on June 14 Fleming told the House that he would be fired; on June 20 he announced that there would be a royal commission on banking and finance; on June 23 Diefenbaker introduced a bill by which the office of the gover-

7 Stursberg, *Diefenbaker ... 1956-62*, 240.

nor of the Bank of Canada would be deemed to have become vacant; on July 13, following stormy scenes in the Commons and distressing ones in the Senate, where the governor shed tears before the legislators, Coyne at last resigned. On July 24 the government appointed Louis Rasminsky to succeed him. At once Rasminsky issued a statement that gave the government the ultimate responsibility for monetary policy. While it was true that Graham Towers, the first governor, and even Coyne himself, had issued similar statements, it was already clear that the third governor, like the first but unlike the second, would work in close co-operation with the government of the day.

What difference had Coyne really made? Even now it is hard to tell. No doubt his 'tight money' policies raised Canadian interest rates, both absolutely and relative to American rates. Hence the policies encouraged Canadians to borrow abroad. As the exchange rate was floating, these foreign borrowings raised the exchange rate when the borrowers exchanged their US dollars for Canadian dollars in the foreign exchange markets. Imports of goods were encouraged, and exports discouraged, at least to some extent. On the domestic scene, Coyne's influence may have strengthened the forces within the government that wanted to control borrowing and outlays, so as to prevent inflation, while working toward a more nearly balanced budget. But some ministers, such as Donald Fleming, had similar desires, and so did some of the senior Finance officials. Scanning Diefenbaker's spending programs, one sees little sight of fiscal rectitude on the 'Coynesian' model. As for the crusade against foreign investment and the reduction in the exchange rate, by 1960 the Prime Minister himself was talking of the former, while important ministers, such as Alvin Hamilton, were arguing for the latter. In 1960-1, commentators often examined the entrails of government and ministerial statements in an effort to discover whether Coynesianism or Keynesianism was in the ascendant. But Coyne probably had little effect on the course of government fiscal policy. Indeed, it may have been because he himself realized this fact that he began his ill-starred program of public pronouncements.

In the 1962 campaign, and thereafter, Liberal publicists such as Walter Gordon made much of the Coyne affair. Few observers thought that the government had been wrong to ditch a recalcitrant governor; although some thought it would have been more tactful to let the man serve out the remaining six months of his term, many thought he should have been eased out long before. Some held that the government had mismanaged the ejection by concentrating excessively on the pension question instead of on the more general and important questions of economic policy that Coyne's line had raised. These charges were certainly justified. Others believed that the Coyne affair had sapped business confidence, thus depressing investment and helping to cause the outflow of funds in 1961 and the exchange crisis of 1962. As to investment, it is hard to believe that any businessman foregoes a chance of profit just because he thinks that the government is inept. With regard to capital flight, however, only Diefenbaker doubted that the Coyne affair made financiers very nervous indeed.

In June 1961, having disposed of Coyne, the government began to contrive a depreciation of the floating Canadian dollar. In principle such a thing is easy to manage: the government can buy foreign money in the market and supply Canadian dollars to the market, thus changing the supply-demand balance. The Canadian dollar would decline because there were more Canadian dollars on offer relative to the demand for them; if we look at things from the foreigners' angle, there is less foreign money on offer to private buyers because the Canadian government is absorbing some of the supply. In the June budget of 1961 Donald Fleming announced that the government would do exactly this. But he did not say how far the dollar would go. Therefore he set up a one-way option for speculators. Everyone knew that the dollar would fall. Hence everyone wanted to sell dollars now, not later. For some time the government's Exchange Fund was absorbing foreign money so as to depreciate the Canadian dollar. But as summer 1961 passed into winter the market got the message, and private speculators moved rapidly out of Canadian currency. Where it had once *absorbed* foreign money so as to force our dollar down, now the Exchange Fund was *supplying* foreign money so as to slow its descent. Further, the International Monetary Fund had become worried. A signatory to the IMF agreement, Canada was supposed to maintain a fixed exchange rate, and was definitely not supposed to manipulate the rate so as to gain a competitive advantage. In 1950 the IMF had allowed Canada to float the rate, but only on the understanding that it would not manipulate it. Since June 1961 Canada had been doing exactly that. Clearly in this respect, as in others, Canada was ignoring its international commitments.

In June 1961, an American dollar cost $1.0055 Canadian. The 'exchange premium' had gone. From July through October the price was around $1.03 but in November and December it slid downward, hovering around $1.05 from January through May. That is to say, ninety-five cents US would now buy one Canadian dollar. In June 1961, when Fleming had announced the new policy, our exchange reserves were $1,985 million (US). By December they had risen to $2,056 million. In spring 1962 the reserves fell month by month, from $1,922 million in January to $1,495 million in May. When the exchange rate and the reserves are falling together, it is a sure sign that the Exchange Fund is spending reserves to slow the descent of the currency. Although by mid-March it seemed that the government was trying to stabilize the Canadian dollar at ninety-five cents US, no one could be sure about the future. As Professor Donald Forster wrote at the time, 'many speculated that the massive reductions in reserves might destroy market confidence that the authorities could control the rate.'[8]

On April 10, Fleming explained that although the government would not hesitate to spend its reserves so as to 'prevent sudden or erratic movements in our exchange rate,' it was not willing to fix any particular rate. It would seem that the Prime Minister did not notice what his Minister of Finance was saying; in any event, he later denied any knowledge of the problem. Three weeks later, on May 2, 1962, the exchange rate was pegged at 92.5 American cents. It would remain there until mid-1970.

The government did its best to convince the electorate that the devaluation would do no harm. The external value was one thing; the domestic purchasing power was another. Devaluation, in other words, did not mean inflation. Of course this was absurd. Canada imports almost 25 per cent of what it uses. When the dollar falls relative to other currencies, prices naturally rise. Indeed, this happened almost at once after the devaluation of May 2.

Donald Fleming has since argued that no one in government foresaw the crisis. This statement is hard to accept: anyone could see that to keep the rate at ninety-five cents the government had been spending its exchange reserves. When the problem came to his attention late in April, Fleming conferred with his officials and with Louis Rasminsky, the new governor of the Bank of Canada. Fleming decided that the rate must be pegged. But the officials could not agree on a rate. So Fleming himself chose 92.5 cents. Having dispatched officials to the IMF in Washington, he reported his decision to the Prime Minister. Diefenbaker reluctantly agreed with the action. Already he feared that the Diefendollar would cost his party the election. He was probably right.

Thanks to the election campaign, the cabinet was scattered across the country. The Prime Minister was in Quebec. Alvin Hamilton, the agriculture minister, who had wanted devaluation for more than a year, was in Vancouver, where he knew nothing and cared less about the means by which Fleming had chosen the rate. Nevertheless, on June 8 he announced that it was a compromise between two groups of cabinet members, one group favouring ninety cents and the other ninety-five cents. The speech made Fleming and Diefenbaker very angry. It also sparked a further speculative run because it suggested that the government might not defend the new rate. On June 10 Fleming did his best to repair the damage. His efforts were without effect. The election of June 18, returning as it did a House of minorities, may have made matters worse. Perhaps the financial community assumed that there would be confusion, runaway budget deficits, and inflation; perhaps it was simply nervous. Whatever the cause, in the second quarter of 1962 Canada had to cope with

8 *Canadian Annual Review*, 1962, 178.

an outflow of capital funds that reached $245 million. And it was mainly Canadian residents who were speculating against their own money by moving funds out of the dominion.

Diefenbaker still maintained in his memoirs that he did not know of the problem until April 29. It was wrong of the officials, he implies, not to have told him earlier. As for the decision to peg at 92.5 cents, he argued that this cost him the 1962 election, and that it was unnecessary. Better, he maintained, to have used the national exchange reserves to hold the rate at some target figure until after the election; at that more propitious time the government could have chosen an exchange rate and announced it.

In the Conservative leader's account the whole incident is given an overtone or undertone of conspiracy. The officials, he suggested, might have been influenced by 'partisan considerations.' As for the crisis itself, that too received a conspiratorial explanation from a leader that journalists were already calling the Father of Lies. Diefenbaker wrote in his memoirs: 'The only explanation of the 1962 crisis that makes any sense is that it was orchestrated for political reasons. ... The crisis began with a "spooking" of the New York money market. I believe that it is more than possible, indeed highly probable, that the administration of President Kennedy used its influence to bring this about.'[9]

Diefenbaker admitted that he had no proof. Others have suggested, with no better evidence, that the trouble began with Liberal financiers in Toronto. Presumably we are to imagine that Walter Gordon, who was running the Liberal campaign, instructed all the corporations whose accounts his firms audited to speculate against the Canadian dollar.

Until we have much more documentation no historian can refute such allegations or even discuss them seriously. In any case they are not very plausible. First, they assume that financiers and industrialists readily respond when politicians issue commands for political reasons. All our experience suggests that this assumption is not correct. Second, they ignore the possibility that there were good economic reasons for speculating against the Canadian dollar. But such reasons certainly did exist. The government had said that it wanted the dollar to fall. Noticing that fact, financiers would naturally sell Canadian dollars and buy other moneys so long as the fall had not yet occurred. In so doing they would make the Canadian dollar fall, and this fall would bring further nervous men into the market as sellers of Canadian dollars. Third, these and other conspiracy theories ignore the possibility that, apart from speculation on a fall, there were good reasons for a weakening of Canada's balance of payments. Since the departure of Coyne the Bank of Canada had become much

9 John G. Diefenbaker, *One Canada: The Tumultuous Years 1962 to 1967* (Toronto: Macmillan 1977), 124.

more expansionist. In 1961, for instance, it increased chartered bank reserves by 14.4 per cent, an increase that far outstripped the growth in Canada's GNP. Compared with American interest rates, Canadian interest rates had fallen. Canadian borrowers were therefore far less inclined to seek funds in the United States. Given the fact that Canada's export earnings did not pay for all its imports, to support any particular exchange rate the country needed an inflow of foreign capital funds. If that flow should flag the Canadian dollar would fall. That is exactly what happened before the crisis of April and May 1962.

On June 21 the government was forced to seek foreign assistance – temporary credits from Britain and the United States, and $400 million from the International Monetary Fund. All in all there were lines of credit for $1,050 million. To restore confidence in the dollar the government thought it should also announce an 'austerity program,' although such a scheme ran against the prime ministerial grain. There would be tariff surcharges on almost all of Canada's imports; government outlays would be cut by $250 million; there were cuts in the duty-free exemptions for tourists; if the government's Exchange Fund had to sell foreign money and buy Canadian dollars it would not lend the results to the government.

The crisis was soon over. So as to protect the newly pegged rate the Bank had to become restrictive once again. In 1962 the national output rose 6.8 per cent but the Bank provided only 6 per cent more in chartered bank reserves, thereby applying downward pressure on prices and upward pressure on the cost and availability of credit. This fact, plus the government's demonstration that it was serious about the new exchange rate, brought capital funds flowing back to Canada. Thanks to devaluation and the higher tariffs, the current account improved. As Canadian interest rates were still higher than American, Canadian firms and junior governments were still borrowing in the United States. In a matter of months the dominion could repay its emergency foreign borrowing. By the end of 1962 the Exchange Fund held $1 billion more than it had contained a year before. The tariff surcharges were removed in stages, the last being abolished on April Fool's Day 1963. The dominion civil service, frozen since June 1962, began to grow once more.

In the 1962 election campaign the Liberals made great play with the 'Diefendollar' or 'Diefenbuck.' Doubtless many citizens did believe that the devaluation of May 2 was proof of government incompetence: either the Prime Minister should have told the electorate what was up, or he should not have let the dollar down. As we have seen, Diefenbaker himself maintained that until April 29 he himself had not known what was going on. Incredible though this statement may seem, in fact it is quite plausible. Diefenbaker had no particular interest in financial or economic matters; lacking such interest, he could not expect that officials would keep him posted on exchange developments, and it is perfectly possible that they did not.

As for the fall itself, at the time economists argued that devaluation would be a Good Thing because it would encourage exports and discourage imports. Because the economy was far from full employment in 1962, Canada could readily replace imports with domestic output, and it could quickly expand exports. Indeed, many people thought that for years the Canadian dollar had been worth too much on the foreign exchange markets. As we have seen, that was one of the main elements in the economists' attack on Coyne. Although it was good politics to attack the 'Diefen-devaluation' it was bad economics to do so. No doubt the Liberals realized this, for until 1970 they kept the exchange rate where Diefenbaker had put it.

If one is to believe the picture that Diefenbaker later painted in his memoirs, one has to conclude that until his dying day the Chief never understood the larger issues of economic policy and management that lay behind the Coyne crisis and the dollar débâcle. But he understood the West – the old West of the prairie wheat economy and the new West of oil and gas and potash. And he cared about farmers wherever they lived. From the moment he took office he was anxious to find ways to help them.

There is more than one route to aid farmers. One way is simply to give them money. The Diefenbaker government was quite willing to do so. Another is to try to raise the prices of the things they sell. In 1958, through the Agricultural Stabiliza-tion Act, the government provided new price supports for some twenty-four products. Still another is to provide subsidies for credit and insurance. The Conser-vatives did both. A government might allow farmers to form marketing monopolies, or force them to do so; monopolies, with luck and skill, mean better prices for crops. The Conservatives preserved the Wheat Board's monopoly in the selling of prairie wheat and coarse grains, but they did not set up any new monopolies. This task they left to the provincial marketing boards, whose skills and energies were already apparent. Finally, the government can help the farmer to farm better, or to leave the land. For many decades, through agricultural extension and research, the dominion had been busy with the former; in 1961, under the Agricultural Rehabilitation and Development Act (ARDA), it undertook to help with the latter.

All such devices have obvious political pay-offs. Less obviously, they have eco-nomic disadvantages. Doubtless the civil servants explained these to the cabinet. Certainly there was argument within the cabinet. But as usual in agricultural mat-ters, politics and expediency won. Price supports often produce surpluses, because support prices are typically high relative to demand. A selling monopoly has only limited power if its crop is exported or if imports are allowed. No amount of price-raising can really help the small farmer because he has so little to sell; all price-raising measures tend to help the richer farmer who is marketing a great deal. No matter; farmers have votes.

Until the 1950s Canada could not have afforded the agricultural programs that the Diefenbaker government introduced. The country had not been rich enough, and its farmers had been too numerous. But with the rising prosperity of the forties and fifties went a sharp fall in the absolute number of farm families, and an even sharper fall in their numbers as a proportion of the population. A government can much more easily find a subsidy or build a safety net when the subsidees are few relative to the subsidizers, and when the latter are quickly becoming richer and more numerous. Also, as Canada's city-dwellers became richer they spent a smaller proportion of their incomes on food. Thus farm prices could be raised to help farmers without disrupting city budgets.

In 1957-60 the government could rely on American example and on farm pressure groups for suggestions in plenty. In quick succession Parliament authorized loans for farm-stored grain, other agricultural price supports, acreage subsidies, and fodder subsidies. Many prairie farmers wanted a two-price system by which their wheat would sell for a higher price at home than it would abroad. This they were not given. Diefenbaker later argued that the 'acreage payments' of 1960, by which the dominion simply paid $142 million to the wheat growers, were meant as a substitute. But prairie farmers wanted even more.

Wheat prices were still depressed and prospects were bad; no one had yet envisaged the Chinese wheat sales and it was feared that Europe would buy less wheat in future. Hence the pressure for a compensatory grant and price floor. At the same time there were signs that with respect to tariffs the Conservative government was becoming more protectionist. Certain rates were raised in 1959 and early 1960, while the bases of valuation were changed in ways that raised tariffs and prices within Canada. It seemed that the Tories were returning to their old protectionist ways, and in the West protective tariffs had never been popular. On the other hand, in 1958 the prairies had voted heavily for the Conservatives, and the Prime Minister and other members of cabinet were deeply rooted in the western soil. There is no doubt that they were sincerely interested in agricultural rehabilitation and welfare. But politics pushed them in the same direction, and a mixture of economic and political pressure probably explains the ARDA legislation of late 1960.

The ARDA legislation was actually passed in May 1961, having been introduced in the autumn session of 1960. In spring 1960 Alvin Hamilton, since 1957 the Minister of Northern Affairs and National Resources, took the agricultural portfolio. Although he later said that he spent 60 per cent of his time worrying about wheat sales, he was responsible for the devising of the ARDA legislation. The measure was an odd one. Even when introducing it to the House, Hamilton was unable to give a definite account of what it would actually *do*. The provinces, if willing, would co-operate in a program whose aims were clear enough. Small farmers would be helped to improve the use of their land, to consolidate small farms into more economically viable units, to modernize their houses, and to learn how to farm better. There would be help for those who wished to leave the land; there would be trees and pastures where worn-out or infertile land was still under crops. Other things might be possible; doubtless, the minister explained, they would be. If the provinces agreed, large sums of money would be spent in agricultural areas throughout the dominion. (Later in the 1960s, long after the Conservatives had left office, ARDA blossomed into DREE, the Department of Regional Economic Expansion. Hamilton originally thought ARDA might spend $15 million a year – $6 million in the West and $9 million in the East. DREE spends over half a billion.)

No one knows what ARDA actually accomplished. For one thing, progress of the type that ARDA was meant to encourage was already beginning to be made. Small farmers were leaving the land; arable land was turning to forest and pasture; farmers were finding other things that they could combine with small-scale agriculture to produce a better living. In the sixties such things became more common, but one cannot give ARDA the credit.

Meanwhile there were glimmers of hope with respect to wheat marketing, and the glimmers soon burst into a blaze of light in whose reflection the Tories have been basking ever since. The new light came from an unexpected corner of the world – from Communist China.

Before 1957 Canadian officials had already begun to explore the possibilities of entering this market. In 1958 the Canadian trade commissioner in Hong Kong asked for permission to go to mainland China and sell wheat. The commissioner, C.M. Forsyth-Smith, visited the country and managed to obtain orders for eight shiploads of grain. The grain was sent, but nothing further happened until November 1960, when two Chinese officials arrived unannounced in Montreal, carrying $63 million in letters of credit. Alvin Hamilton, the Minister of Agriculture, at once sent them to visit the Wheat Board in Winnipeg, where a sale was quickly arranged. Canadian officials then went to Peking. This visit, plus a guarantee of credit by the Canadian cabinet, produced an enormous export order. In April 1961 the Wheat Board was able to announce that by December 1963 it would sell at least three million tons of wheat and at least 600,000 tons of barley. In the end, sales totalled 240 million bushels, and Canada earned about $425 million. In those years China was Canada's second-best customer for wheat, and, as Diefenbaker later explained, 'These sales helped to restore our prairie economy to its rightful place in the Canadian scheme of things.' It was he who had made the crucial decision over considerable opposition in cabinet; Canada could safely provide the necessary credit, because the word of a Chinese 'was as good as his bond.'[10]

10 Diefenbaker, *One Canada ... 1957-1962*, 178-80.

Although the American government would not let its own subjects trade with China, Washington does not appear to have opposed the grain sales themselves. However, there were troubles about bunker oil and grain-handling equipment – 'vacuators.' Diefenbaker was not pleased to find that the Americans' Trading with the Enemy Act might prevent Imperial Oil from supplying oil fuel for the grain steamers. At length, after angry discussion, Washington agreed to exempt Canadian subsidiaries from the relevant regulations. The vacuators, however, were actually produced in the United States. The shipowners, not the Chinese government, had ordered them, and they had already been delivered to Canadian ports. When the US authorities tried to get the local representatives of the manufacturers to ship the equipment back to the United States, Diefenbaker went directly to President Kennedy, explaining that this was no business of the Americans. Kennedy agreed to release the equipment, but Diefenbaker believed that this incident ended 'any friendly personal relationship between President Kennedy and myself.'[11]

For prairie farmers the Chinese purchases were a bonanza. The Wheat Board sold all its surplus stocks; wheat prices rose from $1.60 to $2.19 a bushel; the Minister of Agriculture told the farmers to grow all they could; net farm income tripled in three years. It is no wonder that the prairies have voted Conservative ever since. Admittedly the Diefenbaker government deserves little credit for the sales. Neither Diefenbaker nor the Wheat Board caused the two years of crop failures which drove the Chinese onto the world market. Nor were Canadians responsible for the American embargo that gave Canada such an opportunity. At worst, the cabinet might have refused the necessary credits, or refused to deal with Communist officials. There was a political risk, as the cabinet recognized; ethnic votes might be lost because the Conservatives were helping to prop up world Communism. But it was reasonable to hope that Diefenbaker's performances in the United Nations would keep New Canadians in the Tory camp. Anyway, as Alvin Hamilton argued in cabinet, the economic risks were small relative to the pay-offs. In effect the chance was too good to miss.

Although the United States did not really object to Canada's new trans-Pacific grain trade, Washington was very far from happy to find that its northern neighbour wanted to go on trading with Cuba, where, in 1959, the Fidel Castro regime replaced the unpleasant oligarchy of Fulgencio Batista. Canada at once recognized the new regime, but as Cuba moved fairly rapidly into the Soviet orbit the United States eventually severed diplomatic relations and imposed a trade embargo. Although the volume of Canadian-Cuban trade was not large, for some Canadian firms the Cuban market was welcome.

11 *Ibid.*, 180-1.

Equally welcome was the American market for natural gas, where shipments were authorized for the first time in April 1960. Although the Alberta authorities were always nervously anxious to give local consumers a sure supply of cheap gas, by this time there seemed to be plenty of gas in Alberta and British Columbia, and the American market was willing although not eager to buy it. It might now be said that the export was ill advised or that prices were too low. But at the time the prices seemed fair, and there was no sign of an 'energy crisis.' The sales were welcomed not only in Alberta but throughout the country. It was thought that Canada would soon be earning $75 million a year by selling natural gas. In light of our chronic current account deficit, those millions seemed to be a welcome windfall.

It has become fashionable to argue that the Liberal party is 'continentalist,' while the Conservatives protect not merely the monarchy but also the national sovereignty. The gas exports are not the only thing that cast doubt on this easy generalization. The same could be said of NORAD, the Columbia River Treaty, and many other things. But the gas question does bring the point into sharp focus. What could be more 'continentalist' than to connect Canadian gas wells with American households and factories?

Of oil the same things can be said. In the late 1950s the United States was worrying about oil imports, which threatened the profits of domestic oilwell owners and which might imperil national security. The great oil companies, by and large, were eager to import, because South American and Middle East crude oil was cheaper than American; the owners of oil lands, especially in the Gulf States and California, naturally wanted to keep out foreign crude so as to keep their prices up; the Pentagon worried lest too much of American needs were supplied from overseas. Until March 1959 the United States had limited oil imports only through 'voluntary controls,' which the oil companies operated. But on March 10, 1959, the US government imposed mandatory controls, and until April 30 these applied to Canada. The Canadian government was extremely anxious to win a re-entry to the American market, and it argued that in time of war Canada's wells and pipelines would be as secure as America's own. In the background, of course, was the current account deficit, and the government's need to placate Alberta and the other western provinces. As yet it had done little for the wheat farmer, and already it was under attack from the West. Fortunately for the Diefenbaker administration, Washington saw reason, and removed the controls. Hence, for more than a decade, Canadian oil flowed freely south. Continentalism, anyone?

24

Bad Luck and Bad Management: Dominion-Provincial Perplexities, the Columbia, and the Great Defence Débâcle

Like every Canadian government the Diefenbaker administration had troubles with the provinces. Unlike its immediate predecessors it also had trouble with defence policy, and therefore its relations with the United States became very disturbed. This chapter treats first the internal perplexities and then the international ones, where bad luck and bad judgment are inextricably intertwined.

Compared with what it became during the Pearson and Trudeau years the dominion-provincial scene was still relatively tranquil. The blue-eyed sheikhs of Alberta as yet had little leverage. Indeed, by 1960 the dominion had to protect them by giving them a guaranteed Ontario market for their expensive crude and by holding open the taps on the pipelines to the United States. Honouring its promises, in 1958 the dominion began to build the South Saskatchewan Dam, a project that would irrigate immense areas in the arid belt. The Atlantic provinces got special adjustment grants. In the northern parts of the western provinces the dominion's 'Roads to Resources' scheme opened up large areas by road and rail. For Maritime coal production and transport there were new subsidies. But of course the provinces were not satisfied. No junior government, provincial or municipal, ever is.

At Queen's Park the Tories ruled; in Quebec City the Union Nationale was in firm control until 1960. These facts made life no easier for the Tory cabinet in Ottawa, or for its leader. All the provinces wanted more money. More than one was sensitive about autonomy and federal intrusion. Most were unhappy about the tax-sharing arrangements that the St Laurent government had imposed in 1957. Only after 1959 would Quebec allow its universities to accept the federal grants that other universities had received since 1951. Planning to develop the hydro power on the Columbia River, Ottawa found Victoria as obstreperous as Washington, and a good deal less trustworthy.

The dominion's shared-cost programs made matters worse. In 1953-4 the dominion had provided $75 million through conditional grant programs; by 1964-5 it

Tais-toé !

Heil !

Niet !

Le chant du signe.

An obituary cartoon for Premier Maurice Duplessis, who is saying, 'Shut up!'
(Hudon, 1959). Reproduced with the permission of Norman Hudon

distributed $935,500,000. The Diefenbaker government had expanded some old programs and introduced at least fifteen minor shared-cost programs and five major ones, of which the most expensive was the hospital insurance plan. By 1963-4 this plan, enacted by the St Laurent government but accelerated and actually implemented by Diefenbaker, was costing Ottawa $391,297,000 per year. Other large programs were the technical education scheme, assistance for the needy unemployed, old age assistance, and the Trans-Canada Highway – all programs that had been initiated before Diefenbaker took office. Costs were shared on a variety of bases. Commonly the provinces were asked to pay 50 per cent of the costs, but their shares might be as low as 10 per cent or as high as 75 per cent.

It is far from clear that the dominion authorities actually worked out what such things as hospital insurance, the technical education program, or the Trans-Canada Highway would cost the provinces. There was no obvious reason why costs should be split in any particular way. By bearing a larger share, the dominion authorities could have spared themselves the agonized screams of provincial authorities who on the one hand could not say no to federal largesse, but on the other had to raise some of the cost. At the same time all of the provinces faced heavy outlays for such things as road-building and universities, while some provinces wanted to help municipalities with the costs of schools and public utilities. Naturally the provincial governments did not want to impose new taxes, although by 1963 almost all of the provinces were collecting a new sort of tax, the retail sales tax, at rates ranging from 3 to 6 per cent. As for the 'shared tax fields' – income tax, corporation tax, and succession duties – no province liked to impose more tax than the 'abatement from federal tax' which the dominion was prepared to give. Hence all the provinces pressed Ottawa for a bigger share of these jointly occupied taxes. In addition, the poorer provinces pressed for 'equalization grants' that would let them provide the same level of public service as the richer provinces could provide. Differences between federal and provincial priorities further complicated things. Saskatchewan and British Columbia introduced hospital insurance before Ottawa; both were anxious to get federal funds for the schemes they had already set up. But in Ontario and Quebec neither government wanted hospital insurance at all; neither was anxious for Ottawa to set up a shared-cost program that for political reasons they would have to join. There was also a metaphysical-constitutional problem that worried some theorists and politicians, especially in Quebec. By using its spending power to finance a shared-cost program, the dominion seemed to encroach on the provincial sphere. In theory a province might refuse to take part, but in practice it would have to. Thereby, it was argued, provincial priorities were distorted, and the writ of the dominion was made to run within the provinces. Much better, some argued, to give the provinces the money and let them do what they liked with it.

As we saw in Parts II and III, after the Second World War the Liberal government had proposed a system of 'tax rental agreements,' and most provinces had agreed to levy no personal income tax and to limit their taxation of corporation profits. They could tax estates as they wished, and the dominion would treat provincial succession duties as credits against the federal impost. In exchange for their taxing powers the provinces got subsidies. The agreements were renewed in 1957, just before Diefenbaker took office. The Conservatives had promised to give the provinces a better deal, and they did give a special adjustment grant to the Atlantic provinces – $25 million annually for four years. Also, in 1958-9 they increased the income tax rebate from 10 to 13 per cent. Furthermore, the government was attached to the principle of equalization payments, which were meant to supplement the tax powers of the poorer provinces. By 1960 Ontario publicists were loud in their denunciation of equalization payments, although the governments of Saskatchewan, Manitoba, and the Atlantic provinces were understandably extremely attached to them.

In July 1960 there was a dominion-provincial conference. Meant to work out a new plan for sharing tax fields, it ended in deadlock. All the provinces wanted more; no two wanted the same things. In October, when the conference reconvened, Diefenbaker proposed that when the tax rental agreements expired in March 1962 they would not be renewed. The federal government would pump out equalization payments at the rate of $220 million per year, and for five years it would continue to pay the stabilization guarantees that protected provinces against declines in their revenues. So that the provinces could levy their own income, corporation, and estate taxes the dominion would vacate these fields, but only to the extent that it had already done so.

In February 1962, at another session of the conference, Diefenbaker simply told the provinces what would happen with the expiry of the agreements on March 31. Equalization grants would continue, but would be calculated differently. The dominion would guarantee that under the new regime no province's revenue could fall by more than 5 per cent. This was the 'stabilization' provision. Adjustment grants would be continued and increased. There would be a special grant for Newfoundland. As for the three shared tax fields, Ottawa would abate half of its succession duties, 9 per cent of its corporation income taxes, and a rising share of its income taxation: starting at 16 per cent of federal tax in 1962, the abatement would rise to 20 per cent in 1967. Then all provinces could impose their own taxes at their own rates. So long as a province calculated its income tax as a percentage of the federal tax, Ottawa would collect income taxation on behalf of that province.

The Prime Minister announced that he liked this scheme because it would give back to the provinces their constitutional right to impose what taxes they wished. On the whole, the provinces did not like the new regime. Some were disappointed because they had not gained more; others were annoyed because they would get less. Some economists and social theorists were annoyed because in the new regime the dominion alone would not determine the weight of personal direct taxation. Hence Ottawa could no longer be sure that it could manage the level of spending and the pace of economic activity by cutting income taxes or raising them. If Ottawa were to change its tax rates, the provinces might change theirs in the opposite direction, offsetting the effect. In the event, however, the new regime has proved to be much like the old. The provinces have continued to demand that the federal government should vacate more of the shared fields. With the passage of time they have gotten their way. The abatements became larger in 1963, once the Liberals returned to office, and they have been increased many times since. For provinces that opted out of various shared-cost programs there have been special abatements. This arrangement began in 1960, so that the Quebec government could subsidize its own universities. In the mid and late sixties, as we show in Part V, the practice became general. Although the provinces do tax incomes at different rates, and although Quebec has imposed and collected its own income tax, there has not been a return to the 'tax jungle' of the 1930s. No province wants to tax incomes much more heavily than other provinces; every province prefers to demand more of the jointly occupied fields – by 1978, overwhelmingly the income tax, as the dominion no longer taxes estates and as few provinces can raise much money by taxing corporations. As for economic management, although federal taxing and spending have lost ground relative to provincial, relative to the whole economy federal activity has grown a great deal, and nobody would now complain that Ottawa has lost the power to manage the economy. It may not have the *will*, but that is another question. In addition, through federal-provincial conferences and through informal contacts Ottawa often attempts to co-ordinate provincial tax and spending plans with federal and is sometimes able to do so.

Although the disputes about taxing and spending were intertwined with disagreements about constitutional propriety, during the Diefenbaker years there was no great pressure for constitutional reform. In Quebec, the Tremblay Commission thought that things should be tidied up. Doubtless Diefenbaker would have been happier about his bill of rights if it had applied to provincial activities as well as federal. Although the Prime Minister would have liked to 'patriate' the British North America Act so that it could be amended in Canada, as late as June 1960 he did not expect that Canada would quickly devise a formula. At the July dominion-provincial conference, Premier Lesage urged that something be done at once; Diefenbaker then announced that E. Davie Fulton, the federal Minister of Justice, would meet with provincial attorneys general early in October to consider the question of 'patriation.'

The provinces quickly realized that there was no point in patriating the constitution unless they and the dominion could agree on an amendment formula. Ever since 1867 the Parliament at Westminster had amended the BNA Act on request; what would replace this procedure? In November, it was quickly agreed that the language and education provisions, and one or two others, should be 'entrenched.' That is, only if all of the provinces agreed could the dominion amend such provisions. With respect to the rest, there were various proposals aimed at providing greater or less flexibility. Some provinces hoped that if more of the provincial sphere were 'entrenched' there should also be some arrangement by which a province could delegate some of its powers to the dominion. In January 1961 this was agreed to, although Quebec was nervous lest others might delegate too much, leaving her as the only province to cling to the full panoply of provincial pomp and power. Saskatchewan, its CCF government anxious for national marketing boards and comprehensive national planning, was most reluctant to entrench 'property and civil rights.' Quebec, meanwhile, wanted to transfer unemployment insurance back from federal to provincial control. On December 1 Fulton revealed his draft bill. All provincial powers and rights, language, and education were to be entrenched, except that Newfoundland could not veto educational changes. There was some provision for the provinces to delegate functions to the national government. If four provinces wanted to legislate in a federal field, the dominion could consent. Beyond the entrenched clauses, the dominion Parliament could amend the constitution if supported by two-thirds of the provinces containing 50 per cent of the people. The amending formula itself was also to be entrenched.

On December 7, 1961, Quebec rejected the 'Fulton formula' because it did not give the provinces unemployment insurance. And, for the time being, that was that.

Meanwhile there were puzzlements about off-shore oil. In the Yukon, the Northwest Territories, and Hudson Bay, the dominion controlled natural resources, although on provincial dry land control lay with the provinces. But 'Canada' already extended three miles out to sea, and already by 1960 it was obvious that in due course it would advance its seaward frontier. In 1958 and 1960 Canadian representatives had told the Americans that Canada would not always allow American fishing inside a *twelve*-mile limit. Under the waves there might be minerals, especially oil and gas. Who controlled *them*?

The answer was unclear. Ottawa argued that its oil and gas regulations, drafted in 1960 to cover the Arctic, applied to all off-shore waters, and in July 1961 it gave Shell an off-shore exploration permit in the Pacific Ocean. British Columbia was annoyed, claiming that Victoria, not Ottawa, should give the permits and garner the royalties. Premier Bennett proceeded to offer exploration rights for fifteen million acres of the blue Pacific, including the eleven million that Ottawa had assigned to

Shell. Although Richfield had protected itself by taking out both federal and provincial permits, Shell did not do so. When the rights auction occurred on September 1, other bidders bought the province's permission to drill in Shell's area. Soon the Nova Scotia government, hoping for oil off Sable Island, would get excited too. But the federal government did nothing, and late in 1962 British Columbia took the question to the courts, where it lingered until 1979 when the Clark government decided to give off-shore minerals to the provinces. With the Liberal victory of 1980, the issue was unsettled once more.

The same might be said for amending and patriating the constitution. In October 1964 the Liberal government got the provinces to swallow the scheme of 1961-2, now known as the 'Fulton-Favreau formula.' Premier Lesage thought the formula a great achievement; Diefenbaker thought it would make Quebec an associate state, not a province like the others; the NDP thought it too rigid. In many minds the question became entangled with the 'special status' issue: was Quebec a province like the others? One by one the provinces gave their approval. Only Quebec remained uncommitted. In that province the Union Nationale mounted a strong campaign against the formula, while other groups also opposed it. In the end, on October 22, Lesage told the Legislature that he would neither approve the formula nor reject it. Once more, it seemed, the question was dead, or perhaps dormant.

Meanwhile the provinces had taken courage from Diefenbaker's attitude toward disallowance. Theoretically the dominion could disallow any provincial measure; in practice the power had not been used since 1943. In the winter of 1958-9 there was trouble in the woods of Newfoundland. The Smallwood government passed a law that decertified the union of the International Woodworkers of America, who happened to be on strike. When the provincial authorities asked for RCMP reinforcements to help keep order, Fulton and Diefenbaker refused to send them, at least partly because they did not want the RCMP to appear to be strike-breakers. L.H. Nicholson, the head of the RCMP, resigned over the incident, because he thought that the government's decision was a breach of the contract by which the RCMP provided police in the province. Diefenbaker later wrote, 'I was not prepared to sacrifice the reputation of the RCMP to save either Mr Smallwood or the reactionary corporations which owned the Newfoundland forest industry.'[1] After waiting until 1960, however, the dominion would not disallow the decertification measure; indeed, Diefenbaker said that he did not think Ottawa should ever disallow anything. The federal government, he explained, should not be judge and jury over the provincial legislatures that the people had elected. His logic is hard to follow: apparently it is wrong to use the RCMP for strike-breaking when a legitimately elected

---

1 John G. Diefenbaker, *One Canada: The Years of Achievement 1957 to 1962* (Toronto: Macmillan 1976), 317.

provincial government asks for them, and equally wrong to use the pre-eminent power of the dominion to prevent a provincial government from breaking strikes. Although the question of disallowance would surface once more in the late 1960s, in effect the Conservative government's decision had banished it from the constitutional scene. In their own spheres the provinces were now pre-eminent. As John Saywell wrote in 1960, 'It was a far cry from the view of Sir John A. Macdonald.'[2]

Not the least of the dominion-provincial perplexities was the plan for a Columbia River dam, which one journalist thought might better be called the dam' Columbia River plan. This had an international dimension because it required Canada and the United States to co-operate; it also had a dominion-provincial dimension, partly because the British Columbia government had its own plans for power development in the Rocky Mountains. Although Ottawa emerged from the fracas with much credit and British Columbia came out with little or none, it was the dominion that failed to get its way.

Both Diefenbaker and President Eisenhower were anxious to conclude an agreement for the development of the Columbia River, which meandered through British Columbia for hundreds of miles before finally crossing the forty-ninth parallel. As the generating plants were to be in the United States and the water storage in Canada, neither government could proceed without the co-operation of the other. After discussion with British Columbia and with the International Joint Commission, a treaty was completed. It was signed in 1961, three days before Eisenhower left office.

The scheme had been gestating for more than fifteen years. In the early 1940s studies had begun, and the International Joint Commission had been asked to report on the proposal. If the Americans had been allowed to build the dam they first wanted to build, the full hydraulic potential would not have been developed, then or ever. Only when the United States agreed to pay Canada for downstream benefits could Ottawa agree to a draft treaty. The treaty was to last sixty years. Canada would build three storage dams, receiving in return half of the power that the United States would generate downstream. Canada could divert some Kootenay water into the Columbia so as to generate some power within Canada; it would also get $64.4 million for the flood control benefits in the United States.

Because the Bennett government in British Columbia had already proposed a private development of Peace River power, it did not like the new plan. It also quibbled about the sharing of costs between federal and provincial treasuries. What it really wanted was to develop the Peace and Columbia projects, selling the downstream benefits to the Americans instead of importing them in the form of cheap electric power. There was also a chance that the dominion would declare the

2 *Canadian Annual Review*, 1960 (Toronto: University of Toronto Press 1961), 51.

Columbia project to be for the general interest of Canada; it could then control it, importing the power and selling it to the BC Electric Company, the private corporation that then supplied Vancouver and Victoria. To forestall this, in August 1961 Bennett took over BC Electric and also the Peace River Development Company. The United States was prepared to buy the power from the Columbia and it was probably eager to do so, but it did not take sides in the dispute; Bennett hoped that by selling twenty years' worth of the downstream benefits he would garner enough to develop the Peace. Meanwhile the dominion argued that Columbia power would be cheaper power for British Columbia and that if sales were allowed for a term of years Canada might have trouble reclaiming its power when it was needed. As we have seen, the government also hoped to set up a national power grid within Canada, and it feared that by exporting power from the western end of the country it might have trouble supplying power to the prairies.

Early in 1962 the Americans announced that if the Canadians could not settle their row, the United States might have to look elsewhere for power. Bennett, Ottawa learned, would supply Peace River power to a national grid if he could sell Columbia power in the United States. On May 11 the dominion announced that it would soon call for dam tenders, and on May 27 Diefenbaker spoke warmly of the Peace project. On September 27 the throne speech forecast that the treaty would be ratified and power exports permitted. However, there was no legislation before the Conservatives fell from power. It was left to the Liberals, in July 1963, to patch up an agreement with British Columbia. It was decided that the province would get the benefits, sell them back to the United States, and use the proceeds to finance the Peace River project. The verdict was not popular. Many journalists and politicians disliked the new arrangements even more than the old proposal, which General McNaughton, the former chairman of the International Joint Commission, had thought a sell-out. To Ottawa the new arrangement was a humiliation; to W.A.C. Bennett it was a political triumph; to the citizens of British Columbia it meant expensive hydro power from the Peace, not cheap power from the Columbia; to Washington it was a swap of money for energy, a trade that the US government was only too eager to make.

Much more serious and far more alarming were the arguments about defence. In Ottawa no one doubted that Canada should stick with NATO and with an integrated air defence system for North America. In July 1957, with little thought and without cabinet scrutiny, Diefenbaker had committed Canada to NORAD – the North American air defence plan by which Canadian and American officers would jointly administer an integrated air defence force under supreme American command. The St Laurent government had known about NORAD, but had deferred action until after the 1957 election. How was Canada to contribute to NORAD, and what sort of weapons would it use?

The Conservatives had also inherited an embarrassing item. At Malton, Ontario, with government funding, A.V. Roe Canada (AVRO) was building an all-Canadian supersonic fighter plane, the AVRO Arrow, and Orenda Engines was developing the Iroquois engine that would make the plane fly. The two companies had assembled a formidable technical team, and had produced a depressing record of profligacy and budget overruns. Other companies were at work on Arrow weaponry and electronics. The Arrow had been specially designed for Canadian conditions. No doubt the plane and the engine were superb. AVRO said so; the engineers said so; the RCAF said so. But they were expensive, and no other government seemed to want any. The Liberals had intended to cancel the project after the 1957 election. After an embarrassed pause, in 1959 the Tory cabinet decided to abandon both the Iroquois and the Arrow. AVRO complained, and laid off 14,000 workers. Torontonians fulminated. Either on Diefenbaker's orders or on AVRO's, the existing aircraft – all five of them – were destroyed. And for air defence Canada would have to find some other weapon.

Before scrapping the AVRO, the cabinet found the Bomarc anti-aircraft missile. This was an American ballistic device that was meant to intercept Soviet planes, but not rockets. It would be controlled by NORAD's joint Canadian-American headquarters in Colorado Springs. Canada would build two Bomarc sites, and the Americans would supply missiles. The total cost to Canada would be $14 million, far less than the cost of 100 Arrows. Originally the RCAF had expected to order 500 Arrows, but on learning that the reservists would be unable to fly so complex an aircraft it had decided that 100 would have to do.

Meanwhile, the military knew full well that Canada would sooner or later have to buy some new interceptor aircraft for northern defence. The old ones were already obsolete. Every day there were numbers of unidentified aircraft on the radar screens. One could not fire Bomarcs at all of them. At length, in 1961, the government bought sixty-six F-101 Voodoo aircraft from the United States. The government had had to wait until it could do a satisfactory deal with the United States by which American procurements in Canada could provide work for Canada's aircraft industry and offset the cost of the Voodoos. It had also wanted to wait until the hubbub about the Arrow had died down.

These decisions did not kill Canada's aircraft industry. De Havilland and Canadair continued to do original design work; Orenda continued to build engines under licence; most of AVRO was eventually sold to Douglas Aircraft. To assist the aircraft industry the government made various special deals. This industry also gained from the Development and Production Sharing Program, which Diefenbaker and President Eisenhower devised in July 1958. Under this new program, which resembled the wartime Hyde Park Agreement, Canadian firms were able to share in orders from American military procurement. The agreement produced a sharp increase in

American purchases of Canadian arms, which quickly came to exceed Canadian purchases of American. It was in this way that the Diefenbaker government defended Canada against the horrors of continentalism.

The Arrow was a very good aircraft, and many Canadians have wondered why the United States would not buy it. The answer seems to be threefold. First, it did not precisely fit American needs. Second, it was not built in the United States. Third, it was very expensive relative to the alternatives. Indeed, for Canadian defence production the demise of the Arrow and the purchase of the Bomarc represented a sort of handwriting on the wall. For a decade or so, it had seemed reasonable to believe that Canada could produce the most sophisticated military hardware and equip itself therewith. Canada might even expect to sell such things abroad. But by 1958 development costs were rising to insupportable levels, especially if spread over the small outputs that Canada could possibly afford or need. All over the capitalist world the smaller airframe makers and the 'national' airframe industries were in trouble. The economies of large-scale production were very significant, and research, too, had become immensely costly. Closure, merger, or government subsidy – these were the orders of the day, even in Britain, France, and Germany. In 1946 C.D. Howe had hoped that by selling Canada's wartime airframe plants to American and British firms Canada would get some of the international action. To some extent it has done so, chiefly though not entirely by using other people's airframe designs and by building components, such as wings. But in the sixties and seventies the production-sharing arrangements have also made a big difference.

By spring 1960 Canada had begun to build its first Bomarc base at North Bay. Unfortunately, the system was still an untried one, and no one was sure it would work, much less do the job of interception for which it was intended. Also, in the United States the American Army was lobbying in favour of an alternative system, the Nike-Hercules short-range missile. The American Air Force had to defend the Bomarc, its brainchild, against Army sniping. In 1960 there were Congressional inquisitions. To Canada these were intensely embarrassing, as they suggested that Canada might have bought a pig in a poke. More embarrassing was the fact that Canada's Bomarcs would have to carry nuclear warheads. They had not been designed to handle high explosive. Diefenbaker has later maintained that he had thought they could be armed either way. If so, he cannot have read the specifications for Bomarc B. He has also suggested that by 1959 the Bomarc was already junk, because by this time the threat was intercontinental ballistic missiles (ICBMs), not the manned bombers that Bomarc was meant to repel. If he thought this in 1960, it seems curious that he went on with the Bomarc program. In any event, neither he nor his military advisers can have believed that the day of the manned bomber was really over. If North America had dismantled all its bomber defences, there would have been nothing to stop the Soviet Union from building bombers and sending them over the north pole. As the threat was a dual one, the country would need defences against both sorts of weapon. Indeed, the government recognized this in 1961 when it bought the Voodoos.

But the government had still not decided what to do about the nuclear warheads. In 1960 General Pearkes, the Minister of National Defence, reported that he was discussing the matter with the Americans. Thus he revealed that Canada had chosen the Bomarc without deciding to arm it. And as Bomarcs were gradually installed in the two Canadian sites, they were 'armed' with sandbags. The United States was naturally concerned. Although Canada itself had asked to locate the two sites in Canada, both were part of the North American defence system; unarmed, they left holes that made the United States more vulnerable. If the government had decided at once, perhaps no one would have noticed. But by 1960 there was a large and vocal lobby that was arguing for nuclear disarmament. In Britain, Europe, and Canada there was an active 'ban the bomb' campaign. Thousands of people marched to and from Aldermaston, where Britain's atomic research was concentrated. Swimmers defied the American nuclear submarines in Scotland's Holy Loch. Although there was no indication that the Soviet Union would disarm, in western Europe and in Canada the optimistic and the naïve believed that through a great act of self-abnegation they would bring Russia round – or at least, if they did not, their own lands would remain ritually pure until the moment when the Third World War actually began. The Americans and the Russians, it was argued, had plenty of atomic weaponry. Why proliferate the weapons especially since the United States was prepared to shoulder the risk and the responsibility?

In Canada the Liberals and the CCF did not want nuclear weapons. Many Conservatives and some cabinet members felt the same way. After accepting the External Affairs portfolio in 1959 Howard Green laboured mightily, at the United Nations and elsewhere, for the cause of disarmament. How could he do so, if Canada were to accept the new weapons? Rereading the arguments nearly twenty years later, one detects the last gasps of the Protestant conscience in an incompletely secularized disguise. Canada should be pure; by an act of will it *can* be pure; it has no larger responsibilities that might compel it to share in the impurities of the world, the flesh, or its allies. Diefenbaker maintained that the government had not promised anything about warheads, but he never explained why it was spending several million dollars to erect a series of empty metal towers at North Bay.

In 1961 it became clear that Douglas Harkness, the new Minister of National Defence, wanted to accept nuclear arms, both for air and for ground use. That year the first Bomarcs were installed, and in 1962 Canada's NATO ground forces began to deploy the Honest John missiles that were meant for atomic arming. The basic decision had been taken in 1958. Moreover, in 1959 the government had agreed that in Europe the RCAF should play a 'strike reconnaissance' role, one that assumed

Canada's planes would carry tactical nuclear weapons. For this purpose it arranged to produce an American-designed aircraft, the CF-104 Starfighter. In February 1962 Boeing turned over the North Bay base to the RCAF. Still there were no warheads for its twenty-eight Bomarcs. Still the government havered.

Diefenbaker later argued that the real problem was one of control. Under US law, Canada could not acquire title to atomic weapons because these would have to be bought from the Americans. Indeed, they would have to remain in American custody, being released to the Canadians only in time of need. By September 1961, Diefenbaker has written, he believed that President Kennedy would not allow a joint control of such weapons on Canadian soil,[3] although he and everyone else knew that the American government did want to see nuclear arming of Canada's Bomarcs and Voodoos. It is certain that Diefenbaker was wrong about control. In March 1962 the American Secretary of State stated: 'The United States is willing to work out arrangements for joint control consistent with national sovereignty.' With other countries such as Britain the Americans had already devised 'two-key' systems which amounted to a mutual veto. In Canada, however, there was really no will to solve the problem. The Prime Minister seems to have believed that if war should break out there would be time to bring in the nuclear arms and install them for use. He liked the plan for a 'missing piece,' by which part of a warhead would be stored in Canada and part would be flown from the United States in case of need. But it was already known that a Soviet ICBM could reach North America in seventeen minutes. If war did break out there would be no time for such foolishness. Also, to keep such a transfer system in constant readiness would be immensely expensive.

By mid-1962, when the election occurred, nothing had been done. In the campaign the NDP said that it wanted Canada to leave NORAD, abandon NATO if pressed to take nuclear arms, and form a non-nuclear club. Lester Pearson, the Liberal leader, did not want to take nuclear weapons, and his party sat on the fence, while his wife joined the anti-nuclear Voice of Women.

As La Presse observed, 'O shades of Mackenzie King! ... Not necessarily nuclear arms but nuclear arms if necessary.' Diefenbaker explained that Canada would not acquire nuclear warheads for the present, although 'We are in a position to defend ourselves if war breaks out.'[4] By what means he did not explain. Nor could he do so after the election. The second Bomarc base was almost ready. The new aircraft was leaving for Germany. These facts did not sway him. In October 1962 the Americans detected Soviet missiles in Cuba and risked world war to force a withdrawal. The cabinet refused to place Canada's NORAD force on alert; it refused to let America fly

---

3 John G. Diefenbaker, *One Canada: The Tumultuous Years 1962 to 1967* (Toronto: Macmillan 1977), 74.

4 *Canadian Annual Review*, 1962, 4.

nuclear-armed fighters to arctic bases; it did not arm the Bomarcs or the Voodoos. As Professor Spencer explains, 'Fear of adding to the tension and of sharpening the crisis appears to have held the government back; and Canada emerged from it [the Cuban missile crisis] with its defence policies in disarray, its reputation a little tarnished, but its nuclear virginity intact.'[5]

By this time some cabinet members rated survival – military and political – ahead of virginity or ritual purity. Thanks to Green's meditations and Diefenbaker's indecisions the country was defended only by the Americans, and the Tory party was in peril. The Prime Minister must decide, or leave office. As Peter C. Newman later observed, 'In acquiring the CF-101B, the Bomarc, the Honest John and the CF-104 and then refusing to arm them, Canada under John Diefenbaker's management had spent $685 millions for the most impressive collection of blank cartridges in the history of military science.'[6] Something would have to be done. Meanwhile, the Prime Minister was ever more moody and erratic, while the business of Parliament remained undone.

In November 1962 a group of ten cabinet ministers began to consider the future of Diefenbaker and the Tory party. George Hees was their leader. Nothing came of their discussions, but Douglas Harkness, since 1960 the defence minister, was increasingly disinclined to follow Diefenbaker on his trek through Wonderland. In February 1963, following a dramatic cabinet session, Harkness resigned. Canadian-American relations broke down; Canada recalled its ambassador following an American revelation that Canada had 'not yet proposed any arrangement sufficiently practical to contribute effectively to North American defence.' In the Parliament Buildings the conspirators were active once more. They would bid for Social Credit support, replace Diefenbaker with George Nowlan, and hold a leadership convention.

The Social Credit party agreed to support a Conservative government, but only if the cabinet would at once explain its defence policy while behaving responsibly in other ways. Dief the Chief refused to co-operate or to give any assurances. Instead, he mobilized his supporters in cabinet and on the back benches. But the Social Crediters, NDPers, and Liberals could combine and defeat him. On February 5 they did so. For the second time in this century, a vote in the House had brought down a government.

The Prime Minister tried to unite his cabinet behind him for the coming election battle. But in the middle of the campaign he had to digest the resignation not only of Hees but also of Pierre Sévigny, the Acting Minister of National Defence. Both were unhappy about Diefenbaker's anti-American posturing; neither could stand his shilly-shallying on defence.

---

5   *Ibid.*, 136.
6   Peter C. Newman, *Renegade in Power* (Toronto: McClelland & Stewart 1973), 354.

In the 1962 election campaign Lester Pearson and the Liberals had tried to evade the nuclear question. In effect they had been as evasive as Diefenbaker had been. But on January 12, 1963, distressed both by the Cuban crisis and by American military revelations that had revealed the full weakness and dishonesty of the Canadian position, Pearson had promised that if elected he would honour the Diefenbaker commitments: he would accept nuclear arms.

This meant nuclear weapons for Canada, but only for a short while. After a Pearson government was elected, it would 'begin to negotiate Canada into more appropriate roles, ones which would not require Canadian forces to use nuclear weapons.' Coming nine days after retiring NATO commander General Lauris Norstad's declaration at Ottawa's Uplands Airport that Canada was not keeping her promise to accept nuclear weapons, Pearson's statement responded to a growing clamour in the Canadian press against the Diefenbaker government's evasive responses to questions about its commitments. The timing seemed perfect. The Tories quarrelled; the cabinet split, with Douglas Harkness leading the dissidents. After Diefenbaker described Conservative nuclear policy in a debate on foreign affairs, Harkness issued a statement 'clarifying' his leader's remarks. Initially Harkness had welcomed Diefenbaker's speech but then he had had second thoughts. Harkness's Monday statement was followed on Wednesday, January 30, by a US State Department press release – drafted in the White House – repudiating Diefenbaker's comments of the previous week. 'It's a shocker,' a cabinet minister wrote in his diary by way of summation. And it was.

Most Canadians and many Americans deplored the American intervention in the Canadian debate. In the House Diefenbaker denounced the 'unprecedented' American action which, he claimed, was 'an unwarranted intrusion into Canadian affairs.' A fair comment, but then Diefenbaker went too far, claiming that Pearson and the US State Department had colluded and that the Americans had no right to speak of a commitment. Diefenbaker shone a spotlight squarely on his own credibility. Under its glow he became a great deal less credible, as defence officials and even leading Conservatives argued that there *was* a specific commitment. The Ottawa *Citizen* reflected this perception when it wrote: 'Granted the extraordinary ... nature of the State Department intervention ... the essential fact is that the Canadian government has given every appearance of dishonour.'[7] More outspoken was Pierre Berton, who supported Pearson's *volte-face* on nuclear weapons in the language of Kennedy realism. In Berton's view, as in Robert Kennedy's, he who is not for us is against us: 'To earn a reputation we must stop the pretence, the indecision, the fence straddling, the welshing and the double-dealing which have characterized our relations with our partners.' We were not looking at our new world directly, Berton claimed:

7 Ottawa *Citizen*, Jan. 31, 1963.

The nuclear weapons crisis of 1963: Minister of Defence Douglas Harkness quits (Macpherson, 1963). Reproduced with the permission of the *Toronto Star*

National sovereignty is on the wane. If this election proves anything it proves that anti-Americanism is finished as a political issue. We have cast our lot with this continent for better or worse and the people know it. The world is re-assembling itself into larger units and I doubt we could escape the tide even if we wished to.[8]

Reading these words reminds one how much Pierre Berton and Canada changed during the Pearson years.

8 Pierre Berton, untitled article, *Maclean's*, LXVII, 7 (April 6, 1963), 62.

On polling day, April 8, the Conservatives won only 95 seats and the Liberals, 129. Thanks to the NDP and Social Credit members, neither major party had a majority. But John Diefenbaker had lost power forever, and the nuclear question was to be settled. Pearson and Kennedy quickly agreed on a system of joint control and Canada began to acquire the nuclear weapons for which its delivery systems had been designed.

There had been other election issues. There were other examples of Conservative indecisiveness and confusion, with which the opposition parties had made great play. But the historian must find the weapons question the most important, and the most alarming, of all the matters that the Diefenbaker government bungled. First Diefenbaker had made commitments without understanding their import. Then he had refused either to honour the commitments or to withdraw from them. In the end he had succeeded only in dividing his party, infuriating Canada's allies, weakening its defences, and disrupting its alliances. He cannot even have won many votes: Canada's 'ban-the-bombers' presumably voted NDP or Communist, and the opinion polls showed that most Canadians wanted nuclear arms.

In his memoirs Diefenbaker explained that he was the victim of a plot. According to him, Washington set out to manipulate Canadian politics. It suborned Pearson, who changed his tune at Kennedy's behest; the Pentagon had a 'supra-governmental relationship' with the RCAF, which had suborned Harkness and Sévigny; and, in the basement of his embassy, the American ambassador was giving secret lectures to Canadian newsmen, so that they could best 'undermine my government's policy on nuclear weapons.'[9] All was orchestrated from the American Department of State. Diefenbaker believed this in 1963; he still believed it in 1977, fighting once more in his memoirs for the causes that served him so ill in that election campaign. The Conservatives were defending Canada's sovereignty against the big bad wolf to the South; the Liberals, we are told, were Kennedy's running-dogs.

Of course the Americans wanted Canada to decide, and, if possible, to arm the weapons it had willingly acquired; and of course they tried to change Canada's behaviour. However, they did not compel Canada or try to compel it, to do anything in particular, and therefore did not infringe its sovereignty. Nor was Diefenbaker consistent when he criticized the American government, or American soldiers, for making public statements or granting interviews that embarrassed his government. With respect to South Africa and the Commonwealth, or Britain and the EEC, Diefenbaker himself had done exactly the same thing. Indeed, he and his ministers had threatened the British, adopting a tactic to which Washington did not stoop. In any event it was the Canadian voters, not the Toronto media, the old Bay Street gang, or the Washington establishment, that decided to turn the rascals out. Diefen-

9 Diefenbaker, *One Canada ... 1962 to 1967*, 3.

baker believed he spoke to and for the ordinary people. In April 1963 they told him that they no longer trusted him to do so.

On the other hand, Diefenbaker was right when he claimed that in Canada the press did not treat him fairly. Indeed, they handled his foibles in a way that was both insulting and cruel. While he was in office the media developed a habit that is probably now unalterable. Having constituted themselves a sort of popular tribune, they attempt to destroy the reputations of political leaders. This is not to be confused with old-style political partisanship. It is applied with malice but without discrimination to the leading figures of both major parties, no matter which is in power; it serves to conceal matters of substance not only from the public but from the journalists themselves. Minor parties get the same treatment from time to time, although for some reason the CCF and NDP leaders have always been exempted, perhaps because in the federal House they are so powerless that it is no fun to make them look ridiculous. Reporters wrote of Diefenbudgets, Diefendollars, Diefenbubbles, and Diefenbabble, as later they were to write about Peter Elliott Waterhole; no one converts Broadbent into Narrowtwist, or Coldwell into Warmspring. Of course the glossy young media people of Toronto and Montreal did not understand the elderly populist orator from Prince Albert. His style was not theirs; to them his interests and his worries were more foreign than those of Ho Chi Minh. By 1963 it was they, not the Bay Street plotters within the Conservative party, who were Diefenbaker's most dangerous enemies.

Certainly Diefenbaker had little reason to fear that the New Democratic Party (NDP), the retreaded version of the old CCF, could replace him in office. With money from the unions and with a broader organizational base, in the federal sphere it might hope for great things. Nevertheless, it did not do as well as its promoters had hoped. In the 1962 election, it raised its share of the popular vote from 9.4 per cent to 13.4 per cent, and it took nineteen seats, compared with twenty-five for the CCF in 1957 and eight in 1958. In 1963 and thereafter, the NDP vote would be one of the awkward things that could deny a majority to either major party. But most observers think that it was erstwhile Liberal voters who moved into the NDP. For the Tory vote, especially in 1962 and 1963, a much more serious threat came from the Social Credit party.

In 1957, Social Credit won nineteen seats, all in Alberta and British Columbia. In 1958, it won none. In 1962, it rebounded to a new and much higher level, winning thirty seats, largely because in rural Quebec voters turned from the Tories to the colourful leadership of Réal Caouette. Unlike the Albertans and British Columbians who ran the federal party, Caouette actually believed in the 'funny money' ideas of Major Douglas, the inventor of Social Credit doctrine. Among small businessmen and on impoverished farmlands these doctrines had a natural appeal. If Caouette and Social Credit had not existed, presumably some Quebec voters would have stayed with the Tories, in spite of the Diefenbaker disarray, while more would have gone back to their former Liberal affiliation. Certainly the Liberals expected this outcome, only to receive a painful surprise. In Alberta and British Columbia, Social Credit's traditional happy hunting grounds, in the absence of Social Credit the Tories would have gotten the Socred voters, who were emphatically anti-Socialist and generally anti-Liberal as well. Some Albertans and British Columbians must also have voted Socred because the party, based and led in the West, was 'theirs.' Such voters must have worried about the sudden appearance of francophone Socred members, and of a French-Canadian deputy leader. Through the 1960s the Social Credit party would be a source of distress to the two major parties, and especially to the Tories, for, though responsibly led, it did help to prevent any party from getting a clear majority. But with the passage of time it became less important. In Quebec it was unable to make much progress in cities, and with the dwindling of the rural population its support dribbled away. In the far West, as the provincial Socred administrations lost first credibility and then office, so in federal elections voters drifted back to their natural homes in the Conservative party. It was unfortunate for Diefenbaker that before this drift was well under way he had lost the Tory leadership.

Perhaps it did not really matter very much. The last few Diefenbaker years saw a profound change in style, a change that made the Chief's ideas less and less compelling, his own style more and more repellant. The country was turning from old ways to new, and we must now proceed to chronicle that turning.

25

From the Old Ways to the New:
The Changing Atmosphere of the Early Sixties

In 1960, as John Kennedy hailed the passing of the torch to a new generation in the United States, the sixty-three-year old John Diefenbaker still held a torch lit three years before, a torch whose flame now flickered weakly. Canadians were thus diverted by the brilliance of the American blaze, of that new Camelot in Washington which had finally lifted the Republican pall from the American capital. There was something symbolic when Beverly Baxter wrote his last London Letter for *Maclean's* on July 30, 1960, declaring that he hoped he had made Britain more understandable for Canadians 'far across the sea.' This British *ave atque vale* was followed soon by a special issue: 'America 1960' – a '100-page report on the people all the shouting is about.' The issue celebrated American variety; the incredible women of Madison Avenue, a 'vision of energy, neuroses and high income'; Wall Street, 'the damned and exalted canyon'; and Flora, Illinois, or Middletown, 'where the bull sessions were at Honest John Throgmorton's drugstore instead of the barbershop these days, but the bull sounds the same, the white paint on the veranda rails looks as clean, and the piano lessons last as long as they always did.' Small wonder the Americans shouted; no wonder Canadians listened. From Britain the noises were already feeble and plaintive.

Naturally there were Canadians who did not like what they heard. Hugh MacLennan lamented the 'Americanization' of Canada, the 'swamping of our national purpose by that of the United States and of our habits by a state of mind totally American.' There had been no conquest; it had been 'more like a seduction in which the lady keeps murmuring that she can't help herself.' Canadian intellectuals were as always more wary of the American pandemonium than businessmen, bureaucrats, and, above all, the young. In the past Canada's intellectuals had accepted the criticism of American mass culture and politics which American intellectuals themselves had so eloquently delivered. But the new style and the new intellectuals troubled Canadians. There was the popular economist John Kenneth

Galbraith ensconced in Washington; there were the poets Archibald MacLeish and Robert Frost too; the historian Arthur Schlesinger was settled in the White House and sometimes swam in the presidential pool. Where was academic distance, much less alienation, in all this?

The picture was certainly confused. Scepticism was difficult when Kennedy talked to Americans in language almost Periclean in its balance, simplicity, and purpose, while Diefenbaker hectored Canadians in the fashion of a tiresome fire-and-brimstone evangelist. Frankly, Dief the Chief was embarrassing for Canadian intellectuals. Could one imagine Diefenbaker discussing the fashionable Protestant theologian Reinhold Niebuhr with Schlesinger? Or with anyone else? The image quickly became comic. Diefenbaker himself knew that a teetotalling Baptist could not live on the new frontier. Wisely he did not try; less wisely, he let his resentment of the new way turn into a bitterness that affected Canada's relations with the United States and that ultimately speeded his own decline.

America, then, was a land to shout about. *Maclean's* had seen the future, and it seemed to work. And not only for Americans. The stream of technology ran broadly, easily crossing over the undefended border; so too could American wealth and life. *Maclean's* recognized that Canadians would share the icons and legends of Camelot, and to prepare them it listed on its first page 'ninety things and people to watch for from the US.' The list lacks neither amusement nor irony. Mack Jones, the new 'slugger' for the Milwaukee Braves, soon could be watched again in the minor leagues. The Desert Rat (gin and lemon bitters) never quite made it as a cocktail, although Quincy Jones and Buddy Rich certainly did as musicians. Lighted wallpaper intended to replace light bulbs remains a seductive idea but nothing more, yet frozen orange juice in paper cartons is now a part of daily life. The irony in the list would not be understood for over a decade, but it was there. Among people to watch for was Sam (Mooney) Giacana, 'a Chicago hood who is taking over from gangster czar Tony Arcado.' No one watched Sam until it was learned, a decade and a half later, that he and the new president had shared the same mistress. But by that time Camelot was only a memory tinged with sadness and ambivalence. The dynamic young president was soon dead; the American scene soon turned sour.

The immediate impact of Camelot was on politics and especially on the relations between politics and the media. In a sense, however, the Quebec election of June 1960 had anticipated the American election of November. Quebec intellectuals had become closely involved with political life, and effective use was made of the media, especially television. Underlying the appeal of the Liberals was a sense that change was inevitable and, more important, that it was good. As John Saywell pointed out, 'The Liberal leaders – Jean Lesage, Georges Lapalme, Paul Gérin-Lajoie, René Lévesque, and others – gave the impression of intellectual ability, progressive view, youth and vigour, and lent strength to the plea that it was "time for a change".' This, of course, was the stuff of Camelot. The early successes in Quebec suggest that Canadians were ready to sympathize with the New Frontiersmen even before they had ridden into battle.

Lester Pearson and Walter Gordon realized this fact as they began to reconstruct the federal Liberal party from the rubble of 1958. Two important events occurred in 1960. Richard O'Hagan, a Toronto advertising executive and Gordon's friend, became Pearson's special assistant. O'Hagan saw what Kennedy's media people had done, and in similar fashion he began to shape Pearson's rather ragged and soft image into something smoother, harder, and more progressive. Pearson soon stopped wearing bow ties and began speaking simpler and shorter sentences. But Pearson could never have the Kennedy style, and his refashioners wisely refrained from any attempt to recast him in that image. Much was made of his interest in hockey; little or nothing was said of his university background. Meanwhile, another event also sought to attach the progressive label to the Liberal party. In early September the party held a thinkers' conference in Kingston to which they invited numerous 'liberal' Canadians. This was the first such conference since the early thirties – apparently thought was not required in the meantime, while the Liberals ruled – and the tone, as in the thirties, was distinctly to the left of the party's when it had been in power. Tom Kent attracted most attention when this new Pearson adviser called for a state medical system, sickness insurance, more unemployment benefits, retraining programs, subsidization of industries in depressed areas, and an urban renewal plan. This was a forecast of a future that Kent would help shape. Less accurate as a prophet was non-Liberal James Eayrs, who reminded the audience that the Soviet danger remained and that we should contribute to its containment by increasing our contribution to NATO and NORAD. Eayrs would change his mind, but in 1960 most thought with him that his remarks were progressive, a Canadian reflection of what one heard in Boston or Berkeley or Foggy Bottom. Power was still an opportunity, not a threat.

The thinkers' conference was followed by a giant Liberal policy rally in January 1961. The Conservatives too held larger and more enthusiastic conventions. Both parties' conventions had a similar theme: political participation was no longer for only a few. The 'process,' as it came to be called, must be open to all. This view was endorsed even more heartily by the New Party, then being brought to birth from the marriage of the labour movement and the CCF. During 1960, seminars proliferated, spawning New Party organizations throughout Canada, all in preparation for the party's founding convention on July 31, 1961. The enthusiasm was immense, although the new infant was not quite so much unlike the other parties as the CCF had claimed to be. Over 2,000 delegates assembled in Ottawa's Coliseum and debated vigorously and long, passing resolutions as regularly as they wiped their brows in the sweltering August evenings. The party decided to call itself the New

Democratic Party, and delegate Ramsay Cook termed it 'symbolic because [the convention] represented a victory of the rank and file over the officials and what better word than "democratic" to describe such a victory.' Living with 'democracy' in the sixties proved harder than the 'moderate majority' of the NDP realized at the time. Some of them, including leadership candidate Hazen Argue and Ramsay Cook himself, later left the party when the majority lost its moderation.

But the convention was not a prayer meeting worshipping the saints of the socialist past as had happened so often before, and as would occur again. There was still ritual but, as Cook reported, the platform was 'Galbraithian in terms,' the 'music folksy and the liturgy strongly American in flavour.'[1] Because the United States seemed to be pioneering in the adaptation of social democracy to Galbraith's affluent society, the American flavour appealed to the NDP in 1961. Nor was it yet time for the socialists to come in from the Cold War, with the Russians flaunting their abuse of basic human rights in the new concrete and barbed wire barrier dividing Berlin. NATO was endorsed by the NDP, and although NORAD charmed neither the new party nor the Liberals the attack was mainly directed toward nuclear weapons, not the American alliance.

The Bomb was an easy, albeit genuine, target for leftist fear and rage. In July 1960 the spirit of public action exemplified by the broader party conventions led to the creation of the Voice of Women, a peace movement that was dedicated to the abolition of nuclear weapons. The Voice created little controversy at first; when it called on Howard Green in January 1961, the External Affairs minister warmly greeted the delegates, congratulating them on the service they were rendering mankind. The women left with little comment. In the autumn of 1961, however, the women dispensed with the friendly social call on the minister. Together with the Combined Universities Campaign for Nuclear Disarmament they organized a large seventy-two-hour anti-nuclear demonstration on Parliament Hill and presented a 142,000-signature petition to government officials. The nuclear question is discussed elsewhere in Part IV; what is of interest here is the shift in the emphasis of this political pressure group from direct contact with policymakers to 'media events' designed to influence public opinion. This technique, honed to perfection by the civil rights marchers in the United States, became characteristic of public action during the sixties. 'Participatory democracy,' it came to be termed, although the participation was decidedly selective and the democracy questionable at best. But as the American leftist Tom Hayden, who originated the term, later said, 'it was a call to action when students wanted to take action.' The action, then, was rebellious whatever the role might be. Form was as important as content. In the end, for many

1 Ramsay Cook, 'The Labor-Socialist Wedding: Moderation Wins Down the Line in NDP,' *Saturday Night,* LXXVII, 18 (September 2, 1961), 9-12.

North American movements only the husk of form counted; the core of content was dead.

In the early sixties, however, the 'citizen movements' were invariably earnest and their cause generally well defined. There was perhaps a too simple belief in the efficacy of such movements, a belief that led to later frustration and, in a few cases, violence. The belief in the possibility of change through direct action enlivened and complicated the political process, and it was a reflection of a new willingness to test limits, a thirst to taste what was new.

Among things new in 1963 was 'pop art,' which appeared in three Toronto shows late in the year. Pop art puzzled Toronto's critics and attracted few buyers, yet it presaged an important debate among artists, writers, and critics about the nature of culture and the meaning of the avant-garde. But this debate came late to Canada, and in the early sixties Canadian critics continued mainly to lament Canada's isolation and consequent conservatism. As Robert Fulford, surveying the literary landscape in 1962, said of those times, there was a sense in which Canadian literature reflected the fact that Canadians were not living in the twentieth century. We had, Fulford observed, a habit of learning about cultural events a decade after they occurred. Elizabeth Kilbourn discussed art in terms that echoed Fulford when she spoke of the 'spell which for so many years ... locked Canadian painting into perpetual isolation from the rest of the world.'[2] The recognition accorded the Canadian painter Jean-Paul Riopelle at the 1962 Venice Bienniale was a happy exception, but the embarrassing failure of the National Gallery to detect the fakes when it exhibited a large collection of purported old masters in the same year afforded further testimony in support of the general rule.

The Canadian artistic community was nevertheless in a generally optimistic mood. These years were marked by a confidence, surprising in retrospect, that the solution to Canada's cultural deprivation was a more educated public and a more beneficent government. The solution seemed near, for never had universities expanded so fast and never had the government's and the public's support for the arts been so strong. In 1963 alone, the Molson Foundation established several $15,000 awards for outstanding Canadian achievement in the fields of arts and letters; the province of Ontario established its own Arts Council; the federal government announced plans for a $9 million arts centre in Ottawa that eventually cost over $40 million; a new Place des Arts opened in Montreal; Brian Doherty founded the Shaw Festival at Niagara-on-the-Lake; and on Dominion Day in Halifax the Neptune Theatre welcomed its first visitors. Extraordinary beginnings that lasted.

2 Elizabeth Kilbourn in John Saywell, ed., *Canadian Annual Review for 1962* (Toronto: University of Toronto Press 1963), 416.

The Neptune found its home in an old movie theatre, but other efforts required new structures to house them. Sometimes these simply mimicked the uninteresting buildings about them, but occasionally the architect was more adventurous and the building became an ornament to the downtown area and a happy contrast to the dross of nineteen-sixties development and redevelopment. Whole sections of cities disappeared, the Victorian touches that so marked Canada's downtowns until the fifties destroyed forever. In the early sixties there was still little objection to this kind of destruction except from a few specialists, and it must be admitted that many of the old buildings were pretty undistinguished. Toronto, for instance, would have little cause to regret the vanishing of Shea's Theatre and the clutter of tumbledown shops and doss houses that lay around it. Architects on the whole were too busy drafting new plans to concern themselves about the old, and the obligations to their predecessors seemed less important than the legacy that would be left by their own generation, not only in city centres but also on the university campuses, which became laboratories for architectural experimentation. Unfortunately the results of the experiments were mixed at best. Simon Fraser University was placed in a group of elegant pavilions on a mountaintop. The University of Toronto devised a suburban campus that attracted international attention, while on its downtown site it erected a row of tasteless and uncomfortable monoliths that did not even have the virtues of homogeneity. At Massey College and at Trent, Ron Thom experimented with modern adaptations of Oxbridge collegiality. And in London, the University of Western Ontario, eschewing innovation, continued to build in 'collegiate gothic.'

Perhaps the results were so mixed because architects had to draft hastily and contractors had to work as fast as they could. The universities faced extraordinary pressure to expand after 1960. By 1961 the number of university students had reached 113,000. This was 50 per cent higher than in 1956, and 200,000 were expected by 1966. In fact, the number was closer to 300,000. Surveys consistently showed that Canadians thought this expansion a remarkably good thing, but of course they expected that their children would be part of that good thing. The federal government responded by increasing its grants in support of higher education. In their campaign platform of 1963, Liberals offered a system of national scholarships that would open higher education to able but needy students. The willingness of the federal government to become involved with this traditionally provincial area met with few objections, even in Quebec. Indeed, one 1963 poll indicated that 72.5 per cent of Canadians thought that education should be a federal responsibility.

The most important federal in initiative in education during the Diefenbaker years might well have been the Technical and Vocational Assistance Act, mentioned above in connection with economic policy. This provided for a type of conditional grant whereby the federal government paid 75 per cent of the total a province spent on the building and equipping of vocational training schools. By late 1963 Ottawa had approved new construction, additions, or alterations to 538 technical schools. Of this total, 265 were totally new institutions. To serve national needs the new technology demanded its own servants. The Technical and Vocational Assistance Act was a partial attempt to provide them. Although it stressed the classroom rather than the work experience, the Act deserves little criticism on that score. Canadian schoolchildren and their parents were no longer prepared to accept the dependent relationships and the low wages of the apprenticeship system, which in any event had never worked very well anywhere in North America. Government policy did not destroy apprenticeship; Canadian middle class values were effective enough in erasing this ancient avenue to technical and vocational skill.

The pervasiveness of middle class values was clear in all the studies that examined Canadian society in the early sixties. Raymond Breton and John C. McDonald found that in 1961 the majority of Canadian male and female students with four or more years of secondary schooling wanted and indeed expected a high status occupation. There were regional differences, to be sure, but the trend held true in all regions. Another 1963 study of adolescent high-school culture concluded that 'Canadian high school youth act in a conventional manner and are bearers of a conventional culture.' Yet another 1963 survey indicated that Canadian high-school students shared the values of their parents, esteeming heterosexuality, sports, and 'having fun.' There was scarcely a sign of a generation gap in 1963 high schools – and precious little indication of a flowering of interest in high culture.

University students, too, exhibited much less anti-establishment emotion than anti-Diefenbakerism. The fundamental goals of Canadian society were scarcely questioned by the student body. To Canadians who went abroad to graduate schools in the mid-fifties and returned to university appointments in the early sixties the scene was much the same as the one they had known as first-year students – bigger and more challenging in terms of intellectual demands, but not fundamentally different. There was some concern that the students came too much from the upper middle classes. Evidence seemed to support this belief. In 1961 the Dominion Bureau of Statistics showed that although 31 per cent of all families had incomes over $5,000, 70 per cent of students reported parental incomes in that range. What this meant was hard to say: students often did not know what their parents' incomes really were, and the parents of students naturally belong to an age group whose incomes are very much higher on the average than the incomes of families as a whole. Nevertheless, the numbers were disturbing because they seemed to suggest that the benefits of higher education flowed chiefly to the children of the prosperous. The answer urged by university administrators and governments was, naturally, enlargement of the universities, combined with more generous student aid. If fees were kept low and bursaries were generous, there could be a spot for everyone no matter how poor his or her original state. The solution seemed easy; its pedagogical consequences were too obscure to consider. There were some objections, to be sure. Frank Underhill and Peter Dale Scott lamented the loss of 'community' in the new large university, but Robin Mathews in reply praised the American university in which he had begun but not completed his doctoral studies. In that institution of 25,000 students, he wrote, he had not been 'one whit less in touch with faculty' than 'as one of twelve honours students in a Department with half a dozen graduate students in Canada.' A larger university meant more diversity and thus more stimulating minds. According to Mathews, Canada need not fear the 'Ohio States' in its future.[3] Nor had Mathews yet begun to fear the Americans who would come in such numbers to staff them.

Although Claude Bissell has suggested that there was 'a widespread popular radicalism in the early sixties,' this radicalism was apparent only in scattered traces within the English-Canadian writing of the pre-1963 period. Most of these traces were no more than notices of the Beat poetry of Allen Ginsberg, the philosophical anarchism of Paul Goodman, or the founding of the Students for a Democratic Society in 1962, at Port Huron just across the bridge from Sarnia. Seemingly more important for Canadians was Frank Underhill's *In Search of Canadian Liberalism*, a record of Underhill's intellectual migration and an investigation of the authenticity of the Canadian liberal tradition. For Underhill the rounding of the Canadian circle came in the joining together of the radical and liberal traditions. Where did this leave Underhill and other Canadians? Certainly far from the radicalism of the middle sixties which eschewed both the historical approach and the liberal tradition.

Another work derived from the same tradition was *Social Purpose for Canada* (1961), an anthology of essays on the need for continuing social change in Canada. The tone was pragmatic, optimistic, 'responsible,' and managerial, rather than radical. Michael Oliver's preface rather unconvincingly disavowed any direct connection between the appearance of the book and the founding of the NDP: 'The ideas contained in this book will, we hope, influence not only the New Party but all political parties in Canada.' They did so more directly than Oliver imagined: seven years later one of the authors became Canada's prime minister and Liberal leader.

Pierre Trudeau was like many French-Canadian intellectuals and literary figures in being more directly involved with political life and political publicity than his English-Canadian counterparts. The Quiet Revolution did, perhaps, accompany a widespread popular 'radicalism' in Quebec. Books such as Jean-Paul Desbiens's *Les impertinences du Frère Untel* and Abbés Gérard Dion and Louis O'Neill's *Les Chrétiens et les élections* influenced action in a fashion unknown in the rest of Canada.

---

3 Robin Mathews, 'The New University: An Old Role,' *Canadian Forum*, LXXVII (May 1963), 35-6.

There was often a scatological, ribald tone to French-Canadian satire in this period, one that carried over easily to the new radicalism later, and to the unique political/cultural nationalism of Quebec. Among new writers Marie-Claire Blais captured most attention with her remarkable *La belle bête* (1959), an experimental and lurid tale of rural Quebec. Her style, too, passed easily into the bold and surreal attack upon limits in art and life so characteristic of the new left. Still, these works seem more like early shoots rather than solid growths; only watering and nurturing would assure survival of the plants. In 1963 no one yet knew what form that nurture would take.

There were too many early shoots to know what the future would bring. The early sixties were mainly a period of transition in which optimism mingled with uncertainty, and social liberalism accompanied middle class conformism. By 1963 Canadians seemed to be embarrassed about their conservative reputation, and one heard much less of the gleeful comparisons of Canadian and American divorce rates. Even the churches, especially the mainline Protestant churches, sought to cloak themselves in new, more colourful raiments. For some there was a return to the social gospel with a call for an 'activist' Christianity, one that lived in the streets and the slums. The Student Christian Movement, which had branches at almost every college campus in English Canada, was most receptive to such notions, and endless nights were spent discussing how Christians should live in this particular world. Most concluded that they should not live as they had. Even the moderator of the United Church could describe his organization as 'too pietistic and irrelevant in the face of the real stuff of life and great issues of our day.' The church, the Very Reverend Angus MacQueen continued, was merely 'the feeble guardian of personal decency and the fount of tranquillity and optimism.' These virtues counted far less than commitment and change. To spur their complacent parishioners, the head offices of the United and Anglican churches sponsored popular publications that excoriated 'the comfortable pew.' One of these publications, by agnostic Pierre Berton, got much wider distribution than the Bible in some churches, and certainly it was read with more attention. A more lasting and important document than Berton's was Pope John XXIII's 1961 encyclical, *Mater et Magistra*. Yet this historic document also reflected the demand that the church must be less comfortable and more 'involved.' The pope's message was well received by Canadian Catholics, some of whom interpreted it as a call 'to plunge ... into the forefront of the reforms needed in society.' Catholic trade unionists and reformers were particularly pleased at the encyclical's cautious approval of state action and its implied disavowal of the Catholic Church's traditional anti-socialist stand.

Even the Christmas and Easter churchgoer could not fail to notice the change in the faith. The distance between priest and parishioner shortened; familiarity crept into the ritual and liturgy. Folk masses echoed through sanctuaries, and Pete Seeger added his name to the roster as a composer of sacred music. There were study groups where doctrine was to be discussed, not just received. Even the existence of God was debated, and an occasional theological radical could be found to take the negative side. The Anglican, Presbyterian, and United churches seemed to have taken a road that would lead eventually to union, and other churches heeded similar calls for brotherhood. In his 1960 presidential address to the Canadian Council of Churches, the Very Reverend George Dorey proclaimed that 'the fearsome monsters of denominational prejudice and animosity, like the prehistoric monsters whose skeletons we see in the museums, have died.'

But of course the fearsome monsters were still alive. They lingered in the hearts of many churchgoers who resented the liberalizing and ecumenicizing trends in their faiths. Some left old allegiances to join the fundamentalist sects which grew and proliferated throughout the period. Others became dissenters within their churches, modern Jeremiahs warning of new enemies bearing the seeds of moral and spiritual degradation both of the society and of the faith. They could find signs everywhere – in the moral vacuity of Canada's schools, in the disintegration of family life, in the permissive attitude toward sex, in the collapse of censorship. The railings at modern society quickly became tiresome, and the press virtually ignored them, choosing to emphasize the progressive trends in modern religion. The People's Church and the Pentecostals were there, but they were not to be noticed by polite society except when their behaviour found a place in a newspaper's morning or afternoon 'smile.' This reaction was understandable but it led to distortion. Too often the press and even the clergy failed to notice the reservations that accompanied church leaders' professions of reform. *Mater et Magistra*, for example, warned of the serious dangers in the process of modernization at the same time as it revised some of the Roman Catholic Church's traditional attitudes. The latter was usually hailed; the former was generally ignored. Thus many were greatly surprised when the fabric of their faith later did not give way to permit any and every new form of personal and social behaviour.

No topic symbolized this liberal expectation and conservative result so much as birth control, and especially 'the Pill.' The US Food and Drug Administration approved the use of Enovid, an oral contraceptive, in May 1960. Tests showed it to be 100 per cent effective – history's first full guarantee against pregnancy, apart from abstention. No one expected a sudden sexual revolution, and at the time none came, even though birth rates began to fall almost at once. Studies in the early sixties indicated that pre-marital and extra-marital activity had increased very little over that reported by Alfred Kinsey in the late forties. And yet the possibility was there. Earlier, contraception tended to be a male responsibility, and one that was often not accepted. Contraception usually meant condoms, which were normally hidden beneath the drugstore shelf and, with classic hypocrisy, sold 'for the prevention of disease only.' When needed, they were often not to hand. The new freedom for women and the gradual awareness of this freedom is described by Nora Ephron. After her 1962 graduation Ephron moved to New York and immediately decided she must do something about birth control. She was naturally frightened: she told the nurse she was engaged, although she knew she did not have to say any such thing. But within a few minutes, in the 16th Street brownstone that housed the Margaret Sanger clinic, 'a long and happy relationship' began between Ephron and the pill:

When I first started with the pill I would stop taking them every time I broke up with someone. I had a problem making a commitment to sex; I guess it was a hangover from the whole Fifties virgin thing. The first man I went to bed with, I was in love with and wanted to marry. The second one I was in love with, but didn't have to marry him. With the third one, I thought I *might* fall in love. It was impossible for me to think that I might be a person who 'had sex,' so whenever I had no boyfriend it was always a terrible emotional mess. I couldn't start sleeping with someone until I could begin the pill's cycle again. It was awful. Finally, my new gynecologist explained it all to me. 'Dahlink, who knows what's coming around the corner?'[4]

In those days, in so many ways, no one did.

Meanwhile, in Ottawa, the political game was played much as before, but social change had begun to affect the process, the assumptions, and the results. On February 5, 1963, Canada's prime minister walked into the House of Commons with his hands behind his back, his fingers crossed. The old-fashioned gesture was futile, and John Diefenbaker's minority government fell. The crossed fingers seemed to symbolize a superstitious man locked in a prison of his own past and his own narrow beliefs. That, at least, was the way most Canadian journalists saw things. Diefenbaker's political obituaries were written before the campaign began. Only four newspapers remained loyal to the Tory cause, and their defence of the Chief often faltered. The electricity that had startled the nation five years before now seemed mere hocus-pocus. The conjuror's hands had become too slow to fool anyone but the gullible and the senile. To those many Canadians who admired the cybernetic aura of the New Frontier, Diefenbaker had become a national embarrassment.

On the cover of *Newsweek* for February 18, 1963, Diefenbaker's wrinkled, contorted face glowered. The cover story was no more flattering in its description: 'the india-rubber features twist and contort in grotesque and gargoyle-like grimaces; beneath the electric gray of the hairline, the eyebrows beat up and down like bats'

4 Nora Ephron, 'The Pill and I,' in Lynda Rosen Obst, ed., *The Sixties* (New York: Rolling Stone 1977), 71-2.

wings, the agate-blue eyes blaze forth cold fire.' Some people claimed that older, female Tories found Diefenbaker's face rugged, kind, pleasant, and even soothing. His enemies need not have been concerned, for in 1963 one saw few young people at Tory rallies, especially in the cities. To younger Canadians Diefenbaker seemed sadly out of tune with their times.

It is all too easy to be sarcastic about Dief the Chief and his merry band of individualists, not least because Diefenbaker's Conservative-populist administration could so easily be made to look foolish and unco-ordinated – no happy posture for any government, especially for so actively interventionist a one. As the above pages have tried to show, so far as economic affairs were concerned the government's record was at best a mixed one, and with respect to defence and foreign affairs its performance was dismal. No wonder that journalists and university people, now as then, have inclined to make fun of the old man from Prince Albert. By 1963 it had become hard to take the Conservatives seriously as an alternative governing party, and the Pearson Liberals were not slow to learn how to compare Conservative incompetence with Liberal wit and dispatch. Nor did they fail to exploit the Kennedy comparison, misleading and inaccurate though that comparison was. Looking back on 1963 from the early eighties, the authors are inclined to think that so far as confusion and incompetence are concerned it is really hard to distinguish between Liberal Tweedledee and Conservative Tweedledum in the years after 1957. What is really sad about the Diefenbaker years is that the Conservatives lost their best chance in this century to become a properly national party, strong in Quebec as well as elsewhere. If the Québécois had a federalist choice in which they could believe, surely Canada's national politics would be healthier in the eighties. But was the choice lost? stolen? mislaid? or did it ever exist at all? Was the 1958 election a fluke from which nothing may be inferred? However real the missed opportunities may have been, two things are clear. Diefenbaker was not interested in party organization. And he did not care about Quebec.

What happened on election day, April 8, 1963, was more complicated than Diefenbaker, *Newsweek*, or the young Canadians who shunned the Tory rallies realized. The Liberals won 129 seats with 41.7 per cent of the popular vote, and the Conservatives took 95 seats with 32.8 per cent. As for the minor parties, the NDP garnered 17 seats with 13.2 per cent of the vote, and Social Credit collected 24 seats with 11.9 per cent of the vote.

Canada had another minority government. This much is clear; its significance is not. Soon after the election political commentators presented interpretations that suggested the election of 1963 had been decisive, at least symbolically. In 1965 the political philosopher George Grant lamented Diefenbaker's defeat, seeing that defeat as definitive proof that there could no longer be 'an alternative to the American republic being built on the northern half of this continent.' Grant admitted

Diefenbaker's weaknesses but honoured his 'telling historical sense' that harked back to earlier days when for 'young Ontarians ... the character of the country was self-evident.' The passion of Grant's argument and its intellectual sophistication and subtlety apotheosized the Diefenbaker government, shielding its contradictions behind a historical dialectic. While Grant's lament told us much about Canadian myths and the discontinuities of Canadian history, it did not succeed in fitting Diefenbaker convincingly into its interpretive framework. A decade later Diefenbaker's memoirs showed Canadians how much the Chief, with his curiously ambivalent attitude toward the Americans and with his banal understanding of political ideas, stood outside the historical pattern that Grant had so cleverly constructed.

Grant's interpretation of Canadian history rightly commands attention, but a more useful analysis of what happened in April 1963 is found in Peter Regenstreif's study of voting patterns between 1957 and 1963. Regenstreif pointed out that the political affiliations had become 'remarkably unstable.' Canadians were casting off their old political raiments as they moved from their parents' homes, from their familiar communities, and from traditional to new forms of behaviour. There was no Canadian consensus in 1963; but, Regenstreif added, Canada did possess an élite population that was reasonably small and localized. By 1963 Diefenbaker had offended most segments of this élite. The 'crucial lesson' of the Diefenbaker period, he argued, was that 'if any party coming to office nationally does not do so with the support of élite opinion, it must gain that support immediately and then hold it if it wishes to remain in office.' This Diefenbaker had not done; relying on rural and traditional support was not enough; his defeat inevitably followed.

If Diefenbaker failed, Pearson scarcely did better. The controversy over nuclear weapons brought credit neither to government nor to opposition. But the Liberals were to have sixteen years in office, during which time they could disentangle the confusion they had inherited, while making mistakes of their own. They would also observe and have to cope with the further evolution of Quebec's Quiet Revolution, which became steadily less tranquil as year followed year through the sixties. If Canada's relationship with the United States was one of the two foci of political change during the early sixties, the other was the place of French Canada and Quebec in Canadian confederation.

Apart from Peter Gzowski's sensitive articles in *Maclean's*, there was little but superficial comment on Quebec in the English-Canadian media prior to 1963. There was much sympathy but little understanding of what the so-called Quiet Revolution might mean. Most important, there was little recognition of the demands that Quebec's changes would make on the rest of Canada. Most English Canadians appeared to think that their country could remain the one they knew. Among Protestant and post-Protestant opinion there was a widespread feeling of relief that Quebec was at last casting off the 'fetters of Catholicism.' No longer 'priest-ridden,' the province would at long last be a fit partner for the progressive and secular forces that had long run English Canada while looking down on their francophone fellow citizens.

But Quebec was not yet a 'province like the others.' The nuclear question underlined the differences. Pierre Berton, in his comments urging Canada to take nuclear weapons, castigated his country for its weakness during the Korean War. Why had Canada been so spineless as to send a 'token' force? Why had conscription not been decreed? To ask the question was to forget the past and misunderstand the future. In fact, nuclear weapons were most unpopular in Quebec. Pearson's announcement led almost all important Quebec newspapers to oppose him. Social Credit received an immense boost, and Pearson lost some valuable potential candidates who became vociferous opponents. In a sarcastic and possibly libellous *Cité Libre* editorial, Pierre Trudeau charged that 'les Hipsters' of Camelot had decided to destroy Diefenbaker:

You think that I dramatize? But how do you think the policy got made? You think that General Norstad came as a tourist to Ottawa on January 3 to call the Canadian government to respect its commitments? You believe it is by chance that Mr Pearson, in his address of January 12, was able to call on the authority of General Norstad? You believe that it is by inadvertence that the State Department had sent to the newspapers on January 30 a communiqué reinforcing Mr Pearson's positions and where Mr Diefenbaker was called a liar?[5]

Trudeau's caustic questions remain unanswered. They are most important for what they reveal about the questioner – cynical, emotional, and thoroughly distrustful of the Ottawa that Trudeau observed from a distance.

Pearson's nuclear weapons policy cost him élite support in Quebec which earlier statements had attracted. In December 1962 Pearson had shown, in a speech drafted by Maurice Lamontagne, that he was prepared to move to meet the new Quebec. This was probably the most important speech of Pearson's life; it was scarcely noticed outside of Quebec. Pearson called for an inquiry to investigate 'the means of developing the bicultural character of Canada.' He admitted that, in the past, English Canadians and the federal government had held a narrow vision of the rights of French-speaking Canadians. 'This meant that, for all practical purposes, there would be an English-speaking Canada with a bilingual Quebec. What is called the "French fact" was to be provincial only....' As a description of the past the statement was fair, but the assumption that the vision of Canada's anglophones could be easily broadened was too facile. The Pearson government and its successor would try to reshape Canada's mentality; the task would prove far more difficult than Pearson himself had imagined possible.

5 *Canadian Annual Review 1963* (Toronto: University of Toronto Press 1964), 32

PART FIVE

The Pearson Years 1963-8

26

Coming Apart and Changing Together

'Even citizens of a South American republic might have envied Canadians in 1963.' The usually dour *Canadian Annual Review* thus began its 1963 issue with this unfamiliar comparison of Canada to a banana republic. The new prime minister, Lester Pearson, might, the *Review*'s editor declared, respond as Franklin Roosevelt had when told he would be the greatest American president: 'either the greatest or the last.' He was neither; but perhaps he was closer to both than we have realized.

In the eighties, we forget how serious the strains upon Confederation seemed in the mid-sixties. Canada had outgrown its old political garments and it had to try out new ones or refashion the old. On the one hand, internal growth had strained the fabric of Confederation and, by the mid-sixties, few thought simple readjustments would ease the strain. There were external influences, too, which forced Canada to change. The gray threads now seemed merely dull, not stolidly respectable, and in any case that respectability which had marked Canada's earlier style was no longer a value Canadians or others cherished. Throughout the country we cleaned out our closets, but we were uncertain whether we would refill them with the new fashions we saw.

Nowhere was this uncertainty more obvious than in the English-Canadian reaction to events in Quebec. The English-Canadian media showed a generosity toward the Quiet Revolution that rested upon too superficial an appreciation of the nature of the social, economic, and political changes occurring in Quebec. The first stirrings of separatism in the form of the Rassemblement pour l'indépendance nationale troubled English Canadians: the bombs in Montreal mailboxes outraged them. Too often, all dissent was lumped into a general mass called separatism. How could one interpret Liberal cabinet minister René Lévesque's warning that 'there must be a new Canada within five years or Quebec will quit Confederation.' Lévesque admitted being 'first and foremost ... a Québécois and second – with a rather growing doubt – a Canadian.' Graduates from the University of Toronto's University College in 1963 applauded Lévesque enthusiastically, but the enthusiasm may have simply masked confusion. The parts of Confederation were no longer fitting into the familiar mental images they had learned in the classroom.

What they had learned created many of the problems, not least Lester Pearson's. Pearson's background made it easier for him to accept the demands for change emanating from within Canada. Conversely, he was ill prepared for the changes that occurred beyond his nation's boundaries. To understand Pearson's idea of Canada requires consideration of his idea of internationalism. Pearson had spent his formative years outside of Canada. His memoirs reveal how important to him were the First World War, Oxford, and, above all, the international anarchy of the 1930s which he observed as a bystander in London and Geneva. He sensed both the fragility of international order and his nation's unwillingness to face the impact upon it of the world beyond its borders. This always distressed him; in the 1930s it frustrated him and formed in his mind strong ideas about the need for internationalism. In the 1950s and 1960s, he determined that he must break down those crustaceous formations that limited the growth of Canadians. Pearson's internationalism and his domestic politics thus were obverse sides of the same coin. By leading Canada into the bracing winds of international activity, Pearson hoped to open his countrymen to fuller awareness of the possibilities of, and threats to, humanity. There could be light in this world, but the dark was always nearby. 'The dark,' he once wrote, 'comes from our fears and our hates, our wrong priorities and our rooted prejudices, the destructive use to which we put so much of our technology, and poisoning and polluting of our environment, weariness, and a declining public commitment to new international responsibilities.' Of these fears and hates, his nation had too many.

Like the turn-of-the-century imperialists, Pearson looked beyond Canada because he did not like the limits he saw within. Yet unlike his critic, George Grant, Pearson was not a part of that conservative tradition. Pearson might have admitted that in earlier days the British connection had been an essential ingredient of a distinctive Canadian identity for English Canadians. For Pearson, however, an identity was not an end in itself; nor was that particular British-Canadian identity whose loss Grant lamented especially congenial to him. His diplomatic career had led him toward a cosmopolitanism which accepted progress, relativism, and liberalism. His direct experience with Europe in the 1930s had made him distrust the irrational in politics and also the values of the past. Canada's past had too many fears, too many hates, and too much memory. Thus, the only historian who became prime minister was, perhaps, the most eager to break with the past. In his view, Canada could not remain a nation if it continued to dwell upon its past. This was the intellectual foundation of Pearson's determination to give Canada a distinct flag, to promote bilingualism and biculturalism, and to heighten the activity of the Canadian state in cultural and social realms. Education, mobility, and affluence would clear the path toward a progressive modern state. In 1963, Pearson could not foresee how many Canadians of his own background would hesitate to take the path that he himself had followed so easily.

THE AMERICANS, THE WORLD, AND CANADIANS

It would be wrong to regard Pearson as an outsider to Canadian intellectual traditions. Like Frank Underhill, J.W. Dafoe, and, in 1963, Peter C. Newman and Pierre Berton, Pearson shared an acceptance of Canada as a North American nation. Like Berton, he believed that Canada had 'cast [its] lot with this continent for better or worse.' Since 1945, that lot had been mostly good. The Americans had made many mistakes; they had shown too little regard for Canadian sensitivities and too much alarm toward the Communist threat. Yet their aims seemed fundamentally decent and beneficent; certainly the benefits of American economic and military leadership in the free world were great for Canada. Like most of his generation, Pearson recalled American isolationism and attributed to it many of the catastrophes of the pre-1939 period. He and his fellow Canadian diplomats took some credit for weaning the Americans away from isolationism and toward responsible leadership. What Peter C. Newman expressed in a pre-election (March 7, 1963) *Maclean's* article summarized Pearson's attitude well.

The future prosperity and even the existence of Canada depend directly on the goodwill of the USA. This doesn't mean we should toady to Washington. But it does mean that we can hardly expect our point of view to carry much weight, if our chief emissary in future bargaining with the US president is a politician elected on the basis of blatant anti-Americanism.

Canada was part of the American team; quarrels over strategy were for the privacy of the clubhouse, not for the playing field.

This was the easy language of Mike Pearson's first official meeting with Jack Kennedy at Hyannis Port in May 1963. Cape Cod in May meant long afternoons of languid conversation, in this case about baseball earned run averages. Pearson quickly proved himself a member of the league, and Kennedy extended to him the kind of comradeship he reserved for those he approved. When Pearson prepared to leave, Kennedy took down the presidential flag and, bareheaded and coatless in a driving rainstorm, handed it to Pearson. The impulsive gesture captured so well the casual elegance of Camelot, the strong whiff of the romantic, and the instinct for drama. Even so, the beaming Pearson departed not much the wiser about what this new political blend in Washington augured for Canada.

For one thing, the rapport between Kennedy and Pearson did not eliminate all differences between their countries. Even the Hyannis Port communiqué expressed Canadian concern about the Canadian trade deficit with the United States as well as American opposition to the Canadian intention of moving to a twelve-mile off-shore fishing zone. More significant was Walter Gordon's first budget, which alarmed American businessmen and officials who regarded the proposed tax on takeovers of Canadian firms as discriminatory and 'protectionist.' Still, ultimately, it was the Canadian reaction not the American protest that led Gordon to withdraw the tax. The embarrassment of Gordon continued when in late July Kennedy proposed to Congress an interest equalization tax to be applied to foreign borrowings in the United States. The Liberals, having ridiculed the ninety-two-and-a-half cent Diefenbuck, could not accept without protest a policy that might cause further dollar devaluation. Thus Canada's most nationalistic finance minister had to beseech the Americans to make Canada an exception to the new tax. The special relationship still held; Canada got its exemption. Ironically, the exemption which Gordon did so much to obtain contributed to greater American involvement in the Canadian economy. To the nationalist finance minister, the incident was 'another sharp reminder of Canada's dependency on the United States.' Further contact with Americans convinced Gordon that 'at least the more junior people in the State and Treasury Departments held decidedly imperialistic views about Canada.' Further contact with Gordon convinced Americans that Canada's finance minister possessed limited competence but abundant paranoia. On the Liberals' second time around, things would not be the same.

That both partners had changed was soon obvious to others. When Secretary of State for External Affairs Paul Martin had his first meetings with Defense Secretary Robert McNamara and Secretary of State Dean Rusk, the Americans' determination to 'go right through' in Vietnam even if it meant 'one thousand years' startled Martin. So did the reports from Canadian officials in Saigon in the fall of 1963 which described the American satisfaction about and involvement in the overthrow of South Vietnam's president, Ngo Dinh Diem. It was as if Canadians had tried on a new pair of spectacles that changed the outlines to irregular and grotesque shapes. They still heard Kennedy's alluring voice calling Americans to bear any burden and meet any hardships, support any friend and oppose any foe. The two peoples were still friends; Canada still believed that the Americans could identify the common foe. Certainly the Canadian officials in Southeast Asia shared the American perception that there was a definite foe. Few in Canada disagreed in the summer of 1963, so soon after the near catastrophe of the Cuban missile crisis. What troubled Pearson and Martin was the Americans' zeal, the impetuosity which obviated a careful weighing of the effects of Asian involvement on allies, on public opinion, and on America itself. These feelings were prophetic, but when they were expressed to American leaders, they were ineffective and the counsel was disregarded.

Kennedy's foreign policy troubled Canadian officials, but his domestic policy commanded respect and imitation. The Liberal party's domestic program drew its spirit, if not its form, from the reinvigorated liberalism of the Kennedy administration. In the early 1960s political liberalism enjoyed its post-war heyday. The unattractiveness of authoritarian alternatives seemed indubitably proven by the wall at Berlin, by Solzhenitsyn's *One Day in the Life of Ivan Denisovich*, and by the affluence and confidence of Western society. The case for civil rights and for the abolition of irrational and archaic restraints on individual behaviour had never been so strong as in the summer of 1963. Canadians applauded and admired the massive, peaceful, and eloquent demonstrations with which American blacks sought to redress ancient wrongs. Martin Luther King's dream of an America where the 'sons of former slaves and the sons of former slave owners will be able to sit down together at the table of brotherhood' stirred emotions because its realization finally seemed possible. The American experience, for all the dark moments of its past, was moving toward the light. Canadians watched more sympathetically and more attentively than ever before. They could see the future working and it could be Canada's as well as America's, even if it came to Canadians slightly second-hand.

The strength of the bond with America was revealed on November 22, 1963 when suddenly the light seemed much further away and blackness so near. On that late fall day, the death of Kennedy in Dallas stunned Canadians. Like Americans, they stopped to watch what they could not believe. That one day is imprinted on the memories of an entire generation. For Peter Gzowski, twenty-nine on November 22, 1963, 'no other event in public history – not V-E Day, not the beginnings of the October crisis in Quebec, not the first landing of mankind on the moon ... stands so clearly in my private memory.' He could never again see the world as it was before. It was not public history but our private selves that changed most. Ten years later, Gzowski remembered:

I guess there are two things that I hope for the son who saw me weep that day. The first is that he will understand why. And the second is that, if something should happen to him, the way it happened to all of us, that he will weep too, and survive.[1]

There was, though, much that did not survive that day.

The extraordinary articulateness of the Kennedy administration had prevented Americans and others from detecting the lack of substance in the rhetoric. Kennedy had not forecast the future; in fact, he had mainly expressed the past. His belief in the possibilities of America were Whitmanesque, redolent of the last century's most lavish visions. His confidence in the capacity of Americans to 'bear any burden'

---

1 Peter Gzowski, *Peter Gzowski's Book about This Country in the Morning* (Edmonton: Hurtig 1974), 155.

derived from those heady post-war days when, with a devastated Europe, America's leadership was craved and her economic muscles barely tested. In fact, the American century was rapidly ending, even as its vitality was being so eloquently acclaimed. European recovery had brought European independence, most obviously seen in Charles de Gaulle's bold truculence toward 'Anglo-Saxons.' The dollar so much prized after the war was becoming too abundant, and the United States faced persistent balance of payment difficulties. And the rapidly appearing Third World was showing a hostility to the American liberal-capitalist model which surprised Americans. In the 1950s Kennedy had been one of the first American politicians to welcome 'the winds of change.' He had shared the Rooseveltian view which decried colonization and which identified decolonization with the American revolutionary heritage. He could understand neither the appeal of the other revolutions nor the inevitable fragility of democratic institutions in non-Western societies. From this misreading of the past and misunderstanding of the future, many of America's calamities of the next decade derived.

Canadians naturally were much affected. Lyndon Johnson, the new American president, had granted Pearson special attention at Kennedy's funeral. Johnson reaffirmed that Canadian-American relations were 'unique' and that Canada would never be taken for granted. He promised to continue what had gone on before. Indeed the first year of the Johnson presidency impressed many Canadians greatly. The Civil Rights Bill, the War on Poverty, the pursuit of détente with the USSR, and the activist use of the courts gave the impression of an energetic, effective administration. The Pearson government's own legislative enthusiasm derived in part from the contemporary American belief that good government could be measured by programs, agencies, and activity. Doubts about Johnson's international activism rarely surfaced in Canada in 1964, not least because he seemed so much more pacific than his right-wing opponent, Barry Goldwater. In February 1965, for example, James Eayrs could argue that Johnson's approach represented a retreat from American activism internationally. Domestic policy was being placed ahead of foreign policy. This was to be welcomed for 'The Great Society ... is not a retreat into unreality and irresponsibility but rather a closer and more realistic definition of objectives.' Eayrs was wrong in this; there would be little realism in Washington in the next few years, and the definition of objectives would remain elusive. America's burdens had become too much to bear.

A decade earlier Canada would probably have lent its strength to share these burdens. Now there was growing reluctance. By late 1964, one could find increasing criticism of American foreign policy, especially in Quebec. Canadian officials also saw that there was some advantage in creating distance between American and Canadian objectives. In that year of the first Chinese atomic test, Canada considered a break with the Americans over the question of Chinese admission to the United

Nations. Martin and his officials soon learned, however, that the domestic gains from such action (polls showed Canadians favoured recognition of China) could not offset the difficulties with the Americans that such an action would create. Canada still had serious balance of payments problems and American forbearance was essential if the difficulties were to be solved easily. Moreover, the chronic problems of the automobile industry seemed finally close to a lasting solution through the Canada-United States Automotive Agreement, the Auto Pact, which was announced on December 11, 1964. This agreement established qualified free trade in automobiles and automobile parts for manufacturers and guaranteed Canada a larger share of North American production. In short, there would be more Canadian jobs and industry; the alternative was a protectionism that even Walter Gordon rejected out of hand.

A second economic area where Canadian policy created difficulties was the attempt by Citibank to take over the small Dutch-controlled Mercantile Bank of Canada. When James Rockefeller, Citibank's president, told Gordon of his intention in July 1963, Gordon warned that he and the government opposed foreign control of any Canadian chartered bank. Citibank went ahead despite the warning. The result was a Canadian decision to include a provision in the proposed revision of the Bank Act which would prevent Mercantile from expansion of its very limited operations so long as it was foreign controlled. The retroactivity of this action profoundly disturbed the State Department and Wall Street, not because of the impact on Mercantile, but because of the implications which retroactivity of legislation might have if applied to other American enterprises in Canada or elsewhere. Dire warnings and subtle hints passed from Washington and New York to Ottawa throughout 1965. By the end of the year, the substance of the case lay submerged beneath the nationalism it had aroused.

Another catalyst to nationalism in Canada was the government's failure to carry out the recommendations of the O'Leary Commission that Canadian control of Canadian magazines and newspapers should be established. In his 1965 budget Gordon brought in legislation which proposed to do this by disallowing income tax deductions for advertising in non-Canadian newspapers or magazines, with the notable exceptions of *Time* and *Reader's Digest*. The exemption of the two leading foreign periodicals which had 'maple leaf' editions arose from Canadian fear of American reaction, but to many Canadians this exemption rendered the legislation meaningless, in the words of the Toronto *Globe and Mail*, merely locking in 'the two biggest wolves with the sheep.' Most in the Liberal caucus agreed, if one can accept the later testimony of Pauline Jewett. It was Gordon's sad task to explain to caucus that, although he personally disapproved of the exemption of *Time*, 'this was the price we had to pay to get approval of the automotive agreement' and to assure that *La Presse* was not sold to 'European interests sympathetic to the Separatist cause,' and the *Globe and Mail* to Americans. Whether the *Globe* and *La Presse* rumours had any substance is unknown. The argument nevertheless convinced the caucus, and the legislation was passed. The controversy illustrated the difficulties inherent in reducing Canada's cultural dependence on the United States. State interference with the press was a taste that once acquired would grow with ominous consequences for intellectual freedom. Thus the *Winnipeg Free Press* denounced Gordon's bill as characteristic of undemocratic countries which sought to control the press 'through the indirect pressure of the state.' For the less literate, the *Winnipeg Free Press* clarified its point by placing Gordon's photo above the story and beside those of Hitler, Stalin, Mussolini, George III, and other historical rascals. Others, however, painted Gordon in the colours of the Canadian patriot. The *Toronto Daily Star*, published by Gordon's close friend and fellow nationalist, Beland Honderich, excoriated Gordon's detractors and let it be known that if Gordon could have had his way *Time* would have been scuppered as well. In the end no one was fully happy with the bill and the problem continued to haunt later governments.

What revealed most clearly the change in Canadian attitudes toward the United States was not an incident but the reaction to a bland report entitled *Canada and the United States: Principles for Partnership* written by two senior diplomats, Canadian Arnold Heeney and American Livingston Merchant. In the aftermath of the assassination, in a mood of sympathetic fellowship, Johnson and Pearson had asked Heeney and Merchant to study how Canada and the United States could 'make it easier to avoid divergencies in economic and other policies of the two countries.' Their report came in July 1965 when the value of avoiding divergency was no longer so widely assumed. The controversies about magazines, banks, and the balance of payments were only a part of the broader interaction that had created new bruises and reservations.

In February 1965 the United States began to bomb North Vietnam, and, in the following month, American combat troops began to fight there. Very soon the evening news showed Americans dying in this most public of wars. During this time and before, Canada, primarily through Blair Seaborn, a member of the Canadian delegation to the International Control Commission, had tried to find the key to peace. Seaborn had warned Hanoi of the violence that would follow if it did not desist, while simultaneously offering, on behalf of the Americans, negotiating points. Seaborn got nowhere. Pearson and Martin fumbled as they saw the United states lurch toward full war in the early spring of 1965. When they met Americans they trusted such as Mike Mansfield, Bill Fulbright, and Scotty Reston, they heard dire warnings about the unreliability of Johnson's judgments. Indeed, one of the senators hinted that Johnson was becoming mad, or, at least, obsessed on the subject of the war. What he heard, read, and saw also disturbed Mike Pearson very much. His son Geoffrey, an officer in External Affairs, voiced criticisms of the war that might have come from *The New York Review of Books*. Maryon Pearson echoed her son. In April 1965, Pearson decided he must raise his voice to express his doubts. The occasion he selected was a convocation address at Temple University in Philadelphia. The speech he largely wrote himself. When, at the last moment, Paul Martin saw it, he threatened to resign. What Pearson called for was a halt to American bombing of North Vietnam, not forever, perhaps, but simply as a test of the possibility of negotiation. It seemed cautious, but Martin sensed that domestic and foreign criticism of American policy had made the Americans inordinately sensitive. The remarks would burn, he said. On the plane to Philadelphia, Pearson decided he would disregard his minister's and his officials' warnings. Thus, in measured words, he called for a halt in the bombing.

Johnson exploded. At Camp David, he grabbed Pearson by the lapels, stopping barely short of physical violence in an angry rebuke. The Canadians were carrying so little of the free world's burden; how dare they tell the overloaded Americans how to carry theirs. Pearson fumbled his reply. He publicly pretended nothing had happened, only to have the Americans leak stories of Johnson's displeasure to their press. Dick O'Hagan, Pearson's press secretary, threatened resignation. He told Pearson that both of them had looked like fools. Pearson did not need to be told. He already knew it. He also knew that this American president was unlike others, a bully who threatened, a vulgar manipulator who tested one's mettle – as he did once to Pearson – by asking the Prime Minister to urinate with him. Disbelief mixed with fear was the major response of Pearson to Johnson and of Canadians to America's very troubled society.

Thus when Merchant and Heeney suggested in July 1965 that 'Canadian authorities must have confidence that the practice of quiet diplomacy is not only neighbourly and convenient to the United States but that it is in fact more effective than the alternative of raising a row and being unpleasant in public,' their case fell flat. Leslie Roberts, the caustic journalist, said that the recommendation meant that Canadians were expected 'to keep quiet and hope for the lollipops which are dished out only to good little boys.' The trouble was, Canadians still liked the lollipops – the auto pacts, the tax exemptions, and the defence support – but looked at the donor differently. He was no longer the clean-faced charmer of five years earlier, but a leering, harder man. Many years later, a senior Canadian official recalled that 1965 was for Canadian-American official relations what 1956 and Suez was to Anglo-Canadian relations. It was like discovering that your spouse had had an affair: divorce was not possible, but neither was trust.

After the Temple University speech, Pearson and Johnson never repaired their relationship. Pearson, knowing that his nation still craved lollipops, apologized to Johnson for his remarks, but the situation improved little. In August Johnson refused to permit Pearson to publish their correspondence on Vietnam, embarrassing the Canadian, who had promised he would do so. If the politicians lost trust in America, so did the population, but more slowly. The August 1965 Gallup Poll revealed that 58 per cent of Canadians regarded the United States as Canada's best friend. In the following spring both Young Liberals and Young Conservatives debated whether Canada should contribute directly to the American effort in Vietnam. They decided that Canada should not, but the rejection of the motion was neither overwhelming nor immediate. Where the change was most noticeable was among the literary and intellectual élite, groups which before Vietnam had been most critical of American influence on Canadian life. Vietnam provided substance for their case. No longer was it necessary to balance censure of America with criticism of the Soviet Union. No longer was the North Americanness of Canada a premise to be granted. As the bombing of North Vietnam continued, as blacks, neither non-violent nor Christian, burned Watts, and as many American intellectuals accepted as serious analysis the charge that their nation was a cancer upon human history and that tolerance itself was the most effective form of repression, Canadians became confused.

The kaleidoscope of confusing images created in Canada a fear that the nation might fall prey to the virus sweeping the United States. After all, the smoke from Detroit's riots drifted very quickly over the river. This time the defenders of Canadian independence came, not, as in the past, from the right, but from the left. The change was sudden. In 1964 the new leftist periodical *Canadian Dimension*, edited by former American Cy Gonick, still looked instinctively south for leadership in social matters. The United States has discovered poverty, Gonick wrote in May 1964; 'it is curious that this subject is being ignored by Canadian counterparts.' The defeat of the Saskatchewan CCF government in the spring of 1964 was attributed to the fact that after the introduction of medicare there was nothing left for a socialist government to do. Two years later the left had a program: the protection of Canada from the malignant wave sweeping America. A *Canadian Dimension* poll of 'leading Canadian thinkers' in the early part of 1967 revealed that most expected that Canada would soon be ruled by a nationalist-socialist government, one that would derive its force from its success in insulating Canada from the American sickness. Two books of essays by Canadian intellectuals revealed the new mood: *Close the 49th Parallel* and *The New Romans*. The Canadian consensus, these books declared, could only be found in opposing the liberal capitalism of Canada's neighbour. Canadians could only finally be free when they rejected the economic system that had created the American virus. So strong was the current that even those who, like Mordecai Richler, had looked forward 'to the day when [Canada] might disappear and we would join fully in the American adventure' resisted no longer: 'Vietnam and Ronald Reagan, among other things, have tempered my enthusiasm. Looked at another way, yes, we *are* nicer. And suddenly that's important.' As Robert Fulford observed, the post-war generation had grown up believing that 'if we were very good or very smart, or both, we would someday graduate from Canada.' Now such graduation was to be feared; we must stay in this *nicer*, more familiar class of our own. Having left Sodom, we would not look back.

But Sodom still absorbed our thoughts. Perceptive observers of the first 'teach-in,' at the University of Toronto, against the Vietnam War in 1965 commented on the striking absence of Canadian material. Others remarked upon the derivative quality of anti-American criticism in Canada: were Canadians saying anything different about America than Herbert Marcuse and Robert Wolff, or, for that matter, J.K. Galbraith and Walter Lippmann? No, there was little originality in the Canadian critique of America; there was mainly the satisfaction for a Canadian that the critique somehow made us feel 'nicer.' This new self-confidence, this sense that Canada was a better nation and Canadians a better people, struck us suddenly. Since the war Canadians had not thought this way. Now Americans told us, and because they did, we believed.

Those who bore the message most effectively and regularly were Canadian intellectuals and bureaucrats, members of the 'new class' which Galbraith then argued would transform society making it more liberal in terms of personal behaviour and more collectivist in terms of economic goals. For the first and perhaps the last time in Canada, the educator became a prophet, teachers seemed to affect eternity. The ideology that so facilely identified education with a broadening of the human spirit and an enrichment of material life was seldom challenged. Canada, this ideology held, must have its own universities, its own culture, its own way of life. With the United States roiled by Vietnam and racial violence, the attractiveness of this vision was obvious.

The role of the educational-cultural élite is best evaluated when we discuss education and culture. What is important here is the effect nationalism had upon policy and popular opinion. Polls clearly showed that public opinion had shifted toward a nationalistic stance by 1967. In 1965, a *Maclean's* poll had shown a strong disposition toward free trade with the United States and a relatively benign attitude toward foreign investment. In 1967, nationalistic responses dominated a *Toronto Daily Star* poll: 67 per cent thought that 'the Canadian government [should] take steps to reduce foreign control of Canadian industry'; 47 per cent believed that 'foreign control of Canadian industry' was an issue of major importance; and 63 per cent believed that Canada did not show enough independence in its dealings with the United States. For Pearson and Martin, this nationalism presented major policy difficulties. Pearson had been literally shaken by Johnson's treatment of his dissent on the question of bombing. He feared the consequences of further and broader dissents not only on Canadian-American relations but on the Atlantic alliance, which he continued to believe was the best guarantee of world peace. To dissent openly and vigorously would be to lose influence on the United States in its most irrational international moment. Was this not, in a nuclear age, an irresponsible act?

Pearson never decided upon the correct answer to this question. One night in 1967, he and Martin debated the war with its most distinguished American critic, Senator William Fulbright. They found they agreed and that they shared the frustration of not knowing what to do. Fulbright consoled the Canadians with the statement that he too could do nothing to tame the American war machine now out of control. This, however, gave little assistance to Pearson and Martin in dealing with their critics. They had to show more independence even if that term was a jelly which could be moulded to any shape, but which, when grasped firmly, could slip quickly and messily through the hand.

To the government's critics, independence meant cutting most of the links Canada had built up with the United States. NORAD was a prime target; so too was NATO, which the critics charged was a European extension of American imperialism. For Canada NATO meant, Kenneth McNaught declaimed, 'acquiescence in Washington's ideological anti-communism.' The Cold War was over, its symbols must end. Written before Russian tanks rolled over Prague and soon after the test-ban treaty, at a moment when apparent Soviet restraints in Asia contrasted with apparent American zeal, and when de Gaulle's short-lived European vision challenged the bi-polarity of the post-war world, McNaught's analysis seemed to bear more weight than it actually did. Those who followed McNaught's fashion included Walter Gordon, Dalton Camp, the New Democratic Party, and some influential Liberal MPs, notably Pierre Trudeau, Donald Macdonald, Jean Marchand, and Gérard Pelletier.

Even policies that had little to do directly with the United States became involved in the debate. Defence minister Paul Hellyer had assumed office in 1963 as a staunch supporter of the American and NATO alliances, of nuclear weapons for Canada, and of modernization of the Canadian armed forces. In March 1964 the *White Paper on Defence* had called for integration of the armed forces and a single chief of defence staff. Naturally some members of the military saw this as an attack on the traditions of the Canadian armed forces. The admirals and generals rallied the opponents of unification, arguing that Hellyer was reducing Canada's armed forces to 'a special peacetime force to undertake small police actions in foreign countries.' This was not Hellyer's intention, but some were delighted to think it was. The NATO-NORAD commitments were made in another day, in different circumstances: they could now lead us down mine-strewn paths where Canadians need not tread. Thus, armed forces integration became a means which could attain the greater end of an independent foreign policy. There were other examples. In the Mercantile Bank case the government refused to back down when, in April 1966, the Americans officially protested against 'discrimination against American-owned banks.' In November the message was tougher, threatening retaliation against the Canadian banks' lucrative American activities. Over the next six months the Liberals fought among themselves about the appropriate response, with Mitchell Sharp, the finance minister, pitted against his predecessor, Walter Gordon. The result was a compromise that irritated the Americans (but they did not retaliate) and that emphasized the divisions within the Liberal party and the cabinet on the nationalist question.

On Vietnam, Martin tried desperately to obtain peace and to establish an independent Canadian position. He sought to do this by sending the retired Canadian diplomat, Chester Ronning, to Hanoi in early 1966. The United States reluctantly approved because, as the Pentagon papers put it, 'there seemed no proper response other than encouragement.' Pearson was unenthusiastic: American ambassador W.W. Butterworth reported that Pearson had said that the Ronning mission was Martin's idea alone, that it was dangerous, and that he had 'scared the hell out of Paul about it last night.' Ronning nevertheless went, although Dean Rusk, the American Secretary of State, made it clear that he could accomplish nothing. He did: the Americans brushed aside an apparent concession Ronning had obtained in his March 1966 visit. On a second Hanoi visit in June, Ronning met low-level officials who were uncommunicative and even cold. Canada had lost credibility not only in Washington but also in Hanoi.

In that same year Canada tried to develop a separate policy toward China. In fact the Ronning trip was part of this plan. He was to go to Peking, where it was thought that his well-known sympathy for the People's Republic would guarantee him a warm reception. It did not get him past the border guards at Canton. Although Ronning brought no new information, Martin and Pearson decided to take some initiative and were surprised when they received American encouragement. This support was short-lived. When the Canadians decided to go ahead and change their vote on Chinese admission at the United Nations, Dean Rusk warned Martin that such an action would greatly offend the United States and many of its allies. In the end, the Canadian 'One China-One Taiwan' resolution failed. The Canadian press, which generally supported an 'opening' to China, offered only faint praise for the Canadian efforts. Privately, the Americans directed sharp criticism. The path toward independence had many tortuous passages.

By early 1967 Canadian-American relations had, in Rusk's diplomatic euphemism, 'deteriorated.' Pearson and Johnson bore mutual suspicion and avoided meetings. Despite the great efforts of aides, neither ever called the other by his first name. In 1966 the two met briefly at a Campobello ceremony, but Johnson seemed much preoccupied. In 1967, the Canadian Centennial meant that Johnson must come. To the astonishment of Canadian officials, it seemed he would not. In Washington, officials whispered that Johnson did not like Pearson nor, for that matter, Canadians. Walter Gordon's speech of May 13, 1967, attacking American policy in Vietnam, had escaped American press attention but not Johnson's. Much offended, he refused to say that he would visit Expo on the US national day. Then, only hours before the supposed arrival of the vice-president, word came; Johnson, not Humphrey, was on the White House helicopter. In an extraordinary one-day dash between Expo and Harrington Lake, Johnson paid his grudging respect to the new centenarian. The visit accomplished nothing, and it was the last time Pearson and Johnson met. Neither had regrets.[2]

In the fall of 1967 Martin echoed Gordon and publicly called for a bombing halt. In the din of American and other international protest, hardly anyone noticed. Johnson by this time had hardened to criticism, and there was no retaliation. To critics of earlier Canadian policy, this American silence proved that Canada need not restrain itself in criticizing the war or in moving out of the American orbit generally. One such critic, Stephen Clarkson, said: 'the more truculent General de Gaulle has become, the gentler has been the Americans' treatment of France. With so much direct investment in Canada, it is unlikely that the Americans ... would want to get rid of a blemish on the finger by amputating the arm.' The analogy is interesting. To consider Canada an arm reflects the exaggerated sense of Canadian importance which both the government's critics and the government itself shared. Neither had yet understood the changes the passing of the post-war time had brought. Secondly, the belief that American retaliation would be rational and limited strikes us now as most peculiar at a time when the United States' resources were being overstrained in a most irrationally fought war. To assume American rationality with Canada but not in Asia was probably illogical.

In that maelstrom of international politics of the middle sixties, 'independence' could seem to many Canadians a life preserver that would save us from drowning or at least prevent us from whirling mindlessly in the patterns of the past. Alas, we did not know exactly what we sought. Independence remained an amorphous substance whose definition eluded common agreement. To the Marxist-nationalists, independence meant closing the forty-ninth parallel, severing forever the ties that had bound Canada to the United States and creating in Canada a socialist society where state ownership predominated. Others regarded independence as a kind of old-fashioned isolationism, and in this respect Stephen Clarkson's concept of independence meaning equality – the right to say no – was not much different from O.D. Skelton's in the 1930s, with the Third World now offering the 'freedom' which the

---

2 Some information on Canadian-American relations in this period is found in Peter Stursberg, *Lester Pearson and the American Dilemma* (Toronto: Doubleday 1980).

United States seemed to offer in the 1930s before the Second World War broke out. But, as in the 1930s, so too in the 1960s: independence for what?[3]

An independent foreign policy, Clarkson argued, is 'ethically just.' Perhaps, but as Peyton Lyon pointed out at the time, it does not mean that 'a policy of non-alignment and tub-thumping diplomacy would augment Canada's influence in world affairs.' We would be most foolish, Lyon wrote, 'to abandon a foreign policy that has been generally helpful, and admired by foreign experts, for a new policy that might prove to be counter-productive, even in helping Canadian intellectuals to overcome their inferiority complex.' In retrospect, it is clear that the debate had meaning only for the moment – for the Vietnam years and after the first misleading glimpses of détente and arms control. When a critic of Pearsonian diplomacy, Pierre Trudeau, succeeded Pearson as prime minister, he discovered not only how little could be changed but also how much the changing circumstances of the world beyond Canada's borders made the premises of the tub-thumpers and their opponents irrelevant. Foreign policy once again went beyond the interest and understanding of most Canadians, and the many tubs thumping now seemed a single hand clapping.

QUEBEC, CANADA, AND CO-OPERATIVE FEDERALISM, 1963-8

'Il faut que ça change.' 'Things have got to change,' the Quebec Liberals declared in the 1960 provincial election. And things did, not only in Quebec but in Canada as a whole. They did so in a way few had imagined in 1960 when the former Minister of Northern Affairs and Natural Resources in the St Laurent government, Jean Lesage, became premier of Quebec. An elegant, imposing man who combined administrative efficiency with strong business and political attachments, Lesage contrasted sharply with Maurice Duplessis, whose vulgarity had been so calculated and whose administrative and political style derived mostly from the pork-barrelling, parish-pump politics of the past. That at least was the first impression. English-Canadian journalists welcomed Lesage as the modernizer that the 'backward' Quebec had so long required. Now, finally, the oldest province might come of age.

In the first few years of the Lesage government, this sympathy persisted. It was an English-Canadian journalist who referred approvingly to post-1960 events in Quebec as the Quiet Revolution. The change that must come would come quietly and conservatively, through the mediation of the modern manager so fashionable then in Ottawa, Toronto, and, of course, Washington. Thus when Liberal senator Tom Crerar, cantankerous and sceptical in his old age, complained that Quebec was

---

3 Stephen Clarkson, ed., *An Independent Foreign Policy for Canada?* (Toronto: McClelland & Stewart 1968). This book contains numerous essays reflecting nationalist criticism of Canadian-American relations.

TABLE 2
Agriculture 1951-71

	1951	1961	1971
Number of farms	134,366	95,777	61,257
Per cent of population on farms	19.5	11.1	5.6

changing too rapidly, that its new self-confidence would threaten the Canadian consensus, the historian Blair Neatby told Crerar that Quebec would have difficulties in passing through these changes but that, in the end, it would become more North American.

As Dale Posgate and Kenneth McRoberts noted much later, for English Canadians, the Union Nationale's traditional nationalism and the 'lag' in political modernization meant that the Quebec 'problem' had 'a deceptive air of manageability.' Indeed, there was a dream that finally a common nationality might come from the 'modernization' of Quebec and the breakdown of the barrier of traditional Quebec nationalism. This was, of course, a dream unfulfilled. Change came to Quebec less quietly than was first thought and, when it came, proved far more resistant to management and government control than political scientists suggested. When Lesage, now the 'prime minister of the state of Quebec,' was asked by his former colleague Mike Pearson where his government and his province were going, Lesage replied 'I don't know.' The reply was honest; and no one else knew either.

Today historians tend to emphasize the continuity of the Quiet Revolution with the past, yet none denies the rapidity of change in the province of Quebec in the 1950s and 1960s. The physical signs were everywhere, from Gaspé villages to Montreal sign paintings, in the churches now become coffeehouses or union halls, in the argot of the street and the jargon of the academy. Some of this change can be measured, and what the available statistics reveal is a society undergoing rapid transformation socially, economically, and culturally.

The image of Quebec as a rural province has not been valid in the twentieth century, but agriculture was for Quebeckers a main occupation as well as a symbol of a way of life until long after the war, as shown in Table 2. This decline in agricultural participation was not matched by a concomitant increase in manufacturing, for that sector of the economy actually saw employment decline from 36 per cent to 31.9 per cent of the labour force between 1946 and 1966. Where growth occurred most rapidly in Quebec, as in Canada, was in the service sector, where employment during the same period rose from 37.2 per cent to 59.7 per cent. These

TABLE 3
Distribution of Male Labour Force, Québec 1951-71

1951

Ethnic group	Total (%)	Proprietary & managerial (%)	Professional (%)	Clerical (%)	Industrial (%)	Agriculture (%)
French	79.9	65.4	63.9	67.2	79.1	91.7
British	13.3	19.0	27.2	26.5	12.3	7.0
Other	6.8	15.6	8.9	6.3	8.6	1.3

1961

Ethnic group	Total (%)	Managerial (%)	Professional & technical (%)	Clerical & sales (%)	Industrial (%)	Agriculture (%)
French	77.5	63.8	72.9	72.3	80.2	91.1
British	11.8	19.0	22.5	17.1	8.8	6.1
Other	10.7	17.2	14.6	10.6	11.0	2.8

1971

Ethnic group	Total (%)	Managerial/ administrative (%)	Professional & technical (%)	Clerical & sales (%)	Industrial (%)	Agriculture (%)
French	75.8	61.9	69.2	72.7	79.5	87.9
British	11.7	22.8	15.9	14.5	8.6	7.9
Other	12.5	15.3	14.9	12.8	11.9	4.2

SOURCE: 1951 *Census of Canada* Volume IV, Table 13 (p 13.9), and Dale Posgate and Kenneth McRoberts, *Quebec: Social Change and Political Crisis* (Toronto: McClelland and Stewart 1976), 38

changes in employment meant (especially for French Canada) changes in the way people lived. The city was an irresistible siren to young French Canadians wanting employment. In 1941, 55 per cent of the French-origin population of Quebec lived in urban areas; by 1951, 63 per cent did; and in 1971, 78 per cent did. City air brought some new freedoms perhaps, but it also created a propinquity which identified inequities. The French Canadians found themselves facing barriers that seemingly prevented them from reaching the heights in those occupations that a liberal capitalist society most esteems.

The figures in Table 3 can readily be misread, misunderstood, and misused. In the recent past they have been. In any event, they speak less eloquently than

Gabrielle Roy's *Bonheur d'Occasion*, Roger Lemelin's *Au pied de la pente douce*, or Pierre Vallières's *Nègres blancs d'Amérique*, which revealed so well the sense of exclusion of the Québécois in the city in their own province. Worse, acquiring the appropriate raiments – education, language, and experience – did not guarantee francophone entry to the boardrooms where economic power lay. Wallace Clement found in 1972 that only 8.4 per cent of the Canadian economic élite was francophone, only 1.7 per cent higher than in 1951 (according to and using John Porter's analysis of the economic élite). Another study by economists argued that, in 1961, 60 per cent of the difference in income between francophones and anglophones in Quebec derived from the discrimination in favour of anglophones for high-level positions. Some institutions changed little, but others did very much and in a fashion that created new tensions within the society.

The Lesage victory in 1960 was the triumph of the city over the country, the articulate over the mute. It had been easy to believe that Quebec was 'backward' and rural under Duplessis because the style of so many of the Union Nationale members was redolent of the barnyard. Lesage's ministers struck one immediately as 'street smart,' men for the city season. Indeed, journalists in 1960 often remarked that the Quebec government was much closer in style to Kennedy's Camelot than to Ottawa. René Lévesque strode easily from the television screen into politics, leaving the impression that every policy could and should be explained in a thirty-minute spot. Some policies had as much substance as the puffs of smoke that surrounded him, but with Lévesque the medium was the message, the image of vitality, exuberance, and commitment. The Minister of Youth, Paul Gérin-Lajoie, had the habits of Oxford common rooms, and the new bureaucrats who began to move into offices where party jobs were previously the major concern brought with them very sharply honed technical skills. They were the equals, if not the betters, of those in Ottawa in talent, in suavity, and, above all, in commitment.

Lesage drew electoral support as well as talent from the anglophone and francophone middle class. Workers and farmers did not take so quickly to the Lesage program and style. But as we have seen their numbers were dwindling, and their doubts about change were drowned out by the very articulate spokesmen who were urging a fundamental transformation of the society. By 1962 the momentum was clear, and the Lesage government knew it had to move beyond where it had stood. What this implied was a more direct commitment to the use of the state than Quebec had ever known. 'Anti-étatisme' (anti-statism) was a Quebec tradition, but this tradition did not pass to the younger, more secular generation that influenced the Liberal party in Quebec at the time. The central debate occurred over the issue of nationalization of hydro in the province. Without the consent of the cabinet or the premier, Lévesque called for such nationalization on February 12, 1962. St James Street trembled only slightly at the news; the presence of George Marler, a financial conservative, in the cabinet, as well as Lesage's own corporate law experience seemed to guarantee that this was one more whiff of smoke that would pass. Nationalization was not popular; it reeked of the musty socialism of the 1930s about which even socialists (including the newly formed New Democratic Party) seemed embarrassed.

On the Labour Day weekend in 1962, the Quebec cabinet met at Lac-à-l'Epaule to consider its general unease, and, more specifically, Lévesque's disregard of cabinet solidarity in promoting nationalization. Drinks flowed freely, and so did opinions. The importance of nationalization to its proponents transcended the action itself. It had become, former Liberal leader Georges-Emile Lapalme later wrote, Lévesque's Long March, a test of faith for believers. The reluctant Lesage let impulse lead him. Turning to his predecessor Lapalme, he asked if Lapalme approved of nationalization and of an election on the issue. Lapalme did at once: 'an election on nationalization would be the answer to a virgin's prayer.' Elections, of course, are not won by prayers alone – and rarely by virgins. The experienced Liberal leadership thus cleverly exploited the nationalistic feeling it had done so much to arouse.

Those who denied the need for nationalization, even if their argument was merely economic, attracted the sting of nationalist rhetoric. When Daniel Johnson, the Union Nationale leader, suggested partial nationalization, Lesage accused him of 'refusing to collaborate in the most important task of economic liberation.' Johnson, Lesage declaimed, was 'taking sides with those hidden interests which are attempting to subjugate us.' It was simple: 'He who is for the people of Quebec is against the [electric] trust.' Rhetoric passed easily from the colonial struggles so much in the news at the time to the Liberal campaign. Political freedom was not enough; now the state, which alone of all major institutions the Québécois could control, must grasp the levers which could bring 'economic liberation.'

The campaign obscured the question of what came next, and it proved to Canadians generally that nationalism in Quebec was not a casualty of the Quiet Revolution but rather a beneficiary. Yet this nationalism possessed a different flavour, one which English Canadians could not so easily identify. When the results of the election came in on November 14, 1962, the Liberals had won a solid victory with sixty-three of the ninety-five seats in the Legislature. Workers and farmers remained resistant to the Liberal appeal, but the anglophone and francophone middle class had combined to give Lesage his victory.

In an analysis of what it all meant, Albert Breton argued that nationalization of hydro and, by implication, most of the projects of the Lesage years were patronage or 'public works' for the francophone middle class. Nationalism in Quebec, Breton wrote, 'is a tool used by the new middle class to accede to wealth and power.' The workers derived no economic benefits; only their employers changed. The francophone engineers, managers, and technicians reaped the rewards of nationalization as they secured positions anglophones had previously held or would have held.[4] Whether the francophone middle class perceived its economic gain so rationally is perhaps questionable, but there can be no doubt that Breton's analysis of the impact of reform has considerable validity. The activist state became the focus of francophone middle class expectations and for very many the provider of economic livelihood. The rapid expansion and secularization of the educational system, an almost inevitable step following the 1962 election, worked the same way. The details of these reforms are discussed elsewhere. Here we need only note that they swelled the ranks of the foot soldiers of the Quiet Revolution over the next decades. For these people, the government's slogan to promote education had a special meaning: 'Qui s'instruit, s'enrichit.'

Sometime in 1962 or 1963, the Quiet Revolution became the Quebec Problem. To English Canadians and to federal politicians generally, what had been expected in Quebec had not occurred. The federal Liberals had expected to benefit from Quebec's disillusionment with Diefenbaker, but in the election of 1962 the twenty-six seats won by Réal Caouette's Social Credit confused and disappointed them. As in the Quebec election, voting patterns revealed fear and resistance to change, as well as serious divisions within Quebec society. Fortunately for the Liberals, Prime Minister Diefenbaker, who had lost most of his Quebec members, seemed neither to know what to do nor to care to do it. When the new Minister of Mines and Technical Surveys, Paul Martineau, met Diefenbaker after the 1962 swearing-in ceremony, he asked what he should tell reporters when they asked what Diefenbaker intended to do about Quebec. Diefenbaker replied curtly: 'Look, you didn't make too much trouble before you were in the cabinet: I hope you're not going to start making trouble now.'[5]

Even without Martineau, trouble was there; but there was also opportunity. Pearson made an attempt to seize it, even though by background he seemed almost as unsuited as Diefenbaker to do so. In the forties when he was first discussed as a possible Liberal leader, an American diplomat had reported to Washington that Pearson's greatest liability was his lack of knowledge of French Canada and his centralist disposition. In 1962 his French still sounded as if it had been learned – badly – in a Methodist manse, but his sympathies for Quebec's demands were much greater. There were other advantages: Jean Lesage was his former parliamentary secretary; Maurice Sauvé advised both federal and provincial Liberal parties; and

---

4 Albert Breton, 'The Economics of Nationalism,' *Journal of Political Economy*, LXXII (August 1964).
5 Quoted in Peter Stursberg, *Diefenbaker: Leadership Lost 1962-67* (Toronto: University of Toronto Press 1976), 9.

Maurice Lamontagne, another Pearson friend and adviser, realized how serious the Quebec Problem was. It was Lamontagne who drafted Pearson's December 1962 speech in which he called for an inquiry which would and should tell us what already seemed clear to Pearson: 'It is now clear to all of us, I think, that French-speaking Canadians are determined to become directors of their economic and cultural destiny in their own changed and changing society ... they also ask for equal and full opportunity to participate in all federal government services, in which their own language will be fully recognized.' This meant, in Pearson's view, 'the greatest possible constitutional decentralization and ... special recognition of the French fact and the rights of French-speaking Canadians in confederation.' Pearson's 'doctrine of federalism' was 'to decentralize up to a certain point as the way to strengthen, indeed to establish and maintain, unity.'

This speech and the policy it foretold won widespread support, even though many of Pearson's caucus, including Walter Gordon, opposed its delivery at that time. Bilingualism became an election plank for the Liberals in Quebec, but what it gained there for the Liberals, Pearson's nuclear weapons policy probably lost. The French press in Quebec quickly turned against Pearson generally, choosing to support no one in the campaign, though *Le Devoir* backed the NDP and others noted with approval that the Créditistes opposed nuclear weapons. More important probably was the disaffection of some intellectuals who, because of the weakness of Quebec representation in Ottawa, were considering running for the Liberals. Jean Marchand, Pierre Trudeau, and Gérard Pelletier decided they could not run, and in Trudeau's case the decision was accompanied by an angry denunciation of Pearson as immoral. Instead of scrub-faced reformers, the Liberals fought the Créditistes with a brawling bush fighter, Yvon Dupuis, who confronted the Créditiste reaction with the methods of the past. The Liberals scarcely seemed the party to deal with Quebec's future. During the campaign, Lesage, although friendly toward the Pearson Liberals, made it clear that his increasingly hard stance against 'Ottawa' would not change. No longer would Quebec Liberals believe in 'Rouge à Quebec, et rouge à Ottawa.'

Both parties had separate identities, and both capitals, Quebec City and Ottawa, had to have their separate attraction for the Québécois. After his victory of April 8, 1963, Pearson, with forty-seven Quebec members, moved to make French a language of caucus and of cabinet discussion. In External Affairs, he and Paul Martin decided that a francophone must succeed their old friend Norman Robertson and that the department must present to the world an image more reflective of Canadian dualism. In the civil service as a whole, bilingualism and the hiring of francophones were to be encouraged. Finally on July 22, 1963, Pearson announced the membership of the Royal Commission on Bilingualism and Biculturalism that he had promised as opposition leader. The co-chairmen were André Laurendeau, the distinguished journalist, and Davidson Dunton, the president of Carleton University. There were, in all, ten bilingual commissioners, four francophones, four English-Canadians, and two representing other ethnic groups. Critics and supporters soon noted how the make-up of the commission reflected a dualistic view of Canada. The Vancouver *Province* denounced it as simply a bicultural crusade, blaming Lamontagne who, it claimed, 'is doing more to destroy Canadian unity than to save it. He is a dangerous man.' Premier Manning of Alberta agreed that the commission had 'the potential of doing Canada more harm than good.' More restrained critics worried that it was less an inquiry than an agent of instruction, a means by which Canadians would learn a particular point of view on the future of Confederation. In Quebec, reactions were mixed. Liberal MP Maurice Sauvé believed the commission 'would only give more ammunition to all the people who are opposed to Canada, and it would only help the strong separatist and nationalist element in Quebec with arguments to fight against Canada in favour of the isolation of Quebec.'[6] Lesage too thought it useful as a gesture, a token of understanding, but not as a response to fundamental constitutional and economic problems. For Lévesque, flirting publicly with separation, biculturalism was a 'fairy godmother' springing full-blown from the Ottawa imagination: 'Il y a deux cultures distinctes, et il est impossible de fusionner les deux en une seule.'

That biculturalism remains an elusive concept, that the commission knew from the beginning what it would report, and that its formation aroused passions are not items meriting condemnation. Moreover, the implementation of bilingualism in the federal civil service had only an indirect relationship with the commission: the Pearson government made that commitment prior to and independently of the appointment of the commission. The B & B Commission in fact did what it was intended to do: alert Canadians to the gravity of their national crisis. Its February 1965 preliminary report put the point bluntly and accurately: 'Canada, without being fully conscious of the fact, is passing through the greatest crisis in its history.' To its credit, the commission contributed to making Canadians more fully conscious of the fact. It contributed little directly to a solution to the crisis, but one may certainly ask what kind of direct contribution it could have made. Events moved too quickly; the commission reacted too slowly. In the end discouragement with the commission reflected pessimism about the future of Canada. The commission began with a bang, punctuated by the explosions in Montreal mailboxes; it ended in a rallentando of whimpers – about its cost, about its purpose, and, most of all, about the future of the country.

6 On this general question see Peter Stursberg, *Lester Pearson and the Dream of Unity* (Toronto: Doubleday 1978).

FEDERAL-PROVINCIAL DIPLOMACY

Jean Lesage believed that the fundamental grievance of Quebec in 1963 was its inability to have 'full exercise of its powers under the Constitution.' In his first federal-provincial conference in July 1960 Lesage had called for an end to shared-cost programs and for appropriate compensation to the provinces. At each succeeding conference he repeated his demand, and in the 1963 campaign the federal Liberals had vaguely supported his 'opting out' of some established programs. Lesage wanted a more specific commitment. Three days before the April 8 election Lesage strengthened his ultimatum:

Twelve months will go by before the next budget speech. Either the federal government, whatever party is elected on April 8, and I repeat, whatever the party elected on April 8, the central government will have made use of the 12 months to make allowance for Quebec's needs or else we in Quebec will have taken steps on our own side to make the required decisions in fiscal policy. And the decisions will be those imposed on us by the aims of economic, social, and cultural affirmation we have set ourselves at the request of the people of Quebec.

In Pearson, Lesage found a sympathetic listener and a skilled mediator, but one whose knowledge of international law and practice far exceeded that of domestic constitutional law and practice. He was, as he later said, 'prepared to make substantial concessions to Quebec (and to the provinces) in the interests of national unity.'

The provinces, especially Quebec, did not need any extra powers merely because they were taking a more active part in the domestic, social, and economic life of their people. But they did need more money, and some, including Quebec, aspired to an international role also. Adding to the problem was the minority Pearson government's need to show that it too was a progressive government, as the spirit of the times demanded. In the 1963 campaign a Liberal slogan declared 'Better Pensions for All.' Once elected, the Liberals moved quickly – too quickly – to put the pension resolution on the order paper of the House of Commons. The minister responsible for the plan, Judy LaMarsh, dubbed it an 'instant plan.' Little resistance was expected, but it came none the less, first from Ontario, where John Robarts became irritated when provincial Liberals drew the issue into a provincial campaign, and then from Quebec, where the objections struck more strongly at Canadian constitutional practice. At the September and November 1963 federal-provincial conferences, the federal government was in a weak position because of the clumsiness of the first 'sixty days of decision' and because the provincial responses had not been anticipated. Quebec had passed a unanimous resolution of the legislature declaring that the province would not accept the federal plan. It had its own plan and would only support a constitutional amendment if it could 'opt out' of the federal plan. Judy LaMarsh, her cherished plan threatened, warned that there might be a 'vast exodus from Quebec' if it remained out of her plan. Why, she asked, could not the Quebec government simply translate the plan into French?

The deadlock continued and the deadline on Lesage's taxation ultimatum loomed nearer. Lesage seemed to take the initiative when he invited the premiers and Pearson to Quebec for a federal-provincial conference from March 31 to April 3, 1964. The welcome was not as warm as expected. The Château Frontenac had a bomb threat; federal ministers had guards with them everywhere. Lesage was more confident and, to the astonishment of the conference, he presented his own pension plan in lavish and full detail. Its benefits were better, and, for provincial governments, its funding most lucrative, because they could borrow from the fund for their social programs in the future. The response, Pearson aide Tom Kent recalled, was electric and 'the federal government position was destroyed. ... The most extraordinary thing about the whole situation was that the federal government had been so completely unprepared for it, for the whole aggressive, powerful stance of the provinces in relation to the federal government.' On the plane returning to Ottawa, some passengers reportedly predicted Confederation's death.

Within a few days, both sides decided to heal the wounds opened at Quebec. Maurice Sauvé and Tom Kent for the federal government and Claude Morin and Claude Castonguay for Quebec worked out a compromise which essentially adopted Quebec's plan and accepted the right of any province to have its own plan. Although Morin later claimed that Quebec gained no more than was its due, that was not the reaction at the time, nor was it the case. Jean Lesage dramatically told the legislature: 'I have lived for the past month a terrifying life. I have worked for my province as no man has ever worked for it. I have made use of all the means which Providence granted me ... so that Quebec, finally, could be recognized as a province which has a *statut spécial* in Confederation, and I have succeeded.' Not only did Quebec secure its pension plan but it also obtained an Ottawa commitment to negotiate, first, Quebec's 'opting out' of many shared-cost programs, and second, a larger share of the personal income tax for all provinces. Together with the creation of a pension fund and its distribution among the provinces, this increase in the share of personal income tax provided to Quebec, and other provinces, the funds they needed for the expanding social programs they supported. By the end of 1964 the federal government knew that it was seen as the loser. As for Lesage, the events of 1964 were and still are a triumph. He did recall later that Judy LaMarsh never spoke to him again, but one suspects Lesage lamented this silence very little.

Aware of the weakness of his government's position, Pearson decided that he had to strengthen the influence of Quebec in Ottawa. The pension controversy had revealed how talented the Quebec public servants were and how Quebec was attracting the loyalties of the brightest French Canadians. Lionel Chevrier, the senior Quebec minister, left early in 1964. Pearson then promoted two younger Quebec members, Guy Favreau to Justice and Maurice Sauvé to Forestry, but he knew this was not enough. In January 1965, he met Lesage in Florida and, in the hospitable climes of Hobe Sound, he asked Lesage to come to Ottawa. It was his duty as a Canadian. The answer was no. Pearson and Lesage parted, with Pearson more uncertain of the future than ever before but more aware of the difficulties facing him and his government.

Pearson carried his search for new men further, but at the moment when the need became clearer, recruitment had become more difficult. Even before the conversation with Lesage, a series of scandals had profoundly damaged Quebec Liberalism. Guy Favreau, who Pearson believed might be to him what Lapointe had been to King, stumbled badly when confronted with evidence that a narcotics-peddling thug named Lucien Rivard had prominent Liberals act on his behalf to prevent extradition. Raymond Denis, an executive assistant, had tried to bribe a Montreal lawyer; Pearson's own parliamentary secretary, Guy Rouleau, had unwisely, if not illegally, interceded on behalf of Rivard. Knowing these things, Favreau's Department of Justice did little. Inevitably the opposition learned about it, and when Tory MP Erik Nielsen pressed his charges Favreau seemed to deny knowledge. The next day Pearson fired Rouleau and in the House said he had only learned of the scandal two days before, on November 22. He then left on a tour of the Canadian West. In his absence Favreau told the cabinet that he had in fact discussed the Rivard case with Pearson on September 2. Moreover, he demanded an inquiry and got one. On Pearson's return, the cabinet agreed that Pearson must rise in the House and disclose the September 2 conversation. But when the House met Pearson remained silent. The debate among his advisers became more heated – should he speak? What should he say? He finally admitted the conversation in a letter to Frédéric Dorion, the judge heading the inquiry Favreau had demanded. It was too late; the gesture seemed insincere and evasive. Pearson appeared to be too ready to abandon his ministers, letting them face the taunts of Diefenbaker and his forces alone. Favreau did not last long. He became almost at once a ghostly figure whose sallow skin and hollow eyes eerily and accurately foretold his death in 1967.

The Favreau tragedy, as it was soon called, was followed by a charge that two other Quebec ministers, Maurice Lamontagne and René Tremblay, had received free furniture from a now bankrupt Montreal furniture company. Lamontagne had been indiscreet in his dealings. Tremblay, however, was guiltless but justified his actions poorly. At the same time, December 1964, Pearson learned that the recently appointed Minister Without Portfolio, Yvon Dupuis, faced charges of corruption. On January 17, 1965, Pearson asked Dupuis to resign. He refused. After a few embarrassing days when no one knew what to do, Dupuis finally went. There were

Crossing the Styx.
Prime Minister Pearson, Minister of Transport Jack Pickersgill, and Minister of Justice
Guy Favreau confront a sea of Diefenbakers (Macpherson, 1964). Reproduced with the
permission of the *Toronto Star*

other troubles, too, such as the curious disappearance of labour leader Hal Banks
just as he faced charges – but the Favreau, Tremblay, Lamontagne, and Dupuis
incidents had the most effect and left the bitterest taste. When Dorion reported in
late June 1965, Favreau immediately offered his resignation because the report
questioned his judgment. Pearson encouraged the resignation. What he did not
understand was the resistance of his French-Canadian ministers to Favreau's resignation. For them the resignation was a symbol of the persecution of French Canadians in Ottawa, an admission of guilt where there was none. Even men of the best
will, of the warmest heart, could not escape the fire. Some English ministers supported Favreau's resignation; the French ministers strongly opposed it. Neither
group could seem to understand the other's motives or feelings. At a moment when
Quebec's attitude toward Confederation was becoming more and more ambiguous,
the collapse and isolation of French-Canadian cabinet members possessed ominous
possibilities.

What can one say of Pearson's performance? Perhaps the opinion of Tom Kent, his aide, is fairest and most revealing.

Mr Pearson was a diplomat. His skill was in settling differences and sometimes that perhaps meant evading the expression of differences. There was an element of escapism, and no question, Mr Pearson could be an escapist. He found it very difficult to say anything unpleasant to anybody face to face, and most people who talked to Mr Pearson tended to leave him thinking that he'd agreed with them. That was true even if the views of A and B in succession were rather diverse, and that sometimes left lots of problems to sort out afterward.

There were always so many problems to sort out afterward. The Pearson government in its first years never possessed a coherent image, never managed to let Canadians know what it intended to do. Whether the government itself knew clearly what it hoped to do seems highly questionable. In the 1920s, in appraising Lester Pearson, Vincent Massey had spoken of Pearson's obvious abilities and sincerity but noted that there was something 'curiously loose-jointed and sloppy about his mental make-up.' The same, alas, might be said of his government.

The decision to call an election in 1965 had little to do with Quebec. The advocates of an election came from Ontario, and they tended to blame the government's malaise upon its minority status. Walter Gordon, fearful that a more popular leader might replace Diefenbaker, had begun to urge an election in the spring and summer of 1965. By early September he had convinced Pearson, if not all his colleagues. The election would be held on November 8.

The Liberal party entered this election with John Diefenbaker as its major issue. Diefenbaker in turn dwelt upon the scandals. The result was an election as bitter as any Canada had yet seen and the creation of a sense among the electors that there could be no escape from the miasma that surrounded Ottawa. The Liberals entered the election knowing they would carry Quebec. To many Quebec Liberals that was simply not enough. This popular support would be for ministers who Quebec thought were wronged but who Quebec knew could no longer have much influence in Ottawa. One of these ministers, Maurice Lamontagne, thought it essential that Quebec's influence in Ottawa be strengthened lest Quebec City become even more the focus of francophone attention and loyalties. He and Sauvé agreed that Jean Marchand, who had not run in 1963 because of Pearson's acceptance of nuclear weapons, must run in 1965. Sauvé, and Marchand himself, believed that Gérard Pelletier and Pierre Trudeau must run with Marchand. This was not so easily accomplished: Pelletier's and Trudeau's acid pens – Pelletier had recently compared the Liberal party to a garbage can – were not forgotten or forgiven by Liberal MPs. Nevertheless, Marchand insisted, and on September 10 the three announced that they would run for the Liberals. Their commitment to Liberalism was weak, but to Quebec and Canada strong. Marchand recalled what they said to each other

'Now for my next act –'
Prime Minister Pearson displays the art of government (Macpherson, 1965). Reproduced
with the permission of the *Toronto Star*

then: 'Well, there is a vacuum [in Ottawa], and if we believe in this country and we
want to do something for the country, we have to do it in Ottawa – and we have to do
it in the party which has a chance to be in power.'

Although the presence of the so-called 'three wise men' probably won few votes,
their entry into federal politics was the most significant event of the election. Ironically, as the left wing of the party was strengthened in Quebec, the right wing gained
in English Canada. In the campaign Diefenbaker drew upon the final drops of
Conservative loyalty while Pearson's expected appeal to the young middle class
proved less enticing than originally expected. Thus on November 8 little had
changed; the Liberals had two more seats (131) than in 1963, but the Conservatives

TABLE 4
Results of 1965 General Election

Seats	Liberal	PC	NDP	Créditiste	Socred	Ind.
Newfoundland	7 (7)	–	–			
PEI	0 (2)	4 (2)	–			
NS	2 (5)	10 (7)	–			
NB	6 (6)	4 (4)	–			
Quebec	56 (47)	8 (8)	–	9 (0)	0 (20)	2 (0)
Ontario	51 (52)	25 (27)	9 (6)			
Manitoba	1 (2)	10 (10)	3 (2)			
Saskatchewan	–	17 (17)	–			
Alberta	0 (1)	15 (14)	–		2 (2)	
BC	7 (7)	3 (4)	9 (9)		3 (2)	
Yukon	–	1 (1)	–			
NWT	1 (0)	0 (1)	–			
Popular vote	40	32	18	5	4	1

also had two more (97). There was no majority, and, for Pearson, no relief. (See Table 4.)

Gordon accepted responsibility for the failure to achieve a majority. He resigned, and so did national organizer Keith Davey. Others drifted away, Tom Kent to the bureaucracy, Dick O'Hagan to the Washington embassy. Most troubling, though, were the departures of Lamontagne and René Tremblay. After the furniture revelations, they had remained in the cabinet. There were no alternatives, but, in the case of Tremblay especially, the charges were unfair. Yet after the election, without proper consultation, Pearson fired them. They were, Pearson said, honourable men; unfortunately his actions did not lead others to see this. What they saw was Marchand, a new member, becoming immediately the most important Quebec minister. However clumsy Pearson's actions were, they made one thing certain: there would be a new look to French Canada in Ottawa.

That at least was Pearson's hope. In late winter 1966, however, the new look seemed old indeed. Once again there was scandal; once again a French Canadian was at the centre – the new Minister of Justice, Lucien Cardin. John Diefenbaker found an issue that he believed might destroy the new minister. The issue was Vancouver postal clerk George Victor Spencer, a most unlikely Russian spy whom the government fired but did not prosecute. Any reader of Le Carré would recognize Spencer, the grey little man who watched games he feared to play, and near the end of the day, ran onto the field and became both victim and fool. Canadians felt sad even though they knew he had served 'the devil.' It was probably wrong not to charge Spencer. It was certainly wrong and foolish when Cardin on national television gave Spencer's name and said he would be watched for the rest of his life. Diefenbaker saw civil liberties infringed and demanded an inquiry. Cardin refused; he stood by the decision of his legal officers. Moreover, Spencer did not want an inquiry. But then on March 4 David Lewis phoned Vancouver to talk to Spencer's lawyer and found that he now did. Pearson quickly reversed himself and told Cardin and the House that there would be an inquiry. Cardin agreed, but late in the day he decided he must resign. The word spread quickly, and soon Jean Marchand was speaking openly of resigning with Cardin. If this was the way Pearson backed his ministers, there was no place for him in government. On March 9 the Quebec caucus exploded, and for the first time Pearson's leadership was questioned. But Cardin defended the Prime Minister. He would stay on, for his party, and for Quebec. Later, he said the same thing to the national caucus. The caucus ended in unexpected unity and, unrealistically, with hope.

On the next day, March 10, the futility of such hope became obvious when Cardin at a press conference was asked to explain what he had meant the previous Friday (March 4) when he spoke about Diefenbaker's participation in the 'Monseigneur case.' The Press Club was already alive with rumour: 'Monseigneur,' a stunning German who was spying for the Russians, had slept with a former Tory minister who sported a moustache. Most guessed the wrong minister. Finally Canadian journalists could match their British counterparts, who had titillated their readers a year before with tales of one-way mirrors, whips, and delectable teenagers involved in the Profumo scandal. Now dull Canada had a scandal of its own. On March 10, under harsh questioning, Cardin blurted out that Mrs Munsinger was a German spy involved with more than one Tory minister. Diefenbaker had known this, but had done nothing. Now Mrs Munsinger was dead. She could tell no more, but Diefenbaker and his colleagues must not be excused. The Liberals, Cardin declared, had a 'working arrangement' to make sure that Diefenbaker did not escape punishment. 'We are going to fight and fight hard and, if we have to, use the same methods that are being used and have been used against us for the past three years.'

It was an unfortunate statement laced with inaccuracies. Gerda Munsinger was soon discovered, very much alive, and working as a hostess in a Munich bar. When *Toronto Daily Star* reporter Robert Reguly found her she said simply, 'I suppose you want to ask me about Sévigny.' The man with the moustache was now known. Reporters thronged before his door before he had a chance to shave. An emotional Sévigny appeared with his wife and children beside him, admitted seeing Gerda 'socially,' and then cited his fine war record as proof of his loyalty to Canada. The defence was a bit embarrassing and hardly to the point, but Sévigny did win much sympathy when Larry Zolf, with a cameraman behind him, beat upon the

Sévignys' door. Sévigny opened it and then answered Zolf with his cane which came down squarely on Zolf's imposing nose.

Soon Gerda became familiar to all Canadian viewers over the age of sixteen (the networks discreetly saved her for the later hours). *Maclean's* sponsored a limerick contest. This one won.[7]

There was a young lady from Munich
Whose bosom distended her tunic.
Her main undertaking
Was cabinet making
In fashions bilingue et unique.

Though now a bit shopworn, her charms were there for all to see on the CBC: the husky dark voice, the luxuriant body, the deep eyes, and the sly smile that always hinted, temptingly, that there was much more there than there really was. Alas, she proved garrulous, too eager to recall past conquests. She identified George Hees as the other minister she knew. Reporters, Christian or not, took this to mean the biblical 'to know.' Hees protested, accurately, that he had simply had lunch with her. But the press continued to hint, in defiance of most human experience, that men and women who eat together must sleep together.

In the House of Commons, Cardin declared that because Gerda was sleeping with a Russian spy and the Associate Minister of National Defence, this was a clear security breach, worse than Profumo. There must be a full-scale security investigation. Diefenbaker defended himself and alleged that Munsinger had been used by the Liberals to blot out their own numerous scandals. He had some proof: incredibly, during the Spencer debate, Guy Favreau had threatened Davie Fulton with revelation of Munsinger if the Conservatives continued to attack the Liberals. The whole business smelled. In retrospect, Gordon Fairweather's comment during the debate seems especially apt: 'it will be hard to explain in the years ahead what we have been doing in these days.' It is. Gerda said it best. 'I knew Pierre as a man. He knew me as a woman. That's all there was to it.' And that's all there should have been.

Pearson had taken little part in the Munsinger debates. He talked of resignation; he did not resign, but most knew his time was short. With Diefenbaker, too, it was clear that the end was approaching. Indeed some Conservatives had approached Pearson during the Munsinger debate asking for help in removing their leader. After the spring, what remained of Pearson's and Diefenbaker's time was really an inter-

7 Quoted in Peter Newman, *The Distemper of Our Times* (Toronto: McClelland & Stewart 1968), 403.

Two solitudes.
John Diefenbaker has problems with his 'Quebec lieutenant,' Léon Balcer
(Berthio, 1965). Reproduced with the permission of Roland Berthiaume

regnum. It was for this reason, perhaps, that the expected damage to Quebec from the Cardin difficulties never materialized. Marchand stayed, as did all the other Quebec ministers. It was, in fact, a show of strength.

Journalists later would divide the Pearson government's relationship with Quebec into the pre-1965 years when the emphasis was on 'co-operative federalism' and accommodation and the later period when a 'harder' line was followed. The influence of Marchand, Trudeau, and Pelletier, who strongly opposed 'special status' for Quebec, is usually deemed to be paramount in the post-1965 period. This interpretation misleads in the sharp distinction it draws between Pearson's supposed 'soft' attitutde and the new Quebec ministers' intransigency. One might better describe the 1963-5 period as one in which the federal government, unprepared for what it faced, simply reacted to events in Quebec. Compromise was thus an instinctive, natural response. By 1966, however, Pearson knew better what he faced, feared it more, and was much less inclined to appease the Quebec government, although he had become even more willing to commit the federal government itself to bilingualism and biculturalism. In April 1966 he announced that all future university graduates joining the federal public service would have to be bilingual or willing to become so. Every Canadian, he declared, must have the right to service by federal officials in the citizen's official language. The prime minister's office itself took on a Gallic air as Pierre Trudeau became parliamentary secretary and Marc Lalonde and Jean Beetz moved into important positions in that office.

But toward Quebec's demands for special treatment Pearson was less sympathetic. No longer reactive, the federal government in 1966 seized the initiative in federal-provincial financial negotiations. The new finance minister, Mitchell Sharp, announced in September 1966 that the federal government would no longer 'make room' for the provinces by turning over tax 'points' as it had done earlier. Shared cost programs would also be reduced in scope. This was mainly a device intended to reduce Quebec's special status. For the first time since the Quiet Revolution, the federal government began a federal-provincial conference with the best-prepared case on its side. The conference in October 1966 was, in the words of a participant, a disaster, yet it revealed that Ottawa had finally found the limits of its generosity.

There was yet another area where the limits of Ottawa's patience and constitutional capacity were most severely tested. This was, of course, the extraordinary liaison between Quebec and France.

THE FRENCH CONNECTION

Quebec's Quiet Revolution almost immediately captured attention beyond Canada. In 1960, Charles de Gaulle, restored to the presidency of France by the generals two years before, visited Canada; on his return he told his cultural minister, André Malraux, to watch for 'interesting events' in French Canada. Malraux's sharp eye soon spotted what he termed 'un climat nouveau' in Quebec and in relations between Quebec and France. From October 1961 when Malraux made this observation at the opening of the Quebec délégation générale in Paris, Gaullist France wooed an increasingly receptive Quebec, and the seductiveness was not merely one-sided. De Gaulle saw in French Canada a French people infused with the spirit which, twenty years after the liberation, France so obviously lacked. Quebec, too, was a modern nation, part of the North American technical miracle and yet French: the lure was irresistible. As the trans-Atlantic romance warmed, the Canadian mixed marriage seemed more strained than ever before. The Gallic flirtation was, to Ottawa, the most serious threat to Confederation of the middle and later 1960s.

That Mike Pearson's government should be so disturbed about Quebec's interest in international ties is not surprising. Pearson himself had seen in the 1920s and 1930s how Canada's step-by-step road to autonomy had led Canada away from Britain and toward independence in all aspects of foreign as well as domestic affairs. The Pearson government thus moved to assure that there was a federal presence in the France–Quebec relationship. Ottawa had to represent French Canada abroad, and Canada' international personality had to be a fusion of Canada's bicultural character. If it were not, many Ottawa officials believed, independence for Quebec was both inevitable and logical. As one official later remarked, one day we would awaken and suddenly realize Quebec had left not through a declaration of independence but quietly through the back door. Then it would all be too late.

During the 1963 campaign Pearson added Paris to the traditional London and Washington visits which began a new prime minister's tenure. He kept this promise on January 15, 1964, and early suspicions about the warmth of de Gaulle's welcome soon disappeared as the French president spoke eloquently of the special and natural solidarity between France and 'votre Etat Fédéral.' Officials worked out new arrangements for technical, cultural, and educational exchanges. The mood, however, was deceptive: de Gaulle, increasingly isolated from his allies, needed Canada's voice and help in 1964. He wanted to buy Canadian uranium and to sell French Caravelle jets to Canada. In NATO, Canada was taking a more understanding attitude than most to France's criticisms of the alliance. Thus, despite the growing differences between Canada and France in 1965, differences that grew out of de Gaulle's new audacity in international policies, the French showed little interest in offending Canada: Quebec was not yet worth a mess.

But propinquity bred affection, especially for Quebec. Jean Lesage and several of his ministers luxuriated in the banquets, the champagne toasts, and the affection that accompanied their Parisian visits. For provincial politicians, these whiffs of the glamour of international diplomacy were intoxicating. By 1964 the Quebec government had begun negotiations for an educational accord. As Ottawa watched Quebec warily, the French displayed a proper hesitation. It took ten months before final agreement occurred. On February 27, 1965, Quebec and France signed an 'entente' and Canada and France exchanged 'notes' to give the curious specimen diplomatic authenticity. The Quebec signatory, Paul Gérin-Lajoie, sought to give it much broader meaning. He declared in Paris that the agreement was the first step toward a francophone cultural commonwealth in which Quebec would represent French Canada. Later in Montreal, Gérin-Lajoie advanced this argument further, claiming that the Quebec state was 'the political instrument of a distinct cultural group.' It should therefore possess the right to sign international agreements in realms of provincial jurisdiction and to participate in international organizations (such as the International Labour Organization) which dealt with provincial matters. Laurier La Pierre, who approved Gérin-Lajoie's claims, pointed out that, if Gérin-Lajoie's beliefs were reality, Canadians 'should recognize that they would be keeping only the form of the Confederation, of the country they know.'[8]

Martin and Pearson shared La Pierre's interpretation though not his attitude. They therefore moved quickly to protect the federal position through the creation of

8 Laurier La Pierre, 'Quebec and Treaty-making,' *International Journal*, XX (Summer 1965), 366.

'umbrella agreements' with foreign powers whereby provinces could reach agreements with foreign governments under the protection and signature of a covering federal umbrella. This, it was hoped, legitimized Quebec's dealings while simultaneously treating Quebec as a province like the others. What was not clear was the part Ottawa would play in what went on under the umbrella. In Quebec's view, federal officials would form the audience; in Ottawa's view they were part of the team.

This difference in perception caused acrimony when France and Canada signed their umbrella agreement ('accord cadre') in November 1965, following by a second, broader Quebec–France entente. Quebec explicitly refused to submit the entente to accord. Quebec would not accept a federal role in Quebec–France dealings. Claude Morin, the Quebec senior civil servant most closely connected with this stance, later wrote: 'Ottawa only realized later that, in its direct relations with France, Quebec was now poised not only to hatch new exchange programs or even simply discuss political problems with French representatives, but also to consult with Paris as if it were a virtually sovereign state and, thanks to French support, be bidden to international gatherings on the same basis as the other nations of the world.'[9]

Morin, who by 1965 was considered a separatist by Ottawa officials, is only partly correct. Ottawa was not so ignorant as he suggests, but it is true that French support of Quebec's attitude had become much stronger. In 1965 France's withdrawal from NATO operations became final. Moreover, Canada would not sell uranium to France nor would Air Canada buy France's Caravelles. Internationally, de Gaulle's purposes were more elusive and, as a biographer has said, it seemed 'as if new and ingenious ways of causing displeasure [to his allies] kept on occurring to him.' Certainly there was much Canadian displeasure. The French ambassador to Canada, François Leduc, a personal de Gaulle appointee, ambled mischievously through Quebec. Ottawa warned him that they must be told what he was doing and whom he was seeing. He promised he would tell them; he didn't. As a result, the Canadian government eventually decided it must invoke certain provisions of the Vienna Convention on diplomatic immunities which required that all diplomats must file notice of their visits. France would be treated as a nation like all others even though it was now acting differently. The diplomats from other countries understood.

In Paris, too, Canadians were being treated differently. Canadian ambassador Jules Léger had faced continuous snubs from the Elysée Palace. He apparently had offended de Gaulle when he presented his credentials. After that, he missed invitations, was denied meetings, and when Quebec ministers received warmest

9 Claude Morin, *Quebec versus Ottawa: The Struggle for Self-Government 1960-72* (Toronto: University of Toronto Press 1976), 37.

head table toasts, Léger, if present, sat too far away, probably with the coldest plate. Other Canadians felt the Gaullist cold shoulder in 1966 and early 1967. Governor General Georges Vanier, distressed by the Franco-Canadian difficulties, thought that a personal visit to his war-time colleague and, he thought, friend might ease tensions. De Gaulle's old friends were not necessarily his present ones. On a technicality, de Gaulle refused to see Vanier or at least offer him head-of-state treatment. Privately French officials warned Canadians that Vanier was not welcome. Neither was Jean Marchand in November 1966. As minor Quebec ministers trod upon the lushest Elysée rugs, the senior federal minister from Quebec cooled his heels in his hotel. Marchand at least got to see Paris; Vanier, the war hero, never saw Paris again. To his funeral in 1967 the French sent a low-ranking representative.

Other French actions seemed also deliberate attempts to repudiate past ties. On February 21, 1966 de Gaulle demanded that Canadian forces leave French soil. Infuriated, Pearson asked 'a high-ranking French public servant' whether Canada would have to take its hundred thousand dead in French graves to Germany along with its planes and soldiers. In a similar vein, de Gaulle refused to attend April 1967 ceremonies at Vimy Ridge because the Canadians had invited Prince Philip. On that spring day at Vimy only a few French local officials honoured Canada's greatest military triumph. Despite enormous irritation, Pearson remained mum. Events had made protest too dangerous.

On 5 June 1966, the Lesage government fell. As in 1962, Lesage called an election to regain his hold on the turbulent forces around him. The device failed, and the Union Nationale under Daniel Johnson took power with a platform of 'Québec d'abord.' Quebec, the platform declared, should possess extended powers and sovereignty internationally. For a while, though, little happened. Federal officials thought that the 'politics of grandeur' might have passed with Lesage. Once again, they were wrong. By the fall the Johnson government had grasped international activity as a means of binding together its diverse caucus. A ministry of intergovernmental affairs was created to 'co-ordinate' Quebec's dealings with 'foreign governments.' Johnson also proposed to convene an educational and cultural conference in Quebec, a meeting which would confirm international recognition of Quebec sovereignty in the fields of education and culture. Johnson was raising the stakes.

The bluff came over General de Gaulle's 1967 visit. Canada's centennial celebrations meant that all heads of state must be invited to come to Canada. De Gaulle received his invitation in spring 1966. On August 4, Pearson learned that Johnson had extended two personal invitations to de Gaulle and the pope. He was immediately suspicious and became more so as some Union Nationale ministers spoke publicly of France's willingness to treat Quebec as a 'sovereign' state. As for de Gaulle, his foreign policy in late 1966 was ever more theatrical and infused with

President de Gaulle receives a state visitor in style: Quebec's Minister of Education Jean-Guy Cardinal (Macpherson, 1969). Reproduced with the permission of the *Toronto Star*

symbolic gesture. He was, in short, unpredictable, and for Ottawa, an unwelcome guest who could not be provoked.

Naturally, both Quebec and Ottawa wanted to establish primacy in preparing for the visit. Ottawa insisted it had a role in all aspects of the tour. Quebec, on the other hand, denied that Ottawa should have a pre-eminent role in the Quebec portion of the visit. André Patry, a constitutional law specialist, was placed in charge of official visits in the Quebec government's Department of Federal-Provincial Affairs, soon to become – significantly – Intergovernmental Affairs. In fall 1966 Patry refused to heed federal demands that he not deal directly with foreign states. By the spring of 1967 Patry was speaking publicly and privately to baffled foreign diplomats about reciprocal rights and privileges for Quebec 'diplomats.' France already appeared to be offering special privileges. In March 1967 Ottawa learned through a rumour of a plan worked out between Quebec and French officials whereby de Gaulle would come in a warship to visit Quebec first and alone. Pearson angrily told his officials that there could be no visit unless de Gaulle came to Ottawa. Moreover, the federal government should control the entire visit which, barring exceptional circumstances, must begin in Ottawa.

A few days later, Leduc confirmed the rumour to Martin. Martin decided to see de Gaulle, Pearson, and Johnson. The Pearson–Johnson conversation was friendly and Pearson recorded in his diary that Johnson was 'prone to excuse his own lapses from common sense and moderation by the necessity of handling carefully his "wilder men".' But the fundamental disagreement was not discussed. This amiable meeting clarified little and settled nothing. The same was true of the Martin–de Gaulle visit, although the French did then agree that de Gaulle should come to Ottawa first.

Within two weeks this agreement disappeared, as did the amicability. The French, clearly after consultation with Quebec, presented a new itinerary in which de Gaulle visited Montreal first. At the same time, in early May, Ottawa and Quebec had a bitter argument over the signing of a Belgian-Canadian cultural accord. Quebec and the other provinces had been informed only one week before signature. Quebec bitterly objected; the federal government declared that Quebec could be involved in implementation but not in signature. André Patry wrote to Ottawa warning that 'Canadian' officials must not accompany Prince Albert of Belgium when he toured Quebec. Pearson wrote to Johnson protesting both the tone and substance of Patry's letter. Johnson sarcastically replied that his 'functionary' Patry had the full support of his government. In the Quebec Assembly Johnson accused Ottawa of duping and using the Belgians. Nevertheless, he agreed that the Canadian ambassador to Belgium could accompany Prince Albert in Quebec. With the Belgian incident both sides had formed ranks and come to order. Only the site of future battle remained in doubt.

In May Johnson went to Paris and the lights of the city had rarely shone so brightly. The welcome, Johnson declared, was 'glittering.' In this atmosphere, the Quebec premier persuaded de Gaulle to begin his historical visit in Quebec and then to travel the *chemin du roi* to Montreal. Ottawa could only agree; dissent would court disaster. In the remaining two months, Quebec and Ottawa quarrelled continually over the length of receptions, seating plans, and the height of flagpoles. Such trivia suddenly bore much meaning. The game was played secretly; the public knew nothing.

De Gaulle came on board the *Colbert* the morning of July 23, 1967. The welcome, *La Presse*, assured the visitor, would be 'royal.' For the Québécois the world would now learn what they had not forgotten. 'Le monde,' Johnson announced on July 21, 'saura que nous éxistons.'

As de Gaulle left the *Colbert* at Quebec, he heard a thunderous roar; for Governor General Roland Michener, there were scattered boos. Soon, Johnson took away the General. They passed through the streets of old Quebec, to the shrine at Ste Anne de Beaupré, and then back to the old city, all in an open car, through seas of waving flags and ceaseless chants – 'de Gaulle, de Gaulle, Vive la France.' That night at a banquet de Gaulle talked eloquently of the return of France to North America. The next day along the historic north shore trail, now christened the *chemin du roi*, de Gaulle responded in kingly fashion to the regal welcome. The long caravan snaked its way to Montreal where half a million thronged the streets and squares before the Hôtel de Ville.

Finally he was on the balcony, arms outstretched to embrace the crowd's warmth. He hesitated, then spoke.

C'est une immense émotion qui remplit mon cœur en voyant devant moi la ville française de Montréal. Au nom du vieux pays, au nom de la France, je vous sabre de tout mon cœur. Je vais vous confier un sécret que vous ne répéterez pas. Ce soir, ici, et tout le long de ma route, je me suis trouvé dans une atmosphère du même genre que celle de la Libération.

The liberation, his most cherished memory, could live once more. France, he dramatically concluded, would know, watch, and listen to all that passed in its oldest offspring: 'Vive Montréal! Vive le Québec! Vive le Québec libre.'

The cries reverberated; but they struck different keys. By evening Pearson was declaring the remarks intolerable: 'The people of Canada are free. Every province of Canada is free. Canadians do not need to be liberated.' The anglophone press agreed, questioning de Gaulle's mental stability. The francophone press and the Quebec government saw it differently. Claude Ryan in *Le Devoir* denounced the anglophone and federal government reaction as excessive, hysterical, a betrayal of fear and animosity. Daniel Johnson confessed he found Pearson's reaction inexplicable: De Gaulle's purpose was blameless. He had simply evoked 'le problème de l'identité distincte du Québec et son immense effort d'affirmation. Le Québec n'a jamais été une province comme les autres.' Polls indicated Quebec agreed: 69.3 per cent thought the voyage worthwhile; 58.7 per cent disagreed with Pearson's statement. Only 20 per cent thought de Gaulle wanted to encourage separation.

Frenchmen, however, had a different view; even the Communist *L'Humanité* thought de Gaulle had interfered, and the conservative *Le Figaro* deemed the intrusion in Canadian affairs disgraceful. That de Gaulle's French interpreters were correct he soon made clear. On his return he expanded upon his encounter with a people possessing 'a unanimous and indescribable will for emancipation.' In a historic and histrionic November 26 press conference the General relived his passage along the *chemin du roi*, claiming once more that the spirit of liberation still dwelt in these people, Frenchmen thousands of miles away. They would inevitably attain the rank of sovereign state and become masters of their own destiny.

The echo did not have the force of the original. Within a year de Gaulle was gone; so were Pearson and Johnson. So much had changed. The spectacle at the Hôtel de Ville had merely ended the prologue to the drama. In September 1967 René Lévesque issued 'Option Québec,' a disjointed but direct appeal for Quebec sovereignty. The Quebec Liberals fumbled, uncertain how to handle the renegade. This time there could be neither compromise nor excuse and at the Quebec Liberals' October 1967 convention Option Quebec was defeated. On November 18, 1967, the Mouvement Souveraineté-Association was formed in a Montreal monastery, its leader René Lévesque. The debate about Quebec was now on different ground; the debaters, too, were different.

That de Gaulle contributed to the spirit of Québécois nationalism and separatism cannot be doubted. That he created a French popular consciousness of Quebec is also true. He and Lévesque also alerted other Canadians to the crisis of Confederation. As Centennial Year came to an end, the century to come seemed as uncertain as the first had been at its beginning.

Illustrations

Prime Minister King (in English) and Justice Minister St Laurent (in French) broadcast to the nation announcing the end of the war in Europe (May 8, 1945).

Courtesy Public Archives of Canada, National Photography Collection, C-22716

Prime Minister King leads his cabinet across a parking lot at the National Liberal
Convention (August 1948).

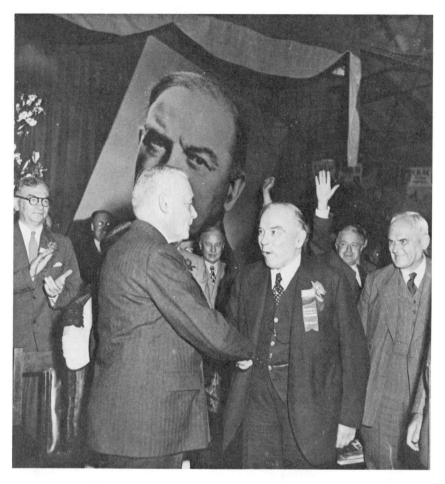

Prime Minister King congratulates Louis St Laurent on his accession as Liberal leader. In the background C.D. Howe beams, Brooke Claxton applauds, and Lionel Chevrier waves (August 1948).

Claude Jodoin addresses the second convention of the Canadian Labour Congress (April 1958).

Courtesy David Portigal and Company Limited, Winnipeg

Prime Minister and Mrs Diefenbaker meet President and Mrs Eisenhower at the American embassy in Ottawa (July 9, 1958).

Photo by D. Cameron. Courtesy Public Archives of Canada, 7518-21

The aftermath of a terrorist mailbox bombing in Westmount in which an army sergeant-major was maimed (May 1963).

Prime Minister Pearson and Premier Jean Lesage confer at a federal-provincial conference. Finance Minister Walter Gordon is in the background between them.

Photo by D. Cameron. Courtesy Public Archives of Canada, PA-117101

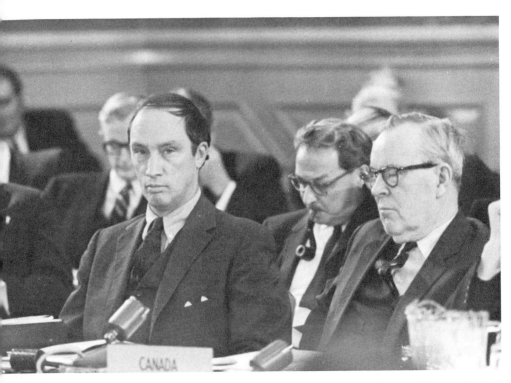

Prime Minister Pearson and Justice Minister Trudeau contemplate the constitution at the first constitutional conference (February 1968). The adviser in the background is Carl Goldenberg.

Photo by D. Cameron. Courtesy Public Archives of Canada, PA-117463

Prime Minister Trudeau greets two visitors from the world of popular culture: John Lennon of the Beatles and Yoko Ono, his wife (December 22, 1969). After this meeting the prime minister's hair noticeably lengthened.

Photo by D. Cameron. Courtesy Public Archives of Canada, PA-110804

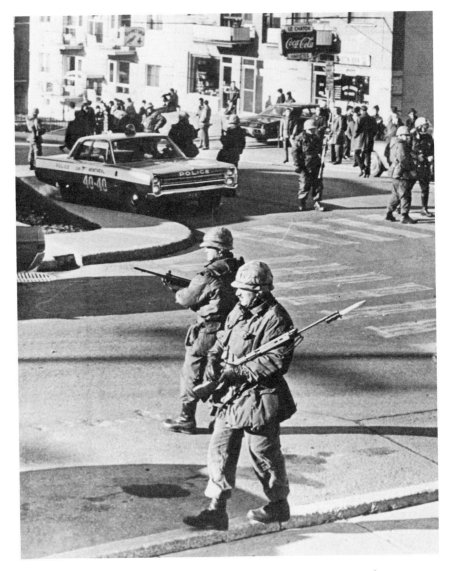

The October Crisis: soldiers patrol a Montreal street (December 1970).

Canadian Press photo. Courtesy CP Picture Service

John Diefenbaker celebrates his eightieth birthday in the House of Commons
(September 1974).

Canadian Press photo. Courtesy CP Picture Service

John Diefenbaker makes a point to
reporters (January 1976).

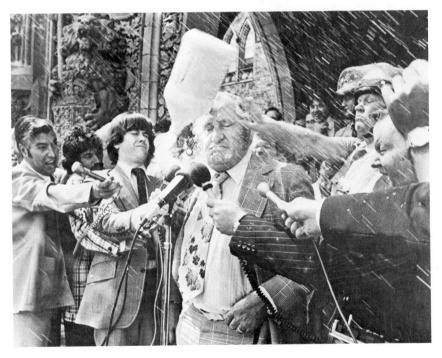

Agriculture Minister Eugene Whelan receives a milk-bath from angry dairy
farmers (June 1976).

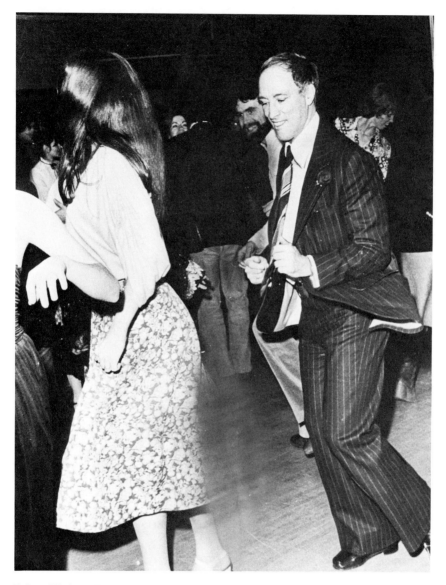

Prime Minister Trudeau boogies at Toronto's O'Keefe Centre (February 1979).
Photo by Doug Griffin. Courtesy the *Toronto Star*

Prime Minister Trudeau addresses a roomful of Alberta Liberals (May 1979). The sign in the background may well say 'Help!!'

Photo by Doug Ball. Courtesy CP Picture Service

The Economy and the Flowering
of the Social Service State

The tension between Quebec and Ottawa derived in part from the claims that both capitals were staking in the area of social reform. The sixties finally brought to Canada that social service state whose first glimmerings had been seen during the First World War but whose form had remained inchoate so long. During the decade many streams merged to create a torrent of legislation that surprised even the optimistic reformers of the 1950s. Prosperity, the sense of security arising from the stability of post-war society, and the general reformist orientation of the media made this full measure of reform possible. So did the need of politicians to win elections. In Ottawa it became fashionable to throw money at problems. Thanks to inflation and economic growth the government discovered that its take was increasing. Because employment was growing and unemployment was falling, unemployment insurance became self-financing once more, and the government did not concern itself about a 'bankruptcy' of the fund. Governments could turn to other needs.

In the election campaign of 1963, Mike Pearson caught this new mood. He promised 'sixty days of decision,' and talked about a health plan, a two-price system for wheat, a $1.25 minimum wage, a forty-hour week, portable old age pensions, a municipal loan fund, a department of industry, and a national development corporation, later known as the Canada Development Corporation (CDC). He also promised to help the Atlantic provinces. One by one, in the difficult years of his administration, the pieces of this ambitious program took on legislative substance.

In 1963 the Municipal Development and Loan Act provided $400 million for municipalities to be lent at 5.25 per cent interest. There was a new measure to subsidize housebuilding in winter; the provinces were creating planning bodies of their own, with co-ordination or urging from Ottawa. To make medium-term forecasts and to advise the government the dominion invented the Economic Council of Canada, which replaced the National Productivity Council that the Tories had formed in 1961. The NPC had been notable chiefly for the elaborate rejoicings that marked its regional conferences; the ECC was to be notable chiefly for the self-conscious earnestness of its *Annual Review* and for the quantity of its research work. Nevertheless, it was the council that helped to launch Canada's own version of the American War on Poverty. By 1963 it was already clear that the wind was blowing in that direction. Inside the new Liberal cabinet Walter Gordon and Judy LaMarsh led the 'progressive' forces. Already in 1962 Saskatchewan had forced its doctors to operate a medicare plan; in 1963 Alberta introduced voluntary medicare, and Ontario proposed to do the same. And most important of all, both Quebec and Ottawa were planning to introduce new pension plans.

In Quebec it was hoped that the pension scheme would provide finance for provincial development. Hence the rates of contribution would be large enough to build up a sizable fund in the first decade. Ottawa, on the other hand, wanted a pay-as-you-go plan, whereby current contributions would pay for current pensions. As the real cost of a pension plan is the consumption of the pensioners, the real economic burden would be the same in either case, whether or not a pension plan was 'funded.' But the Quebec plan had an obvious attraction to a capital-poor government, and other provinces were quick to notice this fact. As we saw earlier in this Part, after a lengthy wrangle with the provinces, legislation was introduced early in November 1964 and passed in March 1965. Quebec and the provinces got their way. Any province could opt out, so long as there was interprovincial 'portability' of pensions. Quebec at once did so. Employers and employees would each contribute 1.8 per cent of earnings up to $5,000. From these contributions a $4 billion fund would accumulate in the first decade, and it would be shared among the provinces in proportion to their contributions. Thus the plan had turned into a mechanism for forced saving, besides its principal announced purpose, which was to provide, for the elderly, widows, dependent children, and the disabled, pensions that varied with the contributions and with the general level of income. In other words, the pensions were partially indexed against inflation, and they would also rise along with average real incomes. They would co-exist with the old flat-rate pension, soon to be raised first to $75 per month and then, via an income guarantee, to $105.

After the pensions came medicare. In 1963 Pearson had promised to introduce it within four years. To do so he needed the provinces' co-operation. Already some provinces had universal medicare, while others had voluntary programs. But some did not want medicare at all. At last, in July 1965, Pearson announced that the federal government would contribute funds to any provincial scheme that was 'universal and portable,' so long as it covered all general and specialist services without using private firms or groups. The final rule was important. In some provinces, such as Ontario and British Columbia, the doctors operated large and successful medicare plans; in some provinces private insurance firms had been active. Almost everywhere there was Blue Cross. In the provinces with more conservative governments the natural tendency was to provide medical insurance through these 'private carriers.' But Ottawa wanted the provinces themselves to administer medicare. One by one, often after much grumbling, the provinces accepted the federal scheme. It would have been political suicide to refuse. Anyway, as several provinces were already running their own medicare schemes while others proposed to do so, the federal money would come in handy. In 1968 nation-wide medicare began.

Medicare was welcomed as a triumph of 'progressive' politics and thought. During the sixties 'progressive' thinking was increasingly critical of the status quo. It was not enough that real per capita output was rising; now more and more Canadian publicists and politicians worried about *inequality* of incomes, about the relations between Canada's affluent whites and much poorer native peoples, and about the nation's responsibilities in world economic and social development. Although Canada escaped the serious disturbances of American and German universities, there was much academic activism and dissent which helped to create a widespread mood of unease and a questioning of social and economic institutions which, before 1962, nearly everyone had accepted.

During the 1940s and 1950s, the national authorities had put their faith largely in macroeconomic monetary and fiscal policies. They appeared to need little more. But such policies had disadvantages. They were too complicated for many politicians and most citizens to understand, and only a strong and self-confident administration could enforce them; nor could they be used for political patronage as social reform measures sometimes could. Further, after 1958 certain intellectual currents were pulling strongly in a contrary direction. As we saw in Part IV, by the late fifties some officials had noticed that Canada was depending strongly upon skilled migrants at a time when unemployment was concentrated almost wholly among the unskilled. These officials, the educational establishments, and the more 'structurally' inclined economists were convinced that the unemployment problem was chiefly or wholly a mismatching of supply and demand: raise the level of education and skills and everyone would find a job. Here was an area where academic dissenters and the politicians could find common ground. Governments had also begun to notice that in the agricultural regimes where population was falling, many individuals were stranded, unable to move, yet unable to make decent livings under changed price-cost conditions.

Diefenbaker's Technical and Vocational Training Act had provided massive national funding for provincial efforts in the field of secondary technical education, and money for the retraining and educational upgrading of adults, especially the unemployed. The Pearson government continued the program, and added to it. In 1967 it took full responsibility for the training and retraining of adults, while it agreed to continue construction grants until every province had received at least $800 per capita. It also offered allowances to any adult who enrolled in a retraining course. By 1971 the national government had spent $1,100 million on the construction of technical schools, and the provinces had spent many millions more.

In 1965, intergovernmental ARDA agreements were revised so as to concentrate upon the relief of rural poverty. In 1966 the government created a $50 million Fund for Rural Economic Development (FRED), which would make grants in rural areas, especially for schools, adult education, land purchase, and re-establishment. This fund began to offer guaranteed minimum incomes to elderly farmers who would agree to leave the land. The spending ceiling was quickly raised: in 1967, the fund spent $300 million. In 1968, it was used to underwrite far-ranging provincial plans for eastern Quebec and Prince Edward Island.

These agricultural and educational plans were not meant to help the poorer regions as such. But since the agricultural problems were concentrated in the low-income districts, and since education was especially bad in the eastern low-income provinces, they inevitably had this effect. Paralleling these plans were new government subsidies for depressed areas. First applied in 1960, these subsidies rapidly proliferated.

In December 1960, and thereafter, the Conservative government had provided tax concessions for firms which might be established in designated high-unemployment areas. In 1962, it had set up an advisory Atlantic Development Board, and in 1963 its Liberal successors gave the board $100 million to spend on capital construction in the Atlantic provinces. When, in 1966, all the money was spent, the government provided another $50 million. In 1963 the Liberals granted a new package of tax concessions which replaced the Conservative ones, and they created an Area Development Agency to watch over the thirty-five designated 'development areas' within which the concessions could be claimed. In 1965 the government began to make grants when firms established themselves in the areas; they also greatly increased the number and extent of areas so designated. By this time 16 per cent of the labour force lived in these 'development areas,' which covered much of Quebec and almost all of the Atlantic provinces. In 1966, faced with a contracting coal industry in Nova Scotia, the nation established a Crown corporation which would buy up the privately owned mines and phase them out while developing alternative local employment. In 1969 the designated areas were further extended, and in 1970 twenty-two 'special areas' were marked off: in these, the national treasury would pay for infrastructure, and primary and service industries could share the grants and tax concessions which in other development areas were paid only to manufacturing.

Further, there were grants to persons. In 1965 the Manpower Mobility Program appeared. It offered loans and, in certain circumstances, grants to would-be movers. At first the scheme did not amount to much. In its first year it disbursed only 1,207 grants and 982 loans. But in 1967 it was made more liberal; grants replaced loans, and the government said it would finance more kinds of movement. Hence, in 1968, 10,000 people received assistance.

All these schemes raised government spending substantially. In 1950 Canada's governments spent just over $1 billion on health and social welfare. In 1971 they spent some $9 billion. They consistently spent some 24 per cent of their total outlays in this way, thus accounting for some 9 per cent of national product in the late 1960s.

These developments should be seen as extensions of the welfare state and of the paternalistic, interventionist state with which we have become so familiar in the 1970s. They should not be seen as socialism, either creeping or revolutionary. In most respects the private sector grew and flourished as never before, although of course businessmen disliked taxation and complained about it. Most new housing was still privately owned, although the CMHC and the provincial housing corporations were more active than they had been in the 1950s. Most industrial output came from private factories. In retail trade and in finance private enterprise predominated, although consumer co-operatives were making some progress. As for the protection of the consumer and the protection of competition, the Pearson government was less active than its successor, although somewhat more vigilant than its predecessor. It did not amend the Combines Investigation Act, and it rarely invoked it. Hence mergers and the construction of conglomerates proceeded with little check from Ottawa. Nor did the government appear to worry about the power of the trade unions. Indeed, it seemed to welcome the extension and expansion of unions and their rights. Strong unions, it seemed, were a palliative to capitalist guilt.

After the end of the Second World War, Canada had returned to the divided jurisdiction in labour matters which it has maintained ever since. The national government has power to legislate only with respect to the workers in certain industries, while the residual power, covering almost 95 per cent of the labour force, rests with the ten provinces. Hence one cannot give any compact and accurate account of the eleven codes of labour law, or of their evolution. Only a few points can safely be made. First of all, because the several provinces began the post-war period with the general national regulation of the war years, they started with similar codes. Employers were obliged to recognize and bargain with unions which had been certified as bargaining agents by the relevant government board. The authorities provided compulsory mediation and conciliation, but not arbitration except when the national government might impose such arbitration ad hoc, as was done several times, especially in railway disputes. Strikes could legally occur only after both unions and managements had passed through the several steps of negotiation which the law prescribed. Contracts were legally binding for a stated term. Hence, compared with some other countries, in Canada strikes were relatively few but relatively lengthy, and were almost always 'official.'

This legal code protected labour unions, although it did little to assist their growth; but, under its aegis this growth had continued – from 711,000 members in 1945 to 1,459,200 in 1960. After a slight decline in 1961-3 union membership expanded again, reaching 2.2 million in 1971. Throughout the period, nearly 70 per cent of all unionists belonged to 'international' unions. Between 1946 and 1971 there was only a slight change in the union membership relative to non-agricultural employees. The unionized percentage rose only from 28 per cent to 33 per cent. But since agriculture became much less important during these years, unionism became much more important for the labour force as a whole. In 1946 only 17 per cent of Canada's labour force belonged to unions, while in 1971 the percentage was 27.2.

Union organization changed in two respects. Following the merger of the American Federation of Labor with the Congress of Industrial Organisations, the Canadian cognate federations had united in 1955 to form the Canadian Labour Congress, a body which also contained several 'national' unions that had no American cognates. By the late sixties, the CLC contained three-quarters of all Canadian unionists. The Canadian and Catholic Confederation of Labour changed its name and orientation, becoming the Confederation of National Trades Unions (CNTU). By the late sixties it had 10 per cent of the unionists.

The unions also changed their relationship with the political parties and movements somewhat. In the early 1960s the CLC had become closely connected with the New Democratic Party, which depended heavily upon union financing. In the mid-sixties the CNTU became very deeply involved with political and linguistic agitation in Quebec, where its membership was concentrated. While unions might deliver the money they still could not deliver the vote.

In 1963 the unions, worried because their membership was not growing, began to ask themselves how they might advance from the blue-collar trades into the white-collar occupations where most new jobs were appearing. In that year two unions merged to form the Canadian Union of Public Employees (CUPE). As yet most government employees were forbidden to join unions or to bargain collectively; however, both in Ottawa and in many provincial legislatures the laws would soon change. CUPE would soon be joined by a horde of what one might call 'white-collar craft unions,' most of whose members worked for government. Many of these unions were very small, mainly because so many based themselves on occupational affinity, not on industry. Thus, for example, on every airport there was an air traffic controllers' union and a host of other specialized unions, not a union for the airport industry. Because the Canadian system of labour relations is good at defining and certifying a network of 'bargaining units,' outside Quebec there were not many of those jurisdictional disputes in which two or more unions fight for the right to organize the workers or represent them. But by the late sixties there were plenty of simple old-fashioned strikes over wages, working conditions, fringe benefits, and the like. And because the bargaining units were often so small and specialized, a tiny group of public employees could cause a good deal of trouble, bringing large industries or government departments to a halt. Before 1963 such strikes could only occur in private services as such. It was in the Pearson years that this changed.

The worries of 1960-2, when the unions had wondered if they could even penetrate the expanding industries – chiefly service trades and the various public services – proved premature. In the Pearson years unionists became much more numerous, and the unions penetrated ever more pervasively. In 1963 Ontario gave civil servants bargaining rights, although it withheld the right to strike; instead it provided binding arbitration. The federal government agreed to the same thing in principle, and Ottawa set up a committee to draft proposals. Already, however, the postal workers were pressing for the right to strike. For hospital employees there was discussion of compulsory arbitration, largely because some hospital strikes were already occurring. In Quebec the government proposed that there should be compulsory binding arbitration for civil servants. But in 1964 there was a long strike in the Quebec Liquor Board, and in 1965, 500 Quebec teachers struck. Submitting to pressure from the public employees, the Quebec government gave most civil servants and all teachers the right to strike over wages, thereby setting the stage for some protracted and bitter disputes in the late sixties and seventies. Already the teachers had formed the Quebec Teachers' Corporation; teachers and other public employees were co-operating ever more closely with the CNTU, which, in turn, was growing ever more nationalistic, and which competed ever more fiercely with the Quebec Federation of Labour, the provincial arm of the CLC.

In 1965 Ontario also set up an arbitration system for civil servants, while banning hospital strikes. For federal civil servants the Heeney Committee recommended bargaining with binding arbitration, not strikes. But by that time the customs workers, like the postal workers, wanted to be allowed to strike. In 1966 the federal government introduced legislation along the Heeney lines. But for the leaders of the public services and their cabinet supporters, this was not enough. The federal cabinet debated at length whether they should go further. The 'liberals' of the cabinet, like the former labour leader, Jean Marchand, and others anxious to woo the urban worker from the NDP, decided that civil servants should be allowed to strike like everyone else. The former civil servants – Bud Drury, Mitchell Sharp, Jack Pickersgill, and Pearson himself – did not much like the idea. But in February 1967 they gave way, and Parliament quickly gave its assent.

The extension of the right to strike did not quell labour unrest. It seemed that strikes were everywhere – in municipal services in Vancouver and Toronto, in hospitals in Quebec, in the post office, in 1968, and, of course, in the traditional areas. Many blamed a seaway workers strike in 1966 for these troubles. In that strike, a majority conciliation board recommended a 14 per cent wage increase over two years. The union rejected this, but, before the strike could begin, the government-appointed mediator announced that a settlement had been reached which granted a 20 per cent increase retroactive to January 1 and 10 per cent more on January 1, 1967. Certainly this encouraged others to push negotiations to the final stages and to seek higher settlements, but it would be wrong to attribute too much influence to it. Bystanders had already begun to suspect that there might be something wrong with the Canadian system of labour relations. The system of compulsory conciliation certainly averted many strikes, but when strikes did occur they tended to be long and bitter. Because a minor dispute was usually settled through negotiation and arbitration, a strike signalled a really serious disagreement. Because the labour relations boards worked hard at the certifying of bargaining agents and at forcing employers to bargain in good faith, the battles over recognition and the nastier battles about jurisdiction that had once been common both in Canada and in the United States did not occur. Nevertheless there were some disputes about jurisdiction. At Inco, there was bitter argument between the United Steelworkers and the Mine-Mill and Smelter workers; in Quebec, there was vicious competition between the QFL and the CNTU. The Canadian arrangements did nothing to keep unions honest. When it suspected that the Seafarers' International Union was mismanaged, Parliament had to step in, setting up a trusteeship to manage the union's affairs. Although the CLC could expel the Teamsters it could not effect any reform in that union. Finally, in vital services – the post office, hospitals, and airports – strikes were becoming more common. The day was not distant when, in New Brunswick and in Quebec, firemen and policemen would go on strike.

These developments were not generally popular. In a sense, admittedly, they were not really new. There had always been railway strikes from time to time, and in several provinces such vital services as city transit, telephones, and even electricity had potentially been at risk. But in the past governments had usually acted quickly to prevent such strikes or stop them. Indeed, it had long been argued that on the railways collective bargaining was a fraud, because in case of any real dispute the federal government would impose a solution sooner rather than later. But in the 1960s such disputes became more common and more disruptive; also, because a small group could now cause so much trouble the strikes looked less sensible, while because there were often no alternatives they also looked more irresponsible. When glue workers or car assemblers strike, it is clear that they are striking against their employer; the public does not really suffer. But what of those who work in government monopolies? The public loses all the service but the employer does not suffer any financial loss because governments do not make profits, and in the end the public pays through higher taxes. And what of strikes in such 'essential services' as hospital, police, and fire services? Not only does the public pay for the settlement through higher taxes; it also pays for the strikes through unnecessary deaths, illnesses, crimes, and fire losses. Hence it was easy to argue that such strikes were really 'strikes against the public.' On the other hand, workers suspected that if they were refused the right to strike they would lose leverage, whether or not governments offered to accept arbitration instead. These fears were hardly surprising, since in several provinces the authorities were already trying to limit the powers and effectiveness of unions. At least, union leaders thought that this was so. The debate continued into the 1970s with neither resolution nor winners.

THE DOLLAR, TRADE, AND BUDGETS

Looking through the newspapers of the middle and late sixties, one might quickly conclude that those were years of economic turmoil. Alarms sounded regularly, but the crises they foretold passed surprisingly quickly. The crises normally arose from our investment and trading patterns and characteristics.

The Pearson government inherited a dollar that its predecessors had pegged at 92.5 American cents in 1962. That exchange rate outlasted Lester Pearson. Indeed, it was maintained by his successors until May 1970. At no time in these years would any minister or any official admit that the rate might be changed – Ottawa had learned a lesson from the Tory mishaps of 1961-2. But the rate was maintained only with difficulty. Year after year Canada imported more than she exported, covering the difference by importation of capital, chiefly from the United States. In the boom atmosphere of the 1960s such foreign money was not really hard to attract. Foreigners were anxious to invest in Canada and Canadians were anxious to borrow abroad. Nevertheless, the waters that had been so tranquil in the 1950s were now scattered with reefs and shoals, around which Canada's monetary authorities had to navigate with care. For the first time in more than sixty years the American government was worried about its own payments position. Although the United States economy regularly produced a current account surplus, American firms were so eager to invest abroad that the gold in Fort Knox, once so massively impregnable, was melting away, while foreigners were heaping up ever-larger holdings of US dollars, all of which were convertible into gold, on demand, at the fixed price of $35 per ounce. Thus the US government began to discourage the export of capital funds just when the Canadians had become very dependent on capital import.

The first crisis occurred in July 1963, when the US government announced that it would ask Congress to levy an 'interest equalization tax.' This tax was based on the cost of credit in the United States, where loans were cheaper than in most countries. Its purpose was to discourage foreigners from borrowing so much in the United States by equalizing the cost of domestic and foreign funds. The US government wanted it because Americans were lending more than America's current account surplus would cover. Although Canada was not a special target, the original idea was to cover *all* foreign borrowing, and Canadians believed that the tax would have the effect of adding a full percentage point to the cost of any new loans they might raise in the United States. Canada could offset the tax by raising its cost of credit, but the result would be a painful monetary contraction. The Canadian government and central bank therefore asked for an exemption, and the US government agreed. Three days after Washington had proposed the tax to Congress, it announced that so long as Canada would not try to increase its reserves of foreign money, it would ask Congress to exempt new Canadian borrowings. That is, so long as Canada borrowed just enough to cover its own current account deficit the United States would not subject it to the tax.

Because Canada–US trade accounted for all of the Canadian deficit, it was obvious, even in Washington, that by borrowing just to cover its deficit Canada could not possibly hurt the American balance of payments. But if Canada borrowed to increase its reserves it would pull gold from American vaults, or add to its holdings of US dollars, the two things the US government wanted to prevent.

Until Congress had actually legislated there was great uncertainty about the actual impact of the tax. Although in the end Canadian borrowings were exempted, for the rest of 1963 and for much of 1964 the American bond market was virtually closed to Canadian borrowers. Fortunately, and unexpectedly, the USSR started to buy Canada's wheat on a large scale. Without that windfall, the Canadian balance of payments would have been in deep trouble. Even so, the Bank of Canada pursued a cautious monetary policy. It allowed chartered bank reserves to rise only by 5.8 per cent in 1963 and 0.5 per cent in 1963, while output rose 5.2 per cent and 6.7 per cent.

More shocks were ahead. In December 1965 the American government published guidelines that were meant to reduce the flow of American direct foreign investment and speed the repatriation of profits by American-owned businesses. At first finance minister Mitchell Sharp did not object, believing that the new rules were consistent with Canada's own policy of discouraging further direct investment. To help the Americans, he had already reduced the target for Canadian reserves of foreign money. But in Montreal the financial world complained loudly, and Sharp soon explained that he disliked the guidelines.

In March 1966, therefore, Minister of Trade and Commerce Robert Winters published some Canadian guidelines. Foreign-owned businesses were asked to do many things, in particular to keep enough profits in Canada for the financing of Canadian expansion. And the Americans told Sharp and Winters that 'the United States government was not requesting United States companies to induce their Canadian subsidiaries to act in ways that differed from their normal business practices.'

In 1965 and 1966 American interest rates were rising, and the Bank of Canada had to keep Canadian rates high enough to ensure an adequate import of capital. In 1967 Governor Rasminsky wrote that he would have liked to move toward more monetary restraint at an earlier time. However, it is not clear how he could have done this, given Canada's promises to the United States with respect to its reserves. If he had kept credit tighter and forced interest rates higher in Canada, he would probably have produced an uncomfortably large inflow of capital funds, more than Canada needed to cover its trading deficit. Indeed, precisely because he was trying to prevent this from happening, through October 1967 the Bank allowed the quantity of money to grow quite rapidly.

There was another crisis late in 1967, when the British pound was devalued. The pound had been under pressure for some time, and more than once others had helped with emergency finance. In November 1967 London at last admitted it would have to devalue the pound from $2.80 US to $2.40. Although the Canadian dollar had been strong, following the British devaluation it did experience some problems, and the more nervous international investors moved funds out of Canada in the expectation that it might follow Britain downward. There was no question of Canada's doing so, however, and Mitchell Sharp, the finance minister, insisted that the dollar would stay at 92.5 American cents. Nevertheless, for no very good reason, speculators began to suspect that other relatively weak currencies, such as the Canadian dollar, would be devalued too. The Canadian currency was a weak one in the sense that every well-informed person knew Canada needed regular borrowings to cover its regular deficits on current account. Hence funds began to flow out of Canada and the flow continued well into 1968.

By year-end the speculative pressures had spread to the American dollar itself. Everyone, especially the French, expected that the United States would have to raise the price of gold. There was, accordingly, a flight from American dollars into gold, and into such strong currencies as the mark. On January 1, 1968, the American government announced new and more stringent guidelines. American-owned firms would have to repatriate 30 per cent of their earnings. American banks were to lend no more than 103 per cent of the amount they had lent abroad in 1967. As for external investment from American funds and from retained earnings, this was restricted to 65 per cent of the average level in 1965-6.

Canada had been consulted about these guidelines and was not much worried, because Sharp thought the curbs would really not affect the behaviour of American-owned firms in Canada. However, it appears that, within days, there was an unexpectedly large transfer of funds from American-owned firms back to the United States. In addition, the Canadian dollar was still under some speculative pressure because of the nervousness about the international monetary situation. By January

21 the government had begun to make emollient pronouncements and to take defensive moves. But as the world financial system moved ever more deeply into speculation against gold, Canada's position became ever more uncomfortable.

Rasminsky later wrote: 'for most of the first half of 1968 the Bank gave top priority to the defence of the exchange value of the Canadian dollar.' What he wanted, and got, was another confidence trick. On March 7, 1968, the Americans gave Canada some new exemptions. They had been trying to discourage US multinationals from transferring funds abroad and to encourage them to bring profits back home. Now these rules would not apply to Canada. Canada arranged to borrow from the International Monetary Fund, and also to borrow $500 million from the American Export-Import Bank, $100 million from the Bank of International Settlements, and $150 million from central banks in West Germany and Italy. In effect the government was mobilizing its resources so as to defend the dollar, and by telling the public how strong its defences were it hoped to end the speculative pressure. The trick worked: the drain slowed at once, and stopped on March 17.

Nevertheless the world-wide speculation continued, reaching a crisis in mid-March, when it was necessary to close the gold markets both in London and in Canada. The speculation had gotten completely out of hand. After three days of frantic negotiation the countries of the western world announced that there would be a new regime. Among themselves, the world's central banks would trade gold at the old price of $35.00; on the open market, gold could be bought and sold at any price; the central banks would neither buy new gold on the open market nor supply gold to it. In effect newly mined gold was now a commodity like wheat or copper. Canada welcomed this innovation, and early in April allowed its own gold markets to reopen.

Canada liked the new arrangements, if only because they would end the speculation. Immediately the Bank of Canada returned to an expansionary course. The chartered banks' primary reserves were allowed to grow rapidly, until at year-end they stood 8.7 per cent higher than in December 1967. Nevertheless, the monetary expansion did not keep interest rates low enough to prevent an accretion of foreign exchange, as capital funds flowed into Canada. By December 1968, for the first time, these holdings were above the 1963 ceiling.

As speculators moved from gold and foreign money back into Canadian dollars Canada's position quickly improved, and by the end of 1968 Sharp had wound up most of the emergency loans and lines of credit that he had negotiated in the first three months of the year in an atmosphere of political crisis. (See above.) Underlying this improvement were two things: the current account balance was improving, and Canada was still importing long-term capital funds, both to finance new foreign direct investments and to expand Canadian businesses and governments.

But now the exemptions of July 1963 and March 1968, once so eagerly sought, had turned into a straitjacket, one that placed the Bank in an impossible position.

Whenever capital came flowing into Canada with especial speed, the Bank would have to make credit easy (thus creating inflationary pressure, about which the Bank and the government were increasingly worried) so as to discourage Canadians from borrowing abroad, lest holdings of foreign money should rise. Once more Canada's monetary mandarins made a pilgrimage to Washington. At last, late in December 1968, the American authorities, who now understood the position, discarded the 1963 rule. Once more Canada could let its foreign exchange holdings rise if it wanted to. Thus after five years the Bank recovered a modicum of freedom with respect to domestic credit policy, which no longer had to be conducted with both eyes firmly glued on the national holdings of foreign money.

Having shed the straitjacket, Canadians did not always remember that in 1963 they had designed it themselves, and willingly donned it. At that time inflation had not seemed to be much of a danger, and the balance of payments seemed much more precarious than in the late sixties, by which time everyone was much more worried about inflation. As circumstances and perceptions had changed, the warm and comforting security blanket of 1963 had become a too-restricting swaddling.

Whatever the long-run impact of this monetary policy, the Pearson era itself was a time of boom, based upon a rising tide of exports and a wave of domestic investment, both domestically owned and foreign owned. And what a boom it was! The list of projects is almost endless. Quebec was building a steel mill and Montreal and Toronto were digging subways. In Nova Scotia the government was manufacturing heavy water, or trying to, and bribing Clairtone Radio to move from Ontario to Pictou. New Brunswick was building the Mactaquac hydro project, and Newfoundland began work at Churchill Falls. Manitoba, too, was building new hydro-electric capacity on the Nelson River, and British Columbia on the Columbia and on the Peace.

Saskatchewan battened on the new wheat sales, and its potash deposits, where production had begun in 1951, began to bulk large. In 1964 Great Canadian Oil Sands began to build its Alberta plant. In the Northwest Territories the Pine Point lead-zinc complex began to produce, and Canada Tungsten reopened its mine. In Quebec there was to be a government-owned plant that would assemble Renault and Peugeot cars; in Nova Scotia there was hope that a Japanese car firm would join Volvo. And alongside these dramatic and newsworthy schemes were developments less picturesque but equally important. Rapidly the country was building its new urban framework – the factories, houses, commercial buildings, shopping centres, roads, sewers, and universities.

In the export trade many things were happening. The Communist states were buying Canada's wheat; and Americans began to buy its cars. In 1963 the Soviet Union signed a massive wheat contract. Never before had Canada shipped more than 400 million bushels a year, but in 1963-4, thanks to this contract, it would have to ship 550 million. In 1965 the USSR bought another 187 million bushels. China, having contracted in 1963 to buy up to 187 million bushels by 1966, reached that figure in June 1965 and at once signed another contract to buy up to 187 million bushels by mid-1969. The United States was not happy about these deals, but Ottawa paid no attention to its complaints. Meanwhile, in November 1963, Canada introduced an export incentive scheme to encourage car exports. Studebaker promptly shut down its American plant and shifted to Canada; Washington as promptly complained. The Canadian government was worried because Canadians were importing more cars and parts than they exported; the Americans objected because the Canadian government was proposing to subsidize exports, thus diverting jobs from American auto cities to Canadian ones. In 1964, therefore, at Canada's initiative, the two governments began to discuss an alternative – a kind of free-trade arrangement for cars and parts – whereby North America would be a single market. In January 1965 an agreement was reached. The United States would eliminate tariffs on Canadian-made cars and parts; Canada would allow the car companies to import cars and parts duty-free from the United States so long as they satisfied certain conditions – a definite minimum level of work in Canadian plants, and a definite ratio between Canadian manufacture and Canadian sales. At once the car companies began to rearrange their production so as to get the benefits of continental specialization. In Canada production went up, and so did employment. By the early 1970s cars and parts were the largest single export, although they were more than balanced by imports. In Canada, thanks to government pressure, car prices fell a little relative to American cars, and car-buyers hoped for a larger pay-off in due course.

The Auto Pact was not genuine free trade, because Canada continued to protect the relatively high-cost Canadian production and because Canadian citizens were still not allowed to import cars duty-free: only the car firms could do so. Although the Pact might eventually reduce Canadian costs and prices to the American level, there was no sign that the government would ever abandon the 'safeguards' which it had built into the 1965 arrangements. For decades Canadian government have tried to win new vents for our exports while conceding as little as possible with respect to importation. The Auto Pact is another example of this tendency, and so are the other initiatives with respect to international trade that were taken during the Pearson years.

On the trading horizon there were two kinds of clouds. The European Economic Community (EEC), established in 1958, was still shaping its common agricultural policy, but by 1963 it was already obvious that this policy would be highly protectionist. Along with the United States, Canada pressed for a more open market in continental Europe; predictably it got nowhere. Meanwhile Oriental goods were providing awkward competition, especially for Canada's textile producers. In 1963, new and more stringent import quotas on Japanese and other textiles were imposed, thus providing more effective protection while reducing certain tariff rates.

In 1963 the Kennedy administration had proposed that all tariffs should be cut by 50 per cent. It wanted multilateral negotiations through GATT – the General Agreement on Tariffs and Trade. In Ottawa, the cabinet was split. Should Canada accede to the American initiative? After all, since 1944 the government had supported much multilateral tariff bargaining, and in a general sort of way Canada wanted other people to reduce their tariffs so long as it did not have to concede very much. Walter Gordon was afraid that Canada could not bargain without making concessions; Mitchell Sharp believed the bargaining could be turned to its advantage. In 1964 Canada agreed to take part in the talks, which had quickly been labelled the Kennedy Round. Canada won an exemption from the across-the-board cuts. Its heavy exports of numerous primary products, on which other countries' duties were already low or non-existent, meant that if everyone were to reduce tariffs by 50 per cent Canada could not possibly hope to gain as much as it would have to give. Instead, a list of 'offers of concessions' was prepared. Canada also hoped, through the Kennedy Round discussions, to maintain its pressure on the EEC. Bargaining went on until September 1966, by which time the EEC had fixed its agricultural policies on basically protectionist lines; this fact was especially alarming to Canada in that Britain was once more seeking to join the Community. Canada supported British membership so long as its own export interests could be safeguarded, but it was already obvious that in the future Britain would not be a large market for Canadian goods. Indeed, when the Kennedy Round negotiations ended in May 1967 it was with the Americans that Canada had done best. Gains in other directions, although valuable, were not nearly so large. Tariff cuts covered $3 billion worth of export trade, of which $1.9 billion went to the United States. Canada's own concessions covered $2.5 billion worth of imports, $2 billion of which came from the United States. The agreements were far from 'unrestricted reciprocity,' and all tariff cuts were extended symmetrically to all fifty GATT members. But it was obvious that, so far as Canadian imports and exports were concerned, the new arrangements would integrate the Canadian economy more closely with the American.

Nowhere was this interpretation more obvious than in energy. On balance Canada was still importing oil. But during the Pearson years its hydrocarbon exports went steadily up, and the United States was the only market. Natural gas exports rose from 86 trillion cubic feet in 1958 and 319 trillion in 1962 to 607 trillion in 1968, while exports of crude oil rose 83 per cent between 1962 and 1968. In the American midwestern and far western states, Canadian oil and gas had become quite important. Something similar had happened with electric power. In the early sixties the Diefenbaker government had hoped for a Canadian national electricity grid. By 1965, however, it was clear that the connections would run north and south, not east and west. Regional electricity systems were connected with their American opposite numbers so that loads could be shared and power could be imported or exported whenever the need arose. The results could be dramatic, as Canadians learned in 1965, when a mechanical failure on the Niagara Frontier blacked out everything from Toronto to New York. In energy, at least, continental integration had come to stay. Or so it seemed by 1968.

THE BUDGETS OF THE PEARSON GOVERNMENT

Present-day governments normally use their taxing and spending programs to steer the economy. In Canada the practice began during the Second World War. We have seen that, in the Diefenbaker years, there was a good deal of budgetary tacking, and it was often suspected that the helmsman did not know where he was going. But when Lester Pearson took office he installed Walter Gordon as his finance minister. The Toronto accountant had written eloquently of the need for 'confidence.' He had helped to form the economic planks of the Liberal platform. The country expected that he would devise a businesslike budget, one that would help to revive the economy. When Gordon brought down his first budget on June 13, 1963, however, the country received a rude shock.

So as to stimulate investment and cut unemployment the finance minister imposed an 11 per cent sales tax on machinery, equipment, and building machinery and made various minor tax changes that were meant to reduce the budget deficit. Economists were agreed that these measures would tend to *increase* unemployment and *reduce* investment, other things being equal. Gordon did not care. He was much more interested in a series of tax tricks that were meant to discourage foreign takeovers and encourage foreign subsidiaries to place shares on the Canadian market. At once there was a horrendous outcry from the stock exchanges, and on July 8 Gordon, having retreated in disorder, produced a second budget. He cancelled the tax on takeovers and diluted the proposals to tax the remittance of interest and dividends to foreigners. As for the new sales tax, he exempted some buildings and decided to impose the tax in stages, rising to the full 11 per cent only in 1965.

Both Parliament and the public were most distressed by the fact that Gordon had relied on three financial advisers whom he had brought from Toronto; the financial community was worried by the foreign investment measures; only economists seemed to notice how foolish it was to *raise* taxes, especially on capital goods, when the economy needed more investment so as to absorb the unemployment and raise the growth rate. In later years Gordon still defended his budget. Admitting that it was inconsistent, he wrote that this did not matter; because he was trying to do two things at once, naturally his budget had contained contradictory measures, and observers were wrong to object. When the first budget appeared, Mel Watkins remarked that it was not merely pre-Keynesian but positively pre-Cambrian. The description still seems to apply.

In his 1964 budget speech Gordon was still worried about the budget deficit, although in 1963-4 this had been smaller than he had expected. In the United States, Congress had cut the income tax so as to stimulate the economy. Gordon refused to do likewise. He made only minor tax changes, but he did abandon his plan to impose a special withholding tax on foreign-owned firms. Then in 1965, doubtless with an eye on the election that he had urged Pearson to call, Gordon cut income taxes by 10 per cent (to a maximum cut of $600). This measure, he said, would 'encourage and stimulate our working force.' In other words, he cut taxes not to stimulate demand but to increase supply.

If we take the three and a half Gordon budgets together, we can see that they provided exactly the sort of medicine that Canada did not need. One budget discouraged new spending on plant, equipment, and structures; another encouraged households to consume more. Yet Gordon was eager to encourage Canadians to save and invest in Canada so as to drive out the foreigner. Fortunately for the Pearson government the forces of economic expansion were strong enough to defeat the regrettable manoeuvres of the finance minister. And on December 17, 1965, following Gordon's resignation, Mitchell Sharp became Minister of Finance. In the St Laurent years Sharp had been Deputy Minister of Trade and Commerce. Soon after the Diefenbaker victory in 1957 he had left the civil service, first for the business world and then for politics. He distrusted Gordon's gimmickry, and, except in respect of banking, he could not have cared less about foreign investment. He thought the Canada Development Corporation, which Gordon had promised but never produced, a waste of time and money.

With Mitchell Sharp at the finance department Canada experienced another period of macroeconomic management along the standard lines that Keynesian economics prescribes. To the professional economist Sharp's budget speeches seemed like echoes from the last years of the King administration and from the St Laurent years, when Ilsley and Abbott and Harris had tried to explain the modern principles of Keynesian economic policy. To social reformers in the Liberal cabinet and outside it Sharp's policy was less attractive. Taking office when inflationary pressures were beginning to worry the nation, he was often obliged to raise taxes and to oppose, defer, or reject new spending programs, especially on the social services. To socialists and economic nationalists, such as Walter Gordon, Sharp was, of course, anathema. Not only did Sharp force the cabinet to defer medicare for a year, but he opposed the publication of the Watkins Report on foreign ownership that Gordon had sponsored, and he did not establish the Canada Development Corporation.

In his first budget, on March 29, 1966, Sharp introduced a series of measures that were deliberately meant to moderate the boom. He proposed to cut federal outlays on construction by 10 per cent and to ask the provinces to follow his example. He raised the income taxes that the middle income and more affluent households would have to pay. He imposed a refundable 5 per cent tax on all but the smaller corporation profits; he reduced capital cost allowances on many kinds of building and machinery. Taken together these measures would reduce the pressure of demand in the economy. Admittedly Sharp extended the term for some special investment incentives, and he proposed to remove Gordon's 11 per cent tax on production machinery and equipment. But, because he did not want to add further fuel to the expansionary fire that was already alight, he planned to remove the tax in stages so that business would respond gradually and gently.

In early autumn 1966 Sharp had become very worried about the risk of inflation. Because the cabinet had decided to raise the old age pension he expected that he would need to raise some taxes. He thought that prices were rising because demand was growing too fast. Price and wage control would not work, and an incomes policy would work only if people understood and agreed with the policy. Seeing no such consensus, Sharp could only defer some government programs and threaten the electorate with more taxes.

By December 19, when Sharp introduced a second budget, he believed that matters were less serious than he had thought in September or in March. Although he now foresaw a budget deficit of $340 million instead of $150 million, he imposed just enough extra taxation to collect the funds the government would need to pay higher old age pensions. As he explained, he was trying neither to stimulate nor to restrain the economy.

The first budget of 1967 reflected the same assessment of the economic situation. On June 1, Sharp told Parliament that he thought the economy was 'in a state of approximate balance.' He foresaw a deficit of $740 million but he did not want to cut spending or raise taxes; there was no case for special stimuli and no case for special restraint. Business was planning to spend less on plant and equipment, but there was still plenty of inflationary pressure. Already, in March, Sharp had restored certain capital cost allowances, and he proposed to cancel the refundable tax on business profits. In June he cancelled the remaining 6 per cent sales tax on production machinery and equipment, which had been meant to last until April 1968. Provincial Crown corporations would no longer pay the 11 per cent federal sales tax when they bought building materials. All these steps were obviously meant to stimulate spending on plant, equipment, and certain sorts of structures. But the stimulus would not be very great. As for taxes on corporation profits and personal income tax rates, these remained as before. Drugs would no longer have the 12 per cent federal sales tax and imported drugs would pay lower duties. But as the opposition was quick to point out, this was not a budget that brought the consumer much joy.

Worse was in store. Early in November Sharp told the House that there would shortly be higher taxes. The cabinet had decided that it must try to borrow less and to make prices rise less quickly. After discussing the situation with the provincial treasurers and finance ministers, on November 30 Sharp introduced a mini-budget. For all individuals who paid more than $100 in tax there would be a surtax of 5 per cent with a maximum of $600. For spirits, beers, wine, tobacco, and tobacco products there were higher excise taxes. Corporations would pay their taxes earlier. Soon afterward the Minister of National Revenue told the House that the government proposed to reduce spending in several directions and to ensure that the civil service would grow much more slowly. With luck, if everything went right, the government would only have to borrow $750 million in the current fiscal year.

This was an orthodox anti-inflationary package of the sort that any academic economist would have applauded. Naturally it was unpopular; even in good times nobody likes to pay extra taxes and nobody wants government to spend less on the services one actually uses. It was easy to make fun of the fact that Sharp kept changing his mind and changing the taxes also. But Sharp could and did explain that he was doing the right thing. When the economic climate changes in unexpected ways the government *should* change its taxing and spending plans. On the other hand, it might be argued that Sharp was too eager to 'fine tune' the economy. When tax rates change households and businesses may not change their ways at once. But governments and politicians want fast results.

To everyone's surprise, on February 19, 1968, the House rejected the budget measures on third reading. Sharp then had to design a new tax package that would do the same things. Now, however, he had new reasons for haste and for concern. In January 1968 the Canadian dollar had begun to fall. To hold it close to the peg that had been fixed in 1962, the government was borrowing abroad and spending its reserves of foreign money. If the government could take a firm anti-inflationary line speculators might be more willing to hold Canadian dollars. Indeed, money might flow back into the country. Hence, on March 6, Sharp proposed to impose a two-year, 2 per cent surcharge on personal and corporate income taxes and to freeze the number of civil servants. He planned to cut the spending plan by $75 million in 1968-9. Thus far it was an 'austerity' package much like his November mini-budget, or like the Conservative measures of 1962. In addition, however, he now proposed to create a review board that could discourage wages and prices from rising too fast. Ever since 1966 some Canadian publicists had wanted an anti-inflationary 'incomes policy.' In 1966 Sharp had seen little hope for such a device. Now he was willing to try. But the thing would be voluntary; it might urge and complain but it could not make anyone do anything.

By 1968 Canada's finance minister faced a much harder task than in 1962 or 1957. The civil service had acquired a vegetable life of its own: unless carefully watched it would grow by 4 per cent or more every year for no very obvious reason. But much more serious was the enormous range of new spending programs to which the Pearson government had committed itself. Many of these – medicare, Canada Assistance, aid for universities, decent old age pensions, and a whole range of shared cost programs – were virtually uncontrollable. For this depressing fact there were two reasons. First of all, many were propelled by 'need' or by demography. Second, most were really run by the provinces. Ottawa provided much of the money, but it did not control the standard of service or its cost, and neither the federal nor the provincial governments controlled the demand. In the Trudeau years, federal-provincial wrangling would revolve in large part around the problems of control. The roots of this trouble were to be found in the Pearson years, when the federal authorities set up new programs without any rational assessment of their costs or controllability. In 1966, it was said, federal-provincial medicare would cost $80 million. How wrong can a cabinet be?

What are we to make of the Pearson budgets? Were they expansionary or contractionary, inflationary or anti-inflationary? To answer the question we have to rearrange the budget data from the *Public Accounts* into the more logical categories of the *National Income and Expenditure Accounts*. When we do this, we find that from January 1963 until December 1968 the dominion government took in $56,922 million, spent $18,908 million on current operations, and distributed $36,044 million in transfer payments to persons, businesses, and junior governments. Thus it 'saved' $1,970 million. On the other hand, it spent an additional $2,190 million on buildings and equipment. Setting this 'gross capital formation' against the savings, we find that the government's true deficit was only $220 million – 0.06 per cent of total gross national product in the years 1963-8. However, these figures do not cover the Canada Pension Plan which ran a surplus of $1,917 million in 1966-8, far exceeding the small federal deficit. Obviously government spending can hardly have been inflationary.

From year to year the changes are quite revealing. In 1958-63, government saving was negative but in 1964 and 1965 saving rose sharply, and although it fell off in 1966-8 it was still positive. In other words, the dominion was taxing enough to finance all the new social welfare schemes and almost all the new bridges, structures, and equipment that the dominion was building and buying. Obviously in 1962-5 revenue was growing faster than expenditure, and it was transfer payments that accounted for much of the extra spending. In 1966, however, current outlays increased by 15 per cent, outgrowing revenue by a wide margin, while capital outlays rose 22 per cent, and in 1967 and 1968 expenditure grew more quickly than revenue. It is no wonder that Mitchell Sharp was worried by new spending programs, medicare, and the like. Over the whole period GNP grew 69 per cent, federal revenue 75 per cent, current expenditure 44 per cent, capital outlays 85 per cent, and transfer payments 73 per cent. The budget was outgrowing the economy, but as yet the divergence was small, and some of the new federal outlays may have replaced outlays that would otherwise have been made in the private sector. Perhaps, if taxing and spending had both been less, the economy would have grown faster, and by 1968 or 1978 Canadians would have been even richer. Many observers think this would have been so, but others believe the idea is nonsense. There is really no way to settle the question. Still, it is reasonably clear that relative to the whole economy the year-to-year movements of revenue and outlay were too small to have much macroeconomic impact. The conclusion is clear: the economy grew because business investment and exports were growing, not because of government policy.

28

The Sixties: Nationalism and Culture

In another day, Walter Gordon's fumblings as finance minister, his unpopularity with the business community, with American investors, and with nearly all economists, would have doomed him to political obscurity and disgrace. This was not so in the sixties. This tweedy scion of the Canadian 'establishment' became a patron to an economic-nationalist movement, which was itself a part of a rambunctious ferment that disrupted what many Canadians thought of economics and society. In a period in which traditional standards and ideas stood condemned because they were traditional, Gordon's visionary quality and his rejection of the economics of the academy became an emblem that permitted him to pass where few others of his kind could go.

Gordon wanted to limit the amount of foreign investment in Canadian business and to control the activities of foreign-owned firms. The times seemed propitious as America's Vietnam adventures spread an ever-denser fog of suspicion and dislike that soon shrouded all things American. Tactless American interventions in Canadian affairs and a tendency to claim an 'extraterritorial' control over the foreign activities of US-based firms increased Canadian fury. Gordon had expressed his concern about foreign investment in the 1957 Royal Commission on Canada's Economic Prospects, which he had headed. Gordon's opinions, some critics noted, did not rest upon a strong foundation of commission research and, in some cases, they conflicted directly with what researchers had found. The Diefenbaker government could easily ignore the report; a Liberal government would likely have done the same. But the Liberals in opposition were tempted by this modern Jeremiah's call to end our old ways and doings, especially since this prophet brought with him money and friends to rebuild a shattered party.

In 1963 Mike Pearson appointed Walter Gordon Minister of Finance, and Gordon's first budget and its failure became not a proof of Gordon's political or economic naiveté but rather an indication of the strength of the 'malevolent' forces working against him. Out of the cabinet after the 1965 election, Gordon became ever more the prophet, decrying his country's relationship with the new Babylon. The chorus accompanying him swelled, and in January 1967 he returned to the cabinet as a 'senior member without portfolio.' He immediately set up a 'task force' which would investigate the effects of American influence in the Canadian economy.

Because Gordon's task force was organized by M.H. Watkins, its output was known as the Watkins Report. After many delays, in February 1968 Watkins and his associates reported. They argued that Canada should extract more information from the multinational corporations, while regulating their activities and forcing them to accept orders from Communist buyers. The nation should also make sure that such firms were paying a fair share of taxes, and it should devise new tax incentives which would encourage the multinationals to sell shares in Canada. The report proposed that Canada should prohibit Canadian compliance with foreign anti-trust decrees, orders, or judgments, and also, perhaps paradoxically, proposed that the nation should devise a more active anti-trust policy of its own. Finally the report urged the government to set up an enormous investment trust – a Canada Development Corporation, which Gordon had been demanding for years.

Partly because Gordon left the cabinet in March 1968, the government did not act upon any part of the Watkins Report, which seemed at first to sink without trace. Nevertheless, in succeeding years the report was like a yeast, gradually leavening the lump of public opinion, especially in central Canada. In the next chapter we shall sniff at some of the gaseous bubbles that resulted during the Trudeau years.

Watkins and his associate, Abraham Rotstein, were economic historians who rejected what they termed the sterility of economic thought in favour of a romantic vision that asserted the importance of reasons of the heart. In this case, their hearts led them to a definition of American interests as fundamentally antagonistic to Canadian interests. This led Watkins, personally, to discard the muted business suit of an academic liberal economist with a Bachelor of Commerce degree and assume instead the open-shirted, leather-jacketed garb of a theorist of the New Left. Watkins and historian Jim Laxer became the leading figures in the Marxist-nationalist 'Waffle' movement that very nearly overwhelmed the forces of moderate democratic socialism in the New Democratic Party. The appeal was straightforward: Canada could never possess its own soul so long as it remained a bourgeois-capitalist nation on this bourgeois-capitalist continent. Government ownership of the economy could alone recapture for Canada its purity and its identity.

That the Canadian Left shared so many qualities of the American Left is hardly surprising; politically, both shared a critique of bourgeois democracy and, above all, a profound distrust of 'technology,' a term which often seemed to mean all things that limited what they might want to do. The Canadian and American New Lefts shared another trait: they were both dominated by the young. So was society, and this gave the decade its predominant image, that of a boisterous uprising of the young that threatened and sometimes tumbled over the fundamental institutions of our society.

John Grierson, the noted filmmaker, dubbed the movement 'The Children's Crusade,' and it was as confusing and sometimes as tragic as that remarkable medieval adventure. In the universities the crusade made its deepest mark. Throughout the sixties, the young had left their families for the classrooms as never before. In 1962-3 there were 196,700 post-secondary students, 11.1 per cent of the population aged eighteen to twenty-four; ten years later, there were 513,400, 18.4 per cent of the same age group. This meant more classrooms, and also, inevitably, that what went on in those classrooms would not be the same as before. The numbers of young people, their parents' and teachers' doubts, and the corrosive effects of rapid change all played their part in the explosion that shattered the traditional image of the university. The shock effects were widely felt. Writing in 1969, the novelist Hugh MacLennan despaired at finding his generation of liberal, humane academics 'assaulted and blackmailed by the Youth [sic] with unprecedented contempt as The Establishment.' His generation, MacLennan wrote, had 'embarked on a lifelong Odyssey that took us through more than one cave of the winds, under the legs of more than one man-eating Cyclops, but we never deviated in our unconscious aim, which was to recreate the old Victorian patriarchal world in the image of an indulgent mother wearing pants. Now we find ourselves cursed by the young for all the things we were proud of, for our voyage did not end in the Ithaca we had deserted, but in the land of the Lotus Eaters.'[1]

The new land at MacLennan's McGill was startlingly unlike the old. Even Frank Scott, a poet, lawyer, and civil libertarian, who had long defended socialist and liberal values, was a subject of abuse during 1967 demonstrations which demanded that McGill become 'French,' a part of the ferment about it. These demonstrations were led by Stanley Gray, a Marxist with an academic research grant from the Canadian government. Not surprisingly, there were immediate protests in the media and from legislators. Perhaps for the first time in Canada, the universities became objects of public suspicion. The normal question was: why should the state subsidize these institutions so highly if they contribute to the disruption rather than the enrichment, economic and otherwise, of society? At first this complaint could be easily dismissed, but by the end of the decade the arguments against it were no longer so convincing. 'Standards' in educational institutions obviously were falling, especially in non-professional programs, as student activists demanded – and often

---

1 Hugh MacLennan, 'Reflecting on Two Decades,' in George Woodcock, ed., *The Sixties* (Vancouver: University of British Columbia Press 1969), 28.

got – an end to such symbols of 'psychological oppression' as examinations and required courses. Issues abounded. At Simon Fraser University in British Columbia, politics became theatre in that striking mountain-top university's central mall. Margaret Trudeau, a student there at that time, recalled that 'all hell broke loose' with every local headline proclaiming 'Riots at Simon Fraser.' Summing up the experience over a decade later, she wrote: 'We fought, we protested, we had good times, and in the end we lost.' To outsiders, the reasons for protest were obscure; the good times, however, were all too obvious.

'Good times' meant experimentation – with sex, with drugs, with fashion, with political extremes. Social researchers in the United States in the 1920s (and, of course, F. Scott Fitzgerald) had noticed that college students behaved differently from the general population. In the sixties, too, they were in the vanguard and, because there were so many young, that vanguard was extremely visible. The externals of tradition and convention were first assailed. Academic gowns were an early casualty, and the campuses became a showplace for the eclecticism that marked fashion in the 1960s. Blue jeans were everywhere and, by 1967, the mini-skirt, created by Britain's Mary Quant, abounded on campuses, if not yet in offices. But in offices, at cocktail parties, and in shops, hemlines crept up inch by inch, and the plumage became thinner elsewhere, as well. Even if Rudi Gernreich's topless bathing suits appeared rarely, if at all, on Canadian beaches, skimpy coverings were the rule. Midriffs often were uncovered or barely concealed by filmy gauze. It would be wrong to suggest that such styles were the fashion, for fashion itself ceased to have a clear direction. More than ever, clothes were 'statements' about the 'identity' and personality of the wearer, whether this meant a billowing skirt reminiscent of ages long past or army surplus jackets, reminder of wars we would not fight. Fashion was a reflection of the age, an age of change and chaos.

Measurement of change in and confusion about personal attitudes and behaviour is always difficult. In Canada we have no counterpart to the large-scale Kinsey report on sexual behaviour, or its 1966 update by Masters and Johnson. What evidence we do have suggests that Canada followed the United States into a 'sexual revolution' during the 1960s. One study, carried out by C.W. Hobart and W.E. Mann, looked at university and trade school students in the late 1960s in three Canadian cities and showed an acceptance of increased permissiveness and a feeling of less guilt about sexual activity. In Hobart's survey, two-thirds of the English-Canadian sample said that they were increasingly permissive in their dating habits, but only 39 per cent of the French-Canadian sample reported increasing permissiveness. A majority of both groups, however, accepted premarital sex where 'love' was present. Interestingly, a cross-national survey of 2,230 male and female students from the United States, Canada, England, Norway, and West Germany found

Canadians to be more conservative, both in their attachment to a double standard for male and female behaviour, and in their coital experience, in which Canadian males ranked fourth and Canadian females fifth.

Even if Canadians were more conservative than the English, they were less so than their fathers and mothers. Moreover, they knew more and thought more about sex. This arose not only from the pervasiveness of sex in the magazines at the corner store, but also from the increased concern for sex education in Canadian society. In this case at least, there is good evidence that what was taught in schools, churches, popular magazines, and even newspapers was remembered. One long-term study of sexuality and family planning among married couples in low-income urban areas of Quebec revealed a distinction between the periods before and after 1969-70. In the earlier period two-thirds of pregnancies were unplanned, and one-fourth of the couples used contraceptives after marriage or after the first pregnancy. In the 1969-70 interviews, however, researchers found that 86 per cent of the couples were using contraceptives, with 49.5 per cent of the women taking oral contraceptives.

Birth rate statistics reflect the impact of the more widespread use of contraceptives, among other factors. The crude birth rate for Canada declined from 27.4 in 1959 to 21.3 in 1965 to 17.6 in 1969. Other evidence, too, showed that more families were being 'planned.' In 1961, the percentage of childless married women between twenty and twenty-four was 26.3; ten years later it was 42. This meant more time for education, for careers, and for double incomes, and for society this presaged major changes in what women would do and how they would live.

In 1967, these changes could not be predicted, but many sensed that women's future in Canada would not be like the past. The Pearson government, prodded by Judy LaMarsh and by groups such as the National Council of Women, appointed a Royal Commission on the Status of Women. Many newspapers ignored it editorially, others were condescending, a few were critical. The *Calgary Herald* blamed 'vocal militants who make a fetish of women's rights' for this unnecessary commission. 'Men and women are not equal,' the *Herald* declared. 'Nature has ascribed roles to women which make it impractical for them to be regarded on the same basis [as men] in many instances.' Besides, most women would not trade 'exerting an immeasurable, if subtle, influence on society ... to compete outright in all things with men.' By the time the Royal Commission reported such sentiments seemed as anachronistic as the pleas of the anti-suffragettes.

One area where women were already competing very well was in literature. Margaret Atwood won the Governor General's award for poetry in 1966, and, after intermittent production for some years, P.K. Page and Miriam Waddington began to publish regularly a richer and more reflective poetry. In fiction, the *Literary History of Canada* noted the change from the 1950s where the 'point of view of the time was male' to the 1960s, 'the decade of Malcolm Lowry ... and of Margaret

Laurence.' Laurence, W.H. New wrote, 'explored the essential differences between middle class expectations and other values, articulated a female perspective, and offered evidence to many younger writers that the simple act of being alive was a political act.' Not only for Laurence and other women had writing become a political act.

Canadian literature was not unique in the political spirit of its art in the later 1960s. Still, even though in Canada the stream flowed in a parallel direction to the American stream, its shadings were different. Both in French- and English-Canadian literature, politics in art meant nationalism. The title of Dave Godfrey's first short story collection published in 1967, *Death Goes Better with Coca Cola*, was the cultural counterpart of the Watkins Report. Vietnam, the charnel house of the American dream, marked Godfrey's pages. He decried the Canadian colonial mentality that made Canadians accept the death cloud of Americanism upon our culture. Godfrey, Atwood, Dennis Lee, Robert Kroetsch, and other young writers sought creative freedom through a search for other traditions and through a shrill rejection of Americanism. In French-Canadian literature, such writers as Hubert Aquin and Marie-Claire Blais were equally strident and even more determined to break through conventional language and content. Theirs, of course, was a different kind of nationalism, one that directed its fury at all things Anglo-Saxon and one that often seemed to equate vulgarity and the English influence. There could be no common meeting ground for these two nationalisms, and Canadian literature remained divided at its linguistic core.

The nationalism of art in the later 1960s is easy to understand given the large numbers of new writers who appeared and the disillusionment with American values. Later, writers like Atwood, Lee, and Blais would treat the period as a 'necessary stage' whose importance lies in the foundations it created. In denying America, Canadians were forced to define themselves. They did so not only in novels and poetry, but even in movies and art. The Canadian film industry that had died so many times was given a strong restorative in the form of the Canadian Film Development Corporation. Artists, too, found a government caught up in the self-celebrating mood of Centennial Year much more willing to be a patron. On occasion the patronage was repaid. Before her return to a Canada that was changing quickly, Joyce Wieland created a quilt for a politician who in 1968 symbolized that change and promised to hasten it. In our future, Wieland stitched on the quilt, we would have 'reason before passion.' The man, Pierre Trudeau, would not fully be his message.

PART SIX

Into the Seventies and Beyond

29

Political Culture: The End of the Tenth Decade

Canada's centennial was more than anyone expected. Coming so soon after the scandals that soured Canadian politics and after the first clear threats to the future of Confederation, Centennial Year seemed to promise little. In 1966 the preparations occasioned mostly derision. Expo 67, the first Canadian World's Fair, remained a muddy, incomplete site and the projected deficit rose ever higher. Ottawa's plans appeared similarly troubled; cynics also thought them mawkish and redolent of small-town boosterism. Nor did Canadian leaders inspire excitement or confidence. Both the Liberal and Conservative parties were clearly waiting for a change, for the appearance of a new generation of politicians untainted by the bitter parliamentary battles of the minority Liberal government. And yet, when the new year came, even the cynics changed their mood. In the *Canadian Forum*, one of the authors of this book confessed that he had looked forward to Centennial celebrations with a sense of impending nausea. He later admitted that the nausea had not come and that he shared the peculiar exuberance that was to capture Canadians for those twelve months. The sensation was perhaps like that of the middle-aged man who has saved up so long he does not know how much he is worth. Suddenly he stands back and recognizes that he has done far more than he knew or had a right to expect.

One can only hypothesize about what produced this mood of gentle nationalism, which affected all regions of the country – although it also took on various regional forms. A major factor was undoubtedly the turmoil in the United States caused by the Vietnam war and by racial tensions. In 1960, *Maclean's* had called America the land people are shouting about; by 1967 it was the land people were shouting at. The critical spirit of American intellectuals passed easily over the border, and its echoes could be heard in the university classroom, in the media, and in private laments for the fate of America. The Canadian sense of inferiority was replaced by a strong gust of moral righteousness which exalted many of those values which had embarrassed

Canadians in 1960: their placidity, caution, and even innocence. Perhaps no book illustrates the mood better than William Kilbourn's personal Centennial project, a book of readings on Canada called *Canada: A Guide to the Peaceable Kingdom*. (Like so many centennial projects this appeared three years after the Centennial.) Although Canada had fought longer and lost more men per capita in twentieth-century conflicts than the United States, the authors seemed not to remember this. What mattered was the world they saw in 1967 where the buttoned-up past of our ancestors was fast disappearing and where the relative calmness of Canadian political and urban life contrasted starkly with the apparent breakdown of American civic life. As nationalistic emotion in America became identified with demagoguery and know-nothingness, Canada's nationalism garnered its strength from its apparent simplicity expressed so well in Bobby Gimby's centennial theme, 'Canada.' One could find the more militant forms of nationalist sentiment in *Canadian Dimension* and even in *Maclean's*, but for most Canadians nationalism meant telling the pollsters that they were more concerned about the effects of American influence on Canadian life and waving our new flag.

The red maple leaf became ubiquitous in 1967. The centre of angry debate when first introduced to the House of Commons in June 1964, the flag now seemed an emblem for younger Canadians. They wore it on their backs in Europe to get rides which would be denied the 'uglier' Americans. Charms, icons, and even automobiles bore the imprint of the red maple leaf. The flag seemed to have become what Pearson had hoped it would be: a symbol of Canadian identity, an expression of the willingness of the young to break with their past. John Diefenbaker, of course, would not have agreed; neither would many other Canadians. Yet in 1967 Diefenbaker was to learn how much his land had changed and how much an anachronism he had become.

Diefenbaker's problems had really begun during the flag debate when his French-Canadian colleagues, notably Léon Balcer, broke finally and firmly with him. Balcer demanded a leadership convention in February 1965, and no doubt the movement would have gained impetus had not the 1965 election interfered. Despite Diefenbaker's surprisingly good performance in that election, many of his colleagues had had enough of him. His performance during the scandals debate was notable for its histrionics, but it embarrassed many of his colleagues. Moreover, the 1965 election results showed that the party had lost the youth and the cities. With Diefenbaker, it seemed that the Conservatives could only be a party of an ever more remote past. By the end of 1965 leading members of the Conservative executive were discussing how best the Chief might go. Eventually they found a leader – the party president Dalton Camp. On September 20, 1966, Camp publicly called for an assessment of the leadership of his party. But Camp had a problem. One of the few remnants of conservativism in the party was the absence of a procedure for leadership review. Camp thus disguised his attempt to overthrow Diefenbaker as a movement to reform the party. He staked his own presidency on the issue of reform. At the party's November 1966 convention those who voted for Camp as president were voting for leadership; those who voted for Arthur Maloney were voting for John Diefenbaker. The byzantine manoeuvres involved in making this choice need not concern us. What is interesting is the support Camp received. It was from the young, the urban, the professional, and the French Canadian. Their organizational skills brought them to Ottawa in greater numbers than the rural and traditional Tories who supported Diefenbaker. One moment during John Diefenbaker's address to that angry convention seemed to capture its spirit. When the leader recalled – correctly – that he had always won more seats than any Tory leader since Bennett in 1930, a heckler shouted: 'Don't talk about the past, we want to go forward.' What lay ahead was not clear; the heckler and his friends were sure of only one thing: they wanted to leave John Diefenbaker behind.

Camp won the presidency, and Diefenbaker became from that moment a lame-duck leader. In Parliament, however, he seemed more a wounded bear lunging after whatever irritated him. Polls showed in early 1967 that the nation was as embarrassed as the party. Conservative strength fell below that of the New Democratic Party and far behind the Liberals. This news hastened the calling of the leadership convention which was set for early September 1967. The abundance of candidates revealed that leading Conservatives thought that their party's future was bright without Diefenbaker. It seemed that Dief would not run, but he remained characteristically silent. He kept his silence as the crowd pushed into Maple Leaf Gardens to hear what they thought – and, in the case of most, hoped – would be the Chief's farewell. But Diefenbaker would not go gently into the night. He raved at his detractors, summoned up his own version of Canadian history to deny the claims of the present, and refused to state what he would do. The next day, fifteen minutes before nominations closed, he filed his nomination papers. His opponents included: several of his former cabinet – George Hees, Wallace McCutcheon, Donald Fleming, Davie Fulton, Alvin Hamilton, and Michael Starr; two provincial premiers – Duff Roblin and Robert Stanfield; someone named John Maclean; and someone else named Mary Sawka. On the first ballot Diefenbaker finished fifth, even behind George Hees. He stayed in for three ballots, his total shrinking each time. On that third ballot, Stanfield had 717 votes and Diefenbaker only 114. Diefenbaker withdrew and left the Gardens. He returned to honour Stanfield the winner. Ironically, he called for loyalty to the new leader. He would not heed his own call, but on that night no one knew the depths of Diefenbaker's bitterness.

'Where the devil is that "one nation" speech!'
Opposition leader Robert Stanfield searches for inspiration (McNally, c1968).

As the Tories left for home they had reason to be contented. Stanfield had been an effective provincial premier. His personality was dull, but it was such a welcome contrast to his predecessor that scarcely anyone noticed. Within two months of the convention's end, the Conservatives had moved significantly (9 per cent) ahead of the Liberals in the Gallup Poll. Unlike Diefenbaker, Pearson recognized that his day had finally passed. His health was not particularly good; his wife wanted his time; and Centennial Year had brought emotional rewards that previous years had denied. On December 14, 1967, he announced his resignation. His heirs were already prepared – at least most of them were. The convention would be in April, and the months in between were notable for their confusion. With the Conservative lead in the polls so large, many wondered why so many sought the prize. The

Liberals seemed in disarray. There was no obvious successor as there had been in 1948 and 1958. The Liberal tradition of French-English alternation seemed more necessary than ever before, but Jean Marchand, the best-known French-Canadian prospect, was disinclined, and his personality was unsuited to the task of leadership.

Pearson shared the belief in alternation and tried to persuade Marchand to run, but the former labour leader knew his limitations better than his leader. Pearson then turned to Pierre Trudeau who had in his brief tenure as justice minister attracted the attention of the liberal media with his divorce reform as well as his articulateness in both languages. Pearson did not like Trudeau, his former parliamentary secretary; while Marchand's volubility charmed him, he thought that 'ice water' ran in Trudeau's veins. Nevertheless, in January 1968 he asked Trudeau to run. Trudeau hesitated. He feared the loss of his freedom and was concerned about his lack of experience; probably, too, he feared losing the election that must come so soon after he became leader. But the question he constantly faced from his friends and his admirers – what is the alternative? – became too difficult to avoid. On Valentine's Day 1968 he announced his decision to run. His remarks on that day revealed how, after the tenth decade, candour, novelty, and even inexperience had become political values of considerable weight:

It seemed to me, reading the press in the early stages a couple of months ago, it seemed to me as though many of you guys were saying, you know, 'We dare the Liberal Party to choose this guy Trudeau. Of course, we know they never will, but we'll just dare them to do it and we'll show them that this is the man they could have had as a leader if they had wanted.' ... And what happened, I think, is that the joke blew up in your face and in mine. You know, people took it seriously.

In the next few weeks, many took Trudeau seriously, especially his opponents in the leadership race: Paul Martin, Paul Hellyer, Robert Winters, Eric Kierans, Mitchell Sharp, John Turner, Allan MacEachen, and Joe Greene. Throughout the country, the meetings to choose delegates saw new faces at Liberal gatherings. Most of them were young; many were at universities or taught there. They were a group that had, to paraphrase Robert Fulford, grown up in a country where things happened elsewhere. Now Trudeau seemed an opportunity to have something happen here; it was a chance that could not be missed. With the zeal and commitment of youth, the Trudeau forces were remarkably successful at the local level. Politicians like Paul Martin and Paul Hellyer who had so carefully tended the Liberal party found that the friends they had met at so many fund-raisers, at so many long political evenings, could not control their constituencies. By the opening of the convention on April 4, Trudeau was clearly in the lead. Sharp had already withdrawn, throwing his support to Trudeau. On the first ballot Trudeau led with 752 votes, followed by Hellyer, 330; Winters, 293; Turner, 277; Martin, 277; Greene, 169; MacEachen, 165; Kierans, 103; and the Reverend Lloyd Henderson, 0. Still, it took four ballots; on the final one Trudeau bested Winters 1,203 to 954.

The new prime minister called a federal election for June 25, 1968. What had happened at Ottawa's civic centre in April now swept the country. Mackenzie King's Canada could not have imagined what occurred. While Diefenbaker in 1958 had stirred emotions, he did so in the style of Elmer Gantry. Trudeau was Bogart in the trenchcoat. The offhand kiss, the sideward glance, the flip insult, the smile, and the tears it brought, all seemed perfectly timed. He ran against his own party as well as the opposition. He did it with a style and a grace that even Liberals hardly noticed. He hectored his audiences, blaming them for a past that had 'hamstrung' them and daring them to change. The mood was propitious for the appeal. In the United States Bobby Kennedy and Eugene McCarthy roused the young by striking similar notes. The past was a dead hand that must be lifted; in the jargon of the day, it was irrelevant.

Stanfield never had a chance. His campaign speeches stand up today better than do Trudeau's; but not many listened. By election day Stanfield knew his fate, and so did Tommy Douglas of the NDP. Trudeau won the majority Canadians had denied their government for six years. The Liberals took 45.5 per cent of the vote and 155 seats, the Conservatives 27.3 per cent of the vote and 72 seats (lower than any Diefenbaker total), and the NDP 22 seats and 17 per cent of the vote. The strongest vote for Trudeau, then and in the future, came from his native province. There can be little doubt that his support in the other provinces came partly because it seemed that this Quebecker could speak most easily, most effectively, and most harshly to that troubled province. Within Quebec, critics of Trudeau's anti-nationalist viewpoint cited this fact as evidence that Trudeau appealed to anti-French feelings in English Canada to obtain his majority. This is surely unfair. Trudeau during the campaign had spoken French from the Kootenays to Halifax; every speech was punctuated by sentences in French. The response was invariably cheers from the anglophone audiences, most of whom did not understand the language. The spontaneity of the gesture belies any interpretation of hypocrisy. Comparing it with what happened later makes one realize how fresh hopes were in that early summer of 1968 and how little Canadians realized what fears and hates still lingered. Trudeau's major appeal in English Canada – and in Quebec – flowed from a broader and more salubrious stream. The crusty dowager of the Canadian press, the *Globe and Mail*, expressed it well in its editorial endorsing Trudeau:

The argument most frequently made against [Trudeau] is that he is unknown, that we have no long-term record of Mr Trudeau as an administrator, that we can't be certain how he will react in any given situation.

But perhaps it is one of the facts of life in the sixties that Canada no longer needs the great certainties that are largely born of fear. Canada is willing to adventure. It may be that what Canadians see in Mr Trudeau is this new side of themselves, a readiness to gamble on the unknown, to move into areas not explored before....[1]

Over a decade later, the Trudeau adventure is difficult to evaluate. The final chapters, of course, remain to be written. In his 1978 biography of Trudeau, a year before the Trudeau government's defeat, George Radwanski wrote that Trudeau's record 'thus far makes him not a failed prime minister but an unfulfilled one.' Radwanski's judgment seems largely based on the persistence and, indeed, the exacerbation of the problem that brought Trudeau into politics in the first place – Quebec's flirtation with separatism. But there is much else to judge in the career of a prime minister of Canada that spans ten years. We have tried to assess these other aspects of Trudeau's career in the remainder of Part VI. In this chapter, we can best evaluate his political success and methods.

Trudeau's election reinvigorated the Liberal party. In the fall of 1967, an outside observer might well have concluded that the Canadian Liberal party was likely to suffer the fate of so many of its counterparts elsewhere. When *Canadian Dimension* asked several Canadian academics, politicians, and journalists what party they thought would succeed in the decade ahead, almost half thought there would be a non-Liberal government of the left. Only Ed Schreyer expressed the belief (and perhaps the hope) that there might be a NDP–Liberal coalition governing Canada. The strong NDP standing in the polls before Trudeau and the leftward drift of public opinion in Canada, as in the western world generally, seemed to threaten Liberalism. In a polarized society, there is little room for a party whose appeal is as a mediating force in that society. The victory of 1968 brought youth into the party; it made Liberal committee rooms respectable to youthful idealists as they had not been in 1965. Not surprisingly, the new Liberals were anxious to shrug off what they regarded as old barnacles, and they were not at all upset when Trudeau failed to observe the niceties of political leadership – as, for example, when he did not permit a day for speeches to honour his predecessor in the House. Nor did they dissent when Trudeau attacked the inefficiency and the conservatism of the bureaucracy, an institution so long identified with the Liberal party. In short, Trudeau accepted the Liberal party's traditional mediatory role, but he rejected its style. Liberalism could be tough and direct.

1 The *Globe and Mail*, July 9, 1974.

In this case, the style was definitely the man. Mackenzie King had dominated his cabinet through his experience, through his careful sifting of ministers' emotions, and through delicate intrigue. He judged his men shrewdly and knew those upon whom he could rely and those whom he must simply court, or, in a few cases, endure. St Laurent shunned intrigue, shared responsibilities, and controlled his cabinet through the respect which his intelligence and integrity commanded. Pearson gave his ministers much freedom, and relied upon his ability to charm and to cajole to move his cabinet toward decision. With Trudeau, apparently, there were no favourites. The cabinet atmosphere was not unlike a high-quality academic seminar where one's weaknesses were continuously probed. A minister knew that neither political weight nor personal charm could excuse a weak brief. Thus Trudeau had from his ministers respect but not love, sometimes not even sympathy. One minister once remarked on the difference between Trudeau and Pearson in the House of Commons. When Pearson fumbled and the opposition scored, his ministers rallied behind him in common cause. When Trudeau was under fire, he stood alone. His ministers watched but stood beyond the fray. George Radwanski records the same impression in a different way. Trudeau, he writes, cannot understand why others are not immune to criticism as he is, nor can he admit that he needs or depends on anyone else. Radwanski claims that the result is an austere aloofness in leadership quite remote from the 'informal, pep-talking, manipulative approach most North Americans have come to expect.' The price 'is to make him a leader respected and followed, but generally unloved.'

Trudeau also changed the style and shape of Canada's administrative substructure. Since the Second World War Canadian governments had adopted various devices for coping with the increasing complexity of adminstration. Under Mackenzie King a Privy Council secretariat was created to keep minutes and guide committees and subcommittees of cabinet in their deliberations. The cabinet secretaries and assistant secretaries combined with the new expert generation of senior civil servants ('the mandarins') to keep Ottawa in working order. St Laurent exploited the system to enhance his direction of cabinet business, using his control of the agenda to guide cabinet discussions and conclusions. As a preliminary to cabinet discussions, issues were fought out in interdepartmental committees of senior bureaucrats so that by the time a problem reached the cabinet its solution had usually been determined.

Under Pearson, however, some slippage occurred. 'Pearson let everybody talk,' one of his ministers recollected. 'The trouble was, nobody knew what the conclusions were.' Confronted by the institutional rigidity of the regular civil service, Pearson sought refuge in special task forces and the creation of new departments to stir things up. But these measures were, at best, palliatives.

Trudeau, who became a member of the Pearson cabinet in the spring of 1967, observed the Pearsonian chaos closely. 'I was quite concerned about the machinery of government,' he told a reporter soon after becoming prime minister. 'One of the reasons why I wanted this job, when I was told it might be there, is because I felt it very important to have a strong central government, build up the executive, build up the Prime Minister's Office, strengthen Parliament.' The key to Trudeau's administrative reforms was the cabinet. Under Trudeau, cabinet committees were strengthened and reorganized. Ministers were expected to fight out their problems in committee, bringing only the most critical or the most insoluble to cabinet as a whole.

Cabinet committees proved, in the experience of the ministers and officials who attended them, to be a great equalizer. Because the spotlight was on the ministers, they were obliged to work harder at their departmental jobs, to become 'experts' in their field, as one ex-minister later remembered. The input and influence of the bureaucrats diminished, but so, in an interesting parallel development, did the political influence of the individual ministers. Obliged to stay in Ottawa and tend the store, the ministers as a group came more and more to resemble administrators and less and less practising politicians. But the ministers' bargaining power, at least in Trudeau's early years, was limited: 'We're here because he's here,' they told themselves, looking down the table at the Prime Minister. By solving one problem, Trudeau created another.

The relationship with ministers in some ways mirrored the relationship with the party. Trudeau's people in 1968 had little experience in the party and, like him, they tended to enter from the top. They were naturally resented and responded with distrust. As with the cabinet so too with the party; the Prime Minister's Office (PMO) became the barrier that shielded the political element from the leader. Trudeau would not come to party fund-raisers. He refused to soothe tender egos. Although a politician like Paul Martin continued to have much influence in southwestern Ontario, Trudeau would not hesitate to place him beyond politics and to do it in a fashion that prevented Martin from attaining a record for political longevity. Trudeau sought to change the texture of Canadian politics, to remove it from the concerns of the local constituency and from the sway of traditional belief. No election revealed this better than that of 1972.

Disdaining traditional election machinery and appeals, Trudeau's campaign was managed by three former academics whose direct electoral experience was negligible. They and others around Trudeau in his PMO seemed to shield Trudeau from the emotions that the country felt. Indeed, Trudeau appeared determined to make the contest not an election at all. The slogan was 'The Land is Strong,' and the technique, in the parlance of the day, was dialogue with Canadians. 'We're not fighting any party,' Trudeau said. 'The other parties can fight us if they want, but we're going to be talking to Canadians.' Theoretically, it seemed the technique might work. After all, had not McLuhan and so many others emphasized the immense and direct power of the electronic media? But it did not. Party workers, ignored since 1968, shunned the campaign. The press seemed bored when it was not angry. Although the Conservatives also ran a dispirited campaign, it was the Liberals who revealed too much distance from the electorate. When the results came in on October 30, the Liberals had lost their majority and very nearly the government. They had won 109 seats; the Conservatives, 107; the NDP, 31; the Créditistes, 15; and independents, 2. Clearly the attempted dialogue had not occurred. The land was no longer so strong as it had seemed.

The day after the 1972 election most commentators spoke of a Liberal defeat and a Conservative victory. Although the Liberals had two more seats than the Tories, the trend was clear, and Trudeau, it was thought, might recognize it with his resignation. The Liberal-supporting Ottawa *Citizen* did urge Trudeau to remain on as a lively leader of the opposition and congratulated Stanfield on his 'victory.' But the reports of Trudeau's death were much exaggerated. Disillusioned yet combatant, hurt yet prideful, Trudeau did stay on, and within a couple of months had the press writing about a new Trudeau – more human, more tender, more willing to listen to Canadian complaints. His office was reorganized and made more political, and the Liberal party was no longer the shabby mate one dragged along in the campaign, but a coy maiden for whom the Prime Minister had ample world and time. The popular Martin O'Connell, a defeated MP, replaced Marc Lalonde as Trudeau's principal secretary, and, in the spring of 1973, Keith Davey, Pearson's very political campaign chairman, was named chairman of the next Liberal campaign. These appointments were more important symbolically than practically. On Trudeau's part they indicated an understanding that he must reinvigorate English-Canadian Liberalism and that he could not remain an elusive, aloof political animal because the mood of English Canada would not accept such a leader. The election had made Trudeau more cynical about the democratic process. In an interview with Patrick Watson, 'Trudeau admitted he had changed and that his "faith in the democratic process" had been altered: "I used to think it would be sufficient to put a reasonable proposition to a person, for the person to look at it reasonably, without passion, but that's obviously not true. Nine-tenths of politics ... appeals to emotions rather than to reason. I'm a bit sorry about that, but this is the world we're living in, and therefore I've had to change."'

The press's response to this change could only have confirmed Trudeau's low opinion of that institution. The government scrambled together a legislative program of wide range but of little coherence for the January session. The *Toronto Star* immediately hailed Trudeau as a 'willing learner' and the legislation as the kind that would have brought him victory a few months before. The *Star* called for the NDP, which held the balance of power in the Commons, to stand by Trudeau and the program. This decision wasn't hard for NDP leader David Lewis. The program was loaded with bait – especially in the areas of social policy and nationalist economics – that Lewis's party could easily swallow. Moreover, Lewis remembered what had happened in 1958, and he feared that another election could have the same result as that earlier Conservative triumph – the decimation of the third party. Thus Trudeau won time, but at some cost. At one point, he complained, 'If a government wants to do the popular things, it will ruin the economy – real quick.' And yet for two years his government had to do the popular thing. He was obviously uncomfortable, and as we suggest in our comments on the economy, his apprehensions about the result of doing 'popular things' had considerable substance.

The apparent transformation of Trudeau once more drew attention to this remarkable politician and away from his opponents. The fascination returned if not the adulation. In Parliament Trudeau seemed to take from Stanfield the advantage that an opposition leader normally has. In his attacks on the Tories, he had the assistance of David Lewis's sharp-tongued eloquence, as Lewis sought to justify his party's support of Liberal programs. Trudeau did not always say the popular thing however. After the election he told Parliament that the opposition had exploited anti-French-Canadian feelings, and he implied more than once that the opposition to his bilingualism program was sheer bigotry. He accused some Conservatives of trying to divide the country by using the language issue. English-Canadian editorial opinion denounced Trudeau, but on this matter he would not retreat. In his own words, he wanted 'to put people on notice that I will not be silent on this. I don't want to create hysteria about it, but I want people to know that wherever I find traces of bigotry, I will fight it whether it be in the province of Quebec or in any other province.'

These remarks were not popular, but they were largely ignored. After the trouncing the Parti Québécois received in the October 1973 provincial election, when Robert Bourassa's Liberals won 102 of 110 seats, Quebec as a 'problem' attracted much less attention. Moreover, the Trudeau government had, after the 1972 election, slowed down the bilingualism program. What captured attention instead was the flood of legislation that the government introduced: an election expenses act which fundamentally changed the rules of the political game and not in a way which benefited the Liberals; a Foreign Investment Review Agency which partially quelled the complaints of the Liberal nationalists like Walter Gordon; improvements in all kinds of pensions which Canadians received from the federal government; a tax cut which benefited most Canadians; and, after OPEC's 1973 success in raising oil prices, a pricing policy which sheltered Canadians from the impact of the world price increase. Because of the tendency to identify social legislation with a broad concern for humanity, the press began to see Trudeau as 'someone who cared,' a man who understood human needs better than before. No matter that Trudeau himself was obviously embarrassed by the political inspiration for much of this legislation and probably believed that human needs in the longer term would have been better served by a less hectic pace of social welfare expansion; the public perception of the government had changed.

Both Tories and New Democrats were confused. Trudeau was daring them to defeat his government in the spring of 1974. That year's budget was calculated both to please an electorate and to force the New Democrats to make a choice. Lewis, whose pre-budget demands had obviously been ignored, could not back down. On May 8, 1974, the Trudeau Liberals were defeated. They were delighted.

In the campaign that followed Trudeau kept his opponents on the defensive. For Lewis it was difficult to attack the government's legislative record when he was claiming that he was its intellectual inspiration. It was much easier to turn on Robert Stanfield, the apparent front-runner, whose party was committed to a badly-thought-out wage and price control scheme. Trudeau revelled in his fate; the insider as outsider, slashing away at his opponents with a freedom he had never had since those days when he tried to bring Duplessis down. He ignored the media, refused interviews, and staged encounters with the press. Harking back to the campaign style of old, he took a train through the small towns and into the hearts of the large cities, all the time promising a brighter future and revealing, it seemed, a new Liberalism with a human face. There was a new kind of unpredictability. He admitted he had changed: 'I have a train and I have Margaret.' Mrs Trudeau, who previously had largely shunned public attention, campaigned at his side, a beautiful mother with her child, a certain denial of those who thought this man cold and austere. After all, how could one who, in Mrs Trudeau's words, taught a stunning young woman so much about loving be anything but human in the broadest sense of that word?

Many were not convinced in the editorial rooms as the newspapers strongly favoured the election of Stanfield's Conservatives, but the newspapers' readers did not agree, especially in the industrial heartland of Ontario, and in British Columbia. Here Stanfield's proposed wage and price freeze hurt him badly. So too did his blandness, which contrasted sharply with Trudeau's energy and flamboyance. Later analyses of the election revealed that leadership was decisive in 1974 and that Stanfield was not perceived as a leader. On July 8, 1974, urban and industrial Ontario and British Columbia swung decisively behind the Liberals and gave Trudeau his majority once more. He won 141 seats (43.2 per cent of the vote), the Conservatives only 95 seats (36 per cent of the vote), and the NDP 16 seats (15.4 per cent of the vote). The *Globe and Mail*, which had supported Stanfield, was impressed:

In spite of the pundits, in spite of the polls, in spite of the most vigorous campaign ever staged by a Conservative leader, the Liberal Party has won a most decisive victory. It is a personal victory for Prime Minister Pierre Trudeau. Not for Trudeaumania, this time, but for the work, effort and energy that he put into his campaign. He went to the country this time and did not, as he did in 1972, wait for the country to come to him.

Trudeau had won – but what? The party was now thoroughly his; even the reluctant now admitted that Trudeau had proven that his political skills were the equal of, if not better than, those of any Liberal leader since King. He thus gained more freedom to shape the party into the mould he required, and his perpetuation of a very political prime minister's office showed that he intended to exercise his power in the party. He also had time. Unlike the minority period when legislative flurry was calculated to keep the opposition off balance, there was now an opportunity for reflection. Trudeau knew that he would be prime minister for a decade and that this would be the best chance to create a program that would be his legacy to his nation.

His first gestures after the election revealed his intentions. In the Prime Minister's Office a policy and planning unit under Michael Kirby was established to co-ordinate medium- and long-range planning. At Meach Lake that autumn the cabinet met and considered where it should go. By January the cabinet had agreed upon a general statement of objectives, and it seemed possible that the lack of direction that had previously characterized policy would now end. The appointment of Michael Pitfield as Clerk of the Privy Council Office and Secretary of the Cabinet gave Trudeau a personal and political friend at the apex of the bureaucracy. His job was to integrate programs and to steer the bureaucracy in the direction that the cabinet and Trudeau had decided it must move. Pitfield's familiarity with and experience in the bureaucracy made him an ideal person to play such a part. And yet, by the autumn of 1975 it was clear that the exercise had failed. As a recent study of the policy and planning experiment discovered, the departments were expected to propose new policies which would help the government accomplish its declared aims.[2] They did not; instead, 'in bureaucratic fashion, department officials sent mainly self-serving responses' which normally said, 'This is how our existing programs and proposals fit your plan for the next four years.' By spring 1976 the attempt to plan had clearly failed, and Michael Kirby was on his way back to Halifax.

Even without the bureaucratic response, the long-range plans of January 1975 would not have been realized. Inflation and rising unemployment bedevilled political planning in that year. The government's attempt to deal with the problems produced growing scepticism and irritation. In his June budget, Minister of Finance John

2 Colin Campbell and George Szablowski, *The Superbureaucrats: Structure and Behaviour in Central Agencies* (Toronto: Macmillan 1979).

Turner began with an ironic paraphrase of Keynes: 'Economics is too important to be left to economists. The choices to be made are essentially political decisions.' In the broadest sense, this was of course true, and the statement is perhaps a reiteration of the faith of January. But as a political decision-maker Turner was not convincing. The *Toronto Star* ridiculed Turner's performance as much show and little substance. He had come 'onto the field of battle like a knight on a white charger. He had promised the country to do battle against the twin dragons of inflation and recession, and here he was Prince Charming before an eager audience. But then he pooped out. With barely a swish of the lance, he turned tail and rode back to his castle, leaving the dragons unscathed and securely in charge.'

A few months later Turner 'pooped out' completely. Turner's department had become a strong advocate of the wage and price controls which Turner and Trudeau had so vociferously and effectively opposed during the 1974 campaign. In early September Turner, who seems to have been undecided about controls themselves, quit the cabinet, causing the press to interpret the puzzling resignation as an indication of impending economic disaster. The plea for controls – never defined and most often misunderstood – became a clamour. Wage settlements were higher than anyone could ever remember; there seemed to be no end to the rate of increase and to the concomitant inflation. Columnists wrote regularly of the possibility that the British 'disease' was crossing the Atlantic and infecting us, but rarely did they note the dismal history of peacetime controls in Britain and in other countries. The cabinet mirrored the nation in its confusion. Finally, the truth of Turner's budget remark became clear: the choice was essentially political. Trudeau was the last to be convinced; he reportedly capitulated when Robert Bourassa informed him that his government intended to grant some civil servants a yearly increase of over 30 per cent. The lack of will was startling enough to show even the most doubtful that controls might be the psychological shock treatment the country so clearly needed. On Thanksgiving Day 1975 Trudeau announced the controls, warning, however, that controls would not be some miraculous palliative for the nation's ills. They would only purchase time 'to understand and adopt the real cure, which is a basic change in our attitudes.'

The effectiveness of controls we assess elsewhere; it is chiefly their political effect that concerns us here. In this respect, they didn't work. Although the press had led the movement for controls, they were not prepared to give Trudeau credit for introducing them. The press and, it seems, the public became more suspicious of the government's direction, if indeed it had one. Even the normally quiescent Liberals had their doubts. At the November 1975 biennial convention of the Liberal party, the opposition to Trudeau was surprisingly open. Corridors were filled with whispers of doom and disgruntlement. In the vote on the question of whether there should be a leadership review, 19.2 per cent voted yes, almost twice as much as the figure after the disastrous 1972 election. Nor could Trudeau impose his choice of Senator Keith Davey as party president. When it became clear that party members regarded Davey as one of the courtiers who had cut off the king from his servants, Davey gave way for the bland figure of Senator Al Graham from Nova Scotia. Ironically, controls themselves were popular with the delegates at the convention as they were with Canadians generally, but their popularity did not transfer itself to the government or its leader.

The reaction to Trudeau's year-end interview, usually an occasion for banalities of the season, compounded his difficulties. The remarks themselves are unexceptional; indeed, they are the commonplace of economic textbooks. In answering a question from Carol Taylor about the evil of 'bigness,' Trudeau said: 'We can't destroy the big unions and we can't destroy the multinationals, we can control them. ... That means the Government is going to take a larger role in running institutions, as we're doing now with our anti-inflation controls.' Tom Cossitt declared that Trudeau had revealed his true intentions, 'namely to take Canada right down the road to a dictatorial form of socialism or a similar form of plain old fascism.' For once, Cossitt found many who agreed, especially in the business community, which even the staid *Canadian Annual Review* described as 'paranoiac' in its reaction to the Trudeau remark. *Le Devoir* asked whether the Canadian Chamber of Commerce had gone mad and whether a collective hysteria had seized business circles. The editorialist correctly saw the reaction to the speech as the culmination of a growing distrust of Trudeau and of the economic aims of the government. The attempt to create long-range plans had produced mainly ambiguity; with ambiguity comes confusion and even paranoia.

For Trudeau the unexpected reaction surely brought further disillusionment with his government and with the electorate. The feeling was mutual. In early 1976 there were widespread rumours that Trudeau would not long remain leader. These rumours partly began because the Conservatives did change their leader in February 1976. As conventions so often do, the Tory convention focused attention upon and attracted support to the party and its new leader, Joe Clark. Before the convention the Liberals had every right to be fairly optimistic about the outcome. The Conservatives were fighting each other with the skill and the vindictiveness characteristic of their internal wars. The frontrunners, Claude Wagner and Brian Mulroney, were subjects of intense scrutiny and criticism, and by the opening of the convention their positions had much deteriorated. Several other candidates could not be taken very seriously: Paul Hellyer, a Liberal retread; Sinclair Stevens, a financier whose record gave rise to some uneasiness; Jack Horner, taken seriously only by himself and John Diefenbaker; Patrick Nowlan; Heward Grafftey; and John Fraser. Although it was fashionable to wear Flora MacDonald's buttons, commitment to her was like the River Platte, a mile wide and an inch deep. This left Joe Clark, whose greatest advantage was that hardly anyone had noticed him. He was young, bilingual and from the West, where Tory strength lay. As Mulroney and Wagner stumbled, Clark moved ahead to take the convention on the fourth ballot. Over-all the effect of the convention was better than the Tories had hoped and, for the Liberals, worse than they had feared. Apart from some individual cases of bitterness, the only regret many had was the loss of Bob Stanfield as leader. On the night he was honoured Stanfield gave the best speech at the convention – witty, intelligent, and probably effective in its call upon Tories to be more loyal to their new leader than many of them had been to him. A cacophonous period ended on a note of grace.

Still, few Liberals feared Clark until the Tories began to pull ahead of the Grits in the public opinion polls in the summer of 1976. By August the lead was eighteen points (47 per cent to 29 per cent), the worst Liberal performance since the Diefenbaker sweep of 1958. It seemed Trudeau could do nothing to halt the slide, except resign. The temptation must have been great. His attempt to explain his policies had been met with misunderstanding and misinterpretation which he no doubt thought was deliberate in some cases. In 1976 he seemed to be afraid to say anything; perhaps he thought it not worth the trouble which any definite statement would surely cause. His family, too, brought pressures of another kind. His third child, Michel, was born in October 1975, and the desire to spend more time with his young family was understandably strong. And then there was his wife and her increasingly bizarre behaviour. In January 1976 Margaret accompanied her husband on a Latin American trip during which she took Peyote in Mexico, wore a Liberal T-shirt with 'Margaret' tattooed on the back in Cuba, and, at what Mrs Trudeau herself described as 'the most formal and pretentious dinner I ever went to in all my years as Pierre's wife,' sang 'a song of love' to Señora Perez, the wife of the Venezuelan president. Within a few months, again in Mrs Trudeau's words, 'Pierre and I had both realized that something had gone seriously wrong with our marriage.' Anyone who has seen a marriage break up – as this one eventually did in the spring of 1977 – can understand the enormous strain Trudeau must have endured. But this and the bad polls and the bad press he did endure.

He probably stayed because in November 1976 the battle he had long feared finally came when René Lévesque won power in Quebec. During the early summer of 1976 the controversy about bilingual air traffic control had alerted Trudeau to the dangerous divisions within the country. On June 25, as pilots refused to fly and controllers to guide unless bilingualism in the air was abandoned, Trudeau told the Commons that 'This country is in danger of very seriously being divided ... as it has not been for 34 years.' While Quebec newspapers interpreted the illegal strike as an irrational anti-French outburst, the *Toronto Sun* blamed the strike on 'a bone-headed, bloody-minded federal government determined to shove French down throats.' Each reaction intensified the other. There is no doubt that René Lévesque's arguments gained much force among francophones as a result of the strike. In terms of English-French relations, this crisis was probably the most serious since 1944, yet, when Trudeau suggested that this might be the case, the *Globe and Mail* accused him of the hyperbole that would create a real crisis. In the House of Commons, Trudeau found a similar disbelief, and the attitudes of Clark and Broadbent troubled him very much. The former he thought opportunistic; the latter, ill-informed and emotionally distant from French Canada. Given Trudeau's perception of himself and his purpose in politics, these events surely steeled his determination to remain.

Stay he did and, after Lévesque's election, English Canadians began to see him once more as the only leader to meet the challenge of separatism. Despite clear evidence in the public opinion polls, non-Quebeckers refused to believe that the Parti Québécois could win. On election night, November 15, 1976, the surge of emotion that swept Paul Sauvé arena as Lévesque spoke jolted Canadians into recognition of the depth of the separatist commitment and the power of its appeal. Clark's response was clumsy, and the NDP's ambiguous, since the Parti Québécois espoused social democracy as well as separatism. Trudeau's eloquent and obviously sincere response won plaudits from all but separatists and obdurate opponents. His popularity and that of his party rose quickly; by mid-summer 1977 the Liberals had the support of over 50 per cent of Canadians, according to the Gallup Poll. In the Conservative ranks there were bitter complaints about the party leadership; there were even questions about whether Clark would survive until the first general election after the convention. The press and social critics were often savage. In autumn 1977 Mordecai Richler wrote: 'while Trudeau is easily the intellectual equal of René Lévesque, Clark, even if he sat on three telephone directories, would still have the fiery Quebec premier looking down on him.' Richler was especially disturbed because Clark had not disavowed Roger Delorme, a Conservative candidate in a May by-election, even though Delorme had claimed that 'only' one million Jews had died in the holocaust and had declared that 'I have dealt with Zionists and Nazis and it was the same thing.' And yet two years after his by-election many Jewish voters marked Conservative ballots for the first time in their lives.

Had the people who remember most forgotten so quickly? The Tory votes were surely not won by Clark's impossible election promise to move the Canadian embassy from Tel Aviv to Jerusalem. It seems more likely that this item is merely further evidence of the discontinuity of Canadian public life in the late seventies. As rapidly as Trudeau rose in the polls in the winter of 1977, he fell in the summer and autumn of 1978. A political study published in 1979 revealed how willing Canadians were to change their political preferences and how far they had come from those days when party affiliation was a badge one wore unto death. Old loyalties faded as did old perceptions, and they did so as rapidly as the changing seasons. So much was not what Canadians had expected it would be.

One thing most expected in late 1977 or early 1978 was an election, but Trudeau, contrary to nearly all precedent, held off. In the late summer of 1977, as the polls showed almost two-to-one support for the Liberals over the Conservatives, Trudeau ignored his leading advisers, but not his nervous caucus, saying: 'As far as I am concerned, just because one is convinced he is going to win an election is not a good enough reason to go to the people.' Mackenzie King would have been horrified. Then, a year later in September 1978 with the Liberals still ten points ahead in the polls (forty-five to thirty-five), Trudeau once again refused to call an election, opting instead for a so-called mini-election of fifteen by-elections. Despite the large Gallup lead, there was more concern in autumn 1978 because private Liberal polls revealed a growing animosity toward Trudeau himself. He was thought to be insensitive and unaware of Canadian needs. There was, moreover, what *Maclean's* termed 'a chilling anti-French bias in parts of English Canada which is aimed at Trudeau personally – although it is often thinly disguised in passionate advocacy of the monarchy.' These perceptions could not easily be changed; and they weren't.

The by-elections were a disaster for the Liberals. Support among the urban middle class dropped precipitously, and soon the polls were showing the Conservatives and the Liberals almost even in support. By this time, January 1979, Trudeau's Queen in the political chess match – the freedom to choose the election date – was almost lost. In September 1978 the press had already begun to question whether Trudeau could long remain as leader, a speculation foolishly encouraged by some Liberals. For example, Ontario Liberal party vice-president Lorna Marsden said in September: 'If we go past Christmas with no clear indication of where we are going, then leadership talk will start.' Of course it did, and it made Trudeau's position much more difficult. Usually John Turner was mentioned as successor, but there was no potential successor so likely to divide the Liberal party as the former finance minister, now a Toronto lawyer. Serious political observers, whatever their political bias, knew that Trudeau would and must stay. To leave the Liberal leadership in response to anglophone pressure when separatists governed Quebec was impossible for Trudeau and, for that matter, for the Liberal party, which might never have recovered. In the late winter and spring of 1979, Trudeau thus played out his part.

He finally called the election for May 22, and, at the beginning of the campaign, many Liberals believed that they would win once more. The issue, they thought, would be leadership, and the polls clearly showed that Trudeau was perceived by Canadians as a more competent leader in nearly every respect. Joe Clark's January world trip during which he almost impaled himself on a bayonet, walked into a door in the officers' mess, and invariably seemed to have left his luggage one country behind seemed proof, in the words of one reporter, that Clark was 'dwarfed on the world stage.' But it really didn't matter. Change – not Clark – became the major issue, and the Conservative organization protected Clark well, as Trudeau and the Liberals assailed Clark's leadership capacity. Clark did make mistakes, especially in his contradictory statements about Quebec's ability to 'vote its way out of Canada,' but Trudeau did too. His moods varied, his style was inconsistent, and his staff showed exceptional qualities only in offending party workers in the constituencies. The Liberal campaign was a disaster.

By the final week of the campaign, the Liberals knew that the Tories had won. The NDP alliance with labour was not swinging votes in industrial Ontario. A television debate a week before the election also changed little. Most thought Clark had been bested (with the exception of the *Toronto Sun*, which, in a throwback to the partisan newspaper politics of the nineteenth century, declared Clark the winner in its headline), but the final poll showed that his party had not lost support.

On May 22, 1979, more Canadians voted for the Liberals than the Conservatives (about 4 per cent more) but the Liberals had too much of their support in Quebec. The Conservatives used the system better than the Liberals, doing poorly in Quebec (two seats), but extremely well west of the Ottawa River, especially in southern Ontario, where cabinet ministers and old Liberal strongholds fell with astonishing ease on election night. In the West, where Laurier and King Liberalism did so very well, Trudeau Liberalism garnered the support of only one out of five voters and carried only one seat west of Manitoba. Only NDP strength in Saskatchewan and, to a lesser extent, in British Columbia kept Clark from a western sweep and a majority. Still, after appointing James Jerome, a Liberal, as speaker, he was only a few seats short, and the pattern of support outside of Quebec offered Conservatives much consolation. They had recaptured the support among the urban middle class that Diefenbaker had lost in the sixties. More important was the remarkable rise in Conservative support among the youth, a segment of the electorate which had tended to vote Liberal since Pierre Trudeau became leader. In 1979, unlike 1968, youth were conservative in their style and, apparently, their political tastes. Voting Conservative seemed to be the counterpart of taking the economics and business courses which the young now so eagerly sought out.

Commentators were quick to find signs of a conservative temper everywhere. Geoffrey Stevens saw 'the story of Canada in the 1970s' as the change from Trudeau's 1970 love beads to the yellow cardigan Joe Clark donned after work. Stevens' newspaper, the *Globe and Mail*, ran an extended story on 'neo-conservatism' in Ottawa and in the Conservative party. Friedman became fashionable; deregulation was most definitely 'in.' Many bureaucrats found the change from the Just Society relatively easy, and their mentors were such disillusioned American liberals as

Daniel Patrick Moynihan, Nathan Glazer, and Norman Podhoretz. Eugene Forsey fumed that no previous Canadian Conservative prime minister could possibly have accepted the American mumbo-jumbo called neo-conservatism, but these young Conservatives in Ottawa could not remember any Tory prime minister except John Diefenbaker and Dief they wanted to forget. When Diefenbaker died in the mid-summer of 1979, the Conservative government presided over an emotional farewell that emphasized the richness of the Diefenbaker personality while ignoring so many personal bad memories of Diefenbaker's political legacy. Indeed, in his cabinet choices, Clark had shown how little he owed to (and, perhaps thought of) the party's oldtimers. Absent from his cabinet were such leftovers from the Diefenbaker era as Alvin Hamilton, George Hees, and Marcel Lambert. In their place were younger, feistier, bystander Tories, many of whom had cut their political teeth a decade earlier in the campaign to rid the party of John Diefenbaker.

Clark probably did want to change his country as he and his colleagues had their party. To them Canada and especially its federal government reeked of Liberalism and Trudeauism. The smell was offensive and its sources had to be found and exorcised. Shortly after Michael Pitfield administered the oath of office to the new prime minister he was dismissed. More controversial was the demotion of William Hood, the deputy Minister of Finance. Hood was replaced by Clark's office (reportedly without prior consultation with the finance minister, John Crosbie) with the Ontario economist Grant Reuber, whose solid credentials muted public protest but did little to quell the unease of civil servants. The Hood dismissal and the anger it created among many long-time public servants probably persuaded the Clark government to desist in its effort to erase the Liberal tinge in the bureaucracy – at least temporarily.

There were other tasks which were more important in consolidating the new government. The Conservative political dilemma since 1917 had been the party's weak presence in Quebec. In 1979, however, western Canada for the first time had more seats than Quebec, and the demographers told us that the western tilt of the political balance would grow in the future. This offered consolation; it was also reflected in the government's policy. Clark and his government seemed to shift the focus of federal politics away from the so-called problem of Quebec. 'Cool it,' was the typical jargon so often heard when Quebec came up in Clark press conferences during the summer of 1979. Unlike Trudeau, Clark said he would take little direct part in the debate that would occur before the referendum. Attacking the 'confrontation' politics of previous federal-provincial diplomacy, Clark promised 'co-operation' with the provinces and vaguely suggested that his 'flexibility' could embrace Quebec's demands as well as those of other provinces. What this flexibility meant remained elusive. During the campaign, Clark had spoken of Canada as a 'community of communities,' which presumably foretold a decentralization unparalleled in Canadian history. Clark did not have time to clarify what he meant, although some signs did appear during his term. He appointed Arthur Tremblay, an authority on the constitution, to the Senate to develop a Conservative constitutional policy. Other actions suggested what that policy might be: the granting of off-shore oil rights to Newfoundland; a move toward provincial status for the Yukon; and federal withdrawal from lottery control. Perhaps there was never to be a definite policy on the constitution and Quebec. In answer to a question of what he would do in the referendum Clark replied that good federal government was the best contribution he could make. Then he added: 'One of the great errors that was made by the former government was their preoccupation with the referendum and their preoccupation with constitutional questions to the exclusion of actions on other fronts. That made the federal government, and consequently federalism, seem ineffective.' By the time Clark said this in early September his own government's effectiveness was being increasingly questioned. On their honeymoon, the Tories found the *Maid of the Mist* running into the rapids.

Troubles came early, most of them arising from Tory carelessness in the courtship of the Canadian electorate before May 22. The first problem was the promise to move the Canadian embassy in Israel to Jerusalem. When Clark made the promise during the campaign the press scarcely noticed, although international relations specialists, had they been consulted, would quickly have pointed to the dangers. Once in office, the new external affairs minister, Flora MacDonald, was warned by her advisers that such a move could have unfortunate consequences which neither she nor Clark had envisaged. MacDonald quickly retreated, telling the press that serious consideration of the move was needed, only to be contradicted by Clark who announced that the embassy would move. Protests flowed into Ottawa from business groups fearing the economic consequences of a move. The press reflected the fears of the population, and finally Clark scrambled to escape from his commitment by asking Robert Stanfield to investigate the question. After touring the Middle East, Stanfield reported that the embassy should remain in Jerusalem. Clark accepted the advice, but his credibility suffered.

Even more serious were the problems with the economy. In the campaign, the Conservatives had promised to 'privatize' Petrocan, to grant a generous mortgage interest deduction to homeowners, to maintain lower interest rates, and to cut income taxes while reducing the budget deficit in the longer run. By September, Jeffrey Simpson was warning that Clark's government was in serious difficulty: 'The government must walk a thin line between restraint and stimulus and goodies, long-term economic considerations and short-term political gain. The scenarios for mighty dustups in cabinet and caucus are already unfolding.' Faced with some internal dissension and, much more seriously, increasing public criticism, Clark hesitated. Parliament did not meet until October, and when it did doubts about

Clark's leadership abounded. The Throne Speech on October 9 reiterated that the Conservatives had been 'given a mandate to change the direction of the Government of Canada, as we enter the 1980s.' But the mandate – debatable even in May – had now been lost. The Clark government would not last until the 1980s.

Aware that many thought him a weak leader, Clark tried to seem decisive. But decisiveness meant decision, and this brought problems. Petrocan had become popular after the election. To many, Petrocan became – quite wrongly – a symbol of low oil prices. Nationalists hailed it as a first line of defence against multinationals. Peter Newman in *Maclean's* (September 17, 1979) claimed that Petrocan 'is the only chance we have of being represented in any major way in the world oil game with a voice independent of the huge multinationals.' If Clark 'privatized' Petrocan, he would 'deprive us of the least costly, most efficient method of achieving Canada's energy goals.' But to leave Petrocan intact would deprive Clark of much political credibility. Again he hesitated, appointing a task force whose report in favour of a distribution of Petrocan shares to Canadians he would not definitely accept. A non-confidence vote on Petrocan was moved in late October, but ten Liberals managed to find other things to do and the government was sustained by 137 votes to 128.

This vote made Clark and his ministers breathe more easily. They thought they had time enough to build their new structure of government. The Liberals were listless, Trudeau strangely ineffective in debate. In the House the Tories had several fine performers who could easily match or surpass Liberal or NDP critics in intellectual debate or parliamentary repartee. Minister of Finance John Crosbie rumbled and roared in a Newfoundland accent which attracted laughter and diverted attention from the many sensible things he had to say. Other cabinet members, such as David MacDonald and Don Mazankowski, impressed in quieter ways. There were disappointments. Ron Atkey as Minister of Employment and Immigration fumbled badly, his reputation sinking quickly as he first offered government assistance for 50,000 boat people escaping the Vietnamese tragedy and then modified that commitment. Roch LaSalle, the Minister of Supply and Services, embarrassed the government with his candour about patronage. This embarrassment could have been expected. LaSalle, the sole Tory francophone elected in May, was not cabinet material, but Clark had no choice. His other francophone ministers, Jacques Flynn, Martial Asselin, and Robert René de Cotret, he appointed from the Senate. They were rarely noticed as they performed their tasks in the Upper Chamber. Their presence served as a reminder of the danger the new government faced unless it increased its representation in Quebec. A strong dose of patronage and provincial rights combined with Quebec's historic fear of exclusion would probably work next time.

Clark himself could be seen as an asset the next time in Quebec. He was the first anglophone leading a major party to speak French. In the Commons he replied in the language of the questioner, and those few who watched Question Period usually gave him good parliamentary grades. Whatever the policy problems the party kept a united front, perhaps feeling that after an election a couple of years hence the elusive majority might be theirs. They needed time and, on November 21, they appeared to get it. Pierre Trudeau unexpectedly announced that 'it's time for a new leader to take up this work.' In the Commons, Clark thanked Trudeau for his past service and hoped he would continue 'to contribute his formidable talents to Parliament and Canada.' Few thought he would remain after the referendum, and even there Claude Ryan was making it clear that Trudeau was not much needed. At the age of sixty Trudeau's future meant Michel, Sacha, and Justin, maybe even Margaret, perhaps a university chair, and surely a large mark upon his nation's history. The political obituaries were predictable. The *Toronto Sun*'s lead said 'Hallelujah.' Others, used to speaking ill of Trudeau, were more respectful – as though honouring the traditions surrounding the dead. Allan Fotheringham declared Trudeau 'the most remarkable Canadian of his generation; he did more than anyone to make this country sit up and take notice. Well, back to the mundane men.'

The mundane Prime Minister told the press it would 'be easier in the next four or five months.' In a little noticed comment which had major implications, Clark said that Trudeau's departure 'will allow us to move more quickly than we might have otherwise in getting some of the legislative initiatives that we have wanted to move on.' The statement betrayed the fears that had made Conservative policy tentative and contradictory and indicated that the government now believed it could take more risks. Without a leader, the Liberals could only watch as the minority Conservatives acted like a majority. According to several reports, it was only after Trudeau resigned that the Conservatives decided they could go ahead with some harsh economic measures which were sure to offend the already troubled and politically volatile province of Ontario.

The Trudeau resignation was, for Tories, an opiate that stilled fears but blurred vision. There was much that should have disturbed the government. The Gallup Poll for November, which apeared just after Trudeau's resignation, showed a startling nineteen-point Liberal lead. The Liberals, moreover, were not the well-disciplined party Canadians had so long known. Trudeau's resignation had come just before a national executive meeting which seemed likely to call for a leadership review which Trudeau forces had not wanted and which Trudeau almost surely could not have survived. Now with Trudeau gone, the two leading candidates to succeed him, Donald Macdonald and John Turner, were scrambling for position; in so doing, their movements uncovered many of the scars of the past. In short, Liberals were troubled, angry, and resentful of Conservative smugness. Most of all they knew that Joe Clark as prime minister was unconvincing. In cartoons Clark's chin receded ever farther. Ethnic jokes became respectable as Clark jokes. 'Have you heard the latest Joe Clark joke?' became an all-too-familiar staple of bar-room and even family dinner conversation. Tories didn't help. Dalton Camp gave Clark a mixed review in his best-selling *Points of Departure*. 'If you were ever in a fight,' Camp wrote, 'the safest man around to hold your coat would be Clark.' Six months later Camp's introduction to another book no longer even granted that Joe Clark was safe.[3]

The members of cabinet measured their condition by what they saw in the Commons – namely, a divided and erratic Liberal party. The country measured the government and its leader by another scale – the higher interest rates, the energy problems, and the sense that, under this prime minister, Canada would be led by a bit player in the increasingly important action on the world stage. Into this setting came John Crosbie (in mukluks) on December 11 to deliver his budget address. 'Don't be defensive,' Crosbie reportedly told the Tory caucus. 'This is an offensive Bodjit' (*Maclean's*, September 24, 1979). It was, but it was not really the 'tough' medicine Crosbie and his detractors later claimed it to be. This budget is analysed in the economics section, but of course its true significance was political. Ontario provincial Conservatives reacted as expected to the budget's provisions for an 18-cent per gallon excise tax and for regular increases of well-head prices which would soon bring Canadian prices to 85 per cent of the rapidly increasing world price. Premier Lougheed, however, beamed on budget night, proclaiming the budget to be proof that Albertans finally had a government in Ottawa they could call their own. Lougheed's glee and Ontario Premier Davis's grumblings were remembered as Liberal MPs began their boisterous annual Christmas party on Wednesday evening, December 12.

The members drank away their doubts and fears as the night passed into morning. There was an NDP non-confidence motion to be voted on Thursday. On the last non-confidence motion, enough Liberals had had political 'flu to allow the government to endure and to taunt them afterward. This time the Tories would face the taunts – or else. The next morning, as the party's late stragglers awoke, they discovered it might well be 'or else.' The Liberal whip, directed by the strong arm of Allan MacEachen, was coming hard. Even Liberal hospital patients felt its sting and Trudeau did nothing to stop MacEachen's skilful directing of errant Liberals into the fold for the night's vote. What made the vote so portentous was Social Credit leader Fabien Roy's decision to demand changes in the excise tax proposal as a price for his five MPs' support. By noon on Thursday, December 13, the young government's survival seemed doubtful. Strangely, it seemed not to care. Clark later said he had never expected the Liberals to defeat him, and for that reason he neither delayed the vote nor bargained with the Socreds. It was a game of bluff, and the Tories thought the high cards were on their side. They weren't.

3 For Camp's comments on Clark, see *Points of Departure* (Ottawa: Deneau and Greenberg 1979).

The Commons filled after dinner on the 13th. Three Tories were missing, Flora MacDonald in Europe, Alvin Hamilton in hospital, Lloyd Crouse, a deserter, in the South Seas. The speaker's call for the vote was an anticlimax. The bluff had been called. The government fell, six months after the election, by 139 votes to 133.

The next morning Trudeau met his caucus and Clark went to see the Governor General. The election would be on February 18. Trudeau told his caucus he would lead them if they could find no other. Conservatives, recalling Trudeau's baggy eyes and listless slouch in the Commons, were already spoiling for the fight. Many Liberals had similar memories. Ontario organizer Judd Buchanan called riding associations and discovered strong hostility to Trudeau as leader. Ontario organizers called local party officials telling them to prepare for a convention on January 18. Donald Macdonald looked like the obvious and even anointed successor, since John Turner, frustrated by the Trudeau Liberals' opposition to his candidacy, had withdrawn. But the caucus was writing another script.

After Trudeau gave his cryptic statement to the caucus, he left for a weekend in Montreal to brood over his future. His caucus, once again guided by MacEachen, made his decision. Since the Pearson years, MacEachen had toiled with little personal celebrity in Liberal party vineyards. He built up a substantial number of credits; more important, his judgment was trusted. That Friday morning he cashed in his credits. Many were wary, especially the Quebec members, who worried about Trudeau's impact on English Canada. Because of their overwhelming numbers and these worries, the Quebec caucus withdrew, leaving the decision to the members from English Canada. The caucus continued into the evening. Some members spoke despairingly of Trudeau's unpopularity with their constituencies, but by late evening these voices had stilled. The caucus 'unanimously' called upon Trudeau to lead them into the next election.

The next morning some members of the national executive fumed, and the meeting carried on to an embarrassing length. Yet it also called upon Trudeau to accept the draft to remain as leader. Liberals outside of Ottawa were astonished. British Columbia Liberals, angered by Trudeau's appearance at a New York disco after pleading illness as an excuse for his failure to attend a BC party meeting, warned that Trudeau could not carry the westernmost province. Leading Ontario Liberals jammed telephone lines to Ottawa, irritated because they knew so little about something that would affect them so much. Macdonald was ready to run, and by Saturday it seemed that Turner might yet reconsider. Support for Turner came from some Quebec Liberals, notably André Ouellet, who saw the former finance minister as a guarantee of a Liberal sweep. Many others thought the same of Macdonald who, on Sunday evening, called Trudeau to tell him that he would replace him, but that he would not run if Trudeau remained although he would, of course, support him. The message was clear; the reply reportedly obscure. Two days later the CBC began the delayed Trudeau press conference with a discussion of the forthcoming Liberal leadership convention. There would be none; Trudeau would stay, but not forever. The Liberal general took off his stripes, but he still stood above his enlisted men. The new 'Liberal team' prepared to face the enemy without a platform, but with a keen awareness of the fatal weaknesses of their Tory opponents.

The Conservatives' greatest weakness was their leader, who, polls soon revealed, was wanted as prime minister by fewer than one out of seven Canadians. As Clark stumbled, too many Tories failed to rush to pick him up. Premier Davis of Ontario, whose treasurer's anti-budget statements Liberals gleefully quoted, found southern climes politically salubrious. Premier Lougheed of Alberta announced that he would remain silent until February 19. He did so even though a Lougheed statement indicating a refusal to accept Trudeau's vague energy proposals would probably have helped the Tories in Ontario. Perhaps nothing would have helped.

Ontario Conservatives hoped that the hostility toward Trudeau that they had found in May would endure, but this hope soon vanished. The early polls generally showed Conservatives twenty points behind in Ontario, the Liberals an astonishing fifty to sixty points ahead in Quebec. The ingredients for a Liberal majority were present even if western Canada would not hearken to the Liberal appeal. The Liberal strategy was to make no mistakes, to arouse none of the old fears of Trudeau arrogance. The promised Liberal platform never appeared nor did any definite statement on energy prices. Liberal strategy was simple. Clark was already fatally wounded. Trudeau became a sniper circling at a distance, refusing contact, never committing himself lest he come too near to the range of return fire. Trudeau read his speeches from a prepared text in which banality and cliché abounded. He became what he had almost never been before – boring. As he walked into one rally, a woman said, 'please be your old arrogant self.' Toward the end of the campaign he did ignite some sparks, but by then it was safe.

If Trudeau lacked arrogance before the crowds, he retained it for the press. At the news conference at which he announced his resignation he had told the reporters – in a wry echo of Richard Nixon – that he would not have them to kick around anymore. Immediately on his return he began kicking again, walking out of the press conference where he announced his decision to remain in the middle of a reporter's question. The press's response, not surprisingly, was generally hostile. Richard Gwyn spoke of two decent party leaders and one who lacked honour and decency. His bitterness did not diminish during the campaign nor did that of Allan Fotheringham, who irritated Trudeau aide Jim Coutts into a lawsuit. The Liberals did not do well in newspaper endorsements either. The *Winnipeg Free Press* finally deserted its long-time political favourite. *Le Devoir* backed the NDP, *Le Soleil* the Tories, as did the *Toronto Sun* and the *Globe and Mail*. *La Presse* and the *Toronto Star* supported the Liberals, the latter in an especially boisterous way. After the election, commentators agreed that the press had opposed the Liberals. The par-

TABLE 5
Results of 1980 General Election

Province	Seats			Liberal popular vote (rounded)	
	Lib.	Cons.	NDP	1979	1980
Yukon/NWT	0	2	1	33	37
BC	0	16	12	23	22
Alberta	0	21	0	21	21
Saskatchewan	0	7	7	20	24
Manitoba	2	5	7	23.5	28
Ontario	52	38	5	37	41.5
Quebec	73	1	0	62	68
NB	7	3	0	45	50
NS	5	6	0	35.5	40
PEI	2	2	0	40	47
Newfoundland	5	2	0	38	47
Total	146	103	32	39.8	43.9

ticular intensity of this anti-Trudeau feeling in 1979-80 might be partly explained by the commentators' awareness that what they said would matter very little.

What did matter was energy prices – especially in Ontario and eastern Canada – and the perception of Clark as an inadequate leader. Not even the famous episode late in the campaign when the Canadian ambassador to Iran, Kenneth Taylor, cleverly managed the escape of six American diplomats from Tehran could establish Clark as an international figure of substance. Canadians gave credit to Taylor, not to Clark. Clark's strong support for a planned Olympic boycott in response to the Soviet invasion of Afghanistan had much public approval and it caused Trudeau to stumble briefly into contradictory statements, but Clark, unlike Jimmy Carter, reaped few political rewards. The supposedly non-partisan National Citizens' Coalition paid for republication in many major dailies of a *Toronto Sun* column which hinted that Trudeau had bussed the Communists too warmly during his world travels. These tired charges stirred few except some Liberals who saw the advertisement as proof that the Election Expenses Act should be amended to prevent groups like the NCC from wearing 'non-partisan' clothes that became invisible at election time.

What was clear during the last week, when the NCC advertisements appeared, was the fate of the Clark government. On February 18, 1980, eastern Canadians had elected a Liberal majority before the Manitoba returns came in. (See Table 5.) With a relatively small shift in the popular vote the Liberals garnered thirty-two more seats than they had in May 1979. Because the Tories had won so many Ontario seats with narrow margins, the Grits were able to recoup many, again with small margins. The Conservatives had, in fact, done much better (5 per cent) than the pre-election Gallup Poll suggested they would, but they would face a Liberal majority. No consolation removed the grief. The NDP too, could point to more seats and more voters (19.8 per cent), but it had remained too much a regional party, the opposition in the West perhaps only while Trudeau led the Liberals.

'Welcome to the nineteen-eighties,' the victor greeted his followers on election night. Eight months before, few had thought he would make it into the eighties; now, just as few could explain how he had. There remains much that is puzzling in Trudeau's survival. If Liberals had polled their party members on leadership in September 1979 Trudeau would surely have lost. As one who entered politics when the Conservatives were ridding themselves of Diefenbaker, he knew how few high cards an electoral loser holds. He thus threw in his cards because he could not bluff and probably was tired of the game. Certainly Trudeau seemed to relish the freedom his resignation brought. The Crosbie budget and the Clark government's political clumsiness meant a new deal with a high trump. He could not refuse; reason and passion joined to give his answer. He became the master of his fate.

What that fate will be is prophecy not history. Yet the past surely determined the present in some ways. René Lévesque's referendum, the promise of 1976, was still to come in December 1979; and for Trudeau, of course, it was still to be fought. There was, too, Trudeau's promise of 1968, the vision of a juster society, and this found its echo – sometimes a hollow one – in the leftish, nationalist tinge of the Liberal campaign of 1979-80. And, finally, there was the Trudeau record after the 1974 majority. His personal life in tatters, he had given too little to public life. In private life in 1979 he was starting over; in public life he wanted a second chance.

Turning for insight from Shakespeare to a B-plus-grade movie, *Starting Over* (playing in Canadian theatres during the campaign of 1979-80), one can suggest that Trudeau may have minimized the dangers of beginning again. In the movie, the unhealed wounds of a bitter divorce are rarely seen or felt; in the political campaign of 1979-80, many old Liberal wounds, too, were glossed over – temporarily ignored, but surely not forgotten. Trudeau's opponents could barely mouth the appropriate courtesies on election night. Some didn't bother. Geoffrey Stevens in the *Globe and Mail* lamented the fates of Joe Clark and Pierre Trudeau. 'The simple decency' of Clark would, Stevens predicted, stop a palace revolt. 'It is a quality that will be as missed in the Prime Minister's Office as it will be welcome in the Office of the Leader of the Opposition.' Some Liberals might have agreed. Trudeau's task was more difficult, but his opportunity was greater. He had already left his mark on Canada's history; he now had the chance to give this mark a clearer shape.

It is too early for historians to judge definitively what Trudeau has already done to our lives and our nation's history. Much depends on what happens to Canada and Quebec in the future, for his most important policies were devoted to strengthening the overstrained sinews which bind the nation together. Some of these policies did effect change. The Ottawa of 1965, to say nothing of the Ottawa of 1945, is utterly gone. French Canadians are no longer token citizens, no longer seriously under-represented at senior levels in the civil service. Despite the many laments about bilingualism's failure – usually from those who never wanted it to succeed – the ubiquity of French conversation in Ottawa is striking. Perhaps francophones still are not completely at home, but they can certainly be more comfortable in their Ottawa surroundings than they ever could before.

In other areas Trudeau's promise was, as George Radwanski wrote, 'unfulfilled.' The Just Society was perhaps a dream that could not be fulfilled; the vexations and vanities of man would forever prevent fulfilment. On a practical level, the means of its accomplishment seemed to move farther away in the 1970s. In the late 1960s and early 1970s the Trudeau government did pass much legislation and took actions designed to redistribute income and to protect those who had less in the society. Its record in this regard is better than that of nearly all European social democratic governments during this period. Certainly government spending in Canada – a tra-ditional measure of the interventionist state – rose at a more rapid pace than in all but one or two western industrialized countries. But these traditional measures and means no longer appeared so effective for achieving the intended results. In the mid-sixties, for example, sociologist John Porter argued strongly for support for higher education as a means of ending inequality in Canada. Spending came; inequality remained. The upper middle class reaped most of the benefits of the massive spending on university education because its children went to university while working class children continued to stay away for reasons that had far more to do with culture than with economics. Again, because of the commitment to redistri-bution, the Trudeau government gave large subsidies to industries to encourage them to locate in disadvantaged areas. The result was higher costs, several business failures, and an over-all reduced growth rate which, in some cases, paradoxically, meant that the disadvantaged areas gained less than they would have if the grants had not been given at all. Trudeau's post-1974 musings about individual responsi-bility and the limits of government surely arose from his experience of government and from his growing awareness that much of any bureaucracy's time is spent in consolidating its own position rather than in serving the interests of the general public.

Trudeau was not alone in his disillusionment and musings. Some of the academic reformers of the 1960s turned to neo-Marxism, which called for a fundamental restructuring of society in order to solve its problems, but which did so not with the apocalyptic rhetoric of the sixties but in academic tomes where the authors' arguments were often buried in footnotes and where the revolution was clearly a task for the next generation. More influential, however, was a disparate group that reacted with calls for less government. At times Trudeau seemed to share this view; at other times he indicated that he believed the problems too great for private initiative to solve. Moreover, because the call for less government intervention came from many who had benefited from the state's role in the economy, Trudeau's ambivalence is hardly surprising.

In so many ways the problem transcended Canada's boundaries, although Canadians seldom seemed to realize this. In his surprisingly popular analysis *The Culture of Narcissism: American Life in an Age of Diminishing Expectations*, Christopher Lasch pointed out that 'even Canada, long a bastion of solid bourgeois dependability' now faced the malaise of bourgeois society, that seems to have lost 'both the capacity and the will to confront the difficulties that threaten to overwhelm it.' If the waves do not roll back Trudeau will not matter; but perhaps neither will history, for so many of the alternatives to our society have shown themselves too eager to abolish the past. If Canadians do not lose their memories entirely, they will probably have many images of Trudeau and the seventies: of a society demanding change yet fearful of its consequences; of a country distrusting its leaders yet craving leadership; of an awesome prosperity whose benefits were questioned once achieved; of a prime minister who brought intellectual content to politics but whose success came mainly from his emotional appeal; of a leader who dared to talk of love during political campaigns but whose relations with other people were frequently marked by distance and marred by personal distrust; and of a man who endured with remarkable stoicism the public exposure of that most private of agonies, the breakdown of his marriage. These are the images that will probably endure; their meaning is for our successors to find.

So much of the material in Part VI is so recent that the making of historical judgment is a risky undertaking, particularly in areas of social history. Nevertheless, three areas require special attention, not least because they received so much attention during the seventies from the press and the politicians. These are: Quebec and the constitution; the economy; and Canada's interaction with the world beyond its borders. In these three areas important changes clearly occurred during the seventies. The meaning of these changes is discussed and their importance evaluated in the following chapters.

30

Canada and the World Beyond

Canada's relations with foreign nations changed in part because so many individual Canadians had closer relations with foreign countries. This was most obviously true of the many recent immigrants to Canada. As the 1971 census showed, 15.3 per cent of the population had been born outside Canada. In urban centres, the percentage was much higher, over 40 per cent in metropolitan Toronto. The change in immigration laws initiated by Jean Marchand's White Paper in the mid-sixties greatly affected the quantity and the kind of immigrants. The White Paper had emphasized training, youth, and, to a lesser extent than in the past, sponsorship and relatives. This opened Canada to Orientals, Blacks, and many southern Europeans, who had been largely excluded by earlier immigration policies. Thus, although Germans were the second largest group of immigrants right after the war, in 1973 Canada took in 14,662 people from Hong Kong, 9,363 from Jamaica, and only 2,564 from Germany. By this time there had been considerable reaction to both the rate and the pattern of immigration. Canadian labour, for example, opposed the former; various groups, ranging from the racist Western Guard to English immigrant-journalist Doug Collins, objected to the latter. Certainly the numbers in the late 1960s and early 1970s were large. Annual immigration in the five years prior to the 1965 White Paper averaged less than 100,000. Between 1965 and 1973, average immigration was well over 150,000. The government reacted by appointing a new committee to study immigration. Its report, 'The Green Paper,' appeared in 1975 and was immediately controversial. Well-organized ethnic and Marxist-Leninist opponents termed it racist; others criticized its ambiguity. Hearings across Canada turned into circuses, and participatory democracy received yet another black eye. The direction of future government policy, however, was decided before any discussion: there would be fewer immigrants. In 1977 there were only 114,914 immigrants, and later years would see even fewer.

Meanwhile, both the 'look' and the tastes of the Canadian city had been considerably changed by immigration. New smells and sights filled the streets of the city. Attitudes changed too, as native Canadians sampled the delights of, for example, squid, which twenty years earlier was as likely to be found on a Toronto restaurant menu as in the Don River. European immigrants especially brought an ease with alcohol that assisted in loosening English Canada's collective (though not necessarily individual) inhibitions about drink. In 1970 Canadians drank 19,471,000 gallons of wine; in 1979 the figure was 37,078,000 – much more of it imported than when the decade opened. Liquor consumption rose more dramatically, from 922,000 to 3,219,000 gallons. It would be wrong, of course, to attribute this increase solely to the presence of new Canadians. Affluence, higher educational levels, and fads also contributed, as did the more numerous contacts of Canadian-born residents with foreign lands.

The domestic transportation system was described as a mess by the transport minister in the early seventies; foreign travel, however, was quite efficient and relatively inexpensive. Charter flights to Europe made European travel accessible to nearly all classes, although by the end of the decade the relative decline in the value of the Canadian dollar affected many travellers' European plans. Just as the sources of immigration moved from northern to southern Europe so did Canadian tourists. And there were so many other places to go – South America, the West Indies, and, naturally, the United States. Florida in winter had more Canadians than most Canadian cities. In 1979 Canadians spent more than $600,000,000 (US) in search of winter sun in Florida. These trips left memories and an awareness of the variety of human experience. English nobles claimed that foreign travel made their sons wiser and better men. We cannot claim that for Canadians, but it is probably valid to suggest that, in small ways, at any rate, it made a difference. For some, especially those who went to the Third World with CUSO and CIDA, it prompted the formation of a new pressure group which clamoured for more Canadian concern and aid for Third World countries. Even so, although Canadians had more contact with the external world in the 1970s than ever before, they had, in a traditional sense, a less internationalist foreign policy than at any time since the 1930s. Certainly this was true of the prime minister.

No previous Canadian prime minister attracted so much international attention as Trudeau, none seemed so well prepared by academic training and breadth of interests to play a large part in international affairs, none was so cosmopolitan in style; nevertheless, Pierre Trudeau has shunned international commitment and action more strenuously than any Canadian prime minister since Mackenzie King. In part he shared King's reasons, believing that his predecessors' concern with the world beyond Canada had diverted their eyes from what was happening in Canada itself.

Like King, Trudeau believed that his greatest contribution to international affairs would be the maintenance of a united Canada. The experience of the First World War and the effects of the British connection had formed King's attitudes. With Trudeau, two wars, the Second World War and Vietnam, appear to have been decisive influences. During the Second World War Trudeau was a dissenter because of that war's demands upon the Quebec in which he lived; and Vietnam contributed to the disillusionment of many Canadians (especially Canadian intellectuals) with the American alliance that had been the foundation of post-war Canadian foreign policy. In addition, Trudeau distrusted the bureaucrats in External Affairs, probably because of that department's long denial of the French fact in both its hiring policy and its diplomatic initiatives.

A comparison with Pearson further clarifies Trudeau's position. Pearson believed that Canada had to escape from the limitations of its domestic concerns because of the new dangers which atomic weapons and the rivalry between the great powers presented. Through involvement in international affairs Canadians would achieve a broader, more liberal outlook and a sense of identity which in the past they had so often lacked. International commitment would give the nation a sense of purpose and, thus, unite Canadians. Trudeau was sceptical. Foreign policy had not united Canadians; he saw instead in the mid-sixties a country arguing, often bitterly, over its relationship to its closest ally's unpopular war. Moreover, the whole concept seemed a hangover from a simpler era when the western alliance had been united and its sway in the 'free world' and the United Nations was paramount. Decolonization and détente had changed the contours of world politics, but Canadian foreign policy had not reflected that change. In a 1969 speech in Calgary for which Pearson reportedly demanded and got an apology, Trudeau charged that 'our defence policy had determined all of our foreign policy. And we had no foreign policy of any importance except that which flowed from NATO. And this is a false perspective for any country. It is a false perspective to have a military alliance determine your foreign policy.' One suspects that neither Trudeau nor Pearson ever understood what the other wanted.

Trudeau was certainly correct in one sense. Canada was having great difficulty in the sixties adapting to changed international circumstances. The rhetoric of Canadian foreign policy did not always reflect reality. External affairs' documents too often were mere cant expressing ill-defined aims. It would be far better, Trudeau argued, if Canada's aims were limited and specific and if it restrained its tendency toward lofty moralizing and helpful fixing. This is not to suggest that Trudeau was incapable of cant: what after all is one to make of his declaration to the US Congress that Canada's break-up 'would create shock waves of disbelief among those all over the world who are committed to the proposition that among man's noblest endeavours are those communities in which persons of diverse origins live, love, work and find mutual benefit'? Even this remark, however, illustrates Trudeau's belief that Canada's domestic unity was its most important contribution to international affairs.

Not long after he took office and during his first election campaign in 1968 Trudeau promised a foreign policy review, the purpose of which would be to devise a new foreign policy for the nation. This promise was made even though he knew that the Department of External Affairs had just completed a thorough examination of Canadian foreign policy and had found that, in most cases, Canada was doing what it should have done. In effect, Trudeau firmly identified himself with the critics of both the department and its policy. He also made clear his suspicion of NATO and NORAD, and indicated that the Canadian commitment to those alliances would become much less generous. Between 1968 and 1970 Trudeau attempted to inaugurate the promised changes in both the substance and the structure of policy.

The changes began before the review was completed. On April 3, 1969, Trudeau announced a 'planned and phased reduction' in the Canadian commitment of forces to NATO that amounted to a halving of the Canadian contribution. At a NATO meeting, Britain's Minister of Defence, Denis Healey, exploded: 'Canada [is] passing the buck to the rest of us.' But the reduction went through despite the opposition of much of the Liberal caucus, several cabinet ministers, 64 per cent of Canadians (according to the Gallup Poll), and leading officials of the Department of External Affairs. External Affairs had already learned that its influence was on the wane. Seven missions had to be closed and personnel had to be reduced by 7 per cent. Even worse, from External's view, the foreign policy review was conducted by large interdepartmental task forces and External's advice was often ignored and, according to some reports, regularly greeted with suspicion. As one observer has written, Trudeau planned to create a new policy-making system which would be based on three elements: 'the participation of many more officials and departments in individual policy deliberations, in order that a wider range of factors and competing proposals might be considered ... a strengthened group of central agencies whose job was to forward the bureaucracy's competing proposals beyond the senior official level to cabinet itself ... and a revised array of cabinet committees and procedures to ensure that the wide-ranging, live discussions below would be re-enacted above and only then arbitrated by political leaders according to self-defined, explicitly stated, well-integrated priorities.'[1] This meant a reduction of External's pre-eminence and autonomy in the area of foreign policy; it also reflected Trudeau's commitment to co-ordination and to the concept of countervailing debate. Nor did Trudeau soften the blow to External; he openly questioned whether diplomacy need exist at all. As

1 John J. Kirton, 'Foreign Policy Decision-Making in the Trudeau Government: Promise and Performance,' *International Journal* (Spring 1978), 290-1.

he told one interviewer, the day of the diplomat had passed: 'I believe it all goes back to the early days of the telegraph when you needed a dispatch to know what was happening in country A, whereas now most of the time you can read it in a good newspaper.' Even Canadian newspaper publishers felt the sting of this remark: he was referring to *The New York Times*.

The Prime Minister's Office took over much of the co-ordinating of the direction of foreign policy; other departments, especially Trade and Commerce, eagerly grasped at the opportunities afforded them by External's decline. The review was genuinely comprehensive, involving departments whose advice and interests External could easily scorn in earlier days. But the mountain laboured and brought forth a mouse: Foreign Policy for Canadians – six brief booklets, four dealing with areas (Latin America, Pacific, Europe, United Nations), one with international development, and one entitled simply *Foreign Policy for Canadians*. They are, frankly, an anachronism today; reading them is embarrassing primarily because, in rejecting the do-good rhetoric of the past, these booklets embraced self-interest with a zeal that would have made Adam Smith blush. The principle that doing good for ourselves is the best way to do good for others is less convincing than the principle that those who try to do good for others more often do good. As Peyton Lyon pointed out in 1970, the new direction was a retreat into irresponsibility, if not fatuity:

We are retreating from Europe, failing to increase our activity in other areas or organizations to any significant degree and taking a giant step in the direction of continental isolationism. If not quite a free ride in world affairs, we are taking one that will be much cheaper, and more sharply focused on national interests.

How accurately Lyon reflected the direction of the report is best illustrated through study of crucial passages in the report itself. 'At times in the past, public disenchantment with Canada's foreign policy was produced in part by an over-emphasis on role and influence obscuring policy objectives and actual interests.' In booklets designed for the general public this passage is remarkably obscure. Cannot influence represent interest? If this means, as one commentator has written, that the comment reflects Trudeau's belief that 'roles' and 'influence' are impositions on others and violate the principle that all states should be permitted freedom to make their own decisions, why is that not simply said? Both this interpretation and Trudeau's remark in 1971 that Canada has 'taken the position that every country is entitled to decide its own policies whether they be military, defence, social, or economic' have troubling implications. Surely an abundance of independent decision has been inimical to Canadian interests in the past and surely, too, all countries must recognize the limits of their right to act without regard to the rest of the world. With one statement, however, all can agree: 'There is no natural, immutable or permanent role for Canada in today's world, no constant weight of influence.' Events were soon to prove how true this statement was.

The booklets ignored Canada's relationship with the United States, but in August 1971 President Nixon's protectionist economic measures startled Canadians and their government into recognition of the dependence of this country upon the United States. The shock was twofold: Canada was not given special treatment, and the measures themselves revealed for all the end of post-war American economic dominance. Many Canadians felt they had been set adrift. Even those who had called upon the government to cut loose the American anchor worried openly about where we would land. The government's response – one of the most curious foreign policy statements in Canadian history – was External Affairs minister Mitchell Sharp's *Canada–US Relations: Options for the Future*, published during the election campaign in October 1972. This became known as the Third Option paper. Option one was maintaining Canada's present relationship with the United States; option two was closer integration with the Americans; and option three, reduction of 'Canadian vulnerability' to American actions. A third-grader of modest intellectual attainments should have been able to choose the right option. Option three, however, presented some problems. The obvious connection to make to reduce our dependence on the Americans was with the Europeans, whom we had recently offended with our NATO withdrawal and whom we had treated rather cavalierly in the 1970 review booklet on Europe. Some did suggest the Third World as an appropriate venue for Canadian action, but as one of the authors has suggested elsewhere, 'it was inherently improbable that public opinion could swallow a facile identification between Canada and the Third World.' So Europe it was.

In April 1974 Canada handed an aide-mémoire to the Commission of the European Economic Community and to the nine member governments. What Canada wanted was recognition of its distinctiveness from the United States, and also some new European trade connections. In October 1974 Trudeau travelled to European capitals in search of substance for his vague policy. The results were not happy. Europeans were displeased with Canada's defence policy, especially toward NATO; the new directions of 1969 had apparently led us the wrong way. Moreover, the Europeans saw little reason to sign a trade agreement with the Canadians at a time when important multilateral negotiations were taking place under the GATT framework. Even Trudeau admitted that Canada's proposals were 'banal.' But Canada persisted, and in June 1975 the European Community agreed to go ahead in its negotiations with Canada for a 'contractual link.' By that time, as a result of the major economic blow to industrialized western nations dealt by the Arab oil embargo and the dramatic increase in oil prices, the value of such a link had much depreciated. By 1979 the contractual link was seldom heard of and Europeans were blunt in stating their refusal to give special treatment to anything but Canadian exports of natural resource materials. What they wanted was the one thing Canadians did not want to give. We were back to options one or two.

Since the 1972 paper, options one or two had become more palatable to Canadians, if only because alternatives were so manifestly lacking. American involvement in Vietnam had ended in 1973, and with it vanished the most useful target opponents of American influence in Canadian life possessed. Moreover, the Nixon-Kissinger policy of détente coincided well with the apparent direction of Canadian policy since 1968. Indeed, since Canada had moved independently to recognize China in October 1970, it now took some credit for the so-called American opening to China. The satisfaction of having acted first was almost all Canada got, however, for with the American initiative most of its hopes for economic advantage from the recognition vanished.

If the 1972 Third Option paper had become no more than a relic which required occasional obeisance, *Foreign Policy for Canadians* had become merely the focus of antiquarian curiosity. The 1972 paper had in fact represented the reassertion of External Affairs' pre-eminence in the field of Canadian policy-making. It signified the failure of the review process which had aimed to reduce External's influence. External's recovery is too complicated to consider here; what is important is what it signified – that is, the return to many of the precepts that had governed Canadian foreign-policy makers since the war. At first the disavowal of the 1970 review was polite and indirect. External officers regularly quoted *Foreign Policy for Canadians*, just as bureaucrats two generations before had cited Mackenzie King's *Industry and Humanity*, but by 1976 (secure in the knowledge that even its authors had either forgotten or regretted what they had said) even the passing references were dropped. Much else had been forgotten too.

By 1977 the polls were showing that the majority of Canadians had 'very great' or considerable confidence in American foreign policy. They also showed that only in the prairie provinces was there a majority of poll respondents who were willing to make an economic sacrifice to buy back Canada. No longer was there embarrassment in pilgrimages to Washington, and, after the 1976 Parti Québécois victory, both René Lévesque and Pierre Trudeau courted the American capital's favour. The debate about Canada's future was carried on most eloquently in the depths of Wall Street and the halls of Congress. Trudeau, who had been called an 'asshole' on the Nixon tapes, developed a good relationship with Nixon's successor, Gerald Ford, and with Ford's successor, Jimmy Carter. In contrast to the Vietnam years, when close ties with an American president would have given rise to charges of sell-out or 'complicity,' Trudeau's warm reception in Washington and his equally warm response garnered press and public approval in Canada.

There was, then, much irony when the Liberal campaign committee decided in 1979 that it must emphasize Trudeau's role on the world stage and the esteem shown him by leaders of other countries, especially the Americans. In 1968 Trudeau probably had won support because of his intention to reduce Canada's international role to a bit part. In the 1979 and 1979-80 campaigns it was clear that a different approach was required. Although Trudeau was less fervent in support of American actions during the Afghanistan crisis than was Joe Clark, he did speak in language that in 1968 would have labelled him a Cold War warrior. Both he and Canadians had become more aware of the dangers of standing aside and more sensitive to the congruity of Canada's interests with those of other states. Occasionally, too, Trudeau had even seemed to revel in his international commitments. His long tenure, his obvious intellectual gifts, and his linguistic skills had won him much respect in the important meetings which, after 1974, brought Western leaders together to face the most serious crisis their nations had faced since the war. In Commonwealth meetings, after initial scepticism, he developed warm relationships with some Third World leaders, and he showed genuine interest in the debates. Yet the image which persisted among many was still that of Trudeau the new prime minister, sliding down the banister at an early meeting. In 1978, *International Journal* published a special issue on 'Trudeau and Foreign Policy,' and the tone was one of sharp disappointment among authors of all ideological persuasions. The first article, by Harald Von Riekhoff, put the discussion in its proper perspective: 'In assessing Trudeau's impact on Canadian foreign policy, we are ... dealing with a residual function of his over-all political activity and hardly the one which will ultimately determine his place in Canadian history.' So far it hasn't. It's likely it won't.

31

Quebec and the Constitution

The Canadian constitution continued to function during Pierre Trudeau's time in office. The Prime Minister was confident that it would, if properly interpreted, and he had written a book, *Federalism and the French Canadians*, to expound his point of view. The book became an unlikely bestseller in the spring of 1968. It was unusual at any time for a politician to write a book on his own, far less to peddle it successfully, but such was the national appetite in that happy spring for things trudeauvian that even the subject of the constitution failed to deter many thousands of would-be readers, at least before they bought the book.

Trudeau rejected any idea that the British North America Act needed fundamental revision. His view was much the same as St Laurent's: the provinces already had all the power they needed to seek their own destinies. Demands for more power and more money were, by the same token, unreasonable, reflecting not so much real needs as the appetite for power of their sponsors – the provincial politicians and the provincial bureaucracies. Such demands took little account of either the national interest or its guardian, the federal government. It was up to the Trudeau government to stand firm and preserve Ottawa's freedom to act as an arbiter in confederation and a leader outside it.

Trudeau's views notwithstanding, there was substantial demand for a change in the country, especially in Quebec where it was most forcibly expressed by the Union Nationale premier, Daniel Johnson. Johnson, too, had written a book, *Egalité ou Indépendance* (Equality or Independence), which preached a new, provincially centred destiny for the French Canadians in their real homeland – Quebec. Johnson's own feelings were ambivalent and, perhaps, vacillating. At times he seemed to be veering toward indépendance; at others he seemed prepared to let events take their natural course toward an unknown destination. But Johnson's position was highly significant, not just for its influence on Quebec government policy, but also for the appeal it had for an increasing number of Québécois – whether Union Nationale supporters or not – who demanded that Ottawa's power over their province be diminished, and that Quebec be accorded a larger influence over whatever federal powers remained. At its crudest, 'equality' meant giving Quebec an equal say in the running of the central government. And that directly challenged the basis of representation – as well as the foundations of political power – across the country.

It is not surprising that this proposition was not taken seriously. In 1968, Quebec had roughly 28 per cent of the population. In wealth and population, it was outdistanced by Ontario alone. English Canadians outside Quebec could see little justice in the demand for equality; as far as most English-language commentators could judge, Québécois enjoyed the same opportunities as other Canadians, as individuals, and it was for them to make the most of things. Any other solution would give the inhabitants of Quebec extra privileges at the expense of other Canadians and their national government.

But Johnson's preaching could not be ignored altogether. The Premier of Ontario, John Robarts, had admitted as much when he summoned the representatives of the provinces to a public think-tank, the Confederation of Tomorrow conference. Ensconced on the fifty-fourth floor of the Toronto-Dominion Centre, overlooking the distant smokestacks of Buffalo, the premiers encouraged one another with centennial good will. Changes might possibly be made, and, Johnson was told, they might be enough to justify Quebec's continued presence in Canada. But it would have to be a modernized sixties version of Canada, a much reformed country.

The Pearson government succumbed to the pressure of Robarts's example. It summoned a constitutional conference to meet in Ottawa in February to consider what needed to be done about the hoary old BNA Act. The mere fact that the conference had been summoned indicated that something new was needed; by tossing the constitution in the pot, the federal government brought it into question: a subtle, but tangible, de-legitimization of the federal position.

The federal government's prescription for constitutional reform faithfully represented Trudeau's commitment to individual rights over those of groups. Guarantees of language rights, entrenchment of a bill of rights in the constitution, binding commitments from all the provinces, and the transfer of the power to amend the BNA Act from Westminster to Canada were the federal government's proposals. In May 1970, the Minister of Justice, John Turner, announced that 'substantial agreement had been reached.' Language rights, access to taxation, regional disparities, and shared cost programs were among the areas of 'substantial agreement.'

The way had been smoothed by the election of a Liberal government in the province of Quebec in April 1970. The new Bourassa government was committed to making federalism work, and to convincing Quebeckers that participation in a federal Canada was a 'profitable' enterprise. While 'profitable,' confederation should also be prepared to accommodate Quebec's particular demands, especially in the field of social policy. Gradually the federal and Quebec positions were clarified. Bourassa wanted concessions in the area of social policy; Trudeau wanted to enshrine such agreement as had already been reached in a definite and irrevocable constitutional formula, one which would end once and for all the necessity to run to Westminster to amend much of the constitution.

A conference was scheduled for Victoria in June 1971. There, after a lengthy negotiating session, a 'Canadian Constitutional Charter, 1971' was proclaimed. The charter was much more modest than Trudeau's original intentions. It entrenched a limited number of personal freedoms, but only 'subject to such limitations ... as are reasonably justifiable in a democratic society in the interests of public safety, order, health or morals, of national security, or of the rights and freedoms of others.' Such a compromise would have guaranteed the courts a busy time in the years ahead as lawyers and judges struggled to penetrate the murky language of the Charter.

Language rights, too, represented a compromise. The right to use French in Parliament and the legislatures was guaranteed, except in Saskatchewan, Alberta, and British Columbia. French could be used in federal courts, and in other courts in New Brunswick, Newfoundland, and Quebec – but not in Ontario, with its 482,000 French-speakers. The constitution of the Supreme Court was to be altered to permit provincial participation in the nomination of judges, and to ensure that any case involving Quebec's civil law would always be heard by a panel with a majority of Quebec justices. There was to be a domestic amending formula, involving varying numbers of the provinces, but giving Ontario and Quebec a veto over any change. And there was to be a compromise on social policy, with Ottawa conceding provincial primacy in the important areas of pensions and social benefits.

It is remarkable that so much could be agreed, even if the agreement was 'tentative.' It was decided that all provinces and the federal government must state their concurrence within ten days. Bourassa, who had not achieved as much as he wanted, returned home with deep forebodings. These proved justified. Within days a storm of protest swept through Quebec. The federal government still had too much power; Quebec had been faced with an ultimatum; equal status, special status, or anything remotely resembling them, was not conceded. The Victoria Charter would not do. And so Bourassa said, on June 23.

'If there isn't agreement, then that is the end of the matter, for now, or for a while, I hope,' Trudeau had said. Although some expressed the hope that all was not lost, it was evident that no new initiatives were likely. To some, Bourassa's refusal meant that no accommodation was possible with Quebec inside the federal system. To some Quebeckers, it meant that no accommodation was possible with English Canada; and that in turn implied that French Canada would never be able to speak to English Canada 'd'égal à égal.' And, if equality meant a province with vastly increased powers inside and outside the federal government, that impression was correct. To English Canadians, Victoria was not a stage on the route to either total decentralization or 'two nations,' but a means to make the existing constitution more workable, and, it was hoped, more palatable to Quebec as well as to themselves. If neither aim could be achieved, then the present arrangements would have to do.

Although federal-provincial discussions over the constitution were suspended for the moment, ordinary federal-provincial diplomacy continued. Fiscal agreements for 1972-7 had to be negotiated; as usual they resulted in further redistribution of federal tax revenue to the provinces, so that the provincial share of the income tax 'take' reached 30.5 per cent. Because Quebec had long since 'opted out' of most federal shared cost programs, the level of federal income taxation remained much lower there than elsewhere, and the provincial share, collected directly by the province, much higher.

Shared cost programs remained a large proportion of the federal budget. Some of them were costly – too costly in the minds of the Trudeau cabinet and its officials. The temptation to apply a 'Quebec solution' to the other provinces was therefore financially tempting and philosophically congenial; once again Quebec would be a province just 'like the others.' Medicare was the first target. The federal government announced that it intended to place a ceiling on its contributions to a scheme which it had itself fathered; the provinces could pay the balance, if they wished, or make cutbacks. As might have been expected, the federal démarche produced a storm of indignation among the provinces. Indignation spawned unity: all the provinces agreed that they wanted more money – much more – from Ottawa if the national government intended to leave them footing the bill. At the end of 1976, when the fiscal agreements for 1977-82 were complete, they had largely obtained what they wanted.

In one aspect of economic management, as we shall see, the federal government compounded its own weakness through concessions to the provinces to manage the marketing of agricultural products. That, added to a pronounced tendency on the part of the provinces to conduct their own economies as far as possible in the narrowest interests of their own workforces or industries, helped to intensify economic divisions within the country. Although still largely intact, the Canadian common market grew ever more limited and imperfect. The provinces, one economist commented, 'have not failed to infringe on the spirit, and sometimes on the letter, of the Constitution. They have thus impaired the Canadian common market.'

It would not seem unreasonable to predict that, left to their own devices, the provinces will most often act to impair the spirit and the letter of the constitution, and where caught out – as the Maritime provinces were over off-shore mineral rights, or Quebec over cable TV jurisdiction – will rely on political pressure to give them what the courts do not. The Trudeau government's over-all record in federal-provincial relations has been mixed: bold in the approach, but sometimes enfeebled and infirm in withstanding the provinces' political demands. The brief Clark government was bold in neither respect, partly because of ideological preconceptions, expressed in the phrase, 'a community of communities.'

Trudeau's return to power was in part the result of the perception in eastern Canada that the competition between levels of government and the frequently incoherent division of jurisdiction in Canada have produced a dangerous weakening of the central power. The Trudeau government's philosophy in this area, if not always its practice, had consistency and, to many, rationality to commend it. A government remote from the people it governs, exercising its mandate through local intermediaries, and depending on the consent and co-operation of those intermediaries, may not be blessed with a long life-span. It may prolong its existence with timely concessions, but in the long run it will suffer, as one commentator has suggested, the Canadian version of the death of a thousand cuts.

Before 1979, for most English Canadians the constitution meant Quebec. Here hopes were brightest in 1968. Canadians outside Quebec expected that Trudeau, a Québécois with a distinguished command of both languages and a reputation for saying the same thing in both, would restore Quebec to a state of harmony inside the Canadian federal family. Some commentators (not to mention the Lévesque government) have interpreted this to be a desire 'to put Quebec in its place,' presumably beside the national coal scuttle, ready to fetch and carry for its bloated anglophone brethren. This was, and is, a misconception. Trudeau hoped to give the Québécois, as individuals, a stronger place in the Canadian federal system; as for their government, that was in Ottawa as well as Quebec City. The same links of patriotism and self-interest that bound the citizen to the one should apply to his relations with the other. Most Canadians agreed.

This perception of the proper relations between the province and the central government did not attract large sections of the Quebec intelligentsia, who were for the most part committed to a conception of 'deux nations' in a single state, with the province of Quebec equalling in the balance of power the 70 per cent of Canadians who lived outside it. And only one step beyond 'deux nations' was its intellectual twin, the 'souveraineté-association' preached by René Lévesque. It might be said that in the final analysis 'souveraineté-association' was the same as 'deux nations'; it was simply that the first required a more drastic rupture of the constitutional balance in order to convince English Canadians that Quebec would in the future occupy a place that was separate but equal inside a confederal state of very limited powers.

It was obvious that Trudeau's ideas were seriously at variance with the conception that Quebec (and all the French-speaking Quebeckers inside it) formed a 'collectivité' animated by collective cravings for separate institutions, jurisdictions, and destinies, focusing on what was local and controllable, and denying that on important matters the Québécois could or should share their experiences or interests with their neighbours. In this conception the contrary also obtained: non-Québécois influence on Quebec society should be reduced to a minimum. And that applied particularly on the touchy issue of language.

Officially, English and French enjoyed equal status in the Quebec legislature (renamed in a grand gesture the 'National Assembly' in 1968) and Quebec courts, as well as in the federal Parliament and courts. The Protestant minority in Quebec and the Catholic minority in Ontario had a right to their own separate schools, thanks to compromises at the time of confederation. But it was not along Protestant and Catholic lines that conflict developed, but along those of language. There were, in 1971, 888,000 persons using the English language at home in Quebec, and 4,870,000 who used French. The English-speakers were and are overwhelmingly concentrated in or around the Island of Montreal; English-speaking pockets elsewhere in the province were and are relatively insignificant – except, of course, to their inhabitants.

The English minority in Quebec has a peculiar composition. As of the 1971 census, 36 per cent of those identifying themselves as English-speaking Quebeckers had been born outside the province; in addition, outside the province, there were some 713,000 persons of English mother tongue who had been born in Quebec (more than the native-born Quebec remnant of anglophones inside the province). Thus, while the English-language group in Quebec has continued to grow, slowly, in absolute numbers, it has suffered a steady haemorrhage of its members, who have departed to what are presumably more congenial climes elsewhere in Canada. It is important to note that this process has been going on for some considerable time, and that it is neither a phenomenon simply of the past decade nor a direct consequence of the emergence of the Parti Québécois as a political force. The list of towns outside Montreal that were once English and are now French provides mute but eloquent testimony to decades of out-migration by Quebec's English residents: Sherbrooke, Magog, Waterloo, Huntingdon, and Ormstown are useful examples.

These facts might have been comforting to Quebec's nationalists if they had not had their eyes firmly fixed elsewhere. The percentage of Quebec residents of French mother tongue dipped slightly between the censuses of 1951 and 1961, from 82.5 per cent to 81.2 per cent, and it dipped again, to 80.7 per cent in 1971 (although it should be remembered that it had been 79.6 per cent in 1931). It did not take long for some demographers to draw a picture of a tidal wave of English-speakers, with their immigrant allies, swamping the French institutions of Quebec, first in Montreal and then in the rest of the province.

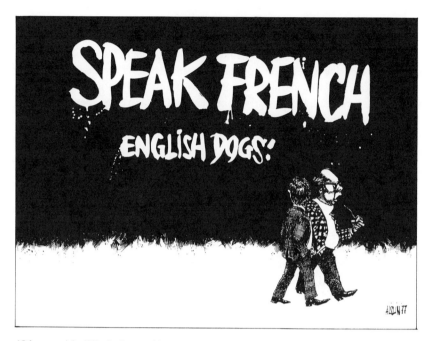

'*Of course it's difficult for outsiders to grasp the subtle complexities of the situation here in Québec*'
(Aislin, c1977). Reproduced with the permission of Aislin: *The Montreal Gazette*

It was in Montreal that the first trouble came. In the autumn of 1969, a dispute over educational facilities offered to the children of Italian immigrants in the Montreal suburb of St Léonard – fanned by extremist elements – turned into a riot. The Union Nationale government of Jean-Jacques Bertrand responded in three ways: it unsuccessfully prosecuted those prominently involved in the riots; it appointed a royal commission to study the whole problem of language in Quebec; and it introduced Bill 63, affirming that parents in Quebec had freedom of choice in their children's language of education. The bill stipulated that every child attending school in Quebec should, as a matter of course, learn French, but that proviso was lost to view in the brouhaha that followed. Freedom of choice, for the nationalists, was the worst solution of all: a heavy dose of legislative coercion was what they demanded. The outcry was loudest, as was to be expected, from the French-language teachers and among students in French-language universities. The latter staged a one-day strike in protest, but the bill was passed all the same.

It is not surprising that the agitation over Bill 63 stirred deep feelings on both sides. There was hostility on the part of those nationalists who believed that

Quebec's French future and identity were threatened, and who drew sustenance from a study for the Royal Commission on Bilingualism and Biculturalism that showed French-speaking Quebeckers clinging to the bottom of the economic ladder and English-speaking Quebeckers clustering near the top. The English-speaking Quebeckers reacted with alarm at the threat to rights and institutions they had always enjoyed and for which, as private citizens and as taxpayers, they had paid.

A provincial election was due in 1970. In January, the Liberal party found itself a new leader. The principal candidates were Claude Wagner, attorney general under the old Lesage government, Pierre Laporte, the former minister of municipal affairs, and Robert Bourassa, a young economist elected for the first time to the assembly in 1966. There might have been a fourth candidate, Jean Marchand, the Minister of Regional Economic Expansion in Ottawa, but Trudeau dissuaded his Quebec lieutenant from running. He did not prevent him from intervening in the Liberal convention, however, and it was with Marchand's strong support that Bourassa became Liberal leader.

Bourassa immediately led his party in the Quebec general election, called for April 29. The Liberals stressed two themes in their campaign. In French-language ridings, they stressed economic development and the economic dangers of separatism; in English-language ridings they had no difficulty using the threat of separatism pure and simple. Immigrant groups, remembering the separatist Parti Québécois's fervent opposition to Bill 63, had no difficulty in voting against separatism. In the election, the Liberals received 45 per cent of the vote and seventy-two seats; the Parti Québécois got 24 per cent of the vote and seven seats.

The Bourassa government was markedly different from its predecessors in style, and, some might argue, in content as well. The new premier fervently believed in keeping in close touch with the grass roots of his party; the telephone was his talisman, carrying out appeals for help and information at all hours and bringing in return advice and warnings. Through the grass roots, and the Liberals' fund-raisers, Bourassa kept close contact with the Ottawa Liberals – this despite the official and public distance maintained between the two parties.

Relations between the federal and provincial Liberals were never simple or easy. It was generally true that Liberals federally were Liberals provincially, and the two parties had a common anti-separatist ideology which drew them closer together. But Bourassa, gawky, young, and inexperienced, cut an unimpressive figure beside the dashing Trudeau; it was easy for opposition propagandists to claim that Ottawa was dominating Quebec through its novice premier.

This became painfully apparent during and after the October Crisis in the autumn of 1970. To all intents and purposes, the federal and Quebec governments stood shoulder to shoulder against terrorism and against extra-constitutional attempts to exploit the crisis in the interests of a Quebec united against Ottawa. But it was suspected that during the crisis Trudeau had operated at long range, imposing his will on a confused and terrified Bourassa through his personal emissary in Quebec City, Marc Lalonde. This image is doubtless exaggerated, but the October Crisis blurred so many images, and this is merely one.

32

The October Crisis and After

Like William Kilbourn, many Canadians considered their country to be 'The Peaceable Kingdom.' There had been little political violence in Canada in the twentieth century. Moreover, Canada was also at peace externally, a happy contrast to its belligerent southern neighbour, then bogged down in the Vietnam war. With as its philosopher-prime minister a man who was known to disapprove of the military (which had just been drastically reduced in size), this state of affairs in Canada seemed likely to continue.

The military, certainly, were discontented, but their opinions counted for little. They found they had new roles to play: in the autumn of 1969, when the police of Montreal went out on strike, the army was called in by the civil authorities to restore order after a night of rioting. In the fall of 1969, however, the Montreal authorities had something else on their minds: terrorism. The cause of an independent Quebec had not yet flourished at the polls, and some of its sympathizers, especially those on the extreme left, thought it was time to hurry things along with a few well-placed bombs. In their view the illegitimate capitalist state was by its very existence in an attitude of war with its subjects. Capitalism could be purged only by violence and, in Montreal, with its highly visible and generally prosperous English-speaking minority, anti-capitalism could easily blend with anti-colonialism. National liberation struggles overseas, especially in Algeria, Bolivia, and Cuba, furnished ready-made models of heroic struggle, and the rest was easy: thefts from armouries, construction sites, or gun stores provided the arsenal of the revolution.

Omelettes are not made without breaking eggs, according to the jargon of the period, and revolutions are not won without at least some incidental deaths: such violence could be justified afterward in press releases, or more often shrugged off. The press was eager to publicize it, and horror was always good copy, so that the terrorists of the Front de libération de Québec (or FLQ) could always be assured of an instant audience. The Front was a self-perpetuating entity. Current evidence suggests that it never had much of a formal organization; rather, small groups of individuals appropriated the title from time to time, thereby preserving the illusion of a continuing, hydra-headed conspiracy.

It was such a conspiracy that the municipal authorities of Montreal depicted in testimony in Ottawa. But their testimony had little effect. Ordinary police procedures turned up terrorists from time to time, and these men were periodically brought before the courts and sent off to the penitentiary. Their crimes, though serious, did not demand more than the ordinary powers of justice for their suppression. It was true that terrorism was growing more frequent: in November and December 1969 there were five separate bombing incidents in Montreal. In June 1970, a plot to kidnap the Israeli consul in Montreal was uncovered. The well-publicized arrests of two revolutionary theorists, Pierre Vallières and Charles Gagnon, contributed to the general excitement. And in August 1970 there was a new twist: FLQ terrorists, training with the Palestinian terrorists, announced that they would soon renew their struggle, using selective assassination as a weapon.

When, on October 5, 1970, the British trade commissioner in Montreal, James Cross, was abducted from his home, terrorism was very much in the air. Before long a press release arrived from the FLQ announcing its terms for the release, unharmed, of Cross. They included a ransom ('voluntary tax') of $500,000 in gold ingots, the release of a list of 'political prisoners' then serving time for their crimes, re-employment of some former post office drivers in Montreal, no police pursuit, free transport out of the country, and the reading of the FLQ manifesto and all subsequent communiqués on radio and television.

The manifesto, a hysterical and abusive potpourri of grievances combined with a distorted view of history, attempted to justify FLQ actions in terms of the rhetoric of colonial revolution and national struggle. In tone and substance it was not greatly different from thousands of bygone leaflets that had passed unhindered from the printing press into the wastebasket. But this time it was different: the FLQ had a hostage, and the price for his life was national attention.

The ultimate responsibility for a diplomat's safety rests squarely in the hands of the federal government. But police power is, for the most part, a local matter, and in this case responsibility lay with the city of Montreal and the Quebec provincial police. There were anxious consultations among the various levels of government as to the proper policy to be adopted, but it is impossible, even now, to say just what proposals were made during these discussions. What is certain is the result: a decision to bargain with the FLQ by agreeing to comply with some of its less dangerous demands. As the terrorists had demanded, the FLQ manifesto was published and broadcast, safe passage was guaranteed for the kidnappers, and the attorney general of Quebec promised that he would support parole for some of the 'political prisoners.'

The partial surrender by the constituted authorities in Ottawa and in Quebec was well intentioned: if Cross's life could be saved, then some concessions, even in the face of terror, were worthwhile. But concessions enforced at the barrel of a gun may tend to give the impression that more can be extracted if the price is raised; and so, while the first kidnapping cell of the FLQ continued to hold on to Cross, another self-constituted group, describing itself as the 'Chenier financial cell,' swept up Quebec's Minister of Labour, Pierre Laporte, as he played ball with his children outside his suburban house on October 10.

Although the Cross kidnapping was taken seriously, the authorities remained calm; but the abduction of Laporte threw many in the Quebec government into a state of panic. Ministers flew their families out of the province: the less timid to Ottawa; others as far as New York. Pierre Laporte was the second minister in the Quebec government; he had been a strong contender for the Liberal leadership only nine months before. Laporte's disappearance affected the innermost circles of Quebec politics.

Events moved quickly to a crisis. As the police pursued the search for Cross and Laporte, the provincial government dithered over what to do. It was speculated that a coalition government might be formed comprising all the parties in a kind of national union in order to find a way out of the crisis. Bourassa himself did not engender sufficient confidence, and it was darkly suspected that he would cave in to hardline pressure from Trudeau. A hard line, in the eyes of many influential Québécois, would mean a refusal to comply with some, at least, of the terrorists' demands, such as the release of 'political prisoners.' The lives of two men were concrete: the legitimacy and authority of the state were abstract. Many intellectuals and journalists and some politicians plumped for the concrete, but the situation is by no means as clear-cut as these individuals then seem to have believed it to be. Terrorism poses both a theoretical and a practical problem to those who confront it (naturally it poses no problem at all to those who sympathize with or support it). As one recent student of the phenomenon of terrorism has argued, 'It is an important, sometimes over-riding, terrorist aim to undermine the political will, confidence and morale of liberal governments and citizens so that they are made more vulnerable to political and social collapse.'[1] More practically, one terrorist act, if one is to judge by experience abroad, will most likely lead to another. Events in Brazil in the same year, 1970, furnish an illustration: in September 1969 terrorists seized the American ambassador. The price for his release was fifteen prisoners. The German ambassador's turn came in June 1970: his ransom was forty prisoners. The Swiss ambassador followed in December 1970: his release was extorted at the cost of seventy prisoners. And, once undertaken, the tactic of conceding terrorist demands takes on a crazed logic of its own: what was given for one must be given for the next.

---

1 Paul Wilkinson, *Terrorism and the Liberal State* (London: Macmillan 1977), 80.

As we know, some of these considerations were in the minds of Canada's federal and provincial governments as they contemplated the difficult question of what to do. Evidence of confusion and demoralization was painfully apparent in the days after the Laporte kidnapping, when it was argued that only a new government (even though the democratically elected government of Quebec was only six months old) could have the authority and legitimacy to deal with the real crisis.

What could that crisis be? In the eyes of many observers, it was the rigid and inflexible attitude that Ottawa was said to be taking in refusing to comtemplate any further concession to the terrorists' demands: for any further concession, as Trudeau and his ministers knew, meant the release, before their sentences were served, of many or all of the 'political prisoners' then held in federal penitentiaries. Bourassa, on the other hand, was said to be inclined to a softer line (although some evidence that has appeared since contradicts this). In order to 'strengthen' Bourassa's hand, therefore, sixteen prominent Quebec personalities, including various labour and business leaders, Claude Ryan, and René Lévesque, urged Bourassa to persevere 'despite and against all obstruction from outside Quebec' in order to negotiate the 'exchange of the two hostages for the political prisoners.' The use of the term 'political prisoners' without quotation marks surprised some, even when Ryan justified it as a 'question of fact and not law,' in itself a curious phrase. The implication that it was up to Quebec to solve its own problems, and that interference from 'outside' (meaning the rest of Canada) was illegitimate, was familiar enough in the separatist camp, but alarming when it came from those not already committed to Quebec's independence.

That same day, October 14, less respectable elements in Quebec society were taking action designed to support the FLQ. The lawyer negotiating on behalf of the terrorists urged a meeting of Université de Montréal students to boycott classes; the boycott began the next day. At another Montreal college, students occupied their rector's office, proclaiming that they would stay there 'until the victory of the FLQ.' That evening, a rally was held in Montreal's Paul Sauvé arena, with an audience of three thousand chanting 'FLQ ... FLQ ... FLQ.' Michel Chartrand, a Montreal labour leader, told the audience that the FLQ was going from strength to strength. 'There is no doubt,' he said, 'that there are infinitely more people now in accord with them, who understand and sympathize with the objectives of the FLQ than there were in 1963 and 1966.' Chartrand was doubtless right. Some of those who, in 1963, condemned the first bombings now remained uneasily silent, either convinced that it was not their fight, or frightened to speak out. One Montrealer who did speak out while in Toronto was reproached by his fearful family when he came home: it was dangerous, they explained, to draw attention to oneself.

By Thursday, October 15, a climax was approaching. That evening, a curious conversation took place between the premier of Quebec and a PQ member of the assembly. 'What do you want me to do?' Bourassa asked. 'You must immediately form a coalition government,' the Péquiste replied. He urged Bourassa to get rid of the more hesitant members of his cabinet and replace them with members of the opposition and other public bodies, including the trade unions. 'That coalition government will oppose Ottawa and negotiate with the FLQ. We haven't a minute to lose. It's your last chance.' Bourassa, however, refused. It was, he said, already too late.

As the two men spoke, the Canadian army was taking up positions around Montreal, Quebec City, and Ottawa. At the invitation of the government of Quebec, the troops had come to reinforce the hard-pressed police. It was the first intimation that the general public had had of the gravity of the crisis, and of the two governments' determination to resist further concessions to terrorist pressures. More was to come. At three o'clock on the morning of Friday, October 16, the federal government invoked the War Measures Act, declaring that an 'apprehended insurrection' existed in Quebec and giving the police extraordinary powers of arrest and detention against anyone suspected of belonging to, or sympathizing with, the FLQ.

That morning the police began a series of raids across Quebec, rounding up anyone suspected of belonging to the FLQ. The size of the round-up seems to have surprised its authors, the federal cabinet, who had seen a list of only some seventy suspects. In sum, some 436 persons were arrested and detained under the authority of the War Measures Act during the whole time of the crisis. The selection of whom to arrest seems to have been left in the hands of the police, and the police did not always proceed with due regard for reasonable evidence. In one notorious case, they entered the home of the federal Secretary of State, Gérard Pelletier, in search of a different Gérard Pelletier. Their source of information in this case seems to have been the telephone book.

The immediate effect of the imposition of the War Measures Act was the silencing of the vocal support for the FLQ which had been so much in evidence in the previous weeks. Of those arrested, 62 were eventually brought to trial, and 20 were convicted. The War Measures Act could not save Laporte or Cross, although it did allow the police to divert more resources to the pursuit of their kidnappers. The FLQ group holding Laporte murdered their helpless victim on Saturday, October 17 ('executed' is the revolutionary cant they employed), and left his body in the trunk of a car to be picked up.

Cross was eventually found and released, early in December. His captors traded the British diplomat's life for their own safe passage out of the country, to Cuba, where they lived, more or less discontentedly, for several years. They later moved to France, which admitted them as 'political refugees.' Eventually some returned to Canada, where they were tried, convicted, and, in view of their stated repentance for past misdeeds, given light sentences. The murderers of Laporte were uncovered in the corner of a country basement later the same month. They too were tried and convicted; because of the gravity of their offence, they received heavier sentences; some are still in jail, although sympathizers periodically demand their release.

Most of the terrorists' demands were not achieved. No 'political prisoners' won their freedom. Despite the raucous rhetoric that surrounded the first stages of the kidnapping crisis, the seizure of the two victims did not touch off revolutionary festivities in the streets of Montreal. Nor was the October Crisis the first of many, as those who believed in the existence of revolutionary conditions in 'oppressed Quebec' had predicted. Instead, there was a decline and then a cessation of terrorist activity. That may have been coincidence, or it may have derived from the vigorous employment of the power of the state to confront and crush terrorism. Once the stakes were raised in the game of revolutionary theatre, once the governments made plain that those who played at parlour revolution faced real and immediate sanctions, the enthusiasm for a day of the barricades, FLQ style, noticeably diminished.

The bases of the government's reasoning were explained in a speech by Prime Minister Trudeau on the night of Friday, October 16. 'Should governments give in to this crude blackmail,' Trudeau informed his television audience, 'we would be facing the breakdown of the legal system, and its replacement by the law of the jungle. ... Freedom and personal security are safeguarded by laws; those laws must be respected in order to be effective.' But under the threat of terrorism, extraordinary dangers required extraordinary measures: 'The criminal law as it stands is simply not adequate to deal with systematic terrorism,' – a discovery which other countries besides Canada have made. Finally, Trudeau emphasized, 'This government is not acting out of fear. It is acting to prevent fear from spreading. ... It is acting to make clear to kidnappers and revolutionaries and assassins that in this country laws are made and changed by the elected representatives of all Canadians – not by a handful of self-selected dictators....'

Trudeau's actions provoked much discussion at the time, and much condemnation since. Some alleged that the government had acted on the basis of inadequate information; it had panicked and used a sledgehammer to squash a gnat. Others suggested that the government knew well what it was doing: and that was to crush separatism, legal and democratic, under the guise of suppressing an illegal revolutionary conspiracy. Still others decried the use of troops to protect public figures and public buildings during the crisis, and complained loudly when Trudeau replied that he would do anything that was necessary to protect constituted authority in Canada. Trudeau was short with the last variety of questioner. 'Yes,' he said, 'well there are a lot of bleeding hearts around who just don't like to see people with helmets and guns. All I can say is, go on and bleed, but it is more important to keep law and order in the society than to be worried about weak-kneed people.'

The first two objections merit serious consideration. In answer to the first complaint, that the government acted hastily and panicked, it is possible to observe that governments are neither omniscient nor omnipotent. The information that the government had to hand indicated that the arms and dynamite thefts of the previous couple of years were largely unaccounted for; that the wild threats of the revolutionaries themselves now had to be taken more seriously than before; and that the will to resist revolutionary violence in Quebec was demonstrably weakening. There was a reasonable basis for all these observations, and it is not surprising that the federal government acted as it did to shore up and restore the political will to resist violence in Quebec.

As for the objection that Trudeau was acting to squash separatism and its most prominent proponents, the Parti Québécois, we have the statements of both the Prime Minister and one of his supporters, Bryce Mackasey, during the crisis. On October 17, Mackasey stressed to the House of Commons that the Parti Québécois was 'a legitimate, political party. It wants to bring an end to this country through democratic means, but that is the privilege of that party.' Trudeau himself made the same point in November to an interviewer. Those who claim that Trudeau was acting to discredit the PQ must fly in the face of explicit public statements by Trudeau and his ministers.

The War Measures Act crisis produced one of the highest favourable ratings in public opinion that any Canadian government has ever achieved. Eighty-seven per cent of Canadians, with no significant variation between English and French, signified their approval of the government's course. Even so, the government's reputation has suffered because of its actions. The benefits have been hard to seize upon, the defects and injustices (and there were many in the way the police applied their powers) easy to criticize. In retrospect it is difficult to understand what else, legally and politically, could have been done. The government was bound to uphold the law and its application. It would have been ultimately foolish to concede much of the terrorist program, and it may have been unwise to concede any. Politically, it is the government's duty to try to manage conditions, including public opinion, so that danger to the fabric of the Canadian state is avoided or repaired. That it also seems to have done, averting the possibility of a coalition government in Quebec City, and uniting with, rather than opposing, the government of Quebec to put down manifestations of support for revolution and terror. In this it acted wisely and properly.

Nevertheless, the crisis caused Trudeau to lose respect for Bourassa. There were other factors which later exaggerated the differences between Ottawa and Quebec: Bourassa's inability to impose an agreement on his cabinet and party over the Victoria Charter; the excursions of some Quebec ministers into federal jurisdiction; and the Bourassa government's attempts to compromise with the nationalists over language policy. Trudeau responded publicly and intemperately, which must have further diminished the esteem in which Bourassa was held inside Quebec.

The most apparent divergence between the federal Liberals and those of Quebec took place over the Bourassa government's Bill 22, introduced into the legislature in May 1974. Bill 22 was designed to affect both the economic life and the language of education of the province: it enacted incentives for firms to expand the use of French in their daily operations ('francization') and in their dealings with customers; but it also abolished the freedom of parental choice that Bill 63 had guaranteed. In future, admission to English-language schools was conditional on whether one's maternal language was English, or on a language test administered to determine if a toddler really had a sufficient knowledge of English to slip through the loopholes of the bill. In a final fillip, French was made the sole official language of Quebec.

As we have suggested previously, the enactment of Bill 22 was probably unnecessary to protect the French character of Quebec or of Montreal, given the steady emigration of English Quebeckers from the province and the probability that there would be fewer immigrants in the seventies and eighties than in the fifties and sixties. It was, moreover, not only the English who were leaving. Of those immigrants who came to Quebec and assimilated to the English community only a minority chose to remain indefinitely. The rest packed their bags and, like their native-born fellow citizens, departed. But politically Bill 22 failed to appease the hysteria expressed in Quebec nationalist circles, as the following editorial on the subject from *Le Jour*, Montreal's separatist daily, made plain: 'A whole people is in the process of being dispossessed of its collective rights by an immigration that is massively anglophone. It has the right to know what is happening.'[2] Moreover, the bill made explicit what many English Quebeckers had long feared: their government intended to rework the context of their lives, from the language spoken in the workplace down to the signs on shops (these were, after a certain delay, to become bilingual, at least in English-speaking areas). They were unhappy about it, and they let the premier and the prime minister know about it. Across the country there were demands that Bill 22 be disallowed, or at least reviewed by the Supreme Court to determine its constitutionality.

Trudeau steered a careful path among the linguistic minefields. He did not like Bill 22, but explained that his government could not disallow a law simply because it was foolish or unjust. That would have depopulated the provincial statute books. Perhaps he sensed that Bill 22, for all its fallacies, was indeed better than any alternative that the separatists could dream up; and, as time would show, he was right.

2 Un peuple entier est en voie d'être dépossédé de ses droits collectifs par une immigration massivement anglophone. Il a le droit de le savoir.

If Bourassa's language policy embarrassed the federal government, events in the federal sphere helped to undermine the position of the provincial Liberals. The occasion was the attempt by the federal government to expand the use of French in air traffic control – to put, as the saying went, 'français dans l'air,' by making several airports in Quebec bilingual. The proponents of French pointed out that 90 per cent of controllers in Quebec had French as their mother tongue, and that most Quebec pilots were French. The Canadian Airline Pilots Association (CALPA) was distressed at the possibility that incoming aircraft, using and understanding only English, might be endangered by French communications between air traffic control and local air traffic. There was no reconciling the two points of view; the pilots went on strike in June 1976 over the issue of 'air safety.' Opinion in English Canada overwhelmingly backed them and, although there was no particular danger in airports outside of Quebec, pilots of foreign airlines professed to believe that any intrusion into Canadian airspace endangered the safety of their passengers. 'This debate,' Richard Gwyn wrote in the *Toronto Star*, 'as everyone knows full well, isn't over safety but over bilingualism,' which most English Canadians disliked, as the massive English-Canadian support for the pilots demonstrated. French Canadians took notice.

Although the air traffic control dispute was terminated by an agreement by the federal government to study the whole matter at greater length, its repercussions undoubtedly lasted far beyond the immediate inconvenience to passengers and public that the strike had caused. Bourassa later singled out the air traffic control dispute as an important factor in his party's defeat in the provincial election of November 15, 1976.

The other reasons were common enough: economic unrest, inflation, Bill 22, and 'pseudo-scandals' promoted by the opposition Parti Québécois. It is difficult not to sympathize with Mr Bourassa, on this last count at least. 'Name one case,' he challenged Lévesque in a televised debate. Lévesque, evidently surprised by the question, referred only to 'generalized cancer' in his reply. But more Quebeckers by then preferred Lévesque's version of recent history to Bourassa's.

Lévesque had learned some valuable lessons in his years in opposition. Independence, immediate separation from Canada, perturbed the electorate. As long as independence remained the party's principal stock-in-trade, the PQ's chances of electoral success were doubtful. But if independence were defused, put, so to speak, in cold storage, the Bourassa government was sufficiently unpopular to be defeated.

The solution was proposed by Claude Morin, who had resigned from the civil service in 1971 and who now publicly proclaimed his adherence to the separatist cause. Morin's experience in federal-provincial relations had persuaded him of the efficacy of gradualism: if the electorate were pushed, a little at a time, to accept that

The Parti Québécois is elected in Quebec (Aislin, 1976). Reproduced with the permission of Aislin: *The Montreal Gazette*

the PQ could govern, it might then be prepared to swallow the PQ's independence option. Morin's reasoning was accepted by the party. Henceforth, independence would be on the instalment plan: first a PQ government, and then, somewhere down the road, a referendum on its special nostrum, souveraineté-association.

The Quebec electorate approved. On November 16, an emotional Lévesque saw his party swept to victory after victory as Liberal bastions fell one after another. Even Bourassa was defeated. The English-language voters did not, it is true, choose the PQ, but they split their votes between the Liberals and a revived Union Nationale. 'The divided anglophone vote,' Bourassa later admitted, 'allowed dozens of PQ candidates to capture their respective ridings.' Without accepting that 'dozens' of seats changed hands according to the whim of the anglophones, it is probably true that the Liberal vote (33.8 per cent and twenty-six seats) would have been more impressive in an election focused more clearly on separatism. Lévesque's 41.4 per cent garnered a majority government of seventy-one seats.

English Canadians were startled. Trudeau had recently assured the country that separatism was dead; now it was alive and well and governing Canada's second-largest province. Observers, including the prime minister, drew comfort from the fact that the real battle was just beginning. This would be the battle of the referendum, now inevitable. In a partial response, Trudeau dredged up the constitution and appointed a national unity task force. His constitutional proposals, revealed with great fanfare in the summer of 1978, were a badly written and worse-conceived potpourri of Senate reform and Supreme Court fiddlings. They fell with a dull thud before an astonished and somewhat bemused populace. The national unity task force perambulated the country after the fashion of its bilingualism and biculturalism predecessor. After much labour and droning, it emitted a report that repeated most of the myths about Canadian history dearly beloved of Quebec nationalists; in token of apology for past injustices (112 years of it) it tendered a decentralized constitution.

The Canadian academic community also rushed to the barricades, but whether to build them up or tear them down no one could be certain. Universities vied with one another in holding national unity rituals: York held a conference, so Toronto, Queen's, even Harvard must hold theirs too; one after another their products marched from the printed presses to accumulate unread on groaning academic shelves. The *Canadian Forum*, the matriarch of left-wing ferment, surprised its readers by publishing the manifesto of a Committee for a New Constitution. This new proposal looked to decentralization and two nations for Canada's (or Canada-Quebec's) salvation. It stopped just short of promoting separatism as a good, desirable in and for itself.

While the rest of Canada talked and bickered, Quebec acted. The Lévesque government sponsored labour reforms, electoral reforms, and encouraged Crown corporations. It also, naturally, passed a law concerning referenda. But its most notorious enactment, in the eyes of the rest of Canada, was its language legislation. The PQ had promised to revise, reform, and improve Bourassa's Bill 22. So it did – in nationalist eyes. In the new version, children of English-speaking parents

were automatically guaranteed a place in English schools for themselves so long as
the parents had been educated in Quebec. Given the rate of emigration of English-
speaking natives of Quebec, this would not be a difficult promise to fulfil. The
younger sisters and brothers of children already enrolled in English-language
schools were also guaranteed an English education. But there the concessions ended.
The children of all immigrants to Quebec, including immigrants from other Canadian provinces, were to attend French-language schools. A partial exemption, for
three years or less, was accorded the children of temporary residents in Quebec.

The language of instruction in the schools was, however, only a part (although an
important one) of the Lévesque government's linguistic policy. That policy was
explained in a white paper issued in March 1977, and stated in legal terms by the
PQ's Bill 1 (later, because of a procedural problem, renamed Bill 101). The bill
started off unequivocally by defining Quebec and Quebeckers as French. French
members of Quebec society enjoyed rights – rights which now had the force of law
behind them; others, including the long-established English community, were
treated as 'exceptions.' They would, nevertheless, have to conform to the PQ's legislation, institute programs of 'francization' in their businesses, rewrite their signs,
and make their municipalities (in some of which the English are still a majority)
conform to the dictates of a law which proclaimed French to be the only legal
medium of public affairs.

The Office de la Langue Française was set up to enforce the new law, and to
devise detailed regulations to speed the task on its way. The white paper described
the widespread appearance of English in Montreal as 'difficult and embarrassing.'
English signs which might offend the public were to be expunged, although signs
which had already been changed to conform with the previous language law were
given a brief stay of execution. Thus, signs on private businesses in English language areas were henceforth to be in French only; internal signs, for example in
English-language bookstores, were also to be in French. One zealous bureaucrat at
one point decided that English-language churches should conform as well and
translate their liturgy and hymnals into French, but a last-minute reprieve was
permitted in this case. The language police were ever vigilant, however. When a
contraband shipment of Dunkin' Donuts bags was uncovered they were immediately subjected to the full rigour of the law – and burned.

It would be comforting to be able to dismiss Bill 101 and its excesses as an
exercise in comic opera bureaucracy straight out of the *Inspector General* but both its
principle and practice have disturbed many. As Claude Ryan pointed out in *Le
Devoir* at the time of Bill 101's first appearance, it is 'rigid, dogmatic and authoritarian,' in keeping with the 'narrow and chauvinistic brand of nationalism' of the bill's
authors. In protecting the language of the majority against improbable terrors, the
Parti Québécois has seen fit to negate the rights of a minority of close to one

million persons, to treat them almost as non-citizens, and their language as a non-entity. In so doing it has violated basic individual rights and has appealed for the first time to the power of the state to coerce private citizens with respect to the language they speak in their private, business lives. That anglophone provinces had also once behaved badly is certainly true but this is, of course, no excuse. In any case, the English-language provinces stopped short of prohibitions on signs and shops.

Many English-speaking citizens of Quebec have responded by voting with their feet. In the last half of 1977 some 50,000 people left Quebec, compared to the 33,000 who left in the corresponding part of 1976 and the 28,000 during the last six months of 1975. Many companies have also left, with the Sun Life Insurance Company as the flagship of the departing fleet.

The effect will certainly be to enhance the French character of Quebec, although at the expense of some hundreds of thousands of the province's well-educated and productive citizens. The large French-speaking population will, for the most part, be spared the strain of bilingualism (although an economic analysis might tell us that knowledge of two languages is a definite economic advantage), and the leaders of Quebec will no longer be embarrassed by anglophone signs as they contemplate the uniquely French character of their diminished province.

In the long run, graduates of Quebec universities and technical colleges will take some of the places of the departing English; as more of these become available (either through migration or through economic growth) the French character of workforce and workplace will be reinforced. There may well be an inflow of skilled and educated francophones from other provinces. These processes will proceed at a somewhat faster pace and with greater disruption than the simple effluxion of time would have brought about. But if the language measures do prove to be the last gasp of nationalist fervour in Quebec, the provincial economy will probably evolve, in the long run, much as if nothing had been done.

There have been economic and social elements of the emerging Quebec nationalism whose impact on economic growth might prove very unattractive. The nationalization of the asbestos industry as an act of linguistic and cultural revenge may prove to be one of these, as may the determination to bring Crédit Foncier Franco-canadien, long controlled by Paris interests, under Québécois control. On the labour front, mobility of construction workers was restricted to those actually living in the province of Quebec, provoking a dispute with the neighbouring province of Ontario. Although it was pointed out that Quebec workers probably derived more benefit from working in Ontario than Ontario workers did from working in Quebec, this was a minor consideration for the government of Quebec, which was, from an ideological standpoint, uninterested in the mobility of labour. Increasingly, such things appeared to be straws in the wind.

The political fortunes of the Lévesque government had remarkably little effect on the strictly political destinies of the Trudeau regime. Trudeau's support in Quebec remained relatively constant throughout the 1972 and 1974 elections, and an attempt to persuade Quebeckers to vote Social Credit in the 1979 election as a protest against federalism fizzled. In the 1980 election the federal Liberals even improved on past performance, taking every seat but one in Quebec and swamping the opposition in the popular vote.

As federal politics eddied back and forth the provincial Liberals took the time to reconstruct their party under a new leader, Claude Ryan. Ryan's selection provoked misgivings among many. He was anything but a doctrinaire Liberal, and had on many occasions in the past opposed the party's federal and provincial policies. His often dry oratorical style provoked misgivings among the electorally-minded. But Ryan was not without his supporters, as by-elections proved. Nor was he without a program of his own.

What Ryan and Lévesque stood for became clearer as the Parti Québécois' promised referendum approached. At the beginning of November 1979 the Quebec government published a White Paper on the referendum in which it outlined its proposed scheme of 'sovereignty-association.' Grandiloquent, tendentious, and emotional, the White Paper chronicled past wrongs to make current points. The history sometimes seemed to be that of another country. Omitting those parts of Quebec history that might have demonstrated co-operation, agreement or mutual advantage between French and English, the White Paper selected events that illus- trated opposition and discord. In 1914, the White Paper inaccurately declared, 'despite firm and virtually unanimous opposition [from Quebec], Canada entered the war.' The National Policy of 1879, which enshrined protection of industry as a fundamental Canadian policy, appeared to the authors of the White Paper to have benefitted Ontario alone. As Senator Maurice Lamontagne, a Liberal critic, noted, the tariff policy of the central government had probably favoured Quebec more than Ontario – and continues to do so. The Quebec government also detected a 'formid- able centralizing attack' on the provinces by Ottawa since the war, one which had intensified in recent years. These misreadings of history were, of course, mere transparent flourishes which underlined the paper's central appeal, in which Quebec was asked 'to choose the only road that can open up the horizon and guarantee us a free, proud and adult national existence'; in other words, sovereignty.

Once sovereignty was achieved, there would be association. The White Paper proposed four Quebec-Canada agencies: a community council, a commission of experts, a court of justice, and a monetary authority. The first of these would be chaired alternately by Quebec and Canadian representatives and Quebec and Canada would possess 'fundamental legal equality.' In some cases these agencies could be 'modifications' of existing institutions such as the Bank of Canada. In all cases the 'adjustments' were made to seem the essence of sweet reasonableness. 'Monetary union' and 'free circulation' of people and goods (already impaired under existing federal arrangements) would remain. For Quebec, sovereignty 'will have a legal impact on the power to make laws and to levy taxes, on territorial integrity, on citizenship and minorities, on the courts and various other institutions, and on the relations of Quebec with other countries.' An adult national existence perhaps, but one might suggest that in this plan the adolescent was leaving home with the keys to father's house and mother's Mastercharge.

That, of course, was the impression that the White Paper sought to convey to a worried and divided Quebec electorate. Knowing that the electorate, even after four years of Parti Québécois rule, would not support independence pure and simple, the Lévesque cabinet sought to reassure its potential voters. There would be no sovereignty without association. Regardless of the frequently voiced warnings of the other nine premiers, Lévesque told an audience, the other provinces would come round – 'on their knees' – in the face of popular mandate for sovereignty-association. Parti Québécois supporters elsewhere in Canada, accepting the inevitability and the righteousness of Lévesque's position, urged their fellow Canadians to 'respect Quebec's right to self-determination' by accepting sovereignty-association.

Most English Canadians, however, looked to Claude Ryan for an alternate vision of the constitutional future. On January 9, 1980, Ryan presented his proposals for 'A New Canadian Federation.' The document was clearly the product of Ryan's logical, intense mind. More wooden and less tendentious than the Lévesque White Paper, the Ryan proposals, unfortunately dubbed the 'beige paper,' hailed the achievements of Canadian federation while demanding fundamental changes in its structure. Central to the constitutional reform was a Federal Council which would serve as a provincially based watchdog over a new, decentralized constitutional structure and numerous government appointments. The importance of preserving and expanding language rights across Canada and of correcting regional disparities was recognized. Nationalist yet Canadian, the 'beige paper' affirmed the Liberals' belief that they were 'a part of the wave of cultural, economic, social and political affirmation which is presently sweeping over Quebec.' Liberals refused, the paper continued, 'to choose between Quebec and Canada, as if one should necessarily exclude the other. On the contrary we choose Quebec AND Canada because each needs the other to fulfill itself.'

To anglophones the rhetoric of this paper was more appealing than its substance. The response to it was tepid. Ontario's premier, William Davis, hesitated to reply and was vague when he finally did. Press comment often ignored the details while lauding Ryan's undeniable commitment to Canada. Péquiste strategist Claude Morin called Ryan's plans a 'mixed up federalism that could lead us to another 40 years of continuing discussion with the rest of Canada.' More disturbing was the political scientist Léon Dion's extended series in *Le Devoir* which echoed Morin's doubts that English Canada would accept much while arguing that the paper would not appeal to francophones. Better no statement, Dion argued, than the over-complex paper of January. For the referendum the 'beige paper' was a clumsy weapon, too heavy to tote into battle, and too scattered in its aim. Ryan's party, reinvigorated through an intensive membership campaign, nevertheless endorsed it unanimously at a convention in late February. As the referendum neared, the debate about Quebec's and Canada's future began. The two papers were but the first step; later the route would become more treacherous for both parties.

At first, however, the Lévesque government seemed to have events running its way. The referendum question was announced and debated in the Quebec National Assembly in March. The question was relatively lengthy:

The Government of Québec has made public its proposal to negotiate a new agreement with the rest of Canada, based on the equality of nations;

this agreement would enable Québec to acquire the exclusive power to make its laws, levy its taxes and establish relations abroad – in other words, sovereignty – and at the same time, to maintain with Canada an economic association including a common currency;

no change in political status resulting from these negotiations will be effected without approval from the people through another referendum;

on these terms, do you give the Government of Québec the mandate to negotiate the proposed agreement between Québec and Canada?

The strategy behind the referendum question was the same that had led to the Parti Québécois' victory in the 1976 election. The electorate was not asked to approve immediate independence or effective change of any sort; but its approval would be a tangible step on the way. Party orators in the National Assembly left their television audience in little doubt of the true symbolism of the referendum. A 'oui' answer to the government's question would be positive, prideful, nationalistic, and assertive. Reading, for the most part, texts prepared for them by others, Lévesque's troops scored a brilliant theatrical success. By contrast, Ryan's deputies, reading speeches they had written for themselves (at their leader's insistence), seemed hesitant, negative, and parochial.

Relying on the momentum of the legislative debate, Lévesque chose an early date for the referendum: May 20. 'Oui' and 'non' committees were established, as required by the referendum law, under Lévesque's and Ryan's respective direction. Lévesque set off on a quasi-sacramental tour of the province, dispensing certificates identifying their proud holders as original supporters of Quebec nationhood. Ryan's campaign meanwhile failed to catch fire in the eyes of the media. The result, until the first public opinion poll, seemed a foregone conclusion.

Yet Lévesque's campaign showed from the beginning some curious features. Although the referendum question itself was clearly based on negotiations for 'sovereignty,' the premier himself tended to avoid the term. 'It is a question of honour,' Lévesque said, 'to demand equality and the first *déblocage* ... at least, dammit, to say that this is the direction we want to go in.' Unfortunately for the would-be voter, these nuances were not present in the referendum question itself. While denaturing the question, the 'oui' supporters also suggested that only by going to the extreme of supporting the option of sovereignty-association could Quebeckers show English Canadians that they were serious in their complaints about the country. Thus, to vote 'non' was also in some fashion to ratify a continuing subordination of French to English in Canada.

Gradually, as April turned into May, it became apparent that Lévesque's message had convinced only a minority of the voters. The premier had failed, in particular, to convince the 18.5 per cent of Quebec's population who spoke a language other than French that they should entrust their destinies to a separate and independent Quebec governed by the Parti Québécois. The negative anglophone reaction was explained away as the result of brainwashing by a media slavishly responding to the dictates of its 'foreign' (non-Quebec) owners. More probably the English-language and ethnic voters were simply interpreting the evidence that the last three years had placed before them. Bill 101, with its limitations on the use of the English and other languages, was hardly encouraging. Some of the expressions of the Parti Québécois' cultural supporters, who voiced their nationalism in vociferously anti-English ways (as in the play *Medium Saignant* or the poem *Speak White*) were particularly disturbing. Those anglophones who proclaimed a new-found allegiance to the cause of a sovereign Quebec had to work with unpromising material in their efforts to persuade the English community that there was positive benefit in abandoning Canada for a future as a minority in an independent Quebec. More negative benefits were stressed by other Parti Québécois orators, who warned the obdurate English of the danger of alienating the francophone majority, or of cheating it of its rightful prize.

Lévesque and his followers also protested against the periodic interventions from outside Quebec of other provincial premiers and of federal politicians. The latter should confine themselves to minding the store in Ottawa, keeping their noses strictly out of a 'provincial' matter (that this provincial matter involved the very existence of the federal government was held to be of small account). The federal politicians not surprisingly ignored Lévesque's strictures. Marshalled by the Minister of Justice, Jean Chrétien, a parade of federal Liberals and Conservatives descended on Quebec to support the 'non' side. (The New Democrats, citing obscure reasons of their own, abstained). Joe Clark made a particularly effective excursion, but the *pièce de résistance* was the prime minister himself. Trudeau made

Prime Minister Trudeau reads a story to his children (Christmas, 1978), as René Lévesque approaches from the rear (Mallette, 1978). Reproduced with the permission of the *Globe and Mail*, Toronto

three speeches in Quebec in the course of the campaign, speeches which were rated among the best he had ever given. Placing Quebec's leaders side by side, even 'oui' supporters leaned massively toward Trudeau; 53 per cent of Quebeckers (and 46 per cent of francophone Quebeckers) placed Trudeau squarely ahead of Lévesque (22 per cent and 27 per cent, respectively) in preference.

Contrary to initial expectations, pride in Trudeau and attachment to Canada both played a significant role in the campaign. The bread-and-butter issues that the federalists had emphasized in the provincial elections of 1970, 1973, and 1976 no longer worked quite the same magic: polls showed that 57 per cent of francophone voters expected that economic conditions would either improve or remain the same if Quebec won its sovereignty-association. At the same time, 72 per cent of francophone voters (and 96 per cent of anglophones) confessed to a deep attachment to Canada.

Up to the last moment the result appeared uncertain. But within minutes of the polls closing on the evening of May 20 the results became clear. The 'non' side seized a decisive margin and maintained it. At the 'oui' headquarters defeat was finally conceded at 9:30 pm, two and a half hours after the polls closed, and an emotional Lévesque informed his followers that the ball was once again in the federal court. He naturally added that the 'non' campaign had been unfair and reprehensible. Watching Lévesque's ungracious concession from a suburban hockey rink, justice minister Chrétien was overheard to mutter, 'Hypocrite.'

Across Canada there was an audible sigh of relief, tempered by a rush of wind as commentators and provincial politicians proclaimed the result to be a mandate for 'renewed federalism' and not for the 'status quo.' Opinion polls from within Quebec tended to confirm this, though what 'renewed federalism' might mean varied greatly from person to person, and place to place. That French-Canadians expected to become more 'equal' in the result seems indisputable, but whether this could be satisfied by constitutional or more orthodox political means remained unclear. For the moment only one thing was evident. A solid 59.5 per cent of Quebec's voters had rejected 'sovereignty-association.' The 'non' vote was widespread within Quebec, where only one major geographic region voted in the majority for 'oui' (the north shore and Saguenay region), and a majority of French Canadians (52 per cent) had voted 'non.'

In Alberta, Premier Lougheed opined that the people of Quebec had really been concerned about economic issues within confederation, all evidence from public opinion polls notwithstanding.[3] More constructively, Saskatchewan called for immediate federal-provincial negotiations on the renewal of national institutions and the redistribution of federal and provincial powers. In Ontario the Simcoe County Council contributed its mite by condemning the provincial government's efforts to 'push bilingualism on Canada,' by opening a French high school in the area.

There were still, obviously, great difficulties to be overcome. In the stampede of provincial politicians for more power there remained the danger that Quebec's real expectations of Canada might well be forgotten, and equally the danger that the remnant of federal power that might be left behind by provincial rightists would not be enough to organize a real country around. As the historian Terry Copp reflected, shortly before the referendum, 'How can we in the rest of the country have the nerve to ask [Quebeckers] to make an emotional or political identification with Canada when we ourselves are in the process of building a consensus on decentralization and emasculation of the powers of the national Government?'[4]

3   *Globe and Mail*, May 21, 1980.
4   *Globe and Mail*, May 10, 1980.

33

Economic Developments

Quebec's concerns were not only emotional but economic. In the seventies the economic fabric of the country was transformed and the part played by government in that transformation was great. Longer-term trends were naturally at work – rising employment, rising real income, rising living standards, increasing economic involvement with the United States. As we argued in Part I, such developments should not be credited to any particular government nor blamed upon it. But the seventies saw profound changes in many directions that made the whole structure different. Ottawa might seem to be increasingly impotent, but it could still affect the economy greatly. Because these structural changes are so many and so important for shaping the Canada in which we now live, the first and longest section of this chapter is given over to them. The second section treats traditional economic management – taxing, spending, money, and the foreign exchanges. We shall see that in wielding these traditional macroeconomic weapons the Trudeau government was relatively unskilled and increasingly diffident, not to say inept. On the other hand, with respect to gimmickry and structural fiddling – the matter of the first section – it was more imaginative and active than any peacetime administration in Canadian history.

THE CHANGING ECONOMIC STRUCTURE

The 1970s saw various shifts in the balance of economic power. In part because of government subsidy and encouragement, life in the Atlantic region improved relative to that in central Canada. By autumn 1979, indeed, thanks to off-shore discoveries, a wave of gaseous and oily enthusiasm was sweeping Nova Scotia and Newfoundland. But the manufacturing industries of Quebec, based so largely on textiles, clothing, footwear, and other rather uncompetitive consumer goods, faced increasingly vigorous competition from imports. Here political events had some effect and new developments did not arrive with sufficient speed or vigour to help meet new conditions, although in the late seventies the Quebec economy was performing surprisingly well. In so far as the Québécois encouraged an exodus of anglophone firms and businessmen they made matters worse for themselves, at least in the short run. In Ontario, although the Committee for an Independent Canada spoke of 'de-industrialization,' the industrial and financial community continued its rapid development. Regrettably, however, neither in Ontario nor in Quebec did labour productivity rise fast enough to provide the extra consumer goods that people thought they needed and should have. Also, the public was probably confused by the ever-growing wave of protest against 'extortionate' corporation profits; one seldom heard that corporations pulled in less than 10 per cent of GNP, and that, on the average, they paid at least 35 per cent tax on the profits they garnered. Hence, doubtless, some of the pressure for extra money wages – a pressure that many blamed for the inflationary trends of the decade. In western Canada, the Trudeau years began with agricultural impoverishment and with flaccid markets for Alberta oil. But in 1973, when OPEC initiative transformed world oil markets, the West found itself more wealthy than ever before. Wheat farmers, too, did well on world markets for several years in the mid-seventies. Paradoxically, as westerners became more prosperous than other Canadians they seemed to resent eastern Canada more than ever. In the mid- and late-seventies, 'western alienation' was a vogue phrase that was also a fact of life.

Another fact of life in the seventies was concern for 'ecology,' a word whose meaning was elusive but whose effect was clear. Influenced by American models, Canadians talked and chattered and regulated and protested and legislated and delayed in an effort to ensure that things would stay as natural as possible – whatever that might mean. Greenpeace tried to safeguard whales and caribou. Brigitte Bardot was not alone in worrying about the baby seals of the St Lawrence. Much was heard about the fragile Arctic environment. Determined to appear to protect that fragility, Ottawa delayed the approval of pipelines, and created Justice Thomas Berger's inquiry to help find reasons for doing so. Some provinces drew up more stringent regulations regarding pollution and tried to undo the ravages of earlier decades. By 1979 the Great Lakes were noticeably less polluted than in 1968, although at Montreal the St Lawrence was still an open sewer. The federal authorities passed new laws and negotiated with the United States. With respect to airborne pollutants from cars, Ottawa adopted increasingly strict American-style regulations. Indeed, given continental free trade under the Auto Pact, it could hardly avoid doing so. Ontario pressed ahead with the development of nuclear power, and Ottawa did its best to peddle Canada's very own Candu reactor from China to Peru, but by 1981 there was widespread nervousness about nuclear safety and the impact of nuclear installations on the environment. Canada could not escape the informational backwash from Pennsylvania's Three Mile Island incident; and in Ontario especially, politicians ignored advisers' insistence that nuclear energy was safe. In many relatively small respects there was a good deal of tidying up, although never enough to satisfy the real enthusiasts. And as usual there was some sign of overshooting. Good though it might be in the abstract to preserve some Ungavan brook against pollution, prevention may also cost society a good deal, and a cost in one direction implies some sacrifice in another. Is it better to have a pure stream in Ungava, or a great big swimming pool in a crowded Montreal suburb? This question was, if anything, even harder to raise and more difficult to answer in 1981 than in 1968.

A government had to care about the environment; it also had to care about people. Hence, presumably, its imaginative and unwise experiments with the unemployment insurance system that had been designed in 1940 and extended somewhat during the 1950s. In 1968 the scheme covered those who earned less than $7,800 per year, on the sensible ground that the more prosperous were unlikely to become unemployed, and that, if they did, they could look after themselves. The St Laurent and Diefenbaker governments extended the system to cover fishermen and farm workers, and added the 'seasonal benefit' for the winter months when persons had not worked long enough to qualify for ordinary benefit. Benefits came out of a fund, which was theoretically self-sustaining and fed by contributions from employees, employers, and the exchequer. For the new world of the Just Society, where problems of poverty and deprivation were much discussed, the old arrangements seemed too restrictive. The government therefore devised a new scheme, which it announced in 1969. Presenting it to the House, the Minister of Labour spoke in terms that made the government's intention perfectly clear: the plan would not simply insure against unemployment but provide 'individual development coupled with adequate income support.' In other words, unemployment insurance would become part of the welfare system. Everyone would be covered. Benefits would be raised, and they would be easier to get, ranging up to three-quarters of average wages with an initial ceiling of $100 per week. Employees would pay a smaller share of the cost, and the national exchequer would contribute more. In 1971 the necessary bill was introduced and passed.

By 1981, some of the results were part of the national folklore. In certain parts of eastern Canada whole communities lived for much of the year on unemployment insurance, just as they had once lived on seasonal benefit; but now they lived much more comfortably than before and had less incentive to seek new jobs in other places. Some of the results were bizarre and unexpected. In the great cities, musicians and artists found that their living standards had a new underpinning, and the system provided a new and hidden subsidy to the arts.

Although unemployment insurance proved to be an income support plan for Quebec and eastern Canada, the Trudeau government was anxious to devise a more organized and purposive plan to help the poorer regions. In so doing, it should be remembered, it was concerned partly to develop a new nation-wide constituency that would naturally look to Ottawa for help, as, for example, manufacturers had looked to Ottawa in the bad old days of protectionism. The ARDA and FRED schemes for rural redevelopment, and also an Area Development Incentives plan that was due to expire in 1970, had been inherited from the Diefenbaker and Pearson years. Before 1968 was out, Trudeau had appointed Jean Marchand to a new portfolio of Regional Economic Expansion, soon christened DREE. In 1969, Parliament transferred ARDA and FRED to DREE, and, under the Regional Development Incentives Act, gave DREE quite remarkable powers. The minister could decide which regions and firms qualified for capital assistance grants. These could range up to $12 million, and they could be made anywhere in the Atlantic provinces (except in Labrador), and in many parts of the other provinces as well. DREE quickly became the vehicle for all sorts of federal-provincial development plans. In 1974, Ottawa signed General Development agreements with all the provinces except Prince Edward Island, whose needs were provided for under an earlier agreement. Thus Newfoundland was sprinkled with 'DREE schools,' New Brunswick acquired 'DREE hydro,' and so on. By 1979, DREE was spending half a billion dollars a year.

Many observers thought that DREE worked with unemployment insurance to make the Canadian economy less flexible and less productive than it would otherwise have been. Ironically, these new arrangements co-existed with initiatives in competition policy, tariffs, and taxation, all of which were meant at first to make us *more* flexible and productive. But nothing much came of these new initiatives; it was 'DREE-ism' that triumphed in the end. In agriculture the triumph was delayed a little, but by 1975 it was complete.

So far as prairie farmers were concerned, the Trudeau government could do nothing right. They blamed it for transport problems, boxcar shortages, and bad conditions on world markets. They never forgot that in a moment of irritation the Prime Minister had said: 'Why should I sell your wheat?' But, given the Canadian Wheat Board, wheat marketing *was* Ottawa's responsibility. And whatever Trudeau may have said or thought in his calmer moments, as a marketer the Wheat Board's performance was not at all bad.

In 1969-70, when markets were unreceptive, grain piled up and wheat prices had to be lowered, partly because the International Grains Agreement had collapsed. In 1969 the government gave new cash advances to farmers, even on unharvested grain. In 1970 it invented 'Project LIFT,' under which farmers were paid for *not* growing wheat. But in the early seventies world markets revived and stocks fell, largely because the USSR had re-entered the market on a really large scale. Farm incomes increased dramatically, and so did the price of wheat. In 1972-3 it was $2.62 per bushel, the best ever. In 1973-4 it went to $5.49 a bushel, and in 1974-5 it was almost as high. Government responded by subsidizing domestic consumption, holding the domestic price at $3.25 and paying the farmers the difference. It also acted to stabilize farm incomes by inventing an insurance plan for western farmers. This was meant to ensure participating farmers that they would never earn less than they had earned in each preceding five-year period.

From 1968 to 1975, the cash receipts from wheat farming rose from $605 million to $1.7 billion, comfortably outstripping inflation and bringing new prosperity to the prairie provinces. Regrettably, in the late seventies wheat prices fell back from the $5 figure, and wheat farmers' incomes shared in the retreat. Also, there were ever-increasing difficulties in the transport of wheat, chiefly because grain-shipping rates were controlled at so low a level that the railways had no incentive to provide rolling stock or to maintain track and stations. In addition, there were troubles in grain handling at the ports. In summer 1979 the situation verged on a national scandal. The Clark administration appointed a commissioner to see what could be done. In the 1979-80 campaign, Trudeau astonished most railway experts and convinced few farmers with a pledge to doubletrack the railways to the Pacific. During all this time, Alberta was awash in oil revenues, and Saskatchewan was doing relatively well out of oil, potash, and forest products. The wheat situation came to matter much less in the late seventies than it had in the late sixties, although naturally the wheat farmers did not see things that way. The wheat problem was difficult because so much of the output was exported under conditions that the Wheat Board might hope to influence but could not control. Further, as in the sixties, a great deal depended on crop results in the Communist world. Thus China and Russia joined Britain as Canada's principal customers, but their comings and goings were erratic and, in the longer run, they were trying to become self-sufficient in grain. As for the British market, its future was uncertain once Britain had joined the European Economic Community in 1973. Europe's agricultural protectionism would eventually drive Canadian wheat off Britain's markets. This problem was not acute by 1979, when prices and market prospects were very good once more; but it would certainly come over the horizon early in the 1980s.

As with wheat, so with other foodstuffs: after some years of reluctance the Trudeau government responded to pressure from producers who wanted more security and higher incomes. Here, however, the medicine was already available – more protection, more subsidy, and more power for the marketing boards. Now and then, the government did show a consumerist bent. At one point it cut some food duties as an anti-inflationary measure, and in 1975 it prohibited beef export for the sake of the Canadian consumer. But most of the time the fence of tariffs, quotas, and import prohibitions was maintained in good working order, and elaborated in ever more protectionist ways. Further, in 1975 the government amended Diefenbaker's price support law, raising the support level from 80 per cent of a ten-year average to 90 per cent of a five-year average adjusted for rising production costs. By 1976 these and similar arrangements covered a remarkable list of farm products – cattle, sheep, hogs, milk and cream, soybeans, non-prairie oats and barley, pears, carrots, prune plums, lambs, potatoes, Nova Scotia apples, Ontario pears, and cherries from Ontario and British Columbia.

Supplementary help came from the marketing boards – 108 provincial entities by 1975, providing 57 per cent of farm cash income. Ottawa did what it could to co-ordinate and strengthen the boards. By December 1975 it had allowed 79 provincial boards to control interprovincial and export trade. In 1972, under the Farm Products Marketing Agencies Act, it provided for new nation-wide marketing boards which could go into effect on the request of producers and provinces whenever the job of control and pricing was too much for the provincial boards. The federal egg-marketing agency began in 1973, and the turkey-marketing agency in 1974. The idea appealed to other farmers, and a queue quickly formed, containing producers of various fruits and vegetables, chickens, corn, tobacco, and – yes – pregnant mares' urine. Eugene Whelan, the Minister of Agriculture, conducted a continuous campaign to convince consumers that they should be glad to pay whatever prices the marketing boards might choose to extort.

Sometimes the results were painful and absurd. At one time there was a mountain of powdered milk that the government could not give away. At another time there was a chain of egg warehouses whose contents the egg agency absentmindedly allowed to rot. One journalist suggested that by combining the rotten eggs with the skim milk the government could bake an enormous custard and use it as a symbol of national unity – or a platform for Arctic oil drilling. Few laughed.

These price-raising policies were especially odd given that the government also claimed to be fighting inflation. But through 1974 urban Canada voted Liberal regardless, and with respect to such matters the NDP policies were no better. Nor was there any evidence during the brief Clark administration that Conservatives would act differently.

Some people argue that in agricultural policy, as in regional development policy, the Trudeau government inherited arrangements and assumptions that it could not really have changed; therefore it was not fundamentally to blame for all the dreary developments described above. Whatever the truth may be, there were three areas – competition, tax structure, and tariff and other protective devices – where one might have hoped for something new and sensible. Indeed, on all three subjects the government did try – for a short time – to do better. But in the end the results were unimpressive.

In competition policy the government evinced a characteristic pattern of advance and retreat. On taking office its members seem to have believed that there could be and should be fundamental reform, and they planned to model that reform on the best textbook principles, as transmitted to the cabinet by the economists on the Economic Council of Canada staff and the Watkins task force. But as time passed the political realities gradually became clearer. Reform would hurt too many vocal interests. Consumers, who would stand to gain, were badly organized and mute. As the government became unpopular it could less readily carry a series of measures that excited so much opposition, especially from the business classes.

A year after assuming office the Trudeau government received a report from the Economic Council. The report, which the Pearson government had requested, recommended much more vigorous measures to create and protect competition. The Watkins Report took a similar line. By that time it was obvious that the old Combines Investigation Act did nothing to prevent mergers and precious little to encourage competition or to protect consumers. Admittedly, it was not clear that the federal government could do much more without the consent of the provinces, which control 'property and civil rights.' But in 1971 the government forged ahead with its Competition Bill along the lines the Council had suggested. The result was a storm of protest. Various special interests objected that they would have to give up their cherished restrictive practices; no businessman liked the thought that the government would have stronger power to prevent monopoly, price fixing, resale price maintenance, and a variety of other things that help producers but hurt consumers and make the economy less efficient. The bill expired with the 1972 general election. Thereafter, the government proceeded much more cautiously, deciding to legislate in stages. In 1974 it introduced a much milder measure, one that said nothing about mergers but that gave new powers to the authorities to prohibit many new things, including the extension of foreign laws and directives into Canada. This measure died, was reintroduced, provoked fierce controversy, and was finally passed. Meanwhile, nothing had been heard of the second stage, which was supposed to handle monopolization and inefficiency. In 1975 the government set up a royal commission to examine the concentration of economic power. At length the commission reported that Canadians had almost nothing to worry about under that heading.

From the Carter Royal Commission on Taxation that Diefenbaker had appointed in 1962, the Trudeau government inherited a 2,600-page report in six volumes (not counting the many research studies that accompanied it). Among specialists in public finance the report excited worldwide admiration. But, because the commission wanted to tax capital gains as income and also to tax the oil and mining industries more heavily, the reception within Canada was rather less joyous. In November 1969 Edgar Benson, the finance minister, tabled a White Paper on tax reform that already represented a partial retreat from the full logical rigour of the Carter plan. Once again there was an outcry. Thus when in 1971 the government actually moved to modify the income tax system there was little relation between its proposals and Carter, and not much resemblance to the 1969 White Paper. Capital gains were to be taxed, but at a concessionary rate, and principal residences would be exempt. Although mining companies were taxed more heavily for the time being, these arrangements were soon changed as the nation worried more about energy. Not much was done about corporation taxation, which retained many allowances, concessions, and special arrangements – devices that would expand later in the decade, and would shortly provide the basis for the NDP cry, 'corporate welfare bums!'

Benson described the whole process – the steps from Carter to the White Paper and then to the Bill – as an exercise in participatory democracy. The historian is much more likely to call it an exercise in futility and a splendid case study of pressure-group activity.

In trade policy, as in tax policy, there were inheritances from earlier governments that at first seemed to place the government's feet firmly on the path of liberalization – fewer and lower tariff barriers, as well as fewer non-tariff obstructions to trade. But here the inheritance was mixed, and the retreat to interventionism and protectionism even more pronounced.

Having committed itself to help the poor countries' exports, the government in 1970 promised to reduce tariffs on many of these items. But it exempted the 'sensitive' goods, those on which Canada had imposed quotas. Charity began at home, chiefly in Quebec and the Atlantic region. In 1969 the government introduced the tariff cuts that had been negotiated under the Kennedy Round, and in the 1970s it participated actively in the 'Tokyo Round' of talks that GATT proceeded to organize. In 1979, when these talks were brought to a satisfactory conclusion, there was much congratulation in Ottawa. In 1971, when President Nixon decided to subsidize American exports and to raise American tariffs, Canada did not retaliate, perhaps in large part because so many Canadian goods were exempted. Instead, while complaining bitterly in Washington, it provided transitional assistance to domestic industries. Recognizing that Commonwealth preferential tariffs now made little difference to Canada's transatlantic trade, when the British entered the European Economic Community in 1973 Canada wished Britain well and did not complain. In February 1973, many food tariffs were reduced as an anti-inflation device. But by October, when there was a chance that American beef imports would really have an effect on Canadian prices, John Turner raised the beef duties, more than offsetting the February reductions. From then on, Canadian trade policy seemed to become steadily more protectionist. The process was more visible with respect to non-tariff barriers. The Pearson government had begun in the sixties to impose import quotas so as to control the flow of cheap textiles, clothing, and shoes from the efficient low-wage countries of Asia and Latin America. In the seventies the quotas were retained, extended, and made more restrictive. Canada did agree to the tariff reductions in the 1979 GATT revision, and the rhetoric of freer multilateral trade con-

High meat prices for Easter
(Wicks, 1973). Reproduced with the permission of Canada Wide Feature Service Ltd

tinued to ring out from Ottawa. But as the unemployment problem became more pressing, Ottawa was less inclined to protect consumers and more inclined to protect farmers, industrialists, and workers in the endangered industries, especially those located in Quebec.

With respect to the foreign investment question, the same sort of shift toward protectionism took place. In the sixties most professional opinion argued that the country had gained by welcoming so much foreign capital and that where harm had been done the fault had been Canada's. The government's proper task, therefore, was to manage things so as to increase the gains relative to the costs, remembering that the former were already much larger than the latter. This line had been taken in the Watkins Report of 1968, by the economist A.E. Safarian, and by almost all qualified observers. Certainly in the late sixties the business community did not want the government to do anything dramatic. It was not businessmen who pushed the government from the benign acquiescence of the late sixties to the systematic screening and interventionism of 1971 and thereafter. The credit – if that is the word – belongs to three groups: nationalist sectarians among the intelligentsia and their echoes in the media; like-minded people within the Liberal party and caucus; and eager officials, anxious to 'regulate' foreign-owned firms in the national interest.

In 1973 and afterward, additional pressure came from the oil price crisis and from later developments on the energy front. In the background was an ever-increasing but unacknowledged echoing of American populist opinion, which held that large business is Bad, multinational business is Worse, and oil companies are Worst of All. Without infuriating its own business supporters in Canada, the government could do little or nothing about the Bad. But by acting to 'control' the Worse and the Worst of All it could pacify its populist supporters and give its bureaucrats more work and more power.

The Watkins task force reported in February 1968. It called for more competition, lower tariffs, more information about the foreign-owned firms, and more taxation of such firms. It thought the government should set up a state trading agency to act as a dealer of last resort in East-West trade; it wanted the government to block the extension of American anti-trust law and trading-with-the-enemy law into Canada, where foreign-owned firms had often felt themselves subject to this kind of extraterritorial influence from Washington; it wanted a Canada Development Corporation. Although the state trading agency vanished without trace, most of the other suggestions eventually made their way into law or regulation, although not soon enough to satisfy Professor Watkins or Walter Gordon.

In 1972, Ottawa officials produced the Gray Report on the costs and benefits of foreign investment. Much more hostile and interventionist than the Watkins Report, it recommended a heavier reliance on ad hoc regulation, and it wanted a tribunal that would review six areas: takeovers; new foreign-owned enterprises; licensing, franchising, and investments by existing foreign-owned firms (and all their other activities); as well as the external investments of Canadian-owned multinationals. At once the government introduced a measure that would have set up a takeover tribunal. At length, in 1974, the tribunal did appear in the form of the Foreign Investment Review Agency (FIRA). Thereafter almost all takeovers and transfers of ownership to foreign interests, or among them, were subject to screening – with ultimate decisions at cabinet level – as were most direct foreign investment in new enterprises and any foreign expansion into any new and unrelated areas of business.

What FIRA actually meant was hard to say. Naturally its promoters thought it did not go far enough, while many Canadian economists and businessmen thought it went rather too far. Late in 1979, the Clark government was muttering about its iniquities. Certainly it was not as all-encompassing as the Gray Report had suggested. Certainly, too, its results could be odd. Most academic observers, Canadian and otherwise, believed that the FIRA procedures were more rigorous and arbitrary than those of any other developed industrial country, several of which have similar schemes. More than two-thirds of all applications were approved, but gradually it became clear that the screening agency and the cabinet were developing criteria that went beyond the explicit letter of the Act (the Act also gave the cabinet a complete discretion that it was certainly willing to use). For example, by 1979 it was unwilling to permit foreign takeovers and transfers in publishing, even when the firm in question was already foreign owned. The Act did not provide a special status for publishing; presumably the government had decided that national virility required a Canadian-owned book industry. In Edmonton, publisher Mel Hurtig doubtless rejoiced. In the 1980 election campaign, the Liberals promised to press on even further in the 1980s as Herb Gray relished his role as finance critic. After the election Gray became the minister responsible for FIRA and immediately promised 'tougher' application of rules.

There was more artillery used in the battle against the foreign firm. There were special rules to extrude foreigners from Canadian broadcasting and cable networks. Although the Canada Development Corporation established in 1971 was not meant to buy back Canada, by 1979 it had purchased control of one multinational firm from American interests, fought takeover battles in Alberta oil, and collected a pharmaceutical firm that in earlier days would probably have passed into foreign control. In 1974 the government bought De Havilland Aircraft of Toronto from Hawker Siddeley of Britain, and Canadair from General Dynamics of the United States, in the hope that it could sell the two firms to Canadians. By mid-1979 it had still not managed to do so. Thus, more or less by accident, Canada had nationalized most of its aerospace industry. Even more striking and most pregnant with possibilities was the arrival of Petrocan.

On December 6, 1973, Trudeau told the House that the government would set up a national petroleum company. This body was meant to arrange for oil imports, work the oil sands of Alberta, and explore for conventional oil and gas – in short, to co-exist with existing multinationals such as Imperial, Texaco, and Gulf. It could refine and distribute, although Trudeau did not think that it would do so for some time. The Venezuelans had already suggested that if Canada had a national oil company they might be able to arrange a long-term supply contract. Thanks to the new tax plans of 1973, the private oil companies were cutting back on their exploration and threatening to stop all development in Canada. The price increases and shortages of 1973 frightened the government and forced it to aim for self-sufficiency in oil. In 1975 an appropriate bill was introduced and passed. The Conservatives thought it was not needed; the NDP (who wanted to nationalize Imperial Oil) thought it did not go far enough.

By 1979 Petrocan had found some oil and gas; it had learned to co-operate usefully with the multinationals in exploration and development; and it had become an important importer. In the 1979 election the Conservatives were pledged to abolish it, and the NDP to elaborate it, while the Trudeau ministers were content to point to its achievements. Had it done more than the multinationals would have done? Had it cost Canada less? No one knew. But in autumn 1979 the Clark government changed its stance. Petrocan's fate was to be not abolition but 'privatization,' along lines that would rejoice any capitalist's heart: the profitable bits would be sold off, and the government would keep the loss-makers.

Although, in the 1980 election, the Liberals and the NDP clamoured to claim parentage, the truth is that in the national energy picture Petrocan had made very little difference by 1979. In the quagmire of federal energy policy it was more like a piece of floating turf than an island of safety and security. Canada could not escape the world-wide disturbances that swept the oil markets in 1973 and thereafter. Many Canadians thought Petrocan would insulate them from the external cold blasts, but *that* it could never do, although Trudeau and Broadbent hinted it could. It was hardly surprising Canadians were confused.

Until 1973 Canada's main problem had been to find markets for its oil. Ottawa worried about restrictive American quotas and preserved intact Diefenbaker's National Energy Policy, by which Ontario and western Canada were sequestered protected markets for high-cost Alberta crude: in the early seventies, Iranian oil landed in Montreal for about $2.50 per barrel, while in Ontario Alberta oil cost $3.00. To keep out cheap foreign oil and gasoline, Ottawa maintained a sort of documentary dyke just west of the Ottawa River and kept the transcontinental oil pipelines well short of Montreal: after all, pipelines can move oil in either direction.

Early in 1973 a surge of American demand threatened Canada's domestic market, and so, in February, the government decided to control oil exports. On the world market demand grew stronger, and prices rose both at home and abroad. By August, Alberta oil fetched $3.80. In September the Prime Minister froze the domestic price at $4.00, planned to extend the pipeline to Montreal, and devised a two-price system by which Canada would levy an export tax to equalize the domestic price with the foreign, now well over the $4.00 mark. In eastern Canada, OPEC had raised the price of crude by 50 per cent between April and September 1973. This, however, was only the beginning. With the outbreak of the Yom Kippur war between Israel and Egypt, OPEC restricted supplies and raised prices by another 70 per cent. By November, imported oil cost $7.50 per barrel, and by the end of the year it was over $10.00. The government was obliged to unfreeze oil prices in eastern Canada. Alberta crude was now moving farther eastward, but without a pipeline it could do so only at high cost and rather slowly. The domestic $4.00 freeze was due to expire at the end of January 1974, but, at NDP insistence, it was extended to April, at which time the price rose to $6.50. Meanwhile the government had spliced together a policy. The Montreal and Mackenzie pipelines were to be expedited. The Alberta tar sands were to be developed. Petrocan was to be invented. Eastern

Canada would use more Canadian crude and import less. The improvisations were desperate; the pressure from the left was consistent; the goal was 'self-sufficiency' – or perhaps 'self-reliance'; the result was a vagueness too common in Canadian public life after 1973.

Now there was a natural conflict between the eastern provinces, which used most of the oil, and the western provinces, which owned it. Alberta wanted to get the world price, and bitterly resented Ottawa's new export tax, even though there was still plenty of room for it to force up its royalty take. Quebec and the Atlantic region bitterly resented the world price and hankered after Alberta's artificially cheap crude, or, if they could not have that, after a subsidy. Canada's oil imports roughly equalled its exports, but there was no convenient way to replace the former with the latter, given the pipeline systems and the long-term commitments to export. For the oil companies there was the chance of windfall profits on their large stocks of oil and refined products. If the provinces did not force up their royalty rates, the companies could also expect large new profits from the oil they were pumping. Early in 1974, the federal Minister of Energy convinced the companies not to raise prices until they had sold off any lower-cost inventories. Thus, although consumers gained, the federal exchequer lost, because the extra profits would have been taxable. Alberta and Saskatchewan agreed that when oil prices went up they would use some of the extra money for development. Alberta said that to make life easier for Ottawa it would put away some of its new loot in its Heritage Fund. The result was to infuriate the poorer provinces, who would otherwise have drawn even larger equalization payments from Ottawa. In the 1980 election the Heritage Fund became, in eastern Canada, the symbol of western exploitation.

All the provinces agreed that to establish a single nation-wide price the federal government could subsidise oil imports for Quebec and the Atlantic provinces. It was agreed that to stimulate domestic exploration and development the Canadian price would have to drift upward, though not necessarily to world levels. Meanwhile, by taxing oil export Ottawa would have some extra funds to help subsidise oil imports. Of course the effect of this package was to ensure that Canada would consume more oil, import more, and export less, than if prices were not held below world levels. Thus by 1979 the country was again a large net importer, and in the 1980 election no party could promise that this situation would change quickly. The subsidies were a new and heavy burden; the country was more exposed than in 1973 to the next turn of the OPEC screw which came in 1979 as the OPEC price rose rapidly toward $35 per barrel. The subsidy now cost over two and a half billion dollars a year.

The Alberta authorities controlled the volume of domestic conventional production, which came from shrinking reserves. Hence in the 1980s Canada would have to depend ever more on the costly oil from the tar sands, on heavy oil, and on new discoveries in faraway places – the Arctic, the off-shore Atlantic shelf, maybe even the Gulf of St Lawrence. In light of these facts it might have seemed sensible to cut domestic consumption as fast as possible by letting prices rise to the world level at once. But there were obvious political reasons for not doing this. The oil-importing zones were the poorer parts of the country; Quebec was solidly Liberal; and the NDP would not stand for any such thing.

If Canada was to be more 'self-reliant,' it would have to produce more. However, the tax studies of the previous decade had produced a suspicion that the resource-based multinationals were getting their inputs too cheaply and paying too little tax. Furthermore, the Alberta and Ottawa authorities had realized that in trying to tax the oil companies they were like two dogs chewing at the same bone. Alberta tended to force up its oil royalties, and so did Saskatchewan. In doing so, they reduced the apparent profits that the federal government could tax, because royalties had been treated as a cost of doing business. In May 1974, Minister of Finance John Turner proposed to end this old arrangement. In November 1974 he returned to the charge. Of course it was oil, and its new and higher price, that had made this issue a really important one. Nor would it have arisen if the companies actually owned the oil they were busy extracting. But by adding provincial royalty and federal income tax, an oil company could readily report no net profits – or not enough to justify new Canadian ventures or to finance them. To the provinces, the federal proposal was an insult added to the injury of the oil export tax, even though the producing provinces were to get half of the export tax cash. Premier Lougheed of Alberta was especially annoyed. But the Prime Minister argued that only by disallowing all royalties could Ottawa assure itself a fair share of revenue from resources. If royalties were to remain deductible, a province could force its royalties so high that there would be no profits left for Ottawa to tax!

In the acrimonious disputes of 1974 Lougheed clearly recognized the implications for development. Trudeau probably did not. By early 1975, however, he had come to understand that there would have to be a compromise. Oil prices would have to rise in Canada; the provinces would have to receive a larger take, and the oil companies would have to get enough to encourage new exploration and development. Thus from 1975 through 1979, although the domestic oil price was kept consistently below the world price it was adjusted upward from time to time, after discussion and agreement with the provinces. Ottawa and Edmonton also agreed to share the loot. Between 1972 and 1978 the net operating income of the Canadian petroleum industry rose by $7.9 billion, an increase of 452 per cent. Of this increase, the provinces got $4 billion, or 52 per cent, the oil companies $3.1 billion, or 40 per cent, and Ottawa got the remaining 8 per cent. The oil companies did better than had been expected in 1974 because both the provinces and Ottawa introduced various special incentives – drilling bonuses, speedy write-offs for exploration outlays, and special exploration allowances for frontier projects. In the end, therefore, the special deals more than offset the 'disincentives' of Turner's 1974 plan.

By early 1979 the universe of oil was unfolding as it should. Domestic oil, which brought $12.75 a barrel, had risen near the OPEC world price of $14.75. Within Canada Syncrude had come on stream, and exploration and development were proceeding apace, even though there was still no pipeline to the Arctic. But in 1979, the Iranian revolution produced a constriction in world supply at a time when world demand was rising rapidly once more. The result was a new upsurge of oil prices by OPEC and its imitators, such as Mexico. Within Canada the phenomena of 1974 quickly reappeared. By late 1979 imported oil already cost as much as $23.00 per barrel, and the price was rising rapidly.

OPEC raised its prices still further, and in summer and autumn 1979 there was a general agreement that Canadian oil prices would also have to rise – although not to world levels, or even to the artificially low American level. Higher prices would be needed to finance new development and to restrain consumption, or so Canadians were repeatedly told. But there was so little connection between rhetoric and reality that the citizens could and did become as confused as the politicians perhaps hoped they would. Once more Alberta argued that it was entitled to the world price, and that it should receive at least 45 per cent of any extra oil revenue. The Trudeau government had established a formula by which, when the oil price rose by $1 per barrel, the oil companies would get 45 cents, Alberta the same, and Ottawa 10 cents. Once the Clark government had come to power, it seemed that everyone except Ontario was anxious to see prices rise by more than the amounts the Trudeau government had planned – $2 per barrel per year in 1980 and 1981.

In autumn 1979 the Clark government argued about energy policy and negotiated anxiously with Premier Lougheed of Alberta and with the other provincial premiers. In November the Prime Minister told the premiers that he would like to raise the oil price by $4 per barrel per year in 1981-2 and to change the share-out, so that Ottawa would get 25 per cent of the gain. He also wanted an energy self-sufficiency bank and a much heavier federal tax on gasoline. The goal, he said, was self-sufficiency by 1990. But no one could be sure if the increases, or the new share-out, would satisfy the Albertans.

John Crosbie, the finance minister, naturally had to work the energy package into his December 11 budget. The proposals attracted fascinated and horrified attention. The government proposed to raise the gasoline tax by 4 cents per litre, or nearly 18 cents per gallon. The oil price would rise $4 per barrel in 1980 and $4.50 per barrel in each of 1981, 1982, and 1983. There would be a new federal tax that would skim off $1 per barrel in 1980 and still more in 1981-3. Much of the new revenue would go into a new energy bank.

Predictably these plans infuriated the consuming provinces, which had hoped to give less, and the producing ones, which had hoped to get more. Unfortunately there was no way to be sure that they would produce Clark's goal – self-sufficiency by 1990 at eighty-five or ninety per cent of the US price. Crosbie's plan implied a Canadian price of $31.25 per barrel by 1983 – up from $13.75 in December 1979. How much oil would Canada itself produce at that price, and how much would its citizens demand? No one could possibly know. If there was excess demand Canada would still be importing some oil. By January 1980 oil was already trading on world markets at well over $30 per barrel. Unless OPEC were to collapse it would cost far, far more by 1983, and Ottawa would still find itself subsidising any imports. On the other hand, if domestic supply were to overshoot domestic demand at $31.25 there would be downward pressure on that price and, lo and behold, a 'surplus' available for export!

In the January 1980 election campaign the Liberals provided an alternative plan. First they promised that they would not let oil prices rise as much as the Clark government proposed, at least not in 1980-1. Also they talked of a 'blended' price that would average the prices of imports, domestic crude, and high-cost synthetic crude from the tar sands and the like. This plan would get government out of the subsidy business eventually, no small matter now that Canada was importing forty per cent of its oil consumption and subsidising every barrel at the rate of $17.25 or more. But because the plan would keep Canada's own price level below world prices so long as the country had any low-cost conventional crude, it would still artificially encourage Canada to consume more and produce less. An odd prescription from an energy-conscious party!

Higher prices were meant to restrain Canada's appetite for oil, which was, on a per capita basis, the highest in the world by 1979. They were also supposed to encourage domestic production and to finance exploration and development, especially in the tar sands and other high-cost areas. But no one knew what such developments would really cost, or what cash-flow would induce the oil companies to undertake them. There was no particular reason why the flow of current revenue should finance all the outlays, or even most of them. What was needed was an adequate return on development outlays, which in principle could be funded partly by borrowing or stock issues. But without adequate investment incentives, both exploration and development would soon come to an end.

Meanwhile, Canada had been working hard to develop unconventional fuels. After the adventures of 1973 there was renewed interest in coal, both in British Columbia and in Nova Scotia, where it was hoped that coal-fired generators would help reduce the province's dependence on OPEC oil. Fundy tidal power, that perennial will-o'-the-wisp, once more made headlines but not electricity. There was some renewed interest in atomic power and in Canada's very own Candu reactor. There were more wood stoves, some bio-gas generators, the occasional windmill, and a few solar water heaters. More interesting and much more promising were the developments in Alberta and Saskatchewan, where oil sands and heavy oil were being tapped at last. The costs admittedly were very high, but so was the cost of conventional oil, especially from OPEC.

Before the price rises of 1973, there was one experimental extractive plant in Alberta – Great Canadian Oil Sands Ltd, whose plant dated from 1967. It was making oil but not money. Late in 1973 the premier of Alberta announced that Syncrude Ltd would start work soon, aiming to produce its first oil in 1978. Early in 1974 a Shell plant was expected to come on stream in 1979 or 1980, and another consortium project was aiming at 1982, by which time it was hoped that the tar sands would be producing 420,000 barrels per day. But by late 1974 government and the companies were much more pessimistic about the prospects, both technical and financial. Costs were higher than expected, but no one seemed to know just how high they might go. Furthermore, no one knew just how far or how fast the domestic price might be allowed to rise. In December one firm withdrew from the Syncrude consortium. Its place was taken by government – Ottawa, Edmonton, and, for a time, Toronto. Nevertheless, the private participants said that unless three conditions were met they would withdraw from the project. Ottawa must allow Syncrude royalties to be deducted from income for federal tax purposes; it must let Syncrude sell oil at world prices, not at the controlled Canadian level; and Edmonton must exempt Syncrude from any prorationing schemes of production control. Early in February 1975 the three governments agreed, and Syncrude went ahead more or less on schedule. As planned, it sold its first oil in 1978, but by early 1980 it was still overcoming its start-up problems and moving haltingly toward its designed capacity.

It may seem an easy step from oil price control to general wage and price control. Indeed, nothing makes the lurch toward interventionism clearer than the imposition of general control in 1975. Nevertheless, all the evidence suggests that the government was reluctant to take this step. When it was formed in 1968 there was already much talk about incomes policies. Britain had experimented several times with wage freezes and wage controls. In many countries it was thought that wage increases were causing prices to rise. But the government then believed that in Canada controls could not work. Much of the inflationary pressure came from abroad via Canada's immense import and export trade. Worse still, there was no consensus about controls; that is to say, the unions would not stand for them. So compulsion was pointless.

In December 1968 the authorities invented the Prices and Incomes Commission and Dr John Young came from British Columbia to head it. The Commission could issue reports and recommendations although it could not actually make anybody do anything at all. Nevertheless, the unions would have nothing to do with it, so Young really achieved very little. He did conduct a propaganda campaign for voluntary restraint, and in 1970 held a national rally at which 250 business and professional leaders promised to raise prices less than they would otherwise have raised them. In 1971 the United States imposed controls, but Canadian ministers continued to insist that Canada did not need them and could not use them anyway. In 1972 the Commission itself asked for general but temporary controls on prices and wages. Many newspapers agreed with Young, but the government abolished the Commission.

In 1973, because food prices were rising especially rapidly, the government restricted the export of meat and subsidized the domestic consumption of wheat; but it was still unwilling to control food prices directly. Instead it invented the Food Prices Review Board, under the chairpersonship of Beryl Plumptre. This board had no power, but, in accordance with then current fashion, it was to monitor price movements. It quickly set up a research division, and 'Plumptre's posses' descended on supermarkets. From time to time Mrs Plumptre announced that the great food chains were *not* the villains, and now and then she crossed swords with Eugene Whelan, whose price-raising activities in the Department of Agriculture should already have been a public scandal. But the result was copy for the journalist, nothing more.

At the same time, house prices continued to rise in most of Canada, and mortgages cost more than ever. The government's response was twofold: it would finance a land assembly and development scheme; and it would support research on cheaper ways to service land. In the short run, both plans would cost money, not save it, and neither could quickly affect the housing market. Meanwhile, to prevent mortgage rates from going sky-high, funds were pumped into CMHC. The extra money raised house prices even faster, and increased inflationary pressure throughout the economy; but at least the government seemed to be 'doing something about the housing crisis.'

As inflationary pressure continued, in 1973-5 there was new militancy among organized labour, especially in Quebec and more especially in public employment. Teachers, postmen, air traffic controllers – all were asking for wage increases that ranged from 20 per cent to 80 per cent. Strictly speaking such demands were not inflationary. Since most of the services in question were not *sold* to anyone, the demands implied higher taxes but usually not higher prices. Still, private employers faced the same sorts of demands, and there it was obvious that the results would be some mixture of higher prices, a weaker dollar, and fewer jobs.

By December 1974 the finance minister was trying to orchestrate a new program of voluntary restraint. Early in 1975 he announced that the chief cause of inflation was now wage push. But by May 1975 it was clear that labour would not co-operate in a voluntary program, and it had long been clear that John Turner did not want a compulsory one. At budget time, in June, Turner told the Commons that he and the cabinet had discussed controls but had rejected the idea. Then Turner left the cabinet in September, and the way was clear. On October 13 the Prime Minister told the House that there would be controls after all.

To evade the constitutional minefields Ottawa asked the provinces to co-operate. Prices were to go up only when costs rose. Wages and professional fees could go up by the inflation rate plus 2 per cent. The guideline for the first year would be 10 per cent, for the second 8 per cent, and the third 6 per cent. Wages could not rise by more than $2,400, and jumps of $600 or less were not to be controlled at all. Farm and fishing incomes were naturally exempt, as were smaller firms; as expatriate Canadian economist John Kenneth Galbraith had recommended, the scheme covered only public employment and the larger private firms – about 1,500 businesses with about four million employees. There would be an anti-inflation review board, whose administrator could roll back price and wage increases.

The plan was to last for three years at least. The CLC planned a national day of protest, but no one paid much attention because the controls were really very popular. The provinces swung quickly into line, some of them using the federal initiative as an excuse for comprehensive rent controls. Prices and wages still rose, but the rate of increase fell, and academic studies suggested that the controls program might actually be credited for some of this decrease. By 1978 prices were rising much less rapidly than in 1974-5, and the extraordinary wage demands seemed to be bad memories from the past. But there was still plenty of wage push, and the money supply was still growing very fast – over 14 per cent in 1977, and over 10 per cent in 1978. The country was running a massive deficit on current account, and the government's financial position had changed from comfortable to disastrous.

Would controls actually end in 1978? The *coup de grâce* was administered after the Prime Minister had visited Germany, whose record of stable prices and rapid growth was the envy of the world. In mid-summer 1978, after his return from Bonn, Trudeau announced that controls would end that autumn. He went on to say that the real problem was the government deficit: this time there would be genuine cuts in public spending!

As for labour relations, the German success offered no solution for Canada. The experience since 1970 suggested to thoughtful scholars that no miracle cures existed for a labour relations system that observers on all sides admitted was close to breakdown. Labour union membership in Canada had grown continuously since the 1960s (unlike the United States), primarily because of the rapid expansion of public service unions. In 1962 there were slightly over one and a half million organized workers, in 1973, well over two and a half. In the 1970s the man days lost from strikes and lockouts soared to levels over four times that of the early 1960s. The Woods Commission which investigated why this happened found many explanations but no easy palliatives. In 1975, the CLC talked much about 'tripartism,' pointing to

(Donato, c1978). Reproduced with the permission of Canada Wide Feature Service Ltd the successful labour-management-government co-operation in prosperous Germany and Scandinavia. After a feeble attempt to initiate this by labour and government, many concluded that such a system could only come to Canada slowly. Most, in labour, government, and the press, concluded it should not come at all.

Meanwhile, as the federal-provincial shared-cost programs had become ever more expensive and alarming, labour began to worry about losing some of their gains. By agreeing to split the cost of health, education, and welfare with the provinces Ottawa had commited itself to make outlays that it could not control. From time to time the federal government would try to negotiate a rearrangement by which its own costs were controlled. In 1977 it was obliged to impose a solution: for the next five years its contributions would escalate automatically in step with the growth of GNP, not with actual spending on higher education and medicare. Understandably the provinces, no matter how much they valued their own financial autonomy, were reluctant to swallow Ottawa's medicine. Over and over again Ottawa had to impose a solution on the provinces. By 1975 the great federal initiatives had come, although their full long-run cost was yet to be digested. Unemployment insurance and welfare had been modernized; health and old age had been provided for; eastern Canada was assured of subsidized oil. Now the bills were coming in. They were horrendous. But again the economic situation made solutions difficult to find.

MACROECONOMIC MANAGEMENT

Year after year the problem was inflation. Or so a succession of finance ministers and central bankers told the Canadian people. There was, in addition, an unemployment problem. Although employment and output went up year by year, unemployment figures also increased both because the labour force was growing quickly and because, as we saw in the last section, structural changes tended to raise them. Not only were the boom babies of the forties and fifties coming on to the job market; but also more women were entering the work force. Furthermore, in spite of the unemployment figures, immigrants flocked to Canada whenever the government would give them visas – and often when it would not.

For inflationary pressure the orthodox fiscal medicine is higher tax rates, lower government spending, or both. But these weapons create more unemployment, at least in the short run. Hence any government would be reluctant to use them when unemployment is already a political issue. Further, year by year federal spending was ever more clearly out of control. Too many uncontrollable items had been built into the budget, both in the federal outlay pattern and in the system of grants and subsidies to persons, junior governments, and businesses. Ottawa could reduce its own capital outlays, but these were small relative to everything else. It could restrict growth in the civil service, but officials could not readily be fired and, in a relatively young service, attrition was bound to be slow – especially given the generous salaries and benefits that Pearson had introduced and that the Trudeau government greatly augmented. There was also genuine doubt among economists in the seventies about the efficacy of traditional fiscal policy. Suppose that the main inflationary pressure came from wage push? If income tax rates were raised, what would happen? Might not workers just demand higher money wages, offsetting the effect of the higher taxes?

At first there was an attempt to use traditional weapons in traditional ways. The federal government ran an over-all surplus in 1969, 1970, 1973, and 1974. The relatively small deficits of 1971 and 1972 were swamped by the surpluses of other years. On balance, therefore, federal taxing and spending were exerting an anti-inflationary effect. In autumn 1968 Minister of Finance Benson announced that he would freeze public employment and control spending; he also raised the taxation of incomes and took other steps that were meant to produce more revenue. In 1969 he did nothing much to taxation, relying on the growth of GNP to raise government revenues enough to cover the 9.5 per cent increase in government outlays that he foresaw. Similarly in his March 1970 budget he raised no taxes, and as the year passed and unemployment became more of a problem he announced several new spending programs. In 1971, income taxation was reduced by 3 per cent (although the budget was chiefly concerned with the tax reforms that were described in the first part of this chapter), Benson's intention being to raise almost as much money with the new system as with the old. Thus the 1971 budget was meant to have some expansionary effect. In fact, income tax revenue continued its inexorable climb, growing more rapidly than outlays and eliminating the over-all deficit between 1972 and 1973. Benson may or may not have been wise, but at least he was trying to manage taxing and spending so as to move the economy in the direction he thought it ought to go.

After 1972 matters became more complicated, and the macro-economic direction became very unclear indeed. The new Minister of Finance, John Turner, raised income tax rates and reduced the taxation of corporations, while raising certain pensions and inflation-proofing all pensions for the aged, disabled, and veterans. To create jobs the government extended the Local Initiatives Programme it had launched in 1971, and it spruced up a variety of make-work projects, apparently in the belief that by directing its money to such projects it could create new jobs without raising prices – a dubious line of thought. In 1973, perhaps responding largely to NDP demands, Turner cut income taxes and raised pensions, and the government was still committed to the cutting of corporation income taxes; at the same time Turner indexed personal tax exemptions, raised veterans' allowances, and cut some excise taxes. The finance minister estimated that the total cost of the changes was $1.3 billion. Nevertheless, in 1974 total federal revenue was several billion higher than in 1973, and the federal surplus was $593 million – 2 per cent of federal revenue, and 0.4 per cent of GNP. The percentage was so small that the impact must have been insignificant. If NDP pressure had not determined the content of the budget, perhaps the finance minister would have brought down a more restrictive budget that would have made a serious contribution to the anti-inflationary fight.

Later that same year Prime Minister Trudeau announced that the government would battle inflation by raising various welfare payments and subsidies – exactly the wrong medicine. In May 1974 the budget was equally perverse. Turner proposed to reduce personal tax rates and to cut some sales taxes, while taxing corporations, vehicles, and alcohol more heavily. The budget, Turner explained, was meant to increase *supply*, thereby fighting inflation. But in the short run supply could not increase much, while inflation must be fought from month to month and week to week. In November 1974, announcing that he was steering a narrow course between inflation and the risk of recession, Turner reduced personal taxation while adjusting corporation tax rates and allowances in ways that were meant both to raise more revenue and to encourage new investment – once more, so as to increase supply. To the same end, some temporary tariff reductions were extended to 1976, and travellers got larger duty-free allowances, although these allowances were still smaller than they had been in the late 1940s and 1950s. In June 1975, price controls not yet having been introduced, Turner presented a 'neutral' budget. To increase supply and maintain investment there were various new gadgets. Some sales and excise taxes were raised and others were lowered, but now the main thrust was toward cost control. The unemployment scheme would be changed so as to save money, and so would the medicare grants to the provinces. Government spending would be restrained in a sense; it would grow only 15 per cent instead of the 20 per cent that had originally been intended. In terms of 1971 prices, GNP had grown only 1.2 per cent in 1975 and would grow only 5.4 per cent in 1976.

The next year saw a new finance minister and another change of direction. Donald Macdonald said he was worried about inflation, but his budget, which included a few tariff increases, larger personal deductions, and lower corporation taxation, did not reflect the fact. Indeed, the finance minister explained that his budget was meant to be mildly stimulative. However, he did take some steps to make the unemployment insurance machine somewhat less generous. In 1977, as unemployment was still rising, there was some public demand for an expansionary budget. In 1977 and 1978, although none of its critics thought it was going far enough, the Trudeau government responded by systematically cutting taxes in the face of its ever-widening budget deficit.

In March 1977, Donald Macdonald provided an extra $458 million on job creation, and distributed $300 million worth of special investment incentives that were meant to encourage business, to fight unemployment, and raise growth. Although the *Globe and Mail* called the result a 'standpat' budget, it would reduce taxes in 1978 by over a billion dollars. In Jean Chrétien's two 1978 budgets the direction was much the same. Those who had expected a bountiful pre-election giveaway in April were disappointed. One Toronto economist called the package 'niggling.' But Chrétien did give yet further encouragement to business investment, focusing this time on research and development, railways, and heavy oil. Also, and most ingeniously, he offered to pay most of the cost if the provinces would cut their retail sales taxes for six months. In November 1978 he went further, cutting Ottawa's own manufacturers' sales tax from 12 per cent to 9 per cent, reducing the unemployment insurance premium scale for 1979, and extending various incentive schemes. As the government had made some spending cuts in August 1978, the second Chrétien budget might be said to balance off the spending cuts with tax cuts. But if the government had been serious about fighting inflation it would not have cut taxes at all.

Although no one would have predicted such a development from the tenor of the spring election campaign, by December 1979 it seemed that the Conservative cabinet had reached exactly this conclusion. When John Crosbie presented his budget on December 11, austerity was the watchword. The problem was inflation; the government would have to manage its affairs with prudence so as gradually to restore a balance between income and outgo; gone without trace was the Clark plan for a sharp but temporary cut in the income tax. Corporations would pay more tax at once, and so would consumers of beer, wine, cigarettes, and gasoline. Unemployment insurance premiums would go up. In spring 1979 the Tories had promised to let houseowners offset their mortgage payments against their tax liabilities. But even before the budget was presented Canadians had learned that this plan had been modified to save money and to appear less unfair; also, they knew that it would come only in stages. Crosbie announced that there would be new energy tax credits, but these would only partly offset the new taxation, and the government intended that in real terms (after allowing for inflation) it would be spending no more in 1984 than in 1980. Did it mean what it said? Could it have honoured its pledges? In January 1980 the electorate deprived the historian of any chance to find out.

When inflation co-exists with economic growth, as in Canada during the 1970s, government revenues will rise automatically unless tax rates are cut. If old programs do not become more costly or if new programs are not invented, the result will be a steady growth in the government surplus, and this surplus will have an ever-larger anti-inflationary effect. But Canada's federal government had gradually adopted many programs whose costs could not easily be controlled. Furthermore, by indexing personal exemptions and by raising so many pensions and other benefits to offset the effects of inflation, the government had connived at an erosion of its own tax base and a further increase in its uncontrollable outlays. To make matters worse, from time to time the government transferred more of the shared-tax fields, especially the income tax, to the provinces. Then there was lavish if temporary expansion of some old programs, such as DREE, coupled with a tendency to invent new programs. One notable example was the oil import subsidy. Meant originally to be self-balancing through the tax on oil exports, the subsidy soon became a heavy charge on the exchequer. There was also a noticeable and increasing tendency to cut business taxes rather than personal income taxes so as to encourage business investment. Even though in 1975-8 federal revenues marched on upward, expenses grew faster. To finance its operations the government had to borrow from the Bank of Canada and from anyone else who would lend to it. Throughout the seventies it was an active borrower because it had to finance so many things – CMHC, extra holdings of US dollars in certain years, and also the investment plans of the CNR and of so many other Crown corporations.

During the years 1968 through 1978, Ottawa had to find $24 billion for the ordinary purposes of government. But on balance there was a cumulative surplus through 1974, and in 1975-8 a budget deficit of $26 billion, of which $11 billion was needed in 1978 alone. This was the fiscal disaster area that the Clark government discovered when it assumed power. During 1975-8, after allowing for the financing of CMHC, the CNR, and the changing reserves of foreign exchange, the government actually had to borrow $22 billion. The Bank of Canada provided $3.8 billion, the chartered banks $1.6 billion, and the Canada Savings Bonds campaigns $7 billion. The rest – $9.6 billion – was raised by selling other kinds of bonds and, in certain years, by drawing down the government's own holdings of cash. Most economists thought that these patterns of financing were uncomfortably inflationary. Because Canada Savings Bonds could be converted into money for their full face value on demand they were thought to be almost like money; when the Bank of Canada purchases government bonds it automatically adds to the reserves of the chartered banks, thus making it possible for the banks to create more money and credit; when the banks themselves buy government bonds they do it by crediting government accounts, thus directly increasing the supply of money.

To sell new issues of Canada Savings Bonds, and to ensure that people would keep the old issues they had bought in the past, the government repeatedly raised the interest it would pay on these bonds, so that by 1979 the yield on CSBs was at last slightly above the current rate of inflation. These increases helped to pull money into the treasury, and sometimes to keep it there. But what really saved the government, especially in the face of the yawning fiscal chasm of 1978, was the sale of foreign exchange – chiefly US dollars – from the national hoard. In 1968, 1970-2, 1974, and 1976, the government had bought US dollars to keep the Canadian dollar from rising too fast and too far in relation to the American. Naturally it had supplied Canadian dollars in exchange for the US dollars that it bought. But in 1977 and especially in 1978 it was *selling* US dollars in exchange for Canadian dollars so as to prevent our dollar from *falling* too fast and too far. Thus in 1977 it pulled in almost a billion dollars this way and, in 1979, $5.5 billion – fully half of the government deficit for which financing had to be found.

Lavish though the developments of the Trudeau years had been, as taxer and spender the federal government had in fact long since lost the primacy to the junior governments. In 1974 the federal surplus was only 0.4 per cent of GNP. It seemed that the government might be wise to ignore the macroeconomic impact of its own taxing and spending, concentrating instead on the manipulation of business investment. In the mid-seventies, indeed, some economists thought that they were foolish to spend so much time analysing Ottawa's deficits and surpluses. But the period 1975-8 saw an explosion of federal spending. Deficits reappeared, and they yawned ever wider, so that in 1978 the federal deficit was 5 per cent of GNP – quite large enough to affect unemployment, inflation, and the value of the dollar.

After 1974 the federal fiscal position went from bad to worse. Every year there were deficits, and these grew steadily. It is no wonder that in the 1979 election the Tories could say that the budget was out of control, and the Liberals could not defend themselves very well. But the problem had complicated origins. Federal revenues grew quite steadily, from $29 billion in 1974 to $37 billion in 1978, a gain of 28 per cent. Federal spending on goods and services – that is on salaries and commodities – rose $5 billion, of which $1.6 billion was extra defence outlays. The cost of the debt more than doubled, rising from $3 billion to $6.4 billion. But transfer payments to persons, such as unemployment insurance, rose from $8.7 billion to $14.6 billion, while payment to the provinces rose from $6 billion to $10.5 billion; subsidies to businesses, including the oil import subsidies, rose from $2.8 billion to $4 billion. In percentage terms, *every* kind of spending was outgrowing revenue. But there was plenty of extra revenue to cover the extra outlay on goods and services. Thus in a sense it is all the other things – subsidies to persons, businesses, and provinces, plus debt-service – that pushed the federal exchequer so very deeply into the red. Indeed, by 1978, to bring the budget back into balance *without* cutting these subsidies and grants would have forced Ottawa to reduce its basic outlays on goods and services from $12 billion to $0.6 billion. In 1979 the new Clark administration would talk of shrinking the public payroll by 60,000 persons. But it could not possibly shed enough public servants to make much of a dent in the deficit.

Whatever the government may have been saying at the time, it would be absurd to maintain that Ottawa was really fighting inflation in 1975-9. If federal taxing and spending were aimed in any particular direction, that direction was anti-unemployment. But we should ask ourselves whether, given the origins of the deficits, Ottawa could really have done much better. To a quite remarkable extent they came from things that the government could change slowly or not at all. Indeed, in real terms federal spending on goods and services was almost constant, and it was certainly rising less rapidly than national output. In principle, of course, Ottawa could have raised tax rates. But in 1978, to balance the budget would have implied a 31 per cent increase in federal taxation. Need we wonder why no one tried or why federal finance ministers came and went?

Whatever the frustrations of macroeconomic management in a federal state where spending is out of control, Ottawa certainly could and did manage the exchange rate and the national holdings of foreign money, the foreign exchange reserves, all by itself. Occasionally a province would bleat that it should be allowed a voice. But although Ottawa politicians certainly listened to the voters all across the country, with respect to the exchange rate they did not listen to the provincial premiers. Nor did they need to heed the Americans with respect to the foreign exchange reserves. As we saw in the last chapter, in December 1968 Canada recovered the power to vary its holdings of foreign money without giving up its preferential access to American finance.

By that time Bank of Canada Governor Louis Rasminsky, seriously worried about inflation, wanted to control the money supply quite tightly. Thus in 1969 national output grew 5.3 per cent, while chartered bank reserves *fell* slightly, and in 1970 reserves and output grew in step with one another. These arrangements were part of an anti-inflation campaign that probably created more unemployment in 1969-70 than either Rasminsky or the government had intended. When unemployment rose still more in 1971-2, the monetary system expanded very rapidly indeed, and it is tempting to suspect that this expansion was an anti-unemployment policy.

The anti-inflation campaign of 1969-70 attracted funds from abroad. Also, in 1970, for the first time in nearly twenty years, we began to run a *surplus* in the current account of our balance of payments. Our foreign purchases fell slightly. Our receipts from abroad jumped sharply upward; the result was a current account surplus of nearly one billion dollars in 1970 – almost exactly the same as the current account deficit Canada had run in 1969.

These developments produced enormous pressures on Canada's monetary system. The government could keep the exchange rate pegged at 92.5 American cents only by massive purchases of foreign money on the foreign exchange market. But, as we have noted several times in earlier chapters, to make such purchases the Bank basically creates Canadian money in the required amount, adding to the money supply and to inflationary pressure. Although the causes were not quite the same as in early 1950 (when the fixed exchange rate had last been abandoned), the manifestations were basically similar, and the authorities responded in the same way: on May 31, 1970, the Canadian dollar was allowed to float away from its 1962 peg.

Obviously the dollar would have to rise, given the strength of world demand for it. Even if the government had wanted to re-peg at a higher figure, it would have had trouble choosing a number, because the world monetary scene was so turbulent and uncertain at that time. One thing was clear: a rising dollar would be anti-inflationary, because it would cheapen imports and discourage exports. Even so, after the float the government tried to prevent the monetary policy, capital inflow, and current account surplus from pushing the exchange rate to politically unattractive heights. For every tourist who rejoiced that his dollar would go farther in Florida, there was a farmer or factory worker who worried about the link between a dear dollar and dismal life at home. Thus in the course of 1970 Canada's US dollar holdings rose 73 per cent even though the Canadian dollar was rising fast on the foreign exchange market. Also, the Bank and the Minister of Finance tried persuasion: to reduce the inflow of foreign capital they asked Canadian borrowers to 'explore very carefully the possibilities of doing their necessary financing in Canadian markets.'

For the rest of the decade the Canadian dollar floated. It floats still.

Late in 1971, the government made a political virtue out of this necessity. When he returned from a meeting at which governments had agreed on a new set of exchange rates for the capitalist world economy, Canada's finance minister explained that Canada had won the right to keep its floating dollar, which was, he said, priced by the forces of supply and demand. But this was not so. Throughout the seventies the float was a very dirty one. Trying to moderate the movements of the floating rate, the government built up reserves at some times and spent them at others. In December 1968 Canada's international reserves were $3 billion US. In December 1970, after a year in which the Canadian dollar had risen from a discount of 7 per cent almost to parity with the American, they were $4.6 billion, having increased almost 50 per cent in a single year. In 1971-2 they rose further, and so did the dollar: in December 1972 the reserves were $6 billion, and the dollar had risen about 2 per cent since the end of 1970. Obviously Ottawa was trying to moderate the rise by buying US dollars in exchange for Canadian. In the mid-seventies both reserves and dollar rate fluctuated. In May 1974, for example, Canadians could buy an American dollar for only 96.2 cents. But throughout 1975 the American dollar commanded a premium, and Canada's American-dollar reserves were declining as government tried to prevent a more drastic rise in its price.

The current account surplus lasted only two years – 1970-1. Thereafter the deficits reappeared. The strength of Canada's dollar depended critically on capital imports. When a lot of foreign money was flowing into Canada, the dollar tended to be bid up, and the government tended to moderate the rise by adding to its reserves. When the inflow slackened or reversed itself the dollar weakened and reserves tended to fall. Meanwhile, the international financial scene grew more disturbed year by year, and Canada's current account deficit was tending to rise in absolute size even though it was not particularly large relative to either production or exports. Thus when, in 1977-8, less capital came in and the import gap widened, the Canadian dollar fell with a thud. The government spent reserves and borrowed abroad, but it did not borrow or spend enough to avoid a slide, first below parity with the American dollar, to the mid-nineties, then to the mid-eighties, and then, for a few days in February 1979, even lower. In 1979 the rate seemed to be more or less stable in the range of 84-87 cents, but nobody could be sure how long it would stay there.

Just as the rise in the early seventies had tended to deflate the economy, so the fall in the late seventies tended to raise prices and stimulate production in Canada, nor did it seem that wage rates rose enough to offset the competitive edge that the depreciation had given the economy. Thus it was inconvenient that wage and price controls ended in October 1978, when the Canadian dollar was already slithering downward. By mid-1979 there were signs that the slide had created new profits, exports, and jobs, and there was still not much sign that it had pushed up wage rates. But nothing final could be said about the effects, because these would only appear gradually, and much later.

Although fiscal policy and exchange-rate policy were sensibly anti-inflationary at least some of the time in the early and mid-seventies, for ten of the eleven Trudeau years the Bank of Canada and the banking system were systematically stoking the inflationary fires. On a narrow definition (currency plus demand deposits in chartered banks) the money supply grew 4.3 per cent in 1968, 7.1 per cent in 1969, 2.3 per cent in 1970, 13 per cent per year in 1970-74, and 10 per cent per year in 1975-8 – an average of 9.5 per cent per year for the Trudeau years. On broader definitions which include such things as chequable savings accounts, the money supply grew considerably faster – 12.7 per cent per year in 1969-78 by one definition, and 15.8 per cent in 1971-8 by another. Only in 1970 did output grow a little faster than money, and then only if the supply of money is defined in the narrowest possible way. But for the decade as a whole it is obvious that money, growing at 9.5 per cent per year or more, was outgrowing output, which expanded only 4.5 per cent per year.

Until after 1974 the government's own deficit was not to blame. We have seen that in 1969-74 there was a cumulative government surplus. But we have also noticed that in 1975-8 the federal deficits were so large that the Bank of Canada had to create a good deal of extra money just to help finance the state. Also, throughout the seventies the money supply was growing because some government projects –

CMHC, the exchange reserves, the Crown corporations – often needed more finance than the budget could provide from current taxation. Furthermore, the inflationary process itself created a need for more money and credit, just to keep the wheels of commerce turning. If the price level doubles, the typical household will need twice as many dollars, on the average, just to bridge the distance between one payday and another. Credit cards, which proliferated in the seventies, provided a considerable cushion offset, but not a complete one.

In principle the Bank of Canada could have followed the same sort of tight-money policy that James Coyne had followed in the late fifties. Since the dollar was floating in both decades, the effect would have been much the same – a more valuable dollar, more imports, fewer exports, a much larger inflow of foreign capital, more unemployment. Prices would therefore have risen more slowly; but these unpleasant side effects would have been unpopular to say the least. However, the Bank and the government might have argued that they were simply following the same sort of expansionary path that other countries, especially Britain and the United States, were taking. Indeed, in 1973-5 it was usual for Ottawa to say that because inflation was a world-wide phenomenon Canada could not really avoid it. This was a half-truth at best. West Germany is as tied to the world economy as Canada is. So is Switzerland. Yet the German mark and the Swiss franc rose ever higher, and in both countries there was little inflation. Perhaps this was one of the many things that the Prime Minister learned on that apparently fateful visit to Bonn in summer 1978.

The Bank knew perfectly well that its policies were adding to inflation. By the late seventies it had begun to announce its targets for monetary expansion, and it said that it would lower these targets year by year so as to convince people that there would not be enough money to fuel further inflation. Regrettably, just when the Bank was announcing this new line of policy the federal budget deficit was moving out of control. It would remain to be seen who would give way – the Bank's governor or the finance minister. By early 1980 some observers were expecting to see a revival of the Diefenbaker confrontations, with a different cast but with the same basic plot.

During the 1970s Canadians all learned new lessons. The Canadian economy became a major topic for debate at dinner parties and for concern in corporate boardrooms. The decade disappointed most Canadians, perhaps because their expectations had been so high in 1970. That was not so in 1980.

34

Living in the Seventies:
Culture, Education, and Social Trends

In 1974 Pierre Trudeau reportedly decided not to make a speech on his government's cultural policy because the topic was deemed politically too sensitive. Twenty-five years before it would have been simply ludicrous. In the quarter century since the Massey Commission, the state had become the major supporter of cultural activity in Canada, and an articulate pressure group had appeared to assure that the source that had brought life continued to nurture what it had created. Through content quotas, direct subsidies, and tax relief, the state recognized that culture was a legitimate area for large-scale operations. Sometimes the contrasts with the past were astonishing. In the mid-seventies the British Columbia Minister of Public Works (a portfolio usually associated with bridges and roads), referred to art as 'the sensitizing object' and 'an essential ingredient in our society.' Alberta's head of the Cultural Development Division in the Ministry of Government Services dreamed of Alberta as 'the cultural capital of the North American continent.' Money builds capitals, and here Alberta's commitment in 1976 to spend $400,000,000 on cultural facilities suggests that there was more than rhetoric in Canada's most prosperous province. Quebec, of course, had less money, but its nationalism and the close ties between the Liberal and Péquiste politicians and the university community meant that the government inevitably took responsibility for promotion of culture. Throughout Canada the munificence was remarkable. In 1964, government support for Canadian museums, art galleries, and related institutions was $6,060,067; six years later it was $22,478,511. Canada's per capita support of the arts in 1971 was almost ten times that of the United States. Canada was no longer a nation whose art collectors embarrassed art's finest critics and whose professional artists were as scarce as palm trees and, like palms in Canada, something to be kept inside in bare corners. In 1952, Canadian artists exported 52 works; in 1962, 1,116; and in 1974, 9,131. Similarly, Canadian buyers imported 1,329 works of art in 1952, 5,222 in 1962, and 32,680 in 1974. State support for artists thus paralleled, and was the corollary of, a public sympathy for the arts that had not been present earlier.

'... *the Canada Council and the* CRTC *are there to make us cultured Canadians, and we've always gone along with it....'*
(Norris, 1977). Reproduced with the permission of Norris, the *Vancouver Sun*

It is hoped that the reader will not necessarily regard as special pleading (although admittedly university professors are given to such activity) the suggestion that the major factor in this creation of new tastes among Canadians is the expansion of educational opportunity in Canada. Leisure and affluence are, of course, important factors; yet when one considers the creation of culture, the part played by education is clear. A survey of artists by *Arts Canada* in 1976 indicated that 10 per cent of artists' incomes came from sales, 10 per cent from direct grants, and 40 per cent from teaching and related occupations (10 per cent also came from unemployment insurance and welfare). The discontent in the artistic community in the late 1970s can, therefore, be seen as directly related to the ailments that afflicted Canadian education; having endured severe growing pains in the 1950s and 1960s the educational system now faces, in the vernacular, a severe mid-life crisis.

Urged by Quebec and the other provinces, the Trudeau government gradually disengaged itself from the educational system that federal money had done so much to build up in the 1950s and 1960s. Ottawa continued to finance much of the training and retraining of adults. Through the Canada Council and the other research councils it still financed a great deal of research in the universities. It still operated the military colleges at Kingston, Victoria, and St Jean. Through DREE, it helped finance schools in the backward regions. But it did not renew the provisions for financing secondary vocational and technical education that it had devised in the early sixties. And in university finance it made a gradual exit. The universities were not happy about this. In province after province, the fiscal net was gradually tightened around them. Provincial authorities now controlled fee scales. Sometimes they treated endowment income as an offset that reduced the provincial grants. Generally they failed to raise grants in step with inflation, although the pattern differed from province to province. In the early fifties, faced with a similar squeeze, the universities had won federal subsidies to supplement provincial grants. By 1977, when in some respects the situation was parallel, it was apparent that Ottawa would not listen.

For the universities the Trudeau years were difficult; and the troubles were not all financial. Full-time enrolments continued to rise, but much less rapidly than in the sixties. Indeed, by the mid-seventies some locales saw enrolments falling, and, especially where enrolments determined grants, there were already some signs of a scramble for students. By 1979 the scrambling was much more widespread. Part-time studies expanded greatly, and much better arrangements came to be made for the part-time student, but the numbers did not explode as the futurologists had forecast in the late sixties. In any case, part-time students did not fit neatly into curricula that had been designed for full-time study, and in general it was the curriculum that gave way, as one university after another, in response to economic and student pressure, adopted some form of the American 'credit system.' This system had already firmly rooted itself in many provincial secondary systems. The credit system was a neat way to meet the demands for 'flexibility' and 'freedom of choice' that were so often heard in the late sixties, when a great deal of time and effort had had to go into redesigning curricula.

At the same time, on many campuses there were disorders that reflected or imitated developments in Europe and the United States. Journalists began to write 'think pieces' about student revolutionaries. Student politicians brooded on an American tract, *The Student as Nigger*, and began to suffer from delusions of grandeur in which terrified administrators often encouraged them to indulge. At Toronto and elsewhere students sat in; at Sir George Williams they occupied part of the building and destroyed the computer. There was pressure to insert students into administration at all levels, from appointments committee to board of governors. There were demands for Black studies, native studies, women's studies, urban and environmental studies, and, of course, Canadian studies. In addition, because some student leaders – and some faculty members – wanted changes that would make university study more flexible and, probably, easier than before, the old curricular arrangements came under attack.

By the late seventies many of these stresses had passed. The revolutionary student had largely vanished, at least partly because it was now clear that a university degree did not guarantee a good job. Students were working harder and opting for the more structured and vocationally oriented courses (such as commerce) where job prospects were thought to be good and where rewards were quicker and more certain. There were demands for a return to a more structured program of study, although there were endless arguments about the shape that structure should take. The old certainties were gone, and the years of freedom had taken their toll.

In 1977-8 enrolments finally began their predicted fall. Everyone had known that a decline was on the way, but the change came more quickly than most people expected. Some universities responded by lowering their entry standards. Others were more imaginative. For instance, in autumn 1979 Karma Buddhist College enrolled its first students. Affiliated with Brock University, Karma had been founded to perpetuate the Kargyu strain of Tibetan Buddhism. Although its courses were not to count for academic credit, Karma claimed (or at least hoped) to bring students 'to a greater, higher level of self-realisation.' To the optimists, it represented a last flutter from the flower people of the sixties. To the pessimists, it looked like a desperate step, meant to bring more students to Brock. Time would tell whether either end, or both, would be reached and whether other universities would adopt equally unusual expedients.

The early seventies saw a boom in Canadian studies and 'Canadianization.' From Carleton University Professors Robin Mathews and James Steele were issuing anti-American manifestos. In Ontario a legislative committee called for measures to bring about a Canadianization of faculties. Gradually the immigration authorities responded, not only to such demands but also to protect the job prospects of Canada's graduate students. As so few universities were hiring by the mid-seventies little Canadianization was possible, but where jobs were available there was a natural pressure to favour the Canadian candidate. And no doubt in some places there was a great deal that could properly be done. Without substantial drafts of foreigners the university expansion of the sixties and early seventies could not have happened. But it is also possible that the recruitment arrangements of the sixties had not always been quite fair to Canadian candidates. Whether or not this was really so, there was a widespread feeling that the universities should be more Canadian, both in staff and in program. Hence the efflorescence of courses in all aspects of Canadian life, literature, and society. The wave of Canadian content even spread abroad. Responding to sarcastic comment and anxious to strengthen Canada's links with Europe and the Far East, Ottawa began to subsidize Canadian studies programs in Japan, Britain, and other countries of continental Europe, as well as in the United States. The results were sometimes funny, and often ineffective, but at least the government was trying to dispel that ignorance about Canada of which travelling Canadians had so often complained.

Besides the universities and their affiliates, which enrolled 374,000 full-time students in autumn 1977, there were the community colleges, which enrolled 240,000. Of these 34 per cent were in university transfer programs, very largely in Quebec. Ten years before, the Quebec Collèges d'enseignement générale et professionel (CEGEPs) had not existed, and in the other provinces there had been little or no higher education outside the universities. But in the seventies an ever-growing amount of university-type work was being done in the community colleges, which also offered a vast range of career programs. In 1966, 14.2 per cent of all Canadians aged eighteen to twenty-four were enrolled in some sort of full-time schooling, almost entirely in the universities. By 1976 the percentage had risen to 19.4 per cent, partly because the community colleges offered so many new and attractive alternatives to university study. Having risen steadily for twenty years, in 1977-8 university full-time enrolments actually fell a little, as did enrolments in community college transfer programs, while the colleges' career programs went from strength to strength. More Canadian students seemed to want easier entrance requirements, shorter courses clearly focused on jobs, and a somewhat less pressured academic environment. All these things the community colleges could offer. Indeed, most of them had been designed to do just that.

Although there had been a few junior colleges in Canada, the decade of the sixties was a time of new foundations – institutes of technology, community colleges of various kinds in the anglophone provinces, and in Quebec the CEGEPs. By 1968 Ontario already had some twenty Colleges of Applied Arts and Technology (CAATs), and Quebec soon came to possess some thirty-seven CEGEPs, of which four operated in English. Some twenty-eight classical colleges had survived in Quebec, but they were now of much less significance than before. In the early seventies, Alberta and British Columbia saw a flowering of junior colleges, while in Saskatchewan, Manitoba, and the Atlantic provinces, governments showed some inclination to adopt or adapt the Ontario CAAT.

What did all this expansion mean in terms of learning? It was hard to say. Many of the institutions, such as Ryerson in Toronto and the BC Institute of Technology in Vancouver, successfully developed rigorous training schemes whose graduates were welcomed in the work world. But the CEGEPs were a very mixed bag, especially in their university transfer streams. In British Columbia, some university people thought that transfer students from the junior colleges were not really ready for senior work in the universities, and some observers regretted the passing of the old senior matriculation system, by which some high schools offered what was in effect first-year university.

Whatever the junior colleges and other community colleges were trying to do, like the universities they were working with students who often seemed to have learned less than expected in secondary school. No one quite knew what had gone wrong, but by 1979 most observers agreed that something had. In Ontario, it was usual to blame the erasure of the old high-school curriculum with its limited freedom of choice, the introduction of a credit system with free options, and the abolition of external examinations for high school exit or university entrance. In other provinces the same general trends could be detected during the seventies, and if these criticisms were proper in one province, presumably they applied in nine or more. In Quebec it was often believed that the state secondary schools had grown too fast, staffing themselves with ill-prepared young enthusiasts whose main interests were political. In the late seventies there were signs of a reaction here and there, partly because parents, discovering what was actually happening in the schools, began to protest. But both teachers and educational establishments had grown attached to the new system, and it remained to be seen how much change they would allow.

The slippage in standards was doubly surprising because for the first time in a quarter of a century the schools did not have to cope with an ever-rising wave of pupils. Enrolments in elementary and secondary schools peaked in 1970, and thereafter they dropped nearly 10 per cent in the course of the decade, reflecting the falling birth-rates of the 1960s. The result was panic in the teachers' unions, and joy in ministries of education. Teachers' colleges closed or reduced their intakes. Ministries raised the standards for certification, especially in elementary teaching. In universities, fewer students concentrated on the humanities subjects that in the fifties and sixties would have led to a secure if demanding career in schoolteaching. In the schools themselves, pupils were allowed to shift away from the more academic or difficult subjects. Thus the free-choice curriculum made things worse so far as many teachers were concerned. These trends were especially noticeable and alarming with respect to the study of French in the anglophone provinces. Although many schools were extending and improving their French instruction, and although some school districts were mounting impressive immersion schemes, fewer anglophone pupils were actually studying the other national language. Trudeauvian bilingualism was unpopular, and French was supposed to be difficult. In francophone Canada, it seems that more pupils were studying English, but chiefly because more teenagers were staying in school. Some observers thought that the average Quebec pupil was actually mastering less English than before. If so, the fact would be further fuel for the separatist bonfire.

As parents came to believe that in the public schools their children would learn little, not enough, or nothing, private schools flourished. Their enrolments rose from 140,000 in 1971 to 182,000 in 1975, even though total enrolment was falling from 5.8 million to 5.6 million. Many new schools were founded, and some old ones managed to raise not only the calibre of their intakes but also the quality of their efforts. Of course some of the private schools specialized in trendy trivia; but others offered remarkably rigorous academic programs. One new foundation, the Lester Pearson College on Vancouver Island, was planned with a view to build international friendship by mixing pupils from different countries.

It was often thought that the separate and parochial schools did a better job than the public schools, even though they had less money, because both pupils and teachers took discipline more seriously. Whether or not this was so, in many cities separate school enrolment went on rising long after public school enrolments had begun to fall. This was largely because so many immigrant families were Roman Catholic. More pupils meant better morale, but the results could sometimes look grotesque, as separate school boards put up new schools while public school boards worried about empty classrooms.

There were still some disputes about the financing of denominational schools. In British Columbia, the Roman Catholics campaigned from time to time to acquire tax dollars. In Ontario, where tax support for separate schools ended with Grade 10, there were efforts, notably by the Liberal party, to extend the support through Grade 13 and to make it more generous. In Ontario, too, there was some agonizing about government financing of church-related colleges and theological faculties. But by the mid-seventies this kind of worry had come to seem increasingly anachronistic. In disputes about schools and schooling, it was now language that mattered; not religion.

What mattered in Canadian social life is not yet clear. We surely cannot say now what future generations will deem significant. Our comments are admittedly eclectic, some might say eccentric, but they represent our impression of some of those trends that might endure and some of those events that will stay in Candians' memories.

The seventies neither roared nor soared nor were dirty. Adjectives shun the decade, but for Canadians, change came quickly yet not in a regular pattern. This was the decade in which the sexual revolution really hit the Dominion of the North. Birth rates, having fallen for almost a decade, stabilized at or slightly below the net reproduction rate. For the first time since the thirties, one-child families were chic. In the great cities there were more varieties of family structure, and these families were far less stable than ever before. Pre-marital intercourse was now reported to be so common as to be commonplace. Divorce was also more common as a result of the 1968 changes in the divorce law. Between 1971 and 1974 divorces rose from 20,685 to 45,019; the latter number almost seven times the number in 1961. The stigma attached to illegitimacy all but disappeared. For the first time, the one-parent family became a noticeable fact in Canadian urban life. On the other hand, the unwanted baby was a vanishing species, as the adoption agencies discovered. In spite of a vocal right-to-life movement, abortion was now frequent, simple, often easy, and getting steadily easier. The Pill was readily available, although its effects worried many women who chose interuterine devices instead. Condoms could be bought almost everywhere, now that it was no longer illegal to display or sell them. As for pornography, although the really hard and nasty material was still not widely sold, there was far more soft porn in the late seventies than ever before. By then there were signs of a change of heart with respect to these materials. In 1978 the government that had taken the policeman out of the bedroom was actively considering bringing him back to the magazine rack. Indeed, its proposals would have let any local authority ban almost any printed material, anything from *Pericles* to *Penthouse*, if local sensibilities found it offensive. What might be done about porn on home video-tape remained to be seen. But whatever might happen to the porn industry, there was no reason to expect any general sexual counter-revolution.

As with sex, so with drugs. During the seventies the drug culture peaked, and parts of it became respectable. In 1969 LSD and STP became 'restricted drugs,' and thereafter fewer Canadians went tripping on hallucinogens. But the LeDain Commission recommended that marijuana should be 'decriminalized,' and although nothing was formally done, the drift of police and judicial action was clearly to de-emphasize the cannabis problem. More and more people came to believe that reefers were no more harmful than rye. There seemed to be less social smoking – the ritual passing-around of a joint. But as the adolescents of the sixties became the young executives and professionals of the seventies, perhaps there was more scope for extended and private enjoyment. As for heroin and the other drugs that everyone admitted were really dangerous, the addiction problem certainly did not diminish, and the crime it generated did not grow less. But by the mid-seventies the teenager was a dying breed, killed off by the Pill. Both absolutely and relatively there were fewer adolescents than there had been ten years before. Also, there were plenty of signs that the young were turning back to the traditional solace of earlier generations – booze. Now most provinces let the young drink at eighteen or nineteen, and sales statistics showed that the young would be even more tempted by John Barleycorn and his friends than their parents had been. Total alcohol consumption increased from 394,532,000 gallons in 1970 to 520,068,000 in 1978.

Nearly all the social indicators that Canadians had traditionally used to measure the stability of their society seemed to reflect instability in the 1970s. The abortion rate rose from 8.3 per 100 live births in 1971 to 17.4 in 1978. Suicides increased from 2,559 in 1971 to 3,317 in 1977; and especially troubling were the rises in rape convictions from 1,019 in 1969 to 1,886 in 1977 and in murder convictions from 342 to 624. What these indicators mean is no longer so certain as it seemed when Sir Wilfrid Laurier proudly compared our divorce and crime rates to those of the decadent Americans. Many commentators followed Christopher Lasch in suggesting that the pattern of changes in social behaviour reflects the narcissism of modern culture. This idea generated the phrase 'the me decade,' a common label for the seventies. Perhaps the label fits and will stick, but it would be unfortunate if these trends, which reflect the decline of restraints upon individuals and a diminished concern for the welfare of the community as a whole, were seen through the narrow focus of a decade and a single nation. Even in Canada itself, regional variation was striking:

the divorce rates in British Columbia and Newfoundland were, in 1978, 326.7 per 100,000 and 75 per 100,000, respectively. In all these things Canada followed the Western world generally and the changes reflected patterns already apparent in earlier decades. Moreover, if so many social critics lamented the way we lived now, there were many positive changes which the critics of an earlier generation had demanded but never really expected. We had artistic and educational opportunities beyond our fondest hopes in 1945, and a much greater proportion of the population took advantage of these opportunities.

The sixties was the great decade of building to house the arts. Alberta built two identical concert halls, one for Edmonton and one for Calgary. Vancouver built the Queen Elizabeth Theatre and the smaller Playhouse. Thanks to the centennial celebrations of 1967, Charlottetown got a theatrical showpiece, Toronto eventually got the St Lawrence Centre for the Performing Arts, and, most important and most valuable, Ottawa got the National Arts Centre. More theatres and halls opened in 1970. Thereafter, little occurred: the last major project was the Shaw Festival Theatre. But the good work had been done. Provided at last with suitable venues, Canada's performing arts blossomed. By 1970 there were repertory companies in Halifax, Fredericton, Montreal, Ottawa, Toronto, every major prairie centre, Vancouver, and Victoria. Some summer festivals, such as Vancouver's, sank without trace. Others, such as Stratford, withered steadily in artistic merit while triumphing at the box office and at the rich subsidy trough. Still others, such as the Shaw Festival at Niagara-on-the-Lake, went from strength to strength. And off the great and very expensive stages there was a flowering of less expensive and less lavish theatre. This kind of thing was most noticeable in Toronto and Montreal, but other cities were affected too. Subsidies helped, of course. So did unemployment insurance. Quality varied, partly because so few companies really had to depend on pleasing the public, and partly because acting had become a form of self-expression, not a form of discipline. There were troubles with directors, too. Some were criticized, especially Stratford's Robin Phillips, who was accused of mingling a disrespect for the classic texts with an interest in gimmickry. Others, such as George Luscombe in Toronto, did well in spite of Marxist and populist obsessions. Not that such obsessions were peculiar to directors. Playwrights shared them, and as subsidies spread and theatres sprang up there were opportunities for the 'genuinely Canadian play' – everything from Merrill Denison's *March Hay* to Robertson Davies' *Pontiac and the Green Man* and Michel Tremblay's *Belles sœurs* and *St Carmen of the Main*, surely one of the most boring pieces of theatre ever thrust upon the public. But at least for Tremblay's play there was a public, both in English and in French. For the outpourings of many other Canadian playwrights this could not be said. Subsidized companies *performed* the plays, yes. But often the audience stayed away in droves. And the Toronto Truck Theatre, which did well at the box office on things like *The Mousetrap*, was vilified by the 'arts community' because it was both popular *and* unsubsidized.

In parallel with all this there was some genuinely commercial theatre activity. In 1970, *Hair* ran for a year at the Royal Alexandra Theatre in Toronto and for twelve weeks in Montreal. Ed Mirvish, having grown rich as a retail merchant, bought the Royal Alex, ran it as a commercial proposition, and appeared to grow still richer. Summer stock companies performed popular plays without subsidy. In some cities, touring companies still came from Britain and from New York. Affluent Canadians were increasingly inclined to use theatre as a decoration to their lives, and the theatres, both subsidized and unsubsidized, mounted massive campaigns to get the public away from the TV screens and into the stalls.

As for theatre, so for opera, ballet, modern dance, and music. Although the subsidies never seemed large enough, the trend was certainly upward, and provinces and cities joined corporations and the Canada Council in underwriting the massive budgets, while, from time to time, the banks presumably carried the massive deficits. Sometimes patience failed, of course. In 1979 the Festival Singers of Canada went messily bankrupt. The Canadian Opera Company stuck largely to things that it knew the public wanted to hear. Admittedly, in 1967 and thereafter it had performed Somers's *Louis Riel*. But this was a special centennial project, with special foundation subsidies. Anyway, Riel was on his way to secular beatification, and no one could deny that he was genuinely Canadian. The three major ballet companies toured and polished and trained, daring to face critical audiences in New York, London, and even the Soviet Union (the same could not be said of the subsidized theatre companies). Ottawa's National Arts Centre, opened in 1969, quickly earned a distinguished reputation as home of a summer opera festival and as year-round base for Mario Bernardi and the National Arts Centre Orchestra. There were more symphony orchestras, too, and more of these were approaching international standing. Vancouver brought Richard Bonynge to run its new opera, and, from a base in Halifax, the Atlantic Symphony Orchestra toured ceaselessly, except when its members were on strike.

Every so often there were nervous twinges about all this. Was the whole thing *too* dependent on subsidy? What would happen if the money ran out? In summer 1979, when the federal government was talking about cutbacks once again, the annual meeting of Canada's 'dance community,' both classical and modern, meditated with some seriousness on possible politicization. One commentator almost wished this would happen, because the result would surely be the most graceful and well-conducted protest march Parliament Hill could ever hope to see.

In cinema, too, subsidy combined with tax gimmickry was working a miracle, both in quantity and in artistic quality. The latter, of course, was mixed: at one extreme, *Mon Oncle Antoine*; in the middle, *Goin' down the Road*; at the other,

Meatballs. The distributing industry was largely Canadianized. Although the number of movie houses was falling, small new houses were still opening, and they usually belonged to local interests. American multinationals still owned Famous Players and Twentieth Century theatres, but in 1978 a Canadian entrepreneur bought Odeon from Britain's Rank interests. By 1979 one might suspect that the Canadian film production industry was doing its best to follow the appropriate line. The Film Development Corporation would lend government money for 'Canadian' films, no matter whether the stars came from Napanee, Beverly Hills, or Lower Slobbovia. But Canadian movie-goers now had the chance to see bits of Vancouver Harbour and slices of Trinity College and gobs of King township on film – although only as background. In Quebec things were much better. And, strangely, hovering on the fringe but making money were such companies as Canukr Films, which made movies in Ukrainian. At first it had trouble because all its casts spoke Ukrainian with Canadian accents. Also there were troubles because the specially constructed Ukrainian village near Oshawa did not look sufficiently weatherbeaten and decayed to be believably Ukrainian. But a little practice and experience cured the first problem, and a couple of Ontario winters cured the second.

There was some pressure for a quota system, like that in Britain, by which a certain percentage of all showings would have to be Canadian. This was not provided for the movies, but the Canadian Radio and Television Commission (CRTC) did persevere with quotas, not merely for television but also for radio. The government had already acted, in 1968, to ensure that in any broadcasting company 80 per cent of the voting shares had to be Canadian and that all such companies had to have Canadians as directors and chairmen. With the boardrooms purified, Canada's electronic media could presumably do their nationalist best, while the CRTC would do what it could to make sure that the public would watch and listen. At first it said it would stress quality not quantity, although, perhaps not surprisingly, that did not last long. It quickly moved to tighten the content rules it had inherited. In 1970 it ruled that, from 1972, 60 per cent of all television material must be Canadian, not just over-all but in prime time as well. Of the remaining 40 per cent, no more than 30 per cent was to come from any one country. As for radio, it ruled that 30 per cent of all music must be 'Canadian' – that is, the song must be sung, played, or written by a Canadian, or produced in Canada. Further, it said that within two years at least 5 per cent of all the material must have been composed or written by a Canadian.

The result was quite complicated. In 1970, following the Commission's ruling, the record companies and the Canadian Association of Broadcasters got together and examined the situation. To their surprise they found that there were already 7,000 discs that could be called Canadian. At that time, Helmut Kallmann wrote, 'the whole effort seemed to be designed as much to promote the employment and marketing aspects of the music industry as to make the listener familiar with the home-grown product.' Indeed, the listener can seldom have known whether any particular singer or disc was 'Canadian.' Yet after the quota was invented there certainly was a flowering of Canadian pop records and pop performers – all sorts, from folk through rock to country and western. Indeed, the popular arts came together in Tremblay's *St Carmen*, about a Québécoise cowgirl singer who goes to Kentucky to improve her yodelling and but whose political consciousness is somehow raised during the process. Meanwhile, the gurus of international pop had their huge Canadian followings, and the tides of musical fashion did not stop at the Atlantic seaboard or the forty-ninth parallel. Nevertheless, there were fewer teenagers, so that the youth culture, which was so largely musical, subtly changed its texture. Side by side with the music of the young ran a trend in instant nostalgia, as young and not-so-young adults relived the music of their own youths, all the way back through the Beatles and Elvis to the big band sound of the forties.

As for the music that was not pop, there was at last some chance for Canadians to buy their own performers on disc. To find Canadian compositions was admittedly more difficult, but few of these outpourings were missed. In 1967 the CBC had begun to produce some records for distribution through ordinary business channels. In the Trudeau years this arrangement continued at first, only to be superseded by a much larger project of CBC recordings. Regrettably, these records were not sold in stores; to get them one had to write to Toronto, thus encountering what had become the worst postal-sorting office in the capitalist world. Besides the CBC's labours, the commercial companies themselves began to seek out Canadian performers and orchestras, especially those whose conductors were known abroad. The Toronto Symphony made several discs; so did the Festival Singers.

One might think that because so many Canadians lived next to the United States the CRTC's labours would be in vain. As the cable systems expanded they could and did carry ever more American TV, and even FM radio. Further, the quality of the American product was rapidly improving thanks to the new and relatively generous funding of American public broadcasting, whose ad-free programming competed directly with the CBC's. But the CRTC had an answer, or thought it did. It would regulate cable as well. Some provinces (Quebec, for one) sought to annex this right, but were not allowed to do so, although both Quebec and Ontario were at length permitted to set up their own broadcasting stations. As for cable, it would have to give priority to Canadian advertisers and sources of programming, and it would have to provide 'community' channels no matter how few people might watch these feeble dribblings of local self-expression. Furthermore, the cable systems could carry American channels only when *all* relevant Canadian channels were already on line, even where the Canadian signals duplicated or triplicated one another. In the event, the cable technology was too much even for the CRTC. For a time the Commission made it illegal to import American signals by microwave; but nothing could stop the cable converter, which could increase the number of channels from ten to twenty or even more, thereby providing room for American signals in plenty. Although the Commission might strain every nerve to make sure that every anglophone family would be watching *The King of Kensington*, all it achieved was a rupture for itself – and, increasingly, a belly laugh from the public.

By 1980 many Canadians were questioning whether CBC television could survive the defection of viewers and the effects of new technology. Few had doubts about the survival of Canadian literature. At the beginning of the decade Margaret Atwood had published a primer on Canadian literature, *Survival*, which argued for the persistence of certain themes (most notably 'survival') in Canadian literature and which, in evangelical fervour, called upon Canadians to recognize a unique literary heritage. As Malcolm Ross pointed out, Atwood's intellectual structure left out a great deal of Canada's heritage – in particular those parts which were not defensive and obsessed with survival. But few read Ross; and many read *Survival*. Indeed, after *Survival* it seemed that Atwood had given a formula to which Canadian authors must conform. Certainly her novel *Surfacing* was an elaboration of what she thought had been and, in the future, must be. Fortunately, by the end of the decade, the stridently defensive tone of *Survival* was no longer necessary, as Canadian writers got increasing and favourable notice at home and elsewhere.

Atwood herself became a critical and popular success, although, interestingly enough, her novels received more praise in the United States than in Canada. About Marian Engel's and Alice Munro's work there seemed to be more consensus, and the latter author's extraordinary sense of time and place put her short stories and novels on both history and literature reading lists. Certain western Canadian authors had similar fortunate fates. Rudy Wiebe and Robert Kroetsch had vastly different styles, but as representatives and interpreters of a distinct Canadian literary tradition they attracted much attention. So did Robertson Davies, whose voice was unique yet Canadian and whose novels sold well in Canada and elsewhere. French-Canadian literature became less nationalist and political as the decade passed. Most writers remained separatist, but, as Marie-Claire Blais admitted, that commitment meant far less in their art. The most acclaimed work in French during the 1970s was a novel by Antonine Maillet that won the Prix Goncourt, and its subject was the Acadians, not modern or even old Québec. Few would read Maillet, and in Canada far more Canadians read the sports pages than the book reviews. The gap between popular and high culture widened in the 1970s, although governments worried about the former as well as the latter, so that in sports, too, nationalism became central to public debate.

When, for example, Canadian football clubs enforced blackouts locally on televised games, they presumably diverted a few bodies into the bleachers but switched many more eyeballs to the telecasts of the NFL games of the week. There was little that the government or the CRTC could do about this. However, they could impose tax penalties for Canadian firms that advertised on American TV. But if enough Canadian sets were tuned to the border stations Canadian business would find that it paid to advertise there, tax penalty or no. Fortunately for the nationalists, the seventies saw all sorts of new initiatives on the sports front. Canada hosted the 1976 Olympics and saved Canadian football from complete Americanization. But it did other things too.

In 1970, Mayor Jean Drapeau announced that Montreal had won out over Moscow. In 1976 his city would host the Olympics. There would be a splendid stadium for 80,000 people. Just in case the Québécois got interested in cycling, there would be a velodrome. For athletes and journalists there would have to be an Olympic village, for which Ottawa would help pay because it would turn into public housing afterward. As for the rest, the Mayor assured his electors, it would not cost Montreal a penny.

Where would the money come from? Gradually the picture unrolled. There would be a national Olympic lottery – the father of Loto Canada. There would be Olympic coins, stamps, and so on – promoted by the dominion, but aimed at financing Drapeau's dream. On ticket sales, one supposes, Drapeau hoped to raise some advance money.

Meanwhile, the country would have to get ready. Canada had already allowed the NHL to grow, but the effect on the calibre of hockey was disastrous, and anyway Canadians were already losing on international rinks to the Russians and the Swedes. Ironically, the nation that had given birth to hockey had no Olympic team between 1968 and 1980. To ready the athletes for competition there would be Canada Games from time to time and Ottawa would contribute funds to help athletes, coaches, and so on. Canada's national self-respect seemed to demand some sort of sporting life, especially after the ignominy of the 1968 Olympics in which Canada ranked fourteenth in the winter events and nineteenth in the summer. There was some consolation: Gordie Howe had scored his 700th goal and he continued to score more; Nancy Greene was great on skis; Karen Magnussen was superb on skates; and Nijinsky, son of Northern Dancer, was a magnificent horse. But none of this was enough.

In the end, the Olympics came near to being a national and municipal disaster. The buildings were overambitious; the workers were not diligent; the money was not forthcoming; and everything cost more than expected. Almost up to the moment the Olympics commenced, people wondered whether they would happen at all. Almost certainly the International Olympic Committee had arranged for some sort of fall-back position. Some structures, including the great stadium, were not finished on opening day; and a few could never be completed as designed. Still, some things went better than expected. In 1970 the superannuated runner, Bruce Kidd, had predicted that the Olympics would bring violence to Montreal. Quebec's poor, he said, would not stand for such a lavish extravaganza when their own needs were so great. Kidd was a poor prophet. For many Montreal workers the construction binge meant good jobs and big money. For everyone, the events themselves meant good spectacle and big excitement. Canada's showing, admittedly, was not brilliant, but no one had really expected it to do very well. As for the financial mess that the Olympics left behind, in 1980 all three levels of government were trying to untangle it.

From the Olympic adventure two things followed. One was the lottery. The other was sporting subsidy. In 1980, both were still very much alive. And if Ottawa could have a lottery, there was no reason why the provinces could not. Thus the Olympic Lottery begat not only Loto Canada but also Lottario, Wintario, the Western, the Provincial, Loto Quebec, and so on. Little or none of the net went into general revenue; most was pumped out as subsidies to sports and culture. In 1979, when the Clark government said it might abolish Loto Canada, the sporting community rose as one and yelped with pain. It then tried to make common cause with the arts community, which was also yelping. (As a political alliance or lobby, the result is certainly a most implausible coupling.) As for the lotteries, people seemed to like them. Revenues far exceeded expectation. The TV spectaculars at which winners were announced attracted large audiences. As a form of tax, a lottery is inefficient because the costs of collection are so high; but at least it is a voluntary tax. It is no wonder that in 1979 the Clark administration was wondering about a lottery for the hospitals. Shades of the Irish Sweepstakes!

In earlier times Canadians might well have resisted the lottery temptation. But the decade of the seventies was a decade of moral change. It seemed that everything went – women's liberation, gay liberation, abortion on demand – you name it, some Canadian offspring of an American organization was lobbying for it. The old certainties were going fast. In Quebec, the Catholic school and welfare systems were quickly secularized as the religious fled from classroom and bedside. In Ontario, the Mackay Committee wanted to abolish religious instruction. The Anglican Church said it could see no reason not to ordain women and homosexuals. The pope was still opposed to birth control, but many Canadian papists were manifestly not. Even the United Church, bastion of conservative radicalism, stopped fighting the good fight against beverage alcohol. Indeed that church seemed to have little fight left.

In the old mainline churches there was a collapse of morale. In Quebec it was not the government's secularizing onslaught that killed the triumphalist church. If the hierarchy and the parishes had not lost their self-confidence, life would have been much harder for Quebec's politicians and officials. Deploring Methodist doctrine with respect to priests and bishops, the Anglicans nevertheless appropriated Methodist practice with respect to female ordination and abortion, and their leaders accepted not only the social gospel, but occasionally, the theology of revolution. By 1978, the Primate of all Canada was explaining on national television why he was quite willing to give money to some African movements that were terrorist as well as revolutionary. Anglicans were scarcely the Conservative party at prayer. Admittedly, in one respect Anglican tradition was intact: there was still one religion for the clergy and another (or more than one) for the people. The difference was that the clergy were trying to redirect and trendify the popular religion. To some extent the same thing was happening in the Roman Catholic church, where vernacular liturgies and theological modernism quickly filtered down from bishops' conclave to catechism class. But there was a difference. The Roman reforms were genuinely about religion; the Anglican reforms were not. Indeed, many Anglican priests were so anxious to be modern that they were quite prepared to abolish the denomination's most cherished and only unique possession – its liturgy. The United Church, having little to lose by way of liturgy or doctrine, had much self-confidence to lose. No longer could it see itself as the Church of Canada. Membership was falling; Sunday school classes were emptying; more and more inner city churches were redundant; and immigrants rarely joined the United Church. Now and then, moderators opined that the government was admitting too many Catholics. But there was not much heat in such complaints, and now no one attended to them. Equally painful was the collapse of the church-union discussions. In the seventies the United Church digested two small protestant sects, but the Anglican Church, the one big fish it had hoped to catch, eluded it, and the union talks, begun decades before on Anglican initiative, lapsed. Soon afterward the Anglicans themselves were facing a minor schism. Following the decision to ordain women, a few Anglican priests and some lay people seceded, affiliating themselves with the new Anglican Church of North America, an American schismatic body. The apparent cause seemed too slight to provoke such a response, and of course the real cause lay far deeper. The schismatics were protesting not just against female ordination but against the whole tendency of 'reform' in Canadian Anglicanism. One schismatic thus remarked: 'Christianity is not about Zimbabwe and the guaranteed annual income. It is about Jesus Christ who died for our sins and who is present in the Blessed Sacrament.' Increasingly this was a minority view.

By 1979 the real competition was not among the big old denominations – Protestant, Anglican, Roman – all of which were stumbling erratically, and most of which had become far too polite to proselytize. It was between the old denominations and the new – the fundamentalists, the Pentacostals, the Mormons, and a vast array of deviant young people's groups, some Christian and some not. The media people, so often agnostic and liberal, did not know what to make of all this. Clearly it was good that the old denominations were shedding 'obsolete dogma' and devoting themselves to good works. What a pity that they were shrinking, while the unreconstructed, roughneck, ill-educated, unpolished fundamentalist sects were growing in numbers and in wealth.

As Christian fundamentalism flourished at one extreme, so did a whole series of movements that seemed to be secular religion substitutes – jogging, consumerism, anti-pollutionism, gay liberation, women's liberation, and pro- and anti-abortion enthusiasm. Under all these headings there were certainly injustices to be remedied and wrongs to be put right. But it was regrettable that the new votaries so often lacked either sense of humour or sense of proportion. There was rapid evolution in the law, especially during the late Pearson and early Trudeau years. The criminal code was changed to allow abortion in certain circumstances, and to permit homosexual relationships among consenting adults. As Trudeau explained, Parliament had taken the policeman out of the bedroom. Province after province passed human rights measures, meant in part to improve the status of women and to outlaw sexual, religious, or racial discrimination. By 1979 it was common to ask whether such measures could, should, or did outlaw discrimination on the basis of 'sexual orientation.' To the annoyance of the fundamentalists but to the applause of many of the media people, all over Canada the gays were coming out of their closets. Women were coming out of the kitchen too. There were many signs of changed attitudes. Many women kept their own names at marriage, or hyphenated them. Women were more prominent not only in the labour force but in many professions and occupations once reserved for men. Law and medical schools saw female enrolment rise, in some cases, to over 40 per cent. It was said that increasingly they were paid as well as men. But this statement was disputed. To help working mothers there were far more nurseries and creches – in the jargon of the period, 'day-care centres.' To help the Inuit and other native peoples, there were new subsidies and new kinds of consultation. In 1969, the government had proposed to abolish the 'Indian Problem' by repealing the Indian Act, integrating the native people into the larger society, and giving the provinces control over their welfare. But the native people did not like the idea, and the government withdrew hastily. In the middle and late seventies there was much concern about native people land claims, not merely in the far north but elsewhere, and about Inuit hunting rights. When the James Bay native residents objected to the hydro-power developments in that region, the Quebec authorities felt constrained to offer a large sum as compensation. By the end of the seventies it could be argued that Canada had made some progress in removing all sorts of old injustice and that the secular religionists had provided much of the push, but that a good deal remained to be done.

Replacing the old exportable religion of the medical missionary was the new religion of foreign aid, complete with ministry, consistory, and pope – the director of the Canadian International Development Agency (CIDA). Canada set up a Canadian International Development Institute, whose purpose was cloudy and whose activities were invisible. CUSO volunteers went overseas, both to anglo- and to francophonie, with special attention to Africa. Canada brought in people for specialist training, and sent experts abroad. It gave more aid – not much, relative to our rising national wealth, but enough to require a large CIDA staff that sometimes seemed to consist chiefly of former CUSO volunteers. Much Canadian aid was unpopular with the clerisy of foreign aid, but it was very attractive to the suppliers and recipients. On the whole, this aid seems to have been welcome, and most of it was probably well applied, although there were some well-publicized disasters. Repeatedly Canadians were told that they were not giving or doing enough. Sometimes they were urged to pay higher prices for imports from poor countries. Often they were urged to untie their aid. Always they were urged to give more. Since nothing Canada could do was likely to make a large impact on world poverty, it could always be argued that Canadians were not doing enough (the devout will readily spot the parallel with traditional religion). By 1979 the foreign aid lobby was large, vocal, and often self-righteous, while the foreign aid interest that battened on Canada's aid program had every reason to be pleased. As an American economist had said fifteen years before, 'There's money in poverty.'

In all these things there was an awareness that the stability Canadians had a generation ago was gone and, for their children, it would not return. The absence of the conservative social behaviour of the 1950s was not regretted by most Canadians. They had shed their greatcoats, buttoned-up vests, and tight corsets; although without them they often feared going into the ever colder blasts outside. And yet they would and they were not alone.

PART SEVEN

Conclusion

35

Conclusion

In 1944 the Canadian Chamber of Commerce undertook to look into the future. It polled Canadians in Kitchener and Vancouver to discover what they hoped for and expected at war's end. The responses indicated a desire for a richer material life: refrigerators, cars, and a house in the suburbs. Possibly because they were not asked they did not express a desire for a new constitution, world government, or international workers' solidarity. They did not get any of these things, but they did get refrigerators, cars, and a house in the suburbs, not to mention television sets, snowmobiles, and microwave ovens. They also got family allowances, unemployment insurance beyond their wildest dreams, health insurance, and contributory old age pensions. Economic progress made all these things possible. The period from 1945 to 1980 was one of almost uninterrupted economic growth whose benefits were widely shared among all levels of Canadian society and in all regions.

Even the unemployed, the native people, and other groups considered disadvantaged in the early 1980s have gained from Canada's economic growth. We are now more critical of deprivation, poverty, and oppression than we could have afforded to be in the 1940s. Those who hoped for more fundamental social and economic change are of course disappointed. Whether or not one shares their disappointment, one must recognize that in fact society has undergone a massive transformation since 1945, and with that transformation has come an unprecedented abundance of material prosperity.

Canadians in 1945 could not have anticipated all the consequences of their desire for a better material life. More of them had to live in larger cities to which were also attracted very large numbers of immigrants. Their lives have consequently become more complicated; in the process they have been forced to become more tolerant of diversity and many of them have actually come to enjoy the variety and freedom the great cities have made possible. What their parents believed has often been discarded. They live differently, behave differently, and presumably believe different things.

The rise in living standards was accompanied by increased organization, larger corporations, larger cities and their attendant problems, and larger government. Most Canadians had more comfort and security than ever before, but they were dependent for these things on distant and impersonal institutions both private and public. The wish for new and expensive services created certain tensions and unhappinesses which may or may not be regarded as inevitable. People distrusted bureaucracy, feared large corporations, and resented the power of larger labour unions and other special interest groups. By 1980 some parts of Canadian public life were visibly malfunctioning, such as the schools, the post office, and the Canadian system of labour relations. At times during the late 1970s, one might have thought that the national mood might best be summed up as a long and ear-splitting whine.

Rising prosperity has nevertheless created new demands and an ability to pay for these demands on a scale inconceivable in 1945. It became relatively easy for governments to imagine they could solve problems by throwing money at them. Pressure groups also came to believe that government could finance their obsessions; indeed, governments themselves often seemed to believe this. This tendency increased in the 1960s and 1970s when the public came to think that budgets need not be balanced and that the supply of money need not be rigidly controlled. For obvious reasons, one found little dissent from this new orthodoxy in the governments or in the media. The results could be seen in the financial disarray of the 1970s.

The services that were demanded – such as education, roads, health care, social assistance – belonged constitutionally to the provinces and had largely been supplied traditionally by the municipalities. Thus only a major constitutional overhaul would have prevented a steady expansion of provincial activities relative to those of the federal government. Decentralization was therefore inevitable given the existing constitutional structure of Canada and the economic and social developments of the period. In addition there was a noticeable tendency for the provinces to offer services which the national government had initiated, and which it was still willing and able to offer. Because of the rivalry between the two levels of government dominion-provincial conferences became a regular feature of Canadian life – all too regular in the opinion of some.

The planners of 1945 tried to avoid this problem by proposing a restructured constitution in which decisive powers would belong to the national government. This was politically impossible, as the 1945 dominion-provincial conference proved; thereafter the King and St Laurent governments largely avoided the problem by abandoning most of the social welfare schemes so popular during the Second World War. But in the heady prosperity of the sixties, it seemed possible to use the federal spending power to resolve constitutional difficulties by throwing money at the provinces in order to produce a welfare state.

Federal incursions into the sphere of social welfare were encouraged by reductions in spending in areas that were unquestionably national in scope, such as defence. If it had been necessary throughout this period to maintain a defence effort comparable to that of the early 1950s, there would have been less room for much of this. The unexpected and unsought result of social welfare planning and accomplishment was that the national government was weaker in terms of its undoubted responsibilities at the end of the period than at the beginning.

In the case of one provincial government, that of Quebec, an activist outlook exacerbated the tensions that would in any event have been present. The federal government feared, with much justification, that it might soon have little or no direct contact with Canadians in Quebec. Moreover, the Quebec government moved into areas of shared jurisdiction with its own deposit insurance, pension plan, and cultural policy. Other provinces were less adventurous and their motivations less ideological, but their actions contributed to the conflict in the same fashion.

One sees this in the field of natural resources where the interest of the national government in the 1940s and 1950s was directed to the solution of national problems such as unemployment, growth, and imbalances of payment. As constitutional conflict intensified, debate over the exploitation of natural resources which had previously been considered to require co-operation became more bitter. Because provincial governments own these resources, they were naturally interested in using them and especially their revenue for provincial ends. But the national government remained interested in resources, and its underlying reasons for such an interest have not changed, although new concerns have emerged in Ottawa also. Of course all conflict is not federal-provincial; provinces differ among themselves with respect to resource exploitation. Ontario and Alberta would have feuded over oil prices if Ottawa had not existed. Indeed, without a strong national government, a rational arbitration of their differences would likely have proven impossible. Similarly, Ontario, Manitoba, and Quebec would have warred over egg marketing and chicken sales.

The courts theoretically might have solved these difficulties; practically they have not. The perplexities of divided jurisdiction have remained unclarified by the courts, and special interest groups have taken advantage of this ambiguity and of the division itself. Business, for example, has often used one level of government to obtain a privilege the other level had refused. But business was sometimes a victim as well. In the cases of cable television permits and mining regulations, both levels of government demanded that companies comply with the regulations of each. What was involved in these disputes was the question of government patronage in its largest and most legitimate sense. It could be argued that some of the federal government's more surprising activities in the late sixties and seventies might be interpreted as an attempt to maintain a clientage. Thus a splendid, empty airport in Quebec was built;

national historic sites appeared everywhere; a Department of Regional Economic Expansion tried to look after those perennial federal clients, the less advantaged provinces; and ethnic groups, recent beneficiaries of Ottawa's immigration policies, benefited again from large grants to maintain the visibility of their various national heritages. Provinces naturally responded with their own historic plaques and their own multicultural grants. Such progress continues still.

The character of the change in public life is relatively easy to describe. The change in the texture of private life occurred mainly behind curtains, and its implications are much more difficult to discern. We cannot psychoanalyze the Canadian people, but we can suggest that Canadians now live different lives than their parents did. Many paths lead to different ends, and many old trails are now overgrown. What this means remains uncertain. Some observers have concluded that since 1945 Canadians have become more Americanized. We think this interpretation is misleading because it is too easy. We were not, in fact, much different from the Americans in 1945. Since that time both societies have developed in similar ways, responding to many of the same ideological and economic developments. We do not mean to understate the very real difference between Canada and the United States. After all, the United States is eleven times larger than Canada, and more than eleven times richer. Its place in the world reflects this difference. Canada still enjoys some of the comforts of a small and closely linked society. Nevertheless, like Americans, we have become less local and parochial in the last quarter century. Like the citizens of Denver, Birmingham, and Munich, our lives have become more varied and broader.

Survey data have shown that Canadian attitudes and values are less diverse in the late 1970s than they were in the early 1960s. This means that anglophones and francophones are more alike today than before. Yet there is an apparent paradox: the people have become more homogeneous as the polity has become less integrated and less organized. People can be pardoned for being confused. According to the best liberal theory, greater similarities and prosperity should lead to understanding and happiness. Few would agree that it has. In 1945 Canadians had relatively little, hoped for much, but did not really expect it. Surely they never expected exactly what they got.

Select Bibliography

Writings about Canada since the Second World War can (and do) fill the shelves of many libraries in Canada and even some abroad. Yet the material is of such variety and complexity that researchers or students are tempted to give up before they get properly started. Certainly there are few short-cuts, but some handy guides do exist through the thicket of information. The purpose of this bibliographical essay is to introduce the reader to some of the books and other materials that are likely to be helpful.

First among the guides is the grandmother of governmental handbooks, *The Canada Year Book*, crammed full of useful information from the statistical to the statutory, in annual editions in English and French. For the period down to 1960 the *Year Book*, literal and tedious though it often is, remains the only consistent guide to legislation and regulations in force throughout Canada, as well as to a host of statistics otherwise difficult of access for the ordinary reader using the ordinary library. In 1960 the *Year Book* was supplemented by the revival of a long-defunct Canadian institution, the *Canadian Annual Review*, published in annual volumes by the University of Toronto Press. Originally conceived on a grand scale to cover everything from provincial politics to mass media and sports, the *Review* has since 1971 focused more narrowly on political and economic happenings. Without these two series our task would have been infinitely more difficult, if not downright impossible.

There is no general account of economic development in Canada since 1945. Some material may be found in William L. Marr and Donald G. Paterson, *Canada: An Economic History* (Toronto: Macmillan 1979), especially Chapters 2, 7, 8, 9, 12, and 13. The older *Canadian Economic History* by W.T. Easterbrook and Hugh G.J. Aitken (Toronto: Macmillan 1956) has only a few pages on the post-war years. Quantitative studies covering part of our period have been published by, among others, Harvey Lithwick (*Economic Growth in Canada: A Quantitative Analysis* (Toronto: University of Toronto Press 1967)) and W.C. Hood and A.D. Scott (*Out-*

put, Capital, and Labour, Royal Commission on Canada's Economic Prospects: Ottawa: Queen's Printer 1957). The most convenient and important source of primary quantitative data remains Statistics Canada (formerly the Dominion Bureau of Statistics). In the notes to Chapter 1 we have mentioned the most significant publications. There is also an annual *Catalogue*, through which the reader can track down a wealth of specialized statistical publications both periodical and regular. Ottawa produces a monthly indexed *Canadian Government Publications Catalogue*, and the National Library issues a monthly and annual compendium (*Canadiana*) listing all new Canadian books. Every year the University of Toronto Press issues its *Subject Guide to Canadian Books in Print*. Scholarly papers relating to economic affairs are published by the Fraser Institute, the C.D. Howe Research Institute, the Economic Council of Canada, the *Canadian Journal of Economics*, and *Canadian Public Policy*. Both of these periodicals review new books relating to the Canadian economy; before 1967 such reviews appeared in the *Canadian Journal of Economics and Political Science*, which for many years also contained a 'Bibliography of Canadian Economics.' From time to time useful papers appear in the *Journal of Canadian Studies*, and the scholarly literature can be searched thoroughly with the aid of the quarterly *Journal of Economic Literature* and its occasional summary in the *Index of Economics Journals* (Homewood, IL: Richard D. Irwin). Much can be gleaned from the various introductory economics textbooks that have been prepared for the Canadian market. Naturally the authors are inclined to recommend the descriptive passages in Ian M. Drummond, *Economics: Principles and Policies in an Open Economy* (Georgetown: Irwin Dorsey 1976). In the late 1970s Statistics Canada issued several volumes entitled *Perspectives Canada*; these contain not merely economic data but also social indicators.

Passing from general treatments and bibliographical aids, we must first note the distinction between semi-popular treatments of controversial topics and scholarly treatments of topics that may or may not be in the public eye. Second, we should observe that in economic affairs both controversial writing and public discussion have concentrated disproportionately on two topics – the foreign investment question and, in the seventies, the energy problem. On each topic an ocean of ink has been spilled, leaving the public not much wiser than it was thirty years before. The controversy over foreign investment is embalmed in: Royal Commission on Canada's Economic Prospects, *Report* (Ottawa: Queen's Printer 1957), M.H. Watkins and others, *Foreign Ownership and the Structure of Canadian Industry* (Ottawa: Queen's Printer 1967), Harry Johnson, *The Canadian Quandary* (Toronto: McGraw-Hill 1963), M.H. Watkins, 'A New National Policy,' in T. Lloyd and J. McLeod, eds., *Agenda 1970* (Toronto: University of Toronto Press 1970), Task Force on Foreign Investment, *Report* (better known as the *'Gray Report'*) (Ottawa: Information Canada 1972), and A.E. Safarian, *Foreign Ownership of Canadian Industry*

(Toronto: McGraw-Hill 1966 and later editions). H.C. Eastman and S. Stykolt, *The Tariff and Competition in Canada* (Toronto: Macmillan 1968) is also relevant. Kari Levitt's account (*Silent Surrender* (Toronto: Macmillan 1970)) can mislead. With respect to energy policy the same could be said of James Laxer, *The Energy Crisis* (Toronto: Lorimer 1975). It would be better to begin with Leonard Waverman, ed., *The Energy Question: An International Failure of Policy* (Toronto: University of Toronto Press 1974), and with the annual reports of the National Energy Board. Something can also be learned from Larry Pratt, *The Tar Sands* (Edmonton: Hurtig 1976). The view from Ottawa can be glimpsed neatly in National Energy Board, *Canadian Natural Gas: Supply and Requirements* (Ottawa: National Energy Board 1979).

Passing to fiscal, monetary, and trading matters, much of the scholarly literature consists of papers that only professional economists can make much of. With respect to trade and international finance there is a good deal of information in the series *Canada in World Affairs* (Toronto: Canadian Institute of International Affairs, roughly annually), which now extends to 1965. The general reader can learn something from textbooks, such as R. Craig McIvor, *Canadian Monetary, Banking, and Fiscal Development* (Toronto: Macmillan 1958) or D.E. Bond and R.A. Shearer, *The Economics of the Canadian Financial System* (Scarborough: Prentice-Hall 1972), from Scott Gordon, *The Economists versus the Bank of Canada* (Toronto: Ryerson 1962), and, after 1960, from the summaries in the *Canadian Annual Review*, especially the excellent treatments by D.F. Forster. For a 'monetarist' view of the Bank of Canada's more recent behaviour, see Thomas J. Courchene, *Money, Inflation, and the Bank of Canada* and *The Strategy of Gradualism* (Montreal: C.D. Howe Research Institute, 1976 and 1977). The Bank's earlier record is treated by E.P. Neufeld, *Bank of Canada Operations and Policy* (Toronto: University of Toronto Press 1955 and later editions). An invaluable treatment of monetary and exchange rate policy is Paul Wonnacott, *The Canadian Dollar 1948-1962* (Toronto: University of Toronto Press 1965).

In matters of economic organization, business, agriculture, and labour, it is hard for the general reader to get much beyond the textbook, and in some areas, such as agricultural organization and policy, there are very large gaps in the literature. Don Mitchell, *The Politics of Food* (Toronto: Lorimer 1975) has some useful material but the tone is polemical and the analysis incomplete. On labour one may consult Gordon Bertram, *The Contribution of Education to Economic Growth* (Economic Council of Canada Staff Study no. 12, Ottawa: Queen's Printer 1966), John Crispo, *International Unionism* (Toronto: McGraw-Hill 1967), J. Hamelin et F. Harvey, *Les Travailleurs Québécois 1941-1971* (Cahiers de l'Institut Supérieur des Sciences Humaines, Québec: Université Laval 1976), R.O. Miller and F. Isbister, eds, *Canadian Labour in Transition* (Scarborough: Prentice-Hall 1971), S. Ostry and

M.A. Zaidi, *Labour Economics in Canada* (Toronto: Macmillan 1972), and Task Force on Industrial Relations, *Report* (Ottawa: Privy Council Office 1968). On industry see D.H. Fullerton and H.A. Hampson, *Canadian Secondary Manufacturing Industry* (Royal Commission on Canada's Economic Prospects, Ottawa: Queen's Printer 1957), Economic Council of Canada, *Interim Report on Competition Policy* (Ottawa: 1969), the books by Safarian and Eastman and Stykolt mentioned above, G.L. Reuber and F. Roseman, *The Takeover of Canadian Firms 1945-1961* (Economic Council of Canada Special Study no. 10, Ottawa 1969), N.C. Stewart, *Concentration in Canadian Manufacturing and Mining Industries* (Economic Council of Canada Background Paper, Ottawa 1970), and Royal Commission on Corporate Concentration, *Report* (Ottawa: Ministry of Supply and Services 1978), along with the staff studies relating thereto. In the literature there is little systematic treatment of the growth and development of particular industries. To find out about such things one must turn to the Statistics Canada materials, beginning with the *Canada Year Book*.

External affairs and defence have inspired a plentiful but variable literature. First, there are the official, scholarly compilations by the Department of External Affairs itself, the *Documents on Canadian External Relations* (Ottawa: Queen's Printer and successors 1967-). For many years the Department also published the useful *External Affairs Bulletin*, later transformed into an opinionated house organ as *International Perspectives*. *International Perspectives* was eventually privatized. Another feature of the post-war years was the appearance of a scholarly journal on international relations, the *International Journal*, sponsored by the Canadian Institute of International Affairs (CIIA). Its French-language counterpart, *Etudes Internationales*, also repays careful perusal. An indispensable source of information is the CIIA's monograph series, *Canada in World Affairs* (Toronto: Oxford University Press and successors 1941 to date), which has been recently revived to cover the post-1963 period. Other documents on external relations have been published by the Carleton Library: R.A. MacKay, ed., *Canadian Foreign Policy, 1945-1955* (Toronto: McClelland & Stewart 1971) and Arthur Blanchette, ed., *Canadian Foreign Policy, 1955-1965* (Toronto: McClelland & Stewart 1977). An often ignored source of information about Canadian external activities is the documentary collection of the American Department of State, *Foreign Relations of the United States*, in its many volumes.

The continuing and important work of James Eayrs, *In Defence of Canada* (Toronto: University of Toronto Press 1964-), contains much useful information. Three prominent figures from the Department of External Affairs have written reminiscences of their careers: John Holmes, *The Shaping of Peace* (Toronto: University of Toronto Press 1979), Escott Reid, *Time of Fear and Hope* (Toronto: McClelland & Stewart 1977) and A.F.W. Plumptre, *Three Decades of Decision*

(Toronto: McClelland & Stewart 1977). For Canada's Commonwealth connection, see Joe Garner, *The Commonwealth Office* (London: Heinemann 1978), Nicholas Mansergh, *Survey of British Commonwealth Affairs: Problems of Wartime Cooperation and Post-War Change, 1939-1952* (Oxford: Oxford University Press 1958) and J.D.B. Miller's excellent volume, *Survey of Commonwealth Affairs: Problems of Expansion and Attrition, 1953-1969* (London: Oxford University Press 1974). Extremely useful for Canadian-American relations are two works by J.L. Granatstein and Robert Cuff, *Canadian-American Relations in Wartime* (Toronto: Samuel Stevens Hakkert 1975) and *American Dollars – Canadian Prosperity* (Toronto: Samuel Stevens 1978). Denis Stairs' unique study of Canada in the Korean War, *The Diplomacy of Constraint* (Toronto: University of Toronto Press 1974), is also useful. Some interesting essays on Canadian foreign policy, reflecting changing styles in the interpretation of international affairs, may be found in Stephen Clarkson, ed., *An Independent Foreign Policy for Canada?* (Toronto: McClelland & Stewart 1968) and Norman Hillmer and Garth Stevenson, eds, *Foremost Nation* (Toronto: McClelland & Stewart 1977). Two collections of essays by John Holmes, *The Better Part of Valour* (Toronto: McClelland & Stewart 1970) and *Canada: A Middle-Aged Power* (Toronto: McClelland & Stewart 1976), offer wise observations on Canadian foreign policy since the war. Despite a profusion of books on Canada, the United States, and the Vietnam war, none presents an adequate account.

The finest source for Canadian political history until 1950 is the Mackenzie King Diary, now available on microfiche (University of Toronto Press 1980), or in the useful and authoritative *Mackenzie King Record*, edited by J.W. Pickersgill and Donald Forster in four volumes (Toronto: University of Toronto Press 1961-70). For King's wartime career, J.L. Granatstein's *Canada's War* (Toronto: Oxford University Press 1975) functions almost as a biography of Canada's wartime prime minister. Louis St Laurent presents a greater challenge for a biographer. Nevertheless, two of his advisers, Dale Thomson (*Louis St Laurent: Canadian* [Toronto: Macmillan 1967]) and J.W. Pickersgill (*My Years with Louis St. Laurent* [Toronto: University of Toronto Press 1975]), have written useful accounts, unlikely to be speedily superseded. Robert Bothwell and William Kilbourn have also written *C.D. Howe: A Biography* (Toronto: McClelland & Stewart 1979) on St Laurent's principal colleague.

John Diefenbaker's memoirs, *One Canada*, 3 volumes (Toronto: Macmillan 1975-7) are fascinating, but also exceedingly badly organized and often misleading. Peter Stursberg's two-volume collection of interviews, *Diefenbaker: Leadership Gained* and *Diefenbaker: Leadership Lost* (Toronto: University of Toronto Press 1975-6) are greatly to be preferred. Lester Pearson's memoirs, *Mike* (Toronto: University of Toronto Press 1972-5) are better written than Diefenbaker's, and better on foreign policy than on domestic political affairs. Two of Pearson's colleagues have written their memoirs. Judy LaMarsh's *Bird in a Gilded Cage* (Toronto: McClelland & Stewart 1968) presents a frequently jaundiced view of her former leader; Walter Gordon's *A Political Memoir* (Toronto: McClelland & Stewart 1977) explains and justifies its author's political career. The best book to date on Pierre Trudeau is George Radwanski's *Trudeau* (Toronto: Macmillan 1978). Joe Clark's career remains to be authoritatively evaluated; current reading on the subject is partisan ephemera.

Some of Canada's provincial figures have also produced or stimulated memoirs or biographies. Joey Smallwood of Newfoundland is best served in Richard Gwyn's *Smallwood* (Toronto: McClelland & Stewart 1968); his own memoirs are best forgotten. Maurice Duplessis has received authoritative treatment in Conrad Black's well-researched book, *Duplessis* (Toronto: McClelland & Stewart 1976). The most useful book on René Lévesque is Peter Desbarats' *René: A Canadian in Search of a Country* (Toronto: McClelland & Stewart 1976). Tommy Douglas of Saskatchewan has received worshipful treatment in a relentlessly favourable biography by Doris Shackleton (Toronto: McClelland & Stewart 1975).

Provincial politics receive comprehensive treatment in Martin Robin, ed., *Canadian Provincial Politics* (Scarborough: Prentice-Hall 1971). Richard Simeon, *Federal-Provincial Diplomacy* (Toronto: University of Toronto Press 1972) is indispensable for federal-provincial relations in the sixties. Extremely useful for the debate on separatism are the Accent Québec series of the C.D. Howe Research Institute, particularly Judith Maxwell and Caroline Pestieau, *Economic Realities of Contemporary Confederation* (Montreal: C.D. Howe Research Institute 1980). Papers relating to federal and provincial politics may also be gleaned from the *Canadian Journal of Economics and Political Science* until 1967 and since that time in the *Canadian Journal of Political Science*. Books relating to the topic are reviewed in the two aforementioned journals, and in the *Canadian Historical Review*, which publishes a comprehensive bibliography on the subject.

Material relating to Canada's cultural, educational, and literary life can be found in Julian Park, eds., *The Culture of Contemporary Canada* (Toronto: Ryerson 1957). The revised edition of Carl Klinck, ed., *Literary History of Canada: Canadian Literature in English*, 3 vols. (Toronto: University of Toronto Press 1976) offers excellent surveys of the various types of English-Canadian writing. Norah Story's *Oxford Companion to Canadian History and Literature* (Toronto: Oxford University Press 1967) and William Toye's *Supplement to the Oxford Companion...* (Toronto: Oxford University Press 1973) also furnish many interesting details. The most recent edition of George Woodcock's *The Canadians* (Toronto: Douglas & McIntyre 1979) is an important social and cultural commentary. Lastly, there are some books on Canadian political culture which cannot be omitted. Donald Creighton's books, *The Forked Road* (Toronto: McClelland & Stewart 1976) is tendentious but readable.

George Grant's *Lament for a Nation* (Toronto: McClelland & Stewart 1965) presents much the same point of view, though at much shorter length. Peter Newman's two popular histories, *Renegade in Power* (Toronto: McClelland & Stewart 1963) and *The Distemper of Our Times* (Toronto: McClelland & Stewart 1968) contain a wealth of colourful detail, though they have now been superseded on many issues. Within the last decade several first-class studies of Canadian political parties have been written. Foremost among them is Reg Whitaker's *The Government Party* (Toronto: University of Toronto Press 1977), based on exceptional access to the papers of the Liberal party; also noteworthy is George Perlin, *The Tory Syndrome* (Montreal: McGill-Queen's University Press 1980). More speculative and less reliable is Walter Young's account of the CCF, *Anatomy of a Party* (Toronto: University of Toronto Press 1969). All three books prove that political scientists can on occasion still write English.

Index

Olympics, the (1976) 450-1; boycott of (1980) 366

Ontario 19-20, 57, 64, 74, 121-2, 124-5, 154, 157, 162-3, 192, 236-7, 257, 312, 352, 365, 367, 384, 400, 402, 406, 441-3, 448, 451, 459; conservatives in 150, 152, 162, 234, 364, 366; economy of 23, 158-9, 179, 317, 364, 408-9, 412, 418, 421; position of in Confederation 91, 93, 95-6, 98, 150, 152, 291, 380-1

O'Neill, Louis 260

Orange Order, the 114

Orenda engine, the 243

Organization of American States (OAS) 208-9

OPEC (Organization of Petroleum Exporting Countries) 42, 351, 408, 418-19, 422-3

Ottawa Agreements (1932) 204

Ouellet, André 365

Ozawa, Seiji 446

Page, P.K. 336

Painters Eleven 173

Pakistan 58, 140-1, 208; immigrants from 32

Parti Québécois 351, 356-7, 377, 384, 386, 391-2, 394, 396-9, 400-4. See also separatism

Patry, André 305-6

Patterson, Tom 168

Peacekeeping 5; in Suez 144; in Vietnam 274

Pearkes, George 197, 245

Pearson, Geoffrey 276-7

Pearson, Lester B. 89, 106-7, 134, 140, 178, 208, 210, 219, 254, 264-7, 284, 323, 342, 344-5, 348-9, 365, 380, 414, 428; domestic policies of 274, 289-301, 311-15, 317-31; foreign policy of 105-6, 135, 143-6, 270-2, 274, 276-7, 279-83, 300-8, 373; leadership of Liberals and 246, 248, 250, 255, 293, 296; philosophy of 165-6, 270-1

Pearson, Maryon 277, 344

Pellan, Alfred 173

Pelletier, Gérard 289, 300, 392

Pensions. See old age

Pentecostals. See religion

Pépin-Robarts Task Force on National Unity (1978) 398

Perry, J.H. 67

Petersen, Len 112

Petrocan 362, 417-18; 'privatization' of 361-2

Petroleum Products 29, 50-1, 71-2. See also energy, national gas, oil

Phillips, Eric 76

Phillips, Robin 445

Pickersgill, J.W. 134, 141, 148-9, 166, 317

Pipeline debate (1956). See Trans-Canada Pipelines Limited

Pitfield, Michael 353, 360

Plumptre, Beryl 424

Pollution 13, 25, 408

Population. See demography

Pornography 173, 443-4, 447

Porter Commission. See royal commissions

Porter, John 286, 369

Powell, R.E. 76

Posgate, Dale 284-5

Post office 318, 458; postal workers and 317-18, 424

Potash 219, 323

Presbyterians. See religion

Prices 34, 41-2, 44; controls on 42, 178, 423-8. See also inflation

Prices and Incomes Commission 423